DISCRIMINATION AGAINST WOMEN

Bowker/CIS Congressional Document Series

Women and the "Equal Rights" Amendment
Discrimination Against Women

DISCRIMINATION AGAINST WOMEN

CONGRESSIONAL HEARINGS
ON EQUAL RIGHTS
IN EDUCATION AND EMPLOYMENT

Edited by Dr. Catharine R. Stimpson, Barnard College,
in conjunction with
the Congressional Information Service,
Washington, D.C.

R.R. BOWKER COMPANY
New York & London, 1973
A Xerox Education Company

Published by R.R. Bowker Co. (A Xerox Education Company)
1180 Avenue of the Americas, New York, N.Y. 10036
Copyright © 1973 by Xerox Corporation
All rights reserved
Printed and bound in the United States of America

No copyright is claimed for the Testimony and Documents
reprinted in this volume. The material was issued by the U.S.
Government Printing Office in the publication *Discrimination
Against Women. Hearings before the Special Subcommittee
on Education of the Committee on Education and Labor,
House of Representatives, Ninety-First Congress, Second
Session, on Section 805 of H.R. 16098*.

Library of Congress Cataloging in Publication Data

United States.   Congress.   House.   Committee on
    Education and Labor.   Special Subcommittee on
    Education.
  Discrimination against women.

  (Bowker/CIS congressional document series)
  Selections from the original ed., 1971, have been
rearranged.
  1. Woman—Employment—United States. I. Stimpson,
Catharine, R., ed. II. Congressional Information
Service. III. Title. IV. Series.
KF3467.E35   344'.73'014   72-13703
ISBN 0-8352-0608-4

CONTENTS

FOREWORD

On June 17, 1970, the Special Subcommittee on Education opened hearings on discrimination against women—the first hearings ever held by a Committee of Congress to consider the subject of discrimination on the basis of sex.

When the hearings began, I did not consider myself naive about the discrimination within our society. Nevertheless, throughout the course of the testimony, I found myself frequently surprised and even at times overwhelmed at the degree of discrimination documented in education, in the labor market, in the professions, in government, and even in the law itself.

We are told that in 1848 a small group of women at Seneca Falls, New York, passed a series of resolutions demanding the right to vote, to speak in public, and to have full equality under the law. Along with these practical demands was a simple statement of principle: "That woman is man's equal—was intended to be so by the Creator, and the highest good of the race demands that she be recognized as such." Clearly, the women of Seneca Falls recognized that a recognition of their worth, and of the discrimination they were experiencing must necessarily accompany any practical reforms.

It is my hope that the hearings held by the subcommittee will awaken in us a consciousness of the problems confronting women in our society and will induce us to work to overcome discrimination through practical reforms in the law and in our institutions.

The Special Subcommittee's hearings were based on a consideration of Section 805 of House Resolution 16098, a very broad higher education bill I had introduced. Section 805 was directed at discrimination against women. Although the bill died at the end of the 91st Congress, and Section 805 along with it, I introduced another education bill with a very similar antisex discrimination Title in the 92nd Congress. In this instance, happily, the major substance of the Title was enacted and is now in our statutes as part of Public Law 92-318.

There is much to be accomplished, much that can be improved, and many inequities that can be righted—but only if we take the time for awareness and for action.

We become aware that, in the area of education,

41 percent of the girls graduating from high school go on to college as compared to 59 percent of the boys;

women get $518.00 annually for scholarship and financial aid as compared to $760.00 for men;

85 percent of the teachers in elementary education are women but only 21 percent of the elementary school principals are women;

the percentage of female high school principals is only 3 percent.

The remark has been made (not altogether facetiously) that if a woman wishes to become a college president, she is well advised to become a nun because nearly all of the meager 1 percent who become college presidents are heads of Catholic institutions.

I do not wish to convey the false impression that discrimination is limited to education.

No federal agency has ever had a woman as general counsel.

No state has ever had a woman as attorney general.

Women constitute only 10 percent of our nation's more than 350,000 scientists.

Only 7.6 percent of our nation's medical practitioners are women.

Indeed, the great value of the hearings is the breadth, the depth, and the general pervasiveness of discrimination on the basis of sex in our society which they document.

One educator is said to have searched at length recently to find literature suitable for children which conveyed any sense of equal representation of the sexes. In despair, she went back as far as the Old Testament—to the story of Noah and his ark—as the only really equal representation of male and female she could find. This is indeed a sad state of affairs.

It is a pleasure to know that the information gleaned during our hearings will now be available to a much wider audience. I would hope that all readers will find reading the condensed hearings as personally profitable as I found my participation in them.

Edith Green
Member of Congress

PREFACE

Discrimination against women in education and employment was the subject of special congressional hearings in 1970. The substance is presented here in this edited version of the two-volume Government Printing Office (GPO) edition in order to make the material available to as large a public as possible in an orderly fashion. The GPO volumes include oral testimony and written documents in the order in which they were placed into the record, followed by a number of prepared statements and supplemental materials. Our text, although reproduced from the GPO publication, has been rearranged into two parts.

Part 1, "Testimony," has been put together so that the reader will follow the sweep and drama of the oral testimony. Written documents have been inserted only if the oral testimony seems confusing without them.

In Part 2, "Documents," we have arranged the written material into seven categories: "Women and the American Scene," general essays about women and discrimination; "Women and Work," facts about all women as workers; "Women and the Law," analyses of the legal identity imposed upon women, which has affected their status as workers and vice versa; "Women and Education," descriptions of the education of women and of the treatment of women in educational institutions; "Women and the Professions," reports about women in specific professions, some of them academic; "Women and Government Action," comments about what the federal government had either done or failed to do before the hearings; and finally, "Model Remedies," some programs for change.

Reducing two volumes to one demanded some cuts. Some cuts were easy: written material that either duplicated oral testimony, remained under copyright restrictions, or was printed elsewhere several times. (An index of omissions, as well as of inclusions, is at the end of this volume.) Other deletions were difficult and were made regretfully. We were particularly sorry to eliminate several reports documenting discrimination on specific campuses, which were drawn up during 1969 and 1970 by local women's groups, since these reports were a basis for suits against the campuses and were valuable blocks for building a picture of national patterns of discrimination. Some of the reports have been included, and others are alluded to in testimony, but unfortunately space limitations have made it necessary to exclude the great mass of detail from Brandeis, the University of Buffalo, California State College at Fullerton, the University of California at Berkeley, the University of Chicago, Columbia University, Cornell University, Kansas State Teachers College, the University of Maryland, and the University of Wisconsin.

Three Representatives—the Honorable Margaret Heckler, the Honorable Catherine May, and the Honorable Patsy Mink—sent statements of support to Representative Edith Green, their colleague from Oregon who chaired the hearings. Their full statements have not been reproduced, but their good will cannot pass unnoticed.

My thanks go to the editors at the R.R. Bowker Company and to Alan Searls, whose editorial work was essential, and whose support of the moral and legal purpose of the hearings was consistently sincere, sincerely consistent, and always useful.

Catharine R. Stimpson
Barnard College

INTRODUCTION

During the summer of 1970, the Honorable Edith Green, a Democrat from Oregon and a member of Congress since 1955, held a series of hearings before the Special Subcommittee on Education of the House Committee on Education and Labor, which she chaired. The purpose of the hearings was to consider Section 805 of House Resolution 16098, the Omnibus Post-Secondary Education Act of 1970.

The title of the legislation was deceptively bland. Its intent was nothing less than to help remedy painful, pervasive discrimination against women, an ameliorative reform through the expansion of the protection of federal law. Its method was to extend certain civil rights measures to women, among them those in education, and certain equal pay for equal work measures to women, especially those in higher echelon positions. The scope of Section 805 was such, however, that it would affect women of all economic classes, and of all races. On June 17, the first day of the hearings, Representative Green described Section 805:

> Section 805 would amend the Civil Rights Act [of 1964] to prohibit discrimination on the basis of sex in federally financed programs and would remove the exemption presently existing in title VII of the Civil Rights Act with respect to those in education. It would authorize the Civil Rights Commission to study discrimination against women and lastly would remove the exemption of executive, administrative, and professional employees from the equal pay for equal work provision of the Fair Labor Standards Act.

Moreover, the hearings themselves were the first ever to be devoted to the discrimination against women in higher education.

The hearings took place on seven days in June and July. They were held in Room 2261 of the Rayburn House Office Building in Washington, D.C. According to one of the women who testified there, Professor Ann Sutherland Harris, then of Columbia University, now of Hunter College, the air-conditioning was almost too efficient, making the room very cold in contrast to the humid air outside. At one end of the rectangular room were subcommittee members and counsel, who sat at a long, raised semicircular table with Representative Green in the middle. Although the subcommittee had fifteen members, all of them men, no more than four of them ever appeared at one time to listen to the testimony, a comment either on the nature of Congressional subcommittee hearings or on the prevailing attitude of men in government towards the issue of women's rights.

Witnesses, at the right of the room, faced the subcommittee and Representative

Green. A press table was to their left, rows of spectators to their rear. The witnesses could be divided into two major groups: those who were protesting the discrimination against women and those in the federal government who would be charged with the enforcement of new laws against sex discrimination. Some witnesses—women in government—were both protestors and potential enforcers. Representative Green herself dropped the impersonal mask of subcommittee chairperson to mention the prejudice she personally had encountered because she was a woman. One of the most interesting passages in the record of the hearings is a dialogue between Representative Green, one of the two women on the full Committee on Education and Labor, and the Honorable Frankie M. Freeman, the one woman on the Civil Rights Commission. Their comments reveal, not only the experience of sex prejudice, but the ways in which sex and race prejudice in America have both reinforced and collided with each other.

> Mrs. Freeman: . . . I am a Southerner. I speak as a Southern black woman. I have been denied admission to places of public accommodation, not because of my sex, but because of my race. As a member of the Civil Rights Commission, we have conducted hearings in Mississippi and Alabama, and in many of these places we have received testimony from women and men who were denied the opportunity to vote. I do not know of any white woman who has been denied the opportunity to vote, but I know that there are black men and women who were denied that opportunity . . . .

> Mrs. Green: Outside of voting, I know of no discrimination that is greater than the discrimination against women. There are places where I cannot go in the front door—because I am a woman.

> Mrs. Freeman: You can go into many front doors that I can't go into because of color . . . .

The witnesses who protested against sex discrimination were impressive. Clearly and irrefutably, they documented the need for Section 805. In detail, they described the difficulties of women in the labor force as a whole, in the professions, in educational institutions, and in the government itself. Any prejudice is deplorable, but that which Representative Green and her witnesses explored was perhaps even more deplorable than usual because of the institutions that were harboring and perpetuating it: schools, colleges, and universities, in theory the sites of objectivity and of transcendence of pettiness; and the government, in theory the guarantor of social justice for all and the guardian of law. Among the witnesses were women, such as Bernice Sandler, whom historians will recognize as some of the most farsighted, industrious, and effective New Feminists, and other women, such as Dr. Pauli Murray, who had been laboring for years against the brutal irrationality of multiple prejudices. The testimony and supporting documents ran to 1,261 pages when the Government Printing Office (GPO) published it in two volumes called simply *Discrimination Against Women*. The volumes, one of the most valuable sources of raw material about women in contemporary America, have an incremental effect as they are read. A person becomes so sated with evidence of discrimination that he or she begins to experience the oppressive weight of bias that women as a class have carried.[1]

---

[1] Representative Green had 6,000 copies of the GPO edition of the hearings printed, six times the normal run. A member of her Congressional staff told me in a telephone interview in June 1972 that all of them had been distributed.

One of the reasons why the hearings are so effective is that Representative Green and her witnesses place their massive statistics within a cultural context. Figures, vital in themselves, also reveal large patterns of action, attitude, and belief. The Women's Faculty Group at Harvard, for example, in a "Preliminary Report" of March 9, 1970, stated that in the academic year 1969-1970 the Harvard University Faculty of Arts and Sciences had no woman full professor on its regular faculty, no woman associate professor, and only nine women assistant professors out of a total of 194 persons of that rank. These shameful facts were a symptom of the antiquated notion that men, but not women, were capable of rational thought and that men, but not women, were capable of managing our universities. Nor are we allowed to forget the price that people pay in hunger and humiliation because of sex discrimination. One statistic emerges and reemerges throughout the hearings as if it were a *leit-motif* in a novel: 60 percent of the children in families dependent upon a woman, who gets neither prestigious jobs, easy promotions, nor equal pay, are poor.

Another remarkable aspect of the hearings is Representative Green herself. She is tireless, vigorous, and shrewd. She refuses to let witnesses slide away with inadequate, if deferential, replies. Again and again she asks government officials—from the Civil Service Commission, the Civil Rights Commission, the Equal Employment Opportunity Commission, the Department of Justice, and the Department of Labor—what they are doing to see that women have equal rights in their own offices as well as in the nation at large. She is at her pungent best as she pushes the ponderous federal bureaucracy into a greater responsiveness to women's rights within and without its own corridors. She also reminds us of a moral and ideological heritage: the right of each person to his or her own destiny, and the right of each person to have at least an equal chance at life's prizes. This is a legacy that has too long been a masculine prerogative rather than a human right. While her tough-mindedness gives the hearings much of their pith, so her moral reminders and her ambitions for Section 805 give the hearings much of their dignity.

The history of Section 805 is convoluted. Indeed, the story of legislative measures is probably among the most genuinely labyrinthian narratives of our time. The omnibus higher education bill, of which Section 805 was a part, died by the end of the 2nd Session of the 91st Congress, a season of campus turmoil. In 1971 during the 1st Session of the 92nd Congress, the House of Representatives took up another higher education bill. One of its titles, which dealt with discrimination against women and which Representative Green introduced, had many of the same provisions as Section 805. The Senate took up its own higher education bill. Senator Birch Bayh, a Democrat from Indiana, introduced measures on the Senate floor to prohibit sex discrimination. After parliamentary perils and confusion, they were adopted. The House and Senate bills were then reconciled in conference, and President Richard M. Nixon signed a higher education act into law on June 23, 1972. Some areas were exempt from bans on sex discrimination; for example, admissions to private undergraduate schools, training schools for United States military men, and undergraduate public institutions if they had traditionally admitted only members of one sex. However, the antidiscrimination measures were substantially those Representative Green had sought two years earlier.

Between the Green hearings on Section 805 in 1970 and the Higher Education Act of 1972 women had gained several legal weapons to use in national and local struggles against sex discrimination. On December 4, 1971, the Office of Federal Contract Compliance in the Department of Labor (OFCC) issued Revised Order 4 which became effective 120 days later and which strengthened provisions against sex discrimination on the part of federal contractors. In March 1972, the Equal Employment Opportunity Act of 1972 became law. It amended Title VII of the Civil Rights Act of 1964 by banning sex discrimination in educational institutions. This act closed an immense loophole and achieved a goal of Section 805. It also gave the Equal Employment Opportunity Commission (EEOC) new powers. As a result, women, who might have failed to find redress at one government agency, might turn to another. In March 1972, the Senate, by a vote of 84 to 8, passed the Equal Rights Amendment (ERA) to the United States Constitution, guaranteeing equality before the law to persons of both sexes.[2]

Even before the Green hearings, women had begun to use a broad, new federal legal device to dissolve the prejudice against them. In 1965, President Lyndon B. Johnson had issued Executive Order 11246, prohibiting federal contractors from discrimination on the basis of race, color, religion, or national origin. Then, two years later, he issued Executive Order 11375, which became effective October 13, 1968, and which amended his previous Executive Order outlawing discrimination on the basis of sex as well. A pattern—women as the last group to receive legal remedy for discrimination—was repeated. The OFCC was to set policy and to enforce the executive orders. In January 1970, the Women's Equity Action League (WEAL), founded in 1968, filed a class action suit against colleges and universities that were government contractors, charging them with sex discrimination. (WEAL's letter to the Department of Labor is part of the record of the Green hearings.) WEAL's step set off a series of events: the use of federal agencies to insure fair treatment of women and minorities in education. The effect of such action will not be fully understood for some time.

Section 805, if it had passed, would have been among the first, if not the first, of the new tools that women might use to construct sexual equality. It would have made the struggle easier. Yet it is neither disrespectful to Representative Green and her hearings, nor is it callous, to say that the defeat of Section 805 itself was comparatively unimportant. The defeat was of the whole bill, not this section alone, and the aims of Section 805 were realized within the next two years, a short period of time for a measure ultimately so radical and so accessible to the ridicule and contempt of those who fear a radical realignment of sex roles. The importance of Section 805 exists in the fact that Representative Green wanted it at all and in the hearings: a thick history of past error, a documentation of present injustice, and a prophecy of future rectification.

Perhaps the experience of Professor Ann Harris was symbolic. She had worked for several days with a team of women from Columbia Women's Liberation, putting her testimony together. She carried sixty copies of it with her to Washington. Her attitude towards the hearings was ambivalent. In themselves, they seemed

---

[2] In May 1970, a month before the Green hearings began, Senator Birch Bayh had held hearings about the ERA. See my edited version of his Senate subcommittee activity, *Women and the "Equal Rights" Amendment* (New York: R.R. Bowker Co., 1972). For cogent analyses of affirmative action programs against sex discrimination, see Carol Herrnstadt Shulman, *Affirmative Action: Women's Rights on Campus* (Washington, D.C.: American Association for Higher Education, 1972), and the various brief reports of the Project on the Status and Education of Women of the Association of American Colleges, Washington, D.C., Bernice Sandler, director.

useless, particularly when she saw the number of empty chairs at the subcommittee desk. No one in power seemed to be listening. On the other hand, she thought the hearings might prove to be a forum, a way of jarring or inspiring people outside of the room to action. As a witness, she was thorough, lucid, and convincing. The testimony was a good example of the collective effort of the women's movement. Her response to the questions of one subcommittee member, Representative William D. Hathaway, was witty and poised. While he revealed sexual conservatism she revealed the patience necessary for any serious political movement. All sixty copies of the testimony were taken and she returned to New York empty-handed. One wonders who read the testimony and where. One cannot doubt that this and other evidence concerning discrimination against women were read with important results. The very motion of the women's movement is welcome evidence.

Catharine R. Stimpson
Barnard College

PART 1
TESTIMONY

WEDNESDAY, JUNE 17, 1970

House of Representatives,
Special Subcommittee on Education of the
Committee on Education and Labor,
Washington, D.C.

The subcommittee met at 10:20 a.m. in room 2261, Rayburn House Office Building, Hon. Edith Green (chairman of the subcommittee) presiding.

Present: Representatives Green, Hathaway, Perkins, Quie, and Steiger.

Staff members present: Harry Hogan, counsel; Robert C. Andringa, minority professional staff assistant.

(Text of section 805 of H.R. 16098 follows:)

PROHIBITION OF DISCRIMINATION

Sec. 805. (a) Section 601 of title VI of the Civil Rights Act of 1964 is amended to read as follows:

"Sec. 601. No person in the United States shall, on the ground of race, color, sex, or national origin, be excluded from participation in, be denied the benefits of, or be subjected to discrimination under any program or activity receiving Federal financial assistance."

(b) Section 702 of title VII of the Civil Rights Act of 1964 is amended by the insertion of a period after "activities" and the deletion of the remainder of the sentence.

(c) That paragraph (1) of subsection (a) of section 104 of the Civil Rights Act of 1957 (42 U.S.C. 1975c(a)) is amended by inserting immediately after "religion," the following: "sex", and paragraphs (2), (3), and (4) of subsection (a) of such section 104 are each amended by inserting immediately after "religion" the following: ", sex".

(d) Section 13(a) of the Fair Labor Standards Act of 1938 is amended by the insertion after the words "the provisions of section 6" of the following language "(except section 6(d) in the case of paragraph (1))."

Mrs. Green. The subcommittee will come to order for the further consideration of legislation that is under the jurisdiction of this subcommittee.

It is with a great sense of personal pleasure that I welcome to the subcommittee today witnesses who will offer testimony on section 805 of H.R. 16098.

Section 805 would amend the Civil Rights Act to prohibit discrimination on the basis of sex in federally financed programs and would remove the exemption presently existing in title VII of the Civil Rights Act with respect to those in education. It would authorize the Civil Rights Commission to study discrimination against women

3

and lastly would remove the exemption of executive, administrative, and professional employees from the equal pay for equal work provision of the Fair Labor Standards Act.

It is to be hoped that the enactment of the provisions would be of some help in eliminating the discrimination against women which still permeates our society.

It seems ironic that in a period when we are more concerned with civil rights and liberties than ever before in our history—when minorities have vigorously asserted themselves—that discrimination against a very important majority—women—has been given little attention.

Increasingly women are constituting a greater proportion of our labor force. As of April of this year there were 31,293,000 women in the labor market constituting nearly 40 percent of the total.

However, despite the growth in the number of women working today, the proportion of women in the professions is lower in this country than in most countries throughout the world.

While the United States prides itself in being a leader of nations, it has been backward in its treatment of its working women.

Professionally, women in the United States constitute only 9 percent of all full professors, 8 percent of all scientists, 6.7 percent of all physicians, 3.5 percent of all lawyers, and 1 percent of all engineers.

Despite the fact that the Federal Government through Democratic and Republican administrations has given lip service to the equal opportunities for employment of women, the very large majority are in the lower grades of Civil Service and only a small portion in policy-making or administrative positions.

Despite increases in earnings, income and wage statistics illustrate dramatically a deep discrimination against women. The average median income for women working full-time year around is $4,457. The comparable figure for men is $7,664.

We have been concerned, and rightly so, about discrimination against the Negro in our society—about the Negro man who averages $5,603—only 69.9 percent of the average earnings for a white man.

But I hear little concern expressed for women who average only 58 percent in comparison. The average wage in the United States is: Negro women, $3,677; white women, $4,700; Negro men, $5,603; white men, $8,014.

The sorry fact is also that the gap in earning power is widening. In 1956, for example, women's median income of $2,827 was 64 percent of the $4,466 received by men.

Women's median wage or salary income rose to $3,973 in 1966 while men's rose to $6,848. So, although both groups experienced increases, women's income increased at a slower rate and their median income in 1966 was only 58 percent of that of men—a 6-percent drop in the 10-year period.

Many of us would like to think of educational institutions as being far from the maddening crowd, where fair play is the rule of the game and everyone, including women, gets a fair roll of the dice.

Let us not deceive ourselves—our educational institutions have proven to be no bastions of democracy.

Initially many women are required to meet higher admission standards than men. While the Federal Government and the Office of Education, in effect, though their policies, encourage college admission standards to be waived for certain individuals, they have shown absolutely no concern over the higher admission requirements set for women in many institutions.

Our colleague from Michigan, Representative Martha Griffiths, cited instances recently where at the University of North Carolina admission of women on the freshman level is "restricted to those who are especially well qualified." There is no similar restriction for male students.

In the State of Virginia, I am advised, during a 3-year period, 21,000 women were turned down for college entrance, while not one male student was rejected.

On the graduate level, not too surprisingly, the situation worsens.

Sex differences in rank and salary at colleges and universities have also been reported by the Women's Bureau of the Department of Labor. A recent report by the Bureau pointed out that "in institutions of higher education women are much less likely than men to be associate or full professors." And citing a 1966 study by the NEA the report states that in 1965–66, "women full professors had a median salary of only $11,649 compared with $12,758 for men."

Total Federal support to institutions of higher education amounted to $3,367 million in fiscal year 1968. Over 2,100 universities and colleges participated in that support. The President's Executive Order 11246, as amended by Executive Order 11375, specifically forbids sex discrimination by Federal contractors. However, colleges and universities are still receiving Federal contracts, and although forbidden by Executive order from discriminating against women, nevertheless continue in this course. I think this warrants our attention and the attention of the administration.

In Federal civil service, as well as in political appointments, there has been lip service in regard to equal opportunities for women but in reality there has been no change through Democratic or Republican administrations.

The National Congress and State legislatures have always been the best proof that this indeed is a man's world—and too often discrimination against women has been either systematically or subconsciously carried out.

In hearings I expect this to be well documented in our tax laws, in social security benefits, in labor unions which through the years negotiated contracts paying women less than men for identical work. Of course, invariably the negotiatiors for both management and labor have been men.

Women do make up over 50 percent of the population, and yet in civil service we find that the women under grade 3, there are 142,867; they make up 21 percent of all the workers and according to 1968 figures, if we take grades 3, 4, 5, 6 and 7, the lowest paid civil service positions, we find that women make up 86 percent of these grade levels in civil service, and that in grades 8 through 18, women make up only 13 percent of the total civil service labor force.

When we get to grade 13, less than 1 percent—six-tenths of 1 percent women. In grade 14, three-tenths of 1 percent, in grade 15, one-tenth of 1 percent.

In grades 16, 17 and 18 less than 1 percent in each grade—and above grade 18 there are 16 women in the entire Federal civil service.

CIVIL SERVICE STATISTICS

In 1968 667,234 women were employed in full time white collar civil service positions.

	Number	Percent
Under grade 3	142,867	21.0
Grade 4	145,685	21.8
Grade 5	183,168	27.5
Grade 6	53,661	8.0
Grade 7	54,866	8.0
Grade 8	9,781	2.0
Grade 9	39,665	6.0
Grade 10	3,295	.5
Grade 11	16,807	3.0
Grade 12	8,451	1.0
Grade 13	3,824	.6
Grade 14	1,743	.3
Grade 15	695	.1
Grade 16	97	(1)
Grade 17	25	(1)
Grade 18	9	(1)
Above grade 18	16	(1)

[1] Less than 1 percent.

I asked for figures the other day from the Office of Education and HEW, in regard to the number of women employees in policymaking positions. The Office of Education has told me an hour ago that they could not get these figures for me. We do have them for HEW, and we find that out of 15,977 employees in grades 12 and up, 2,666 are women.

In HEW, there are only 10 women employees at grade 16. Out of 72 total employees at grade 17, there are only 3 women, and at grade level 18, there is not a single woman in the present Federal civil service in HEW. The grade levels are in the chart attached.

Employees	Total	Women
GS–12 and above	15,977	2,666
GS–12	5,350	1,151
GS–13	4,900	830
GS–14	3,230	488
GS–15	2,195	184
GS–16	214	10
GS–17	72	3
GS–18	16	0

Mrs. GREEN. As I said before, this seems to me to be ample evidence of the discrimination which does exist throughout our Government. As I said, during the next several days I hope that the various kinds of discrimination against women in our society will be discussed and will be fully documented, and that this can be made available to the men who run the world. [Laughter.]

Today, we will have as witnesses before our committee two of my women colleagues in the House.

When they do come in, I will interrupt and call upon them, because they have other committee meetings which they must attend. But may I now invite to the table Mrs. Myra Ruth Harmon, president of the National Federation of Business and Professional Women's Clubs; Jean Ross, chairman of the National Legislative Committee of the American Association of University Women; Dr. Elizabeth Boyer, immediate past president of the Women's Equity Action League; Commissioner Wilma Scott Heide, Pennsylvania Human Rights Commission, behavioral scientist, American Institutes for Research; and Dr. Ann Scott, of the State University of New York at Buffalo, representing the National Organization for Women. We will ask you to present your statements and then perhaps address questions to you individually.

May I turn to Mrs. Harmon first.

STATEMENT OF A PANEL COMPOSED OF MRS. MYRA RUTH HARMON, PRESIDENT, NATIONAL FEDERATION OF BUSINESS AND PROFESSIONAL WOMEN'S CLUBS, INC.; JEAN ROSS, CHAIRMAN, NATIONAL LEGISLATIVE COMMITTEE, AMERICAN ASSOCIATION OF UNIVERSITY WOMEN; DR. ELIZABETH BOYER, IMMEDIATE PAST PRESIDENT, WOMEN'S EQUITY ACTION LEAGUE; COMMISSIONER WILMA SCOTT HEIDE, PENNSYLVANIA HUMAN RELATIONS COMMISSION; BEHAVIORAL SCIENTIST, AMERICAN INSTITUTES FOR RESEARCH; AND DR. ANN SCOTT, UNIVERSITY OF BUFFALO, REPRESENTING THE NATIONAL ORGANIZATION FOR WOMEN

Mrs. HARMON. Mrs. Green, I represent the National Federation of Professional Women's Clubs, and we are honored to be here today. You have in your hands my testimony which is documented, and in the interests of time, I will cut some of this in my oral explanations to you.

Let us look briefly at the changes that have occurred in the work scene and for working women since 1920, just after our national federation was founded and women had secured the right to vote.

In 1920 the life expectancy of a baby girl was 55 years, today it is 74 years. Today out of every 100 girls who are 17 years old, 78 are graduating from high school whereas in 1920 there were only 20. Today for every 100 women 21 years old there are 19 graduating from college compared to 2 out of every 100 in 1920. Today 43 percent of all women are in the labor force, which is 20 percent more than in 1920.

The average woman worker today is married and 39 years old, whereas in 1920 she was single and 28 years old.

Since 1940 American women have been responsible for the major share in the growth of the labor force. Their representation in the labor force has risen from one-fourth to almost two-fifths of all workers.

In 1900 women were only 18 percent of all workers; in 1940, 25 percent; today 37 percent. In fact the number of women in the civilian labor force increased by 75 percent between 1947 and 1968, while the number of men rose only 16 percent.

You have already indicated the facts of the earning gap and I will not repeat that, although it is in my testimony.

A type of occupation does not make very much difference. In 1968 this same report shows that women professional and technical workers had a median wage of $6,691 compared to $10,151 for men. Women clerical workers, sales workers, operatives, and service workers all had an income from between 55 and 65.9 percent of what men received in the same categories.

This is happening today when more women than ever work, when women clearly work to provide an adequate standard of living for themselves, their families, and their other dependents.

The radical difference in wages for men and women today is revealed also by the fact that only 8 percent of men full-time year-round workers in 1968 earned less than $3,000 while there were 20 percent of the women at the pay level; and that 60 percent of the women, but only 20 percent of the men, earned less than $5,000. At the other end of the scale, only 3 percent of the women, but 28 percent of the men, had earnings of $10,000 or more. These figures clearly reveal that women are discriminated against in the work force. They do not show why or how.

Such statistics do not necessarily and invariably indicate that women are receiving unequal pay for equal work. That is certainly part of the story, but in many cases the lower incomes are the result of the fact that women are more likely than men to be employed in low skilled, low paying jobs.

You need only look around you to convince you of this fact, but the report on the earnings gap goes on to conclude that women are much less likely than men to be associate or full professors in institutions of higher education, that women in the technical field are usually in the lowest category of draftsman or engineering technician, that women are usually class B and men the higher paid class A accounting clerks in the clerical field, that women in cotton textile manufacturing are usually the battery hands, spinners, and yarn winders (lower paying jobs); while men are loom fixers, maintenance machinists, and card grinders (the better paying jobs).

As Dr. Cynthia Epstein notes "* * * no matter what sphere of work women are hired for or selected, like sediment in a wine bottle they seem to settle to the bottom."

The next page of my testimony substantiates these statements.

In these cases we do not have a problem of equal pay for equal work, but as mentioned before, a more subtle discrimination not covered by law by which women are deliberately consigned to different kinds of jobs than men: jobs that pay less, offer little or no advancement possibilities, provide a minimum of creativity and responsibility.

Why should a women college graduate in English be asked if she can type when she applies for a job and a man considered for research or editorial responsibilities? Why are 34 percent of all employed women clerical workers? Yet these are the facts at a time when: (1) More women than ever before are working; (2) Women have more education; and (3) Women are provided with more freedom to work outside the home.

The reasons for this state of affairs are multiple. I would like to list only a few of them and then proceed to the legislation at hand as related to these realities of sexual discrimination.

There are myths concerning women workers that are difficult to dissipate. These are used to establish, to explain and to justify this kind of economic discrimination, this consignment of women to lower paying, less challenging positions. For example, women are accused of a high rate of absenteeism and labor turnover. Yet a recent report indicates that sex is not the determinant of the amount of sickness or the chances of an individual leaving one job for another. A Public Health Service study of overtime work lost because of illness or injury showed an average of 5.6 days lost by women and 5.3 lost by men during a calendar year. It was also shown that women are less likely to be absent because of chronic conditions such as heart trouble and more likely to be absent because of acute illness, with men the reverse.

Another analysis indicates that women's illnesses usually keep them away from work for shorter periods than men's illnesses do. As for occupational mobility, if women leave the job to return home to take care of a growing family, men leave for increased employment opportunities to better themselves.

The report concluded that: All in all, the skill level of the job, the age of the worker, the worker's length of service with the employers, and the worker's record of job stability all provide better clues to an understanding of differences in work performance than does the matter of sex.

Another myth is the idea that women only work for a brief time until they get married. Factually, this is not the case since working women constitute almost 42 percent of all women of working age, 37 percent of the work force. In almost three out of five cases the working woman is married and her average age is 39.

We are also told that women work to afford luxuries, yet the Labor Department reports that millions of the women who were in the labor force in March, 1968, worked to support themselves or others. This was true of the majority of the 6.4 million single women workers.

Nearly all 5.6 million women workers who were widowed, divorced, or separated from their husbands—particularly those also raising children—were working for compelling economic reasons. In addition 2.3 million married women workers whose husbands had incomes of less than $3,000 in 1967 certainly worked because of economic need. If we take into account those women whose husbands had incomes between $3,000 and $5,000 (which is still below the amount considered necessary even for a low standard of living for an urban family of four) about 2.2 million women are added.

Again we are told that women are passive, nonaggressive and so must assume certain kinds of jobs (naturally these are the lesser paying jobs) and avoid others (management, policymaking positions), or quite the contrary women are pictured as tempermental, overly emotional and therefore unable to assume responsibilities. Related to this is the theory that women are not born to compete, which in a free enterprise system necessarily must consign women to the lower rungs of the ladder of success.

Such statements are based upon assumptions and reflect certain sex role concepts which continue to mold our society as well as the expectations men and women have of one another and of themselves. The effects of such attitudes permeate not only the job market, but our educational institutions.

Today even though women can technically enter most of our prominent educational institutions—and the growth of coeducation is very encouraging—there are subtle, but vast areas of discrimination extant, which other witnesses will substantiate and detail.

Section 601 of title VI of the Civil Rights Act of 1964 provides that no person shall, on the grounds of race, color or national origin, be excluded from or discriminated against under any program or activity receiving Federal financial assistance.

Section 805(a) of the bill, H.R. 16098, calls for amending section 601 of the title VI of the Civil Rights Act to include sex as one of the prohibited grounds for discrimination.

In other words, that provision would mean that a person could not, because of sex, be excluded from participation in, denied the benefits of, or discriminated against under any program or activity receiving Federal financial assistance.

At this time we have no such guarantee. We do have sex included under title VII of the Civil Rights Act of 1964 relating to employment opportunities only. Including sex under title VI would cover all programs or activities receiving Federal financial assistance in the form of grants, loans or contracts, and we think that is important.

At the present time Executive Order No. 11246, as amended by Executive Order No. 11375 requires a policy of nondiscrimination (including sex) by Federal contractors and subcontractors and employment on Federally assisted construction.

This Executive order does not cover all kinds of Federal programs and activities as recommended in section 805(a) of the bill before us.

Thus we urgently request passage of this amendment to broaden the present scope of guarantees of nondiscrimination in programs and activities assisted by Federal moneys, which are funded from taxes levied on women taxpayers as well as men; and to strengthen, to give the force of law to this guarantee.

Section 805(b) of H.R. 16098 calls for amending section 702 of title VII of the Civil Rights Act to remove the present exemption of teachers from the equal employment opportunity requirements embodied in this section.

Since women in large numbers major in education and pursue careers in that field, we feel that it is especially important that education be covered.

Thirty-eight percent of bachelor degrees earned by women in 1967 were in education. Education also accounted for 51 percent of master's and 29 percent of doctor's degrees earned by women in 1967.

74.9 percent of all education degrees at the bachelor level were conferred upon women in 1966–67.

Teaching is the largest single professional occupation for women. The 1.7 million women noncollege teachers in April 1968 equaled 42 percent for all professional women.

In 1965–66 about 70 percent of all public school teachers were women. In 1968 in elementary schools, about 85 percent of all teachers were women; in secondary schools, 46 percent.

The earnings gap report notes the unequal pay accorded men and women college professors at the same academic rank. Teachers salaries for elementary and secondary education, reported by the National Education Association are not shown separately for men and women. We do notice, however, an increasing trend away from administrative positions—the better paying and more responsible positions—for women. There has been a definite decline in the percentage of women holding these positions.

My written testimony indicates that the term employee would also have to be changed to include State and local political subdivisions in order to include public schools under this amendment.

Section 805(c) of H.R. 16098 calls for adding discrimination against women as a subject of investigation and study by the Civil Rights Commission. Our organization strongly supports this move. We are familiar with the exceptional research and publications of the Civil Rights Commission, notably the "Jobs and Civil Rights: The Role of the Federal Government in Promoting Equal Opportunity in Employment and Training," published in 1969.

We are aware that the Commission has the power to investigate complaints of discrimination and to study and collect information concerning legal developments constituting a denial of equal protection of the laws, and to appraise Federal laws and policies with respect to equal protection of the laws; to serve as a national clearinghouse for information in respect to denials of equal protection of the laws, and to submit reports, findings, and recommendations to the President and the Congress.

Certainly the instances, implications, and ramifications of sexual discrimination in our society sorely need the objective, respected, and exhaustive study that the Civil Rights Commission offers.

Our organization believes that one of the most effective instruments in our effort to make our society one of full opportunity for persons of all races, creeds, and national origins and sexes is information concerning the actual facts of discrimination.

Many men and women are totally unaware of the extent and nature of sexual discrimination in our society. We believe that the Civil Rights Commission, therefore, should be empowered to investigate, review, and report on sexual discrimination in our society.

Section 805(d) would amend the Fair Labor Standards Act to remove the exemption of executive, administrative, or professional employees from the provision requiring equal pay for equal work.

In a recent Federal court the Equal Pay Act of 1963 was described as "a broad charter of women's rights in the economic field."

We would broaden the charter. The National Federation proudly recalls the days and years during which the legislative battle to pass the equal pay bill was fought and the leadership efforts of the women of Congress, particularly the honorable chairman of this subcommittee.

We believe that the bill should be extended to cover more kinds of employment. There is no more reason for justification for discrimination at this level, in this kind of job than there is in those now covered.

From 1945 until passage of the equal pay bill in 1963, our organization worked with other women's organizations and Members of Congress to secure passage of the equal pay legislation.

As you will remember, Mrs. Green, the original administration proposal, supported by BPW and others, did not attach the equal pay bill to the Fair Labor Standards Act.

Accordingly the supporters of equal pay had no intention of eliminating executive, administrative, and professional positions from coverage.

That was a result of the fact that in the interest of getting equal pay legislation passed the proponents agreed to attach the bill as an amendment to the Fair Labor Standards Act.

BPW only agreed to this in order to secure passage, fully expecting that an amendment would ultimately be added, once the legislation passed, including administrative, executive, and professional positions.

Thus with some urgency we are here today reiterating our support of this badly needed remedy. The discrimination in pay that women suffer at administrative, and executive and professional levels continues, as our previous statistics indicate.

The extension of the equal pay act to these positions would be very important because it would encompass those individuals who have the same background, experience, and education but make different wages.

Here it is not so much a problem of different jobs, of being secretaries rather than managers, but of receiving different pay based on sex.

At present title VII, section 703(a)(1), of the Civil Rights Act of 1964 prohibits employment discrimination in hiring, discharging, terms, conditions, or privileges of employment, including that of compensation.

However, the EEOC, which is burdened with administering title VII has an overload of casework. Moreover, the EEOC has very little power, a situation we have sought to remedy by testifying in support of legislative efforts to grant the EEOC the right to issue judicially enforceable cease-and-desist orders, to back up its findings of discrimination based on race, color, religion, sex, or national origin, which currently it does not have.

The EEOC's authority is limited to conciliation efforts.

On the other hand the Equal Pay Act is administered by the Wage and Hour Division of the U.S. Department of Labor. This agency is generally able to obtain compliance.

If there is a refusal to comply or deliberate violation of the law, the Secretary of Labor may obtain a court injunction to restrain continued violation or withholding of back wages legally due.

The Secretary of Labor may also bring suit for the back wages upon written request of an aggrieved employee. Also important is the fact that complaints are treated in strict confidence and unless court action is necessary, the name of the aggrieved party is not revealed, whereas under the protection of title VII such anonymity is impossible.

Indeed the strength and effectiveness of enforcement proceedings under the Fair Labor Standards Act was one of the compelling reasons for BPW's support for attaching the equal pay bill to the Fair Labor Standards Act.

Finally, although not included in the legislation at hand, we should like to indicate our support for the extension of child care facilities throughout our Nation.

We also recommended an increased child care deduction (an increase in the amount of the deduction as well as the income level allowed for taking the deduction) for those who would hire someone or otherwise provide for care for their children while both parents work.

We do not consider this special legislation for women, but for families. Although the mother traditionally has been the one to stay home, the responsibility for child care certainly belongs to both of the parents, especially when both are contributing to the family income.

Equal employment opportunity is not and cannot be a reality unless this need for various kinds of improvement in the types of child care and the ability of families to use these plans are forthcoming.

These measures are very specific legislative remedies for particular problems of discrimination affecting American women today.

They will not solve all our problems, but we believe they will help to balance the scale of justice and to provide legal remedies for present inequities.

Thank you.

Mrs. GREEN. Thank you very much, Mrs. Harmon. I would like to make two brief comments and then turn to the next witness.

I do recall the necessity of equal pay for equal work to make that modification to exempt administrative, professional, and executive positions from coverage of the equal pay because colleagues on the committee and labor unions and others would not vote for it unless this exemption was agreed to, although you, I, and others did not like it.

The other comment I would make refers to page 12 of your statement. You are right that in section 701 of the Civil Rights Act the term "employer" excludes a State or political subdivision.

We had witnesses who testified to classes that were arranged under title III of the Elementary and Secondary Act in high schools, and they were for boys only, and I wrote letters to the enforcement division of the Civil Rights and others, and they said they were sorry, but the schools were not covered by it.

That certainly needs to be corrected. Thank you very much. Mr. Hathaway, do you have a question to direct to her, or shall we hear all of the witnesses?

Mr. HATHAWAY. I think, Madam Chairman, I would like to hear all the witnesses first.

Mrs. GREEN. All right.

We will turn to Jean Ross, chairman of the Legislative Committee of the American Association of University Women.

Mrs. Ross. Thank you, Madam Chairman.

I am Mrs. Jean Ross, chairman of the Legislative Program Committee of the American Association of University Women. The association has a membership of approximately 175,000 and is organized in over 1,600 branches in the 50 States, Guam, and the District of Columbia.

We have obviously become aware of the statistics presented by Mrs. Green and the previous witness, and I will not repeat them, but I will request that our written statements be entered into the record completely.

Several members of this committee are our old friends and quite familiar with our longstanding support for legislation which advances the status of this Nation's most valuable asset, its human resources.

For members less familiar with our work, we point out that since 1882 our most vigorously supported goal has been improvement of educational opportunity for all Americans.

Equally important goals which are to be found in the Association's statements of purpose and policy are the advancement of women, the promotion of equality of opportunity in education, employment and housing, and the ending of poverty and discrimination.

The early records of the Association are full of what now seem to be amusing justifications for support of legislation which would improve the status of women.

This action ranged from support of local sanitation regulations and improvement of working conditions for women, to support for enactment of child labor laws and early support for equal pay for equal work.

In the early part of this century AAUW supported creation of the Woman's Bureau, opposed exclusion of women from the Federal civil service examinations and the payment of lower salaries to women for the same work.

It supported independent citizenship for married women, since women in the early 1920's automatically acquired the citizenship status of their husbands.

AAUW not only supported suffrage for women, but as far back as 1922 it was supporting the principle of appointment to office regardless of sex and urged the introduction of women into the diplomatic service.

In World War II years AAUW supported the creation of women's units in the Armed Forces, the commissioning of women doctors and nurses, and equal pay and rank for women in the Armed Forces. We are happy to see this policy seems to be advancing.

From the mid-forties until its enactment in 1963 AAUW was in the forefront of the organizations active in the struggle for passage of the Equal Pay for Equal Work Act.

We are here today to speak particularly in support of section 805 of the bill H.R. 16098, which we believe would work toward the elimination of discrimination against women, discrimination which we regret still exists in many areas.

As staunch friends of the academic world of which many of our members are a part, we are particularly aware of a situation in which proportionately few occupy top positions in either administration or teaching.

In fact the percentage of women on faculties has dropped seriously in recent years from 30 percent in 1940 to 19 percent in 1969, probably because women find advancement and higher pay more easily found elsewhere.

We are deeply concerned that women in Government service at all levels suffer the same disadvantage.

We also call your attention to one of the many statements, articles, and tables which have appeared recently, the April 13 issue of the U.S. News and World report.

An article in that issue states that 64 percent of approximately 30 million women working today are employed in clerical, service, sales or domestic jobs, most in the lower salary scales.

Mrs. GREEN. Could I interrupt you there? Would you like to have that article included in the record following your statement? Do you think it would be worthwhile?

Mrs. ROSS. Yes.

Mrs. GREEN. Without objection, I would ask that the full statements of all the witnesses be included in the record, and that this article be included with your comments.

Mrs. ROSS. Unfortunately for women, education does not appear to enhance their earning capacity to the same degree as is true for men.

The U.S. Department of Commerce report on income in 1968 indicates that women over 25 with a high school education earn approximately $3,500 annually less than men with the same education.

Those with a college degree earn $5,100 less than men with a degree and $1,600 less than men with a high school diploma.

We are not here to tell you that we think legislative action will bring an end to this unequal employment situation, but we do believe it can help.

There is nothing in the 14th amendment which precludes treatment of women as first-class citizens, and in fact, it seems to us that there is reason to question the constitutionality of any other treatment.

But as in the case of Indian, the Mexican-American, or the Harlem Puerto Rico, the additional protective acts of recent years, such as the Equal Pay for Equal Work Act and the Civil Rights Act are required and need strengthening to insure the equal protection under the law which we are promised under the Constitution.

Such legislation must also contain adequate enforcement authority and must be funded to allow reasonable implementation.

We support section 805 of H.R. 16098 which amends section 601 of title VI of the Civil Rights Act to include sex as one of the prohibited grounds for discrimination.

We urge the immediate enactment of the provisions of section 805 of H.R. 16098 which would correct the unfortunate exemption under section 702 of title VII of the Civil Rights Act with respect to those individuals working in or connected with an institution with educational activities; under any program or activity receiving Federal financial assistance and which would permit the addition of discrimination against women as a subject of investigation and study by the Civil Rights Commission.

We are of the opinion that given adequate enforcement authority the EEOC can make great strides toward the elimination of the discrimination covered under title VII and we regard the amendment in section 805(d) to section 13 of the Fair Labor Standards Act which would remove the exemption of executive, administrative or professional employees from the provisions of the act requiring equal pay for equal work as a most realistic and fair provision.

It seems ludicrous to us that people found capable of doing similar work should receive any differential in their recompense.

AAUW is currently making a study of the status of women on the campuses of its corporate member schools results of which will be available in September.

We also wish to point out our keen interest in and approval of the work of another House Education and Labor Subcommittee in voting to give the EEOC cease and desist power to enable it to order an employer accused by an employee or by the commission to stop the alleged discrimination and to bring school and college teachers under the act's coverage for the first time.

Although our understanding is that today's hearing are to center on section 805 H.R. 16098, the Association wishes to go on record in support of the Higher Education Act which is now up for extension.

We urge its extension, as so much progress has been made under it and other higher education legislation enacted by the Congress in recent years.

We also hope to have the opportunity to appear again before this committee in support of student financial assistance programs, library programs and institutional aid.

Today in conjunction with the earlier part of this statement on the status of women, we again bring to your attention a proposal which we have made to this subcommittee in earlier years.

The Association urges that specified sums be designated to be reserved as loans and grants to be used by women who wish to enter or return to college to either acquire or refresh skills which would make it possible for them to qualify for professional or status positions.

We wish to point out to you a relatively untapped source of very able women power. Many intelligent, able women leave college to become homemakers, and later find themselves unprepared for the type of positions they could fill if training were available to them.

Because there are other pressing demands upon their family budget, further schooling is a financial impossibility for most of them.

As we said to this committee in other years, we recognze that most of the avenues of financial assistance open to other students from private sources as well as those listed in these provisions of the Higher

Education Act are closed to such women.

But who can blame the admission officer, the student loan officer or the faculty counselor who selects the student who is just graduating, or who is now at work in a job requiring further training, instead of someone who has been out of school for some years?

We recognize that it is the responsibility of these administrators to be certain that these limited funds are spent where the greatest expectation of return exists.

Therefore we again wish to ask this committee to add language in the bill or in the report which would provide for special consideration for those women who, with financial assistance in the form of both loans and grants, could enter the job market at higher levels.

We suggest if this vast source of woman power could improve its earning capacity through this proposed opportunity for educational advancement, the Federal Government would soon be reimbursed through the substantial increase in income tax payments which would result.

In May 1969 the Association Legislative Program Committee addressed the following letter, which is included, on an advisory body on education to President Nixon, the Secretary of HEW and to the U.S. Commissioner of Education.

This highlights the need for an understanding of the complex problems and recognizing the needs of students, teachers and educators, providing programs of equality which will allow the members of our democracy to participate in a unified society and provide training and experience for an understanding of and participation in international society.

We believe the events of recent months make the appointment of such a body even more pertinent today.

(The document referred to follows:)

AMERICAN ASSOCIATION OF UNIVERSITY WOMEN,
Washington, D.C., June 16, 1970.

The PRESIDENT,
The White House,
Washington, D.C.

MR. PRESIDENT: At its recent meeting, the Legislative Program Committee of the American Association of University Women discussed at length the several proposals for creation of an advisory body on education to the President. It now wishes to urge the establishment of a U.S. Council of Advisors to the President on Education, comparable to the council of Economic Advisors, for the following reasons.

There is a need to respond to the social and economic changes which are making an impact on education at all levels. These changes call for an understanding of the complex problems involved in:

    (a) Providing equal opportunities for education

    (b) Recognizing the rights of students, teachers, and administrators

    (c) Meeting the special needs of identifiable groups in our society

    (d) Providing programs of quality that will prepare the members of our democracy to participate in a unified society

    (e) Providing educational training and experience for an understanding of and participation in international society.

No longer can realistic solutions to problems in education be recommended only on the basis of past practices. In the interest of innovative growth and progress, new forms of cooperation in education have emerged, and more should be sought. Inter-governmental agencies, voluntary organizations, corporations, foundations, and other public and private institutions and agencies are now involved more than ever before in education. These new forms of cooperation are furnishing a broader and different basis for making decisions about the character and organization of education.

A national commission of advisors to the President on Education could recommend needed research and open avenues of communication between all the relevant institutions in our society. Such a body would have the additional obligation to alert the public to the total responsibility resting upon our society for implementing the goals of universal education, and international understanding.

Sincerely yours,

Mrs. Ross. Thank you very much for again giving us the privilege of appearing before this subcommittee.

Mrs. GREEN. Thank you, Mrs. Ross.

The next witness before the committee is Dr. Elizabeth Boyer, immediate past president, of the Women's Equity Action League.

Dr. Boyer.

Dr. BOYER. I am a lawyer from Cleveland named Elizabeth Boyer and——

Mrs. GREEN. What is your position in Ohio now, Mrs. Boyer?

Dr. BOYER. I am immediate past president of WEAL, and a lawyer. I have been asked to testify in Columbus a number of times and I have been asked to testify in the Senate here on the Equal Rights Amendment.

I have written testimony that is limited strictly to the field of higher education, but since I have been asked to reschedule today, I am limiting myself to testimony that I don't believe will otherwise appear.

We are here in support of H.R. 16098, section 805 (a) through (d). I would like to say that we are in entire agreement with everything that has been said by the two preceding speakers, Mrs. Harmon and Mrs. Ross.

Second, I want to say that these four sections of House Resolution 16098 were submitted by me to the plenary session of the Women's Bureau's 50th anniversary meeting this last weekend, which was attended by over 1,000 women from all over the country.

All four sections were approved by that body without, I might say, undue debate, and I have been authorized to state that for this record.

My written presentation is confined to discrimination against women in higher education, and I would like to have that embodied in the record, of course.

I have been told since the rescheduling that some observations in other areas of discrimination against women in other areas would be appropriate at this time, and so I will confine my testimony to those areas about which I have had occasion to learn a good bit.

The organization which I represent, the Women's Equity Action League, is only a year and a half old, but we have already again gained representation in 35 States and from the start we received monumental amounts of mail from all over the country concerning discrimination against women.

At times we wished we could apply for a franking privilege. A very considerable number of the complaints we received came from union women. About half, I might say, at first, came from women in education, which did surprise me a bit at the time.

But I would say that almost a third, now, come from union women and regarding their own union's failures to act in their interests.

I had a long telephone call of about an hour just before I left Cleveland from a Louisiana woman in one of the unions, telling of discrimination against women on the part of their own unions.

Some of these cases they are bringing to the courts down there.

In Ohio recently, a male representative of an AFL–CIO group

came to Columbus, our State Capitol, and testified before a legislative subcommittee there, where I had been invited to appear. He came and testified against dropping Ohio's so-called protective laws, while his own women members came in to testify just the opposite.

They said they wanted that overtime and had to have it. Fifty of them came in to contradict him. They were so angry that they went back to Dayton and called a press conference and they accused the man publicly of not polling his 125,000 women members who disagreed strongly with his stand.

As legislators, I urge you to examine such testimony and take it with a real grain of salt when union leaders' testimony disagrees directly with testimony of organizations which are interested in women's advancement.

(The document referred to follows:)

WOMAN CHARGES OHIO AFL–CIO UNION WITH FAVORING MALE MEMBERS

The Ohio AFL–CIO union organization which has 725,000 male members and 125,000 female members has been charged with representing only the male viewpoint in opposing repeal of Ohio laws relating to working women. House Bills 984–87 now before the Ohio Assembly would repeal limitation of overtime hours for women, lift the ban on some occupations now barred to women, along with other provisions originally designed to protect women from industrial exploitation.

Mrs. Laura Walters, an Inland Steel employee in Dayton, accused Ohio AFL–CIO secretary-treasurer, Warren Smith, of placing the union on record against the repeal, without polling its 125,000 women members. Most of the union women "I know are in favor of the repeal," Mrs. Walters said, pointing out that as many as 50 women union members from Dayton "have taken time off work to appear before the House Commerce and Labor Committee in Columbus and ask for approval of the bills."

Mrs. GREEN. If I may interrupt you, one of the classic examples is the protective law which used to be in effect (and perhaps still is) to provide for the women in New York and other States that no woman could work in a restaurant that served liquor after 8 o'clock, because they wanted to protect the women from the horrible things that might happen.

Of course, incidentally, the tips are highest after 8 o'clock in the evening, and the male of the species did not extend their concern to the women charwomen who were scrubbing the floors in the halls just outside the restaurants until 3 or 4 a.m. Surely, they needed so-called equal protection—but coincidentally there were no tips for them.

So I take with a grain of salt some of these protective laws.

Dr. BOYER. These are the patterns and the realities. If the question could even be asked of these union representatives whether their women members have been polled, that would be a very penetrating question.

Another thing I would like to urge is that if laws are passed in these respects they should be concrete, easily understood and easily applied. This would not leave industrial women workers at the mercy of their unions.

Another situation has come very directly to my attention, because I am a lawyer, and I was down here Monday on the issue of sex-segregated want ads. We have pushed a motion up to the circuit court level to intervene in a case which the American Newspapers Publishers have brought against the Equal Employment Opportunity Commission.

I can't possibly go into the intricacies of that case, except to say that it is being brought on a highly technical issue to challenge EEOC's help-wanted guidelines and yet it is being presented in articles in the newspapers as though the substantive issue of help-wanted advertising were being challenged.

It is not.

Since section 704(b) of title VII of the Civil Rights Act is so worded as not to mention the newspapers specifically, the newspapers are still filled with "Male" and "Female" help wanted ads to this day, 6 years after title VII became law, although such advertising is illegal under section 704(b) on the part of employers and employment agencies.

Human relations ordinances have been passed to try to stop this practice. The Pittsburgh N.O.W. group has filed suit on this matter under their human relations ordinance.

These laws make it illegal for employers and employment agencies to place such ads, but I submit that suing anyone's prospective employer is not ordinarily the best way to get a job.

This is not likely to ingratiate one and put one on the right foot as an employee, so to speak. So getting responsible women to file suit against employers who are advertising in these illegal ads, I submit to you, is virtually a closed door.

There have been studies of the discouraging effect of the "male-help wanted ads." Dr. Sandra Bem, of Pittsburgh, has prepared a penetrating study on the damaging and discouraging effect of these ads.

Even though we are told you can technically go in and apply for a "male-help wanted" job, the attitude of the employer of "Oh, my goodness, did it get in the wrong column; we advertised for a man" is enough to deter most women.

This section could have been more clearly drafted, and personally I would like to see it amended, if it is to serve the purpose for which it is intended.

My attached brief to the U.S. court of appeals, which I am incorporating by reference, will show that the abuses in help wanted advertising by the newspapers are far reaching.

By aiding and abetting the violation of section 704(b) they are depriving women daily of opportunities to even apply for jobs for which they are qualified.

In my opinion this flouting of the clear intent of Congress should be the cause for remedial action. The newspapers are mere paid agents of employers who file these illegal ads, and as agents doing an illegal act, they are equally liable with their principals.

Freedom of the press will be the outcry, but it does not apply in a paid contractual situation.

Mrs. GREEN. Do you think society would allow ads in newspapers, "Jobs wanted, blacks only need apply, or whites only need apply?"

Dr. BOYER. That is a very perfect analogy. If there were ads appearing in a small town in the South saying "help wanted, white," there would be a tremendous outcry.

These ads are appearing everywhere except in New York, where the human relations ordinance forbids such advertising.

It stands out in front of the public that these laws protecting women's employment rights don't mean what they say. It is a signal to everyone. I hate to accuse the newspapers of perpetuating misunderstanding on this matter, but we have clippings from newspapers that are flatly inaccurate as to this lawsuit.

I have one right now in my portfolio where someone has written in and inquired of a newspaper, "aren't these ads being placed illegally?"

The newspaper's reply is that the newspaper is "waiting for the outcome" of this case. Well, the outcome of this case will not change the legal positions of advertisers and the newspapers, because these are covered by section 704(b). Only EEOC's guidelines are being challenged. The substantive issue is not before the court as to compliance.

Mrs. GREEN. Would you make any comment about the Equal Employment Opportunity Commission on enforcement as to their response if an ad were to appear "whites only?"

Dr. BOYER. I don't know what their response would be——

Mrs. GREEN. Have you seen any indications of any activity on their part?

Dr. BOYER. In the ad area, no; I have not. Cases being filed in the advertising area are being filed in the Federal district court, and I must not pretend I know all the answers, because I don't know what has happened behind the scenes.

I do know that one of the lawyers from EEOC has been urging women in public speeches to tackle these ads through the courts.

Mrs. GREEN. How many women are there in the enforcement division of civil rights?

Dr. BOYER. I don't know.

Mrs. GREEN. Maybe we can develop that from other witnesses, on both of those comments.

Will you proceed?

Dr. BOYER. Yes, I urge Congress to correct this iniquitous and wasteful situation through amendment of section 704(b) since action through the courts will be a laborious process and will result in a multiplicity of suits.

The Supreme Court, as late as October 1968, declined to accept an appeal, as the attached brief filed by Marguerite Rawalt will show, in a case of sex discrimination under title VII.

A brief was filed, and it was not accepted at the Supreme Court level, so that action in these cases, and—access to the courts is a very difficult thing at this point.

Within the last week, the report of the President's Task Force on Women's Rights and Responsibilities was released. It had been submitted in December.

It was released by the White House and to make sure that this important document is a part of the record, I am asking now that it be included.

Someone else, with better right, may ask later that it be included, someone on the Commission, however I wish to make sure, so I will ask for inclusion now.

Mrs. GREEN. I will ask unanimous consent that this report be included in the record at this point.

Without objection it is so ordered.

Dr. BOYER. I find there are three areas in this report of the President's Task Force that are exactly congruent with areas of this bill. I would like to take a moment quickly to point these out.

This report urges congressional action in 11 areas concerning women, and it is an excellent report.

In its section 3–A through 3–K, action is urged in the elementary school area. Section 3–B 2 of their report covers teachers under title VII, as does section 805 (b) of the bill here at hand, this Omnibus Post Secondary Education Act.

Section 3–C of the report seems to me to be similar in its intent to section 805 (a), and section 3–F similar to section 805 (d), covering three of these sections very clearly that are now in consideration before us.

Therefore, passage of these portions of the Omnibus Post Secondary Education Act would satisfy the interests of a large segment of our female working population who have been pressing for the release of this report and its implementation.

The recent Women's Bureau Anniversary Plenary Session, this last weekend also approved and urged immediate implementation of this report, which I would especially like to have in the record, because this report is similar in its thrust to these sections of the Omnibus Post Secondary Education Act which I have just enumerated.

We therefore urge that sections 805 (a) through (d) be passed and immediately enacted into law.

In my written presentation, I have taken this up in a bit more detail, but since time is of the essence, I will merely repeat our endorsement of the two previous speakers and our strong endorsement of these sections 805 (a) through (d) which we have analyzed a bit more in our written presentation.

I thank you.

Mrs. GREEN. Thank you very much, Dr. Boyer. Your full written statement will be made a part of the record immediately following your comments.

Dr. BOYER. Thank you and may these be addenda?

Mrs. GREEN. Yes, without objection, the briefs and the report will be made part of the record.

Mrs. GREEN. Commissioner Wilma Scott Heide of the Pennsylvania Human Relations Commission.

We are pleased to have you here today.

Will you proceed?

Commissioner HEIDE. Thank you, Congresswoman Green.

First I support the views of the people who have testified this morning, and I am pleased to be here, especially for the significance of the proposed legislation.

For identification I am Commissioner Wilma Heide of the Pennsylvania Human Relations Commission and also an associate research scientist with the American Institutes for Research in the Behavioral Sciences.

Additionally I am chairman of the board of directors of the National Organization for Women, Inc., NOW. NOW is ably represented by Dr. Ann Scott, our campus coordinating cochairman. It is on my experience as commissioner, and insights as a behavioral scientist that I would like to draw for special attention to the need and potential of certain portions of the proposed legislation.

Although I will focus on specific facts and their implications my remarks recognize a social context of time, circumstance, and growing imperatives.

The context of legislation H.R. 16098, section 805, must be seen in the light of today's needs and foreseen as changes vital to our future.

Laws based on yesterday are anachronisms that deserve to be repealed or amended. There are several compelling imperatives that the proposed legislation recognizes implicity if not explicitly.

Overpopulation and its consequences in the United States, threatens the quality of people and our total environment. Contraceptives, modified migration patterns, coercive family limitation, and other superimposed methodology do not get to the heart of the problem.

Unless women have, from the moment of birth, socialization for, expectations of, and preparation for a viable significant alternative to motherhood as their chief adult occupation, women will continue to want and reproduce too many children instead of producing ideas, art, literature, leadership, inventions, and healthier social relationships.

Motivational change will be necessary no matter how safe, effective, or universally available are any contraceptive devices for women and men.

The second imperative for changed laws and practices is the women's rights liberation movement.

Compared to other social movements of humankind, this may be the most profound social movement the world has ever known. It poses a fundamental challenge to attitudes and frank mythologies about sex caste divisions of labor and the subservient status of women. It demands basic structural changes in all of our social institutions in ways that are affecting every women, man, girl, and boy. It promises the eradication of sexism, the creation of an androgynous society to replace our androcentric culture, and finally a viable democracy to replace male supremacy values.

Our country and people are neither healthy or whole until the full personhood of women is fully realized. Now to be specific about legislation. First, I would advocate that section 805, parts (a), (b), (c), and (d) of H.R. 16098 be adopted as proposed with one exception.

Section 805(d) would remove the exemption of executive, administrative, and professional employees from section 13(a) of the Fair Labor Standards Act of 1938 that requires equal pay for equal work.

I strongly favor that amendment. Additionally, I unequivocally urge an additional amendment that would extend the coverage of the Fair Labor Standards Act, without any exceptions, to every job that can be influenced by Federal legislation.

This means those most in need, women in low-paid jobs would be paid not less than the Federal minimum wage. Even that modest step would leave most service workers improverished but would be a step in the direction of recognizing women are seriously disadvantaged by relegation to service jobs.

Indeed, over 60 percent of the poor children in this country are completely dependent on the earnings of women.

Actually the problems of poverty are the problems of women, their dependent children and older women who have had diminished, if any, paid employment opportunities.

Mrs. GREEN. Could I interrupt you there? I am sure if I used this on the floor I would be challenged by my male colleagues. What is your source for your statement that over 60 percent of poor children are completely dependent on the earnings of women?

Commissioner HEIDE. I got the information I received originally from the past president of NOW, Betty Friedan, when she was testifying before the Republican platform committee.

Mrs. GREEN. That is a very startling statement. Can you find for us the documentation, the original documentation or survey or study that was made?

Commissioner HEIDE. I would be glad to.

Mrs. GREEN. I am suggesting something beyond Betty Friedan's statement.

Commissioner HEIDE. Yes; I understand. The original source, I would be glad to.

[Profs. Joy Osofsky and Harold Feldman, Cornell University, Fall, 1969]

FACT SHEET ON WOMEN

Education.—In the U.S. in 1968, 78% of all high school girls graduated; in 1967, 50% of the girls and 71% of the boys entered college after high school. If the girls entered a woman's college, they probably received an education inferior to that of their brothers attending all-male schools; the 1967–68 Gourman Report, which evaluated academic excellence, rated leading American colleges as follows:[1]

Top 5 Women's Colleges		Top 5 Men's Colleges	
Barnard	520	Princeton (went co-ed in 1969)	789
Smith	520	Yale (went co-ed in 1969)	777
Bryn Mawr	513	Columbia	764
Wellesley	509	Notre Dame	740
Mt. Holyoke	464	Dartmouth	719

Traditionally, more men than women have received college educations, but the gap is widening: in April 1940, 3.7% of women 25 years of age and over and 5.4% of men were college graduates; in March 1967, 7.6% of women and 12.8% of men 25 years of age and over had completed 4 or more years of college.[2] Of college degrees at all levels, women earned the following percent:

Year	B.A.	M.A.	Ph. D.
1930	39.9	40.4	15.4
1940	41.3	38.2	13.0
1950	24.0	29.2	9.6
1966	40.4	33.8	11.6

In 36 years, women have not progressed. In fact, they now receive a smaller percent of master's and doctor's degrees than they did in 1930.

Employment.—The more education women have, the more likely they are to seek jobs. Only 24% of women with an 8th-grade education were in the labor force full-time in 1968, compared with 47% of women high school graduates, 54% of college graduates, and 71% (rising to 82% for those over 40 years of age) of women with 5 or more years of higher education.

Myth: It doesn't pay to train or promote a women because she will marry and leave and the investment will be wasted.

But 60% of all women in the labor force are married, 20% are widowed. separated or divorced, and the remainder are single women, mainly young ones.[3] Women comprise ⅓ of the labor force, and many continue working during child-bearing years. ⅓ of all mothers work, including 23% of mothers with husbands and children under 6 years of age, and 43% with children aged 6–17.[4] *Work-life*—Of all women at work at age 35, the single woman can expect, on the average, to be on the job another 31 years, about 2½ years more than the average man of 35. Those who are widowed, separated or divorced can anticipate another 28 years of work, about ½ a year less than the average man of 35. Married

---

[1] The Gourman Report is published by the Continuing Education Institution, cited in National Organization for Women, *Token Learning*, p. 6.

[2] Wage and Labor Standards Administration, U.S. Department of Labor, "Trends in Educational Attainment of Women," April, 1968.

[3] Women's Bureau, Wage and Labor Standards Administration, U.S. Department of Labor, "Sex Discrimination in Employment Practices," Sept. 19, 1968.

[4] Manpower Administration, U.S. Department of Labor, "Womanpower Policies for the 1970's."

women with husbands and children have an average worklife expectation at 35 of 24 years. *Job mobility*—While women sometimes leave jobs for pregnancy and childrearing, a 20-year-old man in 1961 could expect to make about 7 job changes in his life. A Department of Labor study shows that in the survey year 11% of the men, but only 8.6% of the women, changed jobs one or more times.[5]

Myth: Women are too expensive to hire—they are absent so often because of illness.

But a 1968 Public Health survey shows that men, on the average, lost 5.4 days during the survey year because of illness or injury, while women lost 5.3.[6]

Occupationally, women are relatively more disadvantaged today than they were 30 years ago. In 1940, women held 45% of all professional and technical jobs but in 1967, they held 37%; in 1940, women held 40% of all service (less-skilled) jobs while in 1967 they held 55%.[7] Despite their 37% share of all professional and technical jobs, women hold a disproportionately small share of positions in leading professions.

Women by occupation as percent of total workers in field:

	Percent		*Percent*
Librarian	80	Social scientist	10
Social worker	60	Scientist	8
Interior design	50	Physician	7
Newspaper reporter	34	Chemist	5
Recreation worker	33	Lawyer	3
Statistician	33	Physicist	3
Personnel worker	25	Engineer	1
Commercial artist	25	Architect	1
Mathematician	10	Federal judge	1

The proportion of women in the leading professions has hardly increased in the past 60 years. In 1967, only 22% of the faculty and other professional staff in institutions of higher learning were women, but in 1940, 28% were women; in 1930, 37%; in 1920, 26% and in 1910, 20%—only slightly less than the proportion today. The dentistry profession, which had 3.1% women in 1910, had 2.1% in 1960. In other countries, women seem to fare better: 74% of the doctors in the Soviet Union are women, as opposed to only 7% here[8] and in Sweden, 6.1% of the lawyers, 6.7% of the doctors and 24.4% of the dentists are women.[9]

Women are underutilized in relation to their educational achievement. In March, 1966, 7% of employed women who had completed 5 or more years of higher education were working as service workers (including private household), operatives, sales or clerical workers. 19% of employed women with 4 years of college were working in these occupations, as were ⅔ of those women who had completed 1 to 3 years of college.[10]

Women are also underpaid. The National Management Association found in a survey that ⅓ of the firms they checked paid women $5 to $15 a week less than men for the same jobs and the same experience.[11] The median income in 1965 for white men was $6704, for nonwhite men, $4277; for white women, $3991, and for nonwhite women, $2816.[12] In 1966, more than ⅔ of all women working in full-time year-round jobs had incomes of under $5000, while fewer than ¼ of all men working year-round and full-time were in this income bracket; 0.7% of women working earned $10,000 or more, while the proportion of men was almost 20 times higher.[13] The gap between men's and women's incomes is widening; in 1955, the median wage of women working full-time year-round was 64% that of men; in 1967, it was down to 60%.[14]

Women are unemployed more than men: in 1966, the unemployment rate for nonwhite women was 6.6%; for nonwhite men, 4.9%; for white women, 3.3%; for white men, 2.2%.[15]

Myth: Women are pin money workers whose position or pay does not matter very much and so they can afford unemployment.

---

[5] "Sex Discrimination," *ibid.*
[6] *Ibid.*
[7] Women's Bureau, U.S. Department of Labor, "Underutilization of Women Workers," August, 1967.
[8] Richard E. Farson, "The Rage of Women," *Look*, Dec. 16, 1969.
[9] J. Rossel, "Women in Sweden," *Sweden Today*.
[10] "Underutilization", *Ibid.*
[11] Thomas J. Fleming, "Sex and Civil Rights," *This Week*, March 19, 1967.
[12] "Underutilization, *ibid.*
[13] "Sex Discrimination", *ibid.*
[14] "Underutilization", *ibid.*
[15] *Ibid.*

But, the 40% of working women who are single, widowed, separated or divorced must work to support themselves. And of the 16 million married women who work, 1/6 have husbands earning less than $3000 a year, and 1/5 have husbands earning between $3000 and $5000 a year. Six-tenths of all families in which wives work would have incomes of less than $7000 a year without the wives' earnings, and, states Mary D. Keyserling, Director of the Women's Bureau under President Johnson, "we today think of a family income of $7000 as not quite enough to assure a modestly adequate standard of living." [16]

We see the effects of low status, low wages and high unemployment in poverty. 19% of white families headed by a woman are poor, while of those headed by a man, 7% are poor; 53% of nonwhite families headed by a woman are poor, while when a man is head, the figure drops to 29%.[17]

Law.—In some cases, the law prevents women from earning as much as men by what is termed "protective legislation". As of January, 1965, 21 states limit women to a 48-hour week, 21 states limit or prohibit night work, and 12 states have limits on weight lifting (some as low as 25 pounds).[18] In 1965, 35 states (and the District of Columbia) refused to pay unemployment compensation to pregnant women.

Some state laws further differentiate between men and women. In Alabama, Mississippi, and South Carolina, women are not allowed to serve on juries, and in 26 states, women are able to claim exemptions from jury service unavailable to men.[19] Four states—California, Florida, Nevada and Pennsylvania—require court approval for a wife to engage in independent business.[20] Only four states recognize a woman's right to acquire her own domicile without limitation. 19 states permit a married woman to acquire her own domicile for the purpose of voting, 6 for election to public office, 5 for jury service, and 7 for taxation purposes.[21] While most states provide that the natural guardianship of a minor child is vested equally in both parents, 6 states—Alaska, Georgia, Louisiana, North Carolina, Oklahoma and Texas—provide by statute that the father is the preferred natural guardian of a minor child.[22]

Politics and power.—Not only do women exercise the vote less than men, both in the proportion of adults who register and the proportion of registrants voting,[23] but they also hold political office in barely token proportions. Currently, there is one woman senator in Washington; since women got the vote, there have been only 10. And as of December, 1969, of more than 300 Administration posts filled by President Nixon, only 13 have gone to women, and 3 of those are White House secretaries.[24]

Although women have little political power, they are said to "control the purse strings", to have great economic influence. BUT, a New York Stock Exchange study shows that while in 1968 there were 12,187,000 women share holders and 11,710,000 men, three out of four orders were placed by men.[25] Men, it appears, make the decisions.

The university.—Although many women go into teaching, few are found at the college or university level, and fewer have professional rank. In a study of academic women, Dr. Jessie Bernard notes that in 1960, 9.4% of the faculty at 20 leading universities were women, comprising 16.1% of the Instructors, 10.4% of the Assistant Professors, 10.1% of the Associate Professors, and only 4.7% of the Full Professors. Women represented 2.0% of the faculty in the Physical Sciences, 6.8% in the Biological Sciences, 4.5% in the Social Sciences, 9.9% in the Humanities, 23.8% in Education, and 86.4% in Home Economics.[26] Cornell University parallels the national situation, reports J. Farley in Development Sociology. Of 1,395 members of Cornell's faculty (all colleges) of professional rank, only 102—or 7%—are women, and only 21 women are full professors. Of the 102 faculty members of professional rank who are women, 3% are full professors, 10% are associate professors, 11% are assistant professors. 51% of all Lecturers and Instructors are women. There is only 1 woman full professor in the College of Arts and Sciences, 2 in Hotel, and none in Law, Engineering, or Business and Public Administration.

[16] "Sex Discrimination", p. 22.
[17] "Underutilization", *ibid.*
[18] M. Mead and F. B. Kaplan, ed., *American Women—A Report of the President's Commission on the Status of Women,* (New York : Charles Scribner's Sons), table 7.
[19] *Ibid.*
[20] *Ibid.*
[21] *Ibid.* p. 156.
[22] *Ibid.* p. 157.
[23] *Ibid.* p. 72.
[24] Farson, "Rage", *ibid.*
[25] Gerald M. Loeb, "Women Share Owners Top Men", Syracuse *Herald Journal,* July 14, 1968.
[26] Jessie Bernard, *Academic Women* (Cleveland : World, 1966), pp. 190–1.

What do women do as professors? A study cited by Bernard rates academic productivity—the number of papers read at professional meetings, the number of articles, books and technical reports written : [27]

	Percent who are highly productive	
	Women	Men
Age group:		
Under 40	19	30
41 to 50	39	60
Over 50	44	68

In discussing bioscientists, Bernard notes that while 94.3% of the men and 91% of the women belong to professional societies, 89.0% of the men attend professional meetings as opposed to 77% of the women. While 72.6% of the men visit other laboratories, 55% of the women do. However, 12% of the women as opposed to 8.9% of the men found discussion to be the prime source of "a recent research idea," and 46% of the women as opposed to 43.3% of the men found discussion with colleagues in the laboratory to be a source of information.[28]

NOTE.—Special appreciation is extended to Deborah Spitz, who compiled and arranged these statistics.

Commissioner HEIDE. Indeed the older the population of students and the greater the prestige of the profession, the greater is the predominance of men and the lesser the opportunity for women.

Women as administrators of higher education are virtually non-existent. Now this picture produces several untoward effects.

It suggests and actually demonstrates to children that the teaching of younger children is for women but that leadership in education and training of older youth and adults is for men.

We don't know precisely how much this contributes to second-class self-images and self-expectancies of girls and women and contributes to untrue male supremacy notions of boys and men.

Female intellectual inferiority is still implied and tragically believed by some females as well as males although the idea has no visible means of support.

Actually, at Yale, which only recently admitted women to undergraduate schools Yale women are outdoing men by every measure of academic achievement as reported in the forthcoming fortnightly newsletter, "Women, the Majority Report."

This states that Yale University has released a study of undergraduate marks wherein 27.5 percent of the women and 22.9 percent of the men received honors.

This is true in spite of the predominance of men in a still male-oriented, male-administered institution within an androcentric culture.

Exclusion of the exemption of educational institutions from coverage of title VII of the 1964 Civil Rights Act promises more role models of women in leadership roles, and men and women in a diversity of roles that are individually not sex determined, and it is with enthusiasm that one must view the potential of egalitarian educational institutions to demythologize the sex role caste stereotyping in educational materials, especially textbooks.

The educator role and student role in terms of compatible scheduling is a particularly viable model of the combination of the occupational parental role for women and men.

Parenthood and career need not be mutually exclusive choices for

[27] *Ibid.*, table 10/1.
[28] *Ibid.*, table D/5.

men or women when we need the talents of and options for both parents within and outside the home.

It is the responsibility of the Federal Government to act when States have not done so. Only a couple States have or currently contemplate any prohibition of sex discrimination in educational institutions so the Equal Employment Opportunity Commission (EEOC) needs jurisdiction.

In this regard, the need of the EEOC itself for enforcement powers is relevant here and I refer you to my testimony before the Senate Subcommittee on Labor dated September 10, 1969 for a statement on the urgency of the agency's mandate.

(The testimony referred to is appended to this testimony.)

Finally I want to focus especially on the potential of amending section 104 of the 1957 Civil Rights Act as proposed in section 805(c) of H.R. 16098 so that discrimination based on sex will be the subject of study and research by the U.S. Civil Service Commission. I want to emphasize first the reasons and then most importantly the potential of the research on sexism.

The price of sex bias is actually greater even than the tragic price of race bias in purely quantitative terms.

The qualitative psychological and sociological consequences figuratively boggle the mind and literally escape precise numerical measurement both in individual and societal terms even if seen in all its dimensions.

Present studies by other agencies require a teasing out of the relevant differentials by sex. For instance, the median earnings of white men employed year round full time is $7,396, of black men, $4,777, of white women, $4,279, of black women, $3,195.

Women with some college education, both white and black earn less than black men with 8 years of elementary education. Women are the economic heads of 1,723,000 impoverished families, and black males are the economic heads of 820,000 poor families.

One-fourth of all families economically headed by white women, more than one-half of all black families economically headed by black females are in poverty; 7 percent of those families economically headed by white males are impoverished.

The unemployment rate is higher among girls than among boys, among women than men whether black or white, and even these figures do not include women on welfare who like other women want to be employed for pay.

Diminished opportunity and absence of child care facilities precludes their actually bothering to seek work and only those actually unsuccessfully seeking work are included in the revealing figures.

The unrest, resentment and sheer outrage of aware women cannot forever be ignored.

For instance from 39 to 50 percent of these who rebelled in Detroit, Watts, and elsewhere were women. The recent significant Golden Jubilee Conference sponsored by the U.S. Labor Department's Women's Bureau was attended by women leaders throughout the country with a theme of "American Women at the Crossroads: Directions for the Future."

The President of the United States could not even be present to greet this great gathering of serious American women in the White House.

The women were relegated to a punch and cookie party on the White House lawn to be greeted by Mrs. Nixon, forever gracious, but neither now nor forever representative of women who have our own identity and personhood independent of the men in our lives.

Responsible women, representing millions of others either boycotted that reception in barely controlled outrage, actively considered a White House sit-in including handcuffing ourselves to some stable accoutrement, or simply refused the charades of the reception line.

Others were apparently grateful for even token recognition, but expressed keen disappointment at the President's continued cavalier ghettoizing the priority of the concerns of women as people.

Indeed, only the respect for the office of the President and of the White House as the symbol of authority prevented an activist dramatization of women's fury. Responsible people expect responsible leadership.

The President saw nonvoting Boy Scouts the day before.

The Girl Scouts were only one of some hundreds of organizations represented at this important conference.

Now allow me to list without elaboration additional reasons for the U.S. Civil Rights Commission to study sex discrimination.

The Commission's work would recognize, legitimize, and document the problem and potential solutions in ways current voluntary groups, victimized by sex discrimination can't marshal very easily.

It could provide the data base and the mandate to educate the public, hopefully in innovative ways, about the reality and seriousness of de facto patterns of sex discrimination whatsoever the causes.

The facts of institutional sex bias are not generally known but however blatant or subtle must be studied and revealed beginning with the U.S. Civil Rights Commission itself.

Even agencies of Government in past and current studies often obscure the differential data on men and women by only detailing race data, by studying only males, or by subsuming the particular data on women by combining information on women and men.

The U.S. Commission on Civil Rights' insight and understanding about sex role stereotyping would have to be very sensitive and knowledgeable. It would have to understand that sex is not a bona fide occupational qualification (BFOQ) for over 99 percent of jobs. Their conceptionalization needs to be very sophisticated and minus the usual stereotyped orientation.

It would go like this: That the only job for which no woman can or could be qualified is sperm donor.

The only job or jobs for which no man is or can be qualified would be human incubator or wet nurse, period.

The more sophisticated problem of research premises, design, methodology, and interpretive analyses requires some insightful attention to sexism as it would influence the work of the Commission. The very questions which research asks often reflect researcher bias, for example, the research always asks the women why she works and the man is never asked. Any research that accepts the status quo as the given, the "natural," and full potential introduces a systematic bias into the research at this point in time.

Indeed, any assumption that any behavior is either innately "feminine" or "masculine" contaminates research. Any assumption about appropriate role behavior based on sex beyond the purely biological is already biased.

Aside from the pervasive and promiscuous bias among researchers in terms of sex role stereotyping in expectations and analyses is the failure to accurately distinguish between sexual behavior and sex role behavior.

Moving up the phylogenetic ladder, sexual behaviors themselves become less stereotyped and more a product of learning. On the other hand, sex role behaviors are entirely learned and dependent on cultural conditioning and societal expectations.

A role is an ascribed status not an inherent characteristic.

One trusts the sophisticated attention of the Commission to sex discrimination would extinguish questions like the following which are not research questions.

If women and men were given the same opportunities and incentives would their accomplishments differ?

As with other minority groups, to ask that question in a time when this culture is so slanted toward men with women unprepared (not unable) for achievement is to ignore, with insensitivity the real present disadvantages to personhood of being brought up female in our culture.

As a matter of fact, one real and immediate value to the Commission's study of and publicity about sex discrimination would be to qualify more women for training and education programs for the disadvantaged under various manpower training projects. In fact it might prompt a change in name from manpower to personnel or human resources and remove one more way our language and thus our thought excludes women as over one-half of our adult population.

The proposed legislation is needed specifically to remove the barriers to development and recognition of the talents of women. Its contributions to the real needs of men cannot be ignored. The often fragile male ego must be strengthened to accept the experience and reality of women as generally equal persons often with talents superior to men.

The traditional male-oriented value system that sanctions violence as the final assertion of mankind, synonymous with nationhood, must be eradicated as dysfunctional and anachronistic.

There are alternatives to the adversary system of human relations. Winning a game or a war or even initiating either is not so laudable as attention to superbowls and patriotism so narrowly conceived and defined mandates.

Indeed national honor on analysis becomes a euphemism for perpetuation of chauvinism.

The proposed legislation in section 805 of H.R. 16098 is no panacea but offers significant potential to facilitate the emergence of the voice and authentic image of women as people.

The Nation and males need that voice and reality. The hand that has rocked the cradle must now rock the boat and guide the ship of state in significant numbers and healthier ways.

The only pertinent questions are: Are men really brave enough to care and do women care enough to bravely assert these imperatives?

As responsible legislators, you can do no less than effect this legislation in the national interest.

I would respectfully request to add some additional statements for the record on H.R. 16098, section 805, and I thank you very kindly for the opportunity to testify and for your attention.

Mrs. GREEN. Without any objection, the additional statements will be made part of the record.

Mrs. GREEN. I agree with you, Commissioner Heide. I think no woman who wants to go into a career or profession can grow to maturity without being keenly aware of the discrimination based on sex.

Our next witness before the committee is Dr. Ann Scott, of the State University of New York at Buffalo representing the National Organization of Women, NOW.

Dr. Scott, we welcome you also.

Dr. SCOTT. Thank you, Madam Chairman, and members of the committee.

My name is Dr. Ann Scott. I am a member of the National Organization of Women (NOW), Chairman of NOW's Campus Coordinating Committee and member of its Federal Compliance Committee.

I am also a member of the English faculty of the State University of New York at Buffalo (SUNY/Buffalo, or SUNY/B). I am here today, however, to speak to you as an individual and as a member of NOW in behalf of section 805 of H.R. 16098.

I agree with everything said here today, and I would like to add one item on the help wanted ads.

When President Nixon issued the task force report he also issued the sex discrimination guidelines which state that no Federal contract for work can put advertising in segregated columns for men and women.

Because of the nature of the OFCC it is possible to file a class action complaint against any employer with a Federal contract with $50,000 or 50 employees or over who does so and this is a very useful tool.

I mention this, because that is one tool, and seems to be the only legislative tool which women now have when they are anxious to end discrimination at universities.

Mrs. GREEN. Without objection, Dr. Scott, that will be made part of the record at this point and we will incorporate it with your testimony.

Dr. SCOTT. Thank you, Madam Chairman.

(The document referred to follows:)

TITLE 41—PUBLIC CONTRACTS AND PROPERTY MANAGEMENT

CHAPTER 60—OFFICE OF FEDERAL CONTRACT COMPLIANCE; EQUAL EMPLOYMENT OPPORTUNITY; DEPARTMENT OF LABOR

PART 60–20—SEX DISCRIMINATION GUIDELINES

On January 17, 1969, proposed guidelines were published at 34 F.R. 758 to amend Chapter 60 of Title 41 of the Code of Federal Regulations by adding a new Part 60–20. Persons interested were given an opportunity to file written data, views or argument concerning the proposals. Also, public hearings were held on August 4, 5, and 6, to receive oral presentations from interested persons.

Having considered all relevant material, 41 CFR Chapter 60 is hereby amended by adding a new Part 60–20 to read as follows:

PART 60–20—SEX DISCRIMINATION GUIDELINES

Sec.
60–20.1 Title and Purpose.
60–20.2 Recruitment and Advertisement.
60–20.3 Job Policies and Practices.
60–20.4 Seniority Systems.
60–20.5 Discriminatory Wages.

60–20.6 Affirmative Action.

60–20.7 Effective Date.

AUTHORITY: The provisions of this Part 60–20 issued Under Sec. 201, E.O. 11246, 30 F.R. 12319, and E.O. 11375, 32 F.R. 14303.

60–20.1 Title and Purpose.

The purpose of the provisions in this part is to set forth the interpretations and guidelines of the Office of Federal Contract Compliance regarding the implementation of Executive Order 11375 for the promotion and insuring of equal opportunities for all persons employed or seeking employment with Government contractors and subcontractors or with contractors and subcontractors performing under Federally-assisted construction contracts, without regard to sex. Experience has indicated that special problems related to the implementation of Executive Order 11375 require a definitive treatment beyond the terms of the Order itself. These interpretations are to be read in connection with existing regulations, set forth in 41 CFR Chapter 60, Part 1.

60–20.2 Recruitment and Advertisement.

(a) Employers engaged in recruiting activity must recruit employees of both sexes for all jobs unless sex is a bona fide occupational qualification.

(b) Advertisement in newspapers and other media for employment must not express a sex preference unless sex is a bona fide occupational qualification for the job. The placement of an advertisement in columns headed "Male" or "Female" will be considered an expression of a preference, limitation, specification or discrimination based on sex.

60–20.3 Job Policies and Practices.

(a) Written personnel policies relating to this subject area must expressly indicate that there shall be no discrimination against employees on account of sex. If the employer deals with a bargaining representative for his employees and there is a written agreement on conditions of employment, such agreement shall not be inconsistent with these guidelines.

(b) Employees of both sexes shall have an equal opportunity to any available job that he or she is qualified to perform, unless sex is a bona fide occupational qualification. (Note: In most Government contract work there are only limited instances where valid reasons can be expected to exist which would justify the exclusion of all men or all women from any given job.)

(c) The employer must not make any distinction based upon sex in employment opportunities, wages, hours, or other conditions of employment. In the area of employer contributions for insurance, pensions, welfare programs and other similar "fringe benefits" the employer will not be considered to have violated these guidelines if his contributions are the same for men and women or if the resulting benefits are equal.

(d) Any distinction between married and unmarried persons of one sex that is not made between married and unmarried persons of the opposite sex will be considered to be a distinction made on the basis of sex. Similarly, an employer must not deny employment to women with young children unless it has the same exclusionary policies for men; or terminate an employee of one sex in a particular job classification upon reaching a certain age unless the same rule is applicable to members of the opposite sex.

(e) The employer's policies and practices must assure appropriate physical facilities to both sexes. The employer may not refuse to hire men or women, or deny men or women a particular job because there are no restroom or associated facilities, unless the employer is able to show that the construction of the facilities would be unreasonable for such reasons as excessive expense or lack of space.

(f) An employer must not deny a female employee the right to any job that she is qualified to perform in reliance upon a State "protective" law. For example, such laws include those which prohibit women from performing in certain types of occupations (e.g., a bartender or a core-maker); from working at jobs requiring more than a certain number of hours; and from working at jobs that require lifting or carrying more than designated weights.

Such legislation was intended to be beneficial, but, instead, has been found to result in restricting employment opportunities for men and/or women. Accordingly, it cannot be used as a basis for denying employment or for establishing sex as a bona fide occupational qualification for the job.

(g) Women shall not be penalized in their conditions of employment because they require time away from work on account of childbearing. When, under the employer's leave policy the female employee would qualify for leave, then childbearing must be considered by the employer to be a justification for leave of absence for female employees for a reasonable period of time. For example, if the female employee meets the equally applied minimum length of service requirements for leave time, she must be granted a reasonable leave on account of childbearing. The conditions applicable to her leave (other than the length thereof) and to her return to employment shall be in accordance with the employer's leave policy.

If the employer has no leave policy, childbearing must be considered by the employer to be a justification for a leave of absence for a female employee for a reasonable period of time. Following childbirth, and upon signifying her intent to return within a reasonable time, such female employee shall be reinstated to her original job or to a position of like status and pay, without loss of service credits.

(h) The employer must not specify any differences for male and female employees on the basis of sex in either mandatory or optional retirement age.

(i) Nothing in these guidelines shall be interpreted to mean that differences in capabilities for job assignments do not exist among individuals and that such distinctions may not be recognized by the employer in making specific assignments. The purpose of these guidelines is to insure that such distinctions are not based upon sex.

60–20.4 Seniority system.

Where they exist, seniority lines and lists must not be based solely upon sex. Where such a separation has existed, the employer must eliminate this distinction.

60–20.5 Discriminatory wages.

(a) The employer's wages schedules must not be related to or based on the sex of the employees. (Note. The more obvious cases of discrimination exist where employees of different sexes are paid different wages on jobs that require substantially equal skill, effort and responsibility and are performed under similar working conditions.)

(b) The employer may not discriminatorily restrict one sex to certain job classifications. In such a situation, the employer must take steps to make jobs available to all qualified employees in all classifications without regard to sex. (Example: An electrical manufacturing company may have a production division with three functional units: one (assembly), all female; another (wiring), all male; and a third (circuit boards), also all male. The highest wage attainable in the assembly unit is considerably less than that in the circuit board and wiring units. In such a case the employer must take steps to provide qualified female employees opportunity for placement in job openings in the other two units.)

(c) To avoid overlapping and conflicting administration the Director will consult with the Administrator of the Wage and Hour Administration before issuing an opinion on any matter covered by both the Equal Pay Act and Executive Order 11246, as amended by Executive Order 11375.

60–20.6 Affirmative action.

(a) The employer shall take affirmative action to recruit women to apply for those jobs where they have been previously excluded. (Note. This can be done by various methods. Examples include: (1) including in itineraries of recruiting trips women's colleges where graduates with skills desired by the employer can be found, and female students of co-educational institutions and (2) designing advertisements to indicate that women will be considered equally with men for jobs.)

(b) Women have not been typically found in significant numbers in management. In many companies management trainee programs are one of the ladders to management positions. Traditionally, few, if any, women have been admitted into these programs. An important element of affirmative action shall be a commitment to include women candidates in such programs.

(c) Distinctions based on sex may not be made in other training programs. Both sexes should have equal access to all training programs and affirmative action programs should require a demonstration by the employer that such access has been provided.

60–20.7 Effective date.

This part is effective June 9, 1970. Signed at Washington, D.C. this 2nd day of June, 1970.

GEORGE P. SHULTZ,
Secretary of Labor.
JOHN L. WILKS,
Director, Office of Federal Contract Compliance.

Dr. Scott. I will proceed.

Although my survey is limited to the one university, I find from my experience as chairman of NOW's campus committee that my study faithfully reflects the typical conditions under which women labor and learn throughout the United States.

Therefore when I speak of my own university, it is by way of illustration of general conditions, and not for the purpose of indicting the SUNY-Buffalo for what are, after all, standard practices.

It also reflects the way women labor in industry.

When I speak of our university, it is not to indict them. I have added an affirmative action program to end discrimination against women that has been drawn up in connection with the OFCC guidelines.

It is the only affirmative action program so drawn, as far as I know, in the United States, though affirmative action programs to end discrimination against women are required of any Federal contractor as Mrs. Green mentioned in her remarks in quoting the remarks from Congresswoman Griffiths.

You will hear later in these hearings some very striking testimony from Dr. Bernice Sandler, who has been using the Office of Federal Contract Compliance to bring compliance complaints against over 100 universities in this country for discrimination against women.

She has filed on the entire system of California and Florida, and she will tell you about these actions.

I would like to return to Buffalo because I know it the best, and it is very typical and I can point out some practices at the State University at Buffalo which would come under the jurisdiction of the OFCC if the legislation were extended.

The State University of New York is a large one, because it is the largest of all the State universities systems in the entire world. It has 67 campuses, something which is not very well known. It has 67 campuses and an astronomical budget. It is tax supported, and like all tax-supported education it is dedicated to equal educational opportunity for all.

Since 1965, Buffalo has pioneered in some of the most innovative programs under Martin Meyerson in the country with regard to minority education, and yet I discover that the great university system discriminates against half the population of the State it serves by not offering women the equality they pay for through their taxes; that this discrimination is by oversight, and not by design, makes it no less effective.

Mrs. Green. Would you agree that because women have not been in policymaking positions, because women have not been represented in State legislatures and in the National Congress and in administrative positions that a lot of the discrimination is really something that men simply are not aware of?

They go blithely about in a man's world, and it is never brought to their attention?

Dr. Scott. I can agree with that. We find it in the universities, just as we do in the legislative and governmental structure of the United States, where I think one representative once said that there are five times as many whooping cranes in America as there are women in the Congress of the United States.

The number of women in Congress is going down as dramatically as the number of whooping cranes.

I think you see this in examining Federal income tax laws where the single woman has historically paid a much higher rate; in the differences in social security benefits for men and women.

Mrs. GREEN. There is a difference in the way benefits are figured for beneficiaries, the survivors, of a woman Member of Congress and the benefits to a survivor of a male Member of Congress. I think the fact that there have not been women on the committees drawing up the legislation is part of the answer.

It has just never been called to their attention, and they go on assuming that it has always been this way, so that is the way it should be.

Dr. SCOTT. I am glad you brought this out because although I don't refer to this directly in my testimony or report, the benefit structure at most universities, I believe, and certainly the State University of Buffalo is so organized that women are separated in the actuarial tables, and statistics for them are very different. This is not true of other minorities. Blacks are not separated in actuarial tables, although the statistics would be strikingly different for blacks than they would be for women.

As a result, women pay more in fringe benefits and receive less. I believe in the entire insurance picture this is the truth, one truth which is very difficult to explain and therefore does not receive much attention.

At times this is by official policy, as you have heard in the University of North Carolina which says in its publications this year that women must be more qualified than men, and this is a State institution.

On the other hand, it can also be policies which are unwritten and therefore very difficult to combat. For instance, in graduate school, the admissions are often determined by the department which may have an unwritten policy but one which everybody knows about, of course, that only so many women are allowed to enter.

This is particularly true, I believe, in male-oriented fields, in medicine, in law, engineering, and business administration. It is not something we can prove, but it is something we can show to exist as a pattern.

For instance, at the graduate school of business management at the University of Buffalo, there are over 450 graduate students.

One is a woman. She is a black and I think she gets counted twice when the statistics come up.

Our university has no official quotas for the admission of women, because in the freshman class women slightly outnumber men.

Unlike Clemson, the University of Buffalo does not reserve many scholarships for "deserving male only"; unlike the University of Maryland, it no longer refers women students to waitresses jobs.

I have one student who grew up on a farm and is an expert tractor operator and was anxious to operate a bulldozer, but she can't get herself referred to a job to even enable her to do this, and earn about four times as much as she could as a waitress.

Yet in spite of no conscious policy to discourage we find on the campus a progressive evaporation of women as we climb the ladder. This is merely a carbon copy of patterns in the United States.

While women comprise 14 percent of the faculty, they are only 5 percent of the full professors and these will bear out the figures that you heard today. In none of the seven faculties in which the University of Buffalo is divided is the number of women even equal to the number of men, either among teachers or graduate students.

Out of 43 departments, schools and faculties, 17 have no women faculty and 25 have no tenured women at all. Even the social sciences which include those disciplines we would suppose to be professionally concerned with social change and minority problems reveal a significantly lower percentage, that is 10 percent of faculty women, than the university as a whole.

Even in the school of social welfare, which is traditionally a woman's profession, faculty men outnumber faculty women 23 to 15, and of course the chairman of the department is a man.

The faculty of arts and letters, which includes many of the disciplines in which women tend to concentrate, has at present not a single woman as a full professor, in spite of the fact that it is the second largest faculty in the entire university.

On the other hand, arts and letters exhibits a startling disparity between faculty and graduate students ratios of men to women. In each of the departments, therefore, there is a very considerably higher percentage of women graduate students than of women faculty members.

This points up a highly suggestive pattern, and I believe the testimony you will hear will show that this is a general practice. There are almost always more women as graduate students than there are in faculties.

What does this mean when we apply this nationwide?

In department after department, the percentages of women graduate students are higher than the percentages of women faculty.

Of the 17 departments with no women faculty, 14 have anywhere from 14 to 18 percent women graduate students.

In department after department overwhelmingly male faculty are earning their living out of what has been referred to, very unkindly I am sure, as the pimping system. That is, by training women for professions in which they are unwilling to hire women as colleagues and equals. What do these women do? They drop out. What else can they do?

A situation like the history departments, for instance, where 24 percent of the graduate students are women, but no woman is on the faculty, strongly indicates underutilization of women. That is, women professionally trained are available now in the working pool, but are not hired. Among the faculty, generally, we find that women comprise 20 percent of the assistant professors, 17 percent of the associate professors, but only 5 percent of the full professors. Elsewhere in the university women are concentrated in the lowest ranking jobs with the least security and are neither hired nor promoted according to availability.

I would like to discuss a series of practices by which the university restricts itself from considering available women. First of these is the nepotism rule. The nepotism rule means that a university or a department, as a matter of policy, will not hire both halves of a married couple. It is also extended to mean they will not hire their nephews or brothers and sisters, but where it applies in an overwhelming number of cases is in the matter of hiring husbands and wives in the same family.

Almost every professional women's organization has gone on record against the nepotism rule. While it applies to men also—if a woman is working in a faculty and her husband applies for a job, the nepotism rule can be invoked there, but I would say in maybe 1 out of 250 cases is it ever invoked against a man.

It has recently been called—it is the official policy of the State University of New York and the name has been changed, because nepotism has become a bad word, to the favoritism rule.

This sounds more like a sultan's harem to me than hiring. We have heard arguments that it works against men as well as women, that it is a dead letter, and, that it will prevent a hypothetical department chairman and a hypothetical college from hiring hypothetical students or relatives to create a hypothetical voting block.

Or we hear also that it provides a social covenience for a chairman reluctant to turn down one of a couple. But, making the name does not change the rule, and dead letter or no, because we do have couples serving in these same departments by dispensation from above. The nepotism rule was instituted in the 1930's against the hiring of wives, and it remains to penalize women.

Since it is acceptable for husbands to put their careers first, but not for wives, the advantage is almost entirely with the husband. Thus, the many academic women who marry academic men, many girls who marry their professors, the many women who are graduating getting their Ph. D.'s marry a college professor, themselves have a Ph. D. are prevented from working in the university. Their opportunities of combining both career and marriage at what may be the best or only university in the area are denied by the nepotism rule.

For husband and wife teams, particularly in the sciences, and we can think of the Curies as a very good example, having a nepotism on the books can discourage qualified couples from applying. The Curies would not be eligible at the State University system of New York. There is a no-inbred hiring policy. That means the university won't hire its own graduates. Now there were originally very good reasons for this when departments were small, but I do not believe that they hold true any more.

Women who marry faculty men and move to universities where there their husbands have been hired may want to start or complete their graduate studies. On being awarded their degrees, however, they find the university will not hire them. This is also true of a growing number of graduate students who marry faculty members.

The policy also discriminates against women who want to turn to graduate studies married to men who are already established in the community because their husbands cannot or will not move. These women are discouraged because no university job will be open to them, even if they do earn their degrees.

Finally, the no-inbred hiring rule discourages women from coming back to degrees at all, because there seems to be no way of using long and expensive training.

I believe that under title VII if the educational exemption were removed that this would no longer be possible. This constitutes a selection system which seems to me to be on the face of it invalid. The no-inbred hiring policy was established and accepted in an era of academic life different from today, mostly during the depression. Universities and faculties were smaller, there was much less movement from campus to campus, and so forth.

Today's universities, however, need no such discriminatory restrictions. It is in the university's best interests to include all applicants including its own, and to choose from the widest field possible.

The no-inbred hiring policy is by extension also true in terms of graduate students. Many universities will not take a graduate student, their own BA's, into their graduate programs. This works a very strong discrimination against girl graduate students, since in the academic professions graduate work and graduate study constitute what we might think of as apprenticeship programs. This is very unfair discrimination, and I would like it to be considered that possibly under the provisions of title VII, referring to apprenticeship programs, this could be considered as a discriminatory measure.

Mrs. Green. Is this different for women than for men?

Dr. Scott. No, it is not, but what happens is that it is often much harder for a girl to move than it is for a man. It is also because many departments have unwritten quota systems or written quota systems about giving girls—about entering them into the graduate programs, or about giving them scholarships. It works a hardship and——

Mrs. Green. Is there any current information on the quota system in medical schools, law schools, and graduate schools for women and men?

Dr. Scott. There is not, to my knowledge, information that has to do exactly with this, partly because universities do not keep information segregated by sex.

One of my great problems in compiling this report was that there was very little information available. I had to send a questionnaire out to every single department and browbeat the secretary until she filled it out before I could get the information.

Among the information that does not exist, and partly because it has not been thought worthy of recording, are the records comparing the number of men to women receiving scholasrhips or loan assistance and they do not keep it. I was told the record even of the graduate degrees awarded by our university are not broken down by sex.

Mrs. Green. Why shouldn't the Office of Education have this?

Dr. Scott. It should, indeed, and one of the provisions of the President's task force calls for the Office of Education to compile this data from universities.

If sex were included, it also would require this data, and I know it, and the New York office of the U.S. Civil Rights Commission is already asking these questions.

So part of our problem is that we simply do not have information. There is no government body which acts as a clearinghouse for sex discrimination except the Women's Bureau. You have to dig through thousands of tables, and all of us at this table have done it innumerable times.

Mrs. Green. Does any one of the three of you at the table know why this information was not gathered after the executive order was issued in 1967?

Commissioner Heide. I would like to comment, and I would like to interpret as a supposition.

First of all, I think it took a while to get this executive order. Then it was written so that it would not take effect until 1968. Then it was only after a great deal of persuasion that there were hearings held on it. Then there was a good deal of persuasion and pressure applied so that the guidelines on this were to be issued, and finally released only immediately prior to the recent conference sponsored by the Women's Bureau.

Why it was issued at this point in time, I suppose your guess is as good as mine, but I think that part of it is that it would not be too far afield to suggest that this is not considered a serious problem, and that there is simply no priority now on the concerns of women as people.

Mrs. GREEN. Nevertheless it was an executive order, which would seem to absolutely require it; Commissioner Heide.

Commissioner HEIDE. The basic Executive Order 11246, did not forbid sex discrimination.

It was only after a good deal of work that the amending Executive Order 11375, was issued. So I think the whole pattern without knowing the details of everything that again happens, is that the concerns of the Federal Government have not placed very high priorities on the condition for women at work.

Dr. SCOTT. I should like to add to that if I may, Mrs. Green, because there were no guidelines on sex discrimination, sex is not an automatic part of compliance, and there is no clear mandate from the Secretary of Labor requiring that every compliance review include the analysis of discrimination on the basis of sex.

We are very anxious to have such assurances from the Secretary of Labor, and it is absolutely required, because I know that there is a great deal of confusion among the compliance review agencies as to whether or not they should support these executive orders in the matter of sex.

Some of them have literally decided not to interrupt it, partly because their procedures are set.

Mrs. GREEN. May I interrupt at this point and ask Mr. Hogan, the council of the subcommittee, to confer with you, Dr. Scott, and to prepare a letter for my signature to the Department of Labor asking for a specific answer on this, and why it has not been done.

Dr. SCOTT. Thank you.

May I also, while I am conferring on this matter, may I also ask your permission to discuss certain provisions of the new OFCC guidelines which are different from the proposed ones, which I think are not as strong as the proposals?

Mrs. GREEN. Yes.

Dr. SCOTT. Thank you.

Mrs. GREEN. And I will ask for unanimous consent that you be allowed to extend your remarks at this point on that particular matter.

Dr. SCOTT. I have a letter to the Assistant Secretary of Labor on this matter, Madam Chairman.

(The document referred to follows:)

DEPARTMENT OF ENGLISH,
STATE UNIVERSITY OF NEW YORK,
Buffalo, N.Y., June 17, 1970.

THE HONORABLE ARTHUR A. FLETCHER,
Assistant Secretary of Labor,
Department of Labor,
Washington, D.C.

DEAR MR. FLETCHER: This letter is to confirm our conversation after the Women's Bureau luncheon, and to comply with your request that I set forth for you in writing the objection of the National Organization for Women (NOW) to the new OFCC guidelines on sex discrimination.

As you will recall, we discussed the vital need for an immediate, express statement from the Secretary of Labor assuring the federal compliance agencies and the general public that the affirmative action goals and timetables required by Order #4 must be enforced in regard to women. There is a great deal of misunderstanding about this among compliance agencies; some agency compliance officials just plain intend to ignore women in enforcing goals and timetables.

NOW has reviewed your guidelines on sex discrimination and is anxious to bring the following objections to your attention:

1. Section 60–20.3(c): This provision permits contractors to discriminate against women *or* men in pensions, welfare programs, and important benefits *so long as* the contractor does not directly profit from his disparate treatment. Thus he is permitted to make conditions of employment distasteful to one sex or the other, while allowing the victim no recourse under your Orders, despite the plain words "equal employment opportunity." NOW recommends the deletion of this section.

2. Section 60–20.5(b): This provision, originally drafted to give wage relief to the blue collar women trapped in underpaid, semi-skilled work (described in the *proposed* guidelines as "ghetto departments") is now meaningless. It merely restates rights women already have under other provisions. NOW urges a return to the original wording.

3. Section 60–20.3(b): NOW has discovered with great dismay that the section on bona fide occupational qualifications has been severely weakened, and the door opened to loose interpretation by the phrase "limited instances."

NOW recognizes no valid bona fide occupational qualifications in the kind of work done by federal contractors, nor in any kind of work except for sperm donor and wet nurse. Your administration has expressed a firm resolve to have uniform civil rights requirements. We therefore would like your firm assurance that this provision will be interpreted consistently with the Equal Employment Opportunity's Commission's definition of bona fide occupational qualifications.

These objections notwithstanding, NOW has found one genuinely valuable improvement over the originally proposed guidelines in § 60–20.3 (g), on leave of absence for childbearing. This is clearly an important step forward in the struggle of women for freedom from biological penalty.

In our conversation on these points, I assured you that NOW recognizes that the best interests of women lie in the OFCC's continued independence from the EEOC. We intend to pursue this position publically. Our final resolve in respect to this will be greatly aided by your response to this letter.

Sincerely yours,

ANN SCOTT,
Federal Compliance Committee,
National Organization for Women.

Commissioner HEIDE. May I ask one other point in relation to any proposed letter? The last look that I took at any agencies that had Federal contracts, the poster on the coverage of OFCC and OECC does not include and this is a large poster, about this large, does not include any reference to the amended Executive Order 11246, to specify the Executive Order 11375 which has exactly the same area of coverage, so that agencies that have Federal contracts can say, "We don't have anything issued that shows that this is covered." So I would recommend this be part of that communication.

Dr. BOYER. There is a revised poster out. We have just mailed it to colleges in the country. It has only been made available in the last month, if that. I am sure a lot of industries do not have it.

Commissioner HEIDE. I know there are agencies and organizations that simply do not have that.

Dr. SCOTT. Referring to industry, by the way, I would like to add that industry may be ahead of the Government, particularly now in the matter of the OFCC.

I know Bethlehem Steel in Buffalo has already come up with a way of getting around the provision in the OFCC guidelines which prevents advertising for—advertising under male and female headings.

That is they're now putting their ads on the sports page, which, of course, has primarily a male readership.

Mrs. GREEN. I suggest that the National Organization for Women undertake a campaign to get women to read the sports and financial pages, as well as the society page.

I think it would be a vast improvement anyway.

Dr. Scott. One other thing on the OFCC guidelines, as far as I know there is no directive requiring, as is now under the EEOC that every compliance team have a woman.

This is also something that should be considered.

Mrs. Green. The Equal Employment Opportunities Commission does have this?

Dr. Scott. Yes, but the OECC compliance guidelines do not——

Mrs. Green. I thought their exclusion, as in the absence of a black, would be prima facia evidence of discrimination.

Dr. Scott. Let me go back to tenure.

Tenure is awarded after—well, tenure—the original purpose of tenure was to assure faculties of jobs after a suitable period and production. It is usually awarded in the 7th year at the university, and it prevents you from being fired. It is job security, and it acts I think as a seniority system here.

However, a glance at the tables and patterns to do with tenure shows again a familiar pattern and at the University of Buffalo, tenured women represent 5 percent of tenured faculty and men represent 50 percent.

Fifty-three percent of all men in the university are tenured. From zero to 5 years and tenure can be granted earlier, 38 percent of the members have tenure, the men, 38 percent, but only 17 percent of the women.

The percentages are interesting, but the figures are, also. Zero to 5 years, 169 men have tenure, but from zero to 5 percent, now only 8 women out of 47, which gives you an indication. Among tenured faculty, women tend to concentrate at the lower end, the lower rank of associate professor. Of tenured men 59 percent are full professors, and only 30 women are full professors. So that even within this category, women are huddled at the lower range.

Mrs. Green. Thirty percent of the women are full professors and/or 30 percent of the full professors are women?

Dr. Scott. I am sorry. Thirty percent of the women, tenured women, are full professors. Thirty percent of the tenured women. Associate professors and full professors are tenured and almost 60 percent of the tenured men are full professors.

Mrs. Green. What percentage of the full professors are women?

Dr. Scott. I think 5 percent.

Tenure now has become something more than promotion systems based on merit. It is, in effect, and at its worst, a mechanism which can be used to regulate faculty size in line with the general economic situation.

This practice can assure universities of a low level turnover and a cheap demand labor supply. It can also be a means of weeding out troublemakers, and it is also a means of rewarding the safe, dull teacher who has the safe, dull book.

Mrs. Green. Let me stop you there. More and more often I am hearing the statement made by colleagues and people in the academic community that tenure is the system to preserve mediocrity.

Dr. Scott. I believe that. I believe my remarks will show that to be true. The only supremacy that I can see it rewards is male supremacy. Perhaps the most distasteful aspect of it is that it is a star chamber proceeding.

A person's fate is decided by a committee which does not know him or her, in a closed session, in which he or she cannot be present and cannot hear evidence or plead his or her own case, and which increasingly denies tenure over the more informed recommendations of the person's own department. All of the criteria are unclear, and the most commonly cited one is publication; people can be granted tenure for service. Tenure means promotion, and patterns clearly show that as presently practiced it is discrimination against women, as a selection system.

I believe that, under EEOC guidelines, the whole tenure procedure could be subjected to a validation study on this basis alone, but only if the protection of EEOC is extended to academics.

Faculty women are not the only people who are discriminated against at universities.

The administration shows that there is a great deal of room at the top. For instance, of the 47 top administrative posts at the University of Buffalo, only one and a half are held by women.

One is held by the dean of the school of nursing. The half is held by the woman who works half time in charge of the office of equal opportunity. This is Barbara Simms, who is black, and therefore can be counted twice.

Again with the staff, we find that you have a problem of starting at the bottom and staying there. The faculty directory, which gives us the only information on the subject, shows that while service and administration departments are overwhelmingly headed by men, they are largely staffed by women.

If the equal pay for equal work act were extended, we would have a startling change in administrative salaries at the University of Buffalo.

Of a series of administrative salaries, we have found—we analyzed them in terms of degree, age, and sex—we discovered a clear pattern of discrimination.

For instance, women in the same job categories, administrative job categories, with the same degrees as men received considerably less money as a group, and as the salaries increase so does the gap.

Among those who were working in administrative jobs with no degree, the average difference was $200 a year more for men. In those who were working in administrative jobs with a bachelor's degree, the average gap was $400 a year more for men, but when both men and women had a master's degree in administration, the average gap was a shocking $1,200 a year more for men than women. This clearly would come under the equal pay act.

Again, we have a problem of students, and I was very happy to hear you bring up the problem of part time. The University of Buffalo has a strong policy against allowing women to come back part time. Many women who want to return to work can do so only if they can come back part time.

Now many women's last child is in school when the woman is 35, and this means she has 30 years of working life ahead of her.

If she cannot come back to school and raise her educational level, she cannot compete equally on the job market and when a university has this kind of policy, it is a de facto segregation policy, because it does discriminate mostly against women who return to universities, and very rarely is it in terms of men.

Part of this we can see by the records which show that where part time is available in the few instances women use it a great deal more than men.

We feel that the universities can undertake a number of procedures which will do something toward offering women equal employment opportunity.

Mrs. GREEN. May I ask you a question? With respect to policy on the return of women, is that written, or unwritten?

Dr. SCOTT. I can't honestly say. I know the department of admissions practically refuses to allow women in part time. I don't know whether it is written or not, but it is a very widely held policy, and it is in the office of admissions. I know this is true throughout the country. Even though much student assistance comes from Federal funding and loans, there is virtually none for part time. This would seem to me also to be a pattern which suggests discrimination under title VI.

Mrs. GREEN. Let me ask you another question. In the education associations that all have representatives here in Washington, has any study ever been made by any of the women's groups about how many women are on the boards, the policymaking boards of these associations? I have been thinking as you were speaking, about the National Education Association, the Association of Land Grant Colleges, the Association of Colleges, or the Association of Junior Colleges, and other such organizations. I can't ever recall having seen a woman as a witness at the table representing any one of these organizations. Occasionally they have guest professors but not association personnel whom they occasionally invite to appear with them. But is there a single woman lobbyist, a woman representative in Washington for any association for education or higher education?

Dr. SCOTT. I don't know if there is or not.

Mrs. GREEN. It would be interesting for one of your groups to make a study of this.

Dr. SCOTT. I have testimony from a woman, dealing with a survey of libraries, which shows that the situation of women librarians in the Civil Service is becoming worse, also.

Could I enter that into the record?

Mrs. GREEN. Yes.

(The document referred to follows:)

GRADE CHANGES IN NUMBER OF FULL-TIME LIBRARIANS (1410 SERIES)[1] OCTOBER 1967–68

Grade	Total	Male	Female
GS-1 to 4	0	0	0
GS-5	−41	−5	−36
GS-6	+5	−2	+7
GS-7	−26	−11	−15
GS-8	+5	+3	+2
GS-9	−13	+13	−26
GS-10	+10	0	+10
GS-11	+64	−7	+71
GS-12	+43	+26	+17
GS-13	+26	+16	+10
GS-14	+8	−1	+9
GS-15	+10	+10	0
GS-16	+3	+2	+1
GS-17	−3	−2	−1
GS-18	+1	0	+1
Executive level	0	0	0
Nongraded[2]	−1	+1	−2
Tota	+91	+43	+48

[1] Excludes employees of Central Intelligence Agency, National Security Agency, Board of Governors of Federal Reserve system, and Foreign National Overseas.

The grades or levels of the various pay systems have been considered equivalent to specific general schedule grades solely on the basis of comparison of salary rates, specifically, in most instances, by comparing the 4th step GS rates with comparable rates in other pay systems.

[3] Includes employees in the Judicial Branch in unique positions for which no grade or salary was reported.

Mrs. GREEN. I will ask that all your materials, plus your statements, be added at this point.

Mrs. GREEN. I do want the materials to be complete and full.

Dr. SCOTT. I would like permission merely to reiterate that because the formation of the self-esteem of human beings is so intimately connected with our educational experiences any measure which encourages the women to make the best use of our intellectual powers will benefit every human being.

This bill is such a measure, and in the interests of equal opportunity for all, even women, I urge you to consider it favorably, for to resist the logic of equality is to be deprived of its rewards.

Thank you.

Mrs. GREEN. Thank you, and I really want to express my appreciation to all five of you, and I am looking forward to the testimony that others will give. Until the second bell I am going to turn to my——

Mr. HATHAWAY. It is the second bell now, Madam Chairman. The first bell rang about 5 minutes after.

I want to say thank you. You can be assured that the male members of the committee will look at this very objectively.

Mrs. GREEN. Again, my thanks. The committee will adjourn until tomorrow at 10 o'clock.

Tomorrow we will hear the testimony of five college presidents from the great State of Maine and then on Friday at 10 o'clock we will resume our hearings on the provisions in 16098 dealing with discrimination against women.

Dr. Ann Harris of Columbia University—I noticed by a shake of her head this morning that she was in disagreement with one point; she will be at the hearing.

Dr. Pauli Murray, from Brandeis University, who served with me on President Kennedy's Commission on the Status of Women, will be with us.

Dr. Bernice Sandler, representing Women's Equity Action League, will testify, and then we will have further discussions about future witnesses whom we can call in other areas.

Thank you again for your testimony here today.

Mrs. GREEN. I would ask unanimous consent that the statement of our colleague Catherine May, be inserted in the record. Without any objection, that is also ordered. The meeting is adjourned.

(Whereupon, at 12:25 p.m. the Special Subcommittee on Education adjourned, to reconvene at 10 a.m., Friday, June 19, 1970.)

FRIDAY, JUNE 19, 1970

House of Representatives,
Special Subcommittee on Education
of the Committee on Education, and Labor,
Washington, D.C.

The subcommittee met at 10 a.m. in room 2261, Rayburn House Office Building, Hon. Edith Green (chairman of the subcommittee) presiding.

Present: Representatives Green and Hathaway.

Staff member present: Harry Hogan, counsel.

Mrs. Green. The meeting will come to order for the further consideration of legislation that is now before the committee. I am delighted to welcome as the three witnesses this morning testifying primarily on section 805, of H.R. 16098: Dr. Ann Harris of Columbia University, representing Columbia Women's Liberation; Dr. Pauli Murray of Brandeis University; and Dr. Bernice Sandler, chairman of the Action Committee for Federal Government Contract Compliance in Education, Women's Equity Action League.

We are delighted to have the three of you here. I would ask unanimous consent that the full statement of Professor Harris be made a matter of record at this point.

STATEMENTS OF DR. ANN SUTHERLAND HARRIS, ASSISTANT PROFESSOR OF ART HISTORY, COLUMBIA UNIVERSITY, REPRESENTING COLUMBIA WOMEN'S LIBERATION; DR. PAULI MURRAY, PROFESSOR OF AMERICAN STUDIES, BRANDEIS UNIVERSITY; AND DR. BERNICE SANDLER, CHAIRMAN, ACTION COMMITTEE FOR FEDERAL CONTRACT COMPLIANCE IN EDUCATION, WOMEN'S EQUITY ACTION LEAGUE

Dr. Harris. I am Ann Sutherland Harris, assistant professor of art history in the Graduate Faculties of Columbia University in the city of New York. I am also active in Columbia Women's Liberation and I am a member of N.O.W. I do not represent Columbia University in an official capacity, but I am a spokeswoman for Columbia Women's Liberation, which supports this testimony and helped to prepare the report presented here today.

Madam Chairman and members of the committee, I am here today to testify to the urgent need to extend the protection of the Civil Rights Act of 1964 and the Equal Pay Act of 1963 to women in institutions of higher education by means of the amendments proposed by the Honorable Mrs. Green in section 805 of the Omnibus Post-Secondary Education Act of 1970 (H.R. 16098).

Much of my evidence concerning discriminatory practices against women in higher education is drawn from my knowledge of the situation at Columbia University. My research merely confirms my long-held suspicion, however, that the situation at Columbia is merely typical of comparable high-endowment, high-prestige private universities in the United States.

That the overall distribution of women in institutions of higher education in the United States is highly suggestive of discriminatory practices and of attitudes prejudicial to women no one can deny. Research into the problem of sexual discrimination in higher education is handicapped at present, however, by the scarcity of sex breakdown statistics for individual institutions.

A great deal of the data now available has been collected by groups of concerned women students, staff and faculty, and is not yet available in published form. I have been astonished—as disheartened—to discover how uniform the pattern is. In whatever proportion the women are to be found, the women are always at the bottom.

The rule—and it applies to outside higher education as well—the rule where women are concerned is simply this: The higher, the fewer. The higher in terms of level of education, the higher in terms of faculty rank, the higher in terms of recognized responsibility, the higher in terms of salary, prestige and status, the fewer are the women.

Dr. Bernice Sandler will present testimony regarding the overall distribution of women, and the evidence these statistics provide of a general pattern of sexual discrimination. My testimony, therefore, will concentrate on Columbia University and on other institutions, principally the University of Chicago, from which I was able to obtain good statistical data and/or evidence of discrimination against women.

I should add that my 40-page report is a summary of several hundred pages of information that I have accumulated over the past year, and that I have selected the material for presentation here because it was typical, not because it was exceptional. The report that Columbia Women's Liberation prepared on the faculty of Columbia and Barnard will be read into the record as an example of the kind of statistical and sociological report now being prepared in many institutions of higher education throughout the United States, both to document the widespread existence of sexual discrimination in the academic world, and to prepare the way for remedial measures.

I am only one of many thousands of women who believe that Congress will be increasingly preoccupied in the next decade with the legislation necessary to insure women equal rights, equal opportunities, and equal status with men in the United States. Women are organizing now as they have not since fighting to win the right to vote 50 years ago. More and more women are realizing that they are treated as second-class citizens.

The word "sex" was added to section 702 of title VII of the Civil Rights Act as a joke, and women will not forget that insult. Equality for women is not a joke. It is a serious issue, although many otherwise fairminded individuals still refuse to believe that discrimination against women is a serious problem, or is a problem that deserves to be taken seriously.

I believe that the best and most convincing evidence of discrimination against women, in the academic world and outside, is statistical, but I know that statistics are tedious to listen to, and I will trust the committee to read at their leisure the substantial body of my evidence.

Here I would like to try and convey to the committee by means of some quotations made by academic men about academic and nonacademic women the sexually negative atmosphere in which women live and work as students, staff, and faculty. These kinds of comments are familiar to all women. If they seem to the men in this audience a trivial form of opposition, I hope they will try to remember that they are not and have not been on the receiving end of such psychological warfare. They have not been subjected to daily propaganda with regard to their intrinsic weaknesses and inferiority. Nor have their ambitions been limited by anything other than their native ability and energy.

No man would be content to be only a husband and a father. Men have not organized political movements demanding the right to be house-husbands supported by their working wives. Thus tacitly men have recognized the limited world to which they still seek to confine women, and to which they continue to seek to limit them by making access to professional careers difficult.

Women's weaker physical constitution has never exempted them from hard physical labor in the United States in the home, in factories, in the fields. It has long been the most valued forms of human achievement from which men have sought to exclude women, and in this the academic world is no different from other spheres of prestigious professional activity.

When President Nathan Pusey of Harvard realized that the draft was going to reduce the numbers of men applying to Harvard's graduate program, he exclaimed:

We shall be left with the blind, the lame, and the women.

At Yale, when the new women undergraduates protested the quota on women and made the modest demand for 50 more women undergraduates the coming year at an alumni dinner, an alumnus was cheered when he said:

We're all for women, but we can't deny a Yale education to a man.

Charles de Carlo, who recently succeeded Esther Rauschenbusch as president of Sarah Lawrence, one of many examples of a women president being succeeded by a man—I know of only one reverse example— said the following, shortly after his appointment:

Feminine instincts are characterized by caring qualities, concern for beauty and form, reverence for life, empathy in human relations, and a demand that men be better than they are.

What is a man who does not think that women are people, doing as president of a women's college? Charles de Carlo thinks that women are myths, muses, madonnas, but not human beings with the potential and full range of characteristics ascribed to men.

Other academic men think that women are chickens. The following statement appeared in a respectable sociological periodical this winter:

Some years ago, a colleague and I shared an office with a great view of the campus. When we were not consumed by teaching, research and/or community service, we would on occasion observe some of the comely girls passing beneath our window. While male scholars will dispute most generalizations, they will readily agree that there just aren't enough chicks in their area of specialization, to put it in professional sociological language [sic]. Hence, my friend and I determined to print some handbills or perhaps put up a sign inviting some of the sweet young things to consider doing advanced work in our field. Alas, we never followed through, and many a pretty girl still walks the street who could have been saved. This clear-cut case of creativity [sic] followed by indecision was duly noted by our professors, however, and we were both awarded doctorates shortly thereafter.

The article was headed: "Have You Ever Considered a Doctorate in the Sociology of Education, My Dear?" It is not my impression that those men were primarily interested in the intellectual capacities of the women they idly thought of attracting into their profession, nor do I think that they would have written a similar piece suggesting that blacks be recruited because of their soft voices and sexy sense of rhythm revealed as they walked past the window.

Sexual discrimination is, as has been said before, the last socially acceptable form of discrimination. (See AAUW questionnaire results cited in report.)

Women students regularly encounter the following kinds of statements during their meetings with male faculty—all quotations come from students with the highest academic qualifications:

"The admissions committee didn't do their job. There is not one good-looking girl in the entering class."

"No pretty girls ever come to talk with me." "You're so cute. I can't see you as professor of anything." "A pretty girl like you will certainly get married. Why don't you stop with an M.A.?"

"We expect women who come here to be competent, good students, but we don't expect them to be brilliant or original." "Women are intrinsically inferior." "Any woman who has got this far has got to be a kook." "Why don't you find a rich husband and give all this up?"

"Our general admissions policy has been if the body is warm and male, take it; if it's female, make sure it's an A— from Bryn Mawr." "How old are you anyway? Do you think that a girl like you could handle a job like this? You don't look like the academic type." "Somehow I can never take women in this field seriously."

The effect such comments have on women students and the attitudes of mind behind them are analyzed at greater length in my testimony where the source of the following quote is given:

Comments such as these can hardly be taken as encouragment for women students to develop an image of themselves as scholars. They indicate that some of our professors have different expectations about our performance than about the performance of male graduate students—expectations based not on our ability as individuals, but on the fact that we are women. Comments like these indicate that we are expected to be decorative objects in the classroom, that we're not likely to finish a Ph. D., and if we do, there must be something "wrong" with us. Single women will get married and drop out. Married women will have children and drop out. And a woman with children ought to stay at home and take care of them rather than study and teach.

Here I should only like to say that when women drop out—and published evidence suggests that their attrition rate is only slightly greater than that of men—I call that discrimination against women, and not, as some do, women discriminating against themselves. What astonishes me is that so many women put up with this kind of sick humor and persist with their intention of getting a B.A., an M.A., a Ph. D. or a law degree, or medical training.

Had I encountered such opposition as an undergraduate or graduate student in London, I doubt that I would be an art historian today.

Indeed, it is my anger and frustration with the male faculty—and they exist on all campuses—who try systematically to discourage women students in the guise of such "jokes" that partly explains why I have changed from being a passive into an active feminist.

I should add that women faculty are not immune from such remarks. One of the first women at Princeton to attend a departmental faculty meeting was introduced with the condescending word, "I'd like you to meet Mrs. X, who is actually very well qualified to be here today."

I am well aware that the universality of this phenomenon means that we are dealing with instinctive, partly unconscious attitudes, and that making laws that forbid sexual discrimination will not solve the problem. Such laws will help, however, to create the kind of social climate in which men and women can learn to respect each other and learn also not to limit the humanity of each other. It will take a long time, but I for one look forward to the end of the battle of the sexes, in academe and elsewhere.

Although I am pleased that Congress is at last beginning to consider legislation that help women obtain fair and equal treatment, this bill contains one section that in my opinion, and in the opinion of Columbia Women's Liberation, will more than offset the benefits of section 805. We wish to express our opposition to title VII of this same bill.

The "disruptive acts" which title VII deals with are so broadly defined as potentially to stifle expression of justifiable grievances by powerless groups: minority groups such as black and brown people, majority groups such as women.

Section 701 places the power to define "disruptive acts" with "trustees, administrators, and other duly appointed officials." The last-named group is not at all defined and could be interpreted as officials of any level of government. This set of people may not be responsive to claims for equitable treatment made by unrepresented groups: racial minorities—for most of these officials are white; and women—for most of these officials are men.

For example, we spoke earlier (in the report attached to this statement) about the lack of adequate gynecological services available to women students. Columbia Women's Liberation undertook to remedy this situation at Columbia and found the administration willing to deal with the issue. However, an administration that did not wish to concern itself with the needs of their own women students might define as disruptive actions taken in the pursuit of fair treatment in this area.

The harsh provisions for punishment in title VII give a person deemed guilty by any court of record a "double punishment": She or he is given a sentence by the courts and then a further sentence by the Federal Government. He or she is blacklisted at all universities by virtue of being unable to receive any Federal money for 5 years, not even a loan.

The effect would be to purge universities of all dissident voices, of those who have given, and will continue to give universities and societies the impetus to change. We believe that women like ourselves are one such group. Our dissent at Columbia has not only been tolerated, but has been welcomed by many of those at whom it is directed.

At other educational institutions, women who have criticized their faculties for sexual discrimination have been "censured for conduct unbecoming," a rare procedure in academe normally reserved for actions such as outright plagiarism. As women who may in the future find our problems turned aside by those who refuse to recognize the existence of sexual discrimination, we cannot turn our backs on the grievances of the oppressed, the powerless, and the dissident, for women are among those people.

You may ask if we are not concerned with disruptive acts. We would answer yes. We are saddened and horrified by the disruption by the powerful, not by the dissidence of the powerless.

The war in Indochina, racism and sexism in America, the punitive repression of groups such as the Black Panthers, these are all examples of the use of disruption, unconstitutional acts, inhumane treatment, brutalization—all acts by the powerful, not the powerless.

The exploitation of black and white women in the labor market is the "public order" upheld by the powerful, just as putting students in front of a de facto firing squad is violence by the powerful. Because Women's Liberation is a movement to end all human oppression and exploitation, we do not advocate violence. We therefore find it inexcusable that violence is visited upon the powerless by the powerful.

We urge Members of Congress to recognize that the true problems in our society are war, militarism, exploitation, racism, and sexism, and to work for the elimination of these problems, rather than to attack those who protest these cancers on the public order. We urge Congress to investigate and cure the causes of militarism, racism, and sexism, rather than repress the dissidence which is merely the symptom of the just grievances of the oppressed groups.

The advancement of women through this bill would come at the cost of the repression of all progressive groups working for change, including women's liberation groups. Because of the repressive aspects of this bill as it stands with the inclusion of title VII, we of Columbia Women's Liberation and I as an individual cannot give it the wholehearted support that we would wish to give it at this time.

Mrs. GREEN. May I say to you, Dr. Harris, that I have been most impressed with the statement that you have made. I fully agree with you that generally boys and men have not been subjected to the psychological warfare that has existed against the girl and the woman. There are two or three points I would like to raise.

On page 2 of your summary statement you make the statement:

In whatever proportion the women are to be found, the women are always at the bottom. The rule—and it applies outside education as well—the rule where women are concerned is simply this: The higher, the fewer.

There certainly is adequate evidence to support this in testimony that was given last Wednesday and in figures which we have from the Department of HEW. In the Office of Education itself, where you are dealing with a profession that has traditionally been open to women you find that when you get to grade level 18 there is not a single woman in a policymaking position.

I put in the record the other day information illustrating that it is the same in HEW, that out of many hundreds of women in HEW, when you get up to the top level, 99 percent of the positions are held by men; the disproportion of members of an ethnic minority is the criterion by which discrimination is confirmed. It seems equally applicable here.

But I would like to add a note to that, too, that when we consider some of the so-called lower positions, and I refer especially to the apprenticeship program, which is supposed to train individuals so they will be equipped to enter the labor market, the best information I have is that in 1968, the year of the latest figures available, of 278,000 registered apprentices under the Bureau of Apprenticeship and Training, 1 percent were girls; 99 percent of the positions held by boys. Of 370 occupations, women were only able to take part in 47, which means that well over 300 occupations have been closed to women working up through the apprenticeship program.

I do not have the most recent data—and I would ask the staff to obtain it and put it in the record at this point—but certainly a short time ago the highest unemployment rate in the Nation was among nonwhite girls between 16 and 21, and here we find even the apprenticeship training positions are closed to them.

So it is not only in the higher education that we find this discrimination, but also in many other areas.

(Document follows:)

EMPLOYEES OF OFFICE OF EDUCATION AS OF JUNE 31, 1969

Grades	Total	Men	Women	Percent who are women
13 to 18	1,150	986	166	14.41
13	432	351	83	19.1
14	441	370	71	16.1
15	240	231	9	3.8
16	25	24	1	4.2
17	9	7	2	22.2
18	3	3	0	0

Note.—Women are a majority of the employees of the Office of Education. Most of them are in grades below GS–9. They remain in grade longer than men in all the posts above clerical and secretarial. There are no women in the major policy-making posts as of 1970. All Bureau heads and all top staff-level office heads are men. In the spring of 1969, a sample of Office of Education employees asked their opinion on their working status and conditions revealed great dissatisfaction among women particularly in the professional posts. A job audit in the Bureau of Elementary and Secondary Education revealed that the male Division chiefs discriminate against the women professionals when it comes to field trips.

Mrs. Green. I would agree with your remarks on page 3. I would agree with you in hoping that Congress will be increasingly preoccupied in the next decade with the legislation necessary to insure equal rights, equal opportunities, and equal status for human beings of both sexes.

On page 4 I might add a little comment to what you have said as to the "house-husband." I have found myself using that word in years past. When I entered politics a thousand and one times in a condescending tone I heard, "How did it ever happen that you went into politics?"

When I first came to Washington, there were four women who entered the Congress that year and all the papers called up and said "We would like to take a picture of you." Every single time they wanted me to be whipping up pancakes or a cake.

Finally, I just said, the congressional job is not making a cake perfectly. I will not have any more such pictures! I asked: When you ask a new male Member of Congress to have his picture taken, do you say, "We want a picture of you painting the window or driving some nails to prove that you are a man?" This is again exemplary of the psychological warfare.

If I might add one other comment, I remember the first time that I ever ran for office I attended a meeting at which a very charming gentleman came up to me. My opponent and I both had spoken and the gentleman said,

You know, I agree completely with what you have said. I agree 100 percent. You are absolutely right, but I am not going to vote for you.

I said,

Well, that is interesting—I am curious why.

His answer was,

Well, you know, we had a woman mayor here in Portland and I voted for her and just see what an awful job she did.

He said,

I am never going to vote for another woman as long as I live.

I said,

I understand that. We had a sheriff and I worked for him and he turned in such a bad performance that I helped to circulate petitions for his recall. I understand what you are saying and the judgment you are making. This sheriff did such a bad job that I am never going to vote for another man as long as I live.

This is a part of the psychological warfare to which the women are subjected and, I think, really, that men are not aware of it. I would like to add one little additional item referring to page 5, which has always dismayed me.

I have always looked with great interest at the newspaper pictures of all of the peace conferences that have ever been held. Supposedly women whose sons go to war and are killed would have equal compassion and concern about the war. But I have yet to see a woman in a U.S. delegation at any peace conference at any time. I asked the Library of Congress to do research on this. Legislative reference has advised me—in research back to 1912—not one woman has ever been a member of a U.S. peace delegation except the U.N. Conference in 1945 in San Francisco.

You would think that women, being concerned about war and peace as much as they are, that somehow they might deserve representation at these great peace conferences. They might also bring viewpoints that would be invaluable in such discussions.

I would also like to add on page 7 regarding the psychological warfare to which you refer, "the sick humor." I agree with you. I think that I would add TV. I do not understand why women don't boycott products that are promoted by advertising depicting women as supercilious idiots.

The American public would certainly no longer tolerate a black pictured as a Step-n-Fetchit.

Dr. HARRIS. The media are beginning to get the message on this. I have seen a recent survey done by an advertising firm listing the 10 commercials most offensive to women on the television and telling those companies if they go on advertising like that, they are going to lose a lot of women's business.

We have to find a new way to get the message across to women.

Mrs. GREEN. I must say I saw an ad the other day, for a product I have used most of my life, and I made the mental note that I will never buy that product again. I am tired of this kind of advertising—representing women as brainless and acting or reacting exclusively on her emotions.

Mr. HATHAWAY. If the gentlelady will yield, I think it is true of men also on television, the pictures they paint, the Marlboro ads and what-not.

Dr. HARRIS. Yes; the masculine mystique is quite hard to live up to.

Mr. HATHAWAY. Probably any man who ran against Margaret Smith in Maine would experience reverse discrimination.

Mrs. GREEN. I don't follow.

Mr. HATHAWAY. Well, because he was a man, he would probably not fare as well.

Mrs. GREEN. I also recall in connection with your remarks on page 7, a time in Congress when I was infuriated over something and got all of the women Members of Congress to sign a letter. I was later called by the male administrative assistant of one of those women Members who asked if I would remove that Member's name.

I said, "Well, if she wants it off, of course, she can take it off." Then I added, "I am curious why she wants her name removed." He said, "Well, in the South we like our women to be quiet."

So in the views of some, even a woman Member of Congress was not supposed to speak out.

Dr. HARRIS. You know, Simone de Beauvoir said in this thinking like a man business, "Man is defined as a human being and woman is defined as a female. Whenever a woman tries to behave like a human being, she is accused of trying to behave like a man."

Mrs. GREEN. Congressman Hathaway, do you want to go on with the next witness or would you like to ask Dr. Harris some questions?

Mr. HATHAWAY. Dr. Harris, there is no question that women are discriminated against in many instances, but I just wonder what limitations we are going to place upon it. Would you consider that in hiring a man and a woman, that you pay the man who has a wife and children to support more money than the woman who is single and has no dependents for the same job?

Dr. HARRIS. If you are going to work on that same principle, I am all for a total revision of all salaries, all distributed on the basis of who needs exactly what. But that is communism and it doesn't go over very well in the United States normally.

Mr. HATHAWAY. It is practiced in the United States, even between a married man and a single man. I know of many congressional offices that do that.

Dr. HARRIS. I think if you compare the salaries of bachelors with the salaries of single women, you will still find that the bachelors are making a great deal more than the women. It is always suggested that the women help to distribute income fairly, and it is generally assumed that men "need" more money than women do.

I believe in equal pay for equal work.

Mr. HATHAWAY. We had it on the floor yesterday in regard to the postal reform bill, and the bill called for a higher salary scale in the large cities than in the smaller towns, because the cost of living was higher, yet the work was the same.

I believe an amendment was offered and accepted to knock that out and left it up to collective bargaining, but that is the thinking of the committee that reported the bill. Isn't that the same situation where you are taking into consideration the needs of the individual employees?

Dr. HARRIS. That is applying to everybody, after all, men and women living even in New York City where indeed it is much more expensive than living in some small town. I say I am not against equalizing wealth, but, as I say, you need to watch because this becomes a double standard which benefits men but doesn't benefit women.

Also men tend to forget when a woman works, she has to "buy" a wife on the open market, she has to buy the people to look after her children, she has to buy housekeeping help, she has to buy more expensive ready-prepared foods, and this all amounts up. I have a section in my testimony laying out the budget of a working woman with a child.

Mr. HATHAWAY. You don't object to paying on the basis of need as long as there is no sex discrimination?

Dr. HARRIS. A man with a private income should perhaps earn less than a man who doesn't have a private income, but it will be a long time before you get that going in the United States, I think.

Mr. HATHAWAY. I presume, too, you don't go on the thesis, that someone raised here yesterday, that the only difference between men and women as far as jobs are concerned is women cannot be sperm-givers and men can't be incubators. Other than that, they can all hold the same jobs.

Do you think women could be stevedores, for example?

Dr. HARRIS. They are in Russia; aren't they?

Mr. HATHAWAY. Can they lift the weights and so forth?

Dr. HARRIS. Nowadays there are so many machines, there are very few men that have to do a lot of heavy lifting.

Mr. HATHAWAY. What about small business where they can't afford the machines so the woman would have to lift heavy bundles?

Dr. HARRIS. There should be no difference in pay. The work woman are doing could be quite as valuable. It tends to become a distinction that results in the men being paid a great deal more for something which is essentially of the same worth to the company in the long run.

Mrs. GREEN. Would my colleague yield?

Are you putting aside qualifications? You are saying that the pay ought to be on the basis of need entirely rather than qualifications for the job in question?

Mr. HATHAWAY. In my earlier question; no. If you have two qualified people, without the sexual difference at the moment, is an employer justified in paying a different wage scale to the person who has more dependents and more need than he is to the other person, even though they both have the same qualifications and are both doing the same job?

I gather your answer to that was "Yes," provided there is no discrimination?

Dr. HARRIS. If you really sit down and work out what the job involves, but too often this becomes a false distinction and the women are allowed to lift 35 pounds and are paid very little and the men get to use machines to lift 45 pounds and they get paid more.

Mrs. GREEN. Would you yield further?

Mr. HATHAWAY. Yes.

Mrs. GREEN. If need is the basis of pay, as you suggest, then I think we ought to probably present some amazing facts. One that I recently came across: 60 percent of all children in the United States living in households headed by a woman are living in poverty.

Now if this is an accurate figure, it seems to me that it might completely revolutionize all of the programs we have, because historically the median income for women has been less than the median income for men. Most women work for the same compelling economic reasons that men do. Yet a very high percentage of working women are in the lowest income brackets.

Dr. Harris. A third of all women who work are heads of families.

Mrs. Green. The facts are that a woman who is the head of a household and is supporting children has historically in the United States been paid less for doing identical work than the man. In one study made a few years ago, in an electrical appliance producing firm, the most skilled woman worker was paid less than the men doing the most menial jobs.

Mr. Hathaway. It seems like most of the testimony is based on the premise that the discrimination based on sex is no different than the discrimination based on color. Yet if we are to believe some of the anthropological studies manifested in such books as "African Genesis" and "Territorial Imperative" and the more popularized "Naked Ape," there is more than just a biological difference between men and women.

Now, of course, you can disregard those books out of hand, I suppose. That is the basis of my knowledge to date. There may be other anthroplogical studies that show these are not true and if that is so, I will change my thinking on it. But it indicates that men's instinct and so forth are different than women's and perhaps for that reason there are certain jobs that men should hold that women shouldn't hold and certain jobs that women should hold that men should not hold.

Dr. Harris. With Mrs. Green's permission, I might include two articles in the testimony. One is the "Kinder, Küche, Kirche, as Scientific Law: Psychology Constructs the Female." It demolishes most of those arguments. Another one is "Building the Gilded Cage" by Jo Freeman, which examines a much broader range of arguments concerning women's vote. Both make use of new scientific research on behavioral psychology.

Most of the evidence that you cited is contaminated by the prejudices of the authors, and this fact renders invalid a great many of their conclusions.

Mr. Hathaway. I will have to look for a book like this written by a woman.

Mrs. Green. I would ask unanimous consent to add those articles.

Dr. Harris. Yes. I have "Building a Gilded Cage" with me and I can send you the other, if you like.

Mrs. Green. Both will be included at this point.

Mr. Hathaway. You know, there are a lot of benefits that women get under various State laws with respect to divorce, to alimony, whatnot, which I presume women would be willing to give up if they had these?

Dr. Harris. The women I know would be willing to have those things examined and adjusted.

Mr. Hathaway. Where a man could cut his wife out of a will and she would get no alimony from divorce and so forth, no laws on night work.

Dr. Harris. Divorce and alimony laws are unfair and in my opinion need reform. Women should be given the opportunity to do night work if they wish to do it.

Mr. Hathaway. Many States don't allow them to under the guise, at least, that they are protecting them from some evil that lurks at night or perhaps it is because they are supposed to take care of the children.

Dr. Harris. They are not allowed to do the jobs at night in which they can earn a lot of money, but they are allowed to do charring jobs, which means they start work at 4 o'clock in the morning; again, double standards, I am afraid.

Mr. HATHAWAY. There is one other problem. On the admissions to schools, in particular, it has been shown statistically that many schools do discriminate against girls in their admissions policies. But on the other hand, there is a certain percentage with girls who just want to get married and have children and don't care for any career whatsoever, whereas most men have to get a career. They have to support themselves and a family.

So aren't the schools warranted, if their objective is to prepare people for jobs later on, in taking in a greater percentage of men than women?

Dr. HARRIS. You must look at the attrition rates before making judgments of that kind. The attrition rate is the proportion of men and women who drop out of college, or of graduate school. It is always assumed that men don't drop out and that women do drop out.

I have included in my testimony evidence which suggests that the attrition rates for men and women are not very different, especially at graduate level. Women who just want to get married and have children don't go to graduate school. They dropped out long ago.

Many women, in fact, have been raised to believe in their inferiority. They think that it is their job to be man's companion and man's servant, and they don't even try to compete. They rarely reach the level where they will be discriminated against.

There is a great deal of evidence suggesting that the motivation of women who do go on is higher than that of men who do. It has to be, in fact, because women are not encouraged to go on.

Mr. HATHAWAY. If you take the college administration and they have just so many kids that they can take into school and they know that 90 percent of the men, for example, in our society have to get a job and, say, only 50 percent of the women are going to have to get it, and they have a limited number they will take in, aren't they warranted in taking in 9 out of 10 men and fewer girls?

Dr. HARRIS. They have no way of telling from these people's applications whether or not they are the women who are going to drop out. They have to judge from the attrition rates and if the attrition rates for women are very, very much greater than men's, maybe they might be justified.

But all too often they assume that the attrition rates are very much greater, but they don't have any evidence. They have not checked the attrition rates for their schools, for that particular problem. At Chicago Graduate School, for example, the difference is only 5 percent.

Mr. HATHAWAY. I don't think the attrition rate would be quite relevant to their responsibility of letting them in in the first place.

Dr. HARRIS. Then you want to look at the number of women who go on and work, and a number of studies have been done in the United States and other countries that show the more education a woman has, the more likely she is to use her education. A study has been completed recently of women Ph. D.'s 10 years after they got their degree; 91 percent of them were working. That is a very high percentage, because the overall statistics of working men in the United States show that just under 70 percent of all men of working age are working full time.

Mrs. GREEN. Would you yield at that point?

Mr. HATHAWAY. A lot are gigolos and some just can't get jobs, but still the percentage is probably higher of men because they marry a woman who doesn't work, because they have to provide for the family.

Mrs. GREEN. Would my colleague yield?

It seems to me there is an analogy—and I would like your comments on it—which the American society has rejected today. That at least some books have been written that in the black community that historically more of the higher paying jobs have been open to black women than to black men. Therefore, in a family with limited funds available where a decision has to be made by the family whether the black daughter or the black son would go to college, the assumption was that the woman could get the job and therefore they would spend the money on her education rather than on the son's education.

American society has completely rejected this and has said this is not fair to either the man or the woman and that each person ought to be treated as a human being and given the right to develop to full potential. Does that seem analogous to you with Mr. Hathaway's question?

Dr. HARRIS. Yes, except I am a little worried about the basis of that. Perhaps you should ask Dr. Murray to answer that, because the average median salaries of the black man are higher than those of the white woman.

Mrs. GREEN. But I am thinking back in previous years, that the black woman has earned more. Do you want to comment on that, Dr. Murray?

Dr. MURRAY. I want to comment on it. I think it is a myth. The population figures show that from 1860 to 1960—we don't know yet the results of the 1970 census—there has been a steadily increasingly display in the sex ratio between males and females within the Negro community and this has grown to the point that I think the latest estimates were something like 700,000 or 800,000 excess females over males.

Mrs. GREEN. In the black community are you speaking of now?

Dr. MURRAY. In the Negro community or black, if you prefer. I am old enough and secure enough to be able to use the term "Negro" without difficulty, since my generation fought to capitalize the term and for the benefit of the young militants I often say "Negro/Black," but I will continue to say Negro.

I have been very much interested in this particular phenomenon because of its consistency and the increasing disparity. The Census Bureau argues that there is not really so much of a disparity, but that there is a loss in counting "floating" Negro males. But if you analyze the Census figures of 1966, you will note that in the age group under 15 years the ratio between males and females within the Negro group is much smaller than within the white group. In the white group the sex ratio is 104.3 percent. In the Negro group it is 100.5. So that by age 15 you have just a balance, 100 males per 100 females, and then you begin to get the attrition.

So when you get into the child-bearing age—25–44 years—the ratio drops down to 86.6 for nonwhites as compared with 96.9 for whites.

Mrs. GREEN. 86 percent male?

Dr. MURRAY. 86 males for every 100 females.

This phenomenon has been commented upon periodically since the late 1890's, but I know of no sociologist who has really studied it to see whether or not in American society there is literally a physical absence of Negro males, whether or not there is something in the American society which is hostile to the survival of the black male.

We know, for example, that male babies are more fragile than female babies and that boys are harder to rear than girls, that it is said that nature compensates for this by producing more males at birth and then at maturity the sex ratio begins to balance. But this is not true within the Negro group.

What I am coming to is this, that this is one of the pressures translated into family life, combined with the fact that the entire black community has been discriminated against, particularly the male in the sense of attempting to assert the patriarchial image alone with the white male.

A Negro girl knows that she will probably have to support herself. A black mother knows her daughter may for a large part of her life have to support herself.

What I am saying is that there is a special incentive for the Negro girl to go to school; it is more likely that she will be self-supporting or that she will carry a heavier economic responsibility in her family than a white girl.

Mrs. GREEN. The question I wanted to ask, Dr. Murray, was: Is it true or not in your judgment that in a family of blacks where there is limited money that the advantage is given to the girl rather than the boy in opposition to the white family historically where, if there is limited funds, the money has been given to the boy instead of the girl, on the basis of future income?

Dr. MURRAY. I am not prepared to accept the premise, first of all. I still think that it is a false premise and that it is a myth. If you ask me where money should go, if it is limited, probably I would say it should go to the one who has the greatest possibility of success. By this I mean the one who shows the greater intellectual promise.

Mrs. GREEN. Whether it is a boy or a girl?

Dr. MURRAY. That's right.

Mrs. GREEN. Mr. Hathaway, do you have another question?

Mr. HATHAWAY. The question in simple terms, say there are 10 women and 10 men in a society and there are only 15 openings in a school and we know, statistically, to make it easy, that all 10 men have to get a job and only five of the women are ever going to get a job: Isn't the school warranted in taking in more men than women?

Dr. MURRAY. Do you want another answer to that?

Dr. SANDLER. I think one could almost make the same analogy and see if it holds with blacks, or Negroes, and say, "Well, since so many of them really aren't going to be professionals and many of them are going to be stuck being janitors and cleaners and in low-paying jobs, why waste time educating them?"

Mr. HATHAWAY. I am not doing it on the basis of what has happened before as far as the jobs have gone. I am just doing it on the simple fact that more men than women have to get a job to support a family, no matter what kind of job it is.

Dr. SANDLER. This is changing, this gap between women who work compared to men.

Mr. HATHAWAY. Many work after their children grow up and so forth, but for the immediate problem, it would seem to me, a college would be warranted in allowing more men in than women, because they know that more men than women have to get a job.

Mrs. GREEN. Dr. Harris?

Dr. HARRIS. I might point out that while women are 51 percent of the population, they are now almost 40 percent of the working population. They only have another 10 percent to go to reach 50 percent of the working population.

So, in fact, there are more women working than not working, so it is the majority of the women who will use their training, not the minority, which is often the implication behind the kind of comments you are making.

What happens to women who work, as you know, is that they are discriminated against.

Mr. HATHAWAY. There is no question that they are discriminated against. I am just talking about the college entrance statistic that shows that colleges do discriminate by taking more men than women. They probably take far more than the immediate difference between the jobs they have to get afterward warrants—in some instances it is 10 to 1—and obviously that is not the case.

Dr. HARRIS. I agree with the previous statement. It becomes a self-fulfilling prophecy if you don't allow the women to get a decent education. Also we know that the majority of women do use their educations, and I think it is wrong therefore to discourage them from getting that education.

The trend now is for more women to get an education and use it. That is a trend to encourage and not discourage. Half of the talent in America today is female talent. It is a pity to waste it.

Mr. HATHAWAY. That is true.

Dr. HARRIS. Most Danish dentists are women.

Mr. HATHAWAY. That is a long way to go to get my teeth fixed. I wish they were closer.

Mrs. GREEN. Am I correct that there is a statistic showing that 90 percent of the women who graduate from college do work?

Dr. HARRIS. Women who get Ph. D.'s, I don't know what percentage of the other degrees, but the latest study of Ph. D. women is 91 percent of them work.

Mrs. GREEN. I think there is probably no statement that could be made with which I disagree more vehemently, to suggest men continue to be given the advantage in educational opportunities because they have to work. I think it is really saying that the woman is not a human being and that she is a second-class citizen and that, when she is 18 and applies for college, some college admissions offices or student financial aid officer is going to make the judgment whether she is going to use the training or not. Can such a person really make a valid judgment this girl will be using her education at 35; this girl will not; this man will; this boy will not?

I think the most shocking figure I have seen is that in the State of Virginia 21,000 girls who applied for entrance to college were turned down and not one single male applicant was rejected. Who in heaven's name is able to play God with a human being at 18 years of age and say this person is entitled to an education and this one isn't because he is going to use it and she isn't going to use it!!

I have seen so many men that never use their college education. They train to be engineers, and end up politicians!! Or they train to be teachers and become real estate operators!

Mr. HATHAWAY. That might be good training for a politician.

Mrs. GREEN. Then, according to the logic suggested of not admitting girls because some of them won't use their education, he should not have gone to 5 years of engineering school! It is a waste of space and money at the college. Somebody ought to have made the judgment at 18 that person should not be admitted to an engineering school because he will never use that training.

Mr. HATHAWAY. From the figures I cite, it is obviously discrimination, but I think a college is warranted to have a policy that says they will take in slightly more men than women, because more men than women are going to be required immediately after graduation to get a job and support a family and, if they are limited in the number of people they can take in, I think they would be warranted in that policy.

Obviously many are going far beyond that and take in only the very brightest women and take in even the dullest men.

Mrs. GREEN. Why don't we play God at 13 and decide—as has been done in other countries and here 100 years ago—that girls are just going to be homemakers and not have them go to high school? What Neanderthal thinking.

Dr. HARRIS. Do you believe in sexual equality?

Mr. HATHAWAY. In some, but not all matters in both ways. I don't think men should be allowed to work in the women's locker rooms, for example, do you?

Dr. HARRIS. No, as long as the women who work in women's locker rooms are paid the same as men who work in men's locker rooms.

Mr. HATHAWAY. There are many jobs that women can't handle that men can handle better and, until I read these articles you have put in, I am not convinced that there isn't more of a difference.

Dr. HARRIS. We are not living a primitive hunting society any more. Then the greater physical strength of men certainly counted, but I think that is the case now in only a very extreme minority of jobs. We all know the problem we have now dealing with unskilled male labor. There are just not enough jobs in which sheer physical strength is necessary any more, even for men.

Mrs. GREEN. We will turn to Dr. Sandler. Would you present your statement?

Dr. SANDLER. Madam Chairman and Mr. Hathaway, I am Dr. Bernice Sandler of the Women's Equality Action League—WEAL—where I am chairman of the Action Committee for Federal Contract Compliance in Education. I am also a psychologist with the Department of Health, Education, and Welfare, and a former visiting lecturer at the University of Maryland in the department of counseling and personnel services. However, I am not speaking as a representative of HEW, but as an individual and as a member of the Women's Equity Action League.

Mrs. GREEN. May I interrupt you for the benefit of those present to read the figures in terms of HEW. I made reference to these the other day. In the total employees in HEW, the GS–12 and above, there are a total of 15,977, and out of that, women number 2,666. When we get up to GS–16, there are a total of 214 employees, only 10 women; in GS–17, 72 employees, three women; and GS–18, 16 employees and no women at this policymaking level.

Above that I am sure that if there were women they would have given me the figures. In the Office of Education the highest number, the same as with all civil service employees, are down at the GS–3, 4, and 5 levels. When we get up to grade level 13, out of the total of 432 employees, only 83 are women, 19 percent; and when we get up to grade 16, out of a total of 25 employees, there is only one woman. When we get up to grade 18, there is no woman in a policymaking position, which I think bears out a discrimination in our own Government and in this Department as well as others.

You may proceed.

Dr. SANDLER. Yet, this is a field in which women are often counseled to enter because supposedly they will not experience as much discrimination as in other fields.

I have submitted a written statement for the record on behalf of section 805 of H.R. 16098, and with your permission I would like to summarize the highlights of that statement, and tell you about the vicious inequities and discriminations that women suffer from our universities and colleges.

Mrs. GREEN. Without any objection the entire statement will be made a part of the record.

Dr. SANDLER. Since January 1970, formal charges of sex discrimination under Executive Order 11246, as amended, have been filed against more than 100 universities and colleges by the Women's Equity Action League (WEAL). The Executive order forbids Federal contractors from discriminating against race, creed, color, national origin, or sex.

As Federal contractors who receive about $3.3 billion per year, universities and colleges are subject to the provisions of this order. WEAL submitted more than 80 pages of materials documenting our charges of an industrywide pattern of sex discrimination in the academic community.

Half of the brightest people in this country—half of the most talented people with the potential for the highest intellectual endeavor are women. These women will encounter discrimination after discrimination as they try to use their talents in the university world.

They will be discriminated against when they first apply for admission. They will be discriminated against when they apply for financial and scholarship aid. They will be discriminated against when they apply for positions on the faculty. If they are hired, they will be promoted far more slowly than their male counterparts; and furthermore, if hired at all, women will most likely receive far less money than their male colleagues.

And all of this is legal!

Columbia University violates no law when only 2 percent of its tenured faculty are women, although 25 percent of its doctorates go to women. Harvard violates no law when, of the 411 tenured professors in its graduate school of arts and sciences, not one—not one is a woman, despite the fact that 22 percent of the graduate students are women. The University of Maryland violates no law when only one woman in the department of psychology (or 3 percent of the psychology faculty) has tenure, while nationally women earn 23 percent of the doctorates in psychology.

It is legal for the University of California at Berkeley to simply hire no women at all in its department of psychology. Statistics like this cross my desk almost daily. The position of women on the campuses is steadily worsening. The proportion of women graduate students is less now than it was in 1930. The University of Chicago has a lower proportion of women on its faculty now than it did in 1899.

Mrs. GREEN. Could I interrupt you there?

It is my understanding, in fact I have letters and various documents and briefs to prove this, that HEW itself and the Enforcement Division of Civil Rights have ruled that the absence of blacks or the evidence of a certain ratio, a number of blacks to the number of whites, is in and of itself proof of discrimination. Would you agree with that?

Dr. SANDLER. Absolutely. Statistical absence of a group is often *de facto* evidence of discrimination. Discrimination by omission is just as bad as discrimination by commission.

Mrs. GREEN. I think it is so well documented over the last few years that if in a classroom there is not a black child, it is *per se* proof of discrimination. I have letters from the Enforcement Division of Civil Rights with respect to plants in Portland that the absence of a certain percentage of blacks is in and of itself proof of discrimination, and they are ordered to hire a certain percentage of blacks. Yet when the statistics are given in terms of the number of women, as you say, it is perfectly legal and the Enforcement Division of Civil Rights is apparently unconcerned.

Dr. SANDLER. Yes; they are not as concerned as they ought to be but I think they will be, particularly if we can get section 805 through.

Somehow, women qualified enough to earn doctoral degrees are not considered qualified enough to teach. And women qualified enough to teach in the university or college are not considered qualified enough for promotion and tenure.

It is completely within the law to discriminate against women on the campus. There is no law forbidding the University of North Carolina from maintaining its quota systems for the admission of women—and I quote from an official university publication: "Admission will be restricted to those who are especially well qualified."

Such official and unofficial quota systems restrict the number of women entering our colleges, but they break no law. Section 702 of the Civil Rights Act of 1964 exempts educational institutions. Title VI of the same Civil Rights Act forbids discrimination, but only applies to discrimination based on race, religion, and national origin—not sex.

The Equal Pay Act excludes "executive, administrative, or professional employees." Even the U.S. Commission on Civil Rights has no jurisdiction whatsoever concerning sex discrimination—it is limited by law to matters pertaining to race, color, religion, or national origin—not sex.

At best, Executive Order 11246 under which WEAL is filing its charges of sex discrimination is an administrative remedy for discrimination in our universities and colleges. Unfortunately, as you well know, the Executive order does not have the status of law. It can be amended or suspended at the pleasure of a particular administration.

The very rules and regulations adopted by the Department of Labor arbitrarily require far less from public institutions than from private institutions. The very guidelines issued last week concerning sex discrimination are far weaker than those originally proposed last August by the Department of Labor itself. All of us wonder why.

Indeed, until WEAL filed its complaints, the Department of Labor and all other compliance agencies of the U.S. Government virtually ignored those aspects of the executive order that applied to sex discrimination, despite the fact that the order went into effect in October 1968. Sex was simply not included in any of the compliance reviews concerning universities and colleges, or indeed, in any compliance reviews with any Federal contractors.

Mrs. GREEN. Could I interrupt you there, Dr. Sandler?

The Equal Employment Opportunities Commission does have something to do with the enforcement of the section VII of the Civil Rights

Act and the Enforcement Division of Civil Rights has something to do with it, if in fact the Equal Employment Opportunities Commission and the Enforcement Division of the Civil Rights of the Federal Government does rule that the absence of a black is *per se* evidence of discrimination. Could you tell me how many women are in the Enforcement Division of Civil Rights and how many women are in the Equal Employment Opportunities Commission?

Dr. SANDLER. I don't know how many in the Equal Employment Opportunities Commission. I do know that in the Department of Health, Education, and Welfare in the Office of Civil Rights there is exactly one woman.

Mrs. GREEN. How many men?

Dr. SANDLER. I don't know, but many more than one. When our complaints first went to the Contract Compliance, she—the one woman—was switched from Civil Rights to the Contract Compliance Division because she was a woman. She is the only one I know of.

Mrs. GREEN. If they live by their own established rules, they are guilty of discrimination?

Dr. SANDLER. Yes.

Mrs. GREEN. The division itself that is supposed to enforce it?

Dr. SANDLER. Yes, they have made an admirable effort to integrate their own staffs in regard to race and they have a good many Negro people on the staff, but only one woman.

New legislation is vitally needed if women are to be accorded the fair treatment and education that is the birthright of their brothers. Section 702 of the Civil Rights Act excludes teachers and administrative personnel in public and private schools, thereby depriving nearly 3 million people of coverage. This is particularly ironic in light of the Government's strenuous activities to integrate student populations of elementary and secondary schools, and in institutions of higher learning. Thus educational institutions of all sorts are in the peculiar position of being forbidden by virtue of title VI to discriminate against pupils and students, but lack the statutory incentive to cease discrimination among its faculty. It is difficult to see how an institution which is allowed to discriminate against all minorities, including women, on the faculty can possibly provide effective leadership in eliminating discrimination at other levels.

It is also imperative that along with eliminating the educational exemption of title VII, that section 701(b) be amended so that instrumentalities of the State are covered by title VII. State educational institutions might possibly be construed as being governmental units, and as such, would still be exempt from the provisions of the Civil Rights Act.

Mrs. GREEN. They already have. Your point is well taken.

Dr. SANDLER. Thus the aim of eliminating the educational exemption would be severely undermined. It would be tragic to leave the State universities free to discriminate in their educational employment practices while requiring private institutions to have higher standards of nondiscrimination.

Title VI must be amended to forbid sex discrimination in federally assisted programs. In fiscal 1969 Federal aid to State and local governments alone exceeded $20 billion—and in all of these programs, as well as in nongovernmental federally assisted programs, sex discrimination is completely legal.

On moral grounds alone, all federally assisted programs should be administered so that all citizens enjoy equal participation and equal benefits from these programs. Yet half of our citizens—women—be they black, Spanish-speaking, white, Indian or whatever—can be denied this basic right of equal participation on the basis of their sex alone, unless title VI is amended to include the prohibition of sex discrimination.

Indeed, all legislation pertaining to discrimination against minorities must include sex. The U.S. Commission on Civil Rights must have its jurisdiction extended so as to include sex, so that it can legitimately study and collect information regarding sex discrimination, so that it can confer with representatives of State governments and with universities and colleges regarding sex discrimination, so that it can submit reports on this to the Congress, and so that it might act as a clearinghouse for information, and to perform the "watchdog" function for women in the same manner that it does so well for other minorities.

The Equal Pay Act needs to be extended to cover executive, administrative, and professional employees. In study after study, women—particularly in education—earn less money than their male colleagues. I know of one full professor who is earning less than a newly hired male assistant professor in her department, who is fresh out of graduate school.

I know of another woman, an associate professor for more than 10 years, who discovered she was earning more than $1,000 below the bottom of her university's scale for associate professors.

Just recently I have heard of several women, in different disciplines and in different institutions, who work for nothing. I doubt if this is the new "volunteerism," because these women would prefer to be paid. The chairman of a department sees nothing wrong with paying a woman less because "she is married and therefore doesn't need as much," or paying her less because "she is not married, and therefore doesn't need as much." Without an extension of the Equal Pay Act, academic women will continue to earn less for equal work.

If section 805 is passed, the psychological effect of such legislation on women would be enormous. Women have been loath to complain about discrimination in their institutions because they risk academic suicide if they do so. I know of two women who did protest and who were promptly and officially censured. They may well lose their tenure, if not their jobs.

I know of several other women without tenure, who openly struggled against sex discrimination on their respective campuses, and who subsequently have not had their contracts renewed. Women need moral and legal support if they are to have the courage to fight for their rights in the academic community.

Section 805 would state loudly and clearly that the time has come to end sex discrimination in America's universities and colleges.

When I first started exploring sex discrimination in higher education, I naively thought that there were merely isolated individual instances of discrimination, and that where such discrimination existed, it was merely a matter of a particular department or a particular individual chairman or administrator.

Certainly every professional woman has anecdotes about discrimination, but there has been little that has been written or documented in terms of the total picture within the university community. As

WEAL's activities and filings have become known, women and men from all over the country, from small and large colleges and universities, from public and private institutions, from institutions of all sorts have contacted WEAL, sending statistical data and asking WEAL to file on their behalf against their college or university.

Let me add here that none of WEAL's filings have been based on anecdotal material. About 20 have been based on discriminatory advertising; the remainder and majority of the complaints have been based on hard statistical data.

As more and more information has been collected, there is no question whatsoever that there is a massive, consistent and vicious pattern of sex discrimination in our universities and colleges. On campus after campus, women are almost always restricted to the lower academic ranks and in some instances not hired at all. Departments that hire women in any numbers equal to the amount of qualified women available (based on the number and percentage of doctorates awarded to women in each field) are indeed a rarity, and truly an exception to the general overall discriminatory pattern.

Essentially our universities punish women for being women. They punish women not only for having children, but even for having the potential to bear children. Such blatant discrimination against women has gone virtually unchecked for years, for in every sector of university life women are losing ground.

Sex prejudice is so ingrained in our society that many who practice it are simply unaware that they are hurting women. It is the last socially acceptable prejudice. A professor in my own department—I should say my own former department, counseling and personnel services—sees nothing wrong in telling his students, men and women, that "women shouldn't be professionals."

Many of the most ardent supporters of civil rights for blacks, Indians, Spanish-speaking Americans and other minorities simply do not view sex discrimination as discrimination. No university today would advertse for a "white assistant professor," yet these same concerned humanitarians see nothing wrong with still advertising for a "male assistant professor." These same humanitarians fail to notice that half of each minority group are women.

In a little noted development all over the country, on both small and large campuses, women have begun to form groups across departmental and professional lines. They are beginning to do more than complain. They are examining the role of women on their campus, and their university's treatment of them.

In various professional groups, such as the American Psychological Association, the American Sociological Association, the American Historical Association, the Modern Language Association, the American Political Science Association, and others, women are forming pressure groups and demanding an end to discrimination within their respective professions. Women are tired of second-class citizenship on the campus.

We live in a rapidly changing world, one which is threatened by the problems of population growth. There is little reason to expect a woman to limit her family if the only realistic alternative to childbearing is a job far below her capacities, coupled with extensive educational and occupational discrimination. Extensive reform of abortion laws, and the dissemination of birth control information will have little impact unless women have something else to do with their lives. The education of women is crucial if we are to do this.

All of the provisions of section 805 extend existing legislation to conform with our stated national policy and goals of equality for all citizens. Women have been discriminated against in many areas of life, of which the university is but one. We need to begin to redress these wrongs.

Section 805 is a symbolic and actual beginning that would give hope and dignity to women, the second-class citizens of our nation. As a member of the Women's Equity Action League, as an educator of counselors, and as a psychologist, as a teacher, as a woman, a wife, and a mother, and above all as a human being, I urge you to support section 805.

Thank you.

Mrs. GREEN. Thank you very much, Dr. Sandler. As the country was very, very slow to do anything about the discrimination against blacks, we saw an increased polarization, we saw an increased militancy.

Let me state it another way: I see an increased polarization and an increased militancy coming about because of the failure of our society to recognize the tremendous amount of discrimination against women. Would you agree with that?

Dr. SANDLER. Yes; I am in contact with a great many women and they are angry and I am concerned about many of our younger women on campus who are perhaps even angrier than the women of my generation.

Mrs. GREEN. We also see blacks today forming voting blocs, which I don't happen to think is healthy in terms of good government. I never have felt that it is good to vote for a white or a black because of race, neither do I feel it is good to vote for a male or a female just because of sex. But do you think that this will happen, that as we see voting blocs of blacks born out of necessity, that we are going to have the same thing as far as women are concerned?

Dr. SANDLER. Yes; it has already begun. I was speaking to a woman in politics yesterday who gave me the figure that for every black male there are 10 women in this country of voting age. That includes black women and other minority women as well.

She is already thinking of how to mobilize women to vote for other women regardless of party, and she gave me a list of candidates of both parties who would be running in the fall elections.

I want to add something in terms of polarization. So often the whole women's movement is seen as an antimale thing and undoubtedly there will be polarization along these lines. I do want to add, however, that many of the women, indeed, many of the men in the women's movements are married and, of course, these women are married to men and many of them have children, half of whom are male children.

It is not so much an antimale movement as equal rights for people.

Mrs. GREEN. I agree with you. I also would like to explode the myth, with which I read again just the day before yesterday, that women are women's chief enemies and the reason there are not more women in politics is because women won't support women.

When I first ran for office, this was of concern to me and to my strategy campaign committee. We had in depth interviews and one of the questions was "Whom are you going to support?" My opponent was Tom McCall, who is the present Governor of Oregon.

After the one interviewed said: "I am going to support either Mrs. Green or Mr. McCall, then the next question was, "Why are you going to support Mr. McCall?" and 8 percent-plus, were going to support him "because he is a man." Of those who were interviewed, "Why are you going to support Mrs. Green?" it was amazingly interesting that 8 percent-plus—the figures were extremely close—said, "I am going to support Mrs. Green because she is a woman."

So one canceled out the other. I am convinced that in most sections of the country it is a myth that women will not support women candidates.

Dr. SANDLER. I don't know if there was ever any substance to the myth; perhaps for some it may have been true. It certainly is changing now.

Mrs. GREEN. In quite the opposite way, because there are fewer of them. It seems to me it ought to be a persuasive argument in this session of Congress for male politicians to support an end to discrimination, because historically, if I may be so bold as to say so, all politicians have counted on women to ring doorbells.

Dr. SANDLER. What is happening now is that women are getting tired of just ringing doorbells and in both parties there has been an effort by women to gain more power and control. There have been women's caucuses formed in an effort to get women into more policy-making positions, and to give them a fairer shake other than just ringing doorbells and answering telephones.

Mrs. GREEN. Only to be excluded from policy decisions the day after election.

Congressman Hathaway, I will yield to you, whether you want to question or hear from Dr. Murray. It depends on your time.

Mr. HATHAWAY. I would prefer to hear Dr. Murray's testimony.

Mrs. GREEN. Dr. Murray, will you proceed with your statement? Again, all three complete statements will be made a part of the record.

Dr. MURRAY. Before I go on the record, I have a number of studies and documents, mostly Government statistics, that are relevant to some of the matters I mention. May I submit them in bulk and have the counsel decide which are relevant for inclusion in the record?

Mrs. GREEN. Yes, I would ask unanimous consent that subject to the counsel's review on length and repetition, that they be made a part of the record.

Dr. MURRAY. My second question, you raised certain questions on which you wished information the last time. I have some information, particularly on the question of EEO's position on want ads and at the end of my testimony if we have time, I would like simply to place that in the record.

Madam Chairman and Mr. Hathaway, I am Pauli Murray, a professor of American studies at Brandeis University. I must say to the Committee that I put my credentials in my prepared statement partly out of pressure from my colleagues and partly because I hoped they would make the male members of the subcommittee take me seriously.

I teach legal studies, civil rights, law and social change, and a course on women in American society. My task in a college of liberal arts is to expose undergraduates to an understanding of the legal system in its various aspects—the judicial process, the legislative process, and the administrative process, and my appearance before this committee is in the nature of in-service training.

Many of my students are headed for law school. Others plan careers in education, community organization, or social work. All of them, however, are asking themselves the question whether our legal system is flexible enough to accommodate necessary social change. What I have to say to this subcommittee is influenced by my own desperate need to answer this question in the affirmative coupled with the apprehension that in the area of women's rights, as in other areas of human rights, our lawmakers will respond only when there is violence and disruption of nationwide proportions.

I appear before this subcommittee, however, as a member of the National Board of American Civil Liberties Union to testify in support of the provisions of H.R. 16098 which seeks to extend protection against sex-based discrimination, particularly in education and employment.

The ACLU stands for the principle of equality of treatment under the law and equality of opportunity without regard to sex. It has been active in litigation to apply this principle for the purpose of eliminating sex-based discrimination in jury service, in the criminal law, employment, admission to State universities, and the like, all of which have been fought by ACLU attorneys either representing women or filing *amicus curiae* briefs.

In its most recent policy statement on academic freedom and academic due process, ACLU has declared:

A teacher should be appointed solely on the basis of teaching ability and competence in his professional field without regard to such factors, as race, sex, nationality, creed, religious or political belief or affiliation, or behavior not demonstrably related to the teaching function. (ACLU Statement of Principles of Academic Freedom, etc., September 1966, p. 8.)

On June 7, 1970, the biennial conference of ACLU overwhelmingly adopted a strong policy recommendation to its national board on the rights of women, including the principle that admission to colleges and universities should not be denied on the basis of ethnic origin, race, religion, political belief or affiliation, sex, or other irrational basis. In ACLU's 50 years of experience seeking to protect individual rights, it has come to recognize that all human rights are indivisible and that the denial of these rights to any group threatens the rights of all. I am happy to espouse this principle here today.

From here on in I am on my own. Some of the views I express may not necessarily reflect ACLU position.

Interrelation of race and sex discrimination:

I have listened to the previous witnesses and wish to associate myself with their testimony which I wholeheartedly endorse, particularly the perceptive comments of Commissioner Wilma Scott Heide and her recognition of the urgency of effective legislative action to remove the barriers to the development of the talents of women in the United States. In view of the thoroughness with which my colleagues have documented widespread discrimination against women in the academic process, in the professions and in other employment, I shall attempt to highlight some areas for emphasis.

As a human rights attorney, I am concerned with individuals as whole human beings, being accorded the respect and dignity which is our common heritage. They are first and foremost persons, quite apart from any other identity they may possess, and as persons sharing our common humanity they are entitled to equal opportunity to fulfill their individual and unique potential.

I think there may be an answer to Mr. Hathaway's question on the probability of women finishing college in what I have just said.

This is our starting point, for in my view it is only as we recognize and hold sacred the uniqueness of each individual that we come to see clearly the moral and social evil of locking this individual into a group stereotype, whether favorable or unfavorable. I have learned this lesson, in part, because I am both a Negro and a woman whose experience embodies the conjunction of race and sex discrimination.

This experience also embodies the paradox of belonging simultaneously to an oppressed minority and an oppressed majority, and for good measure being left-handed in a right-handed world. As a self-supporting woman who has had the responsibility for elderly relatives, the opportunity for education and employment consonant with my potentialities and training has been a matter of personal survival.

Moreover, in more than 30 years of intensive study of human rights and deep involvement in the civil rights movement I have observed the interrelationships between what is often referred to as racism and sexism (Jim Crow and Jane Crow), and have been unable to avoid the conclusion that discrimination because of one's sex is just as degrading, dehumanizing, immoral, unjust, indefensible, infuriating and capable of producing societal turmoil as discrimination because of one's race.

Mrs. GREEN. Could I interrupt you there?

I talked to Shirley Chisholm yesterday and she tells me very emphatically that she has suffered far greater discrimination as a woman than she has suffered as a black.

Dr. MURRAY. One spends 50 years of one's life trying to get equal civil rights because of one's race and turns around and finds one must spend the second 50 years, if you should live so long, to get one's rights because of sex.

The marked parallels in the status of women and of Negroes/blacks have been documented by historians and social scientists. Whether the point of departure has been a study of women or of racial theories, contemporary scholars have been impressed by the interrelationship of these two issues in the United States. (Simone de Beauvoir, "The Second Sex"; Myrdal, "An American Dilemma," app. V, 1944; Ashley Montagu, "Man's Most Dangerous Myth: The Fallacy of Race," fourth ed.)

The history of Western culture and, more particularly, of ecclesiastical and common law strongly suggests that the subordinate status of women, in which they were not considered persons under the law, has provided the models for the subjugation of other oppressed groups. (See, for example, Myrdal, *op. cit.*, Daly *The Church and the Second Sex* (1968)). In George Fitzhugh's famous defense of chattel slavery in the United States in 1850,[1] he analogized it to the position of women and children.

Dr. Montagu has noted that the pattern of antifeminist argument against equality is identical with that of the racist argument. He observed that in the matter of equal opportunities for scientific achievement women have had little chance to obtain employment in the science departments of our colleges as instructors—about 1 to 100.

"Deny a particular group equality of opportunity," he says, "and then assert that because that group has not achieved as much as the groups enjoying complete freedom of opportunity, it is obviously in-

[1] *Slavery Justified by a Southerner,* 1850, in McKittrick, ed., *Slavery Defended,* Prentice-Hall, 1963.

ferior and can never do as well." (in the work cited, p. 182.) Moreover, he finds the same underlying motives at work in antifeminism
as in race prejudices, "namely, fear, jealousy, feelings of insecurity,
fear of economic competition, guilt feelings and the like." He reminds
us that this interrelation has persisted right up to the present:

> We know that to gain even so much as a hearing women had to fight every
> inch of the way. Ridiculed, maligned, opposed at almost every turn, and even
> imprisoned, the leaders of the women's movement realized that they would
> actually be forced to fight—and fight they did. They pitched no battles, although
> there were a few clashes with the police, but they insisted on making themselves
> heard—until they succeeded.
>
> The leaders of groups upon whom the egregious epithet "minority" has come to
> be visited would do well to take a leaf out of the suffragettes' book. In the year
> 1963 they (Negroes) finally did. (In the work cited, p. 184.)

The implications of these findings which are confirmed by my personal experiences and observations are irresistible. In matters of discrimination, although it is true that manifestations of racial prejudice
have often been more brutal than the subtler manifestations of sex
bias—for example, the use of ridicule, of women as the psychic counterpart of violence against Negroes—it is also true that the rights of
women and the rights of Negroes are only different phases of the fundamental and indivisible issue of human rights for all.

There are those who would have us believe that the struggle against
racism is the No. 1 issue of human relations in the United States and
must take priority over all other issues. I must respectfully dissent
from this view. The struggle against sexism is equally urgent. More
than half of all Negroes and other ethnic minorities are women. The
costly lesson of our own history in the United States is that when the
rights of one group are affirmed and those of another group are
ignored, the consequences are tragic.

Whenever political expediency has dictated that the recognition of
basic human rights be postponed, the resulting dissension and conflict
has been aggravated. This lesson has been driven home to us time
after time—in the Civil War, the woman's suffrage movement, the
violent upheavals of labor, and in the Negro revolt of the 1960's.

The late Dr. Kyle Haselden, former editor of the Christian Century, once made the perceptive observation that we are all victims of
the disease of prejudice. If it is true that, without exception, each of us
carries the mote of prejudice in our eye, then it follows that prejudice
manifested against one group through discriminatory action may well
seek outlets against other groups when such action is prohibited. This
theory is suggested in Dr. Montagu's sober comment on the racial
crisis in 1964. He observed:

> It is a thought worth pondering whether there may not be some relation
> between the slackening of prejudice against women and the increase in the
> intensity of prejudices against ethnic and minority groups; that is, whether a
> certain amount of displaced aggression is not involved here. Man, it would seem,
> must have a scapegoat, and for his purposes any distinguishable group will do
> against which the exhibition of aggression or prejudice is socially sanctioned. It is
> a likely hypothesis that much of the deep-seated aggression which was at one
> time canalized in an antifeminist direction today serves to swell the tide of that
> which expresses itself in race prejudice. (Op. cit., p. 183.)

The converse of this example is also worth pondering. It seems
clear that we are witnessing a worldwide revolution in human rights in
which traditionally excluded or alienated groups—blacks, women,
youth, various ethnic minorities and social minorities, the handi-

capped, and so forth—are all demanding the right to be accepted as persons and to share fully in making the decisions which shape their destinies.

Negroes and women are the two largest groups of minority status in the United States. The racial problem has been made visible and periodically more acute because of the peculiar history of black slavery and racial caste which produced a civil war and its bloody aftermath.

The acuteness of racism has forced us to engage in national self-examination and the growing militancy of our black minority has compelled us as a nation to reverse our former racist policies, at least in a formal legal sense. In neglecting to appreciate fully the indivisibility of human rights, however, we have often reacted with the squeaky-wheel-gets-the-grease approach and not given sufficient attention to the legitimate claims of other disadvantaged groups—poor whites, women, American Indians, Americans of Puerto Rican, Mexican, and Oriental origin, and the like. In so doing, we have often set in motion conditions which have created a backlash and which, if developed to an intense degree, would threaten to destroy the gains which Negroes have made over the past few decades, meager as these gains may have been for the masses of blacks.

The fact that women constitute more than 51 percent of the population, the very pervasiveness of sex discrimination which cuts across all racial, religious, ethnic, economic, and social groups, and the fact that women have cause to believe they are not taken seriously—all these combine to make the revitalized movement for women's liberation in the 1970's an instrument for potential widespread disruption if its legitimate claims are not honored.

Given the tendency of privileged groups to retain their power and privilege and to play one disadvantaged group off against another, and given the accelerating militancy of Women's Liberation, there is a grave danger of a headon collision of this movement with the movement for black liberation unless our decisionmakers recognize and implement the rights of all.

Dr. Ann Harris in her testimony before the subcommittee has referred to attempts to satisfy the claims of black militants at the expense of women in institutions of higher learning. Her statement can be duplicated in incident after incident in Government, private industry, and in education.

Mrs. GREEN. Do any one of the three of you, Dr. Murray, know how many universities still require a higher grade point average for admission for women than for men?

Dr. MURRAY. I am told my university, Brandeis, does. This is sheer hearsay. I do not have any official information. The reason given for this, however, is a very interesting one.

It is said that the women of Brandeis, on the average, make higher scores on the college boards than do the men. So that if the women were admitted in accordance with their scholastic ability, there would be probably a much greater majority of women than of men, and this would then create social problems.

So there is an attempt to try to keep what you might call a "sex balance." I will submit for the record a table of the number of women and men graduating with honors for the decade 1961–70, from Brandeis University. It was extremely enlightening to me, and it indicated why I had been staying up nights for 2 years, because my students are so bright.

I think in view of the kinds of questions that are in Mr. Hathaway's mind I would like to digress just a moment.

Mrs. GREEN. Do either of the others know how many institutions require higher grade point averages for college admission for women?

Dr. SANDLER. Sometimes it is not done quite that way. They say we will only admit a certain amount of women, so like at Yale they only admit a small number of women. Then, of course, those women who are admitted tend to have very high averages.

Dr. HARRIS. It tends to be an unwritten rather than a written rule. I have heard it many times. The first time I heard of sexual discrimination, was the fact that that it was harder for a woman than a man to get into college and at graduate level this discrimination is even greater.

I do talk about this in my testimony.

Mrs. GREEN. You are a psychologist, Dr. Sandler. Would you please explain to me the psychological reason for requiring a higher grade point average for women for admission to a college and the trend to waive admission standards for other people at college these days?

Dr. SANDLER. I think this is again not seeing women as people. It is completely inconsistent to say that a particular minority ought to get fair treatment and help in getting into college, when it turns out quite often that the members of that particular minority, be it black, Mexican American or whatever, more often then not tend to be practically all males. It is as though there are not many black girls who need education or help. Compensatory recruiting for minorities is often aimed primarily at the male members of the minorities.

Mrs. GREEN. Again if I may use the Office of Education, the Government, by its policies, its programs, and its guidelines, encourages the waiving of admission standards for some for entrance to college and yet are totally unconcerned about requiring higher GPA's for women.

Dr. SANDLER. Because in the first case there is an admission that there has been an injustice done and therefore one must remedy the effects of past injustices, which means you have a quota, but a quota to increase the number of people you already have. In other words, if you have 1 percent, you aim for 5 percent to get more in.

In the second case it is with women, "Why, we really don't want them anyway, so let's let in as few as possible."

Mrs. GREEN. I don't understand the justification for this, just because my grandmother was treated as far less than equal and because my grandmother was not allowed to vote and because there were occupations where my grandmothers could not earn a decent living, I don't know that I need any particular special attention today because my grandmother was badly abused. This hardly seems the logical way to right an historic wrong—and it may create another injustice that we could avoid.

Dr. SANDLER. This is what the psychologists call "cultural lag." It takes us a while to catch up with the realities of life.

Mrs. GREEN. Do you agree with that, that I ought to have special treatment because my grandmother and great-grandmother were treated as less than equal?

Dr. SANDLER. I think if we are to get women in places where they ought to be, I think we will have to make a compensatory kind of push, in that case I agree with you, I think we have to give women more for a while.

Dr. HARRIS. You don't need to waive admission standards for women. The women admitted are already an awful lot better than the admitted men. If women were just admitted on an equal basis, they would be quite happy.

Dr. MURRAY. I have here (indicating) a table showing the number of honor graduates by sex from Brandeis University, College of Arts and Sciences, for the past 10 years. I find this a fascinating document because of the parity of numbers. This is not a case where there are many more women than men or vice versa. I do note, however; that in the number of degrees conferred from 1961 through 1963, there were more women receiving—slightly more women than men.

Then there began to be a drop, slightly more men than women. This would suggest, if my informant were correct, that there began to be something like a limitation on the admission of women in order to keep this balance.

I would like, however, at this time to read into the record the total figures of this decade in terms of the honor graduates which was the question you raised the other day.

For the decade 1961 through 1970 Brandeis University graduated from the liberal arts college 3,583 graduates, of which males were 1,824 and females were 1,759, which means slightly less women than men.

In the honor *cum laude* with no departmental honors, the total number won by men was 193; the total number won by women was 262. In *magna cum laude* with no departmental honors, the total number won by men was 57, the total number won by women was 91.

In just departmental honors, the men went ahead of the women; there it was not a question of scholastic average, but more men did honors papers than women. The men got 76 and the women got 54.

In the combination of *cum laude* with departmental honors men received 185, women received 152. *Magna cum laude* with departmental honors, men received 119, women received 131. *Summa cum laude* with departmental honors, men received 43, women received 29.

In the class of 1970, which graduated just this June, in *summa cum laude* men received eight, women received eight.

These statistics might help us understand something of the fury of young women when they know on the record that they have the capacity when they graduate from college, and they are then asked when they apply for a job, "Can you type?"

Mrs. GREEN. I would have to make a confession that I have not specialized in—indeed I have avoided the so-called women's issues because I can so easily be accused of being only interested in women's issues and not being equally concerned about the great national and international issues.

I have stayed away from discrimination because some might accuse me of being less than objective—of having a bias. But it seems to me no woman can grow to maturity (a woman who wants to have a profession and a career) and not be keenly and very pointedly aware of the innumerable times that discrimination occurs.

I have been aware of this all of my life, though I would remain fairly silent on it. Mr. Hogan, the counsel of the committee, says that things are much worse than I realized and he has just informed me that from personal experience he knows of a large university in this area in admitting students will take the second echelon women and the top men in one of its departments—because the women would show up better. So they will not admit the best women students to this department.

Now this is the first time I have ever heard this and he tells me from personal experience he knows this is the case.

Dr. SANDLER. This is again the old stereotype that the male must be superior, in every way superior to females, which gets translated that *all* males must be superior in *all* ways to *all* females. It is like weight-lifting. Most men can lift more weights than women, but being married to a man with a bad back, I will say this is not true of *all* men and *all* women.

Again with heights, most men are taller than most women, but surely all of us know some short men and tall women. I lift the suit-cases in our family and nobody is very upset about it because I can do it better.

Mrs. GREEN. Before my colleague has to leave, I am going to ask unanimous consent that the remaining parts of Dr. Murray's testimony be placed in the record as if she had read them, so that we might continue to the time when he feels he must leave.

Mr. HATHAWAY. Thank you, Madam Chairman.

My only basic question is just what the limit should be with respect to barring discrimination.

Dr. MURRAY. None.

Dr. SANDLER. As a taxpayer it is very hard to think of supporting any particular institution that would discriminate in admitting my two girls. I just don't feel that is a good use of my money when it comes to that. I feel discriminated against when that happens.

Mrs. GREEN. If I may comment on that, I have never had a daughter, but I have two sons and I feel just as strongly about it as you do, if they are going to discriminate against girls, I don't see any reason why I should support them with my taxes.

Dr. Harris?

Dr. HARRIS. There is another short article, you can decide whether you would like to include it in the record. It is called "The Politics of Housework" and I will send you a copy anyway. I think you will enjoy it.

Mrs. GREEN. Dr. Murray.

Dr. MURRAY. The point I am trying to make here is that the United States cannot afford to repeat the costly errors of the 19th century in the shrunken world of 20th century crises. One of these errors was the failure to grant universal suffrage at the end of the Civil War, a failure the political consequences of which are still being suffered today.

The enfranchisement of the Negro male, while denying suffrage to all females, black and white, in 1870 delayed women's suffrage for a half-century during which period Negro males were almost totally dis-franchised in the South through legal and extra-legal measures—the "Grandfather clause," intimidation, terrorism and lynching.

Viewing the aftermath of the Reconstruction in retrospect, one cannot help wondering if the history of that region might not have been vastly different if women had received the vote along with Negro males in 1870. The political emancipation of women in the South might well have eased the transition from a slave society to a society of free men and women.

Political power in the hands of white women, in particular, could have reduced the fear of Negro domination. Women, black and white, involving half of the population could have brought to bear their influence upon the difficult problems of reconstruction.

It is significant that, whatever other forces may have been at work in the South, a sharp drop in lynching followed the achievement of universal woman's suffrage in 1920 and the subsequent organization of white church women in the South against lynching. From 1919 to 1929, the number of recorded lynchings in which Negroes were victims dropped from 76 to 7, as the following table indicates:
(Table follows:)

NUMBER OF LYNCHINGS

Year	White	Negro	Total
1919	7	76	83
1920	8	53	61
1921	5	59	64
1922	6	51	57
1923	4	29	33
1924	0	16	16
1925	0	17	17
1926	7	23	30
1927	0	16	16
1928	1	10	11
1929	3	7	10

Source: U.S. Commission on Civil Rights, Justice, 1961.

Dr. MURRAY. The humanizing effect of women's participation in the civil rights struggle in the South during the 1950's and 1960's has not been fully appreciated. Negro women led many of the most crucial demonstrations without loss of life and with superb discipline.

I am thinking particularly of Mrs. Daisy Bates, the key adult figure and State chairman of NAACP in the Little Rock crisis of 1957–59, involving the integration of nine children in the Little Rock High School. White women took the initiative in organizing "Save Our Schools" campaigns when the local schools were closed in defiance of the Supreme Court mandate to desegregate Southern schools.

When ACLU attorneys, including myself, were preparing the brief on behalf of the plaintiffs in *White* v. *Crook*, the landmark decision by a Federal court that the 14th amendment prohibits sex discrimination as well as racial discrimination in jury service, we learned that the Department of Justice was persuaded to file an *amicus curiae* brief supporting our arguments because Mr. John Doar had learned through his experience in the civil rights cases in the South that the Department was more likely to get a fair verdict when women were represented on Southern juries.

The emergent revitalized women's rights/women's liberation movement is no historical accident. It was born of the involvement of women in the civil rights movement of the 1940's, 1950's and 1960's. Because it affects a literal majority of the population, it has a revolutionary potential even greater than the black revolt.

It has the compelling force of an idea whose time has come, and neither ridicule nor verbal castigation can delay it. At present it has a controlled fury and a passion which is at times frightening when one realizes the depth of frustration from which it comes.

I do not think the male members of this subcommittee can fully appreciate the extent to which women's liberation has taken hold across the Nation if you attempt to view it objectively merely through the facts and figures which have been presented here. Women are appealing, demanding, organizing for and determined to achieve acceptance as persons, as full and equal partners with men in every phase of our national life.

They sense that we are in a deep national crisis of values, a crisis which makes us more vulnerable to internal disintegration than to destruction by external military attack. Transcending their cry for full equality is the apprehension that nothing less than our national survival is at stake, and they see this crisis in part as the result of our failure to utilize our human resources and release the creative energies which could bring about internal reconciliation and redeem our reputation as a genuine democracy in the eyes of the world.

We, as a nation, have lived through nearly three decades of racial turmoil which at times has approached civil war. I am convinced that one of the reasons we have not solved our racial problem is not so much that all white people are racists in the current rhetoric of black militancy, but rather, that we have not faced the more fundamental problem of the healthy relationship between the two sexes.

Men have become enslaved by their dependency as well as their dominance. They pay a heavy price in shortened lives, military casualties, broken homes and the heartbreak of parents whose children are alienated from them. Many men find themselves unable to live up to the expectations of masculinity which men have defined for themselves, and many are now chagrined to find that women are no longer willing to accept the role of feminity which men have defined for women.

Just as blacks have found it necessary to opt for self-definition, women are seeking their own image of themselves nurtured from within rather than imposed from without. I am led to the hypothesis that we will be unable to eradicate racism in the United States unless and until we simultaneously remove all sex barriers which inhibit the development of individual talents. I am further convinced that the price of our survival as a nation is the sharing of our power and wealth—or rather the redistribution of this power and wealth—among black and white, rich and poor, men and women, old and young, red and brown and all the in-betweens.

This requires more than "objectivity." It demands a sensitivity, a recognition that individual human beings lie behind those depressing facts which have been assembled here. It demands that we women, who are the petitioners before Congress symbolized by this subcommittee, keep before us the goal of liberating our own humanity and that of our male counterparts. It demands from those who hold formal power—predominantly white males—something closely akin to conversion, the imagination and vision to realize that an androgynous society is vastly superior to a patriarchal society—which we now are—and that the liberation of women through legislation, through a restructuring of our political and social institutions, and through a change of our cultural conditioning may well hold the key to many of the complex social issues for which we do not now have answers.

DISCRIMINATION AGAINST NEGRO/BLACK WOMEN

I earnestly hope that this subcommittee will invite representative women from other minority groups and other economic and social sectors of American life to enrich this record with their views and social concerns. I listened to some of these women a few days ago at the Golden Jubilee Anniversary Conference of the Women's Bureau, U.S. Department of Labor and believe that they can provide the members of this subcommittee with valuable insights with respect to the proposed legislation.

It is my special responsibility, however, to speak on behalf of Negro women who constitute about 93 percent of all nonwhite women, and I wish to call to your attention an article which appeared in the March 1970 *Crisis* published by NAACP, "Job Discrimination and the Black Women," by Miss Sonia Pressman, senior attorney in the Office of General Counsel of the Equal Employment Opportunity Commission and an expert in the law of race and sex discrimination.

This document presents the special problems of Negro/black women because of their dual victimization by race and sex-based discrimination coupled with the disproportionate responsibilities they carry for the economic and social welfare of their families compared with their white counterparts. All that has been reported here with respect to women generally applies with particular poignance to Negro women who, as Miss Pressman points out, are at the bottom of the economic totem pole.

In 1966 the median income of a nonwhite woman who had completed high school was less ($2,475) than that of a nonwhite man who had 8 years of education ($3,681) or that of a white man who had not completed the eighth grade ($2,945). (1969 Handbook on Women Workers, Women's Bureau Bulletin 294, p. 141.)

Consider the fact that while women generally in the United States are the responsible heads of 11 percent (5.2 million) of all families, in March 1966 nonwhite women headed one-fourth of the 4.4 million nonwhite families.

I might underscore the fact that the women who are the responsible economic heads of their families constitute as large a minority as the black minority.

Nearly four out of ten (or 1,871,000) nonwhite families were living in poverty in 1965. Of the 3,860,000 white families headed by a woman, 30 percent were poor. Of the 1,132,000 nonwhite families headed by a woman, 62 percent were poor. (1969 Handbook on Women Workers, pp. 130–131; Negro Women, p. 3)

Although on the average, Negro women have slightly more schooling than Negro men at the elementary and high school levels, their depressed wages stem from the fact they are concentrated in low-paying jobs as service workers and private household workers. Of the 2.9 million Negro women 18 years and over employed in March 1966, 58.5 percent held jobs as service workers including private household work.

When the fact that the 1968 median wage of full-time year-round household workers 14 years of age and older was only $1,523 is taken into account (see Labor D.C. (WB 70–193), p. 1), we can understand more clearly why protection against both race and sex discrimination is crucial not merely for the Negro woman as an individual, but also for millions of black youth in families headed by black women.

The Negro woman has a higher rate of unemployment, a higher incidence of poverty, a greater proportionately economic responsibility and less overall opportunity than white women or black or white men. If we are genuinely concerned about removing the causes of racial conflict, we must relate the statistics I have just described to the deep anger of black teenage girls and black women.

The comparative unemployment rates by sex, color, and age, 1954–66, are depicted in chart D, "Negro Women," page 10, which has been introduced as an exhibit. You will note the sharp rise in the unemployment rate of nonwhite teenage girls (14 to 19 years, of age) coupled with a sharp drop in the unemployment rate for nonwhite teenage boys and a gradual sloping for white male and female teenagers. The rates of unemployment in 1966 are as follows: White males, 2.9 percent; white females, 4.3 percent; nonwhite males, 6.6 percent; and nonwhite females 8.8 percent.

The rate of unemployment among nonwhite female teenagers, 14 to 19 years of age, was highest of all: White males, 9.9 percent; white female, 11.0 percent; nonwhite males, 21.2 percent; and nonwhite females, 31.1 percent.

Mrs. GREEN. Could I interrupt there.

I don't understand the lack of concern by women's groups about the discrimination against girls in the Job Corps. I have used these figures of the highest unemployment rate and I fought for an amendment allowing 50 percent enrollment for girls. We have never even achieved that. Girls have never constituted even 30 percent of the Job Corps enrollees. Our Education and Labor Committee of the House has legislated to discriminate.

Two or 3 weeks ago, we had a bill in for a summer program. As it first came to us, it was just for boys, no girls were to be employed for the summer. We finally got the girls included, but if there are any girls in that program, I will be a bit surprised by the time it is implemented.

Dr. MURRAY. It is in part, I think, because much of the organization among women today, that is, the organization for action against discrimination, is taking place particularly among the professional and academic women and women in the higher industrial occupations climbing the ladder to the higher paying jobs.

The lower economically paid women, I don't think, are as well organized. They are not often in trade unions. When they are black women, very often they are organized in the welfare rights organizations to some extent, but the tragedy of black women today is that they are brainwashed by the notion that priority must be given to the assertion of black male manhood and that they must now stand back and push their men forward.

What this means, in essence, is that while the militant rhetoric is that we are rejecting the values of white society; on the other hand, we are holding on very definitely to the patriarchal aspect of white America, and I think it is tragic and I stand against it. But it partly explains why these women aren't coming in here demanding equal opportunities for girls who are threatened with poverty.

Mrs. GREEN. This is one of the places again where I, as a woman, hate to be constantly the one to raise equality for girls—as a woman's issue. But I was very disappointed when in the committee on the Job Corps legislation, we could never get any recognition by the Education and Labor Committee of the House or by the Administration downtown or by the full Congress that girls were entitled to 50 percent of the places in the Job Corps program. We could never get that recognition for fairness and equality of opportunity.

Dr. MURRAY. I would like to tell you a rather poignant story with rather humorous overtones.

Several years ago, I think about 2 years ago, I sat on the advisory committee of women to OEO. There also sat on that committee a Mrs. Ruth Adkins, I think her name is, who is very active in welfare rights organizations, or certainly in poverty community organizations. OEO was up before Congress, I think, for appropriations and I was trying to inquire into the very question that you are talking about.

I think they were going to close some of the camps, the conservation camps, and I raised the question as to why these camps could not be used in a coed sense and that women also have an opportunity for them. Mrs. Adkins figuratively flew at me, saying "You middle-class women can send your daughters there, but we are not going to do this," and the press picked it up and made quite a business of hair-pulling and what-not.

This was in 1967. I met Mrs. Adkins again at the Women's Bureau conference last week and I said rather tentatively, "Mrs. Adkins, are we any closer together than we were the last time I saw you?" She said, "I think so" and it happened that in various matters on the floor we were on the same side.

I did not learn until after the meeting was over that what Mrs. Adkins thought I was talking about in 1967 was not "conservation camps," but "concentration camps." So much for communication.

Dr. SANDLER. I would like to say the Women's Equity Action League is extremely interested in what happens to working women and every one of our complaints regarding sex discrimination on the universities includes a request that the hiring and promotional policies of staff and faculty be included.

We are very much aware that there is a good deal of discrimination against the women who clean the bathrooms, who clean the hallways, and who work in the kitchens of the university. We would be glad to come and testify concerning the Job Corps and other matters relating to young girls and to working women.

Mrs. GREEN. We have had under title III testimony before the committee where high schools have organized classes for boys only. I believe I told you this off the record; if I am duplicating it, I will ask the counsel to take it out.

I asked why there were not special classes for girls and they said, "Well, the boys need it more than the girls." I said, "It seemed to be under the law that it would be required to give special classes for disadvantaged girls as well as boys." One of my colleagues sarcastically asked me if this were carried out, then I would eliminate classes for unwed mothers and I said, "No; I would not, I would make it available for unwed fathers." I thought they needed the special counseling and guidance as much.

But it seems to me that we have a systematic exclusion through programs financed by the Federal Government. We have classes for boys, for disadvantaged boys, we do not have them for girls, and that is amazing statistics that out of the 278,000, whatever it is, of apprenticeships, 1 percent for girls, that we never have gotten up to 30 percent of the Job Corps places for girls and then we are amazed at the high unemployment rate and society points with shame to the girl who become the prostitute or have a baby to get on welfare rolls—when we have given them absolutely no other way of earning a living.

Dr. HARRIS. They can earn more doing that than in legitimate jobs.

Mrs. GREEN. That's right, it is a shocking accusation against society.

Dr. MURRAY. The younger women who are involving themselves in women's liberation are doing many innovative things which they think of as liberation. For example, they are learning to use tools, they are learning many things that stereotyped views have said that women are incapable of doing.

These same young women might well be steered into, let us say, construction work. There are many women who enjoy the whole process of building. I myself like to do woodworking as a hobby. I think that the conditions you describe will not change until women committed to equal employment opportunity are in decisionmaking positions where they can ferret out and block the discriminatory policy, because you here on the Hill may pass the law, but thousands of men in top super-service positions administer that law and the women are down below in nonpolicy-making positions.

This leads me to say that many of us are beginning to think about bipartisan political action, because we have got to get more women in policymaking positions, not merely because they are women, but women committed to women's development.

Mrs. GREEN. I really believe that all anybody is asking is just to be treated the same as men. But I would also venture a guess that if there were the same number of women members of Congress on this Education and Labor Committee, we would have had 50 percent of the places in the Job Corps for girls. I don't think there is any doubt about it.

I think down at the Office of Economic Opportunity if 50 percent of the people making policy were women, that they would not have recommended and enforced a policy giving most of the money and the attention to boys—and ignoring the training, the counseling, and guidance and encouragement for girls.

Dr. SANDLER. Of course, under title VI, it is quite legal to have Job Corps or any Federal program completely limited to males.

Mrs. GREEN. Exactly. That is why this legislation is before us. I thought that just reason and commonsense would bring about fair administration of the law, but I have now abandoned that conclusion. This is exactly the same reason I have always been reluctant to support an equal rights amendment. I thought that fairness and persuasion would bring the change. I have also abandoned that position—because the years have not brought about those changes.

Dr. MURRAY. I will conclude my testimony with a few very brief remarks on the legislation.

In the face of the figures previously given, is it any wonder that a black woman college student at Brandeis University shortly before the Ford Hall crisis in January 1969 was overheard to say, "Black men, get your guns." I am also reminded of my beloved grandmother's constant warning, "Idleness [i.e., unemployment] is the devil's workshop."

It is important to recognize that while the appallingly low economic status of Negro women is related to lack of educational opportunity, it is integrally related to dual discrimination. A week ago, June 12, I listened to the Honorable Arthur A. Fletcher, Assistant Secretary of Labor, addressing the 50th anniversary conference of the Women's Bureau and telling the 1,000 women assembled there from every geographical and social sector of the Nation the moving story of how his own mother carried the heavier economic load in rearing her children, although his father worked hard to do his share.

Mr. Fletcher explained that his mother held two college degrees, but was forced to support her family by employment as a domestic worker.

My own struggle for higher education through college and law school apart from scholarships for tuition was financed by working as a waitress, dishwasher, elevator operator, night switchboard clerk, and bus girl in a large hotel in Washington during World War II. In this last job the waiters whom we bus girls served were all Negro males, but they tipped us only 25 cents per night.

Our salary of $1.50 per night plus a second-class meal supplemented by what we could steal from the kitchen constituted our weekly wage. If anyone should ask a Negro woman what is her greatest achievement, her honest answer would be, "I survived."

Despite these depressing facts, there is a strong tendency throughout Government and private industry to emphasize the underemployment of the Negro male in relation to the Negro female and to perpetuate the myth of the "matriarchal" Negro family. (See, e.g., the Government report attributed to Daniel P. Moynihan, "The Negro Family," 1965.)

It is an open scandal that civil rights groups dominated by Negro male leaders have been instrumental in utilizing manpower programs and other programs of Federal assistance to raise the status of Negro male youth, while all but ignoring Negro female youth. I hope that this subcommittee will inquire into the various programs financed by the Office of Economic Opportunity for a breakdown by race and sex. The results might be enlightening.

Let me offer one typical illustration of "discrimination by oversight" or "discrimination by design." Brandeis University has instituted a transitional-year program for disadvantaged youth whose high school records or college board results do not meet the admissions standards but who, in the opinion of the administrators and faculty of the program, have the potential to do satisfactory work at the college level if given a year of compensatory education and counseling.

The program is financed in large part by OEO. During its first year, 1968–69, 26 students were admitted to the program. Of the 26, 23 were black males and three were white or Puerto Rican males. No women, black or white, were in the program. I do not know whether any women were recruited or applied.

Pressures from women faculty members resulted in some improvement in 1969–70: the ratio of white youth in the program increased, and of the 26 participants in last year's program, about six were women—one of these a young white woman.

Quite apart from the obvious *prima facie* discrimination involved, the presence of 23 black male youth on a campus where all the black women students were regularly admitted on the basis of their scholastic records created certain social pressures. These young men were deeply involved in aggressively asserting their black manhood. They were also involved in developing racial solidarity through their Afro-American student organization.

But, in fact, they were scholastically second-class citizens in relation to their black female counterparts, all of whom held higher educational status. My personal view is that this paradoxical situation was a factor in the social tensions and frustrations which produced the Ford Hall takeover.

It is against this background that I address myself to some brief comments on the provisions of section 805 of H.R. 16098.

Amendment of title VI, Civil Rights Act of 1964 to include "Sex"

I respectfully submit that in light of the widespread discrimination against women in many areas and in light of the need to protect all groups of minority status against actual or potential discrimination, as a rule of thumb all antidiscrimination measures should include sex along with race, color, religion, national origin, age, and other prohibited bases of discrimination. I do not have time to document the assertion that women are discriminated against in housing (particularly single women or women separated from their husbands), in public accommodations, in criminal law, in jury service, as well as in educational and employment opportunities.

The massiveness of the federally assisted programs to which title VI applies permits women to be discriminated against in a wide area of services and facilities, and particularly the women of minority groups. Section 805(a) of H.R. 16098 would close a much needed gap in the fair administration of these programs.

I add a caveat, this will be true only if we can get women on the Compliance Boards, and there are women in the investigative units.

The experience of the Equal Employment Opportunity Commission with the administration of title VII amply demonstrates that "sex" provisions can be administered along with "race" provisions in our Federal antidiscrimination policies and the procedures developed by the U.S. Civil Service Commission, the Office of Federal Contract Compliance, and the Wage and House Administration of the Equal Pay Act provide a body of experience upon which to draw as well as the regulations of the Department of Health, Education, and Welfare under title VI.

In addition, the amendment of title VI is necessary to prevent a backward trend in equal educational opportunity as some local school authorities in the South seek to desegregate schools by race through the device of segregating public school children by sex. At least two Federal district courts in the Fifth circuit—I think they are schools in Mississippi and Louisiana—covering school districts in Mississippi and Louisiana have approved such desegregation plans and I am told that the Department of Justice has acquiesced.

It has been reported that the boys and girls affected by these plans strongly oppose being segregated by sex, and in my opinion a public school segregated by sex contains the seed of psychological damage not unlike the segregation condemned by the U.S. Supreme Court in *Brown* v. *Board of Education.*

Amendment of section 702 of title VII to remove exemption of educational institutions: Section 805(b) of H.R. 16098 would remove the exemption of teachers from the application of title VII (Equal Employment Opportunity) of the Civil Rights Act. The urgent need for coverage of educational institutions by title VII has been made clear by previous testimony.

It should be observed, however, that section 805(b) would apply only to private educational institutions since section 701(b) of title VII defining the term "employer" expressly excludes a State or political subdivision thereof. Thus, the remedy for conditions at a State university which Dr. Ann Scott described on June 17 is not within the terms of the proposed amendment now being considered by this subcommittee.

The amendment needs to be expanded to cover both public and private institutions of learning by also amending section 701(b) of title VII to make an exception in the case of educational institutions.

Mrs. GREEN. If I may interrupt there, am I not correct that this is the pending business in the equal employment bill that is now before the full committee?

Mr. HOGAN. Yes; the next executive session will take it up.

Mrs. GREEN. It is the pending business. If it is done, it will not need to be put in this bill. If it is not done, we will add it.

Dr. MURRAY. Does it still contain the Esch amendment?

Mrs. GREEN. The Esch amendment at this point is being offered, but I think it will be defeated.

Dr. MURRAY. One of the great values of amending title VII to cover educational institutions is that in light of the overwhelming testimony here, clearly there is evidently a pattern or practice of discrimination in many educational institutions. Under title VII the Attorney General is authorized to bring suit where there are cases of a pattern or practice, an industrywide pattern or practice of discrimination.

I might point out that at present the Attorney General's office has never taken a sex case on the basis of pattern or practice, although it has taken something like 40 or 45 racial cases.

The inclusion of "sex" in title VI of the Civil Rights Act of 1964, would not remedy the evil of discrimination against academic women who seek jobs as members of faculties, since title VI as presently written is applicable only to discrimination in any employment resulting from a program with a primary objective of providing employment.

I believe that Dr. Bernice Sandler is placing in the record a memorandum describing the legislative history of section 702 of title VII prepared by Kathryn G. Heath so that I shall limit my remarks to the observation that the language which section 805(b) seeks to delete from section 702 (title VII) was not in the bill as originally passed by the House, but became part of the language of the Dirksen compromise Senate bill.

It shows that this exemption granted to educational institutions was not in the House bill as passed, but crept into the compromise Dirksen Senate bill. This seems to be no basis for it. There seems to be no legislative history for it to indicate any reason for it other than certain special interests.

Possibly it may well be that there are civil liberties organizations that have some problems of academic freedom and faculties may have some problems of academic freedom, so one could expect that there may be resistance to removing this exemption.

You expressed the view of the absence of women being *prima facie* evidence of discrimination and you are aware of the fact that there are colleges who turn out first-rate male and female honor graduates, but if you look at the faculties of these colleges, you will see that the woman, as was said so eloquently the other day, "simply disappear" as the ranks grow higher.

I would now like to make just one or two statements in answer to a question you raised the other day about the EEOC action and help wanted ads, the sex segregation. You also made the comment, you asked the rhetorical question: can you imagine what would happen if there were adverse advertisements, black or white only, and my own experience includes the struggle in the 1930's and 1940's to get "white only" or "black" or "Negro" out of the help wanted ads.

EEOC, as you know, issued the guideline. The American Newspaper Publishers Association went into court and tried to get a temporary restraining order, asserting that EEOC had no authority to issue a guideline and that it was causing irreparable loss of revenues to the newspapers.

The court refused to grant the injunction, but ruled that since EEOC has no authority to enforce its rules, these rulings do not have the force of law because ultimately they must be enforced by the courts. So this left EEOC with the right to issue the guideline, but no enforcement power behind it.

Now a plaintiff by the name of Brush, *Brush* v. *San Francisco Newspaper Publishing*, has gone into court against the San Francisco Chronicle charging discrimination under title VII. As you know, the general notion is that a newspaper is not an employer, when it is not engaging in employment, but EEOC has entered that case amicus and is arguing that when putting ads or publishing want ads, in effect, the newspaper is acting as an employment agency and, therefore, in its capacity as an employment agency it is within the jurisdiction of the EEOC and subject to the prohibition of the act.

I am told by legal counsel in EEOC that they don't think they will win the case in the lower court and it will obviously go up on an appeal to the ninth circuit.

I want to emphasize the great necessity for enforcement powers for EEOC if one is concerned about equal employment opportunity for women. Women as a group carry the largest burden in the country for enforcing equal employment opportunity rights.

For the reason that only roughly about 20 out of the 36 jurisdictions which have FEP laws included sex at the present time. This means that all of the women in the other States have to appeal to the Federal act and since the Federal act has no enforcement powers, this means that economic burden upon women to go into court, to hire a lawyer, and to carry this burden alone is very great.

So enforcement powers for EEOC would be of particular advantage to women.

I also want to point out that the present tendency on the part of some courts to give a broad interpretation to the bona fide occupational qualification, would, if upheld ultimately by the Supreme Court, sound a death knell of title VII and its benefits to women.

There is presently pending before the Supreme Court a case called *Phillips* v. *Martin-Marietta*, certiorari has been granted. This was a case involving the issue as as to whether an employer has the right under title VII not to hire a mother of preschool-age children, and this is the issue that is to be decided by the U.S. Supreme Court.

Recognizing that some 10 million working mothers have children under 18, some 6 million children under six, some 2.2 million children under three, so that should the employer's interpretation prevail, this would be a serious blow to working mothers who have to work.

Mrs. GREEN. Mr. Hogan advises me we have a witness appearing on this particular matter.

Dr. MURRAY. Another case which is very serious is *Dias* v. *Pan American Airlines*. The airlines have fought consistently and vigorously since the inception of EEOC to persuade the Commission and the courts to rule that sex is a bona fide occupational qualification for being an airline stewardess or an in-flight cabin attendant. EEOC has taken the position that the job can be satisfactorily performed by both sexes.

Mrs. GREEN. Have they taken the same position on pilots?

Dr. MURRAY. Yes, yes; there is a case now pending in the California court of a young woman who has sued one of the western-based airlines on this issue.

Mrs. GREEN. I wrote the president of United Airlines on the flight from New York to Chicago, which was called the Executive Flight— for men only.

Dr. MURRAY. They have taken it off.

Mrs. GREEN. This appears in the exchange of correspondence. They first told me, by the way, that obviously the people liked it.

Through the years I have heard of the "cooks' polls" in regard to blacks. You know, "my cook tells me they like it the way it is," and, it would seem none of the cooks objected to discrimination against Negroes.

Now I am pretty wary of people telling me about the wives' polls. "My wife tells me that she doesn't feel any discrimination." Now on the airlines we are told that discrimination is perfectly all right, because the passengers like it that way—men and women. Well, I know many women executives who did not like it that way. They were inconvenienced and felt discriminated against.

Dr. MURRAY. Unfortunately, a Federal district court has bought that argument and I do hope counsel will make that decision available to you to read on a day when your blood pressure is very, very low. The court has come down hard on the fact that customer preference can be a BOFQ, and should that principle stand, it would mean that clients might say they didn't want a woman lawyer and I would be out of a job.

You could go the whole range, wherever women are trying to break through professionally if such a decision stands. It is customer preference, along with some other language which I think you would be very interested in.

Mr. HOGAN. Do you have that case citation?

Dr. MURRAY. It is *Dias* v. *Pan American*, and if you have access to CCH employment practices, you can probably pick it up very quickly in the index. It may be 62 Labor cases, I can't give you the paragraph number.

I think this about covers the questions you had raised and I want to answer them for you.

Mrs. GREEN. I thank you very much and I am deeply indebted to all three of you, and I hope we may have many conversations together in the future. We will go over all the material and, as I said before, I want this the most complete record that has been assembled in terms of the discrimination in both the legislative and executive branches and in all other forms of discrimination against women.

Dr. MURRAY. May I add just one final footnote?

When the task force report was presented the other day, we neglected to point out that the consensus in the plenary session of the

Women's Bureau Conference was not only that there be implementation of the provisions, the general provisions of the task force, but that there be special attention given to the minority views of Dorothy Haener calling for bringing domestic workers and the low-paid workers, bringing all workers within the reach of Federal power under the protection of the Fair Labor Standards Act.

Because it was a minority view, there was danger that it might seem not to be a part of a consensus here.

Mrs. GREEN. Mr. Hogan tells me she is also on the list of prospective witnesses.

Again, I extend my thanks. We may have one day of hearings next week and then we probably will devote most of the week of June 29, to this subject.

Thank you very much.

(Whereupon, at 1:10 p.m. the special subcommittee adjourned, to reconvene at the call of the Chair.)

FRIDAY, JUNE 26, 1970

House of Representatives,
Special Subcommittee on Education
of the Committee on Education and Labor,
Washington, D.C.

The special subcommittee met, pursuant to notice, at 10 a.m. in room 2251 Rayburn House Office Building, Hon. Edith Green (chairman of the special subcommittee) presiding.

Present: Representatives Green and Dellenback.

Also present: Harry Hogan, counsel; and Sheldon Batchelder, minority research assistant.

Mrs. Green. The subcommittee will come to order for the further consideration of legislation pending before it. Specifically, this morning we will be directing our attention to section 805 of H.R. 16098.

The first witness we have before the committee is Sylvia Roberts. Mrs. Roberts is an attorney from Louisiana and is the regional director for the South of the National Organization for Women.

On behalf of the committee, may I welcome you this morning, Mrs. Roberts. We are delighted you are here and appreciate the time that you have taken out of your schedule. Proceed with your statement as you wish.

STATEMENT OF SYLVIA ROBERTS, ATTORNEY, SECRETARY OF THE LOUISIANA COMMISSION ON THE STATUS OF WOMEN, AND REGIONAL DIRECTOR OF THE SOUTH, NATIONAL ORGANIZATION FOR WOMEN (NOW)

Mrs. Roberts. Thank you, Mrs. Green.

My testimony will be directed at litigation under title VII. I am specifically going to describe circumstances arising in the case of *Weeks* v. *Southern Bell Telephone Co.*, 408 F. 2d 228 (5 Cir. 1969). This was the first case on sex discrimination to reach the U.S. Circuit Court of Appeals. I think it points up the real abuse of and delays that are involved in securing enforcement under title VII. This is to point up another fact, that without further enforcement powers, without a method of really getting at sex discrimination in employment, women are truly helpless today under title VII, in my view.

I would like to give a very brief explanation of the facts concerning Mrs. Weeks and her claim. This case arises in Georgia and involves a woman who worked as an operator from the time she left high school in 1947. She was employed in a small telephone office in which she was ready to do everything and anything. She became very familiar with the switching equipment and all the equipment there in the telephone company's office. She was able to meet most any emergency. I wanted to point out one thing about the telephone company. They have a traffic department and a plant department. Traffic means women operators. Plant means men and installers and cable repairmen and this sort of thing. The significant thing there is that the highest paying traffic, or woman's job, pays less than the lowest paying plant job or man's job. There is no flow from one to the other. Women are in the traffic department exclusively and men are in the plant department in Georgia. Mrs. Weeks had sort of broken a barrier as being employed outside as plant clerk in the plant department and then she learned of an opening in the job of switchman.

This is a job which is inside and involves the transmission of calls and making sure that these recorded messages advising the subscriber that the telephone number is no longer in service—these kinds of things are working correctly. Having been commended by her superviser as a very good plant clerk, in March of this particular year, 1966, she applied or learned that the job of switchman was open and she submitted her bid. There was only one other bidder for this job, a man, who was junior in seniority to Mrs. Weeks.

Under the union contract with the Communication Workers of America, the senior employee gets the job. There is no stipulation about sex in the union contract.

The day following the submission of her bid, her supervisor placed an unsatisfactory work performance notice in her personnel folder. The significance of this is that in a bidding on a job, if a person has an unsatisfactory work performance, then their bid is almost doomed to not being accepted. Fortunately, the CWA representative was in her vicinity that day and was able to get this unsatisfactory work record, which was purely spurious and based on absolutely nothing, expunged from her record.

A few more days passed and she was told that her bid was going to be returned. It was returned because the job of switchman was not going to be assigned to a woman. No reason, but it was not going to be assigned to a woman. She had heard of the existence of the Equal Employment Opportunity Commission in 1966, in the early days of that organization. She wrote to that agency and eventually an investigation was conducted. I say "eventually" because this was in the initial stages of the EEOC. They had very little staffing and it was my information from a former commissioner that they didn't really expect sex discrimination complaints in the first place. They were surprised when women did complain. They did investigate her complaint and a finding was made that the job could be performed by Mrs. Weeks; there was no reason she could not perform all the functions of a switchman, and the refusal of her bid violated title VII. The only procedure open then was to conciliate with the company by the EEOC, and this failed. At this stage she was very effectively barred from a job which paid her $51.50 a week more than she was earning as a plant clerk. She had no money so she asked the court to appoint her an attorney. Several months later she had a trial, after which the U.S. District Court ruled that the job of switchman could be denied to her because it involved strenuous activity and the lifting of a 31-pound relay time-testing set and violated a Georgia regulation forbidden women and minors lifting weights in excess of 30 pounds.

The question of whether or not title VII superseded this State law was not passed upon. Then it was ruled that the bona fide occupational qualification exception covered this job.

Mrs. GREEN. If Mrs. Weeks had a 31-pound child would she be forbidden to lift such child? Or if she were a nurse—and the patient weighed well over 31 lbs.?

Mrs. ROBERTS. No. We are not interested in women except when it comes to paychecks. We protect them only when there is money involved. They can lift any amount in a farm or hospital or anything of this sort, so long as there is no paycheck in question.

That is a very interesting point, Mrs. Green, because, as I will get to later, I show in further proceedings that this particular regulation was never enforced, was never invoked at any time against anyone in Georgia. The telephone company had unearthed this unused provision and relied upon it as saying that they were in grave danger of being prosecuted for this misdemeanor of allowing a woman to lift over 30 pounds. It was also shown this relay time-testing set was used once a year. Furthermore, it was used improperly by the junior employee who was shown on a ladder lifting it over his head when the Bell Telephone operating procedure required it be used on a cart, rolling it to the place where it was to be used and using these leads from the relay time-testing set. There was no necessity of really lifting it; this was rather unclear from the District Court record as presented.

On appeal, Mrs. Weeks' attorney refused to file an appeal for her. She then contacted the National Organization for Women. We accepted the case, and Marguerite Rawalt and I represented Mrs. Weeks in the appeal.

Subsequent to the filing of briefs by both parties and the EEOC as *amicus curiae*, the Georgia weight-lifting statute or regulation— it was not a statute really—was rescinded by the Commissioner of Labor. This is quite interesting because it came about through repeated contacts by the Women's Bureau of the Department of Labor, in which it was stressed that lifting was not a function of sex but depended on technique, muscular build and the individual's capabilities.

It is very hard to generalize that all women have the same ability to lift and that all men have the same ability. These assumptions that women cannot lift over 30 pounds when employed were really without reason. Finally, the Commissioner of Labor in Georgia saw the reason of this and rescinded the regulation.

When we got to oral argument, Southern Bell could no longer assert the Georgia weight-lifting provision as a defense. They were left with the strenuous activity feature of their case. I myself lifted all of the equipment in oral argument and I am a little smaller than the average woman. I think it was quite obvious to the Court of Appeals there was not a reasonable finding that the job was too strenuous for a woman. Mrs. Weeks had testimony in the record by fellow employees to this effect, that she was fully qualified to do this job.

The Court of Appeals reversed the lower court. The real benefit, I think, of Mrs. Weeks' whole chain of circumstances is that it made a very important pronouncement on the scope of the bona fide occupational qualification exception. Before *Weeks*, the authorities and much of the writing and speculation about the scope of the bona fide occupational qualification seemed to hinge on a subjective approach of the employer being able to decide that certain jobs were men's jobs, certain jobs were women's jobs, and he could make that determination. The Court of Appeals set down an objective standard and said that the employer has the burden of proving that he has a factual basis for believing that all or substantially all women would be unable to perform safely and efficiently the duties of the job involved.

We all know that women come in all shapes and sizes. Further, we know that the Department of Labor shows women in every kind of classification of job. So that the effect is that every job is open to women, if the individual woman can qualify, because we cannot say that there is any job—with the exception, I believe the statement has been made, of sperm donor and wet nurse—that cannot be performed by some woman somewhere.

Because of the *Weeks* case, the bona fide occupational qualification is severely limited to a completely objective standard. The fifth circuit made a further pronouncement with respect to the stereotyping, the whole idea of an employer being able to say, "I don't believe a woman ought to do this, especially not a southern belle Georgia girl like Mrs. Weeks." They said that this type of classification could not be used. Judge Johnson, who wrote the opinion, used, I think, some immortal language in saying that:

"Men have always had the right to determine whether the incremental increase in remuneration for strenuous, dangerous, obnoxious, boring or unromantic tasks is worth the candle. The promise of title VII is that women are now to be on equal footing. We cannot conclude that by including the bona fide occupational qualification exception Congress intended to renege on that promise." The fifth circuit court told Southern Bell that they should consider her qualifications. They remained adamant in their refusal to do anything for Mrs. Weeks. Now, 4 years later, we are still waiting for some type of relief for Mrs. Weeks.

I would say that although Mrs. Weeks, as a person, an individual, after these 4 years has yet to experience any benefits from her great victory—other women have. Arbitrations have been undertaken by the union and have succeeded in placing women in the job of switchman with back pay and in other jobs as well.

There have been decisions based on the *Weeks* case and I have cited *Cheatwood* v. *Southern Bell Telephone and Telegraph Co.*, 303 F. Supp. 754 (N.D. Ala. 1969), an Alabama case, decided the same as the *Weeks* case, in which a woman was allowed to qualify for the job of commercial representative in which she might have to lift up to 80 pounds. The court found it was not reasonable and not possible to exclude women from such jobs. Nonetheless, Mrs. Weeks' case underscores the need for prompt remedies. It is just not possible to say that a person has a right to end sex discrimination if it takes 4 years to do it. As a matter of fact, we don't know how many years it will take because if we have to appeal again it may be another 2 years and there is an indefinite time span involved.

Further, the mundane matter of attorney fees is involved here. The National Organization for Women undertook this case because of the importance of it. There was no money involved. Attorneys fees may or may not be awarded. There was a very stiff fight on the part of the attorneys for Southern Bell on the question of attorney fees. I myself have never seen attorneys testify against attorneys.

In this case, attorneys in Savannah who looked at our briefs and the record for an hour and a half testified on the validity of the attorney fees that were asked. On the hours spent, they questioned that, and that was the basis of their question, an hour and a half examination of the work product. I would question very strongly the ability of most attorneys to undertake this type of litigation because it simply is a matter of not being able to afford the expenses, not being able to postpone getting a fee for 2 years, 4 years, something of this sort, when it can just drag on endlessly.

If the EEOC cannot enforce it and you cannot get attorneys who are able to finance such cases, then what are the enforcement provisions that are available? What are the remedies? We find that they are chimerical, in my view.

The other aspect, I think, just as an aside about Southern Bell, is that they have been involved in many cases against women; they have lobbied repeatedly in the Halls of Congress and in the States trying to get an exemption for seniority and pension plans. Before this full committee there is going to be a consideration of the Esch amendment which tries to do this very thing. We consider them to have a status of being a public utility and a monopoly, and yet they are allowed to lobby and really bring about legislation or try to push for legislation which is not in the public interest. It is certainly not in the interest of 51 percent of the population of this country which are women.

We would strongly question whether or not they have the right to do this kind of thing.

Turning to another aspect of sex discrimination, and how it is perpetuated, I would like to take a closer look at the EEOC and its workings, which present severe handicaps to women, in addition to just the mechanical aspects of litigation I have described with respect to Mrs. Weeks. First of all, in looking at title VII we find that it sets up a remedy with no effective enforcement provisions. This is, to me, an anomaly, without having rights, without any real way to protect them. It has occurred to me that perhaps this could only be done if we were talking about women and minority groups. In any other type of situation we wonder whether this would really have been tolerated to set up a remedy with no way to get such relief.

The other aspect of the EEOC's workings is that, in my personal experience, and I say this is quite recently, in Houston, hearings by the EEOC, the members of the National Organization for Women have noted that there is an institutional bias, if you will, on the subject of sex discrimination in the EEOC itself. While great attention is given to race discrimination and ethnic discrimination, the field of sex discrimination is virtually untouched.

This came to our attention in two ways. First of all, we had been aware of the fact that EEOC had collected data over a period of years and had compiled a three-volume work. This work never compares men with women; it compares black women with white women and black men with white men and other ethnic groups. However, this does not give any idea of the fact that a white woman does not make what a black man makes. Apparently it assumes as long as all women are paid what white women are making that is all right. It completely obscures sex discrimination in the very design of the study and in the way it is reported.

The National Organization for Women is not alone in this criticism.

It was included in the President's Task Force on Women's Rights and Responsibilities, and I have cited pages 25 and 26 of that task force report, which says:

"One can examine the whole report and never find a table or narrative statement that compares white men, Negro men, white women, Negro women * * * only from such facts that the discrimination, if any, can be spotted and then analyzed."

So that comparing women to women tells nothing about the widening gap between men and women's salaries. Even the EEOC presented evidence at the Houston hearing that women's position in the labor market is deteriorating; we are not making the small advances that race and ethnic groups are.

I want to hasten to say that we want all groups to be free of discrimination. We don't want to take away from race or ethnic groups. We feel that we should have equal time and we feel that we are part of the civil rights movement and deserve to have our needs met also.

The fact that this data is so arranged as to obscure sex discrimination was really evident in these hearings in Houston on the 2d, 3d, and 4th of June 1970. The press releases by the EEOC were all in terms of discrimination against racial groups and the Mexican Americans. All of these statistics dealt with this type of thing. All of the emphasis was on this, whereas women comprise 30 percent of the work force under the jurisdiction of the EEOC and yet there is just this type of closing one's eyes to the situation.

Now, when I found out these hearings were going to be held we requested time to testify and at length we did get this. It was quite difficult to make contact with them and make sure we were going to testify.

We also requested that the data be reanalyzed so that it could be presented at a public hearing because we knew it was not in a form which could be presented to the public and brought out as showing what the sex discrimination was in Houston. We never got any action on this request so we took the initiative and fortunately we had a member now who is the president, Dr. Sally Hacker, a sociologist, who herself reanalyzed the EEOC data.

Here is a picture of the volunteer, unpaid person preparing a 14-page report on sex discrimination in Houston, while the EEOC has this duty but does not make such a report. I would like to offer the committee the report of Dr. Hacker which is of very high professional caliber. It has eight statistical tables attached to it. We did this because we knew unless we did as volunteers these facts would never come to light. This is the experience that we had encountered.

Mrs. GREEN. Without any objection, that will be made a part of the record at this point.

Mrs. ROBERTS. The other disturbing aspect of these hearings was that the questioning of the witnesses was very vigorously pursued by the Commissioner with respect to race and ethnic discrimination, Mexican Americans chiefly. However, the same questions were not asked about sex discrimination. They never asked, did not seem to feel it was an area of concern to propound exactly the same questions. On the second day of the hearings I personally asked the research staff director why these same questions were not asked. After a short pause he, in a very nice way and not at all hostile, simply said, "That is a valid criticism."

I think they had just not thought of it, despite the fact that during our testimony we had literally begged them to ask the same questions on sex discrimination as they had asked on race and national origin. We just simply met a barrier there where we could not communicate our urgency of asking the same questions. We were constantly told, "Well, sex discrimination is included in race and national origin."

If it was included, why not ask the same questions to bring out the same facts? This is an area where we just simply didn't seem to reach any understanding.

As a result of this, we asked that there be separate hearings on sex discrimination because we found that the few questions that were asked about women were met with such answers as "We don't hire women in our refinery because it is shift work." Of course, what would we do if all the women working on shift work suddenly walked off the job? It is a staggering type of picture. So that employers, I think, have a number of these myths in mind, such as women don't work as steadily, whereas the statistics show that they don't have as high an absentee record. These kinds of things need to be conveyed to employers. We feel that since the EEOC does not have enforcement powers, at least there could be an exchange of information here so that we could work out constructively what these employers are facing, how we could meet what they feel are drawbacks to employing women so that we don't have this constant stereotype of a woman who can only do clerical work and frozen in this clerical pool from which there is no chance for upward movement.

There is no chance for jobs which are in the blue-collar field which would free so many welfare mothers from the shame and, I must say, the real, dire poverty that they are in now.

The same thing should be noted about unions, and these types of hearings I think would give us a constructive avenue for working on this type of problem.

I would like to mention just one area of sex discrimination which does not relate to employment; that is, in my home State of Louisiana. We have a jury exemption for women which relates to getting on the rolls. I don't mean after the woman is called and then asks for release from jury service; I mean we have a situation in which women are never even considered for jury service unless they go and personally hand the clerk of the court a written statement that they wish to serve. The personal experience we have had in Baton Rouge is that women who try to do this are severely discouraged by the clerk who says jury service is not ladylike, they will hear all kinds of things that they don't want to hear, they may be in uncomfortable quarters, all these things which would discourage them from participating in our judicial process.

This was unfortunately upheld by the United States Supreme Court in 1961 in the case of *Hoyt* v. *Florida*, which involved a woman convicted of murder of her husband. She was convicted by a jury, found guilty by a jury of all men, to which she made the objection that she should have had a chance to have a jury of her peers, including women. The Supreme Court said it was perfectly reasonable for Florida to exclude women from the jury because women have this role in society of being the homebuilders and the people who must stay at home and care for children.

This ignored this vast segment of women we have working and perpetuated this idea that women have only one role in society, which we find extremely unrealistic and severely limiting to women as individuals.

We still have a need, and I don't know whether this is in the purview of your committee, for jury service not being denied on the basis of sex.

These kinds of things are examples of how women are limited both in the field of employment and as citizens. I would like to point out that women do want to contribute in a positive way to this society in every way possible to the greatest measure of their capabilities. We hope that this committee will do everything possible to give them this opportunity now.

Thank you very much.

Mrs. GREEN. Thank you very much.

How many States have a situation similar to Louisiana in terms of jury service?

Mrs. ROBERTS. As far as I know, Louisiana is the last one. We tried very hard to get a legislative measure passed in 1968 and the legislature voted it down three times.

Mrs. GREEN. It is my understanding that cases have been thrown out of court when it has been proven that there are blacks who live in the community and there are no blacks who serve on the jury.

Mrs. ROBERTS. Yes, Mrs. Green, that is my understanding also.

Mrs. GREEN. Do you know of any case where this has been brought up in terms of women, where the defendant has been a women and women have been systematically excluded from the jury?

Mrs. ROBERTS. Yes, ma'am. The Louisiana Supreme Court passed on a case called *State* v. *Pratt* just very recently, I think the decision was handed down in May, in which this very point was brought up. Our Supreme Court ruled that it was reasonable to exclude women and this did not violate the 14th amendment. This thing would never be countenanced with respect to race.

Mrs. GREEN. Is that on appeal?

Mrs. ROBERTS. I don't know if they are going on up to the Supreme Court of the United States. I hope they will. I have not had a chance to consult with the attorneys in that case. They are finished, as far as the State system goes. They have gone to the end of the line. This is what we see time and time again.

There is a Mississippi case, United States district court case, *Ford* v. *White*, 299 F. Supp. 772 (S.D. Miss. 1969) which was on a writ of habeas corpus, in which this very point was raised about women who were now subject to jury call but not included in the jury trial. The court held that this new law permitting them to serve on juries was of such recent vintage that it was not possible for the clerk to do this tremendous job of getting women on the rolls, so they were making every diligent effort. This was perfectly all right.

I would like to say that the equal rights amendment we think might take care of this situation to some extent, or we think it would correct it.

I would like to congratulate Mrs. Green for signing the discharge petition so that we can get this equal rights measure before the House this session.

Mrs. GREEN. We are going to have the Chairman of the Equal Employment Opportunity Commission here on Wednesday but can you tell me, in regard to the national and regional offices of the EEOC—and also you made reference to it in Houston—how many women are employed by the EEOC at the top levels?

Mrs. ROBERTS. As far as I know, there is one deputy director. There are very few women employed. I think there are under five that are above the G–14 level.

Mrs. GREEN. Five women?

Mrs. ROBERTS. Yes, ma'am. In the whole EEOC. I wish that I had all of these figures for you.

Mrs. GREEN. You mean in the National and State regional offices?

Mrs. ROBERTS. Yes.

Mrs. GREEN. Out of how many?

Mrs. ROBERTS. I think there are 14. The other point is that there is only one commissioner who is a woman, Mrs. Kuck, who will not be reappointed, we have learned. So we really are in limbo as to whether or not we are going to have a woman on this Commission when women are 30 percent of the work force under the jurisdiction of the EEOC. That is just an incredible situation.

Mrs. GREEN. How many blacks?

Mrs. ROBERTS. At Houston there was only Chairman Brown there. There are, I believe, two blacks, and Mr. Holcombe is a white man and Mr. Ximenes is of Mexican American descent.

Mrs. GREEN. You are speaking of the national commission?

Mrs. ROBERTS. Of the national commission. So that we find that right in the EEOC itself it reflects the national condition of discrimination against women.

We find this is just carried right out in its most visible form in its employees.

Mr. DELLENBACK. Would you yield?

Mrs. GREEN. Yes.

Mr. DELLENBACK. I am concerned about this failure to reappoint a woman to this particular Commission. Do you have this on fairly good authority this is to be the case?

Mrs. ROBERTS. I don't know if there is going to be a woman appointed.

Mr. DELLENBACK. No question of competence?

Mrs. ROBERTS. Mrs. Kuck will not be reappointed. She has been notified.

Mr. DELLENBACK. Has there been any suggestion for a woman to replace Mrs. Kuck?

Mrs. ROBERTS. That I don't know. This is a matter of great concern to us. We have been unable to learn, get any of this type of information. We would like it to be not just a woman who is a woman without any experience in the field of employment or sex discrimination. This won't help us. This will not give anyone a personal commitment to end this kind of sexual discrimination. We find that it has got to be someone who is vitally concerned. If we don't get this type of person, we are going to step right back all the distance, I should say the short distance we have gotten with title VII.

I would like to emphasize that women only have three remedies, as I see it, under the Federal law; Equal Pay Act amendment to the fair labor standards, OFCC, which has come out with guidelines, and title VII.

That is all we have. When we see that title VII is weakened by the weight of the EEOC setup, the way it is administered, then we are lost.

We have lost, I should say, over one-third of our armory. We have nothing to confront employers with except perhaps moral grounds of "How can you treat us this way?"

We have not succeeded in shaming any employer into a fair practice. Yet we are still hoping and we don't want to miss this possibility.

Mr. DELLENBACK. I realize that I am part of the group being attacked under the circumstances but I try not to be defensive about this.

Mrs. GREEN. If my colleague would yield, the focus of these hearings is not antimale, just as it is not antiwhite or antiblack; rather, the focus of these hearings is one of equal rights. I want to reassure my colleague.

Mrs. ROBERTS. I want to state that the National Organization has men on its national board and in its membership. We do not hate men. We feel that this attitude is shared by men and women. We are fighting an attitude which is no respecter of sex. We find that we have many very capable allies in the ranks of men.

Mr. DELLENBACK. Not attempting to be facetious on the subject, I want to avoid that tendency and say from a serious standpoint I do recognize with real concern the points that you do raise. I would say this about Mrs. Green, our chairwoman. I think you have demonstrated in what you have done in the times before this subcommittee and the full committee this issue has arisen, your own deep concern and you have done it, let me say, exactly as you have outlined it. There has been no anti involved in any phase of what you have striven to do. I am sure that Mrs. Roberts is aware of the fact that Mrs. Green has played a very significant role in seeing on a series of bases, if I may say, and in a very feminine fashion she has injected the proper phraseology—I was going to say she has injected sex into this legislation, but she has made certain that the language is broadened at the proper time and in the proper way on a series of points, so I am sure that you are aware of this and I commend the chairwoman for what she has done on this. I am concerned about this.

May I ask one question on this matter of the attorney's fees standpoint. Did you ultimately get your award?

Mrs. ROBERTS. No, we have not gotten our award yet.

Mr. DELLENBACK. It has gone on this number of years?

Mrs. ROBERTS. Yes, that is correct. I might say I don't know when we will ever get it.

Mr. DELLENBACK. Is the attack in assessing the attorney's fees on the amount or on the allowance itself?

Mrs. ROBERTS. The allowance itself initially, but this was beaten back with the citation of *Newman* v. *Piggy Park Enterprises, Inc.*, 390 U.S. 401 (1968), in which it was said and it has been said repeatedly that attorney fees are assessable. There is no way to interpret the Civil Rights Act except that it awards attorney's fees. It was said that Mrs. Weeks should have prospective relief only, not retroactive relief, and not be given this job. Therefore if it was prospective relief then no attorney's fees, because really you hadn't done anything for her apparently. That was the idea. There have been recent cases which say prospective relief, retroactive relief, whatever it is, attorney's fees are to be awarded. This is a point where I was attacked quite personally, which I thought was really unprofessional, unethical, and I dare say that many attorneys would not want to get into such a situation. Also it has been my experience that attorneys are motivated by financial concerns. Most people who are in the law are really not in it for humanitarian pursuits such as social welfare or something of this sort. They do see it as a monetary type of profession, so that when you talk about getting your fee eventually 5, 6, 7 years later or something of this sort, this would not be attractive to an attorney. I think this has been a strategy of Southern Bell, to be quite frank, to discourage the participation of attorneys for the only hope for plaintiffs under title VII who do not have access to some groups such as the NAACP for some group that is heavily funded, private individuals just don't stand a chance.

Mr. DELLENBACK. When you had this expert testimony on the amount of your fee, were they attacking again the assessment itself or were they saying that the amount was disproportionate in value arrived as to the hours devoted or the quality of the work?

Mrs. ROBERTS. The witnesses themselves, Congressman Dellenback?

Mr. DELLENBACK. Yes; what were they saying when other counsel spoke with you about this?

Mrs. ROBERTS. The witnesses simply said that it was just on amount. They were saying that it couldn't possibly have taken this long, and I was very unreasonable in asking that each hour that I spent, which I documented hour by hour, and each expense, was legitimate. I mean my credibility was impugned. As an officer of the court, I was supposedly lying about what I had done. Furthermore, it was said that I must be a very inefficient—I mean the assumption was that since these other lawyers could do these things so rapidly, I believe one attorney said that 40 hours of research was all that was necessary, and that this being a case of first impression, well, still it shouldn't matter because this law was passed in 1964. There would be very few cases from 1964 to date.

Of course that wasn't the point. You must look back and have analogies. You must examine when you don't have authority, you must examine the whole field of law for some type of parallel authority, and you must be sure you don't have any authority, so this does take about twice as long in my estimation, but these attorneys, you see, I was put in the position of somehow bilking the court and trying to perpetrate a fraud, which I thought was extremely unworthy of these individuals.

I produced affidavits by other lawyers on what was a reasonable per hour fee, and the fact that a case of first impression lost in the district court where you are left with something where the die is cast, and then you must work with it as it is, is a very difficult task.

Mr. DELLENBACK. I am concerned about Mrs. Weeks. It is unfortunate how frequently in life one gathers the spears in one's own body, does not end up going through the hole that is created in the defense line thereby. As you point out in your testimony, there has clearly been some benefit derived from that which has been accomplished although not directly attributable as yet to Mrs. Weeks.

Mrs. ROBERTS. That is correct.

Mr. DELLENBACK. I want to commend you for what you have been able to accomplish. Thank you very much for your testimony. Thank you, Madam Chairman.

Mrs. ROBERTS. Thank you.

Mrs. GREEN. I put in the record the other day the median salary of men and women, the median salary of white men and black men, and the median salary of white women and black women. It is my under-standing that when we get to the professional salaries that the black women, because of the enforcement provisions, get better salaries and have greater opportunities than white women. Do you know if this is the case, and do you have any figures on this?

Mrs. ROBERTS. No. I can certainly try to get them, though, Mrs. Green. I believe that is true. I didn't bring all of my materials to date from Louisiana. I wish I had these types of information for you. The black woman is better off than the white woman in many instances, and we are very happy that she has some advantage, but by the same token we feel that the whole idea that women should be paid less in the professional ranks is intolerable.

Mrs. GREEN. The only point I make is that she receives this status because she is black and not because she is a woman.

Mrs. ROBERTS. That is correct.

Mrs. GREEN. And the discrimination continues then on the basis of sex, although it is beginning to be equaled out on the other.

Mrs. ROBERTS. I think we find that most every woman who has achieved any prominence, I am speaking of the political, judicial and business world, says that the discrimination on the basis of sex was a much greater obstacle than on the basis of race.

Mrs. GREEN. We are going to have testimony to that effect. Shirley Chisholm, I believe, is going to testify that the discrimination she has suffered has been far greater on the basis that she is a woman than on the basis that she is black. I have had other black women friends tell me the same thing.

Mr. Hogan, do you have any questions?

Mr. HOGAN. You may have covered this, Mrs. Roberts, and I have missed it, but would you tell us, has the Supreme Court ruled at all on the application of the 14th amendment and the possibility that women are entitled to equal treatment under that 14th amendment?

Mrs. ROBERTS. We have never been defined as persons or entitled to protection under the 14th amendment, although it has been brought up and repeated attempts have been made to try to get this point passed upon favorably for women under the 14th amendment by the Supreme Court of the United States. I would just cite one case that I believe is a Michigan case involving a bartender in Michigan, *Goes-sart* v. *Cleary*, 335 U.S. 464 (1948). This was held to be reasonable. Unfortunately there is also a reasonable test under the 14th amendment. You can't discriminate. I would translate into that unless it is reasonable, and unfortunately for women it always seems to be reasonable, so that we have never hurdled that barrier. That is one reason why we are so strongly in favor of the equal rights amendment, because we have never made any dent in this solid wall through the 14th amendment claim. We do have information from a New York case decided just this week, it was announced in the papers today, on public accommodations, which we feel is based on the 14th amendment, and perhaps this is the first weakening of it.

Women have not fared well before the U.S. Supreme Court. We do have a chance in this case of *Phillips* v. *Martin Marietta*, 411 F. 2d 1 (5 Cir. 1969) which was a case after the *Weeks* case, which said that a woman with preschool children could be excluded from a job, while a man who had preschool children would be accepted, and the Fifth Circuit said this was sex plus another factor, the preschool children, so that somehow, if you add something to sex, something that is already prohibited, then that mutualizes the discrimination and it is all right. Judge Brown asked for an *en banc* rehearing in this case saying this had to be discrimination. Who else was a mother except a woman, so that this had to be a violation of title VII. Fortunately, the U.S. Supreme Court granted certiorari. This case again was undertaken by the NAACP. It was a white woman but the NAACP is financing this. We are filing an *amicus curiae* brief, and we are very encouraged by the fact that this is the first case that the Department of Justice has ever been involved in, in any way, and entered into involving women, while the Department of Justice has been in any number of cases involving racial discrimination. Discrimination is a total blank as far as the Department of Justice goes. We have been in a really bad condition legally and in the enforcement area.

Mrs. GREEN. It is my recollection, from serving on the Kennedy Commission on the Status of Women, that there were lower court cases which said in effect that a woman was not a person, and therefore not entitled to equal protection under the 14th amendment. Is that correct?

Mrs. ROBERTS. Yes. There are any number of them.

Mrs. GREEN. And the Supreme Court has refused to hear these cases?

Mrs. ROBERTS. Refused to review them.   *166562*

Mrs. GREEN. In every case?

Mrs. ROBERTS. This is the kind of authority that we faced in the *Weeks* case. There was nothing for women. There was everything allowing a woman to be discriminated against in all these stereotyped things to be said about why it was reasonable to keep women in this category, because we were availing her of so many protections of society, and she was the keeper of the hearth. Well, many women don't have anything to do with the hearth. They are out working, and may not even be married, but many of them have been deserted or they cannot get child support and they are the sole support. As a matter of fact, 11 percent of the households now are headed by women. How these women can keep the hearth is unknown to me, just as in the *Phillips* v. *Martin Marietta* case, this woman had 10 children. She was not allowed to have as high a paying job with Martin Marietta. Instead, because we want to have this idea that women must stay home and take care of their preschool children, because there was no evidence that she was going to be giving time to this pursuit, and taking away from her job, there was no evidence at all for this; but we want to maintain this idea, when the result is that this woman must work all night as a waitress, in a very strenuous job and much lower pay. Is this a social benefit for the children that she must support? We question the utility and the real benefit of such rulings.

Mr. DELLENBACK. Another subcommittee of this committee, as you may be aware, is deeply involved in the study of day care legislation, trying to do something from another aspect which would be not only beneficial to the disadvantaged, but would be beneficial to working mothers, to help make possible the moving out of just the home into the working world the number of women who otherwise just would find themselves, by having preschoolers, unable to do so, so this does not deal directly with the subject matter of his morning's subcommittee hearings but there is another subcommittee which is striving also to be of principal support to women or of support principally to women in this other thrust.

Mrs. ROBERTS. We are very encouraged and heartened by the attention that Congress is giving to these matters, and we feel that it is a breakthrough, and that women will be able to participate in society. We want to give something to this society. That is our point, and Congress is going to apparently allow us to do so.

Mr. DELLENBACK. Unfortunately, being serious in what I say about a facetious subject, I am sure that part of what you run into from a difficult standpoint is that people want to continually be humorous about it instead of being very serious about it, because you are being perfectly pleasant but you are completely serious about that which you are saying. We tend to start to say things which are facetious, and I am sure this diverts us rather than staying with the point you are reaching.

Mrs. ROBERTS. Your comment is so pertinent to our experience in Houston. As soon as Mrs. Kuck started questioning the witness there was a wave of laughter throughout this courtroom where these things were being held, and apparently discrimination against women is a very funny matter, and that everything to do with women's condition and fight to try to obtain equal opportunity is the most humorous subject imaginable, and we don't know why. Of course it is better than being spat upon, but we always wonder why this invokes this reaction.

Mrs. GREEN. They are not mutually exclusive, though.

Mrs. ROBERTS. Yes; I realize that. I realize that it may be a cover for the other, but we find that this not taking us seriously, it is like putting us on a pedestal. If you are on a pedestal you are not looking eye-to-eye. You are away and you do keep insulating yourself from the subject by putting this wall of humor into the thing.

(Discussion off the record.)

Mrs. GREEN. When we were discussing the lower court cases, where a woman has not been recognized as a person and therefore entitled to equal protection under the 14th amendment, was it a Chief Justice who said of woman—"something better than her husband's dog—a little dearer than his horse."

Mr. DELLENBACK. Not Hand. He is one of the greats.

Mrs. GREEN. It was either a Justice or Alfred Lord Tennyson who several years ago made this statement.

Mrs. ROBERTS. This is true, because women are regarded as property. They do not have a status under common law. Of course as soon as she marries her identity disappears and is merged. There is only one identity and that is the man's identity.

Mr. DELLENBACK. Residence is determined by a host of things.

Mrs. ROBERTS. Yes. We find either we are persons or we are not, and we don't understand how it can be denied that we are human beings, but we are not treated that way.

Mr. DELLENBACK. We have looked upon you as human beings for quite awhile.

Mrs. ROBERTS. I am delighted that this subcommittee does.

Mrs. GREEN. Congressman Dellenback indeed does. I wish it were true with all.

Mrs. ROBERTS. Yes; I don't think they realize they are not treating us as human beings.

Mr. DELLENBACK. Again being serious, you tend to start to say I have noticed the difference for quite some time, and this type of thing. We tend to be humorous about it.

Mrs. ROBERTS. Yes; it is almost a conditioned reflex action. We try to take it in good part. We have in our literature in the National Organization for Women a sheet called Vive la Différence, with a question at the end and we show just how costly this difference is. I am speaking in terms of the differential in wages, and the fact that only 3 percent of all lawyers are women, only 1 percent of all women make over $10,000 a year whereas 28 percent of all men do, so that these differences, and such courtly manners as opening doors and lighting cigarettes are just too expensive. We can't afford them. They just cost us so much, and the doors that are opened don't represent the millions of doors that are closed.

Mr. DELLENBACK. I am sure that it is in part attributable to the fact that the mores and folkways of different segments of society are different and those who are basically, if you will, the decisionmakers of society, react from a different background to it; the legislators, the judges, the high officials, who tend to have wives who are not working, and are in a situation where we have a conditioned reflex toward the involvement of a member of the female sex in the working world. It would be different, I think, if you had the decisionmakers from a different background, you see. I think that is part of what, being realistic about this, you are walking into. The man whose wife fortunately or unfortunately, depending upon how you look at it, doesn't work, tends to look upon the involvement of women in the work world as a different situation from the man whose wife is out there with him working all the time.

If you will analytically, and it doesn't help the situation for which you are striving except insofar as it helps understanding it, and it means something about how you must get to it—I am not telling you how to do it——

Mrs. ROBERTS. I wish you would, Congressman Dellenback. We would appreciate any suggestions.

Mr. DELLENBACK. I do think it is a valid comment you seek on part of what it is, you will, fighting under certain circumstances.

Mrs. GREEN. I think this is true and I think a lot of legal discrimination, things that have been written into law by the Congress itself, men really have not thought about. There have been no women who have served on the committees drawing up the legislation to point out the discrimination, for example, in the social security legislation; the difference in the benefits that a woman's beneficiaries get and a man's beneficiary receives in retirement and death benefits.

Mr. DELLENBACK. In this situation I don't think it is a case as sometimes racial resistance has been, that one feels threatened. I don't think it is primarily that although in some instances it is. It is rather a case that you feel women ought to be treated in a very gracious and loving fashion, but that is the attitude toward it, and you must cut through this to get to what it is you are striving to accomplish.

Mrs. GREEN. The parallel of discrimination against minorities, against blacks especially, and the discrimination against women is striking, historically. When we have made the greatest progress to end discrimination against blacks it has been the time when we have had the chance to make the greatest progress in ending discrimination against women. When I first came to Congress, I don't know how many times I heard people opposing civil rights legislation say, "But I asked my cook, and she says they like it this way," and now we have the phrase, "but I have asked my wife, and she says women like it this way." I think the analogy in very similar.

Mr. DELLENBACK. It doesn't apply in my case however. My wife is with you in large part.

Mrs. GREEN. But I have heard this so many times. I have heard men say this, where the wife is not working: "But my wife likes it this way." I am rather wary of the cooks' polls and the wives' polls. In terms of threat to the male ego—or the male job—one of the things that I have many times said is that women must be the innovator, but she must never be caught with the blueprint in her hand.

Mrs. ROBERTS. It is rather difficult.

Mrs. GREEN. And I think this is true in legislation. Women have accommodated themselves to the discrimination. For example, many times if you have an idea for legislation, and if you are willing to say to some man, "I think this would be a good idea, and you introduce it," that same man—and other men—support it much more easily. It is much tougher if you are not the kind who decides "as a woman I have as much right to introduce legislation and push for it as a man does." Women in the executive branch have told me the same thing many times.

Mr. DELLENBACK. There are written into the laws of this land situations which have been carried in the hands, blueprints have been carried in the hands of the chairwoman of this subcommittee. I have carried the blueprints on occasion.

Mrs. GREEN. I have been one who has been unwilling to make that accommodation, but nevertheless I am not blind to the fact that if I were willing to do that sometimes the days might be easier.

Mrs. ROBERTS. I wonder if I might make this comment. These kinds of myths are things that are inculcated in women so young that they naturally think they should be in the subservient position just as blacks did. The myth I find so hard to understand, that women own everything and therefore what in the world do they want now? They already own all of the wealth of this country. Well, all of the wealth in this country in stocks and all of these things are not in the control of women, primarily because she doesn't have the motivation and it is not ladylike to go around controlling stock and this sort of thing and talking in a corporate meeting, and also these things are tied up in trusts, so that she has no way to control this. She is the record owner, but as far as being in control and owning, and have nothing further to ask for of our legislative system, this is so far from the realities.

Mr. DELLENBACK. I am not sure I agree with the use of the word "subservient." I understand what you mean by its use, but I think it is different. I am not sure the words are equal under the circumstances. The roles are different. The present situation talks in terms of different roles rather than master-servant, owner-property, superior-subservient.

Mrs. ROBERTS. We find men can control the lives of women.

Mr. DELLENBACK. The converse is also true.

Mrs. ROBERTS. Oh, yes. Well, I don't know. In 14 years of law practice I have never seen it. I am not saying I am not going to find it when I get off the plane today, but I find that when men can tell women what is natural for them to do, and tell them how they must live their lives, that this certainly must imply some subservience. The very thing that Mrs. Green was talking about, that one must be accommodating, you wouldn't accommodate an equal on the same basis, where you must be in the background. Why is this necessary? What makes it necessary for this type of approach to be used? Women, if they are smart, don't show how smart they are. Why do you have to not be as smart? So that you are not on an equal basis with a man, so that he doesn't feel that you are trying to challenge him in any way. It is not the question of challenge. It is simply being yourself and being able to be as smart as you possibly can be. At this point many women in professions and business must hide this fact. I would say that this perpetuates the idea of subservience. If the word is abhorrent I certainly will withdraw it, but I believe that it implies a little bit more than different roles. I believe that it requires us to admit that there is a submerging of some of the capabilities of women.

Mrs. Green. I would argue on the word "subservient." I think it is fully justified. I don't know how many women I have heard in my life say, "My husband will not allow me to do this." We hear it often in terms of jobs, "My husband will not allow me to take this job." Men constantly say—I'll have "my girl" call him or get this or that. Negroes have objected to the term "boy." Grown secretaries don't like the use of "my girl." Male staff members are not referred to as "my boy," by their employers.

Mrs. Roberts. It is a matter of privileges. If the husband says, "My wife won't allow me to do this" it is because he agrees she should have this privilege. She has no rights. Women have many privileges but they have no rights. This depends on a benevolent person who doles out the rights to you, so that you may be able to work quite a few privileges into the arrangement, but that depends on your ability, and the person you are dealing with, but does not depend on your status as a woman. I am not saying that women haven't been able to work things out very favorably, but it is because they have used this system and manipulated it, not dealing on an equal basis mainly, and in a marriage situation, as Mrs. Green says, I don't believe I have ever seen a situation in which there was a question of: "My wife won't allow me to do something. My wife doesn't want me to do something."

Mr. Dellenback. You are talking in a different social class. That could be, but I don't think that the wife who depends on her husband for support could really make this stick, because the ultimate power of the dollar is there, and any time she says, "I won't allow you to do this," then you say, "By what measure do you think you are going to enforce this?" while the husband has a very effective means of enforcement of simply just putting her out and saying, "I am not going to support you any more. I don't like what you do, and so I won't be paying the bills any more."

We are going into the question of social fabric. You realize this and the legislators realize this.

Mrs. Roberts. Yes.

Mr. Dellenback. We are talking about to what degree a partnership operates in a family situation, and some of us have what we consider a partnership. Sometimes it is two general partners and sometimes it is a general partner and a limited partner, and sometimes it is not a partnership at all. Again, I don't mean to be facetious. I think we are talking about a different type of situation. We are talking about a fundamental change, and whether a small unit like the family will operate the same, if it has two coequal partners, with the roles being interchangeable. I think there is a question. There are some families, some family situations, where the roles are different. I don't think of it as subservience. I think that in many families the principal role is dealing with the children, and I don't put that in a subservient role or back off to the side lines. I think that is as important a thing as the family does. It raises its children and gets them ready to do whatever they do in the next time of the cycle of the generations. In the well adjusted family—that is a broad term—often the principal role is that of the wife, the mother. On the other hand, in that same family the principal role of the "traditional" breadwinner is the father, the husband. It doesn't mean that one is subservient and the other is not subservient.

Mrs. ROBERTS. Then why do we always say, "She is just a housewife"?

Mr. DELLENBACK. I have rebelled against this. We have run into this in the political role. I will constantly run into constituents, when you are meeting so and so, she says, "I am just a housewife," and I don't know how many times quite seriously I have said, "There is no such thing as 'Just a housewife.'" I think it is wrong, and I deliberately said to the person who said this, "You are using a derogatory term that just plain doesn't fit your role."

Mrs. ROBERTS. I am delighted that this is the type of response you have to this type of comment. Unfortunately, I have not noticed this to be a general thing. Perhaps it is a lack of observation on my part. I do think that in the family realm, in relegating the woman to only one role in the family, then she becomes only important in this sphere, and perhaps overemphasizes, and maybe excludes men from participating in the raising of the children. We feel that it ought to be equal. We don't feel that we should have this phenomenon of a man being almost an absentee member of the family, where he is traveling all the time. He is completely absorbed in business, and all the woman has is her homelife. I would just like to point this out——

Mr. DELLENBACK. You keep using the derogative "all she has, she is only"——

Mrs. ROBERTS. I am repeating what has been told to me. I am also a mirror of my upbringing and my experience. I have so many times the idea of the woman who must stay at home and is completely ingrown in this situation. I might point out to you I am not talking about the upper, and upper middle class. I am talking about the woman who stays home and does housework and all household tasks that can be performed by a high-grade moron, with under a 100 IQ. There is not much challenge there and women feel no importance or challenge, and so when they are forced to go out into the work world as I have seen those who have been divorced and deserted, they have no child support. They have the idea they are not able to do anything but be just a housewife.

Mrs. GREEN. Our next witness is Lucy Komisar, a journalist from New York. We are delighted to welcome you to the hearings this morning. You may proceed.

STATEMENT OF LUCY KOMISAR, WRITER AND A NATIONAL VICE PRESIDENT OF THE NATIONAL ORGANIZATION FOR WOMEN, NEW YORK

Miss KOMISAR. Thank you. I am also a vice president of the National Organization for Women.

"Good night, David."

"Good night, Chet."

Sometime soon, David will say his last good night to Chet Huntley as the latter departs to become a gentleman cattle rancher in Montana, but you can be sure as the stag rule at the Washington Press Club that he won't begin saying, "Good night, Helen," or "Good night, Sylvia." Not for a long time—unless the blatant discrimination against women at NBC is abolished by concerted action by the women's movement.

I'd like to dedicate my testimony today to the memory of Margaret Fuller, America's first woman journalist who lived in the 19th century and who would not think we "have come a long way, baby."

I am a freelance writer—freelance not by choice but because it has been the only way I could work as a journalist. A little over a year ago I applied for a job as a reporter at the United Press International Bureau in New York. The bureau chief told me, "I'm sorry, we already have three girls." When I protested that it was against the law to discriminate against women, he said, "It's our policy to have a quota on women." I and the National Organization for Women have filed a complaint against UPI with the Office of Federal Contract Compliance.

Last year I auditioned for a job at WCBS–TV in New York. The news director had told me there was "an opening for a woman." There are 18 reporters at WCBS–TV, three are women—men have five times as much chance as women to be hired there. I also talked with a public affairs director at WOR–TV who told me they were planning to begin a news show and would have "an opening for a woman." They haven't put on the news show yet and WCBS hired a very capable woman who had more experience than I in television journalism. There are women journalists—the point I'm making is that our opportunities are sharply limited and in an industry that helps set public opinion about the issues and problems of our time, that is a critical deficiency.

Many women turn to freelancing because there they face the least discrimination—partly because freelancing is not a very easy way to make a living and, in the past year, I've written cover stories for the *Saturday Review*, the *Washington Monthly*, and *New York* magazine. The men who turned me down for jobs never said it was because I wasn't good enough.

I'd like to give you some idea of what we're up against. NBC–TV Network News has about 45 male reporters; two reporters are women. There are over 100 male writers and 10 women. There is one woman producer.

CBS–TV News has some 35 to 40 correspondents and reporters: two are women; 20 to 25 producers: two are women; 11 writers: one is a woman. At ABC–TV there are 44 correspondents and reporters: two are women; and 10 producers, none are women.

The statistics for management and technical crews is the same, and it holds true at local stations throughout the country where reporters, producers, writers, and management occupy a domain that is almost as stag as the congressional swimming pool. Except, of course, for the secretaries, production assistants and researchers—often college graduates who are told this is the way to "break in" to television.

National Educational Television is as good an example of this as any. When I worked there as a researcher, a producer told me that I could not expect to go further than associate producer. In fact, he told me that he prefers to work with women associate producers because they are usually better than men at that level. Men who are any good are promoted to producer.

National Educational Television has 19 male producers and two female producers—the eight staff researchers and production assistants are all women. I left the job when, after I had been made an associate producer, I discovered that a young male associate producer, who had been brought in with no television experience, was getting paid more than I. The management refused to bring my salary up to his.

My own experiences are mirrored in those of other women throughout the country. The three networks based in New York City account for 80 percent of the industry's white collar employment of 12,500 jobs. According to 1968 EEOC figures, women there are about 10 percent of officials and managers and 10 percent of professionals in radio and television.

Pencil journalism is not much different. The *New York Times* has a total of 485 editors, reporters, foreign correspondents, and copy editors. Of those 53 are women—but a majority of these are society and women's page writers. Even the society editor is a man!

The wire services are a beginning for young writers seeking to break into journalism, but there is not much hope for women there either. At the Associated Press, with a total of 3,300 employees around the world, there are no women heading any of the 38 domestic or 60 foreign bureaus. In New York City, there are seven women out of 52 editors and reporters. United Press International has 26 domestic news editors: the only distaff member of the staff is in charge of women's news. That EEOC study in New York showed over 3,500 professional and executive jobs in newspapers—198 were held by women.

The story in news magazines and radio is the same. *Newsweek* once ran a full page ad with pictures of its "back of the book" writers. It was titled "See What the Boys in the Back Will Have" and it was an apt description. *Newsweek* editor Elliot Osborne probably reflected the predominant male opinion when he made this outrageous comment after women employees charged discrimination at that liberal bastion: "The fact that most researchers at *Newsweek* are women and that virtually all writers are men stems from a news magazine tradition going back almost 50 years," he said. "A change in that tradition has been under active consideration by *Newsweek* and the magazine intends to pursue its plans to expand opportunities for qualified women." That "tradition" happens to be against the law and *Newsweek* had better do its "considering" with more than traditional "all deliberate speed."

The discrimination against women in media employment and the image of women that appears on TV screens, in newspapers, and in magazines are two sides of the same coin. If women are what the media says we are, we obviously don't belong with the "boys in the back"—except, maybe, as typists or researchers.

The image of women is a complete mother, housekeeper, sex-object, and helpmate. Most of what she does outside the home is considered temporary, unimportant, certainly secondary to getting her wash whiter than her neighbor's or polishing her rosewood Danish modern furniture with the lemon-scented furniture polish that throws her into ecstasies.

The *New York Times* once ran a story about two women who had started a committee to combat noise pollution. "All the news that was fit to print" included the names and ages of each of their children. When was the last time you saw that about men involved in civic activity?

Time Magazine once ran a story about the past President of the U.N. General Assembly and the caption under the picture read "Angie." When was the last time *Time* referred to the President of the United States as "Richard"?

Women in the news are constantly described in physical terms. When was the last time the *Washington Post* referred to "the vivacious Robert Finch"?

A national children's television show establishes the rules of the game very early in life. In one, a character was supposed to figure out which of three puppets was the real mother of the family. He asked the man. "Do you comb your children's fur?" and the response was, "No, I work. I drive a truck." He asked the woman if she kept the cave "neat and clean for your family," and the answer was that she had never been in a cave but that she made the beds and did the laundry. That from the extravagantly praised "Sesame Street" which reinforces the old, tired, sex role stereotypes. Where is it written that a uterus uniquely qualifies a woman to wield dust mops and wash dishes?

The image of women in shows for teenagers and adults is that of the soap operas, family comedies and nighttime serials where women's lives revolve around domestic tribulations. Women who work hold acceptable jobs like nurses and secretaries. Why can't Dr. Welby be a woman?

Advertising in print and on the air echoes those themes.

One for Mattel Toys sets the scene. Barbie doll and her friends do "the 'in' things girls should do . . . talk about new places to visit, new clothes to wear and new friends to meet. . . ." Boys meanwhile are occupied with more important tasks. "Because boys were born to build and learn, Mattel makes Tog'l (a set of building blocks) for creative play. . . . Because boys are curious about things big and small, Mattel makes Super-Eyes, a telescope that boys can have in one ingenious set of optically engineered lenses and scopes. . . ."

The image of big girls isn't very different. Parker Pen had this one in *Newsweek:* "You might as well give her a gorgeous pen to keep her checkbook unbalanced with. A sleek and shining pen will make her feel prettier. Which is more important to any girl than solving mathematical mysteries." Or take one in *U.S. News & World Report:* "Our new line of calculators goes through its final ordeal. . . . The dumb blonde test."

Advertisers trade in sex as if it were listed on the stock exchange. "This nice little blonde from Barcelona will romance you all the way to Spain . . ." says an Iberia ad in *Harper's.* Or, "We have a pretty girl who won't let you get in the wrong line" says Chemical Bank in the *New York Times.* Silva Thins adds a twist of masochism, and a male writer for *Ad Age*, the advertising trade publication, declared forthrightly that this is as it should be—women like to be knocked around.

Well, some of us have gotten very tired of being knocked around—women who graduate from college are sick of being given typing tests when boys who were their classmates get aptitude tests. We are tired of being secretaries and researchers—"office wives," in effect while men with lesser or equal skills are executives and editors and producers. Some of us are letting the men who run the media know just how we feel—from that day-long "consciousness-raising" session for *Ladies' Home Journal* Editor John Mack Carter in which I participated to stickers that say "This Ad Insults Women" or "This Exploits Women" which have appeared on buses and subways around the country—or this "Barefoot and Pregnant Award of the Week for Advertising Degrading to Women" that N.O.W. has printed.

We will be instituting boycotts of products that demean and degrade us and we will be talking with television programing executives about the images of women that harm our own self-images and the aspirations of our daughters and that contribute to that image of women that makes job discrimination respectable. I believe that the status of women in television—our position in employment and the image of women that is presented—are closely connected and are a matter for concern and investigation by the Federal Communications Commission. Certainly, racist programs would not be tolerated; sexist programs should not be permitted either.

I urge support of section 805 to the Post-Secondary Omnibus Education Act. It is shocking that women should have to come to Congress to plead for equal opportunity in the first place. And I urge that the status of women in the media—which plays such a crucial part in the life education of American women—be scrutinized more fully so that the images the media present do not cancel out everything our colleges seek to achieve.

What is the use of education for women if we cannot express our talents and reach our potentials? The Chinese used to bind only their women's feet. This society tries to bind our minds.

(The following tables were submitted for the record:)

EMPLOYMENT RATIO OF MEN TO WOMEN AT UNITED PRESS INTERNATIONAL, 1969–70 [1]

	Total men and women	Number of women
New York offices:		
Executive officers	10	0
Domestic news—Editors, etc	26	1
International news department	5	0
International features	1	0
Newspicture department—Managers and edirors	12	0
Commercial photos	10	0
Special services	3	0
Sales	5	0
Comptroller and secretary	3	0
Personnel and purchasing	5	0
Commercial and credit department	3	0
Auditor, labor relations, communications	11	0

[1] Statistics taken from November 1969 directory.

EMPLOYMENT RATIO OF MEN TO WOMEN AT UNITED PRESS INTERNATIONAL TELEVISION NEWS CORP.

	Total men and women	Number of women
New York Bureau: [1]		
Executives and management	5	0
Cameramen, soundmen, electricians	9	0
Reporters	3	1
Desk editors	7	0
Film editors	3	1
Librarians	5	0
Shipping department	.15	0
Clerks, secretaries, production assistants (basically clerical)	8	8

[1] These totals are not fixed; i.e., people come and go; titles change.

Note: The woman who is the executive secretary—with the company for over 10 years—at this compilation makes $140 per week.

Mrs. GREEN. Thank you so very much. I will add some comments after I call on Congressman Dellenback to ask questions.

Mr. DELLENBACK. Did the Chinese bind only the feet? I don't mean physically.

Miss KOMISAR. What do you mean?

Mr. DELLENBACK. In the same way that you say we bind the mind.

Miss KOMISAR. Yes, I suspect that they actually did bind their minds as well as their feet. Take out the word "only" then.

Mr. DELLENBACK. Haven't we today made significantly different opportunities available than were available to the Chinese? What Chinese girl had an opportunity at the time that feet were bound to go on to college?

Miss KOMISAR. I amend that and I take away the word "only". I don't know enough about Chinese civilization to answer you.

Mr. DELLENBACK. This is a catchy phrase, you see, but the point is that there have been great strides made since that time. It is one thing to say there haven't been enough strides made. That is what you are saying.

Miss KOMISAR. But I don't want to be compared to Chinese women. I want to be compared to American men.

Mr. DELLENBACK. You used the analogy. I was merely asking what you meant.

Miss KOMISAR. I am a writer and writers use phrases like that.

Mr. DELLENBACK. Really, if we want to compare, pick your own area or nationality——

Miss KOMISAR. It was just a metaphor.

Mr. DELLENBACK. But it was intended to make a point. You said, in effect, that our society is as restrictive as was the society of "x" years ago or the nationality across the sea.

Miss KOMISAR. I am saying that our society is restrictive of women's aspirations and of women's possibilities.

Mr. DELLENBACK. You would substitute that sentence for this last one?

Miss KOMISAR. No. I will take out the word "only" because I think that women in China obviously did not participate with men on an equal basis, but the point is that we would be very shocked at thinking about binding women's feet, but we are never shocked at binding women's minds and women's potentials and possibilities and lives and nobody thinks that there is anything wrong with the fact that when women—there used to be a joke when I was in high school about going to college to get your "Mrs." and I never really got the joke and realized what a sick joke it was. Women went to college to get husbands.

Art Buchwald had a piece that somebody mentioned to me about questions that you shouldn't ask women in women's liberation and one of them is "Now that you have gotten out of college when are you going to get married?" That is really the point. We are brought up to be mothers, wives and domestic labor, and if we work, we work as helpers to men. We are never brought up to fulfill ourselves in our own rights. I suggested to a human rights agency in New York that they put on some ads which had a picture of a woman sitting behind an executive desk and a man in a chair with a steno pad, and under it was the caption "What Is Wrong With This Picture?" and the answer is "Absolutely Nothing." Why can't we switch those positions? You talked before about the question of women being home and men being the breadwinner, and there is a debate in Sweden going on now about the whole concept of breadwinners. Where is it written that men are breadwinners and that women should stay home and take care of the children? My feeling is that if a woman has gone through 9 months of carrying a child and then bearing a child, fairness would require that the man should stay home for 9 months and let him take some of the responsibility. Men in this country sometimes act as if we had parthenogenesis, and I think that we have to do away with all of these assumptions that it is somehow a woman's role to stay home and take care of children. I just don't see that that is true. I think women should have the same choice that men have.

Women should have the choice to either have children or not have children, and when they have them, they should make an arrangement with their husbands about who is going to take care of the children or whether or not they are both going to work and the child will be taken care of by housekeepers or child care centers. We ought to have a national system of child care centers. I don't see where it should be sexually determined what a woman's role should be. Part of the problem is that in a sense women who work are playing out the same role of a wife, and that is as a helper. When a man leaves a city to take a different job in another city, his wife goes with him, and if she has a job she quits it. Well, what about the other way around? Suppose a woman gets an offer of a better job in another city. What about her going and the man quitting his job, if hers was a better job, and going with her? Why not? I think if we start thinking in those terms and that is what is happening now, the debate starting with job discrimination is getting down to much deeper issues. You mentioned that yourself and you are right. It is becoming a much more basic question of the role of men and women in the society.

What women are saying to men is "The role that you have assigned us is the one that is subservient. Otherwise why don't you want it?" Why don't men decide, if taking care of kids and taking care of a house is so wonderful, why don't men decide to do it?

Mr. DELLENBACK. I am torn between discussing the bill——

Miss KOMISAR. All right, let's discuss the bill.

Mr. DELLENBACK (continuing). And going off freely into discussions which really are very broad and very basic, because they underlie what we are talking about, and both of you have touched soundly on the broad sweep of what really is involved.

Miss KOMISAR. It comes out of our experience. When I was in high school my mother said, "Don't act so smart, you won't have dates", and we talked about what I would do. I should be a teacher, of course. That is what a girl should do.

Mr. DELLENBACK. Have you been married?

Miss KOMISAR. No.

Mrs. ROBERTS. I am married.

Mr. DELLENBACK. I am looking for a fact.

Miss KOMISAR. Among women that I know who are not married, many of us are, when we think about it, have made that decision partly because of looking around and seeing what women have to give up, particularly if we are women who are very much motivated towards careers. We look around us and see that wives often have to give up their careers, and it is a decision that I wouldn't want to make.

Mr. DELLENBACK. I think essentially, basically, what I read you as asking for is the right to make the decision, and, if the wife decides or if the female decides that she wants to play this particular role, instead of playing that role—the phrase is wrong.

If she wants to do this thing as opposed to doing that thing as her conscious choice, you are saying she should have as much choice as——

Miss KOMISAR. Yes; and what we would like to do is establish the agreement in society, except for a very few things such as perhaps bearing children, that there are very few things that only men can do or only women can do. We would like to do away with designation of certain roles as male and female, so that one would not automatically expect a woman just to stay home with children, or automatically expect a man to go out and work. We would like to do away with the whole question of sex-role stereotypes.

Mr. DELLENBACK. I don't think you can completely, and I do mean because of the mores and folkways and traditions and background. I think there are conditions, overgeneralized and oversimplified.

Miss KOMISAR. We have been brought up and brainwashed and acculturated to such an extent that, if there are differences, we really don't know what they are, and what we would like to do is be free to find out.

Mr. DELLENBACK. Thank you.

Mrs. GREEN. I must say, I am in agreement with what you have said. I think it does come from the personal experience that women have and men do not have. I think women are conditioned. I think your comments about toys is absolutely right. Women are conditioned to accept a particular role from the time they are less than 1 year old. They are given dolls to play with, a stove to cook on, and they are told, "Of course you will marry"; and there has somehow always been attached an individual social stigma to a woman if she does not marry. The old spinster term was a word of derision. It has most often meant she was rejected. It isn't, you know, in terms of the man. The "bachelor" is referred to as the "eligible bachelor." I think this condition exists throughout the woman's life. The most appropriate place for a woman is in the home. We like women if they learn to know their place.

I would like to add a few of the things that have happened just in recent years to support what is being said. I remember you talked about the discrimination in journalism. It was not very many years ago that a group of foreign correspondents were invited to the men's press club here in Washington. When they appeared at the door, there was a woman in the group, I believe two women, and they were not allowed to go in the front door. They had to actually go around to the back and go up the back fire-escape stairs in order to go in, because it was a rule. I entered a protest with some of your colleagues when this happened.

There are clubs here in Washington, I know which clubs they are in town, where women cannot enter the front door. I have a rule now that if I am invited to speak and I know ahead of time it is going to be at one of these clubs, I turn down the invitation. I just refuse to be told that as a woman I have to go in the back door or the side door. I see no difference between this and the objection of Negroes to being required to enter through rear doors or riding in the back of the bus. It seems to me it is exactly the same kind of treatment of certain individuals as less than first-class citizens.

I am advised on, I think, absolutely reliable authority, that in one of our great universities here in Washington, D.C. when men and women apply for admission to one of the departments, that the administration officer deliberately chooses the second echelon of women in terms of their GPA and their ability and they choose the top men who apply. Part of it is the threat that is there that the women will get better grades and so on, part of it is in maintaining a quota system; I believe this is the first time I have ever run into this.

For decades, many universities in the country have acquired a higher GPA for admission for women than for men.

Let me give one more serious example before I go to the amusing things. We are living in a period now where there is great concern about war, our involvement in Southeast Asia, and certainly from an emotional standpoint, from a logical standpoint, from a substantive standpoint, it is reasonable that the mothers of the country, the women are concerned about ending the war. It is their sons and their husbands who are being killed. They are as concerned as men. I said the other day, "I have never yet seen a picture of the U.S. delegation in any peace conference where there was a woman member of the U.S. delegation." This seems incredible to me, with women's concerns about peace and war. Maybe they do have a different kind of approach, and maybe a different viewpoint. It seems to me that ought to be represented. Women from different countries might bring a new understanding that would be constructive. Also, I agree with Miss Komisar's remarks about the ads. I have made a personal resolve not to buy certain products advertised by ridiculing women; and I would hope that "N.O.W.," the "Women's LIB," "WEAL," and all of the other groups would really carry on a systematic boycott of products that in their advertising depict the woman as a supercilious idiot. This is what happens in a lot of the TV commercials. I see it and I think this is by design. We have gone past that stage.

We won't allow a Step-N-Fetchit image any longer on the TV screen. In our early efforts to end discrimination against blacks, we determined we would no longer have certain songs and certain remarks, and certain references in school textbooks, but no similar efforts have been made where equally insulting remarks have been made to belittle or ridicule women.

Mr. DELLENBACK. Would you yield?

Mrs. GREEN. Yes.

Mr. DELLENBACK. Your example, Mrs. Green, of delegates to conventions in the nature of the United Nations—I wasn't aware of this and I am not really quarreling with your basic point, but I am interested in knowing whether the objection you raised to it is because you think everybody ought to have an equal chance, and chance should not end up with all men at such a thing? Or are you saying that they do have a different approach, and, therefore, that different approach ought to be represented?

Mrs. GREEN. I think I am saying both. The Equal Employment Opportunity Commission and the Enforcement Division of Civil Rights have ruled that the absence of blacks in a classroom or the absence of a certain ratio of blacks in a classroom or in a manufacturing or industrial plant or a shipyard—or in any other place, is in, and of itself proof of discrimination. I have letters in my file which carry the message that a disproportion in numbers of an ethnic minority confirms the discrimination. If you do not have this percentage of blacks at the plant in Portland, Oreg., or in other places, *per se*, this proves discrimination.

Mr. DELLENBACK. That is not basically my question.

Mrs. GREEN. Let me go on, please. What I am saying is the continuous absence of women, if they are right in setting that up as a criteria, that the absence of a black is the evidence of discrimination, then it seems to me you can also say that the continual absence of women is evidence of discrimination.

Mr. DELLENBACK. Yes; but that wasn't the question. I was asking you whether you were saying that the absence of women in these delegations was discriminatory, so far as sex is concerned?

Mrs. GREEN. Yes; I am making that charge.

Mr. DELLENBACK. And whether the weakness was, therefore, that the women don't have an equal chance with men or whether the weakness is that in order to make the group as broadly representative as possible, it ought to bring in the different attitudes that women do have toward some things from what males have.

Mrs. GREEN. And my answer to you was I am saying both. I am saying that, first, there is discrimination and, second, that this is not good in terms of the unwillingness to use the resources which are available in terms of women's minds. As long as women are more than 50 percent of the population, and if we don't use their abilities, I think that we are making a bad mistake. I do think the woman sometimes brings a different outlook, a different viewpoint. We said this a moment ago. In congressional committees the fact that women have not served on them, we have ended up with discriminatory laws. Part of the reason, I am convinced, is that men do not have this discrimination called to their attention. I don't think they would defend it. At peace conferences, women might well bring new ideas, might bring reconciliation where many times men have failed. Men are more aggressive.

Mr. DELLENBACK. You are not saying in all things men and women and alike. You have just said they are so significantly different in some ways, not in the legislative example, but the reasons given or the reason for inclusion of both men and women in delegations is that they are different.

Miss KOMISAR. There is a piece that I did in next month's *Washington Monthly* which talks about that and which you might like to read. It is called Violence and Masculinity. The point I make there is that the whole training of men is to be superior, to be in charge, to be powerful, to be dominant, and this shows up in our foreign policy where we can't be submissive because that is feminine. We can't withdraw because that is feminine. We have to be superior, and the other country that we are dealing with has to be subservient. I think this may be an extension of the masculine mystique, and I think we would have a great deal to contribute in this——

Mr. DELLENBACK. We are having a philosophical discussion rather than dealing with legislation but I think it is an important point, because the reason for making equality present in certain parts of the national legislative program, in matters of job discrimination, in matters of economic equality, is because we believe they are exactly the same. Men and women are alike and they should be treated the same, that is a very different point. The point we are making here as I read you now, Mrs. Green, is having said the male approach and the female approach may be in some significant degree different, and such a delegation to be broadly representative ought to have the great benefit and strength of all of that input.

Mrs. GREEN. I am saying that because of the conditioning that has occurred, a woman brings perhaps a different viewpoint. I think I would argue the same in terms of blacks and whites. The white male has simply never recognized the extent and degree of discrimination. In fact I have heard many of my white colleagues in the Congress express a similiar sentiment. I was in a meeting the other day when we were trying to get a grant and a Congressman from the South said very humbly, very frankly, "You know, I just have to admit I grew up in this city. I was not aware of the discrimination." I simply say that when a Negro is invited to sit at the conference table, he brings to it a different viewpoint, because of the experience which he has had over a period of years, and I would argue the same thing in terms of women.

Mr. DELLENBACK. Exactly, I agree with this.

Miss KOMISAR. If more women were in Congress you wouldn't have that condition. We deserve equal treatment because we are human beings and citizens of this country, but we are saying that when we get it the country will benefit from it.

Mr. DELLENBACK. Then we really do mean "vive la différence."

Mrs. ROBERTS. No; we are talking about two kinds of differences. There are no innate differences. I believe that is what you are saying Mrs. Green says there are innate differences because women represent a different train of thought.

Mrs. GREEN. I didn't say that.

Mrs. ROBERTS. No; but that is the way Congressman Dellenback is reading you, I believe. That is not what we are saying. There are no differences and we are challenging that there are differences. There are cultural differences that all of us have been given since we were born. These cultural differences are the ones that we are talking about being represented, not innate differences and that is the crucial point.

Mr. DELLENBACK. I think part of the reasons you want women on jury panels is because a woman might look upon a given situation somewhat differently from the way a man would look at that situation.

Mrs. GREEN. Would my colleague yield on this point? I remember a hearing on juvenile delinquency I attended a while back. That morning I had clipped out of the *New York Times* a long article about a woman who was arrested for being a prostitute, and there was a long article about the two that were involved. It identified the woman by name. It said that she had been taken down to the police court to be fingerprinted. It referred to the man not by name. It referred to him as a successful businessman from out of town. There was no further reference. There happened to be a woman judge from New York who was a witness at the hearing I attended that morning, and I said to her, "Why does this happen, if they both are engaging in an illegal act? Why is the blame put on the woman exclusively, and the man not identified." Doesn't "accessory" as the "accomplice rule" apply here?

One of our colleagues leaned over and said, "You know why, don't you?", and I said, "No, I really don't," and he said, "Because there has to be a witness." I said, "Why couldn't the woman sometimes be a witness." Why, in these cases, is it the rule to charge the woman with the crime—and protect the man as the "witness"?

Miss KOMISAR. Why don't we in this country have a national child care system? It is because the people in Congress are men who don't have to take care of children. If half the people in Congress were women who, because of the rules of our system, social system, had to take care of children, you would be pretty sure we would have a national child care system.

Mr. DELLENBACK. I think that is a little simplistic, but I would say that if I were a defense attorney and my client were a prostitute, I would be very interested in having some women on that jury.

Mrs. ROBERTS. In the same way I would be interested in having workingmen. All these different people have different attitudes.

Mr. DELLENBACK. Because it brings different attitudes.

Mrs. ROBERTS. But it is different experiences, not innate differences. This is the kind of things, Congressman Dellenback, that we are so interested in getting at, and we have confronted here this morning, that certain people have the idea there are innate differences that we must perpetuate and that are valuable. We say that we don't know if there are innate differences. We certainly know there are cultural differences, and this is the kind of thing we are talking about.

Mr. DELLENBACK. I am not really, you see, quarreling with the legislation, Madam Chairman. You understand that.

Miss KOMISAR. In terms of advertising there are some women, and women in advertising are fighting this. This was an ad taken out in *Ad Age*, by Francelli Cadwell, President of Cadwell-Davis. It says "The Lady of the House Is Dead." It talks about ads that depict women as barefoot and pregnant, that dumdum in Wichita, and that seem to have a cleanliness neurosis. She did a study to find the 10 ads most hated by women; they were mostly cleaning products and things of that sort. There are women in advertising who are trying to change the image, and she has said that her agency will not do ads that are demeaning and degrading to women. I think that is a good step. There are some other things in terms of media that are both a reflection of our society and a mirror that tells women what their expectations should be. Here is an ad that says, "After a girl has spent 4 years getting a college education, it is a shame not to spend just a few more weeks getting ready to qualify for a rewarding job." It is an ad from a secretarial school.

I would like to give these to you; ads where media pretty much advertise their policy of sex discrimination. Here is one, "The Metropolitan News Staff of the *New York Times* * * * Pick of the Professionals." It is a newsroom with only men in it.

Here is another ad for WOR radio. There are about three women out of a few dozen men, so they don't think there is anything wrong in showing the kind of discrimination that exists. Not only that, but this indicates to women the kinds of opportunities that are available to them.

Mrs. GREEN. Both Congressman Dellenback and I have appointments and I am going to have to adjourn the meeting, but I would like to make one comment and ask for your remarks before we adjourn. Because our country and our society was so long in doing anything to end the discrimination against blacks, it has resulted in a great polarization, and it has brought about the militant blacks. It is my judgment that if our society, which is run by men, in the National Congress, State legislatures, et cetera, does not put more attention to ending the discrimination against women, I think we are going to have an increased polarization in this conutry. I think we are going to have more and more militant women who will not be willing to tolerate this slow progress, I think also as we now are seeing blocs of votes among the blacks, that we are going to have women voting as a bloc. My own personal view is that this is not the most healthy thing for our society. I would wish that we could avoid it, but I think that we will see it if a change isn't made. Would either one of you want to comment?

Miss KOMISAR. I think it is true and I think that some of the more forward-looking legislators are realizing this, because I know that in New York we have numbers of people who have made statements and are running on women's rights issues. For example, both senatorial candidates in New York, Senator Goodell and Representative Ottinger, have made statements on women's rights. They include it in their literature. They appear at hearings and talk about it and they know that it is an important issue, and I think that Senators and Congressmen who see which way the country is moving will be responsive to the needs of the people, and it is not really a question of—a bloc vote I think is only bad when it is based on something irrational or irrelevant, but voting on the basis of issues is the logical way to vote, and I think women have to begin voting for people, for women and for men who support legislation that is aimed at our needs, particularly at job discrimination, at child care and the like. That is the way that our system ought to run.

Mrs. ROBERTS. The militancy will result if we see as the example—the only way the blacks got anything is being militant. If we are told that we must keep silent because that is our role, and therefore we should just keep waiting, but we have learned by example that the only thing that gets Congress' attention in some instances has been militancy. We don't want to do this. We are trying to stress men's stake in women's liberation. We are trying to stress the positive things that men will gain. Men aren't going to lose, they are going to gain, but if it takes too long to get this point across, I think what we are doing is correct. The model that has been established for us will be followed.

Mr. DELLENBACK. We have had two excellent witnesses. Thank you both.

Mrs. GREEN. I thank both of you for being here. You have been very helpful. I am going to ask unanimous consent that a statement by

Congresswoman Patsy Mink be inserted in the record at this point. Without any objection, this will be done.

Mrs. GREEN. The hearings will continue on Monday morning at 10 o'clock.

(Whereupon, at 12:10 p.m., the subcommittee adjourned to reconvene on Monday, June 29, 1970, at 10 a.m.)

MONDAY, JUNE 29, 1970

House of Representatives,
Special Subcommittee on Education of the
Committee on Education and Labor,
Washington, D.C.

The special subcommittee met, pursuant to recess, at 10:20 a.m. in room 2251 Rayburn House Office Building, Hon. Edith Green (chairman of the special subcommittee) presiding.

Present: Representatives Green and Erlenborn.

Staff member present: Harry Hogan, counsel.

Mrs. Green. The committee will come to order.

We are delighted to have as our first witness this morning Mrs. Daisy K. Shaw, director of educational and vocational guidance of New York City, and past president of the Directors of Guidance of Large City School Systems of the American Personnel and Guidance Association.

We are very pleased to have you.

STATEMENT OF MRS. DAISY K. SHAW, DIRECTOR OF EDUCATIONAL AND VOCATIONAL GUIDANCE OF NEW YORK CITY, AND PAST PRESIDENT, DIRECTORS OF GUIDANCE OF LARGE CITY SCHOOL SYSTEMS OF THE AMERICAN PERSONNEL AND GUIDANCE ASSOCIATION

Mrs. Shaw. Representative Green, distinguished members of the committee:

It is a great privilege for me to testify before you today with regard to section 805 (prohibition of discrimination) of H.R. 16098, the Omnibus Postsecondary Education Act of 1970.

Although women represent a majority of 51 percent of our population, they suffer from many of the same barriers to economic and social progress as do the minority groups in our society. They are paid less than men for comparable work, are often consigned to menial or routine jobs, are passed over for promotion, have a higher unemployment rate than men, and are grossly underrepresented in decisionmaking posts in politics, business, and the professions. These facts are well documented in numerous reports published by the Department of Labor, the Department of Commerce, the Women's Bureau, and various commissions and task forces.

Now, as never before, discrimination against women calls for strong new legislative action as well as vigorous enforcement of existing statutes. However, legislative remedies alone are not enough. What is needed is a thoroughgoing reappraisal of the education and guidance of our youth to determine what factors in our own methods of child rearing and schooling are contributing to this tragic and senseless underutilization of American women. For, as long as women perceive themselves as inferior, and as long as men cast them in subservient roles, legislation alone, though helpful, will not produce any substantive change in the status of American women. Fifty years after women's suffrage was won in the United States, we find only one woman in the Senate and 10 women in the House of Representatives. At the risk of being accused of female chauvinism, may I add that their quality is very high.

How do perceptions of sex roles develop? There is an old popular song of the forties that starts: "You have to be taught before it's too late, before you are six or seven or eight * * *." From their earliest years, children are introduced to picture books which practically condition them to accept males as the commanding, dominant figures in their lives. In a fascinating article published recently in the children's section of the *New York Times* book review, Elizabeth Fisher found that there were five times as many males in the titles of picture books as females, and that even animals in books are male for the most part. Furthermore, says Miss Fisher, even when females are depicted, their activities are quite limited—

> They do not drive cars. Though children see their mothers driving all the time, not a single description or picture of a woman driver could I find. In the world today, women are executives, stockbrokers, taxidrivers, steelworkers; in picture books these are nonexistent—Though there have been women doctors in this country for over a hundred years, and pediatrics is one of their preferred specialties, there is not a single woman doctor to be found. Women are nurses, librarians, teachers—but the principal is always male. . . .

Let us move from the preschool years to the kindergarten. Here little girls are still encouraged to "play house" in the homemaking corner, while little boys are building, firefighting, or policing. If one examines the primers used in the first three grades of elementary school, one searches in vain for a woman depicted as a worker (except for the omnipresent teacher and an occasional nurse, waitress, or secretary). Even the most up-to-date basal readers, issued in endless series by the leading publishers, are still presenting Dick and Jane types having endless fun, while mommy waits innocuously at the garden gate or in the apartment to welcome daddy home from a hard day at the office. (By contrast, the wicked queens of the old fairy tales at least displayed some executive talent.) It is true that there has been an effort during the past few years on the part of some publishers to update reading material used in the elementary schools. However, these changes have been largely confined to presenting a more balanced view of ethnic diversity in the urban environment. With a few outstanding exceptions, as in the Bank Street readers, women are still being portrayed in the same old stereotyped roles.

I have brought with me copies of three popular basal readers. If one looks through them, one searches in vain for an illustration of a woman who is engaged in some meaningful occupation. If you will examine these and any others of dozens of similar books, you will find the same pattern.

Rarely do we find a story about a working mother, although 35.3 percent of all mothers with children under 18 were in the labor force—as of 1967. Children who read stories depicting idyllic family scenes must feel somewhat deprived if their own mommies are out working rather than baking a cake at home. Thus, we continue to nurture the "feminine mystique," the image of women developed during the Victorian era, which limited the culturally approved role to that of wife and mother.

These subtle concepts, imprinted on children's minds in the early school years, are reinforced during adolescence by the communications media. Girls are constantly reminded of the need to be attractive, so that they can acquire a mate who will provide them with all the material comforts. Labor-saving devices are advertised as easing the lot of the housewife, rather than that of the working woman—or man, for that matter. Plenty of men use laundromats, but you never see one proclaiming that his wash is "brighter than bright." With the constant and prolonged emphasis on the need to please rather than the need to be someone, it is small wonder that many girls choose easier or less time-consuming courses of study than boys, and frequently give more attention to the social rather than the intellectual aspects of college life. (There has been some deviation from this trend in the recent past, it should be noted.)

Women themselves sometimes help to perpetuate sex-related career stereotypes. For example, note this recent release from a Woman's Program Newsletter:

ATTENTION, ALL BOSSES!

If you've been looking for a way to express special appreciation to your secretary, here's a suggestion from the State Commerce Department Woman's Program—how about saluting her during Secretaries Week, April 21–26, with the State flower to brighten her desk?

How can it escape even a women executive that the "boss" is "he" and the "secretary" is "she"?

American girls who are now in school will constitute 40 percent of the future labor force in our economy. Whatever their reasons for working—whether to support themselves or their dependents, to supplement family earnings, to achieve wealth or status, or to seek self-fulfillment—they will need special help from counselors in career planning. For most girls, work will be supplemental to their major responsibilities of wife and mother during a significant portion of their lives. Their career patterns will include various combinations of work, school, and marriage. Their ability to carry out their dual role successfully will be complicated by two factors: the discontinuity of their attachment to the labor force and the occupational concentration of "women's" jobs.

The sex label would seem to be a cultural rather than a biological factor in the labor market. The concentration of women in clerical occupations, teaching, nursing, sales, and service occupations is based on cultural factors and societal expectations rather than on sex-linked characteristics or aptitudes.

The broadening career opportunities which should be opened to women place upon counselors a special responsibility to raise the aspirations of girls, to assist them in achieving a satisfactory identity both as women and as workers, and to help replace past occupational stereotypes. Counselors must be continually alert to the changing values of the society for which young people are being prepared. While training for a career continues to play a central role in the education of boys, the importance of career planning for girls is less clearly understood. As the role expectations of American women continue to change in this era of technological progress and automation, counselors are faced with an important question: "Should counseling be different for girls than for boys?"

Thirty years ago, before we had counselors in most cases at all, it would not have been uncommon for a well-meaning teacher to say to a girl: "Your work in physics is excellent, but you may as well be practical. In a few years you'll be married and raising a family. Why go into a field which requires so many years of preparation." To another he might have said: "Your grades are high enough to get you into a premedical course, but you know what chance a girl has of getting into medical school. Besides, it would take you 9 or 10 years before you would be ready for private practice. Why not go into nursing instead? It's a wonderful profession now, and when you are married, you'll be able to give the best of care to your family." And to a third: "Why don't you take a business course? You'll only be working a few years anyway before you have a home and family."

The "self-image" of the individual girl is strongly influenced by society's expectation of her role. Although labor market analysts estimate that 9 out of every 10 girls in school today become workers at some time in their lives, many girls are still indoctrinated with the idea that work will be an optional, incidental part of their lives, if indeed they will ever work at all. Some still believe a Prince Charming will carry them off and they will live happily forever after.

Your action to assure equal opportunity for women through section 805 of the Omnibus Postsecondary Education Act of 1970 will encourage the full utilization of our human resources. May I respectfully offer for your consideration several other recommendations directed toward the same objective:

1. The formation of a commission to study the educational needs of girls with special reference to current practices in preschool and early childhood education, the adequacy and relevance of the curriculum in the light of expanded opportunities for women, and the provision of guidance and counseling for both girls and boys in elementary and secondary schools.

2. Authorization of grants to establish guidance institutes (on the NDEA model) for the in-service training of school counselors in the special guidance needs of girls.

3. Support for increased appropriations for guidance and counseling so that both girls and boys will receive adequate educational and career guidance from qualified, professionally trained counselors.

A few weeks ago, I represented our association before Senator Magnuson's Appropriations Subcommittee to request an additional appropriation of $217,500,000 under title III for guidance and counseling. At the present time, the House figure for guidance is $17 million; the Senate figure is $24,500,000. While even the latter figure falls far short of the actual need, it is our fervent hope that you and your colleagues on the House Appropriations Committee will support the higher figure.

There is great interest in the development of innovative programs in education. The greatest innovation of all would be to provide enough counselors to enable us to reach our young people, so that we could help them cope with the multiple problems which they encounter today. The pupil who comes from a disadvantaged environment plagued by discrimination, marginal subsistence, and disruption of normal family relationships, is least prepared to take advantage of cultural and educational opportunities.

In a recently completed survey conducted by our association, we found the following average counselor-pupil ratios:

City population:	Average C-P ratio
100,000–250,000	1–751
250,000–500,000	1–857
500,000–1,000,000	1–815
1,000,000 and over	1–750

However, in many cities the average was substantially higher (up to 1–2,600). The professionally trained counselor is uniquely qualified to work with the individual student, to encourage educational achievement and career development and to maximize human potential. To accomplish this, the counselor must have a realistic caseload. Ten years ago, accepted professional standards called for a counselor-pupil ratio of 1 to 250 in the secondary schools. An even lower ratio is required for students with special needs.

Today we recognize that girls must be prepared for their dual role as homemakers and as workers. The new life pattern of the modern women will include school, work and/or marriage, home, and a career. The two periods when women are most likely to work are during their early twenties and again starting in their early midforties until the age of retirement. Career exploration and planning for girls has equal importance with career exploration and planning for boys. Girls must be encouraged to select careers which will challenge their abilities and bring them self-fulfillment. At the same time, neither boys nor girls should be restricted to stereotyped choices based on traditional male or female role models.

We are not advocating special counselors for girls but, rather, are underscoring the need for adequate guidance for girls and boys. The lack of expert counseling can have devastating results for both, but girls are at a special disadvantage because they are so often frozen into stereotyped roles by social expectations. (Boys are also confronted by subtle psychological barriers when they seek to enter fields which are traditionally feminine, for example, nursing, early childhood education, dancing, secretarial work.) What we seek is an open society, one which offers equal opportunity and freedom of choice to all. If many, or even most, women should eventually select careers as homemakers, nurses, or office workers, it should be as a result of personal decisions, reached after careful consideration of all options, not because they feel restricted to "women's jobs." In the same spirit, those girls who opt for business, politics, or the professions should meet with no obstacles to self-realization. In summary, we plead for good guidance for all, with special attention to the disadvantaged in our society—both the disadvantaged minorities and the disadvantaged majority—our girls.

Mrs. GREEN. Thank you very much, Mrs. Shaw.

On page 3 you give some statistics about the number of women working with children under 18. I have been looking for the source. I came across it recently and forgot to write it down. I wonder if anyone in the room today has it. The figure was that 60 percent of all children in families where the mother is the head of the household are living in poverty.

Mrs. SHAW. This is the reference. It is from the manpower report of the President, January 1969.

Mrs. GREEN. I have that.

Mrs. SHAW. That is the labor force status of married women with children under 18 and the number of children involved as of March 1967.

Mrs. GREEN. I do not think that figure is in there.

Mrs. SHAW. Which particular figure?

Mrs. GREEN. Not too long ago I read—and it seems to me if this is true, that it has tremendous implications in terms of congressional legislation—that 60 percent of all children who are living in families headed by a woman are living in poverty as defined by the Government. The median income for women, of course, is much less than the median income for men.

It seems to me if this is fact it has tremendous social implications as well as implications for title I of the ESEA and some of the other programs. If any of you have that information or can provide it for me, I would like to have it.

Mrs. SHAW. There is an article in *U.S. News & World Report* published in April which offers statistics. I am surprised that the figure is as low as 60 percent. I thought it was even higher.

Mrs. GREEN. I thought 60 percent was pretty startling.

Mr. ERLENBORN. I would join with the witness in saying I would think that figure is rather low, particularly with the type of welfare program we have, which puts a premium on the family without the father. Sixty percent sounds to me as though it might be low.

Mrs. SHAW. Here is a reference from the U.S. Women's Bureau. "Nearly all of the 5.8 million women workers who were divorced, widowed or separated from their husbands were found to be working for compelling economic reasons. In addition, the 4.8 million married women whose husbands earn less than $5,000 per year were presumed to be working in order to provide their families with a better standard of living."

Mrs. GREEN. Let me ask you two or three things in terms of what the schools can do.

Has any attention ever been given in the New York City schools by the guidance and counseling people to the questionnaires that the children bring home from school to be filled out? They are almost always phrased in terms that I think do psychological damage to a child if the mother is in fact working and the father perhaps is unemployed or AWOL. I think it makes the child feel that somehow his family has a social stigma or they are not quite satisfying or conforming to the social norm. It always asks first, "What is your father's occupation?" Very seldom—in fact, I do not think I have ever seen one that puts on an equal basis "What is your mother's occupation?" There may be no reference to the mother—or written in a rather slighting way to the mother—as "Has your mother any other occupation than housewife?"

I have known of instances where small boys especially see this as somehow destroying the father image or giving the impression their family is looked down upon because the mother is the real breadwinner?

It seems to me guidance and counseling should pay some attention to these questions.

Mrs. SHAW. Yes; you are quite right, Representative Green. I would further comment that in most role books, which are printed official documents, they always call for the father's name first, if they call for the mother's name at all.

Mrs. GREEN. Many times the mother is not even to be listed.

Mrs. SHAW. It is generally understood that when the parent's name is called for, unless the father is listed, the family is deemed to be without a father. If a mother is listed as the parent, then this must be a broken home. That is the general assumption.

In our guidance bureau, of course, we constantly alert counselors to the importance of career planning for girls. We issue endless mimeographed brochures, statements, pamphlets, about careers for women.

Mrs. GREEN. We cannot legislate on this, but guidance and counseling people could do a study of questionnaires that are sent out which give the child the definite impression that the only person who is working is the father and that the mother is unimportant—as if the father is unemployed—somehow he is worthless. I also agree with your statement that girls are counseled right out of positions. They are told "You must not take these courses, because a woman couldn't get a job in this area anyhow." This has happened through the years.

One other question which, again, it seems to me the schools can do something about. I ran across a figure not too long ago that of the 278,000 registered apprentices under the Bureau of Apprenticeship Training, less than 1 percent are girls. It seems to me that an effort should be made to rectify this. It seems inexcusable. The highest unemployment rate of any group in the Nation is among nonwhite girls between 16 and 21.

Mrs. SHAW. I would say the unions are quite resistant. Many unions, especially in the construction area, have been 100 percent male.

Mrs. GREEN. And too frequently 100 percent white-Anglosaxon male.

Mrs. SHAW. Yes. It probably would create a furor if a girl wished to be an apprentice plumber, for example, although there is a rather amusing television commercial currently being shown where a little girl asks Jane Withers, the perpetual detergent advertiser, "Can I be a plumber when I grow up?" That struck me as a rather interesting question. In reply to her, I think the adult said, "Why, certainly. You can also help remove all the stains from your sink by using this marvelous detergent," whatever it is. As I watched that, it occurred to me that there are practically no women plumbers.

Mrs. GREEN. It seems to me it is important that every person have the opportunity to be whatever he or she wants to be, rather than to force him into a particular area. Many women do and will continue to choose to be in the home. Many will not; they are asking for the same options that men have.

Aside from the apprenticeship program, I was shocked 2 or 3 years ago when we had visiting school superintendents testifying. They spoke of special classes that were available to boys who were potential dropouts and how successful they had been. In fact they had been so successful they were doubling the number of classes for boys, and were "even starting ONE for girls." I thought this unequal treatment in public schools was a violation of civil rights and I wrote to the Equal Employment Opportunity Commission and the Office of Education. The high unemployment and dropout rate among girls is ample evidence of the need for similar classes—but schools are exempt under title VI.

There was absolutely nothing I could do about such discrimination at that time—since it was and is legal. I hope to correct this in the current bill which is pending before the committee.

I would also think people in the schools as well as the administration could do a better job of bringing girls in the Job Corps up to 50 percent. Legislatively, the highest I have ever been able to get it as far as the law is concerned is 30 percent, over the violent opposition of some of my colleagues. It seems to me 50 percent of the places should be filled by girls if they want in. At times, the waiting list for approved girls has been long.

In the new Conservation Corps there is no quota written in for girls, and I will be amazed if they have any program for them. I repeat these matters that, I've discussed in previous hearings because I believe guidance personnel should be aware of them.

Let me ask you one other question, if I may. Last night I watched a program called "The Advocates."

Mrs. SHAW. I saw the last part of it.

Mrs. GREEN. What is your reaction to that proposal? Let me ask it in two parts: (1) if it were optional, if it were encouraged; and (2) if it became mandatory. Did you see it?

Mr. ERLENBORN. No.

Mrs. GREEN. In the program the suggestion was made to make half-time work available so the man is at work half-time and the woman is at work half-time, and each would spend half of the time at home. They would still have the same income as they had before when the wife was not working.

Mrs. SHAW. I think in theory it is a very good proposal, but practically it would be ineffective for the following reason: As we find the hours of work being decreased in any given occupation, whether it be professional or blue collar, we find people taking second and third and fourth jobs in order to increase their income. Such an option seems quite reasonable and, in fact, it is an ongoing practice, because many firms have part-time workers, but the effect of this would not be to equalize the homemaking responsibilities of men and women, which I gather is the rationale for the proposal. At least, so I gathered from the discussion which followed.

Wasn't it your feeling that there was a sort of hidden agenda that men should participate in child-rearing to the same extent as women and should contribute to the running of the home, and that this would be possible if men and women both worked half-time and gave half their time to the home? If it worked that way, it would be fine. But, again, I can only speak from experience in the field of education where I see a great many people having more than one job.

People who are ambitious and mobile seem to want to do all that they can do.

Mrs. GREEN. I thought one of the main objectives was that with greater flexibility, more women would be able to work half-time or part-time and still fulfill their obligations at home. In so doing they would attain greater personal fulfillment. I thought that was the second major objective. It would also make it possible for fathers to spend more time with their growing children.

Mrs. SHAW. I agree. There is one very important aspect. While there is a good deal of part-time work available today, it does not carry with it the benefits of full-time work. It does not carry pensions, sick pay, health care, and other fringe benefits that the full-time worker enjoys. If half-time work involves those additional benefits, then I think such a practice might be more effective.

Mrs. GREEN. It would seem to me that our schools, which in past years have had a shortage of personnel, could have recruited a great many highly qualified women who would be willing to come back for half a day. Today, when we still have a terrible shortage of health personnel, I do not know why hospital schedules have to be so inflexible. I do not know why nurses and social workers cannot work half-time.

Mrs. SHAW. I think in many instances the practice is in effect. I recall something of the type even in New York City a few years ago, although I have not heard about it recently. I think they have had such a flock of applicants for teaching positions that they did not find it necessary to extend this practice. I believe that this was proposed.

Mrs. GREEN. Mr. Erlenborn?

Mr. ERLENBORN. Might I ask you, Mrs. Shaw, just one question. On page 6, you say "Thirty years ago it would not have been uncommon for a well-meaning teacher to say to a girl," and you give several examples girls were, in essence, discouraged from entering certain professions. Do you means to indicate by that that it is uncommon today?

Mrs. SHAW. That is a good question. There are many teachers who are still speaking in those terms. Let me amplify.

A few decades ago, most teachers and whatever few counselors there were counseled in terms they considered realistic. They were deeply devoted to the children's interest. They did not want to see children hurt. So, it would not have been unusual, for example, to hear someone say to a young Jewish boy "Look, you have a great deal of talent for engineering, but why break your heart? You know perfectly well that there is so much antisemitism in that field that you will never get very far. Go into something else where you can succeed."

In the same way some counselors spoke to black students in this vein. William Booth, who is now a judge in New York, was a high school student probably 30 years ago and he frequently tells the story of how 30 or so years ago in high school he told his teacher or counselor that he wanted to become a radio announcer, and this person said to him "Why prepare to be a radio announcer? There are no black radio announcers. Go into something else. Go into law." He offers that as an example of the discriminatory attitude through the counseling of students, and of course to a degree that may have been true 30 years ago, teachers and counselors did do that sort of thing 30 years ago but they weren't doing it from malice. They were doing this in an effort to spare their students from future hardships. Today there is an entirely different attitude.

Never, for example, would a qualified counselor say to a girl "Don't go on to a Ph. D. because in a university such as Columbia only 2 percent of the tenure professors are women." As a matter of fact, the percentage of Ph. D.'s among women has dropped from about 20 percent in the 1940's to about 10 percent in the 1960's.

I am making a distinction between counselors who have special training in a study of occupations in the changing labor market who are able to reach girls and point out opportunities to them, whereas teachers reflect more or less the same attitudes as parents and other members of society. They advise girls to do what seems practical, and what may seem practical at the moment may result in a tragic under-utilization of women's talent eventually. That is why I attach so much importance to the provision of adequate counseling in the schools.

In a central New York City high school a counselor will be responsible for over a thousand students. Under those circumstances the counselor cannot reach them, neither the boys nor the girls. It is only where we have these special programs, such as the college discovery program, the college-bound program, where we have counselors in a ratio of 1 to 100 that both the girls and boys succeed. They do not drop out. We have demonstrated over and over again through these special Federal projects under titles I, III, and V, and other titles that through a program of counseling the students do well, but having demonstrated that we cannot replicate it because of the lack of funds.

Right now there are 15,000 high school students in New York City who are getting superb counseling at a ratio of about 1 counselor to about 100 students but the remaining 267,000 are getting it in the ratio of about 1 to 1,200. If you lumped them together you get an overall average of about 1 to 800, but this average is meaningless. Ninety-five percent of our students are getting inadequate counseling and while boys suffer from this also there are adequate outside forces which help project boys into career planning. A boy knows that he will have a career some day; girls are not really made acquainted with all the opportunities that there are for them.

That is why we would strongly urge that a special commission or task force be appointed not so much from the civil rights aspect of looking into discrimination against women but looking into the educational practices starting with Headstart and kindergarten to see what practices we engage in that brainwash girls from an early age to see themselves in a subservient role. Why, for example, is there a homemaking corner in preschool and the nursery school, for girls, while there are building blocks and fire trucks for boys?

Mrs. GREEN. While I am in agreement with what you are saying and I feel very strongly on this, my judgment would be that it would be a small percentage of the American people that would agree with the two of us and that therefore such a commission is impossible. I would like to have your comments in terms of the Congress. I don't think it would be receptive. I think the majority of our colleagues see this as the woman's role and why have a commission to study it. I suspect, from public opinion polls, that that sentiment is shared by the American people.

Mrs. SHAW. The American people are disturbed that such a small percentage of lawyers happen to be women——

Mrs. GREEN. Not at all.

Mrs. SHAW (continuing). And that a small percentage of doctors happen to be women. They aren't?

Mrs. GREEN. No.

Mrs. SHAW. I am disturbed by it.

Mrs. GREEN. A small minority of women also are Members of Congress, if the public were really concerned they would vote differently. I think the answer is no in all of the cases you cite—though not to use women's full potential in education, law, medicine is a loss to the Nation.

Mrs. SHAW. You see, women themselves are their own worst enemies, because they are brainwashed from this very early age to see themselves in this role.

Mrs. GREEN. I want to go off the record—as I've seen some studies that dispute this.

(Discussion off the record.)

Mr. ERLENBORN. I have no further questions.

Mrs. SHAW. I agree with you as far as saying that women do like women, but I question the interpretation of that survey. It may be that women did not see themselves as favoring someone because of sex and that men didn't see themselves as favoring or not favoring someone because of sex. It is a question of identification. When people think of a leader they more generally tend to think of a man in that position because of a long process of conditioning. I see this in school systems all over the country. The majority of teachers in any given school are usually women and the principal is usually a man.

Mrs. GREEN. More recently this has been the case. At one time women were predominantly the principals in elementary schools but now they are in the minority.

Mrs. SHAW. I noted, for example, in our own Board of Education that male superintendents usually select male executive assistants. Now, surely there are just as many capable women executives. Even though these superintendents are all for women's rights, when it comes to selecting assistants they feel more comfortable working with men.

Mrs. GREEN. I think this is true.

Mrs. SHAW. And you have heard the expression from both men and women at times that they dislike working for a woman.

Mrs. GREEN. This is the same statement as against the minority—it's been repeated through the years: "How would you like to work under a Negro boss?"

Mrs. SHAW. Yes.

Mrs. GREEN. I thank you very much, Mrs. Shaw. You have been extremely helpful to our committee.

Mrs. SHAW. Thank you very much for hearing me.

Mrs. GREEN. I am going to ask the next three witnesses to come to the table at once and present their statements and then give us a chance to direct the same questions to all three: Virginia R. Allan, chairman, the President's Task Force on Women's Rights and Responsibilities; Daisy Fields, president of the Federally Employed Women; and Dr. Victoria Schuck, professor of political science, Mount Holyoke College. Shall we start out with Miss Allan, chairman of the President's Task Force on Women's Rights and Responsibilities? And let us find out how much progress we have made, if we may.

STATEMENT OF MISS VIRGINIA R. ALLAN, CHAIRMAN, THE PRESIDENT'S TASK FORCE ON WOMEN'S RIGHTS AND RESPONSIBILITIES

Miss ALLAN. Thank you.

Madam Chairman, I am pleased to be here today to testify in support of H.R. 16098, section 805, pertaining to discrimination against women.

Mrs. GREEN. May I say we are very, very pleased to have you, too.

Miss ALLAN. Thank you very much, Mrs. Green. I am strongly in favor of amending title VI to include women under that guarantee of nondiscrimination in all Federal programs and activities; of extending the coverage of title VII's equal employment guarantees to those in the teaching profession; empowering the Civil Rights Commission to investigate and report on sexual discrimination in our society in the same manner in which they now do for other groups with minority status; and extending the coverage of the Equal Pay Act to administrative, executive, and professional positions.

I come before you today to speak for myself and to report on the support of President Nixon's Task Force on Women's Rights and Responsibilities for this legislation. The title of our report to the President accords with the legislative intent of the bill before us. Both are: "A Matter of Simple Justice."

Last fall I was honored and privileged to be appointed by the President as chairman of a special Task Force on Women's Rights and Responsibilities. A group of 11 women and two men were appointed by the President. We represented various fields of interest and endeavor including education, law, labor, private industry, and the news media. Our group met in extended sessions to make legislative and administrative recommendations concerning the role of women in our society.

Those meetings were most interesting, and we learned a great deal. The 13 members of the task force recognized the rights women should have but cannot exercise, and the responsibilities women would assume but are denied as long as women continue to be held in the position of minors, legally. To some on the task force the facts of discrimination documented for us by experts in many fields were well known (to some by actual experience); to others the revelations were new and hardly believable at times. To all of us the total picture of sexual discrimination in a democratic society was startling and intolerable. We are indebted to you, therefore, for introducing legislation that will, I believe, help change this picture.

Three legislative items proposed by the task force appear in H.R. 16098, section 805. I will comment on each of these. First let me say that the task force did not specifically recommend amending title VI of the Civil Rights Act of 1964, to cover women, thus requiring equal treatment for women in all activities and programs receiving Federal financial assistance. However, I can assure you that such an amendment accords fully with the philosophy and the legislative intent of the task force members. I can speak to this point clearly, for we did recommend amending the public accommodations title, title II, to include women. We also recommended amending title IV and IX to provide equal educational opportunity for women with the support of the Attorney General and the Office of Education to achieve this end.

In making these recommendations regarding title II, IV, and IX, our intent was to make sure that women, who constitute 51 percent of our population, are not denied equal protection of the law or equal opportunities in our society.

One of the basic concepts upon which our democracy was founded was the idea that people can only be free and equal where there is equality of opportunity. If women are unreasonably denied access to public places and public educational institutions (which they support with taxes), then women cannot be considered full and equal citizens. Women should be fully integrated into the educational institutions of our Nation as students (and teachers), and accepted as mature individuals with potential and worth. The amendment to title VI that this bill proposes would help achieve that end by a congressional mandate prohibiting discrimination based on sex in any program or activity receiving Federal financial assistance. It is time to add "sex" as one of the kinds of discrimination that will be unlawful. I heartily endorse this amendment.

The other three parts of section 805 of H.R. 16098 were specifically recommended by the task force.

Title VII prohibits discrimination in employment, whether in hiring, firing, in the conditions or privileges of employment. Regarding title VII, the task force recommended extending coverage of that title to teachers, to State and local government (so that public schools would be covered and because their exclusion is unreasonable). We also recommended removing the burden of enforcement from the aggrieved individual by empowering the Equal Employment Opportunity Commission to enforce the law, which power that agency does not have at this time.

In our explanation of this legislative proposal we noted the inadequacy of the current enforcement proceedings of the EEOC as well as certain budgetary deficiencies and additional staff requirements.

The task force went on to say that: "There is gross discrimination against women in education." I believe the testimony of many of the witnesses before this committee has thoroughly substantiated that statement. The members of the task force heard from many knowledgeable individuals in the field of education. We noted the growing body of evidence of discrimination against women faculty in higher education. From the Research Division of the National Education Association we acquired the depressing information that in the school year 1966–67, 75 percent of elementary school principals were men. In 1964–65 men held 96 percent of the junior high school principal positions while a survey of high school principals for the academic year 1963–64 showed 90 percent to be men.

Since our meetings ended that body of evidence has increased enormously. The Fact Sheet on the Earnings Gap, published by the Department of Labor's Women's Bureau this spring, included valuable statistics on variations in salaries and academic rank of men and women.

In institutions of higher education in 1965–66 women full professors had a median salary of only $11,649 as compared with $12,768 for men. Comparable differences were found at the other three levels as shown in the following table:

MEDIAN ANNUAL SALARIES OF TEACHING STAFF IN COLLEGES AND UNIVERSITIES, BY SEX, 1965–66 [1]

Teaching staff	Number		Median annual salary	
	Women	Men	Women	Men
Total	26,734	118,641	$7,732	$9,275
Professors	3,149	32,873	11,649	12,768
Associate professors	5,148	28,892	9,322	10,064
Assistant professors	8,893	37,232	7,870	8,446
Instructors	9,454	19,644	6,454	6,864

[1] "Fact Sheet on the Earnings Gap," Women's Bureau, Wage and Labor Standards Division, U.S. Department of Labor (Washington, D.C., 1970), p. 3.

In addition I would note that Dr. Lawrence A. Simpson, who is currently a placement director and whose doctoral research analyzed academic discrimination regarding women, has reached the following conclusion regarding the present-day woman college teacher:

More than 50 percent of all academic women are in the broad fields of English, fine arts, health, education, and physical education.

Academic women are most frequently employed in private 4-year colleges with small faculties.

Women are predominantly at lower academic ranks—instructor or assistant professor.

Women are more likely to teach beginning undergraduate students— freshmen and sophomores.

Women earn substantially less than men in the academic world.[2]

Such information convinces me that amending title VII to cover teachers is highly important. Although now not associated directly with teaching, I was for many years a teacher. I maintain my interest in the field, actively, since for the last 7 years I have also been regent of Eastern Michigan University in Michigan. This has increased my contact with academic women and my knowledge of the problems women face in employment discrimination in our universities and colleges. The amendment to title VII to cover education in the guarantee of nondiscrimination in employment is of utmost importance. Young women cannot be expected to pursue a college or graduate school education if those who teach them refuse to hire them, promote them, or treat them as academic equals. It is that simple.

Our task force also recommended extending the jurisdiction of the Civil Rights Commission to include denial of civil rights because of sex. As the task force commented: "Perhaps the greatest deterrent to securing improvement in the legal status of women is the lack of public knowledge of the facts and the lack of a central information bank."

We felt that the Commission's authorization to study denials of equal protection of the laws, and to appraise the laws and policies of the Federal Government with regard to equal protection of the laws under the Constitution should be extended to women.

There are a growing number of private individuals and organizations who are endeavoring to collect the facts concerning the political, legal, economic, and social status of women in our society; hearings such as this one help enormously. But, there is a distinct advantage

[2] "Sex Discrimination In The Academic World," summary of research by Dr. Lawrence A. Simpson (Washington, D.C., Business and Professional Women's Foundation, 1970). See also Lawrence A. Simpson, "A Study of Employing Agents' Attitudes Toward Academic Women in Higher Education," unpublished doctoral thesis, the Pennsylvania State University, September 1968.

in legally constituting the Civil Rights Commission to continually add to the information, to acquire totally unknown statistics, and to keep such information updated.

I can give you some graphic examples of this need. Some of us on the task force were shocked to find out in our study that laws in Connecticut and Pennsylvania provided longer prison sentences for women than for men for the same offense. In these two States such laws had been exposed, opposed, and now held to be inconsistent with the equal protection guarantees of the 14th amendment.[3]

However, this happened in the last 2 years. We do not now know how many States have the same, or variations of this kind of law. We do know that in Arkansas the law currently permits women to be sentenced to prison for up to 3 years for drunkenness and drug addiction. Men cannot be sent to the penitentiary for the same offense.[4] Such laws are patently unconstitutional and certainly should come under the purview of the Civil Rights Commission if mandated to survey sex discrimination and equal protection of the laws.

We do not know how many and which States exclude women from the advantages of certain kinds of public education, as was the case at the University of Virginia and at several New York City schools for superior students.[5]

The Women's Bureau performs an invaluable service in keeping up with varying labor laws regarding women, but they cannot undertake to survey yearly all the special State laws—and the changes therein—for women. Indeed there are State laws regulating the contractual obligations and capacities of women *only*. Jury service, the age of majority, domicile rights are different for men and women. Property restrictions are imposed upon married women, but not married men, regardless of their ability, their education, or their experience. In four community property States, community property, including the wife's personal earnings, are managed and controlled by the husband—Arizona, Louisiana, Nevada, New Mexico.[6]

Clearly these are carryovers from our Anglo-Saxon forebears. Many are neither necessary, reasonable, nor consistent with the 14th amendment. But we simply know too little about them. Again, full information on these matters could be provided by the Civil Rights Commission, if given the power to study this subject of discrimination. We also need to know more about the ways in which employers determine to restrict employment opportunity of women; the ways in which colleges and universities establish written or unwritten quota systems based on sex, the ways college placement bureaus and recruiters choose similar quotas. Although, perhaps, outside the jurisdiction of the Civil Rights Commission, I would hope that this kind of information could also be secured.

In order to propose effective remedies for current sexual discrimination, it is imperative that we secure the facts of societal, legal, and economic discrimination based on sex in our society. Much of this could

---

[3] *Commonwealth* v. *Daniel*, 430 Pa. 642, 243 A. 2d 400 (1968) ; *U.S. ex rel. Robinson* v. *York*, 281 F. Supp. 8 (D. Conn., 1969).

[4] Arkansas Gazette, Saturday, March 21, 1970.

[5] *Kirstein et al.* v. *The Rector and Visitors of the University of Virginia, etc., et al.* (E.D. Va., Richimond Div. Civil No. 220–69–R) : The Evening Star, Washington, D.C., May 3, 1969, A–2.

[6] "1969 Handbook on Women Workers," Bulletin 294, Women's Bureau, Wage and Labor Standards Administration, U.S. Department of Labor (Washington, D.C.: GPO, 1969), pp. 282–292.

be accomplished by the Civil Rights Commission.

I am also grateful to be able to testify in support of amending the Fair Labor Standards Act, so that the equal pay provisions of that bill will extend to executive, administrative and professional positions.

In 1963 when the national president of the National Federation of Business and Professional Women's Clubs testified before the Special Subcommittee on Labor of the Committee on Education and Labor of the House of Representatives, the 88th Congress, I accompanied her as the first national vice president of the national federation. When the equal pay bill passed later that year I was around to celebrate a victory that had taken almost 25 years to accomplish and had required untold effort.

At the time that the equal pay bill passed, those of us who had joined in the National Equal Pay Committee to work for passage, had no intention of excluding executive, professional, and administrative positions. We would hardly have chosen a point at which discrimination would be acceptable.

In fact, as you well know, Madam Chairman, the original equal pay bills, the administration-supported equal pay bill introduced in 1963, contained no provision which would have attached it to the Fair Labor Standards Act.

It was the decision to attach equal pay to the Fair Labor Standards Act that resulted in the exclusion of administrative, executive and professional positions from the operation of the Equal Pay Act because these positions are exempted, excepted in the FLSA. That decision was based on political necessity; this seemed the only way to secure equal pay legislation. Thus, equal pay coverage became coextensive with minimum wage coverage.

I might add that those of us working on the legislation at the time fully expected that an amendment would rectify this omission in the near future.

The task force considered this very problem, recognizing the fact that political necessity had resulted in the exclusion of so many men and women workers from the operations of the Equal Pay Act.

We also recognized that although women in professional, executive and administrative positions have the protection of title VII of the Civil Rights Act of 1964, there are several problems with the kind of protection provided. Cardinal among these is the fact that the complainant's identity can be withheld under the Equal Pay Act, but not under the Civil Rights Act of 1964. The task force thought this especially important for women in executive, professional, and administrative positions. Women are hesitant to endanger positions come-by with great difficulty.

We also took note of the fact that the Equal Employment Opportunity Commission as presently constituted cannot require compliance with the provisions of title VII. Generally, individuals must bring their own suit to court. The EEOC cannot institute a suit, they can only support the aggrieved party. Moreover, the enforcement proceedings for the equal pay bill are not only private but extremely effective. In fiscal year 1969, the Wage and Hour Division found 477,434 employees underpaid approximately $89 million in wages. In a substantial percent of these cases the employer agreed to pay the back wages found to be due. In others, court action was necessary to compel compliance with the law, and 1,929 legal actions were instituted in fiscal year 1969.[7]

Indeed, the Secretary of Labor may obtain a court injunction to restrain not only continued violation, but withholding of back wages legally due. The Secretary may bring suit for the back wages or the employee may bring suit through his or her own attorney.

In summary, because the original intent was never to exclude these positions from the equal pay provisions, because the enforcement proceedings are private and effective, the task force supported amending the Fair Labor Standards Act to require equal pay for equal work to individuals of both sexes who are employed in executive, administrative, or professional capacities.

The task force made many other legislative recommendations, regarding equity in the social security law, special child care legislation, amendments to the Internal Revenue Code to allow certain kinds of dependency deductions, equal treatment for husbands and children of women employees of the Federal Government, etc. I would like, with your permission, Madam Chairman, to introduce into the record of the hearings today the full task force report for the committee to review and help us to implement.

Mrs. GREEN. I think that is already in the record earlier.

Miss ALLAN. All right, thank you.

I would like to close my testimony by first thanking you, Madam Chairman, for holding these hearings and so effectively espousing our common cause. I would also like to note that in my letter of transmittal of the task force report to the President, I emphasized the following: "Women do not seek special privileges. They do seek equal rights. They do wish to assume their full responsibilities." The task force also recommended to the President a national commitment to basic changes that will bring women into the mainstream of American life. Madam Chairman, I believe the legislation we are discussing today proposes some of these very changes, moves us toward that commitment and will help free women to assume their mature responsibilities as citizens. I heartily endorse these proposals.

Mrs. GREEN. Thank you, very much. I must say that I agree with you on the equal pay bill. I had introduced that in every session since I came to Congress in 1955 and we finally achieved passage in 1963, but political necessity required that compromise to exempt executive, professional, and administrative positions from coverage which I did not want but it was either that or no bill. Let me ask you one question which we are going to run up against, and I want to have your views on it.

Amending title VI, of course, will have an impact on schools that are all-girl schools and all-boy schools. What is your reply to that?

Miss ALLAN. Of course, on the task force, as you know, we had Sister Ann Ida Gannon, president of Mundelein College and Dr. Alan Simpson, president of Vassar, both private schools. That was one of the reasons that we did not come out with the recommendation putting sex in title VI, because they felt, and particularly Sister felt very strongly, that at this time in the way our culture is set up girls' schools do give women the opportunity for leadership roles that they don't

[7] Unpublished report, "Some Facts About the Wage and House Division," U.S. Department of Labor, 1970.

have in a coeducational college. Also, Dr. Fitzgerald, who is the associate dean at Michigan State University was a consultant for the task force. She, too, feels that through women's organizations like the Associated Women Students, that women can rise to leadership positions, and so we did debate it. I don't know that I can give you an answer. Dee Boersma, who served on the special committee with Dr. Simpson and Sister Ann Ida, is a graduate student at Ohio State. She had served as president of the student council at a coed university and Dee didn't see any problems at all about women rising to leadership positions but Sister did have great reservations and we respected those reservations and did not come out with that recommendation.

Mrs. GREEN. Isn't this, though, the argument that has been used through the years for black schools and white schools, that it would give the chance for blacks to rise to leadership positions?

Miss ALLAN. That is right.

Mrs. GREEN. Isn't it exactly the same now?

Miss ALLAN. I would say if it had come to a vote in the task force, I am sure that the task force would have included the title VI.

Mrs. GREEN. You did recommend that it go into title IV?

Miss ALLAN. Yes.

Mrs. GREEN. What is your rationale for IV and not VI on this particular point, because IV would accomplish it, would it not?

Miss ALLAN. I know.

Mrs. GREEN. It would have the same effect as amending title VI in terms of Federal aid?

Miss ALLAN. Yes, that is correct. I just bring out that the task force did support title IV. Because Sister Ann Ida felt strongly about title VI we shied away from it.

Mrs. GREEN. What did she say on title IV?

Miss ALLAN. She didn't. She didn't object to it for some reason.

Mrs. GREEN. Maybe she didn't understand that it is the same thing.

Miss ALLAN. Well, it could be. I really don't know.

Mrs. GREEN. It seems strange.

Miss ALLAN. As I say, our younger member, who is 22 years old, felt strongly that titles IV and VI should be in.

Mrs. GREEN. I don't know how we can get to the discrimination against girls and women in schools unless we amend title VI.

Miss ALLAN. That is right.

Mrs. GREEN. And I realize the problem on the other, but otherwise it would be difficult in doing it in coeducational schools, public high schools, where they say that they have a right to have special classes for disadvantaged boys only and that the Civil Rights Act does not touch on this. I am powerless. I can object, but they say "We are not violating the law. The law allows this."

Miss ALLAN. Yes. I spoke more trying to explain sister's views but I would say the task force, if I could read them correctly, certainly, as I indicated in this testimony, were for every bit of it.

Mrs. GREEN. On page 3 you accurately portray the number of women who are elementary school principals, and of course this has gone down in the last several years. Let me make a statement and ask you to comment whether you disagree or agree.

Coming from the educational field myself, I am absolutely persuaded that many women leave the elementary and the secondary teaching field because there is no possibility of advancement. In fact, too often, the most capable women leave, the ones who might be in other positions, because they see nothing ahead of them. Would you agree with that? Therefore, we lose them when we close administrative positions to them.

Miss ALLAN. Yes. Where do you go, though? I left myself and went into business but I felt far greater discrimination in business than in education. I was an assistant principal and I felt relatively little discrimination in the Detroit school system. I went up rather rapidly. The thing that I found—and I think this comes from our culture—is that women didn't want to compete. After I left the school system the merit system of promotion was replaced by a series of examinations, and I found, much to my discouragement, that women didn't want to compete in those examinations. To me this goes back to exactly what the guidance counselor was talking about. I mean, women feel that it is unladylike to compete. That concept is part of our culture.

Mrs. GREEN. I want to ask one other question. I am not sure I agree with that. On page 4 you outline, again accurately, the small number of women in various positions as a discrimination. You remain painfully silent on the number of women who hold policymaking positions in the Office of Education under either this administration or the past administration or any prior to that, or the number of women in policymaking positions in HEW. Was the task force aware of this?

Miss ALLAN. It was a matter of time. We had 2 months to do our work. As you know, the report had to be sent to the President by December 15. There are many areas, as you will note from the task force report, that we would have liked to have recommended. Because we couldn't do everything we recognized the very fact that you pointed out here, and what we did was to recommend that an office be set up within the Office of Education because we are well aware of these facts.

Mrs. GREEN. We found out both in the Office of Education and the Department of HEW—this is within the month—that, of course, down at the GS-3, -4, and -5 levels women predominate but when you get up to GS-18 in the entire Department of HEW there is not a single woman in GS-18.

Miss ALLAN. We studied all of that.

Mrs. GREEN. The Office of Education, I think, is even more pronounced in its selection of women for policymaking, higher paid jobs.

Miss ALLEN. But in the task force recommendation 4—what the executive branch of the Federal Government could do—you will note that we have some means in here to get at those discriminations.

Mrs. GREEN. I do not think that they would allow it if it were black versus white.

Miss ALLAN. The task force recommendation 4 deals with this matter. If our recommendations were implemented I think we would get at the very problems you are raising.

Mrs. GREEN. I would like my colleague from the other side of the aisle to know that I am not any more critical of this administration than I am of the last because their records are comparable—and from my standpoint—subject to criticism by career-minded women.

Mr. ERLENBORN. I noticed your evenhanded treatment of the two administrations. I have no questions.

Mrs. GREEN. Thank you very much. We may have other questions if you will stay, but may we turn to Daisy Fields, the president of Federally Employed Women.

STATEMENT OF MRS. DAISY FIELDS, PRESIDENT, FEDERALLY EMPLOYED WOMEN

Mrs. FIELDS. Good morning, and thank you very much. I must begin by apologizing for the fact that I not only prepared the testimony myself but typed it myself and I think that is quite apparent as you go through it with me, that the typographical errors are the fault of my typewriter and not me.

I am Mrs. Daisy B. Fields, president, Federally Employed Women, Inc., better known by the acronym FEW. FEW is a nonprofit organization established in September 1968. As stated in the bylaws, its purpose is to take action to end sex discrimination in employment in the Government service; to increase job opportunities for women in the Government service and to further the use of the potential of women in the Government; to improve the merit system in Government employment; to assist Government employees and applicants for Government employment who are discriminated against because of sex; and to cooperate with and assist other organizations and individuals concerned with equal employment opportunity in the Government without discrimination because of sex, race, color, age, marital status, national origin, political affiliation, religion or physical handicap.

I consider it a privilege to come before this distinguished committee on behalf of H.R. 16098, the Omnibus Post-Secondary Education Act of 1970, to address myself particularly to section 805 of the act, dealing with the problems of discrimination against women. I will limit my testimony to the critical area of sex discrimination in Federal employment.

Discrimination against women in public service antedates the Constitution itself. In 1773, when a woman was appointed postmaster in Baltimore, she faced rather formidable opposition from no less a person than Thomas Jefferson, who said "The appointment of a woman to office is an innovation for which the public is not prepared." Though few would voice such sentiments today, many still harbor the same attitudes, expressing their views more subtly.

Mrs. GREEN. I agree with everything except that "more subtly."

Mrs. FIELDS. A century ago, June 11, 1870 to be exact, Representative Willard of Vermont participated in a debate in the House of Representatives on legislation which was to influence the employment of women in the Federal Government for the next 92 years. The debate concerned an appropriation bill with a rider that would require equal pay for equal work irrespective of sex. In his argument for it, he said "I hold that this government owes it to the women of the country * * * that they shall no longer be held in a subordinate position and treated as inferiors; that it shall say to them there shall be hereafter no position under this Government for which they are fitted which shall not be open to them equally with men; that when they do work of any of their brothers in any office under the Government, they shall have the same pay their brothers have; that their brains are worth as much, that their labor, their energy, their industry are all worth as much as the labor, the industry, the energy, and the brains of anybody. If the women of the country had the ballot today—as I believe they ought to have it—then this House would be found voting unanimously for this proposition * * *." (Sec. 165, Rev. Stat.)

In the final analysis, the provision was watered down to permit appointing officers to employ "female clerks" at the same pay as men.

Ironically, although this 1870 statute was intended to benefit women in the matter of pay, it was construed by appointing officers as giving them unrestricted right to selective hiring on the basis of sex—to consider only men or consider only women. This restrictive clause was brought to light in 1962 by the President's Committee on the Status of Women (Kennedy) and was declared invalid by the Attorney General. In 1965 Congress repealed the law itself.

Another historical reference I would like to include refers to the Civil Service Commission annual report to Congress for the year ending June 30, 1891. The Commission reported 147 women appointed from competitive examinations to the departmental service and 776 men. The ratio of women to men was a little less than 1 to 5. During the year ending June 30, 1892 the number of women appointed was 86 and the number of men 245, the proportion being a little more than 1 to 3. By way of explanation, the report stated "It is difficult to account for this change, but attention is called to the fact as one of general interest and as probably showing that the prejudice which has hertofore existed to some extent against the appointment of women in the classified service is gradually disappearing."

The same report, commenting on an increase in promotions of women, stated "These promotions have been won on the basis of the efficiency records kept in the departments and the close competitive tests which have supplemented those records and show that when women in the public service have a fair and even chance with the men, they win their full share of the more lucrative and responsible positions."

Ladies and gentlemen, had this logical reasoning prevailed through the years I would not be here today and there would be no need for organizations such as FEW, nor for the proliferation of other organizations identified under the broad umbrella as "the women's liberation movement."

With this historical background, let us turn to the era of the 1960's and the 1970's, and look briefly at the employment status of women in Federal service today. The figures I am about to cite are based on the Civil Service Commission "Study of Employment of Women in the Federal Government, October 1968." Regrettably, the 1969 data are not yet available. However, I have been told, informally, that no significant improvements have occurred.

This analysis refers only to white-collar employment:

As of October 1968, total employment of men and women was 1,963,870. Of these, 667,234 were women—34 percent of the workforce. Breaking this down by grade groups, we find women employed as 78.7 percent in grades GS-1 through GS-6; 19.9 percent in grades GS-7 through GS-12; 1.0 percent in grades 13 and above; 0.02 percent ing grades GS-16 and above.

It should be noted that at the supergrade levels, GS-16 and above the number of women dropped from 164 in 1967 to 131 in 1968.

Occupationally, we find the largest percentage of women employees—over 50 percent—in personnel management; general administration, which, of course, includes secretaries and typists; medical, hospital, dental, public health, and library and archives. The majority of women in these occupations are in the clerical and lower grade technician jobs.

The smallest number of women—under 5 percent—are in veterinary medicine; engineering and architecture; investigation; commodity quality control; inspection and grading; and equipment facilities and service. The paucity of women in engineering and architecture—1.3 percent—is attributable in large measure to the fact that colleges and universities discourage women from enrolling in these fields. Women who do enroll find limited opportunities in the labor market as well as lower pay for comparable work. Consequently, through the years, it's small wonder fewer women are matriculating for these professions.

The same report cites a few unique "breakthroughs" in areas previously considered the male preserve; for example, one woman was appointed a tugboat captain, others included an irrigation officer, free gyro repair foreman; structural engineer; customs inspector, and aviation operations inspector. These are the "token" women on display in the showcase labeled "Equal Opportunity."

Admittedly, the number of women who might seek employment in such fields is comparatively small. But that is not the issue. The basic issue is that all qualified persons—regardless of sex—are entitled to choose, of their own free will, the occupation for which they are best qualified by reason of education, training, skill, motivation, physical stamina, personal desire, and ambition.

In November 1969 the Civil Service Commission issued another report entitled "Characteristics of the Federal Executive." This report includes all employees in grades GS–15 and above. Of the 28,000 employees reportedly occupying positions at these levels, 584, or 2 percent, were women. Over one-third of the women are medical officers; one in six is a social scientist, and less than 1 percent of the top executives in supply and logistics; fiscal occupations, including accounting; business occupations, including contracting; engineering and physical scientists are women.

Certainly, it cannot be said that there are not more qualified women who could fill positions at these levels. My colleagues and I can identify many of them. Rather, the root of the problem lies in our social customs, traditions, life patterns, and the perceptions of the male and female roles—the stereotypes we perpetuate; as well as the fact there is no law presently on the books which would prosecute those who discriminate against women in employment.

According to the Bureau of Labor Statistics, 100 million workers will be in the labor force by 1980—presently there are about 85 million. This will include 36 million women and 12 million nonwhites—as compared with 30 million women and 9½ million nonwhites currently in the labor force.

In discussing these projected work force needs by 1980, Assistant Secretary of Labor Jerome Rosow recently stated that "the real squeeze in demand will be for managers and supervisors in the 30–45 age range; the demand for professional and technical workers will increase about 45 percent—twice as fast as the demand for all workers; the demand for white-collar workers will increase by about 50 percent; all levels of government will need 40 percent more workers to cope with the needs of a population of 243 million people."

While these projections are based on the needs of the Nation as a whole public service will continue to grow despite periodic cutbacks such as we are now experiencing for reasons of economy, and it is imperative that the brainpower of women be fully utilized if we are to meet this Nation's humanpower needs.

Let us examine for a moment some of the rationalizations offered for denying women opportunities to advance to higher level positions: We are told that women are not mobile and cannot be considered for positions requiring possible relocation. The tendency here is to lump all women into one mold rather than seek out those who would indeed be mobile.

Women cannot be hired for positions involving travel—especially extensive travel; they cannot travel in remote areas; or travel with persons of the opposite sex.

Women cannot be assigned to positions involving rotating shifts. We might note here that such rotation is common in the nursing profession. The counterargument to that is "Oh, well, that's different."

Women cannot be hired for positions requiring exposure to the elements; for field work; for heavy lifting; or for hazardous duties.

Men won't work for women supervisors.

Women cannot supervise other women.

The list goes on and on.

It would be foolish for me to deny that these are considerations that must be taken into account in employment situations; but these are not problems which are entirely unique to women. I know, and I am sure you do, too, many men who are not mobile, for one reason or another; who are not willing to travel extensively; are not able to do heavy lifting; will not accept hazardous duties; or who cannot tolerate exposure to the elements.

To those of us who are working mothers, the "heavy lifting" prohibition provokes a chuckle. How often have we lifted our 20- and 30-pound youngsters? How many times have we walked the floor at night soothing a sick child weighing 20 or 30 pounds, whose weight seems double at that hour of the night? The briefcase I tote to and from the office every day easily weighs 15 pounds and my husband claims my purse weighs that, too, and I would like to support that.

Now I would like to discuss some specific problems in the area of sex discrimination in Federal employment. In November 1967 the Civil Service Commission, Bureau of Inspections, issued a publication entitled "The Federal Women's Program—A Summary of Inspection Findings." It covered the period May 1, 1966, to May 1, 1967. Although this report is 3 years old, I regret to state that the same conditions prevail today.

A total of 195 Federal installations were inspected. Based on detailed findings, the report concludes with the following statements:

"Generally, agency programs are being carried out in a nondiscrimination framework." (To me, this is a classic example of damning with faint praise.)

The report continues,

Program statements and objectives reflect required non-discrimination factors, but except in a few instances have not been complemented with positive plans and actions to assure fully equal employment opportunity.

As evidence that such is still the case today, I offer the following:

In a survey conducted by FEW among its members, the following questions were asked: (1) Do you know the name of the equal employment opportunity officer for your bureau or agency? (2) Do you know the name of the Federal women's programs coordinator for your bureau or agency? (3) Have you seen or heard of a plan of action for equal employment opportunity, for minority groups or for women in your agency?

With the exception of two or three members, who worked in the equal employment opportunity area, the answers to all questions were a resounding "No."

Within the past 3 years I conducted two sessions on equal employment opportunity for women for the Civil Service Commission, Bureau of Training. At each one I asked the same questions as above. Again, with the exception of one or two hands—people working in the equal opportunity area—the answers were negative.

The prevailing attitude seems to be that once a fancy-covered plan of action for equal opportunity, containing program statements and objectives, is submitted to the Civil Service Commission, as required by regulations, compliance is achieved, and "business as usual" continues.

Another line in the report states that, "* * * no cases of actual discrimination were found." Again, I must pause for a brief discussion.

Can you conceive any management official being so foolish as to admit to a Civil Service inspector, or to anyone else for that matter, that he is guilty of overt practices of employment discrimination against women, or minority groups, or anyone, when he operates under an Executive Order requiring administration of an equal employment opportunity program?

Second, few women have dared to file complaints of sex discrimination for two reasons: (1) it is generally so subtle and covert as to be extremely difficult to prove; and (2) women who have filed complaints have suffered reprisals in the form of having their jobs abolished and being reduced to lower grades on the pretext of reorganization or reductions in force; or have been reassigned to some degrading position far below their capabilities in anticipation they might resign; or they have been ordered transferred to a different geographic area, allegedly "for the good of the service," on the assumption they would refuse the transfer and could therefore be separated. We know of a number of such cases.

The report admits that progress has been limited and that only a small percent of agencies describe solid advancement. It concludes with statements concerning significant problems and reasons for the lack of advancement of women:

(*a*) Continuing absence of qualified available women candidates for substantive professional, technical and administrative jobs.

(*b*) Passive acceptance (by management) of the lack of qualified women applicants.

Elaborating on these two points, the "substantive jobs" are described as engineers, research scientists, physiologists, and "various technician jobs."

On the matter of passivity, the report states:

Management's position was essentially one of passive acceptance—they saw the lack of women applicants as a program problem; they would consider any woman who applied; but there were no plans for action, such as making sure all women's recruitment sources are being reached or assessing internal training and career development activities to assure that women are being given fully equal opportunity.

In another section the report concludes that traditional or negative attitudes on placement of women in jobs historically held by men was common to many agencies and demonstrated in a variety of ways. For example:

A number of reports showed that some managers still cling to a "men only" concept for certain jobs * * * this restrictive attitude was reflected in how managers described the reasons for lack of progress.

To illustrate:

One installation believed that civil engineer and realty appraisal jobs should be filled only by men. The only employment which management felt was really appropriate for women in their installation was clerical or auditing jobs.

Another activity felt their professional scientists jobs which involved worldwide travel should be filled only by men. They did not believe that women would be suitable for such jobs because of the need for travel.

One installation with a number of jobs in the real estate area felt that women would not be suitable because of the field duties involved.

The above examples are illustrative of other reports which cited management-identified problems reflecting similar attitudes, i.e., they were generally willing to consider women, but preferred to employ men for jobs with the following characteristics or requirements:

High mobility; shift work; exposure to elements; extensive travel; hazardous duties; field work; unusual job environment (docks, isolated areas, etc.); heavy lifting; direct clientele contact (predominantly male clientele); extreme work "pressure."

The factors mentioned do present some hurdles to hiring women, particularly where there are very few or no women applicants in the occupational area covered. However, application of logic and the successful experience of some installations show that these are more likely to be examples of "traditional" thinking rather than insurmountable problems.

This "traditional" thinking has not changed, nor will it change until there are statutes to enforce equal treatment for all who choose to work for the Federal Government.

I would like to move on now to April 1969, when the Civil Service Commission conducted a 1-day Federal Women's Program Review Seminar. In attendance were 122 persons representing 49 Federal agencies. Most were personnel officers and staff, equal employment opportunity officers, and Federal women's program coordinators. Out of this meeting came a series of recommendations which, if fully implemented by the Civil Service Commission and all Federal agencies, would go far toward assuring equal opportunity for women. The list is long, and I will not take your time to read it now. Instead, it is attached to this testimony as "Enclosure 1."

Some of these recommendations were included in the Civil Service Commission's instructions to agencies for preparation of their plans of action for equal employment opportunity. From what we have seen, little attention has been paid to it.

In December 1969, four of us from FEW met with Civil Service Commission Chairman Hampton, Commissioner Johnson, and the two codirectors of the equal employment opportunity program. At this meeting we stressed the need for positive action to implement the recommendations which came out of the April 1969 seminar. We also stressed the need for issuing a notification to agencies to designate an individual to be responsible for coordinating the Federal women's program. We further stressed the importance of the incumbent being relieved of other duties in order to devote full time or at least part time to the program. The Commission subsequently issued a letter to agencies (FPM Letter No. 713–15, Feb. 27, 1970), suggesting the designation of a Federal women's program coordinator or committee and that the job be full-time or part-time as the situation demands.

We understand some agencies have not yet complied. Some agencies have assigned the title, Federal women's program coordinator, though not the duties, to individuals who have full-time jobs in totally unrelated fields, and who have not been relieved of any of their regularly scheduled tasks to enable them to devote time to the program.

Other instances reported to us concern people assigned the title of Federal women's program coordinator, with no delegated authority or responsibility for developing or implementing meaningful and workable programs; with no background or program guidelines to follow; and with no training or experience on which to base their actions. Some of these people have turned to members of FEW, desperately seeking advice and guidance in carrying out the assignment.

In many instances little thought was given to the qualifications of the person selected for the task, notwithstanding the fact that, in line with FEW's recommendation, the Civil Service Commission directive states:

In selecting a Federal Women's Program Coordinator for the staff of the Director of Equal Employment Opportunity, particular consideration should be given to persons with empathy for and understanding of the special concerns of women in the employment situation. The right person will provide the kind of input to the Director of Equal Employment Opportunity which will help assure equal opportunity for women employees and applicants.

In checking with our membership across the Nation, we find many field establishments have ignored the program entirely—they have neither a plan of action for equal employment opportunity nor a Federal women's program coordinator.

Over the years I have talked with many directors of personnel and key management officials in many agencies about the whole area of equal employment opportunity. Whenever we discuss the problems of minority groups, it is always in a serious vein. As soon as the subject changes to equal employment opportunity for women, the condescending smiles appear, a few jokes are made about women's socially acceptable role in our society; and I am assured they have some women on their respective staffs in the middle or upper grades and that they are performing their jobs admirably—as though surprised that women could indeed be good workers. I am never told how well tho men on the staff perform their jobs. This is taken for granted, of course.

Discrimination against women in Federal employment comes in a variety of forms. While this is not the forum to air the whole spectrum of discrimination against women, I must, in passing, urge all of you to consider taking action on existing discriminatory legislation: The Civil Service Retirement Act, the Social Security Act, veterans' pensions, and the matter of overseas allowances. Recently we learned, for example, that the salary differential for married women employees of the Panama Canal Company was eliminated in October 1966, and has never been restored. Why should married women be penalized? Being married doesn't change the cost of living in the area.

The Honorable Martha Griffiths has several bills pending on these issues which desperately need the attention of the Congress.

I would like to conclude with a few specific examples. In addition to the numerous oral reports we have received concerning employment discrimination, a number of written reports are in our files from women in Federal agencies across the Nation. For example:

(1) Three women, GS-7, contract assistants, with 22, 17, and 13 years' experience, respectively, were downgraded to GS-4, typists. During the same period men holding identical jobs were promoted. The male employees were permitted to attend courses in procurement. The women were refused the opportunity.

Mrs. GREEN. How recent is this?

Mrs. FIELDS. Within the last 2 years. I think it was December 1968.

(2) Innumerable cases of violation of the so-called merit promotion program have been brought to our attention. Only recently we learned of a case involving the assistant director, who was also acting director of a division (a woman), being passed over for promotion to the director's position, and a young man from elsewhere in the agency brought in to become the director. The woman has numerous commendations on her performance over the years and, in fact, her name was on the promotion register. Defeated and disgusted, she has decided to retire.

A somewhat similar case involves an outstanding public information officer—a lady who has been writing more of the speeches for the head of her agency and other top officials for years, in addition to being senior editor on many important documents. When the director's position became vacant, she, as deputy director, was not promoted to the vacancy. Instead, a young man, from outside the agency, with comparatively little experience, none in Federal Government, was brought in to head the department. With no further incentive, she, too, has decided to retire. I am personally acquainted with this individual and can assure you the Government is losing an immensely talented human resource.

(3) Another case concerns an employee with 28 years' service, last promoted in May 1961 to a GS-6 position, which she still holds. In June and August 1968, she was assigned additional duties formerly performed by two GS-9's. She was told she would be promoted. When time passed and the promotion was not forthcoming, she asked a bureau official about it. He replied her age was against her. She is still working, still doing the additional duties, but she has not been promoted.

(4) A widow working on a temporary position with the Post Office Department was passed over three times in favor of men for career appointment, despite making a grade of 94.1 and 10-point veterans preference on the list of eligibles. She has been trying to get one of three rural carrier routes which have since been filled by men, one of which, incidentally, was her former husband. On questioning why she was not selected, she was told "forget it," she would never get the job because she was a woman.

(5) A woman, working for many years, is now a GS-6, secretary. While holding a full-time job, managing a home, with husband and children, she succeeded in getting a college degree in 1967—a degree she had been working toward intermittently since 1936. She took the Federal service entrance examination and obtained a rating of GS-7. She asked her supervisor repeatedly for an opportunity for advancement, even if only to a GS-7, secretary or staff assistant. Subse-

quently her name appeared on a promotion certificate for a GS–7, secretary. She was not interviewed, nor selected for the job. She discussed the matter with the personnel officer and was told she was overqualified for a secretary's position, GS–7. When she then raised the point of her eligibility on the Federal service entrance examination for an administrative position, she was told by the personnel officer that he did not think she could compete with the young, "sharp," college graduates just coming out of school. When she protested this attitude, the personnel officer suggested she go to the Civil Service Commission to see if they could find her another position elsewhere.

Within the limited time available, I cannot begin to cover all the cases which have been brought to my attention. They are not all at lower levels. I have others at higher grades, too. These are but a very few examples. I cite them as evidence that not only is sex a basis for discrimination, but so is age, when it comes to women. Yet numerous studies have shown that older women are more dependable, have fewer absences than men in the same age groups.

We know of women with degrees in science, education, law, accounting, to name a few fields, who are working as stenographers, clerks, typists, aides, and technical assistants. Many have had to accept such positions for subsistence or to help support families.

Nearly 4 years ago, President Johnson said:

In the next decade alone we will need * * * 1 million additional specialists in the health serrvices; 800,000 additional science and engineering technicians; 700,000 additional scientists and engineers; and 4½ million State and local government employees * * * The requirements in these fields alone will be 110,000 additional trained specialists every month for the next 10 years.

He went on to say:

That requirement cannot be met by men alone; and unless we begin now to open more and more professions to our women, and unless we begin now to train our women to enter those professions, then the needs of our Nation just are not going to be met.

Unless some instrumentality of the Federal Government—such as the Civil Rights Commission or the Equal Employment Opportunity Commission, referring to the bills S. 245 and H.R. 17555—is given the power and authority to investigate and prosecute cases of sex discrimination, fewer women will be attracted to Government service, and the women in Government will continue to remain second-class citizens, occupying the lowest paid, least rewarding, and least significant positions. The Nation will indeed suffer from failure to utilize the enormous talents of over one-half of our population—the women of the United States of America.

Thank you for your indulgence.

Mrs. GREEN. Thank you.

Without objection, the attachment will be placed in the record at this point.

Mrs. GREEN. Before I question you, I will ask Dr. Schuck to come up so we will be sure to hear from her.

Will you come forward and present your statement? Then I do have questions, Dr. Schuck.

STATEMENT OF DR. VICTORIA SCHUCK, PROFESSOR OF POLITICAL SCIENCE, MOUNT HOLYOKE COLLEGE, SOUTH HADLEY, MASS.

Dr. SCHUCK. I am Victoria Schuck, professor of political science at Mount Holyoke College. I am a member of the American Political Science Association Committee on the Status of Women in the Professions. I appear to express my personal support of section 805 of H.R. 16098, cited as the Omnibus Post-Secondary Education Act of 1970.

A number of professional associations are now researching problems of professional women. The American Political Science Association, for example, created a Committee on the Status of Women in the Professions in 1969 in order to obtain information about the problems of women in the profession, to encourage women to become professional political scientists, and to suggest ways of improving the professional position of women.

This committee has met a number of times, has had information conferences with a number of department chairmen in colleges and universities throughout the country, and has designed studies of graduate students in political science and professional women holding positions in the academic community and in government.

The committee has also met with representatives of such professional associations as the Anthropological, the Economic, the Modern Langauge, the Sociological and Psychological Associations, the Historical Society, and the American Association of University Professors, the Civil Service Commission, and the Educational Testing Service.

Reports on its study of academic administrative problems and nonacademic problems, with alternate solutions and recommendations to the association, will be presented next year. One can anticipate both short- and long-range proposals in 1971.

At its 1969 annual business meeting, the association officially disapproved discrimination against women in admittance to graduate study, in fellowship awards, academic employment, and promotion. Here I refer, of course, to the American Political Science Association.

Recently, the APSA has reached an agreement with the American Association of University Professors to investigate individual complaints of discriminatory practices with respect to those relating to graduate and professional women in the academic community and in government.

I should like to submit two studies for inclusion in the committee's report. The first was published in PS in the fall of 1969, pages 642 to 653, entitled "Women in Political Science, Some Preliminary Observations." And the second is to be published in the forthcoming issue of PS—Summer, 1971—entitled "Some Additional Statistics."

The first sudy resulted from an analysis of data from the U.S. Census, National Academy of Sciences, the American Political Science Directory of 1968—data for the year 1967—and from a questionnaire sent to department chairmen in political science in colleges and universities in the spring of 1969. The second study is based on comparative data of advanced degrees and academic positions held by women in selected fields of the social sciences.

We found that although women are increasing at a higher rate of growth than men in economics and political science they still constitute an exceedingly small number. Women receiving advanced degress; that is, Ph. D.'s, in political science averaged only 24 a year from 1958 to 1968, while men averaged 264 a year.

The ratio of women to men awarded the Ph. D. tells another story. The proportion of women reached a peak in the first half of the 1930s, then fell to 6 percent in the 1950's and, although higher since that time, has never exceeded 8.7 percent.

About half of the departments returning the questionnaire sent out by the association in 1969 reported women faculty, but only 8.4 percent of the total faculty in political science are women. Most of the women reported were in small departments teaching undergraduates. Too, most of the women reported were in the lower ranks. Ninety percent of the departments had no full professor, and 88 percent no associate professor. The women clustered in the rank of assistant professor, and yet they constituted only 9 percent of all the faculty in that rank.

Eleven percent of the men on faculties in 1969 were instructors, compared with 25 percent of the women. Thirty-two percent of the women were in the assistant professor rank, and 33 percent of the men were at this rank.

At the full professor rank, 31 percent of the men held this position, whereas only 14 percent of the women were in such rank.

A small ratio of women were in the distinguished departments and those productive of the greatest number of doctorates than in the category of "All other" departments.

Is a pattern of discrimination suggested by these figures? One cannot be absolutely sure without additional data, and these data are now being collected by the association.

The concentration in the untenured ranks may be attributed to fewer advanced degrees among women, to their youth, to the recency of appointment, or the fact that it is not always easy to find a woman in the proper field.

For example, approximately as many women received doctorates in the decade of the 1960's as in all the years from 1910 to 1959. We find that 59 percent of the women are in one field alone—comparative government and political development.

Can it be coincidence that the same pattern of low rank and small numbers appears in other fields? In anthropology and in sociology, for example. In anthropology, a 1965 study showed women were 10 percent of the full-time faculty, and most were in small institutions offering principally undergraduate work. In sociology, a study of 180 graduate departments, made in 1968–69, showed women faculty were concentrated in the lower ranks: one in four were instructors; one in 25, full professors. Even in graduate departments, the majority were teaching undergraduate courses only.

Apparently the problem of women professionals in the social studies is general.

It should also be noted that a women's caucus was organized in the Political Science Association in 1969. The caucus defines itself as a loosely structured participatory organization concerned with the problem women political scientists face.

In this country we usually cope with the problem only when it is widely conceded to exist. By making explicit the recognition of discrimination based on sex, the proposed legislation is a valuable first step in the quest to have all people treated as equals.

Thank you.

Mrs. GREEN. Thank you very much, Dr. Schuck. Those two reports will be made a matter of the record at this point.

Mrs. GREEN. Mrs. Fields, will you tell me more about FEW?

Mrs. FIELDS. I would be delighted to.

Mrs. GREEN. I had never previously heard of it.

Mrs. FIELDS. Oh, my, we will have to get after the press. Some claim we are too vocal. Others claim we are not vocal enough.

Mrs. GREEN. I really hadn't heard of FEW.

Mrs. FIELDS. FEW began really in April of 1968 at the Department of Agriculture Graduate School. Miss Helen Dudley began a series of seminars for women executives, a 3-day program. Out of this, after two sessions, which were held about 2 months apart, some of the women said "You know, we attend these wonderful courses and learn how to be executives but when the chips are down we really never get that opportunity. Why don't we get together and continue as an alumni association, so to speak, and see if we can't do something to see that more women get opportuniteis for executive level jobs?" From this little core developed what has come to be known as FEW.

It is an acronym, of course, very appropriate. We spent many hours sitting in a hot room in the church on Thomas Circle all summer long, planning, developing, setting up the bylaws, decided on what strategy we shall use, and so on. There were 16 of us at the time. We will be 2 years old in September of 1970 as we really began to function in September of 1968.

We now have well over 1,000 members in 41 States. Eight chapters now exist. We had requests for chapter organizing kits from 57 places across the country. Eight are now established as chapters. Others I anticipate will be coming through very shortly, in fact, oddly, one at Weirton, W. Va., I believe it is, the Women's Reformatory, and we are hoping it is the staff, not the inmates, that are going to become members. But that is the nature of the organization.

Now, I believe I have included in that folder that I hope you have with my testimony copies of the newsletters that we have issued to date, indicating some of the things we have done and are trying to do, as well as the program of our First National Conference which we held last weekend at the Statler Hotel. Senator Cook was kind enough to do the keynote speech and really set the tone for the whole Conference, that we must work for equal opportunity for women.

Our main emphasis at first was on growth. We set our membership dues very low. Believing in full equality, we did not want to exclude women in the lower grades.

While most of the officers and the organizers were women at the professional levels, those of us who, shall we say, have the dubious distinction of being among that 1 percent of civil servants at grade 13 wanted all women to be motivated by association to aspire to greater heights and not taking that self-defeating attitude which exists extensively in the Federal service.

Our concentration this past year, in addition to the growth, has been on supporting legislation. We have instructed our members how to write to this distinguished body and I am hoping that most of them have taken the responsibility. I think they have. Through our chapters, I understand they have actually been writing letters. We are informing them what is in the bill—don't just say "I want you to vote for H.R. 468"—what it is all about.

Mrs. GREEN. Then I hope your number will increase.

Mrs. FIELDS. And we are trying very, very hard to educate our members on what it is all about, and to ask for support accordingly.

Mrs. GREEN. Thank you. Do any of the three of you know the figure to which I referred earlier, that over 60 percent of children in families completely dependent on the earnings of women are poor?

Miss ALLAN. I will look it up.

Mrs. GREEN. We will have Elizabeth Koontz testifying. Maybe she has it. I don't understand this business of the enforcement or nonenforcement of parts of title VII of the Civil Rights Act. Maybe one of the three of you can explain it. I have letters in my file from the Enforcement Division in regard to plants and they say that "In your plant you have x percentage of blacks and this is proof *per se* that there is discrimination because if there weren't discrimination you would, obviously, have a higher percentage." Why don't they apply that to women and when there is an absence of any women for instance, in a grade level or the absence of women in certain areas, why don't they do the same thing? They have the same responsibility, don't they, in the Enforcement Division under title VII, in employment?

Mrs. FIELDS. They don't have the authority to enforce. They can only report these cases.

Mrs. GREEN. The Enforcement Division goes into the plants, into shipbuilding, ship conversion plants, construction firms. I have letters in my file. It is the Enforcement Division of Civil Rights. They look at percentage of employees of certain ethnic groups—and even though it may be higher than the percentage of that ethnic group in the area, they advise them unless they have more they will be in noncompliance.

Mrs. FIELDS. I don't know.

Mrs. GREEN. I don't understood this at all, and I have never had a letter, by the way, that has ever come to me from an enforcement division saying an industrial plan—on a contracting firm discriminated against women.

Mrs. FIELDS. There are other built-in prejudices which are rather subtle, too. There is an Institute called the Executive Institute at Kings Point which is run by the Civil Service Commission and they have the Executive Institute in Charlottesville, Va. For the most part, admission to these training courses, which run anywhere from 1 to 2 weeks, is limited to persons in certain grade levels, and above which there is a built-in discriminatory factor because few women achieve this level. here are some programs given at these Institutes which are for people, I believe, at grade 12 or grade 13 particularly.

Over the past several months I have been buying the Federal Times every week and just collecting the pictures which appear every week in the paper, showing the graduating class of these various Institutes and I started making a tally and find that this one has one out of 47, or 50, participants, that is, you might find one or two women. On one of them I thought, oh, goody, I see two women, but then I read the identification and one of those was a member of the staff at the school, but throughout you see this in all of these courses. Now, they are not programs which are limited to men. Here is the 2-week seminar on the Administration of Public Policy and here you have 42 participants, two women.

Mrs. GREEN. Kings Point, and where is the other one?

Mrs. FIELDS. This is Kings Point. There is one in Berkeley, Calif., now, and then, of course, there is the Civil Service Commission Executive Institute in Charlottesville.

Mrs. GREEN. All of them run by the Civil Service Commission?

Mrs. FIELDS. Right; which, of course, has a built-in prejudice right there because it is limited to——

Mrs. GREEN. We are inviting the Civil Service Commission to testify, as well as people from the Civil Rights Section of the Justice Department, EEOC, the Women's Bureau, and HEW.

(Discussion off the record.)

Mrs. GREEN. Back on the record.

Miss ALLAN. Mrs. Green, I strongly believe that legislation does change attitudes. And on the matter of EEOC cases, the task force was disturbed by the fact that at the time we were meeting the Justice Department had participated in more than 40 cases of racial bias and had not intervened in behalf of an individual discriminated against because of sex.

With the fact that Congress is beginning to take note of the women's movement I think we are beginning to see changes coming around industry. A friend of mine who is with a large company that employs many women told me that just the other day the company came through with a whole section on an affirmative action program for women, so as not to get into difficulties with Federal legislation. A great deal had been done on the race question but this was the first time the company came through on the women, so I know we have a long way to go but progress is being made. Don't look at me skeptically.

Mrs. GREEN. I am not looking at you skeptically. I just am skeptical. I have watched the Civil Service. They haven't changed. I served on the Kennedy commission and I still haven't seen change. They have the same percentage of women down at the GS–2, 3, and 4 levels and the same absence of women at the 16, 17, and 18 levels they have always had. Higher education is no different.

Miss ALLAN. When you asked me the questions on HEW, I want you to know that FEW, the organization that Daisy represents, was sure that we got the same information you gave us, so they are very active.

Mrs. GREEN. In a field that is predominantly women not to have women in policymaking positions in either Education or HEW is shocking, I think, and I have been trying to get the figures. Do you have it on the number of women in EEOC? Do you have it here in Washington or across the country?

Mrs. FIELDS. I can find out very easily because I know a lot of people on EEOC, the number of people on the staff.

Mrs. GREEN. No; in policymaking positions.

Mrs. FIELDS. I would doubt if there are any, but I will check.

Mrs. GREEN. Is there one?

Mrs. FIELDS. Elizabeth Kuck.

Mrs. GREEN. And she is not to be reappointed, I understand.

Mrs. FIELDS. So I have heard.

Miss ALLAN. They have recommended Mrs. Walczak from New York to replace her.

Mrs. GREEN. But in other places?

Mrs. FIELDS. Tariff Commissioner Penelope Thunberg is to be replaced and, as I understand it, she is not to be replaced by another woman, rumor has it. I don't know for a fact.

I know back in 1959 I was the deputy director of personnel in a small agency. The director left and the head of the agency, a very distinguished scholar and a man of some prominence, a psychologist who should know better, called me to his office and in his very dignified manner said how well I was doing and what an outstanding job I had done, but he hoped that even though the director was leaving I would not entertain the notion of leaving, myself, because of my valuable contributions but he would like me to assist him in recruiting a replacement for the director because, he said, "I am sure you understand, Mrs. Fields, the head of a department really has to be a man." I have never forgotten that.

Mrs. GREEN. I thank all three of you very, very much for coming.

Mrs. FIELDS. Thank you for the privilege.

Mrs. GREEN. We appreciate your being here, and we will look forward to comparing notes in the days ahead. Thank you.

(Whereupon, at 12:45 p.m., the subcommittee recessed, to reconvene at 10 a.m., Tuesday, June 30, 1970.)

TUESDAY, JUNE 30, 1970

House of Representatives,
Special Subcommittee on Education
of the Committee on Education and Labor,
Washington, D.C.

The special subcommittee met, pursuant to recess, at 10:20 a.m. in room 2251, Rayburn House Office Building, Hon. Edith Green (chairman of the subcommittee) presiding.

Present: Representatives Green and Burton.

Staff members present: Harry Hogan, counsel; Robert Andringa, minority professional staff assistant; and Sheldon Batchelder, minority research assistant.

Mrs. Green. The subcommittee will come to order for the further consideration of the higher education bills that are under the jurisdiction of this committee.

This morning we are pleased to have as our first witness Nancy Dowding, the president of the Women's Equity Action League (WEAL), Cuyahoga Community College, if Nancy Dowding will come to the table. I think it might be well if we had all of the witnesses that are scheduled to be here this morning come to the table and present their statements. Then the members of the committee could direct questions to any of the several witnesses.

May I ask Dr. Laurine Fitzgerald, Michigan State University, in charge of student services; Dr. Frances Norris, Washington; and Susan Ross and Diane Blank, law students from New York University to come to the table?

Now, may I ask Nancy Dowding to present her statement first.

STATEMENT OF DR. NANCY DOWDING, PRESIDENT, WOMEN'S EQUITY ACTION LEAGUE; AND COUNSELOR, CUYAHOGA COMMUNITY COLLEGE

Dr. Dowding. I am Dr. Nancy E. Dowding, counselor at Cuyahoga Community College in Cleveland, Ohio. I am also a member of the American Psychological Association, and am currently national president of the Women's Equity Action League.

I might note that at ths time I do not identify myself as a member of the American Personnel and Guidance Association because as of this date I plan to discontinue my membership since the organization has persisted in using sex segregated help wanted listings in their

153

placement bulletin.

I come before this distinguished committee on behalf of H.R. 16098, known as the "Omnibus Post-Secondary-Education Act of 1970," to ask your serious consideration of changes in the counseling services and career choices for girls and women. In discussing these issues with contemporary college women, they indicated to me that the problems center more on sins of omission, rather than commission, and that in general young women were simply not expected to plan for a serious and fulfilling career, and that they most certainly are not seriously encouraged to do so. The career counseling problems of young women seem to rest more in what is not said rather than in overt discrimination.

Interestingly enough, this is the same thesis set forth by nationally recognized author Caroline Bird, a member of WEAL's national advisory board. In her book "Born Female: The High Cost of Keeping Women Down," she writes of "The Invisible Bar."

Even if a girl tries for a professional career she may be actively discouraged. Educators hold vocational guidance counselors responsible for the scandalous waste of talent. * * * In the 1960's guidance counselors were urged to encourage adolescent girls toward careers. The counselors were told to be positive. Instead of saying, "Have you thought how you would manage to do that if you had children?" they were instructed to say, "Veterinary practice is a good field for a woman, because she can carry it on near her home." A girl who had a reasonably enlightened high-school counselor might not even realize that she had to get much higher marks than a boy to get into a coed college. But the closer she approached paying work, the more she was slowed by the unspoken assumption that a woman really could not be serious about a vocation but must be working to mark time, earn a little money, or if she were obviously gifted "just for fun." This is the Invisible Bar that keeps women down.

The Invisible Bar is unofficial. It is effective because almost everyone accepts it. Officially, graduate and professional schools invite women to apply. In private, their administrators deplore wasting facilities on women who marry and do not use their education, but "throw it away to get married and have babies." * * * Girls who go to women's colleges sometimes crash unexpectedly on the Invisible Bar when they look for their first jobs. * * * Employers seem equally dismayed. They don't always know what to do with college girls. Big companies give a Princeton senior who has majored in English an aptitude test to see where he might fit, but give a Vassar senior who has majored in English a typing test.

A young woman graduate of Wellsley told me of her encounter with the Invisible Bar in these words, "I went to a girls' college, and I just never learned I was inferior."

The problem is stated vividly by Mrs. Elizabeth Koontz, director of the Women's Bureau of the Department of Labor who was recently quoted:

None of the ladies on television seem concerned with anything beyond finding a hair coloring that will keep her looking young eternally, making sure the family brushes after every meal and finding a floor wax that won't yellow over. The girl who suspects that there might be more to life than this has to go her own way more or less against the weight of society's opinions and expectations.

What a sad indictment of an affluent society.

Along with the Invisible Bar, women are often discouraged from attempting career fields because they are regarded as "inappropriate" choices. Thus, it has been noted by Dr. Pauli Murray, a black woman attorney, writer, and teacher, that while violence has been "the ultimate weapon of resistance to racial desegregation, its psychic counterpart, ridicule, has been used to resist sex equality."

Perhaps it would be better if we could just acknowledge the need for changes and new approaches in vocational counseling for young women, and turn our attention to positive action to accomplish these goals. A helpful pamphlet from the women's bureau states:

> * * * the career "sights" of all too many of our girls are still limited and unrealistic. Most girls have a romantic image of life: school, marriage, a family—and they live happily ever after. But this is not the complete picture. A more accurate life pattern of the modern woman includes school, work and/or marriage, rearing a family (sometimes continuing to work by either choice or necessity), and a return to work when the youngest child is in school. This "quiet revolution" in the life pattern of American women presents a special challenge to those responsible for the counseling of girls.

This last sentence is an important observation, for it implies that counselors need to be made aware of the realistic demands that will be placed on women in our society so that they can be prepared to meet them adequately. It would be my educated guess that a great many professional counselors assisting girls today are not really oriented to the new life style that the younger generation has assumed. But counselors must help girls to consider seriously the significant facts, encourage them to prepare for their dual role as homemakers and workers, and assist them to plan now for a total life. It is my opinion that counselors are partly responsible for the fact that in April 1969, the largest number of women workers (9.8 million) were employed in clerical jobs. About 4.7 million were service workers, 4.4 million were operatives, and 4.1 million were in professional and technical occupations.

Women's Bureau statistics show that in 1967 women workers (14 years and over) had median wage and salary incomes of $3,139 compared with $6,584 for men. The median for full-time year-round women workers in 1967 was $4,273 compared with $7,298 for men. Yet women are the numerical majority of our population!

If we were to allow for the proportion of women who neither choose to nor have to work outside their own homes, the percentages noted above are still obviously disparate.

> An important part of the answer to this disparity in women's educational attainment and earnings lies in the goals and aspirations of these women when they were girls. Counselors in particular can and should help women recognize the new realities.

If we might assume, then, that adequate counseling will be provided to encourage the capable to seek additional education and preparation beyond high school, it becomes readily apparent that the next concern is the financing of such education. And that in turn highlights the need to give young women equal opportunity to qualify for scholarship moneys and aid programs, so that their efforts are recognized and rewarded on the same basis as males. In working with mature women who come to the community college, there is a very real need to provide some assistance with tuition when they are feeling the financial stress of raising their families or living on pensions or limited incomes.

If we further assume that a woman has made her way inside the college doors, it would be well to consider what choices she will have for a satisfying career. No doubt women will always tend to choose areas of social service, by the very nature of our culture; but by the same token, some women—when given a truly free choice—will elect careers from a much broader vocational spectrum. When freed of the stereotyped "appropriate" selection, women of quite equal merit with their social service sisters will elect business, politics, law, medicine, pharmacy, and engineering (just as men are increasingly free to pursue notable careers in the gentler social science areas). As the style of dress of the wholesome youth of today (casual, but not unwashed) signals a lessening of stereotyped male and female roles, so too is there an easing of the rigid lines of "proper" male and female career choices. These early signs of vocational progress need to be protected and encouraged.

The statement of Congresswoman Griffiths in the Congressional Record of March 9, 1970, would support the thesis that counseling services for young college women are inadequate. She states:

> The tragic fact today is that women are losing ground in every segment of university life. Their proportion as students in college is not increasing. Their proportion as students at the graduate level is less now then in 1930.

Yet, let us contrast this with our awareness that education and employment have a positive correlation. A fact sheet from the Women's Bureau reminds us, "There is a direct relationship between the educational attainment of women and their labor force participation. The more education a woman has received, the greater likelihood that she will be engaged in paid employment."

To recognize that 20 percent of the girls in our American society do not finish high school seems to me an unacceptably high percentage, especially considering that 20 percent of this group are unemployed (28.6 percent for black girls, 16.9 percent for white).

Mrs. GREEN. Is that for people between 16 and 21?

Dr. DOWDING. This goes through high school age, so I would assume that it extends to 18, to my knowledge.

Women industrial workers and their union representatives report that they are always used as a casual labor pool, being last hired and first fired—as the economy fluctuates—another good reason to protect women with education and working skills.

It may be that part of the problem rests in the way we really see girls and women in our society. When we consider the limited programs and activities that are made available for girls, in contrast with the number of directed activities for boys, it causes one to consider that the lack of adequate and proper planning for girls may result from a kind of psychological invisibility (rather reminiscent of the psychological invisibility that has been so damaging to Negroes in this country). If this is actually the case, it would be one more of many valid similarities in the unhappy conditions of women and blacks. And, if we do not clearly see girls and women as human beings of true and intrinsic worth and importance in our culture, then indeed they may receive only secondary consideration in the secondary school and collegiate counseling programs also. I defer to my colleague, Dr. Laurine Fitzgerald, for her professional opinions as a counselor educator for specific recommendations in this area.

Community and junior colleges have historically recognized the need for counseling services to assist students with the process of understanding themselves and their capabilities—indeed, this is a hallmark of the exciting role of community colleges in higher education. And this is one area where the older university system might learn from the junior colleges; reports coming in regarding those senior institutions indicate serious lacks of counseling services. What business enterprise would push forward without a planned program of goals to justify the daily efforts? Yet many students are asked to pursue their educations without such purposeful planning or assistance with necessary changes and adjustments during the process.

This prompts consideration of needed publications, testing programs, and special materials for use in counseling girls and women. It is difficult to develop any meaningful library of materials for use on the secondary and postsecondary level. Special attention is needed too in extending training programs for women in paratechnical and paraprofessional career fields, extending beyond the opportunity of training to be a file clerk or typist. Let us offer the same range and variety of programs that seem to be necessary for men in our society.

Social scientist Dr. Robert Amundson underscores the gap between the real and the ideal as reflected in different perceptions of males and females in our society, noting.

Rigid compartmentalization of what is masculine and what is feminine in our society is aided and abetted by some very inept counseling in our schools which often are suggested goals to our youth which are unsuited to the second half of the 20th Century. Even the so-called more traditional roles suggested to young women—those of homemaker, nurse, social worker, and teacher—are often described in a pollyanna style about a world that never was.

Dr. Amundson is involved with the unique Research Center on Woman at Loretto Heights College in Denver which seeks new awareness of woman's role in society. Their literature points out the need to offer women alternatives in choosing a life style of work, study, and homemaking, and a comparable need to educate women about the existence of these alternatives.

And interestingly enough, their publications quote from the President's Commission on the Status of Women in 1963, to this effect:

Illumined by values transmitted through home and school and church, society and heritage, and informed by present and past experience, each woman must arrive at her contemporary expression of purpose, whether as a center of home and family, participant in the community, a contributor to the economy, a creative artist or thinker or scientist, or a citizen engaged in politics and public service. Part and parcel of this freedom is the obligation to assume corresponding responsibility.

The Women's Equity Action League strongly supports this approach to the individual's right to choose her own life style, blending education, employment, and homemaking into a meaningful expression of her true worth and being.. And as a professional counselor, I believe young men and women in our society welcome the opporsunity to offer such a choice of life style to women, and that they will responsibly fulfill the obligations and promises that such an approach holds.

Thank you.

Mrs. GREEN. Thank you very much, Dr. Dowding. As a counselor, when you see the statistics that out of 278,000 slots in the apprentice program only 1 percent are held by girls; how does this affect your counseling of young people?

Dr. DOWDING. Well, I don't think that we have many alternatives at this time except to encourage the girls to try for those programs that are available, but I think that we need to increase the number of opportunities. You have to get some running room in there if you are going to encourage girls to go into these different areas and the ceiling just has to be lifted. More room has to be made available.

Mrs. GREEN. What do you do in counseling a girl who wants to go into the Federal Government where the highest percentage of women employees occurs at the GS-3, -4, and -5 levels and less than 1 percent of all the Federal employees in grade levels 16, 17, and 18 are women?

Dr. Dowding. I think her commitment to values other than monetary ones would have to be tremendous for her to choose that. I am sure that it takes the extraordinary woman or the one who is financially able to sustain herself in spite of those limitations to pursue those career choices that they might genuinely hold uppermost in their thinking, and I am sure that there is a real loss in those service areas because of these barriers to women. I think this needs to be changed.

Mrs. Green. I have several other questions that I am going to save for a little while. Congressman Burton, do you have questions now or do you prefer to withhold them?

Mr. Burton. No; I will wait, Madam Chairman, until the other witnesses testify.

Mrs. Green: All right. Then may I call on Dr. Fitzgerald from Michigan State University.

STATEMENT OF DR. LAURINE E. FITZGERALD, ASSOCIATE DEAN OF STUDENTS AND PROFESSOR OF EDUCATION, MICHIGAN STATE UNIVERSITY

Dr. Fitzgerald. Madam Chairman, I am Dr. Laurine E. Fitzgerald, Associate Dean of Students and Professor of Education at Michigan State University, East Lansing, Michigan. Graduate students whom I have advised are serving as counselors at the elementary, secondary, junior college and four-year collegiate levels; I am a member of the American Psychological Association, the National Association of Women Deans and Counselors, and the Association of Counselor Educators and Supervisors.

My appearance before your committee is in support of H.R. bill 16098, the "Omnibus Post-Secondary Education Act of 1970." I share the hope of many other women educators that this bill will make possible some dramatic and necessary changes in the education of counselors at all educational levels, and that it will provide the impetus for the development of guidance resource materials reflecting greater educational/vocational diversification for young women, and for women who chose to continue their education and/or who wish to reenter the work force.

The contributing factors, reasons perhaps, to the current situation relative to the education and training of counselors who will work with women, and the dearth of resource materials available to professionals in the field are doubtless complex. And it may well be that omission and apathy to the problems of counseling women are major contributors. The fact remains that knowledges regarding the special concerns of the condition of women are "caught—not taught."

In fact, there is some evidence, a small but growing body of research and investigation, that the individual counselor reflects—and his attitudes may even be reinforced by current training programs—the prejudices and biases of the larger society relating to woman and her educational/vocational choices. As an example, one recent study indicates that both male and female counselors hold bias against women entering a so-called masculine (engineering) occupation (1). The results suggest that both groups were more biased against females, than for females. In spite of the commonly voiced egalitarian view expressed by counselors that "women should do whatever they want to do"—it appears that female counselees are confronted with prejudices of the larger society within the counseling session; prejudices which are not recognized by the counselor, male or female. In this study, by Pietrofesa and Schlossberg, the coached female counselee method was employed, and the counselor group was composed of 16 male and 13 female counselors.

I might add that this study has been replicated using both male and female coached clients, very bright, able sophomore college students who had high test scores in science and math. They were coached to go into a counseling session and express vocational choice dilemma. The counselors then were to help the young people decide on a future. What happened was the young men were told that education was inappropriate. In fact, in 17 of the interviews they were told, "You can do better than that." The young women with the same test scores were told that engineering, space science, computer technology was inappropriate and this reinforced the original study.

Gurin, Nachmann, and Segal (2) examined the relationship between the social ambivalence, with the additional complicating value connotations of the right/wrong and masculine/feminine, active/passive of the vocational choice process—and the sexual identity crisis of young women. Observations of a high incidence of abrupt termination of counseling by college women originally seeking vocational assistance led to these considerations of counseling women. Their conclusions were that counselor values and attitudes regarding the masculine and feminine roles were distorting influences in the counseling process. One additional study has examined the impact of the sex of the counselor within the role model context, with the following conclusions:

Results seem consistent with other evidence about the culture in which counseling takes place. It seems plausible that males might be perceived as more competent and prestigeful in vocational counseling and might, therefore, possess more reinforcing power in discussing career-planning activities. Female counselors might possibly be perceived as more effective in discussing matters in which they are thought to have superior knowledge, that is dating and etiquette (3).

These few studies take on greater significance in the light of the fact that *no* normal, university sponsored, graduate-level, degree-awarding program in counselor education requires even a one-semester course in social and psychological sex differences which affect development, or provides any focus on sex differences in a practicum or internship in counseling (4).

With 51 percent of the total population female, 42 percent of our college attenders female, only three out of 10 of all personnel workers are women. The 1967–68 Directory of Counselor Educators publication indicates that in 343 departments of counselor education 209, or 61 percent, had no women professors or educators, 82 had only one woman, and that is 25 percent, and only 52 of the 343 departments had two or more women, or 15 percent.

I might add that, to my knowledge, there are only two women counseling center directors of a university or college in the country who are not civil service employees, only two women out of the more than 1,000 to 1,250 counseling centers nationally.

An additional area of concern which relates to counselor training and performance, and their subsequent interaction with women clients is in the realm of resource materials. The paucity of good guidance and counseling tools for girls and women is appalling to counselors of women, and should be alarming to the "consuming" and informed public. In one recent examination of six major publishers of primers and basic texts, first through sixth grade, the readers were examined to determine the extent to which women were shown as workers, having husbands and children in the same proportion as women workers in reality, the range and distribution of women portrayed as employed, and the nature of employment depicted (5). The results show, clearly, a distortion between the women's real labor force and the labor force presented in the children's taxtbooks. Not only were women portrayed as generally at the professional level rather than the one-sixth actual proportion, but the feminine stereotype prevailed. "Dick and Jane" rarely see a woman engineer.

I reviewed the preschool through eighth grade "occupational-vocational" resource books available in two State libraries, and two metropolitan libraries to determine the incidence and nature of vocational roles depicted for women. With the exception of the feminine stereotyped employment areas, for example, airline stewardess, beautician, nurse, and secretary, women were shown only in supporting roles, if at all. Few comments in the context of job function and responsibility referred to women. The "enlightened" publications tended to show members of both sexes in the performing role. For instance, the newer publications on elementary teaching, as an example (6), show approximately one-third of all teachers male. Elizabeth Fisher deplores the stultifying roles for women in children's literature, where girls and women are presented between 20 to 30 percent of the time. She discovered an "almost incredible conspiracy of conditioning." She points out that "only in Noah's Ark does Biblical authority enforce equal representation for males and females. Except for Random House's "Pop-Up Noah," which has eliminated Mrs. Noah entirely and does not show the animals in equal distribution on the cover * * * males have slight edge, of course. And, there appears to be only one picture book about working mothers, Eve Merriam's "Mommies at Work," with a somewhat apologetic conclusion, according to Miss Fisher's interpretation of the ending * * * "all mommies loving the best of all to be your very own mommy and coming home to you" (7).

Moving to the adult and national scene for a view of counseling resources for women does not improve the picture. The new Federal study of job prospects, the 859-page "Occupational Outlook Handbook, 1970–71" may add to the constricting picture:

Replacement needs will be particularly significant in occupations which have a large proportion of older workers and women.

Five of the six fastest growing occupations are in job categories with positions held primarily by women: registered nurses, cashiers, elementary and secondary school teachers, typists, and secretaries/ stenographers. I noticed in the paper yesterday that New York City has received Federal assistance to train for two and a half years retired policemen and firemen and train them as registered nurses in order to change the female image of nursing. The Occupational Outlook Handbook report further notes an increase in white collar workers, with requirements for professional and technical workers being perhaps "one-half greater than in 1968 employment," and a projected rise of 20 percent for managers, officials, and proprietors (8).

You will note that opportunities will exist for women in the traditional feminine fields, and should also be available in professional and managerial areas * * * perhaps. What new counseling tools will be of assistance to the adviser for girls and women? Perhaps a bit facetiously, I ask you to note the 1968, the newest and "best" vocational interest test for women: in pink (9). The "Strong Vocational Interest Blank for Women" originally by Edward K. Strong, revised by David P. Campbell, is in pink, with a blue form for men. Luci Switzer has noted that men and women, but women particularly, are "victimized by stereotyping that begins literally at the delivery room door and persists from pink-lined bassinet to pink-lined casket." (10). The comparison of the women's "Strong" with the men's inventory is disappointing, indeed: for example, the male form has a scale entitled "banker"—the female form has a scale entitled "bankwoman"; the female form also lists "model" and "actress," and omits some of the comparable and viable employment possibilities for women, such as veterinarian, psychiatrist, as examples. It has fewer areas of "basic interest" and "occupational interest" than does the men's form, and thereby contributes to a clearly differentiated, and possibly secondary or inferior roles for women counselees, counselors, and employees. We might return to the earlier question of bias by design, or by omission.

On the positive side, we are thankful for the revision of this instrument, with the greatly expanded scaling and wider vision of women's dual-career roles, with new format and pictures of young women on the front. In addition, the relatively new leaflet series, "Careers for Women" (11) from the Women's Bureau, is most helpful. We need more referent material, from all sources and for all reading and educational levels. We need special emphasis on training programs for women. If we, as counselors and advisers to women, are to assist coeds in overcoming the tendency to underestimate their intellectual, social, and personal strengths, and capacity for leadership—we must have legislative assistance.

The need for counseling need not be debated during this decade. The need for counselor training and performance with clear involvement of the counselee's psychosexual and psychosocial situation is equally important, but must be pressed if it is to be accomplished. The changing role definition of and for women can be impeded or implemented by the guidance worker, the counselor, the teacher, and the professor. As the new "Occupational Outlook Handbook" concludes: "With so much competition from young people who have higher levels of education, the boy or girl who does not get good preparation for work will find the going more difficult in the years ahead" (8).

Thank you.

(The attachment to Dr. Fitzgerald's statement follows:)

REFERENCES CITED

(1) "Counselor Bias and the Female Occupational Role," John J. Pietrofesa, and Nancy K. Schlossberg, unpublished paper, February 1970.

(2) "The Effect of the Social Contest in the Vocational Counseling of College Women," Maizie G. Gurin, Barbara Nachmann, and Stanley J. Segal, "Journal of Counseling Psychology," vol. 10, No. 1, 1963.

(3) "Sex of Counselors and Models—Effect on Client Career Exploration," Carl E. Thorsen, John D. Krumboltz, and Barbara Varenhorst, "Journal of Counseling Psychology," vol. 14, No. 6, 1967.

(4) "The Recruitment and Training of Educational/Vocational Counselors of Girls and Women," background paper for Subcommittee on Counseling, President's Commission on the Status of Women, 1963.

(5) "Run, Mama, Run: Women Workers in Elementary Readers," Buford Stefflre, "The Vocational Guidance Quarterly," vol. 18, No. 2, 1969.
(6) "The Invisible Women: A Girl's View of the Working World," Laurine E. Fitzgerald, unpublished paper, September 1968.
(7) "The Second Sex, Junior Division," Elizabeth Fisher, "The New York Times Book Review," section 7, part II, May 24, 1970.
(8) "Occupational Outlook Handbook," Bureau of Labor Statistics, New York, N.Y., 1970.
(9) "Strong Vocational Interest Blank for Women," Edward K. Strong, Jr., revised by David P. Campbell, 1968.
(10) "This Revolution Asks Something of Us All," Lucigrace Switzer, "College and University Business," February 1970.
(11) "Careers for Women," U.S. Department of Labor, Wage and Labor Standards Administration, Women's Bureau, Washington, D.C.

Mrs. GREEN. Thank you very much. And, before we turn to questions may we hear from Dr. Norris.

STATEMENT OF FRANCES S. NORRIS, M.D., WASHINGTON, D.C.

Dr. NORRIS. Hon. Representative Mrs. Green, you and the members of this Subcommittee on Education have the gratitude of all American women for your investigation of discrimination against women in our educational system, and for your effort to make available to women educational opportunities without which social equality is unattainable. I am glad for this chance to present evidence outlining one facet of discrimination against women; that is, discrimination against women applicants to medical schools. Women and men physicians alike are aware that medicine is a profession agreeably suited to the skills and temperament of women. Yet, only 9 percent of American physicians are women. The rarity of women doctors in our medical community has limited the freedom of women to choose doctors of their own sex, and has deprived women of the benefits of research into diseases peculiar to women by physician-researchers of their own sex.

Women applicants to medical schools have increased over 300 percent in 36 years, men applicants have increased only 29 percent. But the proportion of women accepted over this time has fallen, and that of men accepted has risen (1). These figures indicate that persistence of limited admission of women to medical schools stems from discriminatory medical school admission policies.

The failure to publicize evidence of prejudice against women applicants to medical schools has resulted in a declining status of women in medicine, as physicians and probably as patients.

EVIDENCE OF BIAS AGAINST WOMEN APPLICANTS TO MEDICAL SCHOOLS

An investigation of prejudice toward women by medical school admissions committees was made by Dr. Harold I. Kaplan, professor of psychiatry at New York Medical College (4). Kaplan's study, sponsored by the National Institute of Mental Health, reviewed the attitude toward women applicants in 95 percent of American and Canadian medical schools over a 7-year period beginning in 1962. Although his presentation provides clear evidence of prejudice against women by medical schools, it has remained unpublished. It demonstrates that medical schools discriminate against women medical school applicants. It is apparent that the women rejected from the small female applicant pool were equal to or better than men accepted and that they were rejected because their sex quota was filled. Many schools admit women in only token numbers. Unabashed admission of prejudice and discrimination toward women was recorded from the medical school respondents to Kaplan's inquiries. Some responses by members of admissions committees are directly quoted, while others are not, for obvious reasons. For example, Harold R. Paine, Ph. D., chairman of the admissions committee of the University of Vermont School of Medicine, is quoted as saying "There is some prejudice toward women on the part of admissions committees." It would be interesting to have Kaplan's unquotable responses.

Dr. Marvin Dunn, assistant dean at Women's Medical College in 1969 opposed the school's new admissions policy permitting virtually unlimited male enrollment partly because of information he obtained from interviews with admissions officers at 25 Northeastern medical schools revealing discrimination against women. Of these 25 schools, 19 admitted they accepted men in preference to women unless the women were demonstrably superior (5). Dunn found that women are not judged on an equal competitive basis, but are placed in a disadvantageous sex category requiring special justification for acceptance. This evidence of obvious bias against women applicants was publicly ignored by Glen Laymaster, the male president championing the new, virtually unlimited coeducation policy. Dr. Laymaster has since resigned under alumnae pressure.

I should just like to make an aside here about this. As you know, the caduceus is the symbol of the physician, and consists of a staff with snakes twining up along its length. Since Laymaster pushed through this premature coed policy several women doctors have been overheard referring to him as a "Snake in the Caduceus."

Over the past years, the low proportion of women medical students accepted has fallen in many schools, in some cases to none. A study of the sex distribution of students in American medical schools is available in the annual education numbers of the Journal of the American Medical Association. The American Medical Association's published figures for the year beginning in 1968 (6) showed that 51 of our 99 medical schools had fewer than 10 percent women accepted. Eleven of these schools had from 3 percent to none accepted. This year, the figures are even worse (10).

Certain medical schools have for years displayed pronounced bias against women applying to them for admission, and their female enrollment figures are consistently, patently, discriminatory. Among the worst of these medical schools are the following: The Medical College of Alabama, Emory University, Chicago Medical School, University of Kansas, Creighton University, University of Nebraska, New Jersey College of Medicine, Bowman-Gray School of Medicine, University of North Dakota, University of Cincinnati, Medical College of South Carolina, University of South Dakota, Vanderbilt University, Baylor University, University of Utah, University of Virginia, and the Medical College of Georgia. Last year, Creighton University accepted no women applicants. This year, Vanderbilt University has accepted no women applicants. Can it be that not one qualified woman applicant could be found in all of Tennessee and Nebraska? Our medical schools, all of which are heavily dependent on Federal funds, reflect a nationwide pattern of discrimination against women. This should not be allowed, and it must stop.

The low sex quota for women applying to medical schools is recorded in the Journal of Medical Education published by the Association of American Medical Colleges (13). Here, a comparison of men and women applicants to medical schools between the years 1960 and 1968 shows that the total percent of women entering has been limited in the last decade to a range of 7 to 10 percent. Equal proportions of men and women applicants are rejected despite the huge disparity in respective numbers, on the basis of an arbitrary grouping of applicants by gender. This practice is wrong.

Mrs. GREEN. May I stop you on that? I don't understand your last sentence in the paragraph at the top of page 4.

Dr. NORRIS. Regarding the arbitrary grouping of applicants?

Mrs. GREEN. "Equal proportions of men and women applicants are rejected despite the huge disparity in respective numbers * * *."

Dr. NORRIS. Yes. Let's refer to the reference 13 here. It is a blue pamphlet and shows the number of men and women applicants over the years 1960–68. That is exhibit I.

Mr. BURTON. Roughly the same percentage of women applicants to medical school as male applicants are rejected, and roughly the same percent once accepted graduate.

Dr. NORRIS. I am not speaking about the ones that graduate.

Mr. BURTON. That is what the data in this blue book reflects.

Dr. NORRIS. The data that I am pointing out in table 6, illustrate that there are equal proportions of men and women applicants accepted and rejected. This "equal rejection theory" is cited by some medical spokesmen as evidencing equal treatment of the sexes by admissions committees. This practice is wrong in a right thinking medical educator's eyes because it arbitrarily groups applicants into two sex groups, a criterion which is irrelevant and arbitrary. The women should be judged completely on the basis of their qualifications without regard to sex.

Mrs. GREEN. In other words, you want one listing, the same as women in unions have required now, that there be one roster of people who are eligible?

Dr. NORRIS. Right.

Mrs. GREEN. Is that what you are saying?

Dr. NORRIS. Yes; were this done it would become readily apparent that it is unfair, it is unjust, to reject half the woman applicant pool. It is felt that it is unfair to reject half the women just as are rejected half the men. There is a far smaller number of women applying for example; 1,000 women applying in 1 year compared to 13,000 men applying. Yet they reject half of those 1,000 women equally as they do half of the 13,000 men, because they are women. This is unfair. Sex is a qualification that should not be considered. It places women in a disadvantageous category.

Mrs. GREEN. In other words, you are saying it is the same as if they had a list for blacks and whites?

Dr. NORRIS. That is correct.

Mrs. GREEN. "We will separate them and this will be the criteria by which we will judge their competence to enter their profession"?

Dr. NORRIS. That is the *sub rosa* philosophy used to reject acceptable women applicants.

Mr. BURTON. Will the chairman yield?

Mrs. GREEN. Yes.

Dr. NORRIS. Are there any more questions on this point?

Mrs. GREEN. Mr. Burton has one, I think.

Mr. BURTON. If we didn't keep any data by gender these other facts couldn't be examined for whatever value they may have.

Dr. NORRIS. Right.

Mr. BURTON. If we didn't keep track of the number of applicants, if we didn't keep track of the number of graduates, if we didn't keep track of those practicing that graduate and those that don't practice medicine that graduate, it would be a little difficult, would it not, to make the case that I gather is being made here this morning?

Dr. NORRIS. It would be impossible. We have to collect and document this data. Data must be collected regarding sex groupings. It is a *sine qua non* to solving this problem.

Mr. BURTON. Then I think you are taking issue with a point you made earlier. I think of more interest to some of us would be an explanation of the roughly equivalent sex rejection rate, not saying in this one instance we shouldn't keep the data by sex.

Dr. NORRIS. You said that; I didn't. We must keep the sex data if we are ever to overcome discrimination against women. We must display to the world the low numbers of women accepted and graduated by our medical schools, our law schools, etc.

Mr. BURTON. I don't mean to pursue this. I have only made two statements. One was that the acceptance percentage or proportion among males and females was roughly the same percentage and the percentage of graduates of those accepted was roughly equivalent. You took issue with that. Of course, you are taking issue with something that is in here. I start out as basically in support of your position. I think we may have an identity crisis here. I think we will do better if we don't fight the data. I think it would be better if we stipulate that is the data and then explain it or define it. As to the sex or gender breakdown, which I thought you said some 12 minutes ago was absolutely irrelevant—and 2 minutes ago you said it absolutely has to be kept—a reading of the record will reflect whether or not I misunderstood you——

Dr. NORRIS. You misunderstood. May I repeat my point? Equal proportions of men and women applicants are rejected on the basis of an arbitrary grouping of applicants by gender. It is the judgment of the applicant on the basis of his or her sex that is wrong.

Mrs. GREEN. If you will yield, as I understand it, what you are saying is that the criteria for admission to a medical school should not be the sex of the applicant's acceptability but you also favor keeping facts and figures on how many males and females are admitted?

Dr. NORRIS. That is correct. I strongly support keeping those figures.

Mrs. GREEN. Let me add an additional point, if I may, for my colleague from California who has a long record of fighting to end discrimination wherever it occurs. For decades in many universities and colleges, a higher grade point average has been required of a women for admission to a college or university than of the male. This continues in many of our colleges today, at the same time that we are lowering admission requirements for other people. One startling indication of that is in the State of Virginia. Testimony was submitted—and I've asked staff to check it—that a few years ago 21,000 women applicants for college were rejected and no men who applied for admission to a college or university were rejected. They were apparently admitted somewhere. It is an amazing figure. If this is true—and if the same were true in terms of minority groups, it would not be tolerated by Government or anyone else.

Dr. NORRIS. To the contrary, Federal funds would seem to be restricted from such discriminatory groups.

Mrs. GREEN. Counsel gave me an example of a great university in the District of Columbia, and I repeat this from testimony we heard the other day, that in one of the schools in that university they chose the 200 most highly qualified males for admission, but of the women applied they were only going to admit a few and of those they deliberately and consciously chose the second echelon women. In other words, they did not choose the most highly qualified women but the second echelon down in terms of high school records (college test scores) in terms of general potential ability.

Dr. NORRIS. I have often wondered if this isn't operative in medical school admissions committees where they might not perhaps choose second echelon women to occupy anchormen positions in the class just to be their anchorman.

Mrs. GREEN. Yes, I think again the analogy, if I understand the point you have made, is if they have place in the medical school for 1,000 applicants and if they were black and white they would be on one roster. They would choose the most highly qualified regardless of whether that resulted in a larger percentage of blacks or whites. They wouldn't separate them and then say "We will choose so many of each."

Dr. NORRIS. That is a correct paraphrase of my thesis.

Mrs. GREEN. Does my colleague have further questions at this time?

Mr. BURTON. I am looking for the chart that confirmed the second of the two observations I made.

Dr. NORRIS. Regarding the graduates?

Mr. BURTON. Yes.

Dr. NORRIS. That information I believe is not available to us in my exhibits, since it is actually not pertinent to the discussion at hand, which is with regard to applicants.

Mrs. GREEN. If I may interrupt, I think we have had testimony that the attrition rates is no higher for women than men.

Mr. BURTON. I think it is highly relevant and the chairman is correct in that observation. I think it tends to make the case. That is, if women are given the opportunity to go to medical school they do, roughly speaking, at least as well as men and, relevant or not, some of us like to get as much by way of abstract information as we can to form whatever conclusions we might.

Dr. NORRIS. I am sorry. Information as regards the performance of women physicians in the United States as compared with men has been amply documented in numerous books and monographs, the most pertinent of which I feel is the one published by the Women's Bureau, entitled "Facts on Prospective and Practicing Women in Medicine."

Another very relevant publication in this regard is "Women in Medicine," by Carol Lopate. The Josiah Macy Foundation Conference on Women in 1966 documented women's excellent work in medicine. Numerous publications regarding the fine performance of American women in medicine are available. I feel it is beyond the pale of my current discussion, and I cannot really go into it any further.

Mrs. GREEN. Do you know the percentage or the figure of all the positions held by women Ph. D.'s in the country? Our present information is that 91 percent of all of the women Ph. D.'s are working at the present time. Some of my colleagues in the House, and certainly many in the public, do take the attitude since we have a limited number of places, women are not going to use their education, and so we ought to educate the men. The fact that 91 percent of the women Ph. D.'s are working seems to me to substantially refute that argument.

Do you have the percentage of women medical doctors who are working?

Dr. Norris. Yes. There was a survey conducted by Lee Powers for the Conference on Medical Womanpower reported in the booklet, "The Fuller Utilization of the Woman Physician." His findings show that fewer than 9 percent of women graduated from medical school since 1933 are not employed.

Mr. Burton. As I understand the information before us, women graduates of medical schools comprise some 17 percent of those not practicing medicine, but of the graduates of medical schools between the ages of 30 and 49, women comprise nearly half of the graduates not practicing. That appears on page 23 of the "Facts on Prospective and Practicing Women in Medicine."

Under the age distribution in 1965, 17.7 percent of all inactive physicians are women. Women between 30 and 50 comprise half the inactive physicians in that age group.

Women represent only roughly 6.7 percent of the total number of physicians in the child-bearing or rearing age. Women graduates of medical school represent half the nonpracticing physicians, although in 1965 they are only 6 or 7 percent of those who are medical school graduates.

I think it is this point that medical admissions committees probably look to in making the judgment that as a class, women should be given different treatment because they do not practice during some of their potential professional life. I would accept that figure as valid. I would explain that data away by saying that is still no answer to the inequity facing the individual woman applicant to medical school.

Dr. Norris. I would amplify this statement by saying that Lee Powers has discovered and documented that fewer than 7 percent of women graduates since 1933 are not employed. It is perfectly true that women physicians of child-bearing age are often required to take out from 2 to 5 years of active practice to care for their offspring. This, I may say, reflects the responsibility of the mother-doctor who "cops out" of medical practice, so to speak, instead of the father-doctor. It should be viewed as a strong sense of responsibility on the mother-doctor's side that she does take these 4 or 5 years out during her child-bearing, child-caring years.

I feel this point, however, is related to the child daycare center situation, and when this country, as European and Asian countries have done, provides child daycare centers, this 4 or 5 year cop-out period will no longer be necessary for the woman, who would much prefer participating in her profession.

Mr. Burton. I think you are right in the sense that one ameliorates the situation and alters the data significantly, although not decisively. I think the fundamental point is that the individual who applies to medical school or any other occupational situation is entitled to equitable treatment, and whether or not they are a member of a class that has certain characteristics 5 or 10 or 15 years from now, it is grossly unfair to discriminate against that individual because they happen to be a member of that class. That general information is of no possible relevance to the individual seeking medical training.

I am quite shocked at the data presented to us. I had hoped we had long since done a good deal better, particularly in this field and related fields. The reason I have reacted a little bit to some of your reaction to my question is that I am shocked on the side of eliminating this injustice, and I do not think it helps to ignore the information. I think it is more important that it be interpreted in the light of common experience, rather than shunt it aside as if it did not exist, because if the efforts of Congress and Mrs. Green are to be successful, it is best to be armed with the best explanations of these data, rather than pretend that it is nonexistent.

Dr. NORRIS. I feel all these myths should be exposed.

Mrs. GREEN. I would like to make this point in regard to what Congressman Burton has said. The injustice, it seems to me, is for somebody to play God when a girl or boy applies for medical school and for the admissions officer to make the judgment at that point that the girl is or is not going to practice or the boy is or is not going to practice. He certainly has no way of knowing whether that girl as a woman is going to leave the labor field for 10 or 15 years or not. He makes that judgment arbitrarily. He is certainly playing God with people's lives.

Dr. NORRIS. And ignoring the statistics available to him which show that women do perform well and contribute consistently to the medical labor field.

Mrs. GREEN. I think an interesting statistic—again referring to page 23—is that I notice that among men over age 60, 84.6 percent are inactive, and only 50 percent of the women are inactive over 60. It might be an interesting figure to gather in terms, again, just of having meaningful data, out of how many years of possible practice does the woman in fact practice? If many more women practice after the age of 60, the total number of years that the woman doctor practices may indeed equal the total number of years that a man practices.

Mr. BURTON. I think that a very sound point. If one constructed a physician-year average rather than where the incidence of active and inactive practice came, giving, among other things, the longevity facts of life in terms of men versus women, I suspect that would narrow dramatically whatever physician-years a male graduate of medical school is in practice versus the female.

Mrs. GREEN. I would like to have that, if it is available.

There is a second question I would like to have you respond to. I can document, by chapter and verse, discrimination in the occupation in which I am engaged, but I am also keenly aware of how difficult it is for a woman to enter the medical field, the legal profession, the journalism profession, or, indeed, as has been so well documented, to be promoted in institutions of higher education and become a full professor. The figures are really very shocking.

I wonder if the figures on page 23 have considered—I do not know whether this is true or not, but I am asking it as a question—that because it is more difficult for a woman to establish a successful private medical practice, more trained women medical doctors go into research.

Dr. NORRIS. I do not know if this is documented, but it is known among the medical community that many women are rejected by the practitioners' groups, hospitals, group practices, and have to resort to NIH, or other Federal research organizations for equal treatment.

Mrs. GREEN. Or go into laboratories to do research.

Dr. NORRIS. Right.

Mrs. GREEN. I wonder if these figures on page 23 reflect this at all. The data states "practicing physicians," as I read it. I think Mr. Burton's point is right, that unless we have an explanation——

Dr. NORRIS. I think Isabelle Streidl might be able to tell us. She compiled these figures, and she would know if she included researching physicians among these.

Mrs. GREEN. Would you ask her that?

Dr. NORRIS. I will be glad to.

(The document referred to follows:)

(Excerpt from letter by Dr. Norris to the Chairman)

One of these questions related to the percent of women graduated from medical schools, and another related to the number of women drop-outs from medical practice.

A 1965 study done by 3 agencies, the American Medical Association, the Association of American Medical Colleges, and the American Medical Women's Association, presented data on the professional characteristics of men and women physicians based on a survey of medical school graduates of the years 1931 through 1956, (Facts on Prospective and Practicing Women in Medicine, EXHIBIT A). On page 50 it is stated that professional inactivity was reported by 8.9% of women doctors and 0.6 percent of men doctors responding: i.e., fewer than 9% of women medical school graduates since 1931 were professionally inactive. This is a remarkably good record considering the manifold duties and responsibilities assigned by default to the women of our world. Additional data show that relative inactivity is involuntary and is largely related to child-care during child-bearing years. As you yourself pointed out, among the inactive men physicians, 85% of their group voluntarily retired after age 60, compared with only 50% women retiring after this age. Men doctors retire from medical practice earlier than women do, and this fact, if studied further, might more than compensate for the involuntary temporary retirement of women during child-care years.

With regards to the second query, women were 7.5% of all med school graduates in 1967, and were 8.3% of matriculants. Women do finish medical school, contrary to popular myth. About 91% of the men finish, and 84% of the women finish, a small difference (The Fuller Utilization of the Woman Physician, p. 14). Furthermore, women that do drop out of school do so for nonacademic, domestic reasons the responsibility for which should be equally shouldered by husbands according to marriage contract.

I challenge the accuracy of the A.M.A. source material purporting to constitute data on 273,000 men doctors and 20,000 women doctors in 1965 (Exhibit A, p. 23). The 20,000 women doctors are no doubt very carefully scrutinized, but collation of complete data on 273,000 men is an improbable task accomplished only with great difficulty and expense. Many men physicians do NOT work full time, but take off at least one "golf" day a week. Another oversight in the male performance evaluation is that medical organizational officers, almost all men, devote much or all of their working time to their official duties and political activities, and very little to no time to the practice of their medical profession.

Mrs. GREEN. Both of those are pertinent to the material on page 23.

Mr. BURTON. Without belaboring any given point, on page 8 of the data before us is information on the percentage of women students and graduates of medical schools. To restate the second point I made, women students graduate in roughly the same proportion as they are members of the class. I think page 8 will confirm the observation I made a few minutes ago.

Mrs. GREEN. Will you complete your testimony now, Dr. Norris.

Dr. NORRIS. Among the medical schools listing their admission requirements (16), none admit to racial prejudice, although some schools have never had a Negro graduate. Four medical schools, last year and this year, openly expressed discrimination against women; these schools are Albany Medical College, Yale Medical School, Emory University Medical School, and Loyola Medical School (16).

It has been erroneously argued by a few medical spokesmen that medical schools accept both sexes impartially because statistics over the years show that half of each sex group is rejected annually by medical schools. In regard to this "equal rejection" posture is a response to my letter to the editor of the New England Journal of Medicine (11), in which I accuse medical schools of biased admissions policies against women candidates. The response by Dr. Harry Linde, of the admissions committee at Northwestern University Medical School (12), denied the existence of bias in his admissions committee policies, but admitted that the group of women applicants were better qualified than the men applying. Dr. Linde's honest confession reinforces the probability that unbiased examination of the very small numbers of women applicants now competing for admission to medical schools demonstrates that the qualification of women are equal or superior to those of the men accepted. There is *no* justification for rejecting half of the small group of women applicants *on the basis of their sex grouping*, as is now done by medical schools. Applicants should be judged on an equal basis without regard to sex.

In Russia, 65 percent of physicians are women. The small proportion of women doctors in America has long compared unfavorably with almost every European country (2), and the chief reason for women's low representation in American medicine is prejudice against women applicants to medical schools. In 1905, when women were restricted to the confines of the home, 4 percent of medical students were women. Now, in our emancipated society, still only 7 to 8 percent medical students are women (3). Long ingrained bias exists against women by our medical school admissions committees, and this bias explains why only 9 percent of American physicians are women.

Medical educators resist regulation of school admissions policies by outside agencies. In a letter to me in November 1969 (14), Dr. Donald Pitcairn, Director of Physician Education Branch of the Division of Physician Manpower of the Department of Health, Education, and Welfare, wrote, "There are no legal requirements for the admission of students in any category into the education program of any medical school. Nor do we favor the establishment of such by any Federal agency." This unenlightened opinion Dr. Pitcairn expresses is incompatible with his responsibility toward American women.

The American Medical Association in 1969, published the statement that medical schools are lowering admission requirements in order to accept racial minority groups (7). Today, with Federal scholarship loans to medical students sharply curtailed, increased enrollment of·scholarship students from racial minority groups will further tax our financially strained medical schools. Forty-three medical schools currently threaten to close down and are receiving what Dr. Robert Marston, Director of the National Institutes of Health, calls "disaster grants" from Federal sources (15). Medical schools are now urging passage of a bill calling for a $5,000 Federal subsidy per medical student. Fully half our population, women, represents brainpower virtually untapped by medical schools, and still, despite the twin threats of medical school fiscal disaster and lowered medical school standards, medical school admission committees obstruct just and equal enrollment of women.

Dr. John A. D. Cooper, president of the Association of American Medical Colleges, in a May 17, 1970, New York Times report (17), approved a study group's recommendation that increased numbers of blacks, American Indians, Mexican Americans, and Puerto Ricans be admitted to our medical schools, but Dr. Cooper completely omitted reference to the female half of these minority groups. Despite discrimination against women recorded in its own publications (13, 16), the Association of American Medical Colleges' public posture is that there is no bias against women applicants to medical schools (16). Dr. Cooper should reassess his association's position. The Association of American Medical Colleges shares responsibility for the accreditation of American medical schools (9), and its tacit approval is necessary for the perpetuation of a long, dishonorable tradition of discrimination against women by medical schools.

During fiscal 1967–68, $615 million of Federal funds paid for over half of all medical school expenses in the United States. Teaching and training grants accounted for some $154 million (8). In 1968–69, Federal funds to medical schools totaled $755 million, which again financed over half our medical school total expenses (18). Federal funds have been budgeted for a 50-percent increase in the number of medical students over the next 4 years. The increased number of students, if limited predominantly to men applicants as is anticipated, will be drawn from a level of the male applicant pool that would have been rejected by medical schools under current standards. The current $755 million of Federal funds, now the life blood of nearly every medical school, should be withheld from any medical school which fails to promote compensatory enrollment of women applicants toward a stated goal of an equal sex ratio of matriculants. Schools consistently restricting women by quota to less than half their matriculants should not be given funds. Women applicants with equal or superior qualifications should, through pressure exerted through these funds, be assured acceptance into their medical school of choice.

A resolution to expose discrimination against women applicants to medical schools was presented to the delegates of the American Medical Women's Association last November. As a member of the American Medical Women's Association and the author of this resolution, I am convinced that the following action must be taken to improve the status of American women in medicine.

A federally subsidized medical school admissions-review committee must be established consisting of women physicians of different racial origins. The purpose of the committee would be to review the qualifications of the small numbers of women applicants to medical schools. Any woman found equal to men accepted should be granted admission to medical school. Medical schools not demonstrating willingness to comply with the review committee's recommendations should be denied access to Federal support. Upon attaining its stated goal of approximately equal ratios of men and women students and physicians, this review committee should then be disbanded.

Thank you.

BIBLIOGRAPHY

1.Facts on Prospective and Practicing Women in Medicine, Women's Bureau, U.S. Dept. of Labor, 1968: page 5. (Exhibit A)

2. Ibid, page 40.

3. Ibid, page 5.

4. Women Physicians: The More Effective Recruitment and Utilization of Their Talents and the Resistance to It—A Seven Year Study: Kaplan, Harold I., Professor of Psychiatry and Director of Psychiatric Training, New York Medical College; sponsored by the National Institute of Mental Health. (Exhibit B)

5. (Exhibit C)

6. Journal of the American Medical Association, vol. 210, Nov. 1969, #8, page 1559. (Exhibit D)

7. Ibid, page 1481

8. Ibid, page 1487 (Exhibit E)

9. Ibid, page 1460–61

10. Private communication, Mrs. Dube, Program Director of Medical School Records, Association of American Medical Colleges. (Exhibit F)

11. Norris, F. S.: New England Journal of Medicine, 282, 346, 1969. (Exhibit G)

12. (Exhibit H)

13. Journal of Medical Education, 45, 204, 1970. (Exhibit I)

14. (Exhibit J)

15. (Exhibit K)

16. Medical School Admission Requirements, U.S.A. and Canada; nineteenth edition, 1968–69; twentieth edition, 1969–70, Evanston, Ill. Association of American Medical Colleges. (Exhibit N)

17. (Exhibit L)

18. (Exhibit M)

Mrs. GREEN. Thank you very much, Dr. Norris.

I think the heart of the matter is contained in the two paragraphs on page 5 of your statement, which point out that in many places women are required to have a higher grade point average and greater ability, but in terms of minority groups we lower the admission standards in order to have more numerically. It seems to me that one of the criteria, in fact the major criterion, that has been used by the Enforcement Division of Civil Rights is that the absence of a black, for example, is proof in and of itself of discrimination, or the absence of a certain ratio of blacks to whites, or whites to blacks, is in and of itself proof of discrimination.

I have letters in my files, and there are innumerable documents where the Federal Government has shown the absence of Negroes in a classroom to be in and of itself proof of discrimination. The absence of a certain ratio of ethnic minorities among employees of an industrial plant or of a bank or construction firm has confirmed discrimination and the Enforcement Division on Civil Rights has so ruled.

It seems to me the same criteria should be used insofar as women are concerned. If the criterion is logical in one place, it ought to be in another. If the percentage of women in a medical school is much lower, then it seems to me the same criteria should be applied as in judging minority groups.

Of course, this is the reason for the amendment which I have offered to title VI of the Civil Rights Act, because now colleges and universities, or any schools that the Federal Government supports, are perfectly free to discriminate on the basis of sex whenever they want to, and nothing can be done about it.

I would invite my colleague from California and the group here today to work on a rewording of that amendment so we do not run into the problem of this provision being applied to all-male schools or all-female schools. If this were the case there would be tremendous opposition by those who still hold the view there is a justification for an all-boys or all-girls school.

I must say I have not completely resolved this in my own mind. But in those schools where they do admit both men and women or both boys and girls, then I think there ought to be an end to discrimination, and the same criteria should be applied against such discrimination as we do against discrimination on the basis of creed or race or nationality.

I speak for women who are interested and becoming more vocal and more militant. I welcome that, because I guess it is the only way we can persuade a world which is run by men of the injustices that are occurring and the brain power and energies lost to the Nation through the consistent and systematic discrimination against girls.

I cited a few minutes ago the apprenticeship program. I just do not understand how the Congress, which has been concerned about minority groups not being in the apprenticeship program, can let year after year go by with only token participation by girls.

We have a Conservation Corps proposed. It was originally designed for boys only. We finally got the law changed so girls would be included. But we do not see the establishment of a quota, and I would be willing to predict if there are any girls in it, it will be token representation only.

So, we systematically discriminate against girls or women in every field, whether it be in apprenticeship and Job Corps training or in graduate study at our greatest colleges and universities.

Mr. BURTON. One point I think we should consider in the entire range of public employment is the interaction of the veterans' preference and the women's opportunity to be promoted.

I do not know how extensive veterans' preference is, and I have no quarrel with the disabled veterans receiving preference. I have no quarrel, also, with men who have served some reasonably adequate period of time getting some preference. I am under the impression that if you serve 91 days, you are automatically given a 5-point preference. I may be wrong in that.

During the testimony, and thinking about Mrs. Green's statement on the low number of women in supervisory jobs, I am reminded of the problem we had on postmasters, where we really had almost to walk on water to get a woman as a postmaster. The veterans' preference, in many instances to the exclusion of nonveterans, presented difficulties that were almost insurmountable—for women.

I am not suggesting that those who want to eliminate discrimination against women run into the buzzsaw of veterans' preference, but I do think at least we should examine how extensive this is and whether in all events it is logical. Someone who has been in the service 91 days, in my opinion, may deserve better treatment to get rehired, perhaps, but 15 years after the fact he does not deserve, in some instances, 5 points over anyone else who is competing.

In the area of public employment, I think that quite seriously has a negative impact on the ability of women to get promotions. That in turn may be rooted back in discrimination which took place 20 or 30 years ago on the ground rules of women getting into the service. The fact is, for most of their working lives women in public service do confront the dilemma, and we at least ought to examine this for its implications.

Mrs. GREEN. Your point in terms of the large numbers is valid, and is one that we should pursue. I will ask the staff to pursue that, but the testimony we heard earlier this week is that when men and women both have veterans' preference the women do not get promoted.

Mr. BURTON. I am not really surprised at that. I think it is an enormous waste of the country's talent and resources, and we cannot justify it on any count.

I think Mrs. Green is to be commended for her fight in all these areas, and more particularly in the fight to attain equality for women in the higher education area. I think there is enough support in the country if we set some rather clear yardsticks. If we should find the current level of medical facilities or instructors is so limited we cannot move in this direction, it would increase the pressures to enlarge on our postgraduate professional educational plant and training programs. It is just an outrage.

There is one other question I would like to have you look into and submit information for the record. Do you find any pattern in private as distinguished from public institutions of higher learning? Do public institutions, generally speaking, have a little better performance record than private institutions, or is it more regional than it is private versus public? Have you any opinion on that?

Dr. NORRIS. I can only say that in 1966, 89 percent of our medical schools had fewer than 10 percent women. So, I would say both the public and private sector are guilty of repression of women applicants.

Mr. BURTON. That is all, Madam Chairman.

Mrs. GREEN. I would hope my colleague from California is right in terms of the sentiment across the country. I find any kind of discrimination degrading to the individual and disastrous to the Nation in terms of the resources that are lost. At a time when we have a tremendous shortage of doctors and health personnel, it is a tragic waste of potential resources not to admit qualified women to medical school.

The reason I take a less optimistic view than my friend and colleague from California is that I probably am more keenly aware of the discrimination that has occurred over a long period of time. One of the most recent things which I find discouraging is that the Women's Bureau of the Department of Labor, which keeps statistics on this, and the Department of Labor itself, which is charged with enforcing many of our regulations against discrimination, were invited to testify before this committee about 2 weeks ago. They have known for a long time that hearings would be held and that they were to testify tomorrow. As of today they tell us they have no position. They just do not know how they feel about discrimination against women and the changes in the law. I think this is rather a shocking admission or confession on their part.

I am not blaming my friends of the opposition party. I am equally critical of Democratic and Republican administrations for doing nothing but paying lipservice against sex discrimination. The Department of Labor, which is charged with the responsibility of enforcement under the employment section of Executive Order 11246, still as of July 1, 1970, does not even have a position on whether they are for or against discrimination against women in terms of affirmative action programs.

Dr. DOWDING. May I add on a very limited association with the Women's Bureau, I find this to be equally true. That has been my experience to date. No willingness to give leadership. Repeated statements of "Let us know what you want to do and we will try to help."

Maybe I am wrong, but I would think we would look to the Bureau for leadership.

Dr. FITZGERALD. Which describes what is, not what can be or should be.

Mrs. GREEN. I think they would be highly criticized if there were hearings on violation of the Civil Rights Act—and allegations of rampant, nationwide discrimination against blacks or any other group, by race or color or creed, and they had no position. This is really what leads to militancy. I am one who has always advocated persuasion instead of coercion, but there does come a time when some of those who want to act by persuasion, unfortunately, are led to feel there is only one other way. I am not recommending that. In fact, I have recommended against it.

Dr. DOWDING. May I refer to a question which comes to my attention: What about the public statement of Mr. Hodgson, Secretary of Labor, before the 50th anniversary on June 13? Miss Rawalt asks that question.

Mrs. GREEN. Miss Rawalt is going to testify tomorrow and she may want to cover it at that time. I am not aware of the statement.

Miss MARGUERITE RAWALT. He announced before the conference called by the Women's Bureau celebrating its 50th anniversary, when he addressed it, that he was in favor of equal rights for women. I think he went so far as to say the equal rights amendment. I do not happen to have the clipping with me, but it was published in the newspaper as well.

Mrs. GREEN. I might also suggest that in all of the hearings on higher education, all of the associations representing higher education are interested and usually out in large numbers, but I see an absence of interest on the part of associations of higher education when discrimination against women in colleges and universities is being documented here in great detail.

I have other questions, but I am going to yield to my colleague from California if he has further questions.

Mr. BURTON. No. I am sure you and the staff have considered whether there is a greater problem at the undergraduate or graduate level. I gather from reading the testimony and from listening this morning that a very massive effort has to be placed on the pressure point of the counseling of women before they set themselves on some irreversible course that in effect precludes them from taking the kind of initial training that prepares them for a professional career.

Mrs. GREEN. If I may respond, we have had testimony on other days on the continuity of discrimination and the consistent pattern. We had testimony yesterday in regard to the different approaches used with respect to girls and boys when they are just 1 year of age. You referred to the books this morning. We have had a lot of criticism of Dick and Jane, and the picture role of the woman as a housewife and mother. While the male is portrayed as an engineer or doctor. Girls are persuaded from the time they are very small that their role is different.

Certainly, I personally can testify that girls are actually counseled out of particular professions. I think the discrimination against women is very analogous to the discrimination against blacks. I have known blacks who were counseled out of their No. 1 choice of a profession because they were told, "If you train for it, you will not have any job." Girls are counseled out, as one of you eloquently testified, of engineering. "Don't study to be an engineer, because there won't be a job for you."

This happened to me, as a matter of fact. I wanted to study to be an electrical engineer. I was told "Don't study to be an electrical engineer, because there won't be any job for you." The same advice was given to me when I wanted to study law. Others have this experience in law, medicine, and other areas of study.

One of you made a reference, and I did not get it. It is not in your prepared testimony. I think it was Dr. Fitzgerald who said that there are 1,200 counseling centers.

Dr. FITZGERALD. Yes, to my knowledge. These are counseling centers at 4-year institutions, college, and university campuses, and community colleges. The number of counseling centers is an approximation.

Mrs. GREEN. Run by the colleges?

Dr. FITZGERALD. Yes; run by the colleges and universities.

Mrs. GREEN. Only two have women directors?

Dr. FITZGERALD. Only two non-civil-service appointees—the University of North Dakota and the University of Denver. There are at least two other institutions that have women as directors—the University of California and the University of Minnesota. They are both civil service appointed. There may be one more woman director at the University of Kentucky.

Mrs. GREEN. Have you any information or has anybody in the room any information in terms of the Federal employment centers, where we are doing an expanded job of counseling and guidance, financed by the Federal Government? Has anybody made a study of the number of women in these? I have never seen a woman in one of these employment centers. I do not suggest my information is total. It is a shocking thing that of 1,200 centers on college and university campuses only two have women.

Dr. FITZGERALD. Two that are not civil service. That may not be entirely correct, but that is to my knowledge. I have been very interested in this utilization pattern. I think my major concern is that there has been Federal assistance for special training programs, giving special assistance to the counselors of other minority groups, but there has been no assistance and attention given for the training of counselors of women.

Somewhere in the material I have with me, in some of the training programs for women, and I have the exact title—the range of positions available for which these young women may be trained is strictly within the feminine stereotype range—beauticians, a very narrow scope.

Mrs. GREEN. I made reference a while ago to the fact that only 1 percent of all the apprenticeship slots in the country are occupied by women, and that in terms of occupations, women are trained in only 47 out of 370 occupations.

I thank you very much. You have been very helpful in bringing out some of the areas of discrimination.

Now may I turn to Susan D. Ross and Diane Blank, law students at New York University.

STATEMENT OF MRS. DIANE BLANK AND MRS. SUSAN D. ROSS, WOMEN'S RIGHTS COMMITTEE OF NEW YORK UNIVERSITY LAW SCHOOL; ACCOMPANIED BY FRANCES SCHREIBERG, DEBBIE GINSBURG, NANCY ENNIS, EDITH BARNETT, BONNIE BROWER, MARY KELLY, SUSAN PERLSTADT, MARION DAVIDSON, JANICE GOODMAN, AND LIZ DUNST

Mrs. BLANK. Madam Chairman and members of the committee; my name is Diane Blank. This is my colleague, Susan Ross. I would like to preface our remarks by saying that the women at NYU and at law schools across the country are very much concerned with this problem. There are 12 of us here today. We are all available for questions, and we hope you ask us questions.

I would like to speak briefly about prejudice in the hiring of women faculty members for the law school. We will speak about certain discriminatory policies practiced by the law school against women members, especially in the area of admission and scholarship.

We feel that section 805 of the proposed bill would help to deal with these problems, and we do support it. In our testimony, however, we would like to focus on the practices themselves to help you to understand the extent and nature of the discrimination against women in the law schools and to help you better to deal with discrimination now and in the future.

Mrs. BLANK. On the hiring of women faculty:

New York University School of Law has never hired a fulltime tenured woman professor of law. It has hired a few women in lesser positions. For the school year 1970–71, the women members of the faculty are as follows: an assistant professor in research, a nontenured position; and a research associate professor of judicial administration, a unique title held only by this woman in the entire history of the law school. The title is deceptive, however, for the position is actually a tenured one on the library staff line.

The latest NYU Bulletin lists 149 faculty members; 1.3 percent, two out of 149, of the faculty are women, and they are in the lowest ranking categories.

The situation is no better at other law schools. Harvard has two women professors out of 82; Yale two out of 60; Columbia one out of 63; Michigan one out of 62; Stanford none out of 36. A survey of 36 prominent law schools shows that out of a total of 1,625 faculty members, only 35 are women, and 25 percent of those 35 are classified as librarians. This information is culled from table I attached to our testimony.

Compare these statistics with the following:

1. Women are more than one-half of the Nation's population.

2. Women comprise almost 40 percent of the Nation's work force.

3. Women made up 15 percent of the J. D. candidates graduating from New York Law School in 1969 and 1970.

In the last 1½ years, the law school administration and the faculty recruitment committee, at the insistence of the women's rights committee, have made a series of commitments to hire women faculty. We would like to report on the progress made, namely:

1. One woman was hired to teach a course on "Women and the Law" at a salary of $500 for the entire semester.

2. Last week the school made an offer to Eleanor Holmes Norton,

chairman of the New York City Commission on Human Rights, to teach a course on "Women and the Law" for one semester in the coming year.

3. A female instructor was promoted to assistant professor in research.

4. A subcommittee was formed to recruit women, and that committee has made a few phone calls to a few out of several women who submitted résumés.

This is what has been done in a year and a half. That is, no additions have been made to the full-time faculty, while at least five men have been added.

We have been told repeatedly that "best efforts" are being made to recruit women for the faculty. During this year and a half, women law students have submitted memoranda, have appeared before the faculty subcommittee, have appeared before the faculty recruitment committee, have appeared before the full faculty, and have met with the dean several times, and throughout we have suggested names of prominent women attorneys who might be interested in teaching.

Mrs. GREEN. Could you furnish me with the number of girls who graduate with honors from the schools to which you referred?

Mrs. BLANK. We do not have that information available. I think we could find that out from NYU and possibly from other law schools.

Mrs. GREEN. I find this very interesting. I notice the number of girls who graduate with honors and yet are excluded in hiring.

Mrs. BLANK. It is common knowledge at NYU that the women are very well represented on the dean's list. They are better represented than the men, for instance, who are accepted.

In the last 2 weeks, and as recently as last night, the women law students met with the dean and chairman of the faculty recruitment committee. Again—promises to find qualified women. Yet, both administrators admitted frankly that "if a few good male candidates come along, we will take them." Since there are only a few faculty positions open at this time—we feel that their actions speak louder than their words—they haven't hired any women and they don't intend to.

Why has so little progress been made? We'd like to point out to the members present some of the reasons given:

1. "There are no women attorneys who are qualified to teach," the administration tells us. Yet, we have given them on many occasions lists of women attorneys, and there are several thousands of women practicing law in New York City alone. In addition, over the past 50 years, several hundred women have graduated just from NYU Law School, many of whom were in the top of their class.

2. "We've approached a few women for appointment to the faculty, but those women have turned us down," the administration tells us. What they mean is that they have approached a few women who are already teaching or have prominent positions in Government or in private practice and, because of this, they have received offers from several law schools. Last year they made offers to two women. One is the only female Supreme Court clerk, and the other is one of the three women partners on Wall Street. The top 10 women, it seems, like the top 10 blacks, are in overdemand everywhere.

3. "Hiring women would mean lowering our standards," the administration tells us. Yet the women who graduated from NYU at the

top of their class were graded and ranked in law school by these very same faculty members who now claim they'd be lowering their standards to hire them.

We have discovered that a "Vicious Cycle Syndrome" exists:

The administration says that in hiring new faculty they generally look for certain credentials. The standards most often applied are graduation from a "prestige" law school, impressive clerkship experience, a position at a prominent Wall Street firm, top administrative positions in government and private industry, et cetera, et cetera, et cetera. * * *

But, women by and large have been excluded from all the above, so demanding these credentials of women applicants is completely unrealistic.

1. It was not until 1954 that Harvard Law School even admitted women at all. As of fall 1969, a look at the enrollment from a cross-section of American law schools revealed that 26 out of 54 schools just happened to have between 5 and 8 percent women; 15 had below 5 percent; 13 had above. These figures are taken from table II which is attached.

2. As for clerkships, there have been only two women U.S. Supreme Court clerks so far, and one of them is now deceased. Many clerkships at the State and Federal level are unavailable to women because many judges have openly stated to the law schools that they will not consider women law students for clerkship positions. Women judges who might hire women law clerks number 1 percent of the total number of judges in the country, 2.6 percent of the judges in New York State. I might add, the relatively large number in New York State comes from the fact that most women judges have jobs in family courts, in the lower echelon courts.

3. As to Wall Street firms, out of the 20 leading firms on the Street, there are only three women partners. The numbers of women associates who have been hired by these firms are so few that this is hardly a reasonable criterion to demand of women applicants.

4. As to Government work, we can count on the fingers of one hand the numbers who have attained high level administrative positions. For that matter, women have been totally excluded from some areas of Government practice. The U.S. Attorney's office for the southern district of New York systematically, under its last administration, has refused outright to hire women for its criminal division.

So it's a vicious cycle: Women aren't hired because they don't have the proper qualifications; women can't get the proper qualifications because only men have access to those avenues and experiences which produce the proper qualifications; so, women aren't hired by law schools.

Mrs. GREEN. In the Civil Rights Act, title VII, on employment, we do include discrimination based on sex. You cite specifically cases where they have said they will not hire individuals because they are women, obviously an open violation of the Civil Rights Act. Can you advise me how many cases the Justice Department has prosecuted?

Mrs. BLANK. Absolutely none, although I spoke to an attorney in the southern district a few months ago. He had heard there was some agitation at NYU among the women, and he called up. There was some question of suits against leading Wall Street firms. He said, "Of course, we were thinking of bringing them before the Human Rights Commission," of which Eleanor Holmes Norton is chairman. He said, "We should really be bringing those suits." I pointed out to him, of course his own criminal division under Morgenthau in past administrations had refused outright to hire women, although they do hire a very small number for their civil division.

Mrs. GREEN. We are inviting the Justice Department to testify, and we will be asking them these related questions. It is my understanding they have brought cases in terms of discrimination in employment on the basis of race, but while the firms that you testify publicly acknowledged they discriminate on the basis of sex, not one single case has the Justice Department ever instituted since the Civil Rights Act was passed.

Mrs. BLANK. The final irony in the cycle is that the law school looks for candidates who have had teaching experience at other law schools. How can a woman acquire teaching experience if no law school will ever hire her?

The law schools simply cannot expect women appointees to the faculty to have been former Wall Street partners, clerks, Supreme Court clerks, judges, U.S. attorneys in the criminal division, members of many prominent law firms, graduates of the best law schools, top administrators in Government, or present teachers on leading law school faculties.

The law schools cannot demand these credentials because women systematically have been denied the chance to acquire them. The vicious circle must be broken at some point, just as it has to be for blacks.

The final dishonesty is that these credentials do not necessarily qualify one to be a good teacher. Those of you who have attended law school must certainly remember that those professors with the greatest credentials were certainly not always the greatest teachers. Even the law school has as much as admitted this fact. For example, they have hired male faculty members to teach new areas of the law like poverty law. These men had experience in poverty law, though they lacked the traditional credentials. So, the criteria can be changed. Yet the law school faculty and administration consistently resurrects these standards when it suits their purpose of barring women.

It is absolutely vital that women be incorporated into the educational sphere of the legal profession.

1. Law schools have a unique responsibility to break down the discrimination in the legal profession.

2. It is of great educative value to both male and female law students to be taught by women professors as well as men.

3. It is imperative and long overdue that male professors learn to deal with women professionally as peers.

4. It is most important for women who are presently in or considering entering law school to see women among the ranks of law school professors.

5. It is imperative that practicing women lawyers see teaching as a professional career for them as well as for men.

6. It is high time that law schools conform to the reality of the rising proportion of women in law. For example, 20 percent of the New York University Law School 1971 graduating class are women. And yet, as we pointed out before, the percentage of female faculty at New York University is only 1.3 percent.

Finally, we point out that teaching has always been considered a woman's field. Forty-two percent of all professional working women are teachers; 70 percent of all public school teachers are women. But these figures pertain only to the elementary and secondary school level. The proportion of women teachers at the college and university level is only 22 percent, just slightly higher than their 20 percent proportion in 1910, and a far smaller proportion than their 28 percent in 1940. In the professional schools, notably, law schools, women teachers are the exception rather than the rule. Many male lawyers have pointed out that women shouldn't go into law or cannot be successful in the field because (1) the long hours are too taxing for them, and (2) they can't devote long hours to the profession because of responsibility to home and family. Yet, they are excluded from teaching in law schools where the hours are shorter and more flexible, where the work-week may be only 2 or 3 days, where research work can be done at home as well as on the job. In other words, the professional demands of teaching do not present obstacles for women; if anything, the demands of time and place are very favorable—it is discrimination by male administration and faculty which keeps women out of teaching. Women attorneys constitute a vast reservoir of talent which is grossly underutilized in the legal teaching profession.

Our experience over the past 2 years with the New York University administration, which has been completely unproductive, and the dearth of women law professors at schools across the country have demonstrated to us that discrimination against women in the hiring of law school faculty is so deep-seated that any efforts to obtain women faculty members will fail unless Federal legislation with appropriate enforcement provisions is passed. Therefore, we support the deletion of the exemption for educational institutions from application of title VII of the 1964 Civil Rights Act.

Mrs. Ross. I would like to speak about discriminatory policies against women in other areas in the law school, and particularly on admissions and scholarship policies.

We believe that discrimination against women in hiring is simply one symptom of institutional prejudice against women. The institutionalization of sex discrimination is reflected in many concrete policies and practices in various areas. The admission of women to law schools is one such area. Women law students in schools throughout the United States have received persistent but off-the-record reports of quota systems and higher admission standards for women.

I will tell you later about a National Conference of Law Women which was formed just this last spring where we talked about that in great detail. At New York University, even, we have had students sitting on admissions committees, we have had secretaries working in the admissions offices, and we have even had professors tell us, yes, there were quota systems in the past, and that right now, today, they are imposing higher admissions standards on women than they are on men.

Columbia has reported the same kind of instances. We have women at New York University who are there because they were so insulted by the interviewing process at Columbia where they were told, "We don't like women here very much, frankly."

There was an interesting letter in the Harvard Law Record last fall from a woman who graduated from Harvard in 1967. She reported that the Dean said:

Harvard Law had then reached enrollment for women of 5% for each class; that Harvard would probably not go above the 5% level since that was Yale Law School's percentage; and that, after all, there could never be a great influx of women into the school (read blacks, read Jews, read Catholics) because the policy was *never to give any man's place to a woman* . . . (emphasis supplied).

We believe this shows the low percentage of women in law schools is not accidental, but is an institutional decision. I think statistics comparing percentages of women in the leading professions in the United States with percentages in other countries are especially shocking.

In Russia, women account for 36 percent of the total number of lawyers; in the United States, 3 percent. Thirty percent of the judges in Germany are women; in the United States, 1 percent. Fifty percent of the law students in Denmark are women; here, 5.9 percent last year. That reflected an increased enrollment due to the heavy draft pressures on law schools.

The American Association of Law Schools is presently studying this whole problem. I do not think their awareness is very great. A symptom of that is the reaction of our own school when we said we wanted to go and recruit women more actively. The dean of admissions was horrified at the suggestion and said, "We already have many too many women, and we certainly don't need any more." In other words, women should be flattered and honored to be allowed to go to a school that is 85 percent male, but men are horrified and insulted to go to a school which is 50 percent female.

We believe the law schools must commit themselves to an affirmative action program like the Philadelphia Plan which is being implemented to integrate the labor unions. In other words, they must work to get an enrollment of 50 percent women.

Mrs. GREEN. Why don't you write letters to the Labor Department and ask them about it?

Mrs. ROSS. We would be very willing to. We have been trying to work on a lot of fronts. Interestingly enough, we submitted proposals to the American Association of Law Schools last December in which we didn't even go as far as 50 percent. We only suggested that they work to get an enrollment of women which was commensurate with the level or percentage of women in the labor force, which I think is now only 40 percent. That proposal of ours was circulated as a terribly radical proposal to influence members of the association to vote for a simple statement that discrimination on the basis of sex is wrong.

They certainly were not willing to commit themselves to such a radical thing as opening up the law schools to 36 percent women or 38 percent women.

Mr. BURTON. What is the range of support among the male law students?

Mrs. ROSS. We have a section on that in the testimony. I will talk about the male attitudes in law schools. I do not think all the men in law school oppose us, but we have a very active group at NYU, and there have been some very disturbing incidents. One of them involved the whole moot court competition this year. The two women involved in that are here today. When that competition started out, two women who were competing asked to apply to be on the moot court board as editors. They were told that they were not eligible because they were not staff members at present on the moot court.

Shortly thereafter, two men who were in exactly their position, that is, who were also competing in moot court competition and who were not staff members, were not only told they could apply to be editors, but were actively encouraged to do so and were voted in.

When we protested that, both the students and faculty involved said that wasn't discrimination on the basis of sex; that was simply a matter of a lack of written procedures.

We got that decision reversed, and then we realized that since this lack of written procedures was a serious problem indeed, we asked that written guidelines be set down for judging the moot court competition then in progress. We were very glad we had done so, because after the competition was through, under the written guidelines the women had won both of the two competitions involved, that is, they had been named one of the two best law school teams to compete next year against each other for the best law school team. They had also both been asked to serve on the national team which would go on to the national competition, a three-man or three-woman team.

The moot court board members tried to change the scoring system after the competition was over so that the women would not win one of those competitions. Again, after a long struggle, we succeeded in reversing that whole decision, and the women were named the winners of both competitions.

The interesting sequel to the whole story is that the one man who was asked to be on the national team refused to serve and, as a matter of fact, every man who was eligible refused to serve. Apparently, the idea is if they can't have it their way, they are not going to play the game.

Mr. BURTON. Were any sanctions applied?

Mrs. ROSS. There are no sanctions against that. We hope the women go on to win the national competition, and the men will realize what they have lost.

Another incident was during a student strike when student committees were formed to go talk to corporations about anti-war activities. A student coordinator of that committee who was a male told the woman who was interested in appearing with other students to talk to those corporations, the women, of course, couldn't go because women weren't in the corporate image.

There has been a great deal of hostility between men and women at the law school, I think because we have begun to bring a lot of things out in the open, because we have begun to ask for things that we think are important. I think what is disturbing is that the professors themselves are not taking a firm stand against it, by and large. In the whole moot court competition, we were struggling just as much against the faculty involved as we were against the students. Some of the professors have what they call ladies' days when they call on only the women in the class. They would never dream of having a Jewish day or a black day, but they don't even think it is insulting or demeaning to call on women on a special women's day. In fact, when we pointed that out to one professor, he said, "Well, it is discrimination against blacks or Jews, but you are just being too sensitive."

Mrs. GREEN. May I suggest that the statement of the policy that you have described is that women are fine if they "know their place"— and stay in it.

Mrs. ROSS. Right; exactly. This is a very serious problem, and we think this explains a lot of discrimination.

One more incident I would like to mention on the question of attitudes is the whole question of Law Review participation. Editors, at NYU at least, are selected by other student members, and yesterday I went back and looked at the list of student editors over the last 8 years. I found that out of the women serving on the Law Review who were eligible to be editors, 13 percent had been named to editorships. Of the men eligible, 39 percent had been named to be student editors.

I think that the studies that have been done by psychologists showing that students will consistently rate essays higher if they are told they are written by men than they will if the identical essay is written by women, has an obvious relevance here.

Students are looking at women's and men's written work, and that is one of the criteria used to select editors, and they are rating the women lower than men. I think that is the only thing that can explain this lower rate.

Mrs. GREEN. You should adopt the technique used by the first woman applicant to medical school a hundred years ago.

Mrs. ROSS. What was that?

Mrs. GREEN. She did not tell them she was a woman. She used only her initials. She was the first woman ever admitted to a medical school. She used only her initials because her first name was obviously feminine.

Mrs. ROSS. Unfortunately, the editors are not chosen until after a year of working on the Law Review. By that time, of course, they all know each other rather well. They know which is which sex.

To go back to some of the discriminatory practices, earlier in the testimony today there was some talk about standards, and we do have something to say about that. The law school has begun actively to recruit students from minority groups and has even relaxed standards and set up special programs to correct past injustice to minorities. Yet women, who certainly are considered a minority group in law schools, are not actively recruited. Instead, they are in many ways discouraged from applying and, rather than set up special programs to encourage women to come to law school, the law schools raise standards, thus making their entrance even more difficult.

Another blatant example of discriminatory practices is in the field of scholarships. Until last year, NYU's very prestigious and lucrative Root-Tilden scholarships were closed to women. Our whole group came to be organized around that issue. Those scholarships are very valuable. They are worth more than $10,000 total, because all expenses are paid through law school.

More than 20 of the scholarships are awarded to incoming men each year as future public leaders of America.

Presumably women couldn't be public leaders and therefore NYU is contributing to making that presumption a reality by excluding women from a training program for public leaders.

Mr. BURTON. Let me interject a question.

Mrs. ROSS. Yes.

Mr. BURTON. Do you have any view on the economic level of the family of the women law students vis-a-vis the men?

Mrs. ROSS. Well, that is a very interesting problem. We don't have very specific statistical information on financial aid, for instance, to women versus men, but some interesting things have happened. I myself, for instance, was married in the middle of my second year in law school to a student who was also in the second year. We were both receiving financial aid before we were married. After we were married the school lowered both of our scholarships on the theory that they didn't want to be supporting a marriage. They wouldn't even continue us on the former level. I think what they were really saying was "We think that one of you should quit to support the other and put the other through law school." I think you know which one they thought should quit.

Mr. BURTON. I see that in your statement, but on the general proposition can one make an accurate generalization about the economic level of the families of the women in law school vis-a-vis the men? Are most of the women from middle class and relatively well-to-do families?

Mrs. ROSS. I certainly don't know.

Mr. BURTON. Is there a smaller proportion, if you please, of women from families of the poor than you would find among the male students?

Mrs. BLANK. I don't think that information is really very readily available.

Mr. BURTON. Do you have an impression in that regard?

Mrs. BLANK. I myself am from a very poor family. Do we have any impressions in that regard?

Mrs. GREEN. Let's call on some of the others, and will you identify yourself for the record, please?

Miss GOODMAN. Janice Goodman.

Mrs. GREEN. A student?

Miss GOODMAN. A student at NYU. I think one of the things we could say is probably at law schools we are mainly middle class. It is a middle class profession and the school has not made that many opportunities for people, although there are some. I think what you will find, though, in general is the women are more self-supporting. In other words, the usual tradition is that the men have wives work while they go to law school. Then after they get out of law school they stay home and have the children, and in fact NYU supports this. They have a separate job category that is law school wife, and they work as secretaries but they get $25 less than all the other secretaries and it is basically a way that the school feels, that this is financial support for the law student to get through school, that the school is doing the law student a favor by hiring his wife in an employment situation. I think those women are becoming more and more concerned about their position there but that is the current situation.

Mr. BURTON. Would you say there is a higher proportion of the male students who come from families that are poor than you can say about the female students, or isn't there enough data for you to have a good impression, or is it just the opposite?

Miss GOODMAN. I think there is not enough data, but one other thing we did find is it seems that a higher number of the women have been out working for 2 to 5 years, myself for more than that, and are self-supporting and are emancipated. They state that they go to law school. I think that you might find a higher percentage in that kind of category. I think that whether they are poor or rich is a statistic we don't have.

Mrs. GREEN. Would you identify yourself, please?

Miss DUNST. Liz Dunst, NYU Law School. I think the question of the financial status is really irrelevant. For example, a Root-Tilden scholarship is worth $10,000 a year, which is not a scholarship based on need. Need is irrelevant to getting that scholarship. The fact that they discriminate against women if the women have more financial backing really doesn't hold much water.

Mrs. GREEN. That has been changed, though?

Mrs. Ross. Right; it has been, but we think this whole question of the level of scholarship aid to women and to men should be explored. I mean on a nationwide basis. I suspect strongly that there is the same kind of institutionalized discrimination there as there is in the field of admissions. I remember when I was in college and was appointed to the graduate school I was told that the Woodrow Wilson scholarship was restricted to 25-percent women, and I suspect that you find that kind of systematic exclusion of women in a lot of scholarships.

Mrs. GREEN. I might interject here that a study of the NDEA loans shows that women get their share in terms of NDEA loans. When you get to the guaranteed student loan program, which is administered by the banks, the girls do not get as many guaranteed student loans as the boys.

Mrs. Ross. Another area we wanted to talk about was living accommodations and health services. Again, we had some incidents at NYU. Single rooms until last year were not open to women, and some women protested and that was eventually reversed. We found out recently that 10 years ago when a woman had tried to open up the law school apartment complex to women, that is, at that time it was closed completely to women, not only single rooms but any kinds of rooms, she spoke to the faculty about it and subsequently blackballing letters were placed in her employment file by some of those faculty members without ever telling her.

Mrs. GREEN. May I interrupt you? We have to go to answer a quorum call. I have a friend on the New York University faculty who told me that in public housing there was discrimination against single women. Would one of you people volunteer to make a study of that and provide it for me—that is public housing financed by the Federal Government, there are written and unwritten discriminatory practices against single women?

Mr. BURTON. Is that student housing?

Mrs. GREEN. No; public housing.

Mrs. Ross. That is a persistent problem. I think New York State has just enacted a law even to deal with that problem, discrimination in housing on the basis of sex.

Mrs. GREEN. Would one of you lawyers provide that? I would ask unanimous consent that at the conclusion of your remarks it be made a matter of record.

Mrs. Ross. Thank you.

Mr. BURTON. As a rule, public housing is not available to single persons generaly, unless they are disabled or older, so I am not sure it would be the classic Federal public housing. It might be your own New York or it might be a student housing program. I know in our city no single person, unless he has a disability or an age thing, is eligible.

Mrs. Ross. In private housing it is a major problem, as well.

Mrs. GREEN. I would like to know what the facts are because this New York University professor told me that this was the case. As we were driving by, she said, "If you are a single woman you cannot get in there." She told me if you were a single man you could. There is the assumption that if a single woman is moving in she is doing it for immoral purposes——

Mrs. Ross. Exactly.

Mrs. GREEN (continuing). And, therefore, they oppose her housing application.

Dr. DOWDING. And also that they may more readily be unemployed. I heard just recently this is another reason for their functioning in that unjust way.

Mrs. GREEN. I would like the facts, though, on it so we could have them and not just rumors. Can you summarize the rest, because we are going to have to go, and I would ask unanimous consent that the entire statement be made a matter of the record. I would also ask unanimous consent that the various attachments provided by the three preceding witnesses and these two witnesses be looked over by Mr. Hogan, the counsel for the committee, and that such ones as are not duplication of preceding materials be inserted in the record.

Without any objection, it is ordered. (Material inserted earlier in the testimony.)

Mrs. GREEN. Could you summarize the rest of your statement?

Mrs. Ross. Yes, I will. Just in conclusion, I would like to say that I think there is a growing and strong recognition of this problem among women law students across the country. This last spring we organized a conference at NYU and we had women representatives from 17 schools. Over 100 women showed up at that conference and there was much talk about the discriminatory practices that they are encountering, and I think there is increased militancy among women as they begin to realize that there is institutionalized sex discrimination.

In conclusion, we strongly support the proposed bill pending before your committee because we hope that it will do something about some of these problems.

Mrs. GREEN. Thank you very much. There is also one other request I would like to make of one of you law students. What are the laws in New York and other places, if you wish to pursue it further in terms of the prosecution of prostitutes? This is something which was called to my attention in a hearing, and I mentioned it before. I really would like it researched. It was called to my attention by an article in the New York Times one day that——

Mr. BURTON. It takes two to tango.

Mrs. GREEN (continuing). A man and a woman were found together. The woman was immediately taken down to the police headquarters, fingerprinted, arrested, and was identified by name and address in the press. The man was identified as a well-to-do businessman from an out-of-State location; he was not identified by name. I asked a question about this and one of my colleagues—(my colleague from California may not agree with this)—leaned over to me and said, "You know why, don't you?" And I said, "No, I really don't." As Mr. Burton says, it takes two to tango; I would think, under the law they were equally guilty. He said, "They have to have a witness; so the man is the witness." I said, "Why don't they occasionally have the woman as the witness?" I would like to have that researched.

Mr. BURTON. Maybe the law should be changed.

Mrs. Ross. May I add just one more point on that specific? New York has just enacted recently a law which makes a man guilty of the crime for patronizing a prostitute, and we were in a course on Women and the Law at NYU, and interviewed various people in the whole legal system, and it was the unanimous feeling that that law was only being used as a weapon against the men to force them to testify against the prostitutes and that there had been no prosecutions against the men under the law.

Mrs. GREEN. It would be very helpful if you would research this. We must go now and answer the bell and I have a luncheon meeting, but if any of you are going to be here this afternoon I would welcome the opportunity to discuss informally with you some of the other questions. If you would get in touch with my office, say, at either 2:30 or 3 o'clock, whichever would be more convenient, there may be some other specific areas that you might be able to help us on in terms of research.

Mrs. BLANK. Thank you very much.

Mrs. GREEN. Mr. Hogan has suggested—I think it would be well— and if you would do it and allow me to leave, that the rest of you who are here in this group give your names to the reporter so that you can be identified. Then, if I have requests, perhaps I can direct them to each of you. Mr. Hogan, would you take charge of that?

We will recess until tomorrow morning at 9:30.

(Whereupon, at 12:30 p.m., the subcommittee recessed, to reconvene at 9:30 a.m., Wednesday, July 1, 1970.)

WEDNESDAY, JULY 1, 1970

House of Representatives,
Special Subcommittee on Education
of the Committee on Education and Labor,
Washington, D.C.

The subcommittee met at 10:30 a.m. pursuant to notice, in room 2251, Rayburn House Office Building, Hon. Edith Green (chairman of the subcommittee) presiding.

Present: Representatives Green, Quie, and Scherle.

Staff members present: Harry Hogan, counsel; and Robert Andringa, minority professional staff assistant.

Mrs. GREEN. The subcommittee will come to order for further consideration of legislation under our jurisdiction. Today we are turning our attention specifically to section 805 of H.R. 16098.

Our first witness is our very good friend and colleague from New York, Congresswoman Shirley Chisholm.

STATEMENT OF HON. SHIRLEY CHISOLM, A REPRESENTATIVE IN CONGRESS FROM THE STATE OF NEW YORK

Mrs. CHISHOLM. Thank you, Madam Chairman.

Mrs. GREEN. On behalf of the committee, may I tell you how much we appreciate your coming this morning to give us the benefit of your views?

Mrs. CHISHOLM. Thank you very much.

Most men and not a few women, do not understand the campaign for equal rights for women. They may know that women are a majority of the population—51 percent—and that they are supposed to control a majority of the Nation's wealth.

How then could it be that women are discriminated against? At first glance, the idea may seem silly.

The Department of Labor found that in 1966, white men had an average income of $7,179. Black men had made $4,508 and white women $4,142. Black women, who are almost universally confined to menial services jobs, averaged only $2,934.

My main point in quoting these figures is to show you in dollars and cents, that white women are more discriminated against than black men in the labor market.

This has some very serious and costly consequences for our society, to which I will return in a moment.

In my own experience, I have suffered from two handicaps—being born black and being born female. I remember vividly one incident at Brooklyn College. One of my favorite professors, a blind political scientist named Louis Warsoff, was impressed by the way I handled myself in a debate.

He told me, "Shirley, you ought to go into politics." I told him, "Proffy (that was a pet name we had for him) you forget two things. I am a woman and I am black."

During my entire political life, my sex has been a far greater handicap than my skin pigmentation. From my earliest experience in ward political activity my chief obstacle was that I had to break through the role men assign women.

A young woman, in a newspaper story I read somewhere, defined that role beautifully. She was talking about her experiences in the civil rights movement: "We found that the men made the policy and the women made the peanut butter sandwiches."

Every man in Congress is here because of the efforts of the women who form the backbone, the effective troops, of a political organization.

Without its thousands of women volunteers, the American party system would not work. It would break down in a confusion of unanswered letters, unmade phone calls, unkept appointments, unwritten speeches and unheld meetings.

Men are not aware of the incredible extent to which they rely on women or, to be more precise in my choice of words, the extent to which they exploit women—to handle the details while the men take the credit.

This brings me to one of the main points I want to make. The prejudice against women has gone unnoticed by most persons precisely because it is so pervasive and thorough-going that it seems to us to be normal.

For most of our history the very closely analagous prejudice against blacks was invisible to most white Americans because it was so normal to them.

It was a deeply ingrained, basic part of their personalities. Discovering that fact has been a great shock for many whites. Many others have not yet come that far, unfortunately. When they have, if they ever do, the race problem will vanish.

But if we ever succeed, as we must succeed if we are to survive, in rooting out the racism that is such a prominent part of our American heritage, we will still be very far from being a just society if we are not also ready to accord full human dignity to women.

After all, half of the blacks and every other minority group in this country are women. When we talk about women's rights we are talking about the rights of the majority of the population.

Sex cuts across all geographical, religious, class and racial lines. Every sector of the American population has a stake in eliminating anti-feminist discrimination.

To quote a brilliant black woman lawyer, Dr. Pauli Murray, "Discrimination because of one's sex is just as degrading, dehumanizing, immoral, unjust, indefensible, infuriating and capable of producing societal turmoil as discrimination because of one's race."

In both cases, please note this, exclusion implies inferiority.

The stereotypes are closely parallel. The happy little homemaker, the dumb blonde, the bubble-brained secretary, are the same kind of distorted pictures, drawn by prejudice, as those of the contented old darky and black mammy and little pickaninnies down on the old plantation.

Blacks and women have both been taught from childhood, because our society is run by and for white males, that they are inherently inferior. To keep them in their place, the same, the very same, characteristics are imputed to women as to blacks—that they are more childish, emotional, and irresponsible than men, that they are of lower intelligence, that they need protection, that they are happiest in routine, undemanding jobs, that they lack ambition and executive ability.

The parallels are striking and almost frightening, aren't they?

Stereotypes are no more credible where they are applied to women than they are when they are applied to blacks.

As far as the argument that the woman's place is in the home goes I would like to borrow a campaign slogan from Mrs. Bella Abzug, Democratic nominee for the 19th Congressional District of the State of New York, and I believe this:

Woman's place is in the House and the Senate and the AFL–CIO Executive Board and the Gridiron Club.

The important thing that must be understood is that women are first and foremost people.

A woman who aspires to be chairman of the board or a Member of the House does so for exactly the same reasons as any man. Basically she feels and knows that she possesses the talents, the attributes and the requisite skills for the job. That and that alone should be the criterion in the business world, the professional world and the political world.

The most articulate and active members of the women's rights movement have of course been professional women, and many of the specific amendments being dealt with today deal specifically with the problems of professional women.

These amendments proposed to section 702, title VII of the Civil Rights Act and section 13(a) of the Fair Labor Standards Act are necessary and important changes, but I would like to devote some of my time today to the problems of the working class and poor women of this country.

Our society's attitudes toward women are closely bound up with one of its major problems, that of social welfare. The staggering costs of social services are straining the national budget and threatening to bankrupt most of our cities.

One of the commonest characteristics of welfare families is that they are headed by women. In many cases the problem began with a man who rejected or evaded the role we assign him, of protector and breadwinner—but that is another question which I cannot deal with today.

The result, obviously, is that some women are forced to assume the breadwinner's role in addition to that of mother and homemaker.

Three million eight hundred and sixty thousand white families are headed by women and 30 percent are poor, earning less than $3,000 a year, and one quarter of all black families are headed by women and 62 percent of them are poor.

In toto, women head 1,920,000 impoverished families. Let me recall the income figures I quoted earlier: white women averaged $4,142 in 1966 and black women $2,934. No one can support a family today on such pitiful incomes. One cannot really be blamed for giving up even trying to do so.

But although the problem is most grave when it concerns women who are heads of households, it is not confined to them. Other women who work do not do so because of the personal fulfillment but because they contribute substantially to the family's support.

In one-third of the U.S. families where both parents work, the husband's income is less than $5,000.

It is almost universally true that women are paid less than men for doing the same work. In college teaching as this subcommittee heard on Monday from Virginia R. Allan, women are paid median salaries $400 to $2,000 less than men of the same academic rank.

Women, like blacks, Puerto Ricans, and other groups that are the targets of discrimination, are clustered in the low level, dead end jobs and are rarely in the more responsible ones.

Although 38 percent of the women in the United States work, only 2 percent of them make more than $10,000 a year.

Women are also discriminated against in manpower training programs. First, because they are frequently channeled into training programs for low entry level jobs with no opportunities for advancement and second, because the quota for women enrollees is much smaller than for men.

In 1968 only 31.7 percent of the on-the-job training enrollees were women, the job opportunities in the business sector program had only 24 percent female enrollees and the new defunct Job Corps had 29 percent female enrollees.

If we are sincerely interested in solving our welfare problems and helping our poor and working class families, we must recognize the correlation between their problems and the battle to provide equal opportunities for women.

For these women, their income is not a supplement; it is essential for the survival and well-being of the family unit.

They must have more and better job training opportunities and equal pay and a fair opportunity for advancement.

Finally they must also have adequate day care facilities. Right now we have 5 million preschool children whose mothers have to work, but day care facilities are available to only 2 percent of our women.

Without adequate day care, we have seriously handicapped women and in some cases doomed them to failure in the job market.

Turning now to the legislation before this subcommittee section 805 of H.R. 16098, I would like to conclude my remarks with this observation: The amendments proposed are all just, necessary and long overdue.

Sex is not, any more than religion or race, a valid basis for discrimination. Women are individuals, just like men, or blacks or Polish Americans.

To consider them as a homogeneous group is manifestly unjust. It is prejudging each individual in the group, each woman, which as you know is the origin of the word prejudice.

These changes in the laws will do much to make it possible for a woman to strive, if she chooses, and to succeed or fail on her merits and her efforts, like every other human being.

My only reservation is that the proposed amendments may not go far enough toward putting teeth in the law.

Our experience with State and Federal civil rights agencies has generally been that, unless they have enforcement powers, they are ignored and impotent.

The disgraceful record of the Defense Department on contract compliance with the equal opportunity laws is, I believe, sufficient evidence of this.

It seems to me that the subcommittee should consider adding enforcement powers to the Equal Employment Opportunity Commission or if this is not practical in this bill as a legislative possibility, that the proposal be embodied in another bill and introduced by appropriate members through some other route.

I thank you.

Mrs. GREEN. Thank you very much, Mrs. Chisholm. I think you have outlined very accurately the very systematic discrimination that does occur from very early years in a girl's life, and discrimination to which this Congress gives its approval, in terms of the manpower training program, the Job Corps, the apprenticeship program, and so forth.

One figure that has come to our attention in these hearings is that in the apprenticeship training program, out of 278,000 registered apprentices in the program, less than 1 percent were girls. This despite the fact that the highest unemployment figure in the Nation is among nonwhite girls, who desperately need the training and the resulting opportunities.

On the last page of your prepared statement Mrs. Chisholm you state we should put more teeth in the enforcement of rights provisions. My information is that the Justice Department does have the enforcement powers, but that the Justice Department has never instituted a single case based on sex discrimination, not a single case, when there have literally been thousands of complaints made to the Equal Opportunities Committee.

It seems to me that history is going to record this, as the biggest cop-out of the century. They assert themselves in other cases of discrimination but not in sex discrimination cases. It seems to me since they are required by the law to enforce equally, when they choose to ignore the enforcement of the law based on sex discrimination, they themselves can be accurately accused of discrimination. Congress stated no preference in title VII of one kind of discrimination over the others.

Mrs. CHISHOLM. This is why I feel, Madam Chairman, that the whole question has to be not only in terms of enacting future legislation that will help to eradicate this whole problem of sex discrimination because we have so much legislation on the books for just about every kind of problem in our Nation.

It is a problem of putting into future legislation that will be proposed in this area. I don't have the time now, but I am very much interested in this whole problem of sex discrimination, and as we go through the legislation on the local, State and Federal level, one can really say there are laws on the books if implemented and carried out and enforced and if they were, it won't be necessary to have this hearing today.

That is why I am concerned about additional legislation in this area, unless concomitantly we really do build into that legislation some kind of real enforcement or some kind of followthrough, where initiation is allowed on the part of the agency so that they can go after the departments that say one thing and actually, when their records are brought before the public, it indicates a different story.

Mrs. GREEN. You and I know that until this year there was one gallery in the House of Representatives reserved for "men only."

I had the interesting experience of going into it unknowingly in my first year here with some of my constituents and a man was sent up by Speaker Sam Rayburn asking me to get out.

As you know, we have no women pages, or women doorkeepers, though we do have women elevator operators now. It is also an interesting observation with respect to the Supreme Court, which decides many cases on discrimination, that we had testimony from women law students yesterday on the number of women law clerks in the history of the U.S. Supreme Court. To the best of my knowledge, there are no women or girl pages, and there never have been, in the Supreme Court of the United States which hands down opinions on discrimination from time to time—and tells others how they are to end it.

Mrs. CHISHOLM. I just want to make one concluding comment. Today, our country really needs the creativity, the ability and the intelligence of all of its citizens in order to be able to get so many things straightened out, and it seems to me that the utilization of the talents of the people in this country should not really be based on sex, because if we look at the history of the roles that women have played in this Nation, there is no question in the minds of those of us who can be objective and not be biased about them that women have been driving forces in many things that has made this Nation the great Nation it is.

For the life of me, I can't understand how we can continue to be so uptight about whether a person wears a dress or a pair of pants, as to whether that person can use their God given talents to make whatever constructive contributions they can make to this country.

This country needs the utilization of its best talents, whether they are found in men and/or women.

Mrs. GREEN. Thank you, very much, Mrs. Chisholm for a most interesting and provative statement. There are many other questions, but I will call on Congressman Scherle.

Mr. SCHERLE. No questions, Madam Chairman.

Mrs. GREEN. Thank you very much for coming.

Our next witness is Mr. William H. Brown III, the chairman of the Equal Employment Opportunity Commission.

STATEMENT OF WILLIAM H. BROWN III, CHAIRMAN, EQUAL EMPLOYMENT OPPORTUNITY COMMISSION

Mrs. GREEN. Again, on behalf of the committee, may I express my thanks for your being here this morning.

Mr. BROWN. Thank you very much, Madam Chairman.

Mrs. GREEN. Would you proceed with your statement, please?

Mr. BROWN. Madam Chairman and members of the subcommittee, I am of course pleased to appear before you today to comment on section 805 of H.R. 16098, the Omnibus Postsecondary Education Act of 1970.

Section 805 would amend the Civil Rights Act of 1957 as amended, titles VI and VII of the Civil Rights Act of 1964, and the Fair Labor

Standards Act of 1938 as amended, for the purpose of further assuring equal opportunity for women.

With the exception of title VII of the Civil Rights Act of 1964 which is administered by the Equal Employment Opportunity Commission, the primary responsibility for implementing this proposed legislation would rest with the Department of Health, Education, and Welfare, the Civil Rights Commission and the Department of Labor. Accordingly I shall restrict my comments to the work of EEOC under title VII and a general discussion of the needs of women in our society today.

The Equal Employment Opportunity Commission was established by title VII of the Civil Rights Act of 1964, which prohibits discrimination based on race, color, religion, sex, and national origin in all aspects of employment.

Section 703(a) provides:

It shall be unlawful employment practice for an employer—

(1) to fail or refuse to hire or to discharge any individual or otherwise to discriminate against any individual with respect to his compensation, terms, conditions, or privileges of employment, because of such individual's race, color, religion, sex or national origin; or

(2) to limit, segregate, or classify his employees in any way which would deprive or tend to deprive any individual of employment opportunities or otherwise adversely affect his status as an employee, because of such individual's race, color, religion, sex, or national origin.

The Commission is bipartisan in composition and its members serve 5-year terms on a staggered basis. Commissioners are appointed by the President, with the advice and consent of the Senate, with one designated as chairman.

Title VII authorizes the Commission to make investigations, to compel the attendance of witnesses and the production of documents, and to make determinations as to whether there is reasonable cause to believe an unlawful employment practice has been committed. The analogy to most other regulatory agencies goes no further, however, for title VII contemplates conciliation rather than coercion as the primary mechanism for obtaining compliance with its provisions, and the Commission is not authorized to seek relief either *de novo* in the district courts, or after administrative adjudication, in the courts of appeals. Where conciliation efforts are unsuccessful the Commission may recommend that the Attorney General bring a pattern or practice suit under section 707 of the act, or the aggrieved person may bring his own civil action in the district court.

Not surprisingly this scheme has proven seriously deficient. By placing the burden of obtaining relief on the aggrieved individual, the act tends to operate as a carrot on the end of a stick. Disadvantaged classes of individuals are locked out of the proffered remedy by the very condition that called for its creation, the fact of their being disadvantaged.

I have commented at length on the need for a more efficacious system of enforcement before another subcommittee of this body, and we are still hopeful that Congress will see fit to provide the Commission with the legal tools reasonably necessary to implement its mandate of eliminating employment discrimination.

The problems of women have been of special concern to the Commission since its inception. In 1967, hearings on sex discrimination were held in Washington and since that time detailed guidelines covering a broad range of employment problems confronted by women have been issued.

The Commission, for example, has indicated that it will construe the BFOQ exception of section 703(e) narrowly, and that stereotyped notions of the capabilities of women as a class will not be considered justification for a preference or limitation based on sex. This same attitude has been applied to State "protective legislation," which the Commission declared in August 1969 to be in across the board conflict with title VII, and therefore unacceptable as a defense to an otherwise established unlawful employment practice. The Commission has also decided that differences in optional or compulsory retirement ages based on sex violate title VII, as do separate lines of progression and seniority systems.

These examples are not intended to be an exhaustive treatment of the Commission's position on sex discrimination, which necessarily has been as variegated as the fact situations with which we have been confronted. They do however, indicate an attitude which could hardly be described as either permissive or wavering. Over 12,000 charges received by the commission since its inception have alleged disparate treatment based on sex, and lately the percentage has risen. During the first 10 months of fiscal year 1970, 2,887 charges received were, based on sex with no letup in sight.

These statistics indicate that not only have discriminatory employment practices directed against women not abated, but also that women have become more conscious of their rights under title VII and are starting to assert those rights.

A few observations illustrating the special nature of the problem seem appropriate at this point:

First, discrimination against women is generally practiced in a fashion far more overt, and with much lesser concern for either law or social niceties than is discrimination based on race. A substantial number of Americans—not only men—tend to view the women's rights movement as a frivolous sort of curiosity.

Second, the black women and other female members of minority groups is doubly disadvantaged, and indeed there is substantial evidence to indicate that black women tend to suffer more as women than as blacks. This is of salient importance to any discussion of the problem, for more than half of all blacks and all other racial and ethnic minorities are women.

Third, while pseudoscientific justifications of racist policies directed against black and brown people seem to be of relatively recent origin—nor earlier, certainly, than the 17th century—the subjugation of women has been accepted as both scientifically and morally justified since the dawn of Western civilization. Accordingly not only do many men accept unquestioningly the limited role women are restricted to in our society, but so do many women. Women have been conditioned not only to accept a secondary role but to enjoy it as well.

In the field of higher education, women have long been invited to participate as students, but without the prospect of gaining employment as serious scholars. In their study of the Academic Marketplace,[1]

---

[1] Kaplow and McGee, *The Academic Marketplace*, Anchor Editor (Garden City: 1965).

Theodore Kaplow and Reece J. McGee concluded that prestige and compatability were the primary factors in faculty hiring decisions, but noted that women were generally regarded as being outside the prestige system all together.

The remarks of a senior member of a department with regard to a woman applicant are instructive:

> We had one young woman come down here from one of the Big Ten. She had the MA and was working on her doctoral dissertation and we would have very much liked to have gotten her, but when she saw the Dean, he turned her down. He didn't like the way she was turned out, thought she was too stylishly dressed. We had thought she looked very lovely.*

Thus despite having the requisite paper credentials the female applicant was treated as a potential decoration, a nonuseful object to adorn the premises. This has historically also been true of blacks. Although there is some recent improvement, black scholars have generally been relegated to all black institutions or have not been able to rise to the top of the academic structure when they have been permitted entry into white institutions.

Since title VII does not cover educational institutions, the Commission does not have detailed statistical information documenting the position of women in institutions of higher learning. From the testimony that has been given before this subcommittee, however, it seems clear that little progress has been made in the 12 years since the Kaplow-McGee study, and in view of the widely recognized job squeeze in academia one can reasonably conjecture that the situation has gotten worse.

The time has long since past when we can afford—in either social or economic terms—to subject a large part of our population to the kind of debilitating patronization that has for so long characterized our treatment of women.

I will be happy to answer any questions you might have at this point, and if there is any service the Commission might offer to aid in your deliberations, please do not hesitate to ask.

Mrs. GREEN. Thank you, Mr. Brown.

How many people are there on the Equal Employment Opportunity Commission?

Mr. BROWN. We have five members?

Mrs. GREEN. And you are chairman?

Mr. BROWN. That is correct.

Mrs. GREEN. Of the five, how many are women?

Mr. BROWN. One.

Mrs. GREEN. I understand her term is due to expire.

Mr. BROWN. Her term expires actually today. The indication is that another woman will be appointed.

Mrs. GREEN. How many blacks are there?

Mr. BROWN. We have one black, which is myself, and one presently pending confirmation.

Mrs. GREEN. Across the country in the various offices of the Equal Employment Opportunity Commission, how many women would there be, not as typists, but in policymaking positions?

Mr. BROWN. We have quite a few. Just to give you an example, of the last seven regional attorneys who were appointed three of those were women. In the top positions, and I am talking about——

Mrs. GREEN. How many of them were white, black, and Indian, or

---

*Ibid., p. 107.

whatever?

Mr. BROWN. There was a mixture. I don't believe we have an American Indian who is an attorney, but we have one white woman, and I believe the other two were black.

Mrs. GREEN. And other positions where they would be making policy?

Mr. BROWN. I can give you some very personal indications of my commitment to it.

Mrs. GREEN. I am not questioning your commitment Mr. Brown. I don't question that. But may we have the statistics, the facts at this point, please.

Mr. BROWN. Certainly.

My Director of Administration retired, just about 7 months ago, and he was a male, and the responsibilities for all the administrative aspects of the entire commission were his. In his place I have appointed a woman. One of our regional——

Mrs. GREEN. Did the woman get the same salary?

Mr. BROWN. Yes; she did, same grade, same salary. One of the regional directors is also a woman.

Mrs. GREEN. How many regional directors do you have?

Mr. BROWN. Thirteen.

Mrs. GREEN. And one is a woman. She is black.

Out of the attorneys, how many are there altogether?

Mr. BROWN. I believe we have a total of about 22 attorneys.

Mrs. GREEN. How many are women?

Mr. BROWN. Of that total number—well there are more than that with the regional attorneys. With the regional attorneys, there would probably be about 35, and of that number, I would imagine some 12 are women.

Mrs. GREEN. And how many of those are black?

Mr. BROWN. I imagine about four or five. I am just taking a wild guess at it, but I imagine four or five of the 12 are black.

Mrs. GREEN. I don't want my question to infer to you that I am not in favor of black women attorneys but I wonder sometimes if the selection in some of these instances is made on the basis of race, and not sex in order to meet requirements of title VII?

Mr. BROWN. In my case the selection was made not on either of those but on the basis of the best person for the job.

Mrs. GREEN. I have in my files numerous letters and documents which show discrimination in education, in segregated classrooms, the Government has taken the position that the absence of blacks in a classroom is in and of itself evidence of discrimination. They have ruled that in many cases.

When there is an absence of women, whether it be as pages in the Supreme Court of the United States, or in clerks of the Supreme Court or as policy level jobs in civil service—do you think we could reach the same conclusion? Or when, in the Equal Employment Opportunity Commission we find that out of 35 attorneys, as you say, 12 are women.

Since women are over 50 percent of the people in the country, if we followed that criterion, would we be justified in concluding that it is evidence in and of itself of discrimination?

Mr. BROWN. I would think that under the *Hayes* case,[1] which came

[1] *U.S.* v. *Hayes International Corp.*, 415 F. 2d 1038 (1969).

down, the mere absence of women, like the mere absence of blacks or Mexican-Americans, would raise an inference of discrimination. There is no question about that. Being perfectly candid with you, and I don't think there is anyone who has a greater commitment to the enforcement of the entire act, and this includes, of course, the sex portion of our act, than I do, I would think that part of the problem is that the number of women coming through the professional schools is relatively small. This is understandable, for women have been discouraged from going to the professional schools. There is a tremendous demand for doctors and lawyers and engineers, and for some reason many of the professional schools still discourage women from attending those schools.

Mrs. GREEN. I understand the rationale you are giving, but may I translate it?

Isn't that exactly the case with blacks? The number of blacks who have graduated from the professional schools during the years has been smaller, but it has not been given us as an excuse for not hiring blacks.

Mr. BROWN. I can be honest with you. It has given us an excuse.

Mrs. GREEN. But it is not accepted by the Government.

Mr. BROWN. No; I would not accept that with regard to women either. In Houston we had hearings, and I asked specifically of corporate officers, "Is there any job in your outfit that a woman could not hold?" And many of the captains in industry in Houston admitted that there were very few jobs that they could not hold. We are talking now not just about the secretarial positions, but the whole petrochemical industry, and the industry has been potentially looked upon as having all male jobs. If they say there is no job women cannot hold, there is no question in my mind that the reason women are not in them is that the companies are not recruiting them.

We have asked them this. They have indicated that when they send recruiters out, they don't many times bother to go to women's schools. They don't have a woman on the recruiting team, which is a help if you are trying to get the point across that you are looking for minorities or women.

Mrs. GREEN. Has the Equal Employment Opportunities Commission looked at the apprenticeship program in the United States? We have heard testimony that only 1 percent of the registered apprentices are women, and that out of 370 occupations represented, women were being trained in only 47.

Mr. BROWN. We have not gone into that specifically. That comes more under the aegis of the Department of Labor. Our Commission, as you know, reacts primarily to complaints being filed with us. At the same time, of course, we ourselves can file Commissioner's charges, and I might just point out to you that very recently, as a matter of fact last week, I filed charges against seven companies and two labor unions alleging discrimination because of sex, and we continue this in any area that we find people are not being properly represented in the work force, be they women or Mexican Americans, or blacks or any other minorities.

Mrs. GREEN. You testified before another subcommittee. Which was that?

Mr. BROWN. I have testified before the House and Senate subcommittees having jurisdiction over the enforcement legislation presently pending before the Congress. They are subcommittees of the Labor Committees of both Houses.

Mrs. GREEN. When did you testify, and I wonder also if we might have copies of that testimony? Did you discuss discrimination against women as well as against minorities?

Mr. BROWN. That testimony was geared to enforcement powers rather than discrimination.

Mrs. GREEN. What day was that?

Mr. BROWN. This was last year, before the Senate.

The House would have been sometime in December.

Mrs. GREEN. Would you give Mr. Hogan the dates, so that we can get copies of the testimony in both cases?

Mr. BROWN. Yes, I will do that.

Mrs. GREEN. On page 4 of your testimony, you said that over 12,000 charges received by the Commission have alleged discrimination because of sex, and that the percentage has risen.

On page 3, you say that where conciliation efforts are unsuccessful, the commission may recommend that the Attorney General bring a pattern or practice suit under section 707 of the act, and/or the aggrieved person may bring his own.

Of all of the 12,000 charges that have been placed before the EOC, how many times have you recommended to the Attorney General action as stated on that page?

Mr. BROWN. In the initial days of the Commission, and this goes back prior to the time I have been with the Commission, quite a number of cases were referred to the Attorney General based on sex, with a recommendation from our Commission that suits be instituted. It was never done, and this practice continued up until very recently.

Since I have been here as chairman, I have had a number of discussions with the Justice Department. As a matter of fact, there are two cases that have been accepted by the Justice Department for filing of suits. One is in Ohio. I can't of course, in an open hearing give you the names of the persons prior to the time the suit is actually filed, but I would be very happy to disclose that to you at some other time.

Mrs. GREEN. Do you know the number—how many of the 12,000 charges have been recommended to the Attorney General for action?

Mr. BROWN. I really don't know.

Mrs. GREEN. Would you get the figures and the total number of charges based on race discrimination and sex discrimination and how many in each of those categories have been referred to the Justice Department with an actual recommendation that the Attorney General bring a suit?

Mr. BROWN. I can do that.

(The document referred to follows:)

STATISTICS ON RACE, AND SEX DISCRIMINATION

In the early days of referral, files selected by the General Counsel as meriting recommendation for suit were transmitted individually, after approval by the Commission, to the Department of Justice by formal letter or memorandum. This unilateral arrangement obviously presented some problems since in the final analysis, under Section 707, the discretion to determine the existence of a pattern or practice is one vested in the Attorney General. Moreover, since often the subject of a referral was also the subject of other pending charges before the Commission, and since Commission negotiation as to those charges was undesirable in the face of any pending litigation, the action or inaction of the Attorney

General would have the effect either of suspending possible administrative relief or alternatively being exposed to possible prejudice or mootness.

In 1968, therefore, a new inter-agency system was put into operation with the formal approval of the Commission and the tacit approval of Justice. Under the new system all files in which conciliation has failed are reviewed by the Commission's General Counsel in light of the criteria suggested above. Analysis sheets are prepared briefly indicating facts, issues, and recommendations for and against referral. Cases identified as potential vehicles for 707 action are discussed thereafter jointly at the staff level by attorneys from both agencies. The Justice Department indicates the files in which it is interested and such files are then transmitted—together with exhaustive information as to the number and location of charges against any particular respondent, copies of the other charges and files where relevant or desired, complete employment statistics and any current facts available. Commissioners, charging parties, respondents and Commission Regional Offices are advised as to the transmittal. Regional Offices are advised as to whether negotiations with a respondent at any given location are to be suspended or continued. Periodic reports as to the status of action or litigation are supplied by Justice and relayed to the Regional Offices. Where files are returned to the Commission without action or when litigation is concluded, Commission negotiations are reactivated where necessary.

Since inauguration of this system, EEOC has transmitted files on 152 cases in which the Department has indicated interest to the Attorney General. It is impossible, partially due to the mix of issues involved, to identify a number of cases in which sex was the sole issue. We are happy to say, however, that on July 20, 1970, the Attorney General filed the first pattern or practice case based on sex discrimination in the Department's history. The case is an EEOC referral, and should be a milestone in Title VII litigation.

Mr. BROWN. Let me give you more background information that might be helpful to the committee. What we do is screen all the cases ourselves and refer the strongest ones to Justice. In the past, and this is 3 or 4 years ago, those cases would languish over at Justice, and many times we would get them back 2 or 3 years later with nothing being done.

We have changed our procedures now. What we do is discuss our cases with the Justice Department. The person responsible for this is a woman, Mrs. Julia Cooper, one of the attorneys in our general counsel staff. She now screens them. She discusses the cases with the Justice Department, and then Justice makes their own decision as to which cases they are willing to accept.

This was done for a number of reasons. Most importantly it was done to avoid having the cases sit over there having nothing done. Because when they are in Justice, we can take no further action as far as the case is concerned.

Mrs. GREEN. Then my information is correct that up to this point that the Justice Department has never instituted a single case, though many have been sent over?

Mr. BROWN. I believe that would be correct.

Mrs. GREEN. With respect to sex discrimination, let me ask you, to see if your thinking compares with mine. When the Civil Rights Act was passed, in title VII, it prohibited any employment practice which discriminates on the basis of sex, color, creed or national origin.

Congress has not indicated any preference in enforcement of these.

Mr. BROWN. That is correct.

Mrs. GREEN. And preference for enforcement in any one area would in and of itself be a discrimination against the others.

Mr. BROWN. I believe so. I think enforcement is needed for the entire act.

Mrs. GREEN. And in fact, any preference for enforcement in one area would have to be made by an administrative judgment, rather than the congressional intent, would it not?

Mr. BROWN. Well, enforcement, of course, can only be provided for, and I am talking about our act again, can only be provided for by Congress, since the Congress saw fit not to give us enforcement powers initially.

Mrs. GREEN. I am talking about the Justice Department on enforcement.

Mr. BROWN. Well, as far as the enforcement powers of the Justice Department, they have the right to institute any actions as they deem appropriate and I might say in defense of Justice, and they don't need me to defend them, but they, like us, are very limited in the number of people they have working on this.

Mrs. GREEN. How many cases are there on the basis of race discrimination?

Mr. BROWN. I don't have the exact figures, over the years, I imagine more than 50 cases have been instituted.

Mrs. GREEN. Based on race discrimination?

Mr. BROWN. That would be race and everything else. There may be national origin in there.

Mrs. GREEN. But not a single one on sex discrimination?

Mr. BROWN. Not to my knowledge.

Mrs. GREEN. It seems to me that their preference for pursuing cases involving race or national origin can't be interpreted as anything except discrimination on the part of the Justice Department.

Mr. BROWN. Some of the cases have been a combination. No case has been instituted solely on the basis of sex, but there are combinations where there was discrimination against black women, for example.

Mrs. GREEN. We are inviting the Justice Department to testify.

Mr. BROWN. You had indicated something about the Supreme Court. I might indicate to you that the Supreme Court very recently did grant certiorari in the case of *Phillips* v. *Martin Marietta*, and it is a sex case.

Mrs. GREEN. But my understanding of this case is that Justice Department itself did nothing about it. You are right, they have asked the Supreme Court to take it.

Mr. BROWN. Yes; and the Supreme Court has granted certiorari on that.

Mrs. GREEN. Has the EEOC asked for authority to take its own cases into court?

Mr. BROWN. Yes; we have.

As a matter of fact, that is the administration's proposal, the one which I have supported.

Mrs. GREEN. What has the answer been?

Mr. BROWN. The answer from the Congress is that it is still bottled up in committee. Both have been introduced, and they are both pending in committee, both on the House side and the Senate side.

Mrs. GREEN. Mr. Hogan, do you have questions?

Mr. HOGAN. Chairman Brown, this subcommittee has received testimony several times in the course of these hearings on discrimination against women, that there is a great need for information collection, for data collection, and that, for example, many Government agencies keep statistics on employment that would allow some inferences about their conformance to the antidiscrimination provisions of the law in regard to race, but not in regard to sex.

Does this information-gathering problem seem to be a real one to you? Do you have any recommendations about how to solve it? Does your agency have any program in this regard?

Mr. BROWN. Our agency does have a program. We have a number of forms: the EEO-1, which goes out to about 225,000 employers; the EEO-2 and 3, which deal with the unions and the apprenticeship training program. We have looked at those forms to try to streamline them to get more information.

On the EEO-1 form there is a place for the employer to indicate the number of women and the various categories in which these women are found. I would say the pattern we have found as far as minorities are concerned are related to the patterns as far as women are concerned. That is, as you go up the ladder in any particular company, the number of women and the number of minorities starts dropping off substantially. Most women are found in the secretarial-clerical classifications. Few are found in the semiskilled or skilled blue-collar positions, or in the white-collar positions.

The same is also true of minorities. We have taken steps to make corrections, even without enforcement powers. We did bring quite a number of commissioners' charges against a large number of companies and unions in Houston, and these are presently being investigated. We have also taken steps to identify the various classes which would be represented, so that in the event we are unable to successfully conciliate those cases, the charging parties, that is, the representatives of the class of charging parties, would have the opportunity of taking those cases into court themselves.

Mr. HOGAN. In that connection, what is the record of women who actually take the complaints into court? What has been their record of success? Is that an adequate remedy?

Mr. BROWN. Certainly it is not an adequate remedy, because I don't think we should put the burden on the person being discriminated against. It seems to me the burden of going into court ought to be on the Government. It should be our Commission's responsibility to go into court and get everything title VII says they are entitled to. It is difficult to say what percentage of the cases get into court which involve women. I can say this: We are successful in conciliating a little bit less than 50 percent of all our cases, after we have found reasonable cause. Of that amount, less than 10 percent go into any court. What percentage of that 10 percent of the 50 percent represent women and what percent represents either Mexican-Americans or blacks or some other minority, I really can't say.

Mr. HOGAN. I think the feeling of the members of the subcommittee is that it places a special burden on employees to expect them to pursue a remedy in court against their employer. Women are not in a position to be very aggressive about pursuit of their rights on their own.

Would that be your view?

Mr. BROWN. With regard to the last point, recently, I have seen a substantial change, and our indications are that women are now starting to recognize that they do have these rights, and have started to assert these rights. I think it is a healthy sign. As I look at our statistics, the number of complaints that have been coming into our Commission during the past 10 months of fiscal year 1970 which are based upon discrimination because of sex has increased 12 percent over that of 1969. Presently some 25 percent, approximately, of complaints coming into the Commission are complaints based on sex.

Mr. HOGAN. The other 75 are essentially race?

Mr. BROWN. About 60 or 65 percent are race, and the others would fall into the religious category, or one of the other categories we cover under our act.

Mrs. GREEN. What is the responsibility of the Equal Employment Opportunity Commission with regard to advertisements for help wanted in the papers?

Mr. BROWN. We have control under our act over the employer who does the advertising. Of course, we have no control over the newspapers. As you know, there is now pending a newspaper suit against the Commission. We have filed Commissioner's charges whenever we find that a large employer has violated the guidelines set down by our Commission, and advertises according to sex. He may advertise just for a male, and we have filed charges against him on our own, because many times other people don't bring this to our attention, or see fit not to file a charge.

Mrs. GREEN. In your regional offices do you monitor newspaper ads?

Mr. BROWN. Yes, we do.

Mrs. GREEN. Would you provide for the committee the guidelines which you have for discrimination, including those for newspaper ads, and help wanted columns?

Mr. BROWN. Certainly.

(The document referred to follows:)

TITLE 29—CHAPTER XIV

PART 1604—GUIDELINES ON DISCRIMINATION BECAUSE OF SEX

1604.1 Sex as bona fide occupational qualification.
1604.2 Separate lines of progression and seniority systems.
1604.3 Discrimination against married women.
1604.4 Job opportunities advertising.
1604.5 Employment agencies.
1604.6 Pre-employment inquiries as to sex.
1604.7 Relationship of Title VII to the Equal Pay Act.
1604.31 Pension and retirement plans.

AUTHORITY: The provisions of this Part 1604 are issued pursuant to Sec. 713(b), 78 Stat. 265; 42 U.S.C. 2000e–12.

SOURCE: The provisions of this Part 1604 appear at 30 F.R. 14927, Dec. 2, 1965, unless otherwise noted.

§ 1604.1 Sex as a bona fide occupational qualification.

(a) The Commission believes that the bona fide occupational qualification exception as to sex should be interpreted narrowly. Labels—"Men's jobs" and "Women's jobs"—tend to deny employment opportunities unnecessarily to one sex or the other.

(1) The Commission will find that the following situations do not warrant the application of the bona fide occupational qualification exception:

(i) The refusal to hire a woman because of her sex, based on assumptions of the comparative employment characteristics of women in general. For example, the assumption that the turnover rate among women is higher than among men.

(ii) The refusal to hire an individual based on stereotyped characterizations of the sexes. Such stereotypes include, for example, that men are less capable of assembling intricate equipment; that women are less capable of aggressive salesmanship. The principle of non-discrimination requires that individuals be considered on the basis of individual capacities and not on the basis of any characteristics generally attributed to the group.

(iii) The refusal to hire an individual because of the preferences of co-workers, the employer, clients or customers except as covered specifically in subparagraph (2) of this paragraph.

(iv) The fact that the employer may have to provide separate facilities for a person of the opposite sex will not justify discrimination under the bona fide occupational qualification exception, unless the expense would be clearly unreasonable.

(2) Where it is necessary for the purpose of authenticity or genuineness, the Commission will consider sex to be a bona fide occupational qualification, e.g., an actor or actress.

(b)(1) Many States have enacted laws or promulgated administrative regulations with respect to the employment of females. Among these laws are those which prohibit or limit the employment of females, e.g., the employment of females in certain occupations, in jobs requiring the lifting or carrying of weights exceeding certain prescribed limits, during certain hours of the night, or for more than a specified number of hours per day or per week.

(2) The Commission believes that such State laws and regulations, although originally promulgated for the purpose of protecting females, have ceased to be relevant to our technology or to the expanding role of the female worker in our economy. The Commission has found that such laws and regulations do not take into account the capacities, preferences, and abilities of individual females and tend to discriminate rather than protect. Accordingly, the Commission has concluded that such laws and regulations conflict with Title VII of the Civil Rights Act of 1964 and will not be considered a defense to an otherwise established unlawful employment practice or as a basis for the application of the bona fide occupational qualification exception.

[30 F.R. 14927, Dec. 2, 1965, as amended at 34 F.R. 13368, Aug. 19, 1969]

§ 1604.2 Separate lines of progression and seniority systems.

(a) It is an unlawful employment practice to classify a job as "male" or "female" or to maintain separate lines of progression or separate seniority lists based on sex where this would adversely affect any employee unless sex is a bona fide occupational qualification for that job. Accordingly, employment practices are unlawful which arbitrarily classify jobs so that:

(1) A female is prohibited from applying for a job labeled "male," or for a job in a "male" line of progression; and vice versa.

(2) A male scheduled for layoff is prohibited from displacing a less senior female on a "female" seniority list; and vice versa.

(b) A seniority system or line of progression which distinguishes between "light" and "heavy" jobs constitutes an unlawful employment practice if it operates as a disguised form of classification by sex, or creates unreasonable obstacles to the advancement by members of either sex into jobs which members of that sex would reasonably be expected to perform.

§ 1604.3 Discrimination against married women.

(a) The Commission has determined that an employer's rule which forbids or restricts the employment of married women and which is not applicable to married men is a discrimination based on sex prohibited by Title VII of the Civil Rights Act. It does not seem to us relevant that the rule is not directed against all females, but only against married females, for so long as sex is a factor in the application of the rule, such application involves a discrimination based on sex.

(b) It may be that under certain circumstances, such a rule could be justified within the meaning of Section 703 (e)(1) of Title VII. We express no opinion on this question at this time except to point out that sex as a bona fide occupational qualification must be justified in terms of the pecular requirements of the particular job and not on the basis of a general principle such as the desirability of spreading work.

§ 1604.4 Job opportunities advertising.

It is a violation of Title VII for a help-wanted advertisement to indicate a preference, limitation, specification, or discrimination based on sex unless sex is a bona fide occupational qualification for the particular job involved. The placement of an advertisement in columns classified by publishers on the basis of sex, such as columns headed "Male" or Female," will be considered an expression of a preference, limitation, specification, or discrimination based on sex.

[33 F.R. 11539, Aug. 14, 1968]

§ 1604.5 Employment agencies.

(a) Section 703(b) of the Civil Rights Act specifically states that it shall be unlawful for an employment agency to discriminate against any individual because of sex. The Commission has determined that private employment agencies which deal exclusively with one sex are engaged in an unlawful employment practice, except to the extent that such agencies limit their services to furnishing employees for particular jobs for which sex is a bona fide occupational qualification.

(b) An employment agency that receives a job order containing an unlawful sex specification will share responsibility with the employer placing the job order if the agency fills the order knowing that the sex specification is not based upon a bona fide occupational qualification. However, an employment agency will not be deemed to be in violation of the law, regardless of the determination as to the employer, if the agency does not have reason to believe that the employer's claim of bona fide occupations qualification is without substance and the agency makes and maintains a written record available to the Commission of each such job order. Such record shall include the name of the employer, the description of the job and the basis for the employer's claim of bona fide occupational qualification.

(c) It is the responsibility of employment agencies to keep informed of opinions and decisions of the Commission on sex discrimination.

§ 1604.6   Pre-employment inquiries as to sex.

A pre-employment inquiry may ask "Male _____, Female _____"; or "Mr. Mrs., Miss," provided that the inquiry is made in good faith for a non-discriminatory purpose. Any pre-employment inquiry in connection with prospective employment which expresses directly or indirectly any limitation, specification or discrimination as to sex shall be unlawful unless based upon a bona fide occupational qualification.

§ 1604.7   Relationship of Title VII to the Equal Pay Act.

(a) Title VII requires that its provisions be harmonized with the Equal Pay Act (section 6(d) of the Fair Labor Standards Act of 1938, 29 U.S.C. 206(d)) in order to avoid conflicting interpretations or requirements with respect to situations to which both statutes are applicable. Accordingly, the Commission interprets section 703(h) to mean that the standards of "equal pay for equal work" set forth in the Equal Pay Act for determining what is unlawful discrimination in compensation are applicable to Title VII. However, it is the judgment of the Commission that the employee coverage of the prohibition against discrimination in compensation because of sex is co-extensive with that of the other prohibitions in section 703, and is not limited by section 703(h) to those employees covered by the Fair Labor Standards Act.

(b) Accordingly, the Commission will make applicable to equal pay complaints filed under Title VII the relevant interpretation of the Administrator, Wage and Hour Division, Department of Labor. These interpretations are found in 29 Code of Federal Regulations, Part 800.119–800.163. Relevant opinions of the Administrator interpreting "the equal pay for equal work standard" will also be adopted by the Commission.

(c) The Commission will consult with the Administrator before issuing an opinion on any matter covered by both Title VII and the Equal Pay Act.

§ 1604.31   Pension and retirement plans.

(a) A difference in optional or compulsory retirement ages based on sex violates Title VII.

(b) Other differences based on sex, such as differences in benefits for survivors, will be decided by the Commission by the issuance of Commission decisions in cases raising such issues.

[33 F.R. 3344, Feb. 24, 1968]

Mrs. GREEN. What would be your attitude if newspapers advertised jobs for blacks only, or whites only, or if prospective employers so advertised?

Mr. BROWN. We would take the same position. It would be basically against the person who places the ad as opposed to the newspaper itself. We have jurisdiction over the newspaper if the newspaper itself discriminates against women or minorities, but we would have no jurisdiction otherwise.

Mrs. GREEN. What is your remedy? What do you do?

Mr. BROWN. What we would do is to go against the person placing the ad.

Mrs. GREEN. What do you do?

Mr. BROWN. Most times we file a commissioner's charge and we would then investigate it. If we found there was a violation, then we would attempt to conciliate the matter. Failing conciliation, any person who is a part of the class could bring an action in court, or the matter could be referred to the Justice Department.

Mrs. GREEN. Have you referred any to the Justice Department?

Mr. BROWN. We usually have not, Madam Chairman. The reason for it is that the Justice Department has a very limited staff, and I think the feeling of most of my predecessors, and I share this feeling, that is, we tend to concentrate in those areas where we can do the most good, and we have tried not to waste the time of the Justice Department in handling just a single individual's case. We can get much more benefit if the Justice Department handles a case, as has happened in some of the private cases, a class of some 400 or 500 women have been affected by a particular action of the employer. This is trying to get them upgraded, or more pay.

It is amazing how many times these things happen in trying to make the distinction between male and female. This is especially true in the newspaper ads. You will find in one column the newspaper ad will carry an advertisement for a bookkeeper, and this will be under the "Help wanted female," and the salary may be $100 a week. In another column you find a heading in the "Help wanted male, accountant," and the salary may be $125 or $130 a week. When you look into the matter what they are doing is exactly the same, but, unfortunately, we can't do anything to the newspaper at this point.

Mrs. GREEN. You do not make any investigation until a charge is made?

Mr. BROWN. We have to make investigation only pursuant to a charge, either by a commissioner or by a charging party filing with us.

Mrs. GREEN. Among the 12,000 charges that have been brought charging discrimination against women——

Mr. BROWN. Our law very specifically exempts our jurisdiction from Federal, State, or local governments.

Mrs. GREEN. So you have never gotten into this?

Mr. BROWN. No; we have not.

Mrs. GREEN. Would you recommend that title VII be changed so that educational institutions, for instance, be eliminated?

Mr. BROWN. Yes; I think the change should be made as far as educational institutions. The ironic thing is that we do have jurisdiction over the education institutions if it applies to any one other than the professional staff. In other words, if you have janitors there who are being discriminated against, or cafeteria workers, we have jurisdiction to adjudicate that complaint.

It seems inconceivable to me to say that while you have jurisdiction over the working people that you should not also have jurisdiction over the people on the professional side, the professors, assistant professors, and instructors.

Mrs. GREEN. Thank you very much, Mr. Brown. Would you provide for the committee the precise figures in terms of the number of lawyer positions and policymaking positions in EEOC, and the number held by women and how many of those are black?

Mr. BROWN. Certainly.

The Commission currently employs three females (two black and one white) in non-attorney positions at or above the GS–15 level. They are the Director, Washington, Regional Office; Director of Administration; and Director of Personnel.

Eight female attorneys are employed by the Commission (three black and five white) including three Regional Attorneys (Los Angeles, Kansas City, and Memphis).

Mrs. GREEN. Our next witness before the committee is Dr. Muirhead from the Office of Education.

Dr. Muirhead, we are delighted to have you back. I hope you are representing the views of the Secretary this morning.

STATEMENT OF PETER MUIRHEAD, DEPUTY ASSISTANT SECRETARY, ASSOCIATE COMMISSIONER FOR HIGHER EDUCATION, OFFICE OF EDUCATION, HEW; ACCOMPANIED BY OWEN KIELY, DIRECTOR, CONTRACT COMPLIANCE DIVISION, OFFICE FOR CIVIL RIGHTS, HEW, AND PRESTON M. ROYSTER, EQUAL EMPLOYMENT OPPORTUNITIES OFFICER, HEW

Dr. MUIRHEAD. I would like to represent them to you.

Mrs. GREEN. Does your entire statement represent the views of the Secretary?

Dr. MUIRHEAD. The whole statement represents the views of the Secretary.

I am pleased to have with me Mr. Preston Royster and Mr. Owen Kiely, who is Director of the Contract Compliance Division.

Mrs. GREEN. I didn't get the first name.

Dr. MUIRHEAD. Preston Royster.

Mrs. GREEN. R-o-y-s-t-e-r?

Dr. MUIRHEAD. Yes.

Mrs. GREEN. And K-i-e-l-y?

Mr. KIELY. Yes.

Dr. MUIRHEAD. Madam Chairman, I thank you for this opportunity to appear before you and talk about the status of women in education. I would like to make some brief observations about inequality of opportunity for women in education, describe our present efforts to improve the situation with the means now available, and comment on section 805 as it would affect the field of education.

First, I should say that it is clear to me, as to the witnesses the subcommittee has previously heard, that the record of educational institutions—particularly higher education—in affording to women equal opportunity, equal status, equal pay has been discouragingly poor. The failure of educational institutions to offer equal opportunity to women seems particularly poignant, since we look to education as the master key to nearly all doors of opportunity.

The subcommittee has already heard extensive testimony about inequities based on sex in institutions of education. Although data on women in education is considerably short of being comprehensive and definitive, it is nevertheless abundant enough to make it apparent that women have not achieved equal opportunity in education—either as students or teachers in postsecondary education or as administrators at all levels.

Throughout the levels of higher education, women seem to enter with a background of higher achievement than men, suggesting a tendency to require higher standards of women for admissions. According to the ACE's—the American Council on Education—annual survey of college freshmen, for example, women enter college with slightly better records of high school achievement.

We know that many colleges admit fixed proportions of men and women each year, resulting in a freshman class with fewer women meeting higher standards than it would contain if women were admitted on the same basis as men. At Cornell University, for example, the ratio of men and to women remains 3 to 1 from year to year; at Harvard/Radcliffe it is 4 to 1. The University of North Carolina at Chapel Hill's fall 1969 "Profile of the Freshman Class" states, "admission of women on the freshmen level will be restricted to those who are especially well qualified." They admitted 3,231 men, or about half the male applicants, and 747 women, about one-fourth the female applicants. Chapel Hill is a State-supported institution.

A 1965 OE sampling of degree-credit graduate students in the arts and sciences found that women had on the average better undergraduate achievement records. Sixty-eight percent of the women had undergraduate grade point averages B or better while only 54 percent of the men had B or better averages.

Women are present in smaller and smaller proportions as one goes up the ladder of academic degrees. In 1968, women were 50.4 percent of high school graduates, 43.4 percent of B.A. recipients, 35.8 percent of those receiving master's degrees, 4.6 percent of those receiving first professional degrees, and 12.6 percent of those receiving doctorates.

Evidently, this pattern of dropping percentages of women as the degree scale goes up results from a complex mix of factors. Both the reality and fear of higher admissions standards certainly play a part.

Women are generally encouraged to think of themselves as potential wives and mothers, and discouraged from thinking of themselves as potential professionals. Professors, counselors, and parents often discourage women from taking postgraduate training, except in "women's fields". They may argue that it is too hard for a woman to get a job in the professions, that she'll only get married and stop working anyway, and so on.

In elementary and secondary education, although a large majority of teachers for example, are female—67.6 percent—only 22 percent of the elementary school principals are women and 4 percent of the high school principals are female.

In a recent National Education Association study, it has been reported that only two women were found among 13,000 school superintendents.

In higher education, women are a small minority of the teaching faculty (about 18 percent) and they tend to remain in the lower faculty ranks. A 1966 NEA study found that 18.4 percent of the full-time faculty in degree-granting institutions were women. Women comprised 32.5 percent of instructors, 19.4 percent of assistant professors, 15.1 percent of associate professors, and 8.7 percent of full professors. Although I know of no national statistics showing numbers of women in higher education administration, data on individual institutions suggest that the percentage may be quite low nationally. For example, a survey of 21 New England universities shows that in top administrative positions, the University of Massachusetts, a public institution, at Amherst had 10 women and 140 men; Boston University had seven women and 107 men, and University of Rhode Island had 86 women and 169 men.

At all faculty ranks, women are paid less than their male colleagues, and the differentials increase as rank and salary get higher. According to an NEA study, the median annual salary for female faculty members was $7,732, 16.6 percent lower than that of men, which was recorded at $9,275. This median salary for women as instructors was 94 percent of that of male instructors; female assistant professors earned 93.2 percent as much as their male counterparts; female associate professors earned 92.6 percent as much as males, and female full professors earned only 91.2 percent as much as male full professors.

Women are more likely than men to teach lower level courses and students. The Office of Education's 1963 study on teaching faculty found that while a majority, 53 percent, of the women taught freshmen and sophomores, only 39 percent of the men did. Only 7 percent of the women were assigned primarily to graduate teaching, while 21 percent of the men were. This is not to imply we see anything wrong with the teaching at the lower levels. On the contrary, higher education would benefit from a standard of value that would give higher priority and status to lower level undergraduate teaching. The statistics simply note that by present standards of value among college faculty, women rate much lower than men.

Women sometimes wait longer for promotions than men. Bayer and Astin's 1968 study on "Sex Differences in Academic Rank and Salary Among Science Doctorates in Teaching" indicates that women teaching in the social sciences tend to be promoted less rapidly than men.

Jo Freeman's report on the University of Chicago, "Women on the Social Science Faculty since 1892," demonstrates that few women in the social science faculty stayed more than one appointment, 3 years, and that those who stayed remained in untenured positions abnormally long.

I have already dealt with some of the contributing factors to inequities such as these, such as lower expectations, institutional practices, lack of day care facilities, and so on. But the inequities are so pervasive that direct discrimination must be considered as paying a share, particularly in salaries, hiring, and promotions, especially to tenured positions. For example, despite the present belief that in many academic fields, there are no women qualified to teach, close investigations have discovered that this is often an untenable excuse.

A recent report on Columbia University practices, for example, found that although the percent of doctorates awarded to women rose from 13 to 24 percent from 1957 to 1968, the percent of women in tenured positions at the graduate facilities have remained about constant—at slightly over 2 percent. A report on the University of Wisconsin found the same consistent pattern; even departments giving over 25 percent of their Ph. D.'s to women (ranging from 36 percent in speech to 58 percent in German), hired much lower percentages (from 9 percent to 24.4 percent) of women as faculty. It cannot be argued that many women holding Ph. D.'s stop working; a 1966 OEO study found that 85 percent of women receiving doctorates between 1958 and 1963 were working full time.

Mrs. GREEN. If I could interrupt there, I think the most recent statistics available show that 91 percent of women holding doctorates are working. Could you check this, please?

Dr. MUIRHEAD. I would like to turn here from the subject of inequality in higher education acceptance and employment practices to give you a sketch of how women fare in certain Office of Education programs, since I understand there has been some discussion about that in the committee.

According to our data, student assistance funds seem to go to women in proportions approximately equal to those in which women attend college. Forty-three and three-tenths percent of all students receiving national defense student loans are female; about 43 percent of college undergraduates are women. Forty-nine percent of the students benefiting from the college work-study program are women; we estimate that women are 40.2 percent of those receiving equal opportuntiy grants. Thirty-six and five-tenths percent of those participating in the guaranteed loan program are female.

Mrs. GREEN. Could I interrupt you there, Dr. Muirhead?

Would you give these same figures, and do you have them with you, for blacks and whites under the NDEA? I know that you have said 43 percent of the NDEA student loans go to women. I take it that you give as the rationale for it, that 43 percent of the college undergraduates are women. What percent of the NDEA loans go to blacks, and what percentage of the undergraduates are blacks? What percentage of the EOG goes to blacks, and what percent of the undergraduates are black?

Also, what percent are in the work study program, and in Upward Bound. The last figures I saw indicated that 57 percent, or 58 percent of the Upward Bound students were blacks.

What I am really saying is that if that is a justification for the percentage of loans, I wonder how it is justified?

Dr. MUIRHEAD. I do not have the figures with me, but I would report to you that the percentage of blacks receiving support under the student assistance programs and the Upward Bound program is far in excess of the percentage of blacks enrolled as undergraduates.

Mrs. GREEN. I assume that need is the factor, but I wonder if there isn't a need among women, also.

Dr. MUIRHEAD. Women seem to get support about under the same terms as men do on the student aid programs, and they presumably have the same amount of need as among men.

Mrs. GREEN. But in treating race, it is entirely different. Have you a different approach to it in the Office of Education?

Dr. MUIRHEAD. In treating race, we have to consider a much greater factor of need among blacks than among women, per se.

Mrs. GREEN. Can you document that?

Dr. MUIRHEAD. Oh, I am quite sure we can document that in terms of financial need among blacks and compared to other than blacks.

Mrs. GREEN. But if you take women versus men, can you document it that the women do not need it more?

Dr. MUIRHEAD. I am not at all sure that I can document that. My premise here would be that the need among women is probably equal to the need among men, but I cannot document it any further than that.

Going on, the NDEA title IV fellowship program for graduate students is relatively equitable, with 28 percent of the awards given to women, who are 33 percent of the graduate student population. The proportion of women awarded NDEA title IV fellowships has been improving from a low of 13 percent in 1959–60. Twenty-nine and three-tenths percent of the graduate academic awards granted under NDEA title VI went to women last year; this has risen from 18 percent in 1960, and I think it has grown with the rising percent of enrollment of women in graduate school.

In the Teacher Corps' first group of volunteers 1966–67 half were women. By last year this had dropped to 44 percent. We attribute this to the proliferation of occupational deferments from the draft for teaching, now halted, and efforts to recruit males to the teaching profession, reflecting a growing effort to have male role models in the classroom.

Mrs. GREEN. Dr. Muirhead, we have two other witnesses. Could I ask you because of time, if you could summarize here, and then your entire statement will be made part of the record.

Dr. MUIRHEAD. By all means.

I would summarize this part by saying that although we don"t have as good statistics as we would like to have, that women in general do fairly well under the Office of Education programs compared to men.

The rest of my testimony concerns the existing provisions with regard to sex discrimination in employment in institutions of higher education and the Presidential Executive Order 11246, as amended. We are now moving to carry out the provisions of the amended Executive order, which would see to it that compliance included sex in employment.

Mrs. GREEN. You are moving to do it. May I ask what has been done, so far?

Dr. MUIRHEAD. We have been assigned responsibility as the Federal Compliance Agency for all universities and colleges. During fiscal 1969, when the assignment was made to us, three individual complaints of sex discrimination in employment were received and investigated by our Contract Compliance Division. Two were resolved to findings in favor of the complaint, and satisfactory adjustments, including back pay, were obtained. The third was found to be without merit.

We are now receiving a substantial number of complaints. As a matter of fact, we have received 85 allegations against over 100 higher education institutions, and several against professional organizations relating to education.

We are now gearing up to undertake compliance reviews in the area of sex discrimination.

As you know, as recently as June 9 the Labor Department issued guidelines on the implementation of this Executive order.

Mrs. GREEN. But the original amended Executive order was in 1967, wasn't it?

Dr. MUIRHEAD. Yes.

Mrs. GREEN. Has any progress been made at all since 1967?

You cite three cases.

Dr. MUIRHEAD. That is the extent of it, because a good deal of our contract compliance work has been directed at the original intent of the Executive order before it was amended. We are moving to carry out our new responsibility now. I should say that contract compliance reviews on sex discrimination are currently underway at Harvard University, the University of Maryland, George Washington University, and Manhattan Community College of the New York City college system.

Mrs. GREEN. Have you sent out written instructions to your compliance officers?

Dr. MUIRHEAD. I am quite sure we have. Let me ask Mr. Keily if he could help us with that.

Mr. KIELY. Yes; we have instructed our field staff that each compliance review conducted at a contractor facility shall include an analysis of the employment patterns and practices relating to sex.

Mrs. GREEN. Would you supply for the record a copy of your written instructions to your compliance officers?

Mr. KIELY. Yes.

(The documents referred to follows:)

JUNE 16, 1970.

Re OFCC Sex Discrimination Guidelines.
To: Robert C. Creech, EEO Staff Chief, SSA.

Attached are copies of the OFCC Sex Discrimination Guidelines. You will note that they become effective on June 9, 1970. All reviews from that time should include evaluations of compliance with the guidelines and affirmative action plans include commitments to overcome deficiencies in the area of utilization of women.

ROY McKINNEY,
*Deputy Director, Contract Compliance Division,
Office for Civil Rights.*

JUNE 11, 1970.

————

Re Sex Discrimination Guidelines.
To: Regional Civil Rights Directors.
From: Joseph W. Wiley, Acting Chief, Field Coordination Branch.

Attached is the news release issued by the Department of Labor on June 9, 1970 together with the Sex Discrimination Guidelines which became effective immediately.

In view of this release all compliance reviews should now include coverage of this aspect of the Executive Order. Affirmative action programs should also include assessment of the problem areas regarding women and goals, projections and targets to correct these problems.

If you need further clarification or we can be of assistance please do not hesitate to call.

Mrs. GREEN. Do they provide an affirmative program?

Mr. KIELY. A private institution is required to have an organized compliance program on file at each of its establishments. A public institution is exempt from that specific requirement to have an organized program on file, but in the process of our compliance reviews with any contractor, whether it is a public or private institution, we are bound to investigate the actual patterns and practices and to negotiate for corrective commitments where we find discrepancies.

If we found there was an exclusion of females from certain job categories, or differences in pay even with the private institutions, they would have to make written commitments on the action they were going to take to correct that problem.

Mrs. GREEN. Thank you.

Mr. MUIRHEAD. I shall summarize the rest of the testimony, Madam Chairman.

I would like to direct our attention to the section 805(a), which would amend title VI of the Civil Rights Act by adding sex to the list of grounds for which no one shall be excluded, and to section 805(b), which would amend title VII of the Civil Rights Act by striking out the provision that excludes educational institutions from title VII's equal employment provisions.

I can report that we both agree with and applaud the objectives of these amendments and support fully the principle of equal rights for women in the field of education as well as all other fields. We question whether these provisions are the very best vehicle for expanding existing law in this area. By way of explanation on the matter of amending title VII, we might again call to the attention of the chairman that Executive Order 11246 does cover almost the whole universe of higher education since the order covers those institutions that are under Federal contracts. So that in dealing with the employment practices of colleges and universities, the Executive Order 11246, as amended, would reach almost all of the colleges and universities.

Mrs. GREEN. Do you feel that that Executive order gives you authority to go in when an institution blatantly practices discrimination in terms of hiring faculty members, and awarding promotions?

Dr. MUIRHEAD. We now have that authority, because it applies to any college or university having a contract with the Federal Government. If they are discriminating against women in any part of their employment practices they would then be liable to the provisions of this Executive order.

Mrs. GREEN. Have you sent out any guidelines, rules and regulations to colleges and universities in the country with regard to this?

Mr. KIELY. May I comment?

In addition to individual visitations and admittedly up until recently they were not getting at the issue of sex in employment, we have.

Now, at those particular institutions where we are doing reviews, we have requested detailed data on all the job categories, from low to high, including faculty, and we will be responsible for getting commitments from the contractors on what corrective action they will be taking.

Mrs. GREEN. How many institutions are you investigating?

Mr. KIELY. Approximately four.

Mrs. GREEN. Four out of 2,600.

My question to Dr. Muirhead was, Have you sent out any directions to colleges and universities, and school superintendents? Has there been any broadside mailing to every college and university in the country citing the law and warning them that if they are in violation they are going to lose their Federal funds?

Dr. MUIRHEAD. Not to my knowledge.

Mrs. GREEN. And the Executive order is over 2-years old. It is almost 3 years old, and in 3 years' time no direction has been given to any college or university in the country. Is that right?

Dr. MUIRHEAD. No; I don't think that is quite right. In that period of time no blanket statement has been issued.

Mrs. GREEN. Don't you do this on all other matters? Don't you send out notices to colleges and universities on a variety of programs? Aren't you sending them out all the time?

Dr. MUIRHEAD. Oh, we certainly are.

Mrs. GREEN. I don't understand, if you consider this important, why almost 3 years have gone by and the attention of the colleges and universities has never been called to this.

Dr. MUIRHEAD. I am not quite sure that it is quite fair to report to you that their attention has not been called to it.

There are many other ways of communicating with the colleges and universities than an announcement from the Office of Higher Education. I would expect that the Executive order as such was printed in the Federal Register.

Mrs. GREEN. Yes, Mr. Kiely, do you have another comment to make?

Mr. KIELY. Yes; we have gotten the cooperation of the National Council on Education and the American Association of Universities, in issuing information on the fact that universities are subject to the order as a contractor, through their publications. We have not on our own motion directly communicated it.

Mrs. GREEN. Is this the way that you communicate on other matters that the Office of Education has responsibility for? Do you go to another agency and say, "Will you please let the colleges and universities know about title II or title V of the new act?

Mr. KIELY. I would say no.

Mrs. GREEN. That is not my experience. I know that you are constantly sending out directives and guidelines to colleges and universities on a variety of things and in that your method of communication is directly to the college. If you have not done it in this case, I cannot help but conclude that you don't consider it very important.

Dr. MUIRHEAD. I think we should respond very directly to you, Madam Chairman, and say that has not been handled directly as it should have been. It has not been given the importance that it should have been given, and you can be very sure that such an announcement will go out.

Mr. KIELY. Dr. Muirhead, there is one procedure that we use which generally speaks to the responsibility of the contractor when he receives a Government contract with the contract package that he gets. There is a description of his responsibility under the Executive order, and it includes a reference to sex as well as——

Mrs. GREEN. What are you talking about in the contract?

Mr. KIELY. When the contract award goes out to a particular university or institution, it goes to the contractor, the university, for example, with information that this particular contract makes him subject to the Executive order.

Mrs. GREEN. Yes; but you aren't writing a contract with any university for the hiring of teachers. You don't have any contract there, so you don't do anything about it in the majority of cases.

Mr. KIELY. We haven't.

Dr. MUIRHEAD. May I move ahead, Madam Chairman?

Mrs. GREEN. Yes; please.

Dr. MUIRHEAD. I would like to comment on the amendment of title VII, in which it is proposed to strike section 702.

We would like to underscore the point that this amendment would make title VII applicable to the employment of faculty and staff by private educational institutions only.

We would now like to move forward and comment on the proposal for the amendment of title VI. We feel that a number of problems would be associated with the proposed amount of title VI, though, of course, we endorse it in principle.

Under title VII of the Civil Rights Act, which deals with fair employment practices, sex may be recognized as a bona fide occupational qualification in cases where the employer can demonstrate that this is necessary. This limitation does not appear in the amendment to title VI, and title VI would, to the extent that it is applicable to employment, presumably prohibit all employment distinctions on the basis of sex, even where sex was, in fact, or could be a bona fide occupational qualification.

We would also like to point out that under title VI, school and universities may not discriminate on the basis of race, color, or national origin in admission policies. It seems to me that such a broad prohibition might not be entirely appropriate with respect to eliminating all differentiations based on sex.

The amendment appears to restrict all enrollment qualifications by sex at all private and public and private colleges. Such an amendment would prohibit Federal assistance to noncoeducational institutions. It would prohibit assistance to dormitories housing one sex only, and programs which might be limited to one sex, such as recreational and physical educational activities. We seriously question the appropriateness of the Federal Government in this manner mandating that all institutions receiving Federal assistance should be coeducational.

There is a long tradition of outstanding men's and women's schools and colleges in this country, and while there is a trend toward coeducation, it is voluntary. The voluntary character of such decision is important, I think, to the independence and diversity of our educational institutions.

The third change is section 805(c), which would amend Civil Rights Act to extend the jurisdiction of the Commission on Civil Rights to complaints of certain kinds of sex discrimination.

We have deferred to the Civil Rights Commission as to how it would cope with the special problems of sex discrimination and the additional resources that would be required.

Finally, section 805(d) would amend the Fair Labor Standards Act of 1958 to eliminate the existing exemption in administrative positions and so forth, from the equal pay for equal work positions.

We support the general principle of this extension and its specific application to the educational community. We defer, of course, to the Department of Labor with respect to any problems that may arise.

So in conclusion, Madam Chairman, let me emphasize that we fully concur in your efforts to eliminate discrimination because of sex. We believe this is a legitimate and appropriate action under the general rubric of civil rights. Our reservations with regard to the specific proposals, where they occur, are technical and procedural and not disagreements in principle.

We would like to volunteer our help in working with you to find the most satisfactory means of attacking this pervasive problem.

Mrs. GREEN. Thank you, Dr. Muirhead.

During the first half of your statement you very effectively and eloquently document by chapter and verse the discrimination against women. In the last half of your statement you seem to applaud our efforts to do something about it, but you oppose the specific changes we propose, or defer to other departments of Government.

Dr. MUIRHEAD. I would not state it that way, Madam Chairman.

Mrs. GREEN. Then I do not understand.

Dr. MUIRHEAD. The statement is incorrect in that its tone implies a lack of cooperation on our part.

Mrs. GREEN. I am not persuaded that when an Executive order exists that is two and a half years old and still nothing has been done by the

Department——

Dr. MUIRHEAD. Your point is well taken, and one of the benefits of your hearings is that you may very well move the slow, ponderous bureaucracy to move with more dispatch toward the things that it should do.

Mrs. GREEN. Let me turn to HEW, which has just told me in 10 pages how much they are opposed to discrimination.

Am I correct that in the Department of HEW that in the grade levels 3, 4, and 5, you have many women, that in grade level 18 there is not a single woman? Is this correct?

Dr. MUIRHEAD. That is correct.

Mrs. GREEN. Do you have any women in appointive positions, policymaking positions?

Dr. MUIRHEAD. I can speak with——

Mrs. GREEN. Above grade 18, that is.

Dr. MUIRHEAD. In the Office of Education?

Mrs. GREEN. In HEW.

Dr. MUIRHEAD. I would have to submit that for the record, but if we do, it is not a significant number.

Mrs. GREEN. Is that significant number zero, or one?

Dr. MUIRHEAD. Appointive positions?

Mrs. GREEN. Grade 18 and above, yes. My information is that there are zero.

Dr. MUIRHEAD. Your information is probably right. The reason why I was hesitating, Madam Chairman, is that I wasn't sure whether some of the positions that had been appointed were above grade 18. I have just been informed that Mrs. Patricia Hitt does come under that category that you just mentioned, as a woman grade 18 or above.

Mrs. GREEN. So you have one.

Dr. MUIRHEAD. We have one.

Mrs. GREEN. And how many men are there?

Dr. MUIRHEAD. I didn't bring the figures for HEW with me, Madam Chairman. I will be glad to supply them. But I did come rather well fortified with figures from the Office of Education.

Mrs. GREEN. But you are speaking for the Secretary this morning. Would you supply for the committee the number of women who are in grade 18? In fact, would you supply the numbers in grades 16, 17, 18, and above in the Washington office and in every regional office?

Dr. MUIRHEAD. Yes.

(The document referred to follows:)

FULL-TIME HEW EMPLOYEES, GS-16 AND ABOVE, AS OF MAY 31, 1970

Grade	Total number of employees	Number of women	Percent of women
Headquarters:			
GS-16	208	10	4.8
GS-17	72	3	4.2
GS-18	20	0	0
Above GS-18	19	1	5.3
Regions:			
GS-16	47	1	2.1
GS-17	7	0	0
GS-18	1	0	0

Mrs. GREEN. Do you have any women who head a regional office, in the Office of Education, for example?

Dr. MUIRHEAD. We have no regional commissioner in the Office of

Education, but we do have a woman who is a regional director in one of the HEW regional offices in New York.

Mrs. GREEN. Would you supply the total number of employees, and the number of women?

Dr. MUIRHEAD. Yes.

In the Office of Education headquarters there are 2,252 employees, of which 1,287 are women. In OE's regional offices there are 394 employees, of which 149 are women. So, of a total number of 2,646 workers, 1,436 of them are women.

HEW as a whole, has a total of 113,811 employees. Of these 165,400 are women, or 57.5 percent. This is the most accurate figure available but there is some margin of error, since our records show no notation as to sex for over 1,000 employees.

Mrs. GREEN. Dr. Muirhead, the Office of Education and Department of HEW have conferences and workshops, and you call people from all over the country to discuss things that are important to you. Have you ever had a conference about the problems which you so eloquently describe in the first pages of your testimony, discrimination on the basis of sex?

Dr. MUIRHEAD. To my knowledge, we have not had such a conference.

Mrs. GREEN. How many pages do you think it would take to list the other conferences you have had on every conceivable subject in the world?

Dr. MUIRHEAD. I am afraid many.

Mrs. GREEN. You probably have had thousands, haven't you, over the time you have been in the Department?

Dr. MUIRHEAD. I am quite sure there have been thousands of conferences held in the past 10 years.

Mrs. GREEN. On every conceivable subject, and yet you outline so persuasively and document so clearly the discrimination against women in the country, and the Office of Education and HEW has never had a conference to discuss it. Is that correct?

Dr. MUIRHEAD. I think it is correct. I would have to check the record to see. But there have not been enough. Even if there has been one, it is not nearly enough.

Mrs. GREEN. Dr. Muirhead, you know as well as I do, and I don't mean this personally, it is directed more to the Department, that HEW and OE come up here every year with recommendations for changes in legislation. Every year you make such recommendations.

Have you ever come up here and made one recommendation of what Congress should do about this problem which you define as so critical?

Dr. MUIRHEAD. We have not.

Mrs. GREEN. There never has been a single recommendation by the Department of HEW or the Office of Education about what might be done to end discrimination against women.

When you object to every legislative change we have made, or as I say, do it by deferring to another department which you know is also going to object.

Have you given thought to what steps you think might be taken? What do you recommend, if you object to everything that we suggest?

Dr. MUIRHEAD. I, first of all, want to have the record show that we have endorsed the concept that is embodied in your legislation.

Mrs. GREEN. Dr. Muirhead, I have been in politics for 60 years, and I have heard colleagues a thousand times on the floor say:

Now, I have the greatest admiration for the gentleman from such and such a State, and I think his objectives are great, but I just can't support this "particular" piece of legislation.

Everybody in politics knows this is the way of stating, in a polite way his opposition.

Dr. MUIRHEAD. May I respond in this manner? For example, I feel that changing title VI of the Civil Rights Act by adding sex to the other factors in title VI would bring with it a great many problems that probably aren't necessary. The concept of extending the Civil Rights idea to include discrimination against women is a good one, but there may be a better way to amend title VI.

Mrs. GREEN. How would you do it? What is a better way?

Dr. MUIRHEAD. One way that I was implying in my testimony was that it be written in such a way that it would not, for example, require all women's colleges to stop being women's colleges, or men's colleges to stop being men's colleges, and so that it would provide some bona fide exceptions for dealing with men and women on the campus.

Mrs. GREEN. I think that you probably are aware of some testimony about 3 years ago on ESEA, I believe, where school superintendents talked about the number of dropouts among disadvantaged boys. They pointed with great pride to programs that they had developed to prevent potential dropouts. One of the superintendents, went on to say that this program has been "so good that we have doubled the number of classes for boys" and "we even have started one for girls." The facts are the dropout rate for girls is very high, and the unemployment rate is much higher for nonwhite girls.

How would you get at this if you oppose this amendment to title VI? The agencies have all written and have said there is nothing they can do, because this violates no law.

Dr. MUIRHEAD. I think we would have to see to it that there is equal opportunity for men and women in Federal programs either through some other way of changing title VI, or through some guidelines that could be developed in the administration of programs. If for example, Madam Chairman, I found there was a very small percentage of women in the NDEA student loan program, we would move very vigorously to see to it that women students got an equal opportunity.

Mrs. GREEN. How would you move?

Dr. MUIRHEAD. We would immediately call to the attention of what I would characterize as the offending institution that women as well as men must get equal opportunity for those funds, and if we found— that they were not doing it, we would question whether or not the agreement they had made with us was being violated.

Mrs. GREEN. But this discrimination that you outlined in your first 10 pages has been going on for years!

Dr. MUIRHEAD. Oh, yes.

Mrs. GREEN. When you tell me you will move vigorously——

Dr. MUIRHEAD. I said we would move vigorously if we found evidence of sex discrimination in the administration of student aid programs. This was the illustration I was using.

Mrs. GREEN. These were classes in a high school to which I was referring a moment ago. I don't see how there is any way you can move. In fact, I think in correspondence—I don't like to use the word "you", because I am talking about the Departments, about the Department of HEW and the Department of Labor, their reply was that there was nothing they could do because there was no violation of the law. Therefore, in a public coeducational high school, they could have special classes for boys who were dropouts, but didn't need to have any for girls.

Dr. MUIRHEAD. I think I come back to the point I was trying to make in the testimony, that we are not opposing an amendment to the Civil Rights, but that such an amendment would have to take into consideration factors that would apply to sex discrimination that do not apply to race, color or national origin.

Mrs. GREEN. I agree with you. I think that there is a legitimate question about the schools that traditionally have been all-boy schols, or all-girl schools. I think this is a legitimate question, and we are working on some modifications of the language.

May I ask you, would you get your lawyers to send up to us a recommendation on how the laws ought to be changed?

Dr. MUIRHEAD. I would be very glad to ask our counsel to work with you on a technical assistance basis in this regard.

Mrs. GREEN. On all the amendments we have.

Dr. MUIRHEAD. Yes.

Mrs. GREEN. And I would like more precise answers, if you can get them from the Department.

The Department of Labor has chosen not to testify, because it does not have a position as yet. I know you have deferred to them on the amendment of the Fair Labor Standards Act.

Dr. MUIRHEAD. Yes; we did. You will note that I pointed out in the amendment suggested for title VII that as the law now stands the amendment would be applicable only to private institutions, and I would expect that it would be your desire to have it apply to all institutions, public and private alike.

Mrs. GREEN. Congressman Quie, do you have questions?

Mr. QUIE. Of those few women in the Office of Education, do any of them protest to you about the discrimination against women in the colleges and universities, and in the administration of Federal programs?

Dr. MUIRHEAD. Yes; we have a number of women in the Office of Education who are deeply concerned about discrimination against women in higher education, but who are even more deeply concerned, Congressman Quie, about evidence of discrimination in the Office of Education itself. Our employment practices in the Office of Education certainly lends some support to their concern.

Mr. QUIE. How do you respond to that?

Dr. MUIRHEAD. We respond by indicating that we are going to do all that we can to open up employment opportunities for women and to see to it that in the appointment to positions in the upper levels, where they are not well represented now, they get an open and equal opportunity for employment in those areas.

Mr. QUIE. What is their reaction when you haven't done it?

Dr. MUIRHEAD. Well, I think the best way to reply to that is that they are tremendously concerned. They feel that employment opportunities in the Office of Education are not equal so far as women are concerned.

Congressman Quie, we have appointed an equal employment opportunity officer in the Office of Education, and he has been clearly instructed to see to it that we improve opportunities for women in the Office of Education. Mr. Royster is with me now.

Mrs. GREEN. Is this his sole responsibility, to do something about discrimination against women?

Dr. MUIRHEAD. No; it is not his sole responsibility. His title does imply equal employment opportunity, and it applies both to women and to minority groups.

Mr. QUIE. Do you expect any results in the future, such as additional women hired in the Office of Education because of the protest of some of the women that are terribly concerned?

Mr. ROYSTER. I think it is fair to say that even though there probably will be more women hired, I am not sure that the number will be extremely significant. I think reflective of that is the fact that the Office has not moved to the point in expressing commitment that it has appointed a woman as part of its equal employment program who would have greater insight in the employment of women, and their problems.

Mr. QUIE. You mean you just don't understand the problems of women?

Mr. ROYSTER. I know I have difficulty. I think I understand the problems relative to the discrimination of black women much more than I do white women, and when you say that black women are discriminated against because of race and then discriminated on top of that because of sex, I am not sure I understand it as well as women do.

Mr. QUIE. The greatest discrimination in this country is against the blacks, so maybe they need to have a woman.

Mr. ROYSTER. I am not sure that is really true. I think the protests over discrimination are more vocal by the blacks than other groups, but I would suggest that discrimination against women is equal.

Mr. QUIE. At least they selected you to fill your position. Maybe they need a woman to look after women. We have a little difficulty understanding them.

Mrs. GREEN. I will be glad to spend several hours discussing it with my colleague.

Mr. QUIE. Oh, my wife does that. [Laughter.]

Mrs. GREEN. You do make reference that there is no woman. I might say, of course, that we have had many women as witnesses during the last few weeks who have outlined very accurately the various kinds of discrimination. But when we get to the Government, I asked the Department of Health, Education, and Welfare to send someone up. In fact, I asked the Secretary.

It was entirely up to the Department who they sent, and I call to your attention it is the fact that it is three men, to discuss discrimination against women. It was the Department's decision, not mine.

We did have Dr. Elizabeth Koontz invited to testify from the Labor Department, and as of yesterday morning, I guess the Labor Department had not thought about it sufficiently, and they had no position to take. We do have one distinguished person we are going to call on next, a woman from the Civil Rights Commission, and this I am delighted that we finally have one woman from the Government who is in a position to do something and to testify about it.

If there are no more questions, may I express my thanks. If you would provide the information that has been requested we will be grateful. I would also ask unanimous consent to submit some other questions which we would ask HEW to answer in terms of discrimination.

I am a bit concerned, since you do have a Bureau of Statistics, that you state in your testimony that there are no national statistics available.

Dr. MUIRHEAD. Yes; and in my complete testimony, which has been submitted for the record, we indicated we are going to take steps to correct that.

I would like to say in closing that I am rather pleased that the Department sent up a man to report to you on discrimination, and I think the man's views should be heard before your committee, and I am pleased to bring it.

Mrs. GREEN. Thank you, and I am very pleased to have you Dr. Muirhead. We all have admiration and affection for you personally. Our questions go to departmental policy. Thank you very much for coming and my thanks also to you, Mr. Royster, and to you, Mr. Kiely.

Dr. MUIRHEAD. Thank you.

Mrs. GREEN. Our next witness is Commissioner Frankie M. Freeman of the Civil Rights Commission.

STATEMENT OF HON. FRANKIE M. FREEMAN, COMMISSIONER, U.S. COMMISSION ON CIVIL RIGHTS; ACCOMPANIED BY HOWARD H. GLICKSTEIN, STAFF DIRECTOR; JUDITH LICHTMAN, STAFF MEMBER, AND JOHN H. POWELL, JR., COUNSEL

Mrs. GREEN. We are delighted to have you here this morning.

As I indicated before, you are one of the few women in the Government in a position to speak on this subject about which so many of us are concerned.

Mrs. FREEMAN. I am Mrs. Frankie M. Freeman. I am a member of the U.S. Commission on Civil Rights and a practicing attorney in St. Louis, Mo. With me are Mr. Howard Glickstein, the Staff Director of the Commission; Mr. John H. Powell, Jr., General Counsel of the Commission, and Mrs. Judith Lichtman, a staff attorney at the Commission.

I appreciate the opportunity to testify this morning on section 805 of H.R. 16098, the Omnibus Postsecondary Education Act of 1970. Section 805 would amend the Civil Rights Acts of 1957 and 1964 and the Fair Labor Standards Act of 1938. The bill would give the Commission on Civil Rights jurisdiction over denials of equal protection of the laws based on sex. It would amend title VI of the Civil Rights Act of 1964 to prohibit denials of the benefits of Federal programs based on sex and it would amend title VII of this act to prohibit discrimination in employment based on sex by private institutions of higher learning. The bill also would remove the exemption of certain professional positions from the equal pay for women provisions of the Fair Labor Standards Act.

In general, the Commission favors Federal legislation which would promote equal opportunity for any group in the Nation whose members are oppressed by discriminatory practices and social customs. The civil rights legislation enacted by Congress since 1957 has done much to hold out the promise to minority groups that this Nation is committed to the elimination of legal and social barriers preventing their enjoyment of an equal opportunnity to the rights and privileges, as well as the duties, of full citizenship.

Unfortunately, this promise is not now a reality. There is much yet remaining to be done before minority citizens may be truly freed from the last vestiges of their cruel history in the United States.

As a result of invidious forms of discrimination, women, like minority group persons, in many respects suffer substantial deprivation of the equal protection of the laws. Because of outmoded customs and attitudes, women are denied a genuinely equal opportunity to realize their full individual potential and thereby are prevented from making their maximum possible contribution to improving the quality of life in this Nation. The manifold talents of American women constitute a vast untapped national resource. Legislation removing antiquated barriers based on sex, therefore, would promote the welfare of this Nation.

The experience of the Equal Employment Opportunity Commission makes clear that barriers against women exist. From June 1965 to June 1966, the first year of EEOC's existence, it received a total of 8,854 complaints of discriminatory employment practices. Of these, 2,452—some 27 percent of the total—were based on sex discrimination. In subsequent years the number of complaints based on sex has remained relatively constant, declining in terms of percentage only because of an increased total complaint flow.

Similarly, in its enforcement of the executive orders prohibiting discrimination in employment by the Federal Government, the U.S. Civil Service Commission has received many complaints of discrimination based on sex. In the year ending March 31, 1969, that Commission received a total of 1,809 complaints of employment discrimination. Of these, 184—approximately 10 percent—were based on sex.

Many of the States in their civil rights acts, have recognized the prevalence of discrimination in employment based on sex. Of 37 States, the District of Columbia, and Puerto Rico, having mandatory fair employment practices acts, 22 States and the District of Columbia prohibit discrimination based on sex.

Thus, it is clear that discrimination based on sex, particularly in employment, is a well-recognized social phenomenon in the United States. I, therefore, support the policy against discrimination based on sex as contained in section 805 of H.R. 16098.

I now would like to turn to each of the subsections of the section 805. I will discuss the implications related to the enactment of this section and point to some problems that should be considered if section 805 is to achieve its purpose.

Section 805(a) would amend section 601 of title VI of the Civil Rights Act of 1964 to provide:

No person in the United States shall on the ground of race, color, sex or national origin, be excluded from participation in, be denied the benfits of, or be subjected to discrimination under any program or activity receiving Federal financial assistance.

Assuredly, no person, solely because of his or her sex, should be denied the benefits of or be discriminated against in any program of Federal assistance. There evidently is no definitive statistical information regarding the extent of discrimination based on sex in Federal programs. We know, however, the general attitude of this country toward the capabilities of women. The role that is thought most appropriate for them is that of homemaker and mother, rather than independent professional or business person.

Mrs. GREEN. Could I stop you there, Commissioner Freeman?

You say there is no definitive statistical information, and Dr. Muirhead said they don't have it in the Office of Education. Within the Government, there is information regarding race discrimination, is there not?

Mrs. FREEMAN. That is correct.

Mrs. GREEN. Why are there not statistics on sex?

Mrs. FREEMAN. The Civil Rights Commission does not now have jurisdiction over discrimination based on sex. We have included, as our testimony will bring out when I proceed that our hearings have brought out facts about discrimination based on sex, but we do not have actual statistics. We are not able to get this information. We do not have it.

I do not know whether any of the Federal programs would have this breakdown now. We don't. This is all I am saying.

It is more than likely, therefore, that in Federal programs directed to assistance for business and commercial enterprises, as well as professional occupations, women are not given the same opportunity to participate as are men. While I have no specific statistical information, I am confident that only a very small percentage of the direct loans made by the Small Business Administration to assist persons in starting or improving small business have been made to women. I also am quite certain that because of the occupations for which working women are believed to be best suited, the State employment services do not refer women to job opportunities and training programs leading to jobs other than those which have traditionally been regarded as "women's work."

While again I have no reliable statistical information, I am confident that discrimination based on sex is not unusual in the area of the sale and particularly the rental of housing units. I would expect that such discrimination is found in direct grant FHA programs such as rental housing assistance, rent supplement assistance and the program which aids poor persons to acquire housing through direct cash assistance.

Under the proposed amendment, such programs would be prohibited from discriminating on the basis of sex. Although title VI exempts programs of insurance or guarantee, thus exempting many business loan guarantees of the Small Business Administration and programs of mortgage insurance for housing units of the FHA, many such exempt programs nevertheless utilize regulations similar to title VI administrative regulations to implement equal opportunity objectives. It can be expected, therefore, that if title VI is amended to prohibit discrimination based on sex, programs such as those mentioned above probably will follow this pattern and will prohibit discrimination based on sex.

In the area of higher education, there are many institutions which purport to admit persons without regard to sex, yet in many instances admission standards vary on the basis of sex. Opportunities for special fellowships supporting postgraduate studies and teaching fellowships may vary on the basis of sex. Availability of housing owned or controlled by educational institutions may vary on the basis of sex. All of these discriminatory practices should be ended and I support legislation to achieve this goal.

Some of the results that are likely to occur by amending title VI merely by adding the word "sex" have significant public policy consequences. Congress should be aware of these before legislating. Some examples of what this amendment may result in are the following:

Many colleges and universities, particularly at the undergraduate level, traditionally have limited admission to either men or women. Under the proposed amendment, such institutions would be ineligible to receive Federal assistance and, therefore, unable to continue many of their present and projected operations, unless they become coeducational.

The proposed amendment of title VI also might intrude on the essential nature of certain institutions of religious education where the student body traditionally has been of one sex or another.

The amendment would require that, as a condition for Federal aid, all housing owned or operated by an institution, including the use of such facilities as gymnasiums and lounges, be available to persons of both sexes on a completely indiscriminate basis. There could not be all-male or all-female dormitories and, perhaps, not even all-male and all-female sections of dormitories.

Neither the Boys Scouts of America nor the Girl Scouts, as presently constituted, could continue to receive surplus Federal material and other Federal benefits under the proposed amendment.

Summer camps for poor children which are operated by churches and other institutions receive much of their food from the Department of Agriculture under the surplus commodity program. Such camps which are open to either boys or girls, but not to both, could no longer receive this Federal benefit.

It is important for Congress to consider carefully whether, as a matter of national policy, we wish to achieve the results described above. I believe some bona fide distinctions remain. Accordingly, I respectfully recommend that the committee carefully consider how a statutory provision can be drafted that will achieve the goal of sexual equality without eradicating bona fide distinctions based on sex. Merely inserting the word "sex" in title VI will not achieve this purpose. I do have a recommendation for such legislation, Madam Chairman.

Mrs. GREEN. Very good.

Mrs. FREEMAN. There should be two sections, the first section should read just as the present title VI except it should substitute the word "sex" for the words race, color, or national origin.

We would add to that, a second section, which would read as follows:

SECTION 2. Nothing contained in this title shall be construed to prohibit the reasonable classification, separation or exclusion of persons on the basis of sex where such classification, separation or exclusion is based upon bona fide qualifications or standards of propriety which are not inconsistent with the purposes of this title.

Section 1 is a direct paraphrase of title VI, substituting the word "sex" for "race, color or national origin." Section 2 is intended to prevent the application of the title in an unreasonable manner, that is, by integrating rest rooms and dormitories or by prohibiting certain programs, such as welfare programs, that might be legitimately geared toward persons of one sex.

Mrs. GREEN. Let me ask you about your recommendation, and the committee is glad to have it, because we are working on language similar to that. If we do not do this, if we just do not amend it, as has been suggested, how would we ever reach, for instance, the apprenticeship program, where only 1 percent are girls?

Mrs. FREEMAN. The apprenticeship programs could be reached under the present Executive orders, but they are not being reached either as far as race and sex are concerned. We have had an Executive order for 30 years on race discrimination, and we have not reached it yet.

Mrs. GREEN. What about the Job Corps? I have fought in Congress, and they have never met the law. Presently, only 29 percent of the Job Corps places are filled by girls.

Mrs. FREEMAN. I don't think there is any denial of the discrimination against women.

Mrs. GREEN. No, but unless we have changes in the law——

Mrs. FREEMAN. We are advocating changes in the law. However, we are advocating the addition of another section.

Mrs. GREEN. Yes, I understand.

Mrs. FREEMAN. Because we feel without this section damage would be done. I would certainly feel that the Boy Scouts have a right to remain Boy Scouts only, and the Girl Scouts could remain Girl Scouts. I am not advocating the integration of men's rooms and women's rooms.

Mrs. GREEN. Does your testimony represent the administration's position?

Mrs. FREEMAN. I am here on behalf of the U.S. Commission on Civil Rights. It does not reflect the views of the administration.

Mrs. GREEN. You have not consulted with the administration on your testimony?

Mrs. FREEMAN. No; I have not.

Mrs. GREEN. Thank you.

Mrs. FREEMAN. Section 805(b) would amend section 702 of the Civil Rights Act of 1964, which now exempts educational institutions from the requirements of title VII, with respect to the employment of individuals to perform work connected with the educational activities of such institutions.

The proposed amendment would eliminate this exemption. Prof. Michael Sovern, the new dean of Columbia Law School, has referred to this exemption as being "highly questionable" and has said:

This * * * [exemption] may be the persistence of tradition in this case the traditional hostility to regulation of education by the Federal Government, but a law forbidding employment discrimination seems a most unlikely road to Federal control of education.

The Commission supports the repeal of this exemption in section 702 of title VII.

I now would like to skip to section 805(d). This section would amend the Fair Labor Standards Act to require equal pay for women employed in academic, executive, administrative, or professional capacities now exempted from coverage by the equal pay provisions. Women are not required to be paid on an equal basis with men in such positions.

A report of the National Education Association reveals that in 1966 women in academic positions earned less than men in the same job categories. For example, women professors received an average salary of $11,649, as compared to $12,768 for men. While women associate professors received an average of $9,322, men associate professors received $10,064. These disparities prevail in the lower academic ranks. For women in executive, administrative, and professional positions, the story is the same. A Labor Department study in 1968 entitled

"Background Facts on Women Workers in the United States" revealed that in 1966 women who worked fulltime, year-round as professionals earned $5,826, while their male counterparts earned $8,945. For that same year women executives and administrators received $4,919, as compared to $9,103 for men. In my opinion there can be no valid purpose served by denying women the right to equal reward for equal work in any occupation whatsoever. The concept that women are not entitled to be paid equally while they are required to produce equal work, has no place in American society. Therefore, I support without reservation the enactment of this proposed legislation.

I come now to that part of the proposed bill with which I am most immediately concerned, that is, section 805(c) of H.R. 16098. This section would amend section 104 of the Civil Rights Act of 1957, by adding to paragraphs (1), (2), (3), and (4) of subsection (a) the word "sex" after the word "religion." The effect of the proposed amendment would be to give the U.S. Commission on Civil Rights, in addition to its present jurisdiction with respect to race, color, religion, and national origin, jurisdiction to consider denials of equal protection of the laws under the Constitution because of sex.

This amendment would impose a responsibility on the Commission which it has not had since its establishment by Congress in 1957. Since that time, the Commission has devoted all of its energies and all of its resources to studying, investigating, and reporting to the President, the Congress, and the American people on the continuing racial crisis confronting this Nation from day to day. I believe our efforts have made a significant contribution, and I am proud to be a member of the agency of the U.S. Government having this long history of devotion to the solution of the problem of racism in the United States.

While the Commission has devoted its energies to racial problems, it has collected data and published reports on problems of direct concern to women. At its 1966 hearing in Cleveland, Ohio, the Commission heard testimony from a number of women concerning the federally assisted welfare program, particularly the AFDC program which affects women with children. This testimony, along with information developed by the staff of the Commission, became the basis of a 1966 Commission report, "Children in Need," a study of the federally assisted program of aid to needy families with children in Cleveland and Cuyahoga County, Ohio. At the same hearing, the Commission heard testimony about the problems of domestic workers as well as women involved in MDTA training programs. This testimony was utilized in a 1967 Commission report, "A Time To Listen * * * A Time To Act," a compendium of testimony from various Commission hearings picturing life in the ghettos of the Nation's cities.

In its 1968 hearings in Alabama, the Commission heard testimony from a number of women in black belt Alabama about the operation of the Government-supported food stamp and surplus commodities programs. Also in 1968, at its hearing in San Antonio, the Commission heard testimony from Mexican-American migrant families. Testimony given at these hearings revealed the extent of discrimination experienced by black and Mexican-American women.

Were the Commission on Civil Rights given jurisdiction with respect to discrimination based on sex without such a substantial increase in resources, it could lose its momentum, and its expertise in the area of discrimination based on race, color, and national origin could be dissipated. The result would be a great loss to the Nation. Among other things, it could create within the Commission a problem of confusion of priorities and misallocation of resources similar to that recognized by the Federal Communications Commission in its report and order released on June 3 of this year.

I am, as you see, a black woman. In a society which in many respects still continues to view women and black people as less than full participants, my life has been spent in the constant struggle to overcome the inferior status which both of these categories have imposed upon me. I can assure you that an individual's resolution is tested throughout her life by this double need to prove her strength and to gain her freedom in such a society.

While I do not oppose extension of the Commission's jurisdiction to include deprivation of equal protection of the laws based on sex, I strongly would object to such an extension if it were not accompanied by that substantial increase in Commission resources to which I have earlier referred.

As one whose experience in this regard is not academic, I must add a note of caution. I urge you not to forget that the great issue in this country, the great danger and the great source of despair is the discrimination endured by minority people.

In 1967 in a U.S. Commission on Civil Rights publication, "Racial Isolation in the Public Schools," I expressed my concern when I wrote

* * * We are now on a collision course which may produce within our borders two alienated and unequal nations confronting each other across a widening gulf * * * Our present * * * crisis is a human crisis, engendered and sustained in large part by the actions, the apathy, or the shortsightedness of public officials and private individuals. It can be resolved only by the commitment, the creative energies, and the combined resources of Americans at every level of public and private life.

I obviously am not unmindful of the problems faced by women because of their sex.

If this legislation is going to give jurisdiction to the U.S. Commission on Civil Rights, it must also include an authorization for additional funds. Unless this legislation does so, we would have to take the position that the effectiveness of the Commission would be diluted. We certainly believe that it is the obligation of this Government not to diminish in any way this Nation's ability to deal with the problem of racial injustice in the United States.

Mrs. GREEN. Thank you, Commissioner Freeman, for your testimony, and I welcome your positive recommendations. It is rather refreshing to have this one agency come up and take some definite positions.

I personally would fully support additional authorization of funds. I think you are right—if you are going to have new responsibilities, you must have the funds and you must have the staff to do an effective job.

It does disturb me a little bit, though, if, as I believe, the discrimination against women is as bad as the discrimination against minorities, that you have placed a higher priority in one field than the other, if the funds are limited.

I assume you would not agree with Congresswoman Chisholm, that the discrimination she has suffered has been much greater because she is a woman than because she is black.

Mrs. FREEMAN. I think Congresswoman Chisholm speaks from her own background, and I speak from mine. I am a Southerner. I speak as a Southern black woman. I have been denied admission to places of public accommodation, not because of my sex, but because of my race. As a member of the Civil Rights Commission, we have conducted hearings in Mississippi and Alabama, and in many of these places we have received testimony from women and men who were denied the opportunity to vote. I do not know of any white woman who has been denied the opportunity to vote, but I know that there are black men and women who were denied that opportunity.

So I do not know that we can say that women are equally discriminated against. I cannot give such an answer, because I speak from the standpoint of my background. We know that the racial discrimination is pervasive in places where there is still a struggle for the right to vote. A right which is very basic. I have not heard or read of any white woman who couldn't vote.

But you see, when women were given the right to vote, all white women could vote. But it didn't make any difference in Mississippi. You couldn't go in and say, "I want to vote because I am a woman." If you were black, you couldn't vote.

Mrs. GREEN. Outside of voting, I know of no discrimination that is greater than the discrimination against women. There are places where I cannot go in the front door—because I am a woman.

Mrs. FREEMAN. You can go into many front doors that I can't go into because of color, As recently as 1961 I took the bus to southeast Missouri. I had to speak there on Sunday. They said, "Ride the bus and leave the driving to us."

At the first rest stop I got off the bus and I went into the restaurant. This was in February of 1961. I went into the restaurant, and right away I could feel that there was something happening. The climate had changed, and as I approached the ladies room in the restaurant, there was a woman who was standing there and she said to me, "Don't you hear her?" And it seems that the waitress had been telling me something, and so I stopped because there was this woman blocking the door to the ladies room. I stood and the waitress came over and said, "Colored people go in the rear." Then, of course, you can understand, or maybe you can't understand, that I really had a problem because I had to decide whether to remove her. But you see, it was not because of my sex.

Mrs. GREEN. This was in 1961? Would this be true in 1970?

Mrs. FREEMAN. It would be true in some places in in the South in 1970. The Civil Rights Commission held hearings in Montgomery, Ala., in April 1968. That is just 2 years ago, 4 years after the Civil Rights Act of 1964, and we received testimony from black people who told us about the discrimination that they encountered, about the things that you take for granted—public accommodations, employment, it ran the gamut.

We received testimony from a black woman who worked as a domestic 6 days a week, and she received $12 a week.

Mrs. GREEN. I voted against the amendment to add "sex" to title VII in 1964, and I did it because I thought it was a gimmick to water the bill down and to really defeat the Civil Rights Act, I tried to state my position very clearly on the floor of the House, and I said definitely that I felt discrimination against women was great, and that while I had suffered discrimination, I felt discrimination against blacks was far greater, and therefore I voted against adding "sex" to it.

Since 1964, I have seen a great deal of progress in terms of ending discrimination against blacks, and I think in the median salary, for example, the median salary is now higher for professionally trained black women than for professionally trained white women.

I would have to say if I had my vote to cast over in the Civil Rights Act of 1964, I would vote to add "sex." I think this aspect of discrimination has been completely ignored.

So with the exception of the vote, and in isolated instances, I must say that I would have to say that I would feel today that the discrimination on the basis of sex is an equal problem in this country to discrimination against minority groups, and while I realize your background, and Shirley Chisholm's is different, and all our backgrounds are different, and they do mold our values and goals, nevertheless I think from now on I cannot support any legislation that will leave out sex, and that will not show a Government concern about this discrimination.

Mrs. FREEMAN. We are not in disagreement with respect to the need to legislate, to include this as appropriate legislation. The point that I am making is that with respect to the jurisdiction of the Civil Rights Commission this legislation must be accompanied by additional resources.

Mrs. GREEN. I understand. I fully appreciate this.

Mrs. FREEMAN. There is still pervasive discrimination in education and employment.

Mrs. GREEN. The only disagreement I have is how do you place one discrimination above the other.

Mrs. FREEMAN. Oh, yes, I do. I absolutely believe, and I think the factual situation in this country will indicate that racial injustice is more pervasive.

Mrs. GREEN. I think that could be debated. I think the testimony we have been having for 10 days would raise serious questions about that.

Aren't the facilities available to solve racial discrimination equal to those available to solve sex discrimination?

Mrs. FREEMAN. Yes, if this Commission receives the jurisdiction and has additional funds, there are programs on sex discrimination that this Commission would immediately initiate, and we also have some suggestions on this.

Mrs. GREEN. In the Civil Rights Commission itself, how many members are there?

Mrs. FREEMAN. Six members. It is a bipartisan commission.

Mrs. GREEN. How many women?

Mrs. FREEMAN. One woman.

Mrs. GREEN. How many blacks?

Mrs. FREEMAN. One. I am she, I am it. [Laughter.]

Mrs. GREEN. Again, they get the double bonus if they can find the black woman.

In terms of staff?

Mrs. FREEMAN. There are 132 permanent employees.

Mrs. GREEN. Of those, how many are women?

Mrs. FREEMAN. Of those, there are 74 female, 58 male permanent employees.

Mrs. GREEN. Would you break it down according to classification? Do you use civil service classifications?

Mrs. FREEMAN. The average grades——

Mrs. GREEN. Just give it to me by grades. Let's start at the top and work our way down.

Mrs. FREEMAN. GS–18, we don't get to any women until we get to GS–15, if you are working your way down.

Mrs. GREEN. How many GS–18's are there?

Mrs. FREEMAN. 18, one male; 17, two males; GS–16, three males; GS–15, three female, nine males. Do you want each grade?

Mrs. GREEN. Well, I think this demonstrates it. At 18 there is no woman, and at 17 there is no woman. And at 16 there is no woman, and at 15 there are three women out of nine.

Mrs. FREEMAN. That is correct.

Mrs. GREEN. So out of 15 employees who would be in policymaking positions, or at least would be in a position to direct some policy out of the Commission that looks at civil rights in this country only three are women.

Mrs. FREEMAN. Well, we are not inclusive as to sex. Maybe we certainly need to be more inclusive, and maybe if you give us the funds and jurisdiction, we will do better.

Mrs. GREEN. Out of the funds you have, what keeps you from hiring more women?

Mrs. FREEMAN. Nothing at all that I can think of.

Mrs. GREEN. It is not a lack of funds.

Mrs. FREEMAN. No, no, except that we can say our record is more than twice as good as other Federal agencies. In Federal service the average grade for the male is a GS–9 and for the female, it is GS–4. The average grade at the Civil Rights Commission for females is equivalent to the average grade in the overall service.

Mrs. GREEN. Would you say that again, please?

Mrs. FREEMAN. The average grade in Federal service for males is GS–9 and for females is GS–4. At the Civil Rights Commission, the average grade is GS–9, and male is GS–13.

Mrs. GREEN. But your record, when you get to the grades 18, 17, and 16——

Mrs. FREEMAN. Out of six persons, the Civil Rights Commission doesn't have more than four employees higher than grade 16, there are zero.

Mrs. GREEN. You have zero percent, if we are comparing them, but at least in the Federal civil service there are a few. It is less than 1 percent, but it isn't zero. That is of women employed.

Mrs. FREEMAN. That is right.

Mrs. GREEN. I think this helps to support the feeling on the part of many women's groups across the country that there is just this blatant discrimination against women, and I think it helps to support my feeling that we are making greater progress in ending the discrimination on the basis of race.

Mrs. FREEMAN. This is just not true. There is blatant discrimination against women, but we are not making greater progress in solving the problem of discrimination against race.

Mrs. GREEN. On the Civil Rights Commission itself, of those six employees in grades 16, 17, and 18, how many of those employees are black?

Mrs. FREEMAN. Of the professional employees—perhaps the staff would have that.

Of the professional employees, 36 are black, 42 are white, nine are Spanish surname.

Mrs. GREEN. How many are women?

Mrs. FREEMAN. Of the professional employees, 34 are women, 53 are men.

Mrs. GREEN. Doesn't that support my statement that we are making greater progress in bringing about some equality on the basis of race and not much progress on sex?

Mrs. FREEMAN. No; because I think it would not be taking into consideration the entire picture. It would distort the picture to look solely at the Civil Rights Commission's employment practices, because the whole complex of living in the society includes not just a small agency like the Civil Rights Commission. It includes all of the responsibilities of getting an education, of getting a job, of being able to live.

Mrs. GREEN. I didn't have an answer yet. GS–18, 17, 16, and 15, how many blacks?

Mrs. FREEMAN. They are getting it for you.

Mr. POWELL. The 18 is a black, and one 17 is a black.

Mrs. GREEN. And the 16?

Mr. GLICKSTEIN. Two whites and one black.

Mrs. GREEN. And the 15, the nine employees?

Mr. GLICKSTEIN. I have to figure that out.

Mrs. GREEN. Would you do that and supply it?

Mr. GLICKSTEIN. I will tell you in a minute or two, if I can remember.

Mrs. GREEN. All right, fine. Of the three women, one is black and two are white, and of the nine men, I will figure that out.

What I am really saying is that the Government and the Civil Rights Commission itself and the enforcement divisions have taken the position and, as I have said, and I have many papers to document it, that the absence of a black is, per se, evidence of discrimination. If this be true, then it seems to me the absence of women should also be considered as evidence of discrimination.

Mrs. FREEMAN. I did not know that the Government had taken that position, per se. If this is the case, then I would certainly agree that there would be an affirmative duty to offer, to assure equality of opportunity on the basis of sex as well as there is on the basis of race. I would certainly concur in that.

Mrs. GREEN. This is the policy in the enforcement division—enforcing desegregation in the schools, in various plants, in private industry.

Mrs. FREEMAN. But, you see, as a practical matter, no contract has ever been canceled on the basis of race, and there has been racial discrimination documented year after year after year. But even so, there has been no cancellation.

Mrs. GREEN. The Justice Department has not even instituted a case where there has been discrimination on the basis of sex.

Mrs. FREEMAN. I heard that this morning.

Mrs. GREEN. They instituted at least over 100 on the basis of race.

Mrs. FREEMAN. We would like to see the result.

Mrs. GREEN. So would I. I would like to see it in both areas.

Do you have the figures?

Mr. GLICKSTEIN. Of the nine male GS–15's, six are white, two black, and one is Spanish surname.

Mrs. GREEN. I thank you very much, Commissioner Freeman, and your associates.

Off the record.

(Discussion off the record.)

Mrs. GREEN. The next hearing of this committee will be on Tuesday, July 7. We are adjourned until then.

(Whereupon, at 1:10 p.m. the subcommittee adjourned, to reconvene on Friday, July 31, 1970.)

FRIDAY, JULY 31, 1970

House of Representatives,
Special Subcommittee on Education
of the Committee on Education and Labor,
Washington, D.C.

The subcommittee met at 9:30 a.m., pursuant to call, in room 2261, Rayburn House Office Building, Hon. Edith Green (chairman of the subcommittee) presiding.

Present: Representatives Green, Perkins, Brademas, and Scherle.

Staff members present: Harry Hogan, counsel; and Robert Andringa, minority professional staff assistant.

Mrs. Green. The subcommittee will come to order for the further consideration of legislation under the jurisdiction of this subcommittee.

Our first witness this morning is the representative from the Justice Department, the Honorable Jerris Leonard, Assistant Attorney General, Civil Rights Division.

On behalf of the committee, Mr. Leonard, may I express my appreciation for your taking the time to be here today and to bring us the views of the Justice Department on this legislation. Will you proceed as you wish?

Do you have a statement?

STATEMENT OF JERRIS LEONARD, ASSISTANT ATTORNEY GENERAL, CIVIL RIGHTS DIVISION, DEPARTMENT OF JUSTICE, ACCOMPANIED BY DAVID MARBLESTONE AND MARY GROVE

Mr. Leonard. Thank you, Madam Chairman. I do have a prepared statement. It is short and we have provided it to the subcommittee.

I would like to introduce two of my colleagues in the Department, Mr. David Marblestone and Miss Mary Grove.

We thank you for the opportunity to express our views today on the provisions dealing with prohibitions against discrimination on the ground of sex. We know you have a full hearing schedule, so I am going to turn directly to four specific points that I would like to make.

First, subsection 805(a) of H.R. 16098 would amend title VI of the Civil Rights Act of 1964 so as to make the prohibition against discrimination in federally assisted programs applicable to discrimination on the basis of sex. At present, discrimination on the ground of race, color, or national origin is forbidden by title VI.

While we are not able to support this legislation in its present form, we wish to suggest an alternative which, in our opinion, would effectively meet the needs with which the subcommittee is concerned.

Our suggestion is that, instead of amending title VI of the 1964 act, separate legislation should be enacted which would prohibit discrimination on the ground of sex in any program of elementary, secondary, or postsecondary education receiving Federal financial assistance. This prohibition would extend not only to discrimination against students and other beneficiaries of the Federal grants, but also to employment discrimination. The legislation would make the prohibition inapplicable where sex is a bona fide basis for differential treatment.

The enforcement provisions of the proposed legislation would be patterned after those of title VI of the 1964 Civil Rights Act; that is, each Federal agency which extends financial assistance to education programs would adopt an appropriate, separate regulation regarding sex discrimination. The means of enforcement would be identical to those provided in section 602 of title VI—(1) administrative proceedings leading to possible termination of Federal assistance, or (2) other means authorized by law, including court suits. All of the procedural and other safeguards contained in section 602 would be incorporated into the new statute.

Our proposal would, I believe, cover virtually all colleges, universities, and public school systems in the United States. The agency with primary enforcement responsibility would be the Department of Health, Education, and Welfare. I might add that our proposed approach has the concurrence of that Department.

Among the areas in which sex discrimination would be forbidden are the following: availability of scholarships and fellowships; admission to graduate programs; and hiring, compensation, and promotion of faculty and staff members. It is not our purpose to bar all-female or all-male colleges from receiving Federal grants; such an institution could satisfy the exception regarding bona fide distinctions. Similarly, the exception would, for example, permit schools to maintain separate dormitories and separate gymnasiums for men and women. The scope of the proviso could best be determined by the administering agencies in their regulations and on the basis of particular situations which arise.

Unlike title VI, the measure we propose would not contain an exemption for employment practices. Considering the record established before this subcommittee, such coverage of employment practices by our proposal seems appropriate. Again, it should be noted that this legislation would apply to almost all of the institutions of higher education, both public and private, and to almost all public elementary and secondary school systems.

We recognize, of course, that our proposal would not reach federally assisted programs outside the area of education. Still, we believe it is a proper response to the problems which have been demonstrated before the subcommittee.

Madam Chairman, we hope that our alternative proposal will meet with the approval of the subcommittee.

Second, subsection 805(b) would amend title VII of the Civil Rights Act of 1964 by striking the provision (in section 702) which exempts from the coverage of title VII educational institutions with respect to employment of persons to perform work connected with educational activities.

As I noted earlier, our proposal to prohibit sex discrimination in all federally assisted education programs would apply to sex discrimination in employment. Accordingly, at this time, I see no need for amending title VII.

Third, subsection 805(c) of H.R. 16098 would amend the statute prescribing the jurisdiction of the U.S. Commission on Civil Rights (section 104 of the Civil Rights Act of 1957, as amended) so as to extend the jurisdiction of the Commission to discrimination on the basis of sex.

We favor the objective of authorizing a Federal agency to investigate problems of sex discrimination, to evaluate the effectiveness of Federal laws and regulations concerning such discrimination and to determine the need for new Federal laws. However, for reasons to be discussed more fully by Mrs. Koontz, we believe that the Women's Bureau, rather than the Commission on Civil Rights, should be the agency which has such authority.

Finally, subsection 805(d) would amend the Fair Labor Standards Act [section 13(a)] so as to make the prohibition against wage differentials based upon sex [section 6(d)] applicable to employment of persons in executive, administrative, and professional capacities. Regarding this matter, the desirability of amending the Fair Labor Standards Act, we defer to the Department of Labor.

Madam Chairman, that concludes my statement, but I will be pleased to answer any questions which the subcommittee has.

Mrs. GREEN. Thank you very much, Mr. Leonard.

Mr. Leonard, I wonder, in your suggested change to the amendment in title VI, would you consider as educational programs the manpower training programs?

Mr. LEONARD. I think, Madam Chairman, that those programs unless they were operated in conjunction with an established educational institution, probably would be employment programs as opposed to educational programs.

Mrs. GREEN. But they are training programs.

Mr. LEONARD. That is true.

Mrs. GREEN. Let's take the apprenticeship program, that has 278,000 slots across the country. Only 1 percent of the apprenticeship training positions go to girls. I'm told, 99 percent go to boys, and girls simply do not have a chance to receive the training necessary to get jobs. The highest unemployment rate in the Nation, as you know, is among non-white girls. So this kind of discrimination could still continue.

Mr. LEONARD. Madam Chairman, apprenticeship programs are specifically covered by title VII of the act now.

Mrs. GREEN. Title VII of what act?

Mr. LEONARD. Of the Civil Rights Act of 1964. And if the point that you are making is that there is not enforcement, I just frankly do not have the factual background to be able to respond as to why that condition exists. I think that is something on which the Women's Bureau, under the proposal which we recommended to you, could develop specific facts. Whether this is because the kind of apprenticeship programs we have are aimed more heavily at construction type jobs or heavy labor type jobs, I just do not know. I can tell you that to my knowledge, at least, we have never received a sex discrimination complaint in this area. If we had, we would have investigated it. We would have attempted to determine what the facts were with respect to that particular apprenticeship program.

Mrs. GREEN. How many complaints have you received from the Equal Employment Opportunity Commission with respect to discrimination on the basis of sex?

Mr. LEONARD. I believe we have received two from EEOC to my knowledge. One resulted in a voluntary agreement being entered into with the employer and the other resulted in a law suit. In addition to that, we have at least a couple more active investigations going on at this time.

Mrs. GREEN. I have asked Mr. Hogan to get the testimony of Mr. Brown of EEOC when he was here. He said the Commission had referred a great many complaints to the Justice Department. Until the *Libby-Owens* case in Toledo the other day, the Justice Department had never instituted a case on discrimination on the basis of sex.

Mr. LEONARD. I think, Madam Chairman, he must have been talking about all of their referrals.

Mrs. GREEN. No; he said there were many referrals on discrimination on the basis of race, but that they had also referred many cases to the Justice Department of discrimination on the basis of sex.

Mr. LEONARD. Madam Chairman, the best information I can give you on that is to provide you, and we will be happy to do that, with a tabulation that we annually give to the House Appropriations Subcommittee showing the EEOC referrals and their disposition. I may be a little fuzzy on this this morning, but I would say that there probably have not been, in the last 3 or 4 years, more than a total of 80 referrals of all kinds from EEOC. We will check that out for you, and please do not hold me to that; I could be wrong. But we will give you the tabulation that we provide to Congressman Rooney's subcommittee, which is part of our annual submission for budget purposes.

Mrs. GREEN. I would like to have that.

The document referred to follows:)

EEOC REFERRALS TO THE DEPARTMENT OF JUSTICE

Prior to March 1969, a matter was referred to the Department of Justice by the Equal Employment Opportunity Commission after EEOC had considered the matter and had determined to make an official recommendation that suit be filed. A statistical summary of EEOC referrals for fiscal years 1966 through 1969 is attached.[1]

As of March 24, 1969, an additional and less formal system of bringing matters to the attention of the Department of Justice was instituted. That is, an employee of the Office of the General Counsel of EEOC selects files or parts of files and informs the Civil Rights Division that such files are available for inspection. Under this procedure, no official recommendation is made by EEOC.

The attached chart covers all types of referrals and does not distinguish between them on the basis of the type of discrimination alleged.

During fiscal year 1970, EEOC sent five referral letters, with recommendations for initiation of suits, to the Civil Rights Division. Two of the letters related to charges of sex discrimination. One of the letters resulted in the "pattern or practice" suit against Libbey-Owens-Ford Company of Toledo, Ohio. The other letter concerning sex discrimination combined three separate charges against a single company. After the Department of Justice succeeded in obtaining a satisfactory voluntary agreement from the company involved in the last-mentioned referral, the matter was returned to EEOC.

In addition to the formal referrals, some 60 charges were brought to the attention of the Civil Rights Division through the informal procedure described

---

[1] The Civil Rights Act of 1964 was enacted on July 2, 1964. However, Title VII did not take effect until one year after the date of enactment. See § 716(a), 42 U.S.C. 2000e–15(a).

above. These 60 files involved 44 employers or possible referrals.[2] Of the 44 employers, some 13 were the subject of charges involving discrimination based on both sex and race. The status of the 60 matters varies; a number of them are under investigation by the Department of Justice, EEOC is to supplement the information in certain of the other files, some relate to the issues already being litigated in the Libbey-Owens-Ford case or in other cases, and others were determined, for different reasons, not to present legal issues or factual questions that would justify formal referral to the Attorney General.

EEOC REFERRALS TO THE DEPARTMENT OF JUSTICE—STATISTICAL SUMMARY

	Total number of referrals [1]	Number o fre-ferrals in which suit filed
Fiscal year 1966 [2]	7	2
Fiscal year 1967	16	5
Fiscal year 1968	17	2
Fiscal year 1969	21	3
Total	61	12

[1] A referral is based on an investigation of specific charges filed against the company or union. However, as of Mar. 24, 1969, an informal system of bringing matters to the attention of the Department of Justice was instituted (see the attached memorandum). The total for fiscal 1969 includes both formal referrals and matters handled under the informal system.
[2] Referrals are cataloged by date of referral.

Mr. LEONARD. I do want to state that from my personal knowledge, and I have discussed this matter with the Chief of the Employment Section of the Civil Rights Division, we have received two such referrals. One resulted in a law suit; the other resulted in a voluntary agreement. We know of two other active cases which came to us outside of the EEOC referral process which are in investigation now.

Mrs. GREEN. All of the work in the Justice Department in terms of discrimination on the basis of race, color, creed, national origin, or sex, in employment and education is going to come to your department; am I right?

Mr. LEONARD. That is true, though the Community Relations Service gets involved in such matters, but not from the standpoint of law enforcement.

Mrs. GREEN. When I mentioned that only 1 percent of the apprenticeship slots were held by girls and 99 percent by boys, you expressed surprise that no complaints had been brought to your attention. It seems to me that there is a lack of attention by the Government, by the administration, and I do not mean just during the last 2 years, but certainly ever since I have been in the Congress. If we go to the other end of the financial spectrum in civil service, we find the same low percentage of women in policymaking positions at grade levels 16, 17, and 18. Less than 1 percent of these positions are held by women. Down at the Office of Education, there is not a single woman at that grade level.

Then, Mr. Leonard, if I may use this as an illustration of what seems to be an absence of concern. Your own biography describes a very impressive background, training, and competence for this position. But on page 2 of your own biography, it says:

The Assistant Attorney General for Civil Rights deals with matters relating to constitutionally protected rights of the individual, as well as carrying out

---

[2] In some instances, the employer-companies were related, as parent or subsidiary, to other of the employers against whom charges were made. In arriving at the figure of 44 employers, we treated each company separately, regardless of parent-subsidiary affiliation.

the court's mandates in this area. Specifically, this includes protection against discrimination because of color, race, creed, or national origin in education, employment, housing, public accommodations, facilities, voting.

Mr. LEONARD. Well, Madam Chairman——

Mrs. GREEN. There is one word that is conspicuous by its absence.

Mr. LEONARD. That biography was written by a woman whom I assure you I am not going to fire because of that omission. But I will tell you one thing: We will amend it immediately.

Mrs. GREEN. My experience is that by and large women in Government do what the men tell them.

Mr. LEONARD. I assure you I did not write that. It is a valid complaint and we will amend it.

Mrs. GREEN. It seems to me that it is beyond just typing a biographical sketch, that it accurately reflects the lack of concern. The omission has never even been noticed. Does this symbolically represent the lack of concern?

Mr. LEONARD. Well, if you will not take offense at this, Madam Chairman, I just do not think that is a true statement. I believe that the Justice Department is prepared to act upon complaints. Now, we are tremendously impressed by the background and the testimony that this subcommittee has developed. But we are lawyers, not sociologists. We have to act not on ultimate conclusions, but on facts. The fact that only 1 percent of the apprenticeship trainees are females is obviously a surprising thing. But that does not tell us anything about discrimination. The thing that tells us about discrimination is that we know that Mary Jones applied to be a welder in the apprenticeship program of such and such local union and company and she was refused because the apprenticeship committee exluded all women. Now, that is the kind of fact situation that we as lawyers need to establish cases. That is why we are urging so sincerely and firmly that the Women's Bureau be given the direction to begin to develop the specifics. We cannot act without specifics and we cannot act, for that matter, without persons saying that they have been denied access to a particular job because of sex discrimination.

Mrs. GREEN. But if we just go to the facts; how many suits has the Justice Department instituted where there have been complaints of discrimination because of race?

Mr. LEONARD. One.

Mrs. GREEN. Just one?

Mr. LEONARD. Oh, I am sorry; race. Employment suits?

Mrs. GREEN. Yes.

Mr. LEONARD. Approximately 40 or 50.

Mrs. GREEN. And until the *Toledo* case about 2 weeks ago, has the Justice Department ever instituted a case because of discrimination on the basis of sex?

Mr. LEONARD. No.

Mrs. GREEN. Is that not a rather impressive fact?

Mr. LEONARD. It is a conclusion, Madam Chairman. It does not go behind the conclusion to determine why. As I said, we act on complaints. We have to have a complaint from somebody or some group, or we have to have some blatant activity called to our attention.

Now, conclusions do not prove anything. All they tend to do is to signal that there may be a problem. There may not be a problem. But in any event, the real test of whether or not there has been employment discrimination as I said, is when Mary Jones goes to apply for the apprenticeship program or the job as principal of a high school and the superintendent says, "Mary, I am sorry, you are well qualified, but we want a man because we are not going to hire a female high school principal." Those are the kinds of facts on which law suits are built.

Mrs. GREEN. I have sent up for the testimony of Mr. Brown. He did testify that they have received 2,878 complaints of discrimination against women in the first 10 months of this fiscal year. He did give us testimony that over the years they had referred to the Justice Department many cases and they did complain that there had been none acted upon. But we will get that testimony before the hour is gone.

Le me turn to Mr. Scherle. Do you have any questions, Mr. Scherle?

Mr. SCHERLE. Thank you, Madam Chairman. I can sure sympathize with the witness here this morning. On an emotional subject such as this, it is always easy to feel that you can build a case, but you have to have the facts to try the case. Is this what you are trying to say? You cannot build a case on complaint if you do not have any facts except conclusions.

Mr. LEONARD. That is correct. As a matter of fact, we apply the same standard in a race discrimination case. We would not judge an employer to be discriminating on the basis of race simply from statistics. When we receive a complaint, it is true that the employment statistics will be one of the first things we look at in order to determine whether there may be some prosecutive merit on that complaint. But we certainly do not rely on that as the basis for commencing a law suit.

Mr. SCHERLE. Can you tell me, Mr. Leonard, when I served in the Iowa Legislature, the initial bill that came up would allow the accuser not to have the burden of proof. Instead the accused had to prove that they were not discriminating. This is very irregular in our system of justice. Well, we changed that to where the accuser must have some responsibility as far as complaints and registering complaints so as to get away from the harrassment of the employer.

Mr. LEONARD. Let me say, Congressman, that our activities take place in the Federal courtroom and the burden of proof is upon the plaintiff. The plaintiff in these cases is the Federal Government. We must establish that the particular employer whom we are suing has established a pattern or practice of discrimination.

Mr. SCHERLE. What I had reference to was private cases.

Mr. LEONARD. Even in a private case brought in the Federal district court, the burden is upon the plaintiff-employee to show that he has been discriminated against by the employer. The burden is not upon the employer.

Mr. SCHERLE. Now, why would not something of that type give the accuser a great deal of leverage in harassment by litigation? If I were an employer, someone came into my business to seek employment and I turned them down and they can turn around and say, well, he did not hire me because of sex, because of color, or something else, should there not be some burden on that individual rather than haul me into court right away to say, well, I thought the man was not qualified and in his testimony, he claims that he was discriminated against? What protection does the employer have under that type of litigation?

Mr. LEONARD. The protection that the employer has is that the burden of proof is upon the complainant, the employee, to prove that the employer has in fact discriminated against him. As far as the question of harassment is concerned, I really do not have any facts on that question. We lawyers have a saying that anybody can start a law suit; it is another thing to get relief.

I do not know how many private cases are started in this area per year. I indicated to you that regarding pattern or practice cases, the only authority the Attorney General has, while I do not have the exact figure, I would say that since 1965 when title VII took effect, we probably have started not more than 50 such law suits.

Mr. SCHERLE. Well, as far as your court cases are concerned, if it is your obligation to protect the person who makes a complaint, is there not a certain amount of responsibility upon the accuser, to prove he was discriminated against rather than upon the accused to prove that he was not discriminating? It does not make sense to me.

Mr. LEONARD. Really what I was saying is that you cannot merely take conclusions to the effect that only a certain percentage of an employer's workforce is female or is minority and from that alone determine that the employer has discriminated. There must be thousands of cities and small towns in the United States where, if you were to apply that kind of standard, you would have automatic judgments against employers and unions when, in fact, there may be no minority employment force available.

Mrs. GREEN. Would you yield?

Mr. SCHERLE. Yes.

Mrs. GREEN. Is that not the test that is used in schools—that the absence of blacks or the absence of a certain number of blacks is proof positive of violation of the Supreme Court decisions in cases throughout the South?

Mr. LEONARD. No; that is not the test that the courts have applied to determine whether or not a school district is operating a dual or a unitary system. The test in education is whether or not the children who live in a particular geographic area all go to the same school—that is, the school that is provided for all children who live in that particular area—and whether or not the geographic zone lines have been drawn in such a way as to reduce segregation. It is not the ultimate fact of just counting the numbers.

Now, I am frank to admit that when we receive a complaint, we look at the statistics. They are like a thermometer, Madam Chairman. It tells you something, but it does not tell you the whole story. You must look at the specific facts of the school system.

For instance, we can show you school systems where all the children are black; there are no whites.

Mrs. GREEN. But I have memorandums written by lawyers who went down into some of the Southern States where they wrote directives to the schools which stated that they were to have, for instance, a black teacher in this school or a white teacher here, or they were to have so many blacks or so many whites. There was no other criterion except the ratio and the number.

Mr. LEONARD. Excuse me. Now you are getting into the question of teachers and I have to explain that.

Mrs. GREEN. And students. The memorandums included both.

Mr. LEONARD. I hope those memorandums are not coming from my lawyers.

Mrs. GREEN. They are not coming from your lawyers, but they have come from the Justice Department, in past years.

Mr. LEONARD. We do not believe that is the law with respect to students.

Let me say with respect to faculty that the Supreme Court, in the *Singleton* case, adopted a very pragmatic rule and said where the school system does not come up with a faculty desegregation plan that in fact desegregates the faculty, then the district courts have authority to impose upon them what we call the *Singleton* rule. The *Singleton* rule simply says you must racially balance the faculty. But that same rule of law does not apply to students.

Mrs. GREEN. I do not want to get off the main subject of the hearings this morning, but it seemed to me the absence in other cases was the proof.

Thank you, Mr. Scherle.

Mr. SCHERLE. Only one thing more, when we get into this field, which is very sensitive and very ticklish, I wonder if sometimes we do not create more problems by encouraging litigation and harassment of people who are trying to work this thing out at the present time.

That is all, Madam Chairman.

Mrs. GREEN. Thank you.

Congressman Brademas?

Mr. BRADEMAS. Thank you, Madam Chairman.

Thank you very much, Mr. Leonard, for your testimony. I just have two or three questions.

As I understand it, the bill under consideration, H.R. 16098, would amend title VI of the 1964 Civil Rights Act to make prohibition against discrimination in federally assisted programs applicable to sex as well as race, color, or national origin. You have indicated that you are not prepared to support that proposal, but would prefer a separate bill to prohibit discrimination on grounds of sex and any federally assisted program in the fields of elementary and secondary and postsecondary education. Have I accurately stated your posture?

Mr. LEONARD. I think that is an accurate summary, yes.

Mr. BRADEMAS. Could I then ask you a couple of questions? Maybe it is purely inadvertence; if not, then I wonder what your reason was for omitting to include preschool programs?

Mr. LEONARD. Congressman, if that is the construction which you put on the words in my testimony, that is inadvertent.

Mr. BRADEMAS. I assumed that it was and there is no reasonable reason for it. But at least in the legislation that we consider in this committee, we go to some pains to make distinctions between elementary and secondary and postsecondary, and so on. I am glad that you did not have in mind saying that it is all right to discriminate against women in Headstart programs.

Mr. LEONARD. No, that would not be our intention.

Mr. BRADEMAS. Now, you also said that unlike title VI, your proposal of a separate bill would not exempt employment practices. Do I assume that one of the justifications of your wanting a separate bill rather than an amending of title VI is you are contending that your proposal is thereby stronger in that it would cover employment practices? I do not want to put words in your mouth; I am just trying to understand why you prefer one rather than the other.

Mr. LEONARD. I think that what we are really trying to say is that our suggestion is more directly responsive to the record that this subcommittee has made. I am nitpicking, if you please, but I think what we are really saying is that a separate bill which would include not only the prohibitions as to the programs themselves, but also as to the employment activities that are associated with those programs, would more clearly cover the kind of problems brought out in testimony and evidence which you have developed.

Mr. BRADEMAS. I just have one other observation, Madam Chairman. I must readily confess that it may appear to be a self-serving question, but I am distressed that with all of our concern about discrimination on account of sex, and I happen to agree that we are rather outrageous in that respect in this country, we do not hear very much about discrimination on account of marital status. There is, at least if you look at the tax laws of the United States, the fact that we discriminate against single people more than any other modern civilized or allegedly civilized industrial society. Perhaps someday, Madam Chairman, you and I can talk about amending this or other bills to include outlawing discrimination on that account.

Thank you, Mr. Leonard.

Mr. GREEN. I might say that Martha Griffiths has done yeoman work in the Ways and Means Committee to try to bring to the attention of her colleagues in the discrimination terms of tax discrimination.

Mr. SCHERLE. Madam Chairman, to answer my colleague from Indiana, rather than set up additional legislation, I think it would be easier to find John a wife.

Mr. BRADEMAS. I think one campaign at a time is enough.

Mrs. GREEN. Mr. Leonard, your suggestion, regarding title VI does make sense to me because I think there were some problems in the original wording of it. However, on page 2 you state the legislation should make the prohibition inapplicable where sex is a bona fide basis for differential treatment. The equal rights amendment is scheduled to be on the calendar on August 10. This relates, of course, to equal protection under the 14th amendment. What would this exemption do to the equal rights amendment in terms of the constitutional argument?

Mr. LEONARD. Madam Chairman, that is a very deep constitutional interpretation question and I am frank to admit that, at this point, I could not do more than just skim the surface of it. Because what you are really asking is for me to search the mind of the Supreme Court, I believe, as to how it might deal with specific fact situations. And I think the only way that I can answer that question is to say that it seems to me that there are bona fide distinctions which can be made. I believe all of us are committed to the proposition that "bona fide" should be strictly construed and I even hesitate to give any examples. But I think we can all——

Mrs. GREEN. I wish I could accept at face value that statement "all of us are committed to the proposition that this would be strictly construed."

Mr. LEONARD. Let me say that I am. I certainly would look with great disfavor on an employer who would attempt to set up a distinction which was a strawman and was not bona fide.

Mrs. GREEN. Do you think Dr. Berman's is bona fide!!

Mr. LEONARD. I am advised by my associates to pass that question.

Mr. BRADEMAS. Madam Chairman, will you yield?

Mrs. GREEN. Yes, I will; but I hesitate to at this point!!

Mr. BRADEMAS. I know Dr. Berman, but I am delighted to disassociate myself from his views.

If I may, Madam Chairman, because it is not often that we get the distinguished Assistant Attorney General before the subcommittee, put a question to him on a not directly but not altogether unrelated matter which is also of concern to us in the full Committee on Education and Labor with respect to the whole question of school desegregation in the South.

Do I understand, and this may have some relevance to the question of sex discrimination also, do you in the Department of Justice take the position that you will not move in terms of sending lawyers into the South to carry out school desegregation orders unless the Southern States or southern school districts seek your assistance?

Mr. LEONARD. I think, Congressman, that the President had something to say about the subject last night. I certainly would not be presumptuous and appear before this subcommittee just a matter of hours after he spoke on the subject and attempt to interpret or tell you what he said. I do not have the verbatim quote before me, although I did see the news conference.

Mr. BRADEMAS. I have it. I will read it to you.

Mrs. GREEN. Could I make a suggestion? We go into session at 11 and we are to hear Civil Service and Labor representatives also. Could we confine the questions to discrimination on sex.

Mr. BRADEMAS. This is my last question, Madam Chairman.

Mrs. GREEN. Fine, but I would like after that to direct questioning back to discrimination based on sex—as there are countless hearings on the other—and really none on this.

Mr. BRADEMAS. Here is what the President said last night:

The Attorney General has primary responsibility in this field, and I think a prediction made by him must be given great weight. Whether that prediction turns out, of course, depends in great part on whether there is cooperation in the key Southern districts where the desegregation program is still behind schedule.

Now, as far as the number of federal officials that should be sent to the South, let me emphasize that that will be based on whether those Southern districts or states that have this problem of desegregation ask for the help of either the Justice Department of HEW experts.

Mr. LEONARD. That is what the President said, Congressman, and I assume that those of us who are in Federal executive positions will carry out the President's directive.

Mr. BRADEMAS. So you will not go unless invited?

Mr. LEONARD. I am not so sure that that is what the President said. But in any event, as I mentioned, I think we have to have some discussion about the specifics. The Justice Department has always acted upon complaints in the past, but I think we really need to determine exactly what the President meant.

Mrs. GREEN. If I could get back to title VII, which is before us, when Congress passed title VII which provides that there should be no discrimination in employment based on race, color, creed, national origin, or sex, the Congress did not state a preference of one over the other, did they?

Mr. LEONARD. That is correct.

Mrs. GREEN. Then if any agency of the Government turns its entire attention to discrimination, for instance, on the basis of race, it is an administrative preference and not based on the congressional mandate?

Mr. LEONARD. Madam Chairman, that statement or conclusion, if that is what it is, on your part is based on the assumption that there is equal visibility and in fact equal quantity of the problem. I can think of many other examples in law enforcement, and that is what we are talking about here.

Law enforcement tends to act on those problems which are more aggrevated and those which come to its attention, particularly the Justice Department. The Justice Department is not a Federal police force; it is an agency that acts upon complaints. The truth of the matter is there is, at least as far as what is brought to our attention, far greater discrimination on the ground of race than there is on the ground of sex.

Mrs. GREEN. How have you reached that conclusion?

Mr. LEONARD. Based on the complaints which come to us.

Madam Chairman, let me make this completely clear to you: We have no hesitancy to act in upholding the law, and we will. But we cannot act on conclusions. We have to act on facts. We have to act on complaints.

Mrs. GREEN. But my understanding is that over 12,000 complaints have been made to the EEOC of discrimination based on sex. Now, I do not know how many of those are valid, but there have been complaints.

Mr. LEONARD. But please understand in addition that the Justice Department has only pattern or practice authority. We have no authority to act upon the complaint of one female who may have been discriminated against for a specific job. We can act only where it is shown that the employer has engaged in a pattern or practice of discrimination against women, and we are willing to do that. We have done it. We do not hesitate to do it. But the facts have to be there.

Mrs. GREEN. With respect to preference by any department or agency of the Government, if you want to go back to that, in terms of title VII, we have the executive order that where there is discrimination, the Federal contractors must present an affirmative plan of action. This is not done by the Justice Department, I grant you, but I thought perhaps you would want to comment upon it, because it involved the Enforcement Division and the Compliance Division.

I have a letter directed to a company in Portland. They simply state that when deficiencies, including the absence of a token representation of minority employees, are found to exist in the Federal contractors equal employment opportunity program, the regulations require that the contractor develop a written affirmative action program which includes an analysis of the current work force and the establishment of goals and time deadlines, etc., etc.

Now, it is my understanding that the Labor Department, and we have, I hope, someone who can respond to this question today, has made this Order No. 4 apply only to minorities and not to discrimination on the basis of sex. Now, is that not stating an administrative preference under title VII?

Mr. LEONARD. I think, Madam Chairman, my difficulty in answering the question is that it may be that Order No. 4 in and of itself may relate only to racial questions. But I have before me another guideline which has been published by the Department of Labor which relates to sex discrimination. And although I am frank to admit I have not gone into it to any great depth, it does seem to set out affirmative action responsibilities for employers. And, of course, that is what Order No. 4 is all about. I would have to put the two together and spend some time reading them to determine whether or not there is any difference between the two, either in fact or in intent.

Mrs. GREEN. What is the executive order that you are referring to?

Mr. LEONARD. I am reading from a guideline that was printed in the Federal Register on June 9 of this year, just a little over a month ago. It purports to be an implementation of Executive Order 11375. If I am correct, I believe that is the order which supplemented Executive Order 11246.

Mrs. GREEN. That was at the time of the 50th anniversary?

Mr. LEONARD. I am told that that is correct; yes.

Mrs. GREEN. May I ask you, Mr. Leonard, to supply additional views on that, because it seems to me that Order No. 4 is far stronger in requiring the contractors to have an affirmative action program, and they so far have said this does not involve discrimination on sex; it applies only to racial matters. That is really the basis of my question. It seems to me that the Government has, by administrative action, placed enforcement in ending one kind of discrimination above all others, when Congress did not in any way say that that was to be the case. We are going to hear from the Labor Department and I hope there will be somebody who can respond definitely to these questions.

Mr. LEONARD. I hope so, too.

Mrs. GREEN. Thank you very much Mr. Leonard. Mr. Scherle, do you have any further questions?

Mr. SCHERLE. Madam Chairman, just a little statement. I am not going to judge at this time as to whether or not this type of legislation is necessary. However, there is one thing that always makes me a little gun shy. I had the opportunity not too long ago to ride in with a contractor from Illinois. He was at that time constructing a project under a Federal project. He told me on the way in that his contractors, the carpenters could not complete the job because he could not hire any minorities that were qualified to do the job at that time. So he went out and paid $7.50 an hour for these people to read funny books while they completed that job. Now, I say this only in warning that maybe some of the legislation we get into someday might be much more devastating than that which we contemplate as a cure-all.

That is all, Madam Chairman.

Mrs. GREEN. Could I ask one other thing, Mr. Leonard? Do you have the language for your proposed change in title VI?

Mr. LEONARD. I think we could submit that to you next week.

Mrs. GREEN. Would you do that, and would you also provide additional views in relation to the equal rights amendment which I hope will be approved by the Congress this session, what effect it will have on that?

Mr. LEONARD. Yes.

Mrs. GREEN. "Bona fide" has been, over the past many, many years the excuse for a lot of abuses. Would you suggest how we can word the amendment so that it would in fact, just provide for bona fide differences.

Mr. LEONARD. Yes.

Mrs. GREEN. Thank you.

Mr. LEONARD. Thank you.

(The document referred to follows:)

OFFICE OF THE DEPUTY ATTORNEY GENERAL,
Washington, D.C., August 19, 1970.

Hon. EDITH GREEN,

Chairman, Special Subcommittee on Education, Committee on Education and Labor, House of Representatives, Washington, D.C.

DEAR MADAM CHAIRMAN : At the July 31, 1970, hearing on section 805 of H.R. 16098, you requested Assistant Attorney General Leonard to furnish the Subcommittee a bill embodying our proposed alternative to subsection 805(a). The proposed legislation has been drafted, and a copy of it is enclosed.

You also asked Mr. Leonard to submit statistics regarding referrals sent to this Department by the Equal Employment Opportunity Commission and a memorandum discussing the bearing of the proposed Equal Rights Amendment upon the bona fide distinction exception contained in our proposal. The Civil Rights Division is in the process of preparing that material, and we will forward it to you as soon as it is completed.

We hope that the enclosed draft will be acceptable to you.

Sincerely,

HERBERT E. HOFFMAN,
Chief, Legislative and Legal Section.

A BILL To prohibit discrimination on the ground of sex in education programs receiving Federal financial assistance

Be it enacted by the Senate and House of Representatives of the United States of America in Congress assembled, that this Act may be cited as the —————.

SEC. 2. (a) No person in the United States shall, on the ground of sex, be excluded from participation in, denied the benefits of, or subjected to discrimination under, any education program or activity receiving Federal financial assistance, except where sex is a bona fide ground for differential treatment.

(b) No recipient of Federal financial assistance for an education program or activity shall, because of an individual's sex,

(1) fail or refuse to hire (except in instances where sex is a bona fide occupational qualification) or discharge that individual, or otherwise discriminate against him or her with respect to compensation, terms, conditions, or privileges of employment ; or

(2) limit, segregate, or classify employees in any way which would deprive or tend to deprive that individual of employment opportunities or otherwise adversely affect his or her status as an employee.

SEC. 3. (a) Each Federal department and agency which is empowered to extend Federal financial assistance to any education program or activity, by way of grant, loan, or contract other than a contract of insurance or guaranty, is authorized and directed to effectuate the provisions of section 2 with respect to such program or activity by issuing rules, regulations, or orders of general applicability which shall be consistent with achievement of the objectives of the statute authorizing the financial assistance in connection with which the action is taken. No such rule, regulation, or order shall become effective unless and until approved by the President.

(b) Compliance with any requirement adopted pursuant to subsection (a) may be effected (1) by the termination of or refusal to grant or to continue assistance under such program or activity to any recipient as to whom there has been an express finding on the record, after opportunity for hearing, of a failure to comply with such requirement, but such termination or refusal shall be limited to the particular political entity, or part thereof, or other recipient as to whom such a finding has been made and shall be limited in its effect to the particular program, or part thereof, in which such noncompliance has been so found, or (2) by any other means authorized by law : *Provided, however,* That no such action shall be taken until the department or agency concerned has advised the appropriate person or persons of the failure to comply with the requirement and has determined that compliance cannot be secured by voluntary means.

(c) In the case of any action terminating, or refusing to grant or continue, assistance because of failure to comply with a requirement imposed pursuant to subsection (a), the head of the Federal department or agency shall file with the committees of the House and Senate having legislative jurisdiction over the program or activity involved a full written report of the circumstances and the grounds for such action. No such action shall become effective until thirty days have elapsed after the filing of such report.

SEC. 4. Any department or agency action taken pursuant to section 3 shall be subject to such judicial review as may otherwise be provided by law for similar action taken by such department or agency on other grounds. In the case of action, not otherwise subject to judicial review, terminating or refusing to grant or to continue financial assistance upon a finding of failure to comply with any requirement imposed pursuant to section 3(a), any person aggrieved (including any State or political subdivision thereof and any agency of either) may obtain judicial review of such action in accordance with chapter 7 of title 5, United States Code, and such action shall not be deemed committed to unreviewable agency discretion within the meaning of that chapter.

SEC. 5. Nothing in this act shall add to or detract from any existing authority with respect to any education program or activity under which Federal financial assistance is extended by way of a contract of insurance or guaranty.

SEC. 6. For the purposes of this act, the term "education" includes pre-school, elementary, secondary and post-secondary education.

Mrs. GREEN. Our next witnesses are representatives from the Department of Labor.

Mrs. Koontz, we are delighted to see you.

Is there anybody from the Solicitor's Office?

STATEMENT OF MRS. ELIZABETH DUNCAN KOONTZ, DIRECTOR, WOMEN'S BUREAU; ACCOMPANIED BY CAROL COX, SOLICITOR'S OFFICE; AND MRS. PEARL SPINDLER, WOMEN'S BUREAU

Mrs. KOONTZ. Miss Carol Cox will be here with me at the table from the Solicitor's Office; also Mrs. Spindler from the Women's Bureau.

Mrs. GREEN. Would you proceed, Mrs. Koontz?

Mrs. KOONTZ. Thank you, Madam Chairman and members of the subcommittee.

I am pleased to appear before this special subcommittee to discuss equal opportunity for women. As Director of the Women's Bureau, I am constantly and sadly reminded that in the lives of all too many women, the enjoyment of equality in many realms, notably the economic realm, is a myth. The attention of the subcommittee to legislation designed to extend the principle of equality to women is, therefore, very gratifying to me.

The Women's Bureau was established for the sole and important purpose of assisting in improving the lives of women, particularly working women. In 1920 when the Bureau was established, the working woman, her interests and needs, were in a sense isolated from those of other women. This, of course, has long ceased to be true. The needs and aspirations of working women are the needs and aspirations of most women, since the majority of women do work at some time during their lives.

Our Bureau's goal remains that of improving the lives of women but our focus has widened in recent years. We are concerned with the girl as she prepares for work, the girl as she fares in work, the mature woman as she reenters or prepares to reenter the working world and her versatile role in that world. We are also concerned with the disadvantaged woman and girl, barriers to their economic opportunities, and training to break down some of these barriers.

At any point in the life of a working female and in her educational prospects before she enters the worker's world, it is well established that she is likely to encounter irrational, hurtful discrimination on the basis of sex. Section 805 of the proposal before you has the worthy aim of reducing her chances of being victimized by that discrimination.

We favor legal remedies to prevent discrimination on the basis of sex. In view of the Department of Justice's expertise we defer to that Department's assessment of the effectiveness of the legal remedies proposed in section 805(a) and 805(b) of H.R. 16098, amending title VI and title VII of the Civil Rights Act of 1964.

I wish to direct my testimony to matters within the experience of the Labor Department.

With respect to section 805(c), I believe the Federal Government should have a positive responsibiilty to study, investigate, and report on discrimination on the basis of sex. The Department of Labor, however, respectfully recommends that this responsibility be placed in the Women's Bureau where it can be discharged together with other duties pertaining to the welfare of women.

We like to think that after 50 years of faithful stewardship in the realm of women's protection and women's advancement, the Women's Bureau might reasonably anticipate having the express blessing of Congress to put out some new shoots. The Bureau needs clear-cut authority to bring its functions up to date, to include such important matters as discrimination on the basis of sex.

Mrs. GREEN. Could I interrupt you there, Mrs. Koontz. I understand you are expressing the official attitude of the Labor Department, but if there were discrimination against black women, would they suggest that it be handled by the Women's Bureau of the Labor Department?

Mrs. KOONTZ. I am certain that the enforcement probably would be expected to be within the realm of the enforcement agencies as it stands on an equal basis.

Mrs. GREEN. But it would not be in the Women's Bureau?

Mrs. KOONTZ. Well, certainly, black women would be a part of the general group of women as a category.

Mrs. GREEN. But if the discrimination were based on color and it just happened to be a woman, where would it go? Would it go to the Women's Bureau or would it stay in the Civil Rights Division and the Enforcement Division?

Mrs. KOONTZ. I think that in view of the probable testimony and considerations as given previously, the Civil Rights Commission does this on the basis of race. This is a very huge, severe problem, and the fact is we believe specific attention to it should be given by the civil rights agency.

The Bureau is in a position to give undivided attention to women's concerns. Functions pertaining to women would not have to be fitted in with uncorrelated duties having a different emphasis. At the present time we are recipients of numerous communications from individual women and from organizations about women's problems, including discrimination on the basis of sex, but we do not have the legislative authority to investigate or systematically to compile date on sex discrimination in the manner which H.R. 16098 proposes.

Moreover, we have no express authority to question laws, policies, or actions apparently inimical to the interests of women. We are limited to seeking to exercise a persuasive role when we are informed of matters which relate to sex discrimination. Our results, therefore, hang entirely on the acquiescence of other agencies to our proddings.

The Women's Bureau presently makes studies, compiles and analyzes data, and disseminates information and publications to promote the welfare of working women. Priority areas under our present mandate are labor laws (e.g., minimum wage and overtime pay, equal pay, fair employment practices, etc.), employment opportunities, labor force research, vocational guidance and counseling, special problems of low-income women and girls, continuing education, and promotion of supportive services for working women. It performs these duties from its unique position as the only Federal agency exclusively devoted to the problems of women.

The Civil Rights Commission in testimony before this subcommittee has expressed reservations about adding discrimination on the basis of sex to its existing functions. It will have to gear up for this new subject with additional outlays of money. We believe that the Women's Bureau could undertake the new functions more economically although we, of course, would require a modest increase in resources.

We now are a repository for voluntary information on sex discrimination. We now are looked to by many both inside and outside of Government for advice and direction with respect to sex discrimination. Within the limits of our resources, we give what assistance we can. We would like to do much more.

The legislative recognition at this time of the Women's Bureau as the Federal coordinator of action and data on sex discrimination will enhance the Bureau's prestige in all areas in which we work. In modern parlance, our image will be brightened. This means renewed hope and confidence in the future for the women who now make up its constituency.

We bespeak consideration of our earnest request for your encouragement of our growth. This subcommittee has before it an expression of policy for comprehensive study in the area of sex discrimination. We approve that policy, asking only that the Women's Bureau lead in its fulfillment. We would like in the near future to submit to the Congress language to broaden our mandate.

Section 805(d) concerns executive, professional and administrative employees and outside salesmen who are exempted from the equal pay provisions of the Fair Labor Standards Act. H.R. 16098 would repeal this exemption.

These employees already have statutory protection against discrimination on the basis of sex under title VII of the Civil Rights Act of 1964. Indeed, the scope of protection under title VII is much broader than the equal pay provision in the Fair Labor Standards Act. Title VII covers other employment conditions, such as the right to be hired and to have the opportunity of obtaining rewarding employment, to rise out of low paying tedious jobs. These rights are as important to women as equal pay and, indeed, a precondition to any pay discrimination. The Equal Pay Act does not afford these protections. It is our experience in the administration of that act that seldom do equal pay violations stand alone in a firm's pattern of operations. The equal pay violation is usually just one manifestation of discrimination on the basis of sex and the only one we can reach under the Equal Pay Act.

We believe, therefore, that efforts should be directed toward eliminating the full spectrum of employment discrimination against women through the effective operation of title VII. Consequently, we advocate enactment of adequate enforcement machinery for title VII as recommended by the Administration as a solution to the equal pay and related problems of executive-type employees. This title is now deficient in putting the burden on aggrieved employees to institute their own court proceedings when they are seeking relief from discrimination.

I am looking forward to the time when, with full equality assured, men and women will be united in a national effort to achieve a better life for all workers. Actions now proposed by your subcommittee will hasten that proud day.

Madam Chairman, I am pleased to enter into the record the Secretary's statement on sex discrimination that may in part answer the question that was previously asked.

The Federal Government is convinced that the under-utilization of women in employment throughout the nation constitutes a waste of national resources and talent. In recognition of that fact, sex discrimination in employment is prohibited by Executive Order 11246, as amended by Executive Order 11375. Neither those orders nor the Federal Government in enforcing them makes any distinction in the end result sought between sex discrimination and discrimination based on race, creed, color, or national origin. All prohibited discrimination must be dealt with effectively.

Guidelines on sex discrimination were issued by the Department of Labor on June 9, 1970, to provide new requirements of and guidance to Government contractors in eliminating the barriers to equal employment opportunity without regard to sex. Order No. 4, on the other hand, was issued to eliminate primarily race and color barriers to equal employment opportunity. Both documents are directed to the same result and both require affirmative action on the part of Government contractors to attain that result. The primary procedural distinction between the two is the requirement set forth in Order No. 4 that Government contractors analyze their work force and their potential work force recruitment area and where deficiencies in the utilization of minorities exist, that goals and timetables be set to which the contractors efforts shall be directed to eliminate those deficiencies.

These specific procedural requirements of Order No. 4 are not totally suitable to sex discrimination. It is clear that utilization of the concept of goals and timetables as an anti-sex discrimination tool is appropriate. It is equally clear that the exact goals and timetables development procedure set forth in Order No. 4 is not sufficient to meet the often more difficult and elusive problems of sex discrimination. The work force pattern of women and racial minorities differs in significant respects. Many women do not seek employment. Practically all adult males do. Many occupations——

Mrs. GREEN. Does the Labor Department give that as a justification for Order No. 4?

Mrs. KOONTZ. Within the procedure set forth in the actual guides, a part of this is a consideration in their determining the timetables and the goals.

Mrs. GREEN. Because all men seek employment and only 40 percent——

Mrs. KOONTZ. Generally with the assumption that all males do.

Mrs. GREEN. I really am discouraged now, Mrs. Koontz, if that is the official attitude of the Labor Department.

Mrs. KOONTZ. Maybe you will not be as I go on.

Mrs. GREEN. I am getting more and more discouraged about any real deep concern or intention to act.

Mrs. KOONTZ. Well, please don't.

Many occupations sought after by all racial groups may not have been sought by women in significant numbers. A wide disparity in proportions of racial categories exists among the various labor markets of the nation and this disparity does not exist for women.

Now, accordingly, different criteria must be employed in examining work force patterns to reveal the deficiencies in employment of women than are used in revealing racial deficiencies. Such criteria may well include the availability of qualified women in the employer's own force and the interest level expressed in respective occupations, as evidenced by applications for employment in those occupations. It will be necessary to examine whether the applicant's interest among women for certain occupations might be changed by effective, affirmative action programs, and to properly examine these criteria and review suggestions regarding them or regarding the other applicable criteria. The Department plans to engage in an immediate series of consultations with interested parties. Representatives of women's groups, employers, and unions as well as acknowledged authorities on human resources will be invited to participate. The Women's Bureau is presently assisting in this by identifying and recommending women's groups with major contributions to such establishment of the criteria. The information thus obtained will be utilized by the Department in expanding and further defining its approach toward employing affirmative action to achieve an equal employment opportunity for women among Government contractors and by applying the concept of goals and timetables.

Thank you, Madam Chairman.

Mrs. GREEN. Thank you, Mrs. Koontz. Anything I say should not be interpreted as against you personally. I have had the highest regard for you during the years when you were president of the National Education Association, and I was so pleased when the administration appointed you as Director of the Women's Bureau. I think your capacity, your intellect, your personal concern, and your articulateness qualify you for the position. I make the following statements knowing that you did not write that last bit of rhetoric.

I just have to say it is the biggest bunch of gobbledygook I have heard for a long, long time. Therefore, I would be a bit discouraged about the recommendation that the Women's Bureau become the enforcement division to protect women. Because it seems to me that you would still be under the Secretary of Labor, who in only one instance, back in FDR times, was ever a woman. And the Labor Department—you know, after a hundred years, has apparently yet to find out the widespread pattern of discrimination on the basis of sex. There is not much hope in their future plans of action.

Let me turn to Order 4.

Mrs. KOONTZ. May I make a comment on that?

Mrs. GREEN. Yes.

Mrs. KOONTZ. I think there is some advantage in this, though we would not have the enforcement power. That would remain with the agencies that have been given the enforcement. But we do know that there is discrimination among women expressed by many women who do not know the recourses open to them. The Women's Bureau would have the opportunity of investigating and reporting which would allow those agencies to have before them the cases.

Mrs. GREEN. And Congress would give you about one-fiftieth of the amount of money they would give the other agencies of the Government. I think this recommendation, in and of itself, smacks of discrimination. You, surely, or the Administration would not be in favor of having the Bureau of Indian Affairs be responsible for all the investigation and charges and so on of discrimination against Indians, would you?

Mrs. KOONTZ. No; and we would not have the total——

Mrs. GREEN. And would you have a Bureau of Blacks, and set them apart to investigate discrimination against ethnic minorities? It seems to me we ought to come to a time when we treat all women as human beings and that we not discriminate against women in this case and say, here is all of the machinery of the Government over here, and here is a little part over here for women. Because after all, women are 51 percent of the population and 40 percent of the labor force.

Mrs. KOONTZ. I think we would not advance all of the investigatory functions. They would, I believe as expressed by EEOC——

Mrs. GREEN. And you would be expected as the Women's Bureau to operate in a very ladylike fashion. It seems to me if we are going to end discrimination, it is going to have to be done in a determined—and if I may suggest it—in a very tough fashion.

Mrs. KOONTZ. I think perhaps we might leave that image of pursuing daintily our goals.

Mrs. GREEN. Let's go back to Order No. 4. The two orders you did cite, the executive order and the one amending the executive order, gave great encouragement to women who are concerned about discrimination. But it seems to me that Order No. 4 definitely does state a difference.

Now, I know that the rhetoric that you have been required to repeat this morning tries to rationalize this away. But let me ask you if you can supply for this committee a single letter to any employer, any factory, any industry or anybody, telling them that they have to have an affirmative plan of action under the two previous executive orders which you cited? Do you know of a single letter that has gone out to anybody?

Mrs. KOONTZ. I would be glad to verify that.

Mrs. GREEN. I would like one dated before August 1.

Mrs. KOONTZ. All right.

Mrs. GREEN. Because I have in my files letters that have gone out from the Compliance Division of the Department of Labor in regard to affirmative plan of action in having ethnic groups.

I have one in front of me, dated March 23, saying that you are going to be held in noncompliance if you do not provide us with an affirmative plan of action in terms of the hiring of minority groups.

Now, it is well, you know, to have the other two executive orders, but if no follow-up is ever made and if no employer is ever told to have an affirmative plan of action, then it seems to me it is just idle rhetoric.

Mrs. KOONTZ. I think I can say, Madam Chairman, from this statement that there will be forthcoming the kind of order that will compare with Order No. 4, which was specifically for racial discrimination, and that women's groups are being invited to consult and it is to be done immediately. They will assist in determining the criteria which is designed to prohibit sex discrimination. We have requested this because the Women's Bureau is quite vitally concerned, as women's groups are.

I do have the confidence that this order will be forthcoming and the general concern for the goals and timetables will be built into it with the affirmative action that is expressed in the guidelines.

Mrs. GREEN. Well, I would be more persuaded as to the desire of the Department of Labor if you will supply this committee with copies of letters, if you can find any, that have been sent to any employer under the two previous executive orders which you say require an affirmative plan of action.

Mrs. KOONTZ. The guidelines require affirmative action.

Mrs. GREEN. Let's turn to the equal pay, removing the exemption. I was not clear from your statement whether the Department of Labor is in favor of the amendment which I have to remove the exemption of professional, executive, and administrative positions or not.

Mrs. KOONTZ. I would ask Miss Cox, from the Solicitor's Office, if she could make the comment on this particular item.

Miss Cox. Well, the way we feel about it is that it really does not seem to be necessary.

Mrs. GREEN. Let me stop you right there. You feel it is not necessary. Would it do any harm if it were repealed, then?

Miss Cox. I could not say that it would.

Mrs. GREEN. Let's go further, if the exemption is not repealed, is it not legal to discriminate or to pay different salaries for women who hold administrative, executive or professional positions?

Miss Cox. It is not under title VII. Title VII covers all these people.

Mrs. GREEN. But you have laws in conflict?

Miss Cox. Not in conflict, but in concert, mounted along the same lines. We feel like the relief under title VII is more adequate.

Mrs. GREEN. Tell me what relief professional or executive women have ever enjoyed under it, over the past years since the enactment of title VII.

Miss Cox. We hope with additional enforcement machinery that the program might be more effective.

Mrs. GREEN. But has the Labor Department ever moved into executive, administrative and professional positions where there was a differential on pay?

Miss Cox. No, because we do not have the authority, because of what I just mentioned.

Mrs. GREEN. Exactly. That is why the exemption has to be removed, does it not?

Miss Cox. Well, our idea is that the women who go to EEOC may get other injustices of employment taken care of. She may get her promotions taken care of.

Mrs. GREEN. I recognize that. But you just said, if I understood you correctly, that we do not need to remove this exemption because title VII covers it. Then I asked you what relief any woman has ever had from a differential in pay if she is in an executive, professional or administrative position. You tell me there is no relief because it is not in violation of the law.

Miss Cox. No, I did not mean to say that. The EEOC has equal pay cases. I do not know of any specific ones, but they handle equal pay cases and for executive, professional, or administrative personnel, just like they do for other employees.

Mrs. GREEN. But the law allows a differential?

Miss Cox. No; they would have the same right under title VII to receive an adjustment of unequal pay as they would for other discriminations.

Mrs. GREEN. Mr. Hogan.

Mr. HOGAN. The enforcement procedure that would otherwise be available under the Fair Labor Standards Act is now not available to women.

Miss Cox. That is correct.

Mr. HOGAN. Is there any reason why it should not be available?

Miss Cox. Well, we think that the title VII route is a more effective route.

Mrs. GREEN. Well, cite me one instance when it has been effective.

Miss Cox. Well, I cannot cite specific cases.

Mrs. Green. I can cite you a thousand where it has not, where there has been absolutely no possibility for such a professional or executive woman employee to get any help when she is obviously receiving a different salary than a man doing identical work.

Do you have any other questions Mr. Hogan?

Mr. Hogan. Would it be in order, Mrs. Green, to ask the witness to give us—obviously, she is here under an instruction to take a certain position. But we would like to know why the Department of Labor thinks that the enforcement procedure under the Fair Labor Standards Act is not appropriate for enforcement of the prohibition of discrimination against sex.

Miss Cox. Well, of course, under the Fair Labor Standards Act, you have a number of exemptions other than that one you are talking about. You have, for example, retail exemptions.

Mrs. Green. We are talking about sex discrimination today. The only exception by sex under the Fair Labor Standards Act, where there should be no discrimination based on sex, and there should be equal pay for equal work, is in three categories of professional, administrative, and executive positions. In the other categories, though there are many exemptions, the exceptions are not based on sex.

Miss Cox. Well, if you repeal the professional, administrative, executive exemptions, you would still have these people who would be in other exemptions, such as the retail exemption.

Mrs. Green. But not on the basis of sex.

Miss Cox. No, but you could not get to the sex discrimination, because they are exempt from the Equal Pay Act.

Mrs. Green. But we are talking in this committee about trying to end the discrimination based upon sex and I would like to confine it to that and not to the other exemptions in the Fair Labor Standards Act.

Miss Cox. Another thing about the Fair Labor Standards Act is a discrimination in pay on the basis of sex is prohibited only on an establishment basis. You cannot compare establishments. So in the education line, for example, where there is a single principal in a school and in the same system, there is a male principal in another school who receives a higher salary, you would have no recourse under the Fair Labor Standards Act, whereas you would have under title VII.

Mrs. Green. Well, even though the Labor Department thinks title VII takes care of it, why, what harm would it do to remove this one exemption for professional, executive and administrative positions.

Miss Cox. I could not say it would do any harm.

Mrs. Green. Then the Labor Department is in favor of it or opposed to it?

Miss Cox. The position is as Mrs. Koontz stated.

Mrs. Green. She didn't say it. That was very ambiguous.

Miss Cox. I do not think I can clarify it more than that.

Mrs. Green. Let me turn to the apprenticeship program, Mrs. Koontz. Has anything been done, either in the Women's Bureau or in the Department of Labor, about the fact that only 1 percent of the apprenticeship jobs are held by girls and 99 percent by boys?

Mrs. Koontz. Yes; I suppose we can say that it is an increase over last year's number.

Mrs. GREEN. By one-tenth of 1 percent?

Mrs. KOONTZ. The Labor Department does have, I believe, antidiscrimination clauses in the program. But Federal money is not concerned. It has regulatory power, if I am not mistaken, to approve the apprenticeship contracts or the agreements so that the encouragement of women in apprenticeship programs certainly is one that we have been pursuing and the practice, I should hope, would be improved to a much greater extent.

Mrs. GREEN. Previous administrations have come out against having 50 percent of the Job Corps positions available to girls. The highest we have ever achieved has been 29 percent. I tried to get it up to 50 percent and I think the law is now somewhere around 33 and enrollment is at 29 percent. Has the Women's Bureau, or the Department of Labor taken any position on this, or are we to continue discrimination against girls in the Job Corps?

Mrs. KOONTZ. I believe we are encouraging the increase and I think as to the new Mini-Corps, we are encouraging the cities to develop them or to consider it.

I think the percentage of increase, according to our latest figures out of 1969, do suggest some increases.

Mrs. GREEN. Do you know what—and in manpower training or retraining programs?

Mrs. KOONTZ. In the various programs under MDTA, 44 percent, and on the job, 35 percent. I feel the New Careers program, indicating 70 percent at this time, is one of the most encouraging. With the Job Corps, it is still 29 percent, which indicates room for much improvement and encouragement.

Mrs. GREEN. You heard the Justice Department position on the amendment to title VI, that it should only apply to education. Is it illegal now to discriminate against girls in apprenticeship programs?

Mrs. KOONTZ. I am not sure I can answer that. I know there is an antidiscrimination clause.

Mrs. GREEN. Is this ratio of 99 percent and 1 percent in violation of any law?

Mrs. SPINDLER. I think it is in violation of title VII of the Civil Rights Act. It is also a violation of Labor Department regulations.

Mrs. GREEN. Apprenticeship is not entirely employment. Are you sure that——

Mrs. SPINDLER. Yes.

Mrs. GREEN. Has there been a ruling that this discrimination is a violation of the title VII?

Mrs. KOONTZ. I think the 1966 order. We still operate under, I believe, the 1966 order. Is that right?

Mrs. SPINDLER. Yes. I can read title VII on it:

It shall be an unlawful employment practice for any employer or labor organization or joint labor-management committee controlling apprenticeship or other training or retraining, including on-the-job training, to discriminate against any individual because of sex.

That is part of title VII. It is also a part of the Labor Department regulations.

Mrs. GREEN. What has the Labor Department done about it?

Mrs. SPINDLER. According to our records, as Mrs. Koontz has pointed out, we have improved somewhat. We cannot say we have gone all the way up.

Mrs. GREEN. You still admit it is one percent?

Mrs. SPINDLER. We admit it is low. It is very low.

Mrs. GREEN. It is one percent?

Mrs. SPINDLER. I do not know the percentage. That I do not know. I just have the numbers before me and it is low. But we have improved.

Mrs. GREEN. Mrs. Koontz, I really would like to ask, and I hope you can speak as a woman and as a leading educator in the country: What is your real prognosis of the possibility of success in combating discrimination against women? In 1955, the women's median salary income was $2,719, compared to $4,252 by men. It was 64 percent of men's earnings. But in 1968, the women's median was $4,457 and the man's was $7,664, which meant a drop from 64 percent of that obtained by men, to 58 percent. So in the last decade, women have gone down 6 percent in comparison while we have had this great improvement in ending discrimination!

Mrs. KOONTZ. I think that there is no doubt about it, there has been this decrease. And the fact is that it is at the median level principally because of the low-paying jobs that women are in. If sex discrimination exists that keeps women in the low paying jobs then I think we have an obligation to remove the sex discrimination so that women have the choice of jobs, promotions, etc. I am encouraged by the attention being given to the whole matter of sex discrimination and——

Mrs. GREEN. Attention by whom?

Mrs. KOONTZ. By the Labor Department, about which I am privileged to speak. I think there has been a great deal more awareness of the public in general to the form of sex discrimination, and I can personally say that I am encouraged by the attitude and a promise of action.

Mrs. GREEN. I wish you could persuade me that that optimism is justified by the facts.

Mrs. KOONTZ. I am. That is my personal opinion.

Mrs. GREEN. I recently read a statistic, and I think it came from the pamphlet put out by your bureau, that there were more white women in the lowest income brackets in the United States today— and I am speaking now of year-round, full-time jobs—than all Negro men and Negro women combined, working either fulltime or parttime, in the United States. Do you think that is true? I am not positive but I believe it came from your handbook.

Mrs. KOONTZ. It probably did. But what I would be inclined to say is that as we look at the wage scale, I think you are right in saying that the median wage of white women is probably lower, or is lower than that of Negro males.

Mrs. GREEN. My concern is on the part of the Labor Department itself and the Justice Department and the Compliance Division and the Civil Service Commission and the Civil Rights Commission, that with figures given in these days of hearings—that there has been little if any attention given to the discrimination based on sex.

Mrs. KOONTZ. I believe though, if we use numbers by virtue of the Negro population, this could be entirely so, which would not indicate the true picture.

Mrs. GREEN. I am speaking now of really——

Mrs. KOONTZ. Of numbers.

Mrs. GREEN. I am speaking of the children, the youngsters who are at the poverty level or below, toward whom many of our programs are directed.

Mrs. KOONTZ. Yes.

Mrs. GREEN. As I understand it, 60 percent of the children who live in families headed by a woman are in poverty. And if we have a continual pattern of discrimination based on sex, it does tragic things to our society; their children carry for life the disadvantages conferred by discrimination against their mothers.

Mrs. KOONTZ. Yes, I would agree.

Mrs. GREEN. And I repeat—I see little concern being given to this discrimination based on sex; little effort to end it.

Mrs. KOONTZ. We certainly have hope, with some of the programs being projected and some that are in the Congress, and as the Women's Bureau, to really move in this direction with a greater authority, which makes the changing of the Women's Bureau mandate imperative. There are many, I suppose, reasons why certain conditions are not attended to, like substantive reporting, for which we have not had the capacity.

Mrs. GREEN. I must say, Mrs. Koontz, I look at setting up a bureau in the Women's Bureau to end discrimination against women much as I view churches that have "Women's Day," when we honor women in the church for one day!

Mrs. KOONTZ. I think I should make it clear, though, what this really means. It does not mean that all of the investigatory authority of the Federal Government is going to be placed in the Women's Bureau, but it does add some authority to the Women's Bureau mandate, which it does not now have.

Mrs. GREEN. I understand the Labor Department's recommendation and I hope they understand my position and why I look at it with jaundiced eye.

What does the Office of Federal Contract Compliance propose to do about complaints of discrimination in the area of higher education?

Mrs. KOONTZ. I cannot speak specifically for the OFCC, but we do have, with the guidelines having been established, the implications of that and the prospect of the new Order No. 4, which would, itself, involve those forms of discrimination.

Mrs. GREEN. It is my understanding that two organizations—Women's Equity Action League and the National Organization for Women—have filed with the Labor Department over 100 complaints of discrimination in universities and colleges. On June 22 of this year, Mr. Mathis, the public information officer for the Office of Civil Rights, stated that one investigation had been started at the University of Maryland. Is this the progress that you see?

Mrs. KOONTZ. I would ask Miss Cox, who is from the Solicitor's Office, and probably has more knowledge of the specifics than I on this.

Miss COX. I think they have done a little bit better than that. There have been a number of investigations launched. But that is all my information.

Mrs. GREEN. Could you give us the others? Our information as of June was only one.

Miss COX. No; I do not have it. May I get it and submit it to the committee?

Mrs. GREEN. Yes; I would like the ones before August 1, or July 31.

(The information referred to follows:)

COLLEGE AND UNIVERSITY INVESTIGATIONS RELATING TO EXECUTIVE ORDER 11246,
AS AMENDED

The Department of Health, Education and Welfare has been designated by the Department of Labor as Compliance Agency for colleges and universities with respect to compliance with Executive Order 11246, as amended. Pursuant to this designation, the Department of Health, Education and Welfare in June and July of 1970 completed compliance investigations of Harvard University, the University of Maryland, Manhattan Community College and the University of Pittsburgh. An investigation is now scheduled at the University of Michigan.

Mrs. GREEN. How many women are employed in the Women's Bureau in professional capacities?

Mrs. KOONTZ. Approximately 35.

Mrs. GREEN. How many above GS–16, 16 or above?

Mrs. KOONTZ. Two.

Mrs. GREEN. How many men?

Mrs. KOONTZ. In the Women's Bureau? Presently two.

Mrs. GREEN. Above 16?

Mrs. KOONTZ. None.

Mrs. GREEN. No men above 16?

Mrs. KOONTZ. No.

Mrs. GREEN. Discrimination?

Mrs. KOONTZ. No slots.

Mrs. GREEN. In the Department of Labor, at GS–16 or above, how many women and how many men?

Mrs. KOONTZ. I think I can give it to you from this chart that we have that includes females. Above 16, there are seven.

Mrs. GREEN. Seven total?

Mrs. KOONTZ. Five 16's and two 17's.

Mrs. GREEN. And how many men?

Mrs. KOONTZ. Men—the total number in the Labor Department of 16's and above are 99.

Mrs. GREEN. Ninety-nine in the Department of Labor at 16 and above?

Mrs. KOONTZ. Yes, right.

Mrs. GREEN. And again how many women?

Mrs. KOONTZ. Of these, I believe the seven is accurate.

Mrs. GREEN. Seven women out of 99?

Mrs. KOONTZ. Yes.

Mrs. GREEN. You do better than the Office of Education.

Mrs. KOONTZ. Oh, really?

Mrs. GREEN. The Office of Education does not have any women at GS–16 or above.

I have letters in my files written by the Compliance Division of the Department of Labor which says that the absence of Negroes in a particular plant or construction firm is evidence of discrimination. Does the Department of Labor use the same criteria in looking at itself?

Mrs. KOONTZ. I think I can speak from the record as expressed by the Secretary that this is a priority area in the raising of the level, especially of minorities, and we would consider women as a minority, which we remind persons of constantly.

Mrs. GREEN. Perhaps politically, women might remind the country that they are the majority.

Mrs. KOONTZ. They are treated as a minority.

Mrs. GREEN. Thank you very, very much, Mrs. Koontz. We appreciate your being here. We hope that the other questions which you were not able to respond to, we can have written answers for the record.

Mrs. KOONTZ. We will submit those to you.

Thank you very much.

Let me ask the people who are here from the Civil Service Commission if they could come back, say, at 1 o'clock? Is that possible?

Mr. KATOR. I will be glad to come back here.

Mrs. GREEN. Fine, we shall recess until 1 p.m.

(Thereupon, the committee stood in recess until 1 p.m. that same day.)

AFTERNOON SESSION

Mrs. GREEN. The subcommittee will come to order to resume hearings on the legislation which was discussed this morning. We have as our next witnesses representatives from the Civil Service Commission, Mr. Irving Kator, the Assistant Executive Director, and Miss Helene Markoff, the director of the Federal women's program.

Which one of you is going to lead off?

STATEMENT OF IRVING KATOR, ASSISTANT EXECUTIVE DIRECTOR, CIVIL SERVICE COMMISSION; ACCOMPANIED BY MISS HELENE S. MARKOFF, DIRECTOR, FEDERAL WOMEN'S PROGRAM, CIVIL SERVICE COMMISSION

Mr. KATOR. I will, Madam Chairman.

Mrs. GREEN. All right.

Mr. KATOR. Madam Chairman, members of the subcommittee, we are pleased to respond to your invitation to appear before this subcommittee to discuss the employment of women in the Federal Government. I should make clear at this point that we will not be discussing H.R. 16098 but will be discussing generally the responsibility of women in government. I have with me Miss Helene Markoff, who recently became director of the Federal women's program. She will assist me in answering questions or providing additional information to the committee.

There are few areas in the Federal Government in which women have not made their mark. They have participated in all the Federal Government's many accomplishments, whether in medicine, science, diplomacy, law, or administration, and most recently, as evidenced by Secretary Hickel's commendation, in pioneering underwater exploration. Dedicated employees are the Federal Government's greatest assets and more than one-third of these assets are the women in our workforce.

The Civil Service Commission is dedicated to the proposition that persons regardless of sex, race, color, religion, or national origin will have an equal opportunity to serve in Federal positions at all levels and in all occupations. We want to assure that the abilities of women and their skills are used to the maximum extent. We believe it is an unconscionable waste of human resources to fail to use the skills of all persons, whether they be minority group persons or women, in the demanding tasks that face the Federal Government today.

We don't believe women should be relegated to typewriters and clerical work. We don't believe that the turnover rates of women employees are so different from men, nor is their absenteeism any different given the same levels of responsibility within an organization. In short, we don't believe in the stereotypes of women's place in the workforce or that they cannot handle executive or other top-level positions or that their turnover rate is so much higher or their absenteeism any greater.

What we do believe is that the Government must be broadly representative of the population it serves. We believe that decisionmaking by Federal officials will be better decisionmaking when it derives from a mix of the variety of persons who make up our population. This means we recognize the need for more qualified women to occupy top level, decisionmaking positions in Government just as we believe that additional qualified minority group persons should serve in such positions. The Federal equal employment opportunity program which includes the Federal women's program is dedicated to these ends.

Mrs. GREEN. Could I interrupt there, Mr. Kator?

Mr. KATOR. Yes.

Mrs. GREEN. At the top of the page, the inference is left that the absenteeism and the turnover is much higher for women. How much higher is it?

Mr. KATOR. No; I did not intend any inference.

Mrs. GREEN. Or I should say is higher.

Mr. KATOR. The study which I am familiar with would indicate that at the same levels of responsibility in an organization, the absenteeism rate is pretty much the same. I had no inference.

Mrs. GREEN. Do you have those recent figures or later studies? This is one of the myths that should be dispelled.

Mr. KATOR. Yes; I know it is one of the myths. Our study of 1965— is it there, Miss Markoff?

Miss MARKOFF. Yes; we have a study done at the Civil Service Commission several years ago. The Department of Labor has also published a very informative pamphlet. I do not think the inference was that there is a difference, but that there is no difference in comparable grade levels to occupations. Too often the myth is perpetuated because they are comparing unlike positions.

Mrs. GREEN. I think the part that disturbs me was "or that their turnover rate is so much higher."

Miss MARKOFF. Well, so much.

Mrs. GREEN. Then I misunderstood you. I'm sorry.

Mr. KATOR. It is not intended to be an inference.

Mrs. GREEN. I think the studies show this is wrong.

Mr. KATOR. The studies show that at the same levels of responsibility within an organization, you will find the same absenteeism rate, and this is the only implication I meant.

Mrs. GREEN. And the same turnover.

Thank you.

Mr. KATOR. We have attempted, for one thing, to achieve a legal framework in which women have equal opportunity to work for and to move up within the Federal Government. We support legislation to change laws which now provide different treatment of men and women as regards personnel benefits. For example, we reported favorably on H.R. 468 which would assure equality of treatment for widows and widowers for benefits due because of death in service of the spouse. This will remove the last remaining vestige of any different treatment of men and women in Federal employee benefit legislation, administered by the Civil Service Commission. Our position would be generally supportive of other legislation similarly intentioned as regards Federal employees. The Civil Service Act provides for appointments on the basis of merit and fitness, not on whether you are male or female, black or white. In carrying out our responsibilities for staffing the Federal work force, we do not make any distinction in certifying persons to jobs except in two instances: Law enforcement positions which require use of a weapon and custodial jobs serving persons of a particular sex and we currently have under review this very matter as it relates to law enforcement positions. For these reasons, we supported the recommendation to issue Executive Order 11375, signed by President Johnson in October 1967, which added sex to Executive Order 11246 on equal employment opportunity.

Under this order we established the Federal women's program with a director and staff to provide leadership to the Federal Government's efforts at assuring equal opportunity for women. We had three main objectives:

> (1) To create the regulatory and administrative framework for achieving equality of opportunity without regard to sex;
> (2) To bring practice in closer accord with merit principles through the elimination of attitudes, customs, and habits which have previously denied women entry into certain occupations, as well as into higher level positions throughout the career service; and
> (3) To encourage qualified women to compete in examinations for Federal employment and to participate in training programs leading to advancement.

In August 1969, President Nixon issued Executive Order 11478 on equal employment opportunity. The President had asked the Civil Service Commission for recommendations on the equal employment opportunity program and the new order came about as a result of Chairman Robert E. Hampton's recommendations to the President. Sex was included in the order along with race, color, religion, and national origin as a prohibited ground of discrimination. We consider this order to be the strongest, most comprehensive executive order on equal employment opportunity which any President has ever issued. Through this order and through Commission administration of it, the Federal women's program became an integral part of the equal employment program and the agency's Director of Equal Employment Opportunity was made responsible for progress.

Let me clarify that if I may. In each agency, there is a Director of Equal Employment Opportunity and we have assigned responsibility to him to make sure that the treatment of women employees is comparable to that of all other employees. This is his responsibility.

Mrs. GREEN. Is it always a him or a his?

Mr. KATOR. No; as a matter of fact, Mrs. Green, in a number of cases, it is her.

Mrs. GREEN. How many of the coordinators for women's programs are men?

Mr. KATOR. Twenty of the coordinators of the—women's coordinators—are men. Forty-five are women.

Mrs. GREEN. How many positions are still unfilled?

Mr. KATOR. Well, none to my knowledge. All our major agencies have responded.

Mrs. GREEN. Does HEW have a coordinator?

Mr. KATOR. Yes.

Mrs. GREEN. I thought that was not filled?

Mr. KATOR. No; we have a letter that indicates that they have a male, Mr. Sam Hoston, as the Federal women's coordinator. He is on Mr. Farmer's staff. Miss Markoff had a meeting yesterday with the Federal women's coordinators and HEW did have two women there. But Mr. Sam Hoston is listed as the Federal women's coordinator for HEW.

Mrs. GREEN. How recent was that appointment?

Mr. KATOR. I would say within the past month.

Miss MARKOFF. Mr. Hoston is the Director of Equal Opportunity, and he is serving as the Federal women's coordinator for HEW. In his absence, he requested permission to send two women to a meeting I was having, I said most certainly, "Yes," with the scope of HEW, certainly, two women are welcome.

Mr. KATOR. We believe that equal employment opportunity efforts must apply to all persons, including minorities and women. Under the new order, agency affirmative action plans developed for equal employment opportunity apply to all employees, including women. All actions agencies take to enhance opportunities for employees, minority or otherwise, must also be taken to enhance opportunities for women. This is the road, we believe, to equal opportunity for all persons and one which will strengthen our efforts in assuring equal opportunity for women.

Mrs. GREEN. May I ask you, have you asked for affirmative action plans?

Mr. KATOR. Yes.

Mrs. GREEN. Has every agency filed such a plan?

Mr. KATOR. Yes.

Mrs. GREEN. Are they adequate?

Mr. KATOR. Not in all cases. We have returned those that we considered inadequate. A number were inadequate. After meeting with the agencies and discussing the plans, we got considerably strengthened plans from a number of the agencies.

Mrs. GREEN. How many of the coordinators are full time?

Mr. KATOR. I believe we have six full-time coordinators.

Miss MARKOFF. Approximately six. At agency level.

Mrs. GREEN. Out of the 65?

Miss MARKOFF. Yes, at agency level we are talking about.

Mr. KATOR. I think we should make clear that we are talking just at the headquarters level. We have also required agencies to have Federal women's coordinators in major installations and field activities. We do not know the precise number of coordinators, but they exist across the country and should be in all major establishments.

Mrs. GREEN. Thank you.

Mr. KATOR. To assure that the special concerns of women were considered as a part of the equal opportunity program, we directed each agency to appoint a Federal women's program coordinator or an advisory committee to serve on the staff of the agency's Director of Equal Employment Opportunity who, incidentally, is usually a person at the Assistant Secretary level. The Coordinator must have empathy for and understanding of the special concerns of women in the employment situation. We also directed agencies to establish coordinators in the major organizational units and field installations. We have strengthened the role of the Commission's Director of the Federal women's program by placing her in the Executive Director's office. The Commission's Executive Director serves as Coordinator for the Governmentwide program for equal employment opportunity and effectively uses his position to help move the women's program forward. This is the administrative framework in the Commission and agencies to assure equal opportunity for women.

Where we stand: Now that I have covered some of our overall concerns for assuring equal opportunity for women, let me give a picture of women in the Federal Government today—a picture, incidentally, which we should like very much to see improved in the years ahead through our Federal women's program.

Overall, over 665,000 women were employed as of October 31, 1969, in full-time, white-collar positions. This is 33.4 percent of the total white-collar workforce. Women employees serve in virtually all occupations, including those usually considered the domain of men, such as nuclear engineering or air traffic control specialist or geologist, to name but a few, but most serve in the administrative, clerical and technical occupations.

Grade-wise, 517,000 women employees were in grades through GS–6 and represent 46.3 percent of the total employment at these grade levels. In the middle and higher grades, GS–7 through GS–12, there were 138,000 women or 20.2 percent of total employment at these grade levels. At the senior levels, grades GS–13 and above, there were over 7,000 women or 3.8 percent of total employment at these grade levels. Of all women employed, 77.8 percent are in grades 1–6, 20.1 percent are in grades 7–12 and 1.1 percent are in grades 13 and above.

Mrs. GREEN. Do you have the breakdown for 16 and above?

Mr. KATOR. Yes, we have 173 women in grades GS–16, 17, and 18.

Mrs. GREEN. What percent?

Mr. KATOR. 1.7 percent of all persons in grade 16 and above.

Mrs. GREEN. I had 1968 figures and it was less than 1 percent.

Mr. KATOR. Yes, it has gone up a little bit.

Miss MARKOFF. Excuse me, you had 1968 figures?

Mrs. GREEN. Yes.

Miss MARKOFF. In 1968, we had 147 women GS–16 and above, which was 1.5 percent in that particular grade group.

Mr. KATOR. This is GS–16 and equivalent.

Mrs. GREEN. I have 147. You have that 1.5?

Miss MARKOFF. Yes.

Mrs. GREEN. But at the present time, it is 1.7 of all the people in policymaking positions in the Federal Government?

Mr. KATOR. No, I would not say policymaking, Mrs. Green, because many positions at grades 13, 14, and 15 we would certainly consider in policymaking. That figure would apply only to those persons in the supergrade level or equivalent. It really represents pay more than policy. True, the pay does accord generally with the policy, but at 13, 14, and 15, and other grade levels, we certainly have responsibility.

Mrs. GREEN. What about the GS–18 and above positions, what percentage are women?

Mr. KATOR. I am really not in a position, Mrs. Green, to comment on that. This is really outside the scope of the Civil Service Commission and I have no figures which would indicate the nature of appointive positions. I know the administration has been generally concerned about this area. I have read of appointments of women, Mrs. Koontz and others, to high level positions, but I am really not in a position to give that.

Mrs. GREEN. Do you have those, Miss Markoff?

Miss MARKOFF. I have some data for 1969.

Mrs. GREEN. What does that show?

Miss MARKOFF. For 18?

Mrs. GREEN. Eighteen and above.

Miss MARKOFF. There is a total of 656 positions collected in this survey, and 17, or 2.6 percent, were female.

Mrs. GREEN. This is in appointive positions by and large?

Miss MARKOFF. Yes; executive levels.

Mr. KATOR. That is above 18.

Mrs. GREEN. Above 18?

Miss MARKOFF. Yes.

Mrs. GREEN. Thank you.

Mr. KATOR. The most recent figures indicate some progress from previous years. The percentage of women employees in grades 1–6 shows a decline of 1.1 percent from 1968 employment. The total number of women employed decreased 8,000 in these lower grade levels from 1968 to 1969 but increased numerically and percentagewise at the higher grade levels. While in 1966 women comprised 18.9 percent of total employment in grades 7–12, in 1968 this percentage was 19.7 and in 1969 was 20.2, a small but steady increase at these grade levels. Women held 30,000 more jobs in these grades in 1969 than in 1966. Of total women employed, 20.8 percent are at these grade levels. In grades GS–13 and above, women comprised 3.5 percent in 1966; 3.7 percent in 1968 and 3.8 percent in 1969, representing an increase of approximately 2,000 women in these jobs.

Mrs. GREEN. Do you have the breakdown of the same grade levels for blacks?

Mr. KATOR. Yes; I believe I can do that. You want governmentwide on this, Mrs. Green?

Mrs. GREEN. Yes.

Mr. KATOR. This is full-time employment as of November 30, 1969. May I give them to you by individual grade?

Mrs. GREEN. Fine.

Mr. KATOR. This is Negro employment. GS–1—incidentally, this is total general schedule or similar jobs. GS–1's, 998, or 52 percent. GS–2, 3,093, or 30.5 percent; GS–3, 27,599 or 24 percent; GS–4, 31,562, which is 18.4 percent; GS–5, 24,713, or 16.2 percent; GS–6, 9,849, 13.3 percent; at GS–7, 10,823, which is 9.6 percent; GS–8, 2,453, 9 percent; GS–9, 9,682, 6.2 percent; GS–10, 638, 3.5 percent; GS–11, 5,998, 4.1 percent; GS–12, 3,322, 2.7 percent; GS–13, 2,048, 2.2 percent; GS–14, 702, 1.6 percent; GS–15, 358, which is 1.4 percent; GS–16, 40, 1.1 percent; GS–17, 16, 1.4 percent; GS–18, 7, 1.4 percent.

I think that covers all the grades.

Mrs. GREEN. Thank you.

Mr. KATOR. The figures that I cited on women employment in the Federal Government, while showing progress, also points out the problem which faces us and where we need to focus our fire. While the total number of women employees in our work force continues to increase, there is still a heavy concentration of women employees in the lower grades. This is a situation not unlike that affecting minority group employees and one which we believe will be responsive to affirmative actions by agencies and to their efforts at upward mobility which I will discuss shortly.

While women do not hold a large number of top-level career jobs in the Federal Government or in certain occupations, it is an oversimplification to say that this is due solely to discrimination or to male attitudes about the employment of women. There are many complex factors involved, including expectations of women themselves as demonstrated by their educational patterns and career goals. For example, 38 percent of all women who earned degrees in 1968 earned them in the field of education; 24 percent earned them in the humanities and arts; and 16 percent in social sciences. Only 13 percent earned them in basic and applied sciences and minute numbers in the fields of engineering and related fields. The Federal Government has had shortages in the fields of engineering and sciences where few eligible women or men were available for appointment. Societal attitudes are such that many girls in school conceive of themselves as clerks and typists in the employment field and do not aim any higher in their training. They themselves share the attitudes of society as to their roles. They need counseling as to their potential and this has not always been forthcoming to the detriment of the Nation, although a number of Federal agencies have undertaken programs to provide just such counseling to high school girls, a program we hope to expand and intensify. I would like to interject here that there is a new Commission pamphlet which we have just issued, called "Expanding Opportunities For Women in the Federal Service." This aims to bring to the attention of women the opportunities available to them in jobs which they may never have considered before. What this pamphlet does is describe the jobs and have pictures of the women who are serving in these positions.

Now, this pamphlet will be distributed to high school placement officers and to college placement officers.

Another example, I think, is a film which is about to be launched. It has been developed by the Civil Service Commission for use in encouraging high school graduates to consider a career in Government. It is called "A Good Place To Start, Young People in Federal Service," and of four major characters, two are female. One of the girls is a medical technician, the other a cartographic aid. Both are atypical female-type jobs and we hope this film will have an impact in high schools about making girls aware of the opportunities that are available to them.

There are a number of other publications that I think are significant. We have a large number of publications, but just a few, I think I should point out, because it shows what we are trying to do to encourage women and girls to consider Federal employment. We have a brochure here for college students in nontechnical fields. It is distributed at colleges nationwide and commonly used as a handout to young people seeking employment information.

We feature six recent college graduates working in the Federal service, including three females. The cover of the pamphlet itself shows three females, three women and one man.

We also are trying to encourage women to consider the physical sciences and consider engineering and mathematics. We have a pamphlet which we call the Big Pond, a fairly recent publication of the Commission. It is distributed nationwide to college placement officers. It is to be used in counseling students on careers. Of the nine employees features, again three are female, including an engineer who is a project manager at Goddard Space Flight Center, a landscape architect with the National Park Service and a physical chemist at the National Bureau of Standards.

Mrs. GREEN. Could I interrupt there? I have six pictures from the Federal Times about seminars which I understand the Civil Service Commission conducts. Is that right? Seminars for the training of executives?

Mr. KATOR. Yes.

Mrs. GREEN. July 1, 1970. I judge there are 40 or 45 people in the picture. If there are 45, 44 of them are men and one woman.

Mr. KATOR. I am familiar with it.

Mrs. GREEN. In a July 8 picture in the Federal Times, another seminar on management of organizations sponsored by the Civil Service Commission, I am told. Forty men, no women. The one woman in that picture is a staff person.

In the March 4, 1970, Times, another seminar training executives; 38 men, no women. On April 15, 1970, Federal Times, another seminar down at Berkeley, 42 in the picture, two women.

Another seminar up at Kings Point. Forty-six participants; three women.

How do you square what you actually do in your training programs with what you have described in your propaganda pamphlets?

Mr. KATOR. I did not realize the Federal Times gave us such good coverage. But I do plan to cover that later on if I may. Or if you like, I shall respond at this time.

Mrs. GREEN. Well, maybe you can respond briefly now.

Mr. KATOR. All right. And I will cover it later on, too.

We share your concern frankly, and as recently as last month, Mr. Oganovic, our Executive Director, put out a memorandum to all directors of personnel and training directors emphasizing the need to make sure that female employees have an opportunity to participate in these courses. Frankly, the reason they are not participating to a large extent is that they are not at these grade levels.

Mrs. GREEN. Can't you make some change in that? If you have a seminar and you limit it to people in grade 16 and above, you obviously are not going to have any women. But if you have training for future upward mobility within civil service, it seems to me that you cannot pretend that you are offering equal opportunities where you close it to women by limiting enrollment to the positions where there are only men.

Mr. KATOR. No; we share your concern, Mrs. Green, and your point is well taken, is that at grades 13, 14, and 15, where women are eligible to go to Kings Point Executive Seminar Center or Berkeley, they should be given the opportunity to go there. This is the emphasis we want to make with agencies, that they consider the women at these grade levels, and there are a considerable number of women at these grade levels.

Mrs. GREEN. But the rhetoric and the facts are quite different.

Mr. KATOR. I think we will have to watch the Federal Times for some pictures in the future. I think we will see some action in this particular area. As I indicated, we share your concern. I think it is a legitimate concern. We have much that I will talk about in training later on. This, of course, shows just a minuscule portion of the Federal Government's training effort and I do not think, really, this should be taken as representative of what we are trying to do in the training area.

Mrs. GREEN. If we looked at the other training programs, would we find any more women other than those doing the typing?

Mr. KATOR. I think you would, yes.

Mrs. GREEN. I would be interested.

Mr. KATOR. I will come to those figures and they are pretty good, I think.

Mrs. GREEN. Fine.

Mr. KATOR. At least they are better than the Federal Times' pictures.

Mrs. GREEN. I found the Federal Times' pictures most interesting. I was glad they were sent to me. It's still true: "A photograph is worth a thousand words."

Mr. KATOR. If we have pinpointed the problems of heavy concentration of women in the lower grade levels in regard to the employment of women in the Federal Government, a fair question would be what progress has been made and what are we doing to assure further progress.

There are, in fact, a number of bright spots and we are working to make them brighter still. For example, increasing numbers of women are coming into the Federal service at professional and higher level manager positions. The number of women hired from the Federal service entrance examination—I should emphaize that this is the major vehicle for bringing young college graduates and others who have equivalent education to ender the Federal Government in entry level professional and managerial positions from which they can work upwards—the number of women hired from this examination increased from 1,507 jobs in 1963, 18 percent of the total persons selected, to 3,878 in 1968 or 39 percent of the total persons selected.

Mrs. GREEN. Do you have the same breakdown for blacks?

Mr. KATOR. No, Mrs. Green, we do not, because we do not keep records on the basis of race in terms of examinations. We do not do that. We do not keep applications—applications do not indicate the racial identification of an employee. The way we get our minority statistics is actually by visual identification. So we do not have this.

But I do want to emphasize that the data we show for women coming off the Federal service entrance examinations into these positions is very significant, in our judgment. Our recent data indicated that this upward trend in the selection of women in such positions is continuing. In midlevel positions, grades 9–12, approximately 9 percent of 4,471 persons hired in 1968 were women. This hiring percentage corresponds precisely with the percentage of women who were on the register eligible for appointment. At the senior levels, covering grades 15–18, 8 percent of the persons appointed in the first 6 months of fiscal year 1969 were women.

Mrs. GREEN. Do you have those statistics for blacks?

Mr. KATOR. No. We simply do not maintain statistics that way.

Mrs. GREEN. No, but you surely must have some idea from the visual identity to which you referred a moment ago.

Mr. KATOR. What I could, I suppose, show is the increases that have occurred at these grade levels by blacks as opposed to what they were the previous year. I do have figures of that kind that I could make available to you, or I could read them off to you.

In other words, I could show you how many blacks there were in grade 15 in 1967 and how many there were in 1969.

Mrs. GREEN. Would you do that in 1967 from, say, grade 9 on, just percentagewise?

Mr. KATOR. Just percentagewise?

Mrs. GREEN. Yes; that would be faster.

Mr. KATOR. Would you pardon me just a second while I get these sheets here?

If I may, let me give first the 1967 figures. This will be total general schedule, and I have them lumped in this particular printout by grade groupings. The first grade grouping would be GS 1-4. There were 75,846 blacks, or 20.5 percent. In GS 5-8, there were 40,494 blacks, which is 11.6 percent. GS 9 through 11——

Mrs. GREEN. You do not have those broken down by grade level?

Mr. KATOR. I have them from here on. I have 12 and 13. I am sorry I do not have them individually.

Mrs. GREEN. Let's start at 12.

Mr. KATOR. I do on the 1969, but in 1968, we did not present them that way. The 9 through 11 was 12,631, or 4.3 percent. GS 12 through 13, 188,514—I am sorry. That was a misstatement. The figure for GS 12 and 13 is 3,893, or 2.1 percent. GS 14 through 15, 696, 1.2 percent; GS 16 through 18, 66, which is 1.2 percent.

Now, I believe, Mrs. Green, that I did indicate earlier the 1969 figures, but I will be glad to repeat those. I could group them, I guess, just by adding them up. I just do not have them grouped that way.

Mrs. GREEN. Why don't you supply them to us later?

Mr. KATOR. I will be glad to supply them.

Mrs. GREEN. The reason I ask these questions is that charges have been made to me by various women's groups that considerably more progress has been made in righting the wrongs in terms of discrimination on the basis of race than in righting the wrongs in terms of discrimination on the basis of sex. It would seem to me that these statistics do bear this out. Women are 40 percent of the labor force and blacks are what, 11 percent of the labor force?

Mr. KATOR. Yes; 11 or 12 percent.

Mrs. GREEN. Yet the percentage in policymaking positions and at the highest grade levels is not as high for women as it is for blacks.

Mr. KATOR. I would not—No. 1, I think the number of women in the supergrade jobs exceed the number that we have of blacks as far as our 1969 statistics are concerned. We show 173 women in supergrade positions. In grades 16, 17, and 18, of the total general schedule or similar, there were 63 blacks.

Mrs. GREEN. Sixty-three blacks?

Mr. KATOR. Yes.

Mrs. GREEN. And 173 women?

Mr. KATOR. Yes.

Mrs. GREEN. And this is 1969?

Mr. KATOR. Yes. I am not sure that it is a fair statement to say this rights a wrong. If it is, women are certainly better off in that regard.

Mrs. GREEN. How do you say women are better off in that regard?

Mr. KATOR. Just in those grade levels, they were higher.

Mrs. Green. But women comprise 53 percent of the population and Negroes comprise 12 percent.

Mr. Kator. Mrs. Green, I do not know how many women are really in the work force.

Mrs. Green. Forty percent of the labor force is comprised of women. Over 31 million women are working.

Mr. Kator. So the fact that they are 53 percent, we would not expect to have half of the jobs filled by women.

Mrs. Green. No; but if 40 percent of the labor force is women——

Mr. Kator. You might expect to have 40 percent——

Mrs. Green. I would expect to have more numerically than in a minority group that comprises 12 percent of the labor force.

Mr. Kator. Well, actually, Mrs. Green, I just do not think that the statistics are really good evidence here of what should be expected or where there has been discrimination or not discrimination. Certainly in the past, women have had less prejudice, I would say, exhibited as far as ability to achieve educational degrees, which might put them in a position——

Mrs. Green. Say that again?

Mr. Kator. I am comparing with blacks.

Mrs. Green. Go ahead.

Mr. Kator. I am comparing with blacks in terms of the educational possibilities.

Mrs. Green. That women what?

Mr. Kator. I said it seemed to me and I could be wrong on this, but it seemed to me that women might have had better opportunities over the past 15 or 20 or 30 years in terms of educational opportunities that have been presented to them than have been presented to many of the blacks, who have not had such opportunities. What I am trying to say is that many of the higher level jobs, where we are talking about jobs, being held by women or being held by minority groups, require people who have the necessary skills and qualifications to hold these jobs. I am simply trying to indicate that I thought possibly this played a role.

But my concern, frankly, is simply saying that if you have 53 percent or 40 percent of the work force being women, that therefore, they should occupy such positions and that this would indicate discrimination. I think it indicates a problem. It clearly does. I think what we need to do in the Civil Service Commission is find out really what that problem is so we can take the appropriate measures to correct it. We would share your feeling that there are not enough people—I indicated that at the early part—of either the minority groups or women in our major policymaking positions. And we want to do something about that. But I just feel the statistics themselves, I am not sure are good indicators of that.

Mrs. Green. What would be a good indicator if the statistics are not?

Mr. Kator. I think we need more data and I will cover that later. But I do think we need more data frankly.

We were talking about the Federal service entrance examination. I talked about the increase in middle-level positions. Then I talked about the increase at senior levels. I did want to make the point, talking at the senior levels, which is GS 15–18, 8 percent of the persons appointed in the first 6 months of 1969 were women. This was double the percentage of women who were eligible for appointment. But I do not want to kid you or have you think we are talking in large numbers here. We are not. We are talking in small numbers in terms of total appointments at the higher grade levels, but what we are talking about is the trend is toward an increase.

If women have skills and capabilities which have not been fully capitalized on, and we recognize that they do, then an effort must be made to give women employees an opportunity to compete for higher level positions so that they can use their skills and abilities to the fullest extent possible. The major thrust of our new equal employment opportunity program, applicable to women and men employees in lower level jobs, is upward mobility. We believe that not enough has been done within the Federal Government to provide the training opportunities to employees so that they can qualify to move up the ladder and compete for higher level jobs. This program will have special significance to women. This new program on upward mobility was announced to Federal agencies by Chairman Hampton on May 7, 1970, and we will follow up very closely on its implementation. An important part of the program is to facilitate the movement of employees from clerical into technical and professional positions, a problem which has faced many women in the past. This will require the development of career systems, elimination of deadend jobs, and bridging between clerical and professional occupations. It will also require a significant amount of new training opportunities for all lower level employees. We expect that through this program, all employees in lower level positions will have a significantly improved opportunity to advance within the Government service and that women employees will have expanded opportunities to advance.

This may, Mrs. Green, get to some of the questions raised about training, because I do want to move into that point at this time. The training of women employees in the Federal Government will not be limited to lower level positions, although this has been a neglected area in the past. During fiscal year 1969, 41 percent of the male and 32 percent of the female Federal population participated in some type of training. This was certainly not all at the executive level or the executive seminar centers. But this was some type of training that they received while they were Federal employees. While female employees still receive proportionally less training than males, more female employees received training in 1969 than in 1968 or in 1967 and the gap between male and female employees participating in training is being narrowed. Over 248,000 women employees received training in fiscal year 1969. This was a 15.8-percent increase over the number trained in 1967. The largest gap in training between males and females is at the lower grade levels; as I indicated the upward mobility program will hopefully correct this. I have a breakdown here which shows some of the training by grade level. In grades 1 to 4, 43 percent of the male population received training in fiscal year 1969 as opposed to 33 percent of the females in the same grade groups. In GS 9–12, on the other hand, 71 percent of the male population and 63 percent of the female population received training. In grades 13–15, 63 percent of the males received training and 59 percent of the females received training. So I think there is some significance in those figures.

We recognize that despite the progress in training of female employees, more must be done. Last month, Mr. Nicholas J. Oganovic,

Executive Director of the Civil Service Commission addressed a personal memorandum to personnel directors, directors of equal employment opportunity, and Federal women coordinators, requesting that their personal attention be directed to increasing the participation of women in training opportunities, including on-the-job, apprentice, management, executive, and short-term as well as long-term training. Attendance of women at our executive seminar centers—and these are the pictures you referred to, Mrs. Green, from the Times—and at the Federal Executive Institute is low because of the number of available women in the grades from which selections are made is low but we are urging an increased number of nominations for these training centers by Federal agencies and we expect a significantly increased attendance by women.

While on the subject of training, I should like to remark on the efforts aimed not at training women but at training their supervisors, whether men or women. We believe that equal employment opportunity must be an integral part of the personnel management system and is the responsibility of each supervisor and manager. He or she is the key to equal employment opportunity. The supervisor is the person who hires, fires, makes assignments for training, and is responsible for all actions affecting personnel. This is the individual who must understand equal opportunity; this is the individual whose attitudes about women in the work force must be such as to encourage, not discourage, their participation in the full range of opportunities open to them.

Mrs. GREEN. Could I interrupt?

Do you have questions, Mr. Perkins?

Mr. PERKINS. I am most interested in the testimony being presented, and I am delighted, Madam Chairman, that the witnesses have testified on this subject matter.

I personally wanted to compliment the distinguished chairwoman of this subcommittee for pursuing and persevering in this area. I know that tremendous progress has been made as a result of Mrs. Green's efforts, and more progress will be made in the future. I share with Mrs. Green her belief that women should not be relegated—in government, or in any business or profession in this country.

I want to compliment you for such outstanding work.

Mrs. GREEN. Thank you very much, Mr. Chairman.

There are a few questions that I had on this. I was given the information, and it apparently must be old, that in the Federal women's program, 65 coordinators were listed but only 12 were women.

Miss MARKOFF. I would like to speak to that.

Mrs. GREEN. Yes.

Miss MARKOFF. Madam Chairman, I am very happy to be here today. I am the new director of the Federal women's program. I have been at the Civil Service Commission 2 months. One of the first things I managed to do at the Commission, with the Executive Director's support, was establish an interagency advisory group of agency Federal women program coordinators—that is a very long title. We had a meeting yesterday and I invited the women coordinators and called agencies and encouraged them to send female women coordinators.

Mrs. GREEN. As of what date?

Miss MARKOFF. As of yesterday.

Mrs. GREEN. But prior to yesterday, how many of the coordinators were women? Is 12 right?

Mr. KATOR. No, that is wrong.

Miss MARKOFF. There were 65 originally and 12 of them were men. Seventy-five or 80 were women from the start.

Mrs. GREEN. Where did this 12 come from, that only 12 are women?

Mr. KATOR. Let me try to explain. In the early part of this year, we directed agencies to reestablish Federal women coordinators and we said, we want people who have special empathy and concern with women. At that time, they said they were going to appoint people with special empathy and concern. We got back women as women coordinators in most of the cases. That is why I mentioned the figure that 45 out of 65 is correct.

Mrs. GREEN. It has never been 12?

Mr. KATOR. It may have been 12 at some time in the past, I can't answer that. But it is not 12 now and we will see that it never will be 12. There must be women in these jobs.

Mrs. GREEN. We talk about progress. The median income for women in 1960 was 64 percent of the median income for men.

Mr. KATOR. Yes.

Mrs. GREEN. In 1969, a decade later, the median income for women was 58 percent of that of men, a 6 percent decrease in one decade. Do you consider that much progress?

Mr. KATOR. I have to think about the Federal Government. I think the median in the Federal Government, the median grade level is GS-5 for woman and it is GS-7 for men—the average grade level in the Federal Government—the median grade level is 5 for women and 7 for men. The average grade level is 9.6 for men and for women, it is 5.2.

Now, I do not honestly know how that compares with whether we have been making an increase. But since our figures show an upward mobility on the part of women, I expect that we are closing that gap rather than extending it.

Mrs. GREEN. Could you find out if in fact that is true?

Mr. KATOR. I would be glad to.

Mrs. GREEN. Because it is not in general employment.

Mr. KATOR. I think that is very significant, and we should give that to you.

Miss MARKOFF. It is true based on a study in 1963, that it was a grade 9——

Mrs. GREEN. A couple of quick questions. The Civil Service Commission has one woman Commissioner, is that correct? How many men and women on the Civil Service Commission?

Mr. KATOR. How many men and women?

Mrs. GREEN. Yes.

Mr. KATOR. Total?

Mrs. GREEN. Yes.

Mr. KATOR. This is as of May of this year. The total is 2,315 men, 2,900 women.

Mrs. GREEN. No, I mean members of the Commission.

Mr. KATOR. I am sorry, the commissioners at the present time are all men, all males. We have had several women commissioners in the past. Barbara Bates Gunderson is the most recent.

Mrs. GREEN. Very few; very, very few over the years.

How many women are represented in the top jobs in the Civil Service Commission regional offices?

Mr. KATOR. You mean regional directors, Mrs. Greeen?

Mrs. GREEN. Yes.

Mr. KATOR. None. We do not have a woman as a regional director of the Civil Service Commission. However, we have had women occupying top jobs in our regional offices.

Mrs. GREEN. There is not any woman on the Civil Service Commission or any regional director that is a woman?

Mr. KATOR. No; that is correct.

Mrs. GREEN. Is that an indication of discrimination within the Civil Service Commission itself?

Mr. KATOR. No; I do not think so, because in the past, we have had women as regional directors.

Mrs. GREEN. You mean it is going down. There is no progress upwards?

Mr. KATOR. I think this is always subject to change and it may go up. This is not a static situation.

Mrs. GREEN. Let me ask you, What is the procedure when a complaint is filed? If a complaint is referred to the Civil Service Commission, do they refer it back to the agency in which the discrimination is alleged to have occurred?

Mr. KATOR. May I just take one second on that, because I think this is extremely important.

The way it works is that an employee, male or female, black or white, has a discrimination complaint. He goes to a counselor. It is the job of the counselor in that agency in which he works to try to resolve that problem, and in many cases they are very successful. About 3,000 counseling sessions are held a quarter. We have 6,000 trained counselors throughout the Government, they are part-time jobs. There are 6,000 trained counselors. Of those, 12 percent of the total counseling sessions represent women who are complaining about discrimination on the basis of sex.

Now, if that does not succeed, if the counseling does not succeed in clearing up the allegations, then an investigation is made, also by the agency but by persons in the agency who are not under the jurisdiction of the head of the organization in which the complaint arose. In other words, independent investigation. There is another attempt at informal resolution. If that does not work, the individual has a right to a hearing by a third party trained appeals examiner, who must be outside the agency. In fact, most of the hearing examiners are Civil Service Commission employees. If the individual is not satisfied with a decision at that point, he may appeal directly—he or she may appeal directly, to the Civil Service Commission's Board of Appeals and Review.

Mrs. GREEN. I am going to have to leave. I must get to the House Chamber. I wonder if I could ask you to continue, and would you finish these questions for the record.

Mr. KATOR. I was going to give you the number of formal complaints and what happened on them. There were 105 formal complaints based on sex that were closed since July 1, 1969. We found discrimination in 16 of these cases and corrective action was taken. In addition, corrective action was taken in 44 other cases.

Mrs. GREEN. The point I want to really reach, and I hope Mr. Hogan will follow up on it, if the complaint goes to the people who are at the highest level and they are the ones who were in fact responsible for the discrimination in the first place——

Mr. KATOR. It does not go to them at all.

Mrs. GREEN. Would you pursue that? That was my understanding.

Mr. KATOR. No, no; they are completely heard outside.

Mrs. GREEN. I also ask unanimous consent that certain statements on discrimination and on the higher education bill be made a part of the record at the end of today's testimony.

Mr. HOGAN. There are just a few questions. As I understand it, the Civil Service Commission offers an appeals proceeding?

Mr. KATOR. Oh, yes. I will take that a little slower this time. The individual, under a new procedure which we instituted July 1969, an employee believes that there has been discrimination on the basis of sex, race, religion, national origin, color—he goes to a counselor. That is in his agency, a trained person. We have trained him or the agency has trained him. That individual attempts to resolve the problem.

Now, most of the cases are resolved in this fashion. Most of the complaints are resolved in this fashion, because very few go on, only 5 or 6 percent, actually, go on to a formal complaint.

The individual is not satisfied with the counseling that he received in the agency, he does not like the decision, they did not take any action on his or her behalf, he or she then has the opportunity to file a formal complaint in alleging discrimination. At that point, an investigation will be made by someone independent of the organizational unit in which the employee is located. It will not be made by the supervisor of the employee.

After the investigation is made, the complainant is given a copy of the full investigational report and an attempt with her or him and the supervisor or the Equal Opportunity Employment Office, usually, is made in an attempt to reconcile differences and decide on the basis of the investigation whether resolution is possible.

If resolution is not possible, if the complainant still believes that he or she is discriminated against, then they have the opportunity to ask for a hearing. They can be represented at every level of this proceeding that I am talking about. This hearing is before a third party appeals examiner, someone who is outside the agency in which the complaint arose. If the complaint arose in the Department of Defense, for example, it can't be heard by anybody in any one of the services in the Department of Defense. It will be heard, in nine out of 10 cases, by a Civil Service employee.

The Commission employee makes a recommended decision to the head of the agency, the Secretary of Defense, for instance, and says, this is what we find in this case and this is our recommendation.

The head of the agency may adopt the proposed disposition or he may not. If he does not, however, he has to state his reasons why he does not and then the individual complainant has an opportunity to appeal to the Commission's Board of Appeals and Review for a final adjudication of the matter.

Mr. HOGAN. Does the Federal Women's Program Coordinator play any role in this at all?

Mr. KATOR. Not directly unless she would serve as a counselor, and I am not sure that that would be an appropriate role for her. She should be concerned, really, about affirmative action. I think in the Civil Service Commission as an organization, for example, the Federal

Women's Coordinator sits with the Equal Employment Opportunity staffs and our counselors in a committee so that we can decide what our problems are. But directly, as far as that response to your question, I do not think the coordinator as such would play a direct role in the complaint process. I do not think she should, really.

Mr. HOGAN. Do you review the complaints in the sense of what they might indicate in the way of discrimnation and existing as part of the administration of an agency as distinguished from just the individuals concerned?

Mr. KATOR. Yes, every agency gives us each month what we call a closed complaint report. We know what the facts were in the case, we know the disposition of the case, we are able to go back to the agency if we think they they did not handle the case properly. This is in addition to the individual himself taking up the cudgel in his behalf.

Mr. HOGAN. Are you able to generalize at all from that review? Do you see any pattern of discrimination, anything you can correct?

Mr. KATOR. Well, as far as women are concerned, I think the figures that I have here are probably the best kind of generalization. I would like to enter them into the record if I may.

Let me say that since July 1, 1969, there were 105 formal complaints of discrimination based on sex, female, which were closed. I say sex female, because some of the discrimination complaints are from men.

Mr. HOGAN. On the ground of sex?

Mr. KATOR. That is right. That is why I am talking here only about women who have alleged sex discrimination.

Discrimination was found in 16 of these cases. That is 15 percent of the cases. Corrective action was taken. In addition, corrective action was taken in 44 other cases where discrimination was not found. Now, this is significant. In other words, neither the agencies nor the Civil Service Commission is simply concerned just on whether there is a finding of discrimination and refuse to act in the event there is not. We are concerned about patterns. We are concerned about what was the situation in the agency. That is why we have corrective action taken in 44 cases, 42 percent of the total cases.

Let me give you some of the examples of corrective action. One included the discipline of a supervisor by a demotion. That is a pretty harsh penalty and it was carried out. Promotion or reassignment or reinstatement of the complainant. Training was afforded a complainant; an adverse action was rescinded. A supervisory classification was revised; supervisory practices were corrected. In another instance, male or female dress codes were equally enforced. The woman employee alleged that while she had to conform to certain dress codes, the male employees' dress codes were not similarly enforced and it was found that she was quite correct on this point.

I do not know what other generalizations I can give, Mr. Hogan, other than we want to root out this kind of, any kind of discrimination, whether it is on sex, race, religion, national origin. Our whole Equal Employment Opportunity effort is really aimed at that direction.

I did not get in the testimony with Mrs. Green to the point that I did want to make about how significant we think the training of supervisors is. These are the people who hire, fire, make the assignment, or discriminate, as the case may be. These are the people whose attitudes we must change. That is why we are devoting much of the resources to developing training programs for supervisors so they can understand and be sensitive to the needs of women and to the needs of minortiy groups and others in the employment situation.

Mr. HOGAN. Mrs. Green brought up the subject of executive seminars. Is this sort of discrimination ever the subject of concern in such a seminar?

Mr. KATOR. Yes. As a matter of fact, each one of our seminars has a component on equal employment opportunity.

Mr. HOGAN. On sex discrimination?

Mr. KATOR. Well, including sex discrimination. When we talk of equal employment opportunity, we talk about the total thing, including the discrimination on the basis of sex. I cannot say whether every session that we have at an executive seminar session includes a session on sex discrimination. I would be just hazarding a guess. I know they have included a section, a component on equal employment opportunity as a whole.

Mr. HOGAN. Mrs. Green would be concerned that it covered sex discrimination specifically.

Mr. KATOR. Well, I know that.

Mr. HOGAN. Could we trouble you to take a look perhaps at the recent seminar subjects at, say, Berekeley or Kings Point or Charlotte?

Mr. KATOR. Yes. I think I have a recollection that the most recent one at Berkeley was a session on equal employment opportunity handled by a woman. But I will be glad to check and will report back to you.

Mr. HOGAN. All right. What Mrs. Green, I think, would be concerned about on this point is there is a general pattern, because there is a general pattern of discrimination against women and that something must be done affirmatively to change people's minds about it. One way, as you suggest, is to do it by calling it to the attention of the supervisors as a part of the responsibility they have.

Mr. KATOR. Right.

Mr. HOGAN. A second possibility might be that of making it the subject of speeches, perhaps by the chairman or by commissioners. Has there been any expression of concern in that kind of activity?

Mr. KATOR. Much expression, Mr. Hogan. Mr. Organovic, for example, goes out to all our major cities and talks to our Federal executive boards and Federal executive organizations. These are organizations composed of the heads of the major installations in the area. He has been very forceful on the subject of equal opportunity for women. He talks about equal opportunity for all persons, but he is very forceful on the subject of women.

Chairman Hampton met with the Assistant Secretaries of Administration when the Order 11478 was signed, and a good deal of that meeting was devoted to concerns on equality of sex or avoidance of sex discrimination.

Chairman Hampton, in a letter to the President which preceded the issuance of Executive Order 11478, spoke about women in many aspects, indicating the concern with the concentration at lower levels, indicating the concern that we need to bring more women and minority groups, as well, into the upper levels of professional positions. So there has been this kind of concern.

The President's letter to agencies talks of women as well as men. So I think there has been that. I think it is an excellent point.

I do want to emphasize that while these speeches will help, I feel what we need to do is get to the supervisor, because he is the man, really, or woman who is taking the actions that, if they are not fair, he or she is the person taking it. So each person now who becomes a supervisor is required to take 80 hours of supervisory training, including a component on equal opportunity geared to women and minority groups. This is a long term effort, but a most important one, and this is where we get the opportunity to change attitudes which have been molded by society. This is an effort that we are going to work at and I think one that will pay us dividends.

Mr. Hogan. In reviewing Mrs. Green's notes, I can find only one other subject here that she has indicated an intention to ask a question about, but I think it is one that you may already have responded to. That is what positions are designated to be filled by one sex only? As I recall, you said there were two categories.

Mr. Kator. Only two.

Mr. Hogan. And one was up for review.

Mr. Kator. Yes; law enforcement positions.

Mr. Hogan. Let me ask you in this connection, in advertising openings, do you advertise them so that it is known to people who would be looking at the ads that the position is open?

Mr. Kator. Oh, definitely.

Mr. Hogan. Really, or do you advertise——

Mr. Kator. You talk about advertising. You do not mean newspaper ads? We do a limited number of that. We think of our advertising as brochures of this kind.

Mr. Hogan. You usually post them in post offices.

Mr. Kator. Oh, you mean the announcements?

Mr. Hogan. Yes. Is it clear in those announcements?

Mr. Kator. We always say "an equal opportunity employer." I cannot honestly answer—I just can't for a second think of whether the announcement says "male" or "female." We just say "all persons" and we say "equal opportunity employment." Maybe the announcements do, but let me check and let you know on that.

Mr. Hogan. We would like to know.

Do you know the answer to that, Miss Markoff?

Miss Markoff. The recruitment regulations prohibit limiting to one sex. Jobs are advertised and there is an EEO employer statement on it.

Now, the only two exclusions that have been approved are the custodial in an institution or law enforcement, which we are presently reviewing. Those were not blanket exclusions; those were exclusions where agencies could come in for a sex preference under those particular kinds of jobs. We do have some female guards in the Washington area employed in one agency that carry firearms.

Mr. Hogan. Could we ask you, though, to take a look in fact at the notices that you have sent out and that have been posted to see whether it is clear that it is so composed?

Mr. Kator. I think what you mean by "clear" is whether it says "male" or "female."

Mr. Hogan. That is right, or that it does not say "female," when you advertise for a secretary or when you advertise for——

Mr. Kator. I can assure you of that 100 percent; it would never say "female only." I thought what you were asking, Mr. Hogan, is whether it said "males" and "females." We just would not think of putting out any kind of announcement which was restricted to one sex.

Mr. HOGAN. What she is concerned about is the parallel in your procedure to that which exists in the classified section of newspapers—males wanted, females wanted. You do not have that?

Mr. KATOR. I can assure you that that does not exist.

Mr. HOGAN. I think that is it, then. If she were here, she would thank you.

Mr. KATOR. Thank you, Mr. Hogan.

Off the record.

(Off-the-record discussion.)

Mr. HOGAN. The subcommittee will recess subject to the call of the Chair.

(Whereupon, at 2:30 p.m., the subcommittee was adjourned, subject to the call of the Chair.)

PART 2
DOCUMENTS

WOMEN AND THE AMERICAN SCENE

[K.N.O.W., Pittsburgh, Pa., 1969]

THE BUILDING OF THE GILDED CAGE

(By Jo Freeman)

Hidden somewhere in the byways of the social sciences is an occasionally discussed, seldom studied, frequently employed and rarely questioned subject generally referred to as social control. We have so thoroughly absorbed our national ideology about living in a "free society" that whatever else we may question, as radicals or academics, we are reluctant to admit that all societies, ours included, do an awful lot of controlling of *everyone's* lives. We are even more reluctant to face the often subtle ways that our own attitudes and our own lives are being controlled by that same society.

This is why it has been so difficult for materially well-off, educated whites—women as well as men—to accept the idea that women are oppressed. "Women can have a career (or do something else) if they really want to" is the oft-heard refrain. "Women are where they are because they like it" is another. There are many more. "Women are their own worse enemies." "Women prefer to be wives and mothers rather than compete in the hard, aggressive male world." "Women enjoy being feminine. They like to be treated like ladies." There are just variations on the same "freedom of choice" argument which maintains that women are free (don't forget, we are living in a *free* society) to do what they want and never question why they think they want what they say they want.

But what people think they want is precisely what society must control if it is to maintain the *status quo*. As the Bems put it, "We overlook the fact that the society that has spent twenty years carefully marking the woman's ballot for her has nothing to lose in that twenty-first year by pretending to let her cast it for the alternative of her choice. Society has controlled not her alternatives but her motivation to choose any but one of those alternatives." [1]

There are many mechanisms of social control and some are more subtle than others. The socialization process, the climate of opinion in which people live, the group ideology (political or religious) the kind of social structures available, the legal system, and the police are just some of the means society has at its disposal to channel people into the roles it finds necessary for its maintenance. They are all worthy of study, but here we are only going to look at two of them—one overt and one covert—to see what they can tell us about women.

The easiest place to start when trying to determine the position of any group of people is with the legal system. This may strike us as a little strange since our national ideology also says that "all men are equal under the law" until we remember that the ideology is absolutely correct in its restriction of this promise to "men." Now there are three groups who have been accorded the status and the rights of manhood—blacks, children (minors) and women. Children at least are considered to be in their inferior, dependent status only temporarily because some of them (white males) eventually graduate to become men. Blacks (the 47% who are male) have "been denied their manhood" since they were kidnapped from Africa and are currently demanding it back. But

---

[1] Bem, Sandra and Daryl, "Training the Woman to Know Her Place," unpublished paper, 1969, p. 5.

women (51% of the population, black and white)—how can a woman have manhood?

This paradox illustrates the problem very well. Because there is a long standing legal tradition, reaching back to early Roman law, which says that women are perpetual children and the only adults are men. This tradition, known as the "Perpetual Tutelage of Women"[2] has had its ups and downs, been more or less enforced, but the definition of women as minors who never grow up, who therefore must always be under the guidance of a male (father, brother, husband or son), has been carried down in modified form to the present day and vestiges of it can still be seen in our legal system.

Even Roman law was an improvement over Greek society. In that cradle of democracy only men could be citizens in the polis. In fact most women were slaves, and most slaves were women.[3] In ancient Rome both the status of women and slaves improved slightly as they were incorporated into the family under the rule of *Patria potestas* or Power of the Father. This term designated not so much a familial relationship as a property relationship. All land was owned by families, not individuals, and was under the control of the oldest male. Women and slaves could not assume proprietorship and in fact frequently were considered to be forms of property. The woman in particular had to turn any income she might receive over to the head of the household and had no rights to her own children, to divorce, or to any life outside the family. The relationship of woman to man was designated by the concept of *manus* (hand) under which the woman stood. Women had no rights under law—not even legal recognition. In any civil or criminal case she had to be represented by the *Pater* who accepted legal judgement on himself and in turn judged her according to his whims. Unlike slaves, women could not be emancipated (removed from under the hand). She could only go from under one hand to another. This was the nature of the marital relationship. (From which comes our modern practice "to ask a woman's father for her *hand* in marriage). At marriage women were "born again" into the household of the bridegroom's family and became the "daughter of her husband."[4]

Although later practice of Roman Law was much less severe than the ancient rules, some of the most stringent aspects were incorporated into Canon Law and from there passed to the English Common Law. Interpretation and spread of the law varied throughout Europe, but it was thru the latter that it was brought to this country and made part of our own legal tradition.

Even here history played tricks on women. Throughout the 16th and 17th centuries tremendous liberalizations were taking place in the Common Law attitude toward women. This was particularly true in the American colonies where rapidly accelerating commercial expansion often made it profitable to ignore the old social rules. In particular, the development of property other than land facilitated this process as women had always been held to have some right in *movable* property while only male heirs could inherit the family lands.[5]

But when Backstone wrote his soon-to-be-famous *Commentaries on the Laws of England*, he chose to ignore these new trends in favor of codifying the old Common Law rules. Published in 1765, his work was used in Britain as a textbook. But in the Colonies and new Republic it became a legal Bible. Concise and readable, it was frequently the only book to be found in most law libraries in the United States up until the middle of the 19th Century, and incipient lawyers rarely delved past its pages when seeking the roots of legal tradition.[6] Thus when Edward Mansfield wrote the first major analysis of *The Legal Rights, Liabilities and Duties of Women* in 1845, he still found it necessary to pay homage to the Blackstone doctrine that "the husband and wife are as one and that one is the husband." As he saw it three years before the Seneca Falls convention would write the *Woman's Declaration of Independence*, "it appears that the husband's control over the person of his wife is so complete that he may claim her society altogether; that he may reclaim her if she goes away or is detained by others; that he may use constraint upon her liberty to prevent her going away, or to prevent improper conduct that he may maintain suits for injuries to her person; that she cannot sue alone; and that she cannot execute

[2] Maine, Sir Henry Sumner, *Ancient Law*, John Murray : London, 1905, p. 135.
[3] Gouldner, Alvin W., *Enter Plato*, Basic Books ; New York, London, 1965, p. 10.
[4] Fustel de Coulanges, Numa Denis, *The Ancient City*, Doubleday & Co. : Garden City, New York, 1873, p. 42–94.
[5] Morris, Richard B., *Studies in the History of American Law*, Mitchell & Co. : Philadelphia, 1959, pp. 126–128.
[6] Beard, Mary, *Woman as Force in History*, MacMillan : New York, 1946, pp. 108–109.

a deed or valid conveyance without the concurrence of her husband. In most respects she loses the power of personal independence, and altogether that of separate action in legal matters."[7] The husband also had almost total control over all the wife's real and personal property or income.

Legal traditions die hard—even when they are mythical ones. So the bulk of the activities of feminists in the 19th Century were spent chipping away at the legal nonexistence that Blackstone had defined for women. The path of legal equality for women has hardly been a straight one and at times it seems women have had to run as fast as they could just to keep in one place. Even today there are over 1,000 laws that discriminate against women and some of the most onerous of them are of fairly recent origin.

These laws fall into four categories: (1) legal and political rights, (2) changes in status due to marriage, (3) restrictions on employment, and (4) nuisance laws. We will only consider the middle two here. Nuisance laws (such as the Wisconsin rule that only the male guardian can sign a minor's application for a driver's license) are obnoxious but hardly crucial, and with the enfranchisement of the 19th Amendment political rights are not so severely lacking as they once were. However, it might be noted that full equality in this area has not yet been obtained. Women serve on juries on the same basis as men in only 24 states, although only Mississippi totally excludes them. The Supreme Court has ruled six times (the last time in 1961) that the provisions of the 14th Amendment do not apply to women as the wording specifies *male* persons (the first time sex was inserted into the Constitution). And some inequities in legal procedure are just being removed.[8]

Despite the passage of the Married Women's Property Acts in the 19th Century which removed most of the Blackstonian disabilities, many of the Common Law practices, assumptions and attitudes still dominate the law. The property, real and personal, brought by the woman to the marriage now remains her separate estate, but such is not always the case for that acquired during the marriage.

There are two types of property systems in the United States—common law and community. In the nine community property states (Arizona, California, Hawaii, Idaho, Louisiana, Nevada, New Mexico, Texas and Washington) all property or income acquired by either husband or wife is community property and is equally divided upon divorce. However "the general rule is that the husband is the head of the 'community' and the duty is his to manage the property for the benefit of his wife and family. Usually, as long as the husband is capable of managing the community, the wife has no power of control over it and acting alone, cannot contract debts chargeable against it."[9] In two of the states (Texas and Nevada) the husband can even dispose of the property without his wife's consent. Included in the property is the income of a working wife which, under the law, is managed by the husband with the wife having no legal right to a say in how it shall be spent.

In common law states each spouse has a right to manage his own income and property. However, unlike community property states, this principle does not recognize the contribution made by a wife who works only in the home. Although the wife generally contributes domestic labor to the maintenance of the home far in excess of that of her husband she has no right to an allowance, wages or an income of any sort. Nor can she claim joint ownership upon divorce.[10]

Marriage incurs a few other disabilities as well. A married woman cannot contract on the same basis as her husband or a single woman in most states. In only five states does she have the same right to her own domicile. Traditionally, a woman lived where her husband did—if he were to move and she were not to follow him she would be guilty of desertion. In many states a married woman can now live separately from her husband but his domicile is still her address for purposes of taxation, voting, jury service, etc.[11]

Along with the domicile regulations, those concerning names are most symbolic of the theory of the husband's and wife's legal unity. Legally, every married woman's surname is that of her husband and no court will uphold her right to go

[7] Mansfield, Edward. *The Legal Rights, Liabilities and Duties of Women*, Jewett & Co.: Salem, Mass., 1845, p. 273.

[8] For example, in *Commonwealth of Pennsylvania* v. *Jane M. Daniels* the Supreme Court ruled unconstitutional last year the 1913 Muncy Act which provided that any woman convicted of a felony *must* be sentenced to the maximum term prescribed by law. For similar cases see also *Morgan* v. *State*. 179 Ind. 300. 101 N.E. 6; *People* v. *Huff* 294 I.L.I. 164. 94 N.E. 61; *State* v. *Hetiman* 105 Kan. 139, 1181 Pac. 630, 8 A.L.R. 848; *State* v. *Walker* 326 Mo. 1233 S.W. 2d 124

[9] Francis, Philip, *The Legal Status of Women*, Oceana Publications, NY., 1963, p. 23.

[10] Citizens Advisory Council on the Status of Women, *Report of the Task Force on Family Law and Policy*, 1968, p. 2.

[11] *Ibid.* p. 39.

by a different name. Pragmatically, she can use another name only as long as her husband does not object. If he were to legally change his name, hers would automatically change too, though such would not necessarily be the case for the children. "In a very real sense, the loss of a woman's surname represents the destruction of an important part of her personality and its submersion in that of her husband." [12]

When we move beyond the field of personal law we move to an area in which, until very recently, the dual legal status of men and women has increased, rather than decreased, in the last fifty years. Under common law and in the early years of this country there was very little restrictive legislation on the employment of women. It was not needed. Custom and prejudice alone sufficed to keep the occupations in which women might be gainfully employed to domestic servant, factory worker, governess and prostitute. As woman acquired education and professional skills in the wake of the Industrial Revolution, they increasingly sought employment in fields which put them in competition with men. In some instances men gave way totally and the field became dominated by women, losing prestige, opportunities for advancement and pay in the process. The occupation of secretary is the most notable. In most cases men fought back and were quick to make use of economic, ideological and legal weapons to reduce or eliminate their competition. "They excluded women from trade unions, made contracts with employers to prevent their hiring women, passed laws restricting the employment of married women, caricatured the working women, and carried on ceaseless propaganda to return women to the home or keep them there." [13]

An examination of the state labor laws that apply specifically to women reveals a complex, confusing, inconsistent chaos. Thirteen states have minimum wage laws which apply only to women and minors, and two have laws which apply only to women. Three states require overtime to be paid to women and minors only. Adult women are prohibited from working in specified occupations or under certain working conditions considered hazardous in 26 states; in ten of these women cannot work in bars. [14]

The most onerous of all are the so-called "protective" labor legislation. Most of this was passed at the turn of the century as part of a general reform effort to improve sweatshop conditions. It has since been used to deny overtime pay, promotions and employment opportunities to women.

The worst of these are the "weight and hour" laws. In 41 states and the District of Columbia the number of hours a woman can work is restricted— generally to 8 hours per day and 48 hours per week. Limitations are made in 12 states on the amount of weight that can be lifted by a woman. These maximums range from 15 to 35 pounds (the weight of a small child). Other such protective laws include the prohibition of night work in 20 states, the requirement of special facilities such as seats, lunchrooms, dressing rooms, restrooms, toilets and meal periods in 45 states. [15]

Many of these laws are now being challenged in the courts. In *Mengelkoch et al.* v. *the Industrial Welfare Commission of California and North American Aviation, Inc.* the defending corporation has admitted that the women were denied overtime and promotions to positions requiring overtime, justifying their actions by the California maximum hours law. In *Roig* v. *Southern Bell Telephone and Telegraph Co.*, the plaintiffs are protesting that their current job is exempt from the Louisiana maximum hours law but that the higher paying job to which they were denied promotion is not. One major case which challenged the Georgia weightlifting law is *Weeks* v. *Southern Bell Telephone and Telegraph* which recently received a favorable ruling from the Fifth Circuit Court. This may lead to a legal decision that all "protective" legislation is unconstitutional.

But perhaps most illustrative of all is an Indiana case,[16] in which the company tried to establish maximum weightlifting restrictions even though its plant and the plaintiffs were located in a state which did not have such laws. By company policy, women were restricted to jobs whose highest pay rate was identical with the lowest pay rate for men. Many of the women, including the defendants, were laid off while men with junior seniority were kept on, on the ground that the

---

[12] Kanowitz, Leo, *Women and the Law: The Unfinished Revolution,* University of New Mexico Press: Albuquerque, 1969, p. 41.

[13] Hacker, Helen Mayer, "Women as a Minority Group" *Social Forces,* Vol. 31, Oct. 1951, p. 67.

[14] U.S. Department of Labor, *Summary of State Labor Laws for Women,* Feb. 1967, passim.

[15] *Ibid.*

[16] *Sellers, Moore & Case* v. *Colgate Palmolive Co. and the International Chemical Workers Union, Local No. 15,* 272 Supp. 332; Minn. L. Rev. 52: 1091.

women could not lift over 35 pounds. This policy resulted in such anomalies as women having to lift seventeen and one-half tons of products a day in separate ten pound loads while the male supervisors sat at the head of the assembly line handling the controls and lifting one forty pound box of caps each hour. "In a number of other instances, women were doing hard manual labor until the operations were automated; then they were relieved of their duties, and men were employed to perform the easier and more pleasant job.[17] In its defense, the company claimed it reached this policy in accordance with the union's wishes but the Seventh Circuit Court unanimously ruled against it anyway. It is only one of many instances in which corporations and male-run unions have taken advantage of "protective" legislation in order to protect themselves from giving women equal job opportunities and equal pay.

This review of the major ways in which the law discriminates against women does not even take into account the abortion and birth control laws. This is not the place for a major discussion of these issues apart from noting the obvious that the laws were made by men but apply only to women. Suffice it to say that the abortion laws come out of the same tradition as the rest of our legal system. Originally, abortion was illegal only when performed without the husband's consent and the only crime was a "wrong to the husband in depriving him of children."[18] Laws making abortion a criminal offense were not even passed until the 19th Century; before that it was largely regarded as a Church offense and punishable by religious penalities.[19]

Many of these laws are just vestiges of what has been an entirely separate legal system applicable particularly to women. Other groups in society have also had the law remade to fit them into a special legal category in order that it may be used as a means of social control. Thus an examination of the statutes can clearly delineate those groups which society feels it necessary to control. It does not indicate all the areas of exclusion, as the legal system is not society's first line of oppression. There are no laws made to keep people out of places that they have never considered going. It is when certain perogatives are threatend by an out-group that it must be made illegal to violate them. Thus Jim Crow laws were not necessary when slavery existed and "protective" labor legislation was not thought of until women began to enter the job market in rapidly accelerating numbers at the end of the 19th Century.

The statutes do not necessarily indicate *all* of the groups which a particular society excludes from full participation, but they do show those which it is most adamant about excluding. In virtually every society that has existed, the caste cleavages, as distinct from the class lines, have been imbedded in the law. Differentiating between class and caste is often difficult as the two differ in degree that only at the extremes is seen as a difference in kind. It is made more difficult by our refusal to acknowledge that castes exist in our society. Here too we have allowed our thinking to be subverted by our national ideology. Our belief in the potentiality, if not the current existence, of high social mobility determined only by the individual's talents, can accept the fact that this mobility is hampered by one's socio-economic origins but not the fact that it is made impossible if one comes from the wrong caste. Only recently have we reluctantly begun to face the reality of the "color-line" as a caste boundary. Our consciousness of the caste nature of the other boundaries, particularly that of sex, is not yet this high.

The law not only shows the caste boundaries, it also gives a fairly good history of the changes in boundaries. As the rigidity of caste lines fade into the more permeable class lines, the legislation usually changes with it. The middle ages saw separate application of the law to the separate estates. In the early years of this country certain rights were reserved to those possessing a minimum amount of property. Today, nobility of birth or amount of income may affect the treatment one receives from the courts, but is not expressed in the law itself. For the past 150 years, the major caste divisions have been been along the lines of age, sex and ethnic origin; these have been the categories for which special legislation has existed.

Frequently, members of the lower castes are lumped together and the same body of special law applied to all. Most of the labor legislation discussed earlier applies to "women and minors." The state of New York once worded its franchise

---

[17] Brief for the Plaintiffs/Appellants in the Seventh Circuit Court of Appeals, No. 16, 632. P. 5.
[18] Dickens, Bernard M., *Abortion and the Law,* MacGibbon & Kee, Ltd.; Bristol, 1966, p. 15.
[19] Guttmacher, Alan F.. "Abortion—Yesterday, Today and Tomorrow", *The Case for Legalized Abortion Now,* Guttmacher, ed., Diablo Press: Berkeley, 1967, p. 4.

law to include everyone but "women, minors, convicts and idiots." When a legal status had to be found for Negro slaves in the 17th Century, the "nearest and most natural analogy was the status of women." [20] The Supreme Court went even further in its landmark 1875 decision [21] by declaring that the Constitution did not give women the rights of citizens under the law in language and reasoning borrowed directly from the *Dred Scott* decision.[22] But the clearest analogy of all was stated by the Southern slaveowning class when trying to defend that system prior to the Civil War. One of the most widely read rationalizations was that of George Fitzhugh who wrote in his 1854 *Sociology for the South* that "The kind of slavery is adapted to the men enslaved. Wives and apprentices are slaves, not in theory only, but often in fact. Children are slaves to their parents, guardians and teachers. Imprisoned culprits are slaves. Lunatics and idiots are slaves also." [23]

The progress of "out castes", particularly those of the wrong race and sex, also has been parallel. The language of the Nineteenth Amendment was borrowed directly from that of the Fifteenth. The "sex" provision of Title VII (only the second piece of corrective legislation pertaining to women that has been passed [24]) was stuck into the Civil Rights Act of 1964 as a joke by Octogenarian representative Howard W. Smith of Virginia.[25]

Many of the same people were involved in both movements as well. Frederick Douglass was a staunch feminist and urged the first Convention at Senaca Falls in 1848 to demand the franchise when many of the women were reluctant to do so. Similarly, the early feminists were ardent abolitionists. The consciousness of two of the most active is dated from the World Anti-Slavery Convention in London in 1840 when Lucretia Mott and Elizabeth Cady Stanton were compelled to sit in the galleries rather than participate in the convention.[26] Many of today's new feminists also come out of an active background in the civil rights and other social movements.[27] Almost without exception, when one of the lower castes in our society begins to revolt, the others quickly perceive the similarities to their own condition and start the battle on their own grounds.

Thus it is not surprising that these groups quickly find that they have more in common than having a similar legal situation. All of them, when comparing themselves to the culture of the middle-aged white male,[28] find that they are distinctly in the minority position. This minority position involves a good deal more than laws and a good deal more than economic and social discrimination. Discrimination *per se* is only one aspect of oppression and not always the most significant one. Being subject to separate laws and poorer access to the socioeconomic system are only some of the characteristics of being in a minority group. This point has been well explored by Hacker and the chart she developed to sum up the similarities between women and blacks is reproduced at the end of this article.[29]

The Negro analogy has been challenged many times on the grounds that women do not suffer from the same overt segregation as blacks. This point is well noted. But it is important to realize that blatant discrimination is just one mechanism of social control. There are many more subtle ones employed long before such coercion becomes necessary. It is only when these other methods fail to keep a minority group in its place that harsher means must be found. Given that a particular society needs the subservience of several different groups of people it will use its techniques to a different degree with each of them depending on what they are most susceptible to. It is a measure of the black's resistance to the definition which white society has tried to impose on them that such violent extremes have had to be gone to to keep the caste lines intact.

Women, however, have not needed such stringent social chains. Their bodies could be left free because their minds were chained long before they became functioning adults. Women have so thoroughly internalized the social definition that their only significant role is to serve men as wives and raise the next

---

[20] Myrdal, Gunnar, *An American Dilemma,* Harper : New York, 1944, p. 1073.
[21] *Minor* v. *Happersett*, 21 Wall. 162, 22 L. Ed. 627.
[22] Hodes, William, untitled paper to be published in the Rutgers Law Review.
[23] Fitzhugh, George, *Sociology for the South,* A. Morris : Richmond, Va., 1854, p. 86.
[24] The first was the Equal Pay Act of 1963 which took 94 years to get through Congress.
[25] Bird, Caroline, *Born Female: The High Cost of Keeping Women Down,* David McKay Co. : New York, 1968, Chapter I.
[26] Flexner, Eleanor, *Century of Struggle,* Atheneum : New York, 1959, p. 71. They were joined by one white and one black man, William Lloyd Garrison and John Cronan.
[27] Freeman, Jo. "The New Feminists" in *The Nation,* Feb. 24, 1969, p. 242.
[28] Myrdal, *op. cit.*
[29] Hacker, *op. cit.*, pp. 10–19.

generation of men and their servants that no laws are necessary to enforce this. Where socialization failed, custom sufficed.

The result is that women, even more than other minority groups, have their identities derived first as members of a group and only second, if at all, as unique persons. "Consider the following—When a boy is born, it is difficult to predict what he will be doing 25 years later. We cannot say whether he will be an artist or a doctor or a college professor because he will be permitted to develop and fulfill his own identity. But if the newborn child is a girl, we can predict with almost complete certainty how she will be spending her time 25 years later. Her individuality does not have to be considered; it is irrelevant." [30]

Yet until very recently, most women have refused to recognize their own oppression. They have openly accepted the social definition of who and what they were. They have refused to be conscious of the fact that they are seen and treated, before anything else, as women. Many still do. This very refusal is significant because no group is so oppressed as one which will not recognize its own oppression. Women's denial that they must deal with their oppression is a reflection of just how far they still have to go.

There are many reasons why covert mechanisms of social control have been so much more successful with women than with most other minority groups. More than most they have been denied any history. Their tradition of subjection is so long that the most dedicated feminist scholars cannot unearth a past era worthy of emulation. For the most part even this tradition is purged from the history books so women cannot compare the similarities of their current condition with that of the past. In a not-so-subtle way both men and women are told that only men make history and women are not important enough to study.

Further, the agents of social control are much nearer to hand than those of any other group. No other minority lives in the same household with its master, separated totally from its peers and urged to compete with them for the privilege of serving the majority group. No other minority so thoroughly accepts the standards of the dominant group as its own and interprets any deviance from those values as a sign of degeneracy. No other minority so readily argues for the maintainence of its own position as one that is merely "different", without questioning whether one must be the "same" to be equal.

Women reach this condition, this total acceptance of their secondary role as right and just, through the most insidious mechanism of social control yet devised—the socialization process. That is the mechanism that we want to analyze now.

To understand how most women are socialized we must first understand how they see themselves and are seen by others. Several studies have been done on this. Quoting one of them, McClelland stated that "the female image is characterized as small, weak, soft and light. In the United States it is also dull, peaceful, relaxed, cold, rounded, passive and slow." [31] A more thorough study which asked men and women to chose out of a long list of adjectives those which most clearly applied to themselves showed that women strongly felt themselves to be such things as uncertain, anxious, nervous, hasty, careless, fearful, full, childish, helpless, sorry, timid, clumsy, stupid, silly, and domestic. On a more positive side women felt they were: understanding, tender, sympathetic, pure, generous, affectionate, loving, moral, kind, grateful and patient. [32]

This is not a very favorable self-image but it does correspond fairly well with the social myths about what women are like. The image has some nice qualities, but they are not the ones normally required for that kind of achievement to which society gives its highest social rewards. Now one can justifiably question both the idea of achievement and the qualities necessary for it, but this is not the place to do so. Rather, because the current standards are the ones which women have been told they do not meet, the purpose here will be to look at the socialization process as a mechanism to keep them from doing so. We will also need to analyze some of the social expectations about women and about what they define as a successful *woman* (not a successful person) because they are inextricably bound up with the socialization process. All people are socialized to meet the social expectations held for them and it is only when this process fails to do so (as is currently happening on several fronts) that it is at all questioned.

[30] Bem and Bem. *op. cit.* p. 7.
[31] McClelland, David, "Wanted: A New Self-Image for Women" in *The Woman in America*, ed. by Robert J. Lifton, Beacon Press: Boston, 1965, p. 173.
[32] Bennett, Edward M. and Cohen, Larry R., "Men and Women: Personality Patterns and Contrasts" in *Genetic Psychology Monographs*, Vol. 59, 1959, pp. 101–155.

First, let us further examine the effects on women of minority group status. Here, another interesting parallel emerges, but it is one fraught with more heresy than any previously made. Because when we look at the *results* of female socialization we find a strong similarity between what our society labels, even extols, as the typical "feminine" character structure and that of oppressed peoples in this country and elsewhere.

In his classic study on *The Nature of Prejudice*, Allport devotes a chapter to "Traits Due to Victimization." Included are such personality characteristics as sensitivity, submission, fantasies of power, desire for protection, indirectness, ingratiation, petty revenge and sabotage, sympathy, extremes of both self and group hatred and self and group glorification, display of flashy status symbols, compassion for the underprivileged, identification with the dominant groups norms, and passivity.[33] Allport was primarily concerned with Jews and Negroes but compare his characterization with the very thorough review of the literature on sex differences among young children made by Terman and Tyler. For girls, they listed such traits as: sensitivity, conformity to social pressures, response to environment, ease of social control, ingratiation, sympathy, low levels of aspiration, compassion for the underprivileged, and anxiety. They found that girls compared to boys were more nervous, unstable, neurotic, socially dependent, submissive, had less self-confidence, lower opinions of themselves and of girls in general, and were more timid, emotional, ministrative, fearful and passive.[34] These are also the kinds of traits found in the Indians when under British rule,[35] in the Algerians under the French [36] and elsewhere.

Two of the most essential aspects of this "minority group character structure" are the extent to which one's perceptions are distorted and one's group is denigrated. These two things in and of themselves are very effective means of social control. If one can be led to believe in one's own inferiority then one is much less likely to resist the status that goes with that inferiority.

When we look at women's opinions of women we find the notion that they are inferior prevalent just about everywhere. Young girls get off to a very good start. They begin speaking, reading and counting sooner. They articulate more clearly and put words into sentences earlier. They have fewer reading and stuttering probelms. Girls are even better in math in the early school years. They also make a lot better grades than boys do until late high school. But when they are asked to compare their achievements with those of boys, they rate boys higher in virtually every respect. Despite factual evidence to the contrary, girls' opinion of girls grows progressively worse with age while their opinion of boys and boys' abilities grows better. Boys, likewise, have an increasingly better opinion of themselves and worse opinion of girls as they grow older.[37]

These distortions become so gross that, according to Goldberg, by the time girls reach college they have become prejudiced against women. He gave college girls sets of booklets containing six identical professional articles in traditional male, female and neutral fields. The articles were identical, but the names of the authors were not. For example, an article in one set would bear the name "John T. McKay" and in another set the same article would be authored by "Joan T. McKay." Questions at the end of each article asked the students to rate the articles on value, persuasiveness and profundity and the authors for writing style and competence. The male authors fared better in every field, even such "feminine" areas as Art History and Dietetics. Goldberg concluded that "Women are prejudiced against female professionals and, regardless of the actual accomplishments of these professionals, will firmly refuse to recognize them as the equals of their male colleagues." [38]

These unconscious assumptions about women can be very subtle and cannot help but to support the myth that women do not produce high quality professional work. If the Goldberg findings hold in other situations, and the likelihood is great that they do, it explains why women's work must be of a much higher quality than that of men to be acknowledged as merely equal. People in our society simply refuse to believe that a woman can cross the caste lines and be competent in a "man's world."

[33] Allport, Gordon W., *The Nature of Prejudice*, Reading, Mass.: Addison-Wesley Co., 1954. pp. 142–161.
[34] Terman, Lewis M., and Leona E. Tyler, "Psychological Sex Differences" in *Manual of Child Psychology*, ed. by Leonard Carmichael, Wiley & Sons: New York, 1954, pp. 1080–1100.
[35] Fisher, Lewis, *Gandhi*; New American Library: New York, 1954.
[36] Fanon, Franz, *The Wretched of the Earth*, Grove Press: New York, 1963.
[37] Smith, S., "Age and Sex Differences in Children's Opinion Concerning Sex Differences," *Journal of Genetic Psychology*, Vol. 54, 1939, pp. 17–25.
[38] Goldberg, Philip, "Are Women Prejudiced Against Women?" *Transaction*, April, 1968, 5, pp. 28–30.

However, most women rarely get to the point of writing professional articles or doing other things which put them in competition with men. They seem to lack what psychologists call the "Achievement Motive." [39] When we look at the little research that has been done we can see why this is the case. Horner's recent study of undergraduates at the University of Michigan showed that 65% of the women but only 10% of the men associated academic success with having negative consequences. Further research showed that these college women had what Horner termed a "motive to avoid success" because they perceived it as leading to social rejection and role conflict with their concept of "femininity." [40] Lipinski has also shown that women students associate success in the usual sense as something which is achieved by men, but not by women.[41] Pierce suggested that girls did in fact have achievement motivation but that they had different criteria for achievement than did boys. He went on to show that high achievement motivation in high school women correlates much more strongly with early marriage than it does with success in school.[42]

Some immediate precedents for the idea that women should not achieve too much academically can be seen in high school for it is here that the performance of girls begins to drop drastically. It is also at this time that peer group pressures on sex role behavior increase and conceptions of what is "properly feminine" or "masculine" become more narrow.[43] One need only recall Asch's experiments to see how peer group pressures, armed with our rigid ideas about "femininity" and "masculinity" could lead to the results found by Horner, Lipinski and Pierce. Asch found that some 33 percent of his subjects would go contrary to the evidence of their own senses about something as tangible as the comparative length of two lines when their judgements were at variance with those made by the other group members.[44] All but a handful of the other 67 percent experienced tremendous trauma in trying to stick to their correct perceptions.

These experiments are suggestive of how powerful a group can be in imposing its own definition of a situation and suppressing the resistance of individual deviants. When we move to something as intangible as sex role behavior and to social sanctions far greater than simply the displeasure of a group of unknown experimental stooges we can get an idea of how stifling social expectations can be. It is not surprising, in light of our cultural norm that a girl should not appear to smart or surpass boys in anything, that those pressures to conform, so prevalent in adolescence, prompt girls to believe that the development of their minds will have only negative results.

But this process begins long before puberty. It begins with the kind of toys young children are given to play with, with the roles they see their parents in, with the stories in their early reading books, and the kind of ambitions they express or actions they engage in that receive rewards from their parents and other adults. Some of the early differentiation along these lines is obvious to us from looking at young children and reminiscing on our own lives. But some of it is not so obvious, even when we engage in it ourselves. It consists of little actions which parents and teachers do every day that are not even noticed but can profoundly effect the style and quality of a child's developing mind.

Adequate research has not yet been done which irrefutably links up child raising practices with the eventual adult mind but there is evidence to support some hypotheses. Let us take a look at one area where strong sex differences show up relatively early—mathematical reasoning ability. No one has been able to define exactly what this ability is but it has been linked up with number ability and spacial perception or the ability to visualize objects out of their context. As on other tests, girls score higher on number ability until late high school, but such is not the case with analytic and spacial perception tests. These tests indicate that boys perceive more analytically while girls are more contextual—although this ability to "break set" or be "field independent" also

[39] McClelland, op. cit. passim.
[40] Horner, Matina S., "Woman's Will to Fail," Psychology Today, Vol. 3, No. 6, Nov. 1969, p. 36. See Also: Matina S. Horner, Sex differences in Achievement Motivation and Performance in Competitive and Non-Competitive Situations. Unpublished Doctoral Dissertation, University of Michigan, 1968.
[41] Lipinski, Beatrice, Sex-Role Conflict and Achievement Motivation in College Women, Unpublished Ph. D. dissertation, University of Cincinnati, 1965.
[42] Pierce, James V., "Sex Differences in Achievement Motivation of Able High School Students", Co-operative Research Project No. 1097, University of Chicago, December 1961.
[43] Neiman, Lionel J., "The Influence of Peer Groups Upon Attitudes Toward the Feminine Role" in Social Problems, Vol. 2, 1954, p. 104—111.
[44] Asch, S. E., "Studies of Independence and Conformity. A Minority of One Against a Unanimous Majority" in Psychological Monographs, Vol. 70, 1956, No. 9.

does not seem to appear until after the fourth or fifth year.[45]

According to Maccoby, this contextual mode of perception common to women is a distinct disadvantage for scientific production. "Girls on the average develop a somewhat different way of handling incoming information—their thinking is less analytic, more global, and more preseverative—and this kind of thinking may serve very well for many kinds of functioning but it is not the kind of thinking most conducive to high-level intellectual productivity, especially in science." [46]

Several social psychologists have postulated that the key developmental characteristic of analytic thinking is what is called early "independence and mastery training", or "whether and how soon a child is encouraged to assume initiative, to take responsibility for himself, and to solve problems by himself, rather than rely on others for the direction of his activities." [47] In other words, analytically inclined children are those who have not been subject to what Brofenbrenner calls "over-socialization," [48] and there is a good deal of indirect evidence that such is the case. Levy has observed that "overprotected" boys tend to develop intellectually like girls.[49] Bing found that those girls who were good at special tasks were those whose mothers left them alone to solve the problems by themselves while the mothers of verbally inclined daughters insisted on helping them.[50] Witkin similarly found that mothers of analytic children had encouraged their initiative while mothers on non-analytic children had encouraged dependence and discouraged self-assertion.[51] One writer commented on these studies that "this is to be expected, for the independent child is less likely to accept superficial appearances of objects without exploring them for himself, while the dependent child will be afraid to reach out on his own, and will accept appearances without question. In other words, the independent child is likely to be more *active*, not only psychologically but physically, and the physically active child will naturally have more kinesthetic experience with spatial relationship in his environment.[52]

When we turn to specific child rearing practices we find that the pattern repeats itself according to the sex of the child. Although comparative studies of parental treatment of boys and girls are not extensive, those that have been made indicate that the traditional practices applied to girls are very different from those applied to boys. Girls receive more affection, more protectiveness, more control and more restrictions. Boys are subjected to more achievement demands and higher expectations.[53] In short, while girls are not always encouraged to be dependent *per se*, they are usually not encouraged to be *independent* and physically active. "Such findings indicate that the differential treatment of the two sexes reflects in part a difference in goals. With sons, socialization seems to focus primarily on directing and constraining the boys' impact on the environment. With daughters, the aim is rather to protect the girl from the impact of environment. The boy is being prepared to mold his world, the girl to be molded by it." [54]

This relationship holds true cross-culturally even more than it does in our own society. In studying child socialization in 110 non-literate cultures, Barry, Bacon and Child found that "Pressure toward nurturance, obedience, and responsibility is most often stronger for girls, whereas pressure toward achievement

[45] Macoby, Eleanor E. "Sex Differences in Intellectual Functioning" in *The Development of Sex Differences*, ed. by E. Maccoby, Stanford University Press, 1966, p. 26 ff. The three most common tests are the Rod and Frame test which require the adjustment of a rod to a vertical position regardless of the tilt of a frame around it; the Embedded Figures test which determines the ability to perceive a figure embedded in a more complex field; and an analytic test in which one groups a set of objects according to a common element.

[46] Maccoby, Eleanor E., "Woman's Intellect" in *The Potential of Women*, ed. by Farber and Wilson, New York : McGraw-Hill, 1963, p. 30.

[47] Maccoby, *Ibid.*, p. 31. See also : Julia A. Sherman, "Problems of Sex Differences in Space Perception and Aspects of Intellectual Functioning," *Psychological Review*, Vol. 74, No. 4, July, 1967, pp. 290–299 ; and Philip E. Vernon, "Ability Factors and Environmental Influences" *American Psychologist*, Vol. 20, No. 9, Sept. 1965, pp. 723–733.

[48] Bronfenbrenner, Urie, "Some Familial Antecedents of Responsibility and Leadership in Adolescents" in *Leadership and Interpersonal Behavior*, ed. by Luigi Petrullo and Bernard M. Bass., New York : Holt, Rinehart, and Winston, 1961, p. 260.

[49] Levy, D. M., *Maternal Overprotection*, New York : Columbia University Press, 1943.

[50] Maccoby, *op. cit.* p. 31.

[51] Witkin, H. A., Dyk, R. B., Patterson, H. E., Goodenough, D. R., and Karp, S. A., *Psychological Differentiation* New York : Wiley 1962.

[52] Clapp, James, "Sex Differences in Mathematical Reasoning Ability" unpublished paper.

[53] Sears, R. R., Maccoby, E., and Levin, H., *Patterns of Child Rearing*, Evanston, Ill. : Row and Peterson, 1957.

[54] Bronfenbrenner, *op. cit.*, p. 260.

and self-reliance is most often stronger for boys." [55] They also found that strong differences in socialization practices were consistent with highly differentiated adult sex roles.

These cross cultural studies show that dependency training for women is widespread and his results beyond simply curtailing analytic ability. In all these cultures women were in a relatively inferior status position compared to males. In fact, there was a correlation with the degree of rigidity of sex-role socialization, and the subservience of women to men.

In our society also, analytic abilities were not the only ones valued. Being person-oriented and contextual in perception are very valuable attributes for many fields where, nevertheless, very few women are found. Such characteristics are valuable in the arts and the social sciences where women are found more than in the natural sciences—yet even here their achievement is still not deemed equivalent to that of men. One explanation of this, of course, is the repressive effect of role conflict and peer group pressures discussed earlier. But when one looks further it appears that there is an earlier cause here as well.

As several studies have shown, the very same early independence and mastery training which has such a beneficial effect on analytic thinking also determines the extent of one's achievement orientation [56]—that drive which pushes one to excel beyond the need of survival. And it is precisely this kind of training that women fail to receive. They are encouraged to be dependent and passive—to be "feminine." In that process the shape of their mind is altered and their ambitions are dulled or channelled into the only socially rewarded achievement for a woman—marriage.

Now we have come almost full circle and can begin to see the vicious nature of the trap in which our society places women. When we become conscious of the many subtle mechanisms of social control—peer group pressures, cultural norms, parental training, teachers, role expectations, and negative self concept—it is not hard to see why girls who are better at most everything in childhood do not excel at much of anything as adults.

Only one link remains and that requires taking a brief look at those few women who do manage to slip through a chance loophole. Maccoby provided the best commentary on this when she noted that the girl who does not succumb to over-protection and develop the appropriate personality and behavior for her sex had a major price to pay: the anxiety that comes from crossing the caste lines. She feels that "it is this anxiety which helps to account for the lack of productivity among those women who do make intellectual careers—because (anxiety) is especially damaging to creative thinking." The combination of all these factors together tell "something of a horror story." It would appear that even when a woman is suitably endowed intellectually and develops the right temperament and habits of thought to make use of her endowment, she must be fleet of foot indeed to scale the hurdles society has erected for her and to remain a whole and happy person while continuing to follow her intellectual bent." [57]

The plot behind this horror story should by now be clearly evident. There is more to oppression than discrimination and more to the condition of women than whether or not they want to be free of the home. All societies have many ways to keep people in their places and we have only discussed a few of the ones used to keep women in theirs. Women have been striving to break free of these bonds for many hundreds of years and once again are gathering their strength for another try. It will take more than a few changes in the legal system to significantly change the condition of women, although those changes will be reflective of more profound changes taking place in society. Unlike blacks, the women's liberation movement does not have the thicket of Jim Crow laws to cut through. This is a mixed blessing. On the one hand, the women's liberation movement lacks the simple handholds of oppression which the early civil rights movement had; but at the same time it does not have to waste time wading through legal segregation before realizing that the real nature of oppression lies much deeper. It is the more basic means of social control that will have to be attacked as women—and men—look into their lives and dissect the many factors that made them what they are. The dam of social control now has many cracks in it. It has held women back for years, but it is about to break under the strain.

[55] Barry, Herbert, Bacon, M. K., and Child, Irving L., "A Cross-Cultural Survey of Some Sex Differences in Socialization" in the *Journal of Abnormal and Social Psychology*, Vol. 55. Nov. 1957, p. 328.
[56] Winterbottom, Marian R., "The Relation of Need for Achievement to Learning Experiences in Independence and Mastery" in *Basic Studies in Social Psychology*, ed. by Harold Proshansky and Bernard Seidenberg, New York: Holt, Rinehart and Winston, 1965, pp. 294–307.
[57] Maccoby, *op. cit.* p. 37.

CASTELIKE STATUS OF WOMEN AND NEGROES*

Negroes	*Women*

1. HIGH SOCIAL VISIBILITY

(a) Skin color, other "racial" characteristics	(a) Secondary sex characteristics
(b) (Sometimes) distinctive dress— bandana, flashy clothes	(b) Distinctive dress, skirts, and so forth

2. ASCRIBED ATTRIBUTES

(a) Inferior intelligence, smaller brain, less convoluted, scarcity of geniuses	(a) Do.
(b) More free in instinctive gratifications. More emotional, "primitive" and childlike. Imagined sexual prowess envied.	(b) Irresponsible, inconsistent, emotionally unstable. Lack strong super-ego. Women as "temptresses."
(c) Common stereotype "inferior"	(c) *Weaker*

3. RATIONALIZATIONS OF STATUS

(a) Thought all right in his place	(a) Woman's place is in the home
(b) Myth of contented Negro	(b) Myth of contented woman—"feminine" woman is happy in subordinate role

4. ACCOMMODATION ATTITUDES

(a) Supplicatory whining intonation of voice	(a) Rising inflection, smiles, laughs, downward glances
(b) Deferential manner	(b) Flattering manner
(c) Concealment of real feelings	(c) "Feminine wiles"
(d) Outwit "white folks"	(d) Outdo "menfolk"
(e) Careful study of points at which dominant group is susceptible to influence	(e) Do.
(f) Fake appeals for directives; show of ignorance	(f) Appearance of helplessness

5. DISCRIMINATIONS

(a) Limitations on education—should fit "place" in society	(a) Appearance of helplessness
(b) Confined to traditional jobs— barred from supervisory positions. Their competition feared. No family precedents for new aspirations	(b) Do.
(c) Deprived of political importance	(c) Do.
(d) Social and professional segregation	(d) Do.
(e) More vulnerable to criticism	(e) For example, conduct in bars

6. SIMILAR PROBLEMS

Roles not clearly defined, but in flux as result of social change. Conflict between achieved status and ascribed status.

---

*From Hacker, op. cit. pp. 10–19.

TRAINING THE WOMAN TO KNOW HER PLACE: THE POWER OF A NONCONSCIOUS IDEOLOGY [1]

(By Sandra L. Bem and Daryl J. Bem,[2] Department of Psychology, Carnegie-Mellon University)

"In the beginning God created the heaven and the earth . . . And God said, Let us make man in our image, after our likeness; and let them have dominion over the fish of the sea, and over the fowl of the air, and over the cattle, and

---

[1] Citations should be made to the published version of this article: Bem. S. L. & Bem, D. J. Case study of a nonconscious ideology: training the woman to know her place. In D. J. Bem, *Beliefs, attitudes, and human affairs.* Belmont, Calif. : Brooks/Cole, 1970.
[2] Order of authorship determined by the flip of a coin.

over all the earth . . . And the rib, which the Lord God had taken from man, made he a woman and brought her unto the man . . . And the Lord God said unto the woman, What is this that thou has done? And the woman said, The serpent beguiled me, and I did eat . . . Unto the woman He said, I will greatly multiply thy sorrow and thy conception: in sorrow thou shalt bring forth children; and thy desire shall be to thy husband, and he shall rule over thee." (Gen. 1, 2, 3)

And lest anyone fail to grasp the moral of this story, Saint Paul provides further clarification:

"For man . . . is the image and glory of God; but the woman is the glory of the man. For the man is not of the woman, but the woman of the man. Neither was the man created for the woman, but the woman for the man." (1 Cor. 11)

"Let the woman learn in silence with all subjection. But I suffer not a woman to teach, nor to usurp authority over the man, but to be in silence. For Adam was first formed, then Eve. And Adam was not deceived, but the woman, being deceived, was in the transgression. Notwithstanding, she shall be saved in child-bearing, if they continue in faith and charity and holiness with sobriety." (1 Tim. 2)

And lest it be thought that only Christians have this rich heritage of ideology about women, consider the morning prayer of the Orthodox Jew:

"Blessed art Thou, oh Lord our God, King of the Universe, that I was not born a gentile.

"Blessed art Thou, oh Lord our God, King of the Universe, that I was not born a slave.

"Blessed art Thou, oh Lord our God, King of the Universe, that I was not born a woman."

Or the Koran, the sacred text of Islam:

"Men are superior to women on account of the qualities in which God has given them pre-eminence."

Because they think they sense a decline in feminine "faith, charity, and holiness with sobriety," many people today jump to the conclusion that the ideology expressed in these passages is a relic of the past. Not so. It has simply been obscured by an equalitarian veneer, and the ideology has now become nonconscious. That is, we remain unaware of it because alternative beliefs and attitudes about women go unimagined. We are like the fish who is unaware that his environment is wet. After all, what else could it be? Such is the nature of all nonconscious ideologies. Such is the nature of America's ideology about women. For even those Americans who agree that a black skin should not uniquely qualify its owner for janitorial or domestic service continue to act as if the possession of a uterus uniquely qualifies *its* owner for precisely that.

Consider, for example, the 1968 student rebellion at Columbia University. Students from the radical left took over some administration buildings in the name of equalitarian principles which they accused the university of flouting. Here were the most militant spokesmen one could hope to find in the cause of equalitarian ideals. But no sooner had they occupied the buildings than the male militants blandly turned to their sisters-in-arms and assigned them the task of preparing the food, while they—the menfolk—would presumably plan further strategy. The reply these males received was the reply they deserved, and the fact that domestic tasks behind the barricades were desegregated across the sex line that day is an everlasting tribute to the class consciousness of the ladies of the left.

But these conscious coeds are not typical, for the nonconscious assumptions about a woman's "natural" talents (or lack of them) are at least as prevalent among women as they are among men. A psychologist named Philip Goldberg (1968) demonstrated this by asking female college students to rate a number of professional articles from each of six fields. The articles were collated into two equal sets of booklets, and the names of the authors were changed so that the identical article was attributed to a male author (e.g., John T. McKay) in one set of booklets and to a female author (e.g., Joan T. McKay) in the other set. Each student was asked to read the articles in her booklet and to rate them for value, competence, persuasiveness, writing style, and so forth.

As he had anticipated, Goldberg found that the identical article received significantly lower ratings when it was attributed to a female author than when it was attributed to a male author. He had predicted this result for articles from professional fields generally considered the province of men, like law and city planning, but to his surprise, these coeds also downgraded articles from the fields of dietetics and elementary school education when they were attributed to female authors. In other words, these students rated the male authors as better at everything, agreeing with Aristotle that "we should regard the female nature as afflicted with a natural defectiveness." We repeated this experiment informally in our own classrooms and discovered that male students show the same implicit prejudice against female authors that Goldberg's female students showed. Such is the nature of a nonconscious ideology!

It is significant that examples like these can be drawn from the college world, for today's students have challenged the established ways of looking at almost every other issue, and they have been quick to reject those practices of our society which conflict explicitly with their major values. But as the above examples suggest, they will find it far more difficult to shed the more subtle aspects of a sex-role ideology which—as we shall now attempt to demonstrate—conflicts just as surely with their existential values as any of the other societal practices to which they have so effectively raised objection. And as we shall see, there is no better way to appreciate the power of a society's nonconscious ideology than to examine it within the framework of values held by that society's avant-garde.

Individuality and self-fulfillment

The dominant values of today's students concern personal growth on the one hand, and interpersonal relationships on the other. The first of these emphasizes individuality and self-fulfillment; the second stresses openness, honesty, and equality in all human relationships.

The values of individuality and self-fulfillment imply that each human being, male and female, is to be encouraged to "do his own thing." Men and women are no longer to be stereotyped by society's definitions. If sensitivity, emotionality, and warmth are desirable human characteristics, then they are desirable for men as well as for women. (John Wayne is no longer an idol of the young, but their pop-art satire.) If independence, assertiveness, and serious intellectual commitment are desirable human characteristics, then they are desirable for women as well as for men. The major prescription of this college generation is that each individual should be encouraged to discover and fulfill his own unique potential and identity, unfettered by society's presumptions.

But society's presumptions enter the scene much earlier than most people suspect, for parents begin to raise their children in accord with the popular stereotypes from the very first. Boys are encouraged to be aggressive, competitive, and independent, whereas girls are rewarded for being passive and dependent (Barry, Bacon, & Child, 1957; Sears, Maccoby, & Levin, 1957). In one study, six-month-old infant girls were already being touched and spoken to more by their mothers while they were playing than were infant boys. When they were thirteen months old, these same girls were more reluctant than the boys to leave their mothers; they returned more quickly and more frequently to them; and they remained closer to them throughout the entire play period. When a physical barrier was placed between mother and child, the girls tended to cry and motion for help; the boys made more active attempts to get around the barrier (Goldberg & Lewis, 1969). No one knows to what extent these sex differences at the age of thirteen months can be attributed to the mothers' behavior at the age of six months, but it is hard to believe that the two are unconnected.

As children grow older, more explicit sex-role training is introduced. Boys are encouraged to take more of an interest in mathematics and science. Boys, not girls, are given chemistry sets and microscopes for Christmas. Moreover, all children quickly learn that mommy is proud to be a moron when it comes to mathematics and science, whereas daddy knows all about these things. When a young boy returns from school all excited about biology, he is almost certain to be encouraged to think of becoming a physician. A girl with similar enthusiasm is told that she might want to consider nurse's training later so she can have "an interesting job to fall back upon in case—God forbid—she ever needs to support herself." A very different kind of encouragement. And any girl who doggedly persists in her enthusiasm for science is likely to find her parents as horrified by the prospect of a permanent love affair with physics as they would be by the prospect of an interracial marriage.

These socialization practices quickly take their toll. By nursery school age, for example, boys are already asking more questions about how and why things work (Smith, 1933). In first and second grade, when asked to suggest ways of improving various toys, boys do better on the fire truck and girls do better on the nurse's kit, but by the third grade, boys do better regardless of the toy presented (Torrance, 1962). By the ninth grade, 25% of the boys, but only 3% of the girls, are considering careers in science or engineering (Flanagan, unpublished; cited by Kagan, 1964). When they apply for college, boys and girls are about equal on verbal aptitude tests, but boys score significantly higher on mathematical aptitude tests—about 60 points higher on the College Board examinations, for example (Brown, 1965, p. 162). Moreover, girls improve their mathematical performance if problems are reworded so that they deal with cooking and gardening, even though the abstract reasoning required for their solutions remain the same (Milton, 1958). Clearly, not just ability, but motivation too, has been affected.

But these effects in mathematics and science are only part of the story. A girl's long training in passivity and dependence appears to exact an even higher toll from her overall motivation to achieve, to search for new and independent ways of doing things, and to welcome the challenge of new and unsolved problems. In one study, for example, elementary school girls were more likely to try solving a puzzle by imitating an adult, whereas the boys were more likely to search for a novel solution not provided by the adult (McDavid, 1959). In another puzzle-solving study, young girls asked for help and approval from adults more frequently than the boys; and, when given the opportunity to return to the puzzles a second time, the girls were more likely to rework those they had already solved, whereas the boys were more likely to try puzzles they had been unable to solve previously (Crandall & Rabson, 1960). A girl's sigh of relief is almost audible when she marries and retires from the outside world of novel and unsolved problems. This, of course, is the most conspicuous outcome of all: the majority of American women become full-time homemakers. Such are the consequences of a nonconscious ideology.

But why does this process violate the values of individuality and self-fulfillment? It is not because some people may regard the role of homemaker as inferior to other roles. That is not the point. Rather, the point is that our society is managing to consign a large segment of its population to the role of homemaker solely on the basis of sex just as inexorably as it has in the past consigned the individual with a black skin to the role of janitor or domestic. It is not the quality of the role itself which is at issue here, but the fact that in spite of their unique identities, the majority of America's women end up in the *same* role.

Even so, however, several arguments are typically advanced to counter the claim that America's homogenization of its women subvert individuality and self-fulfillment. The three most common arguments invoke, respectively, (1) free will, (2) biology, and (3) complementarity.

1. The free will argument proposes that a 21-year-old woman is perfectly free to choose some other role if she cares to do so; no one is standing in her way. But this argument conveniently overlooks the fact that the society which has spent twenty years carefully making the woman's ballot for her has nothing to lose in that twenty-first year by pretending to let her cast it for the alternative of her choice. Society has controlled not her alternatives, but her motivation to choose any but one of those alternatives. The so-called freedom to choose is illusory and cannot be invoked to justify the society which controls the motivation to choose.

2. The biological argument suggests that there may really be inborn differences between men and women in, say, independence or mathematical ability. Or that there may be biological factors beyond the fact that women can become pregnant and nurse children which uniquely dictate that they, but not men, should stay home all day and shun serious outside commitment. Maybe female hormones really are responsible somehow. One difficulty with this argument, of course, is that female hormones would have to be different in the Soviet Union, where one-third of the engineers and 75% of the physicians are women. In America, women constitute less than 1% of the engineers and only 7% of the physicians (Dodge, 1966). Female physiology *is* different, and it may account for some of the psychological differences between the sexes, but America's sex-role ideology still seems primarily responsible for the fact that so few women emerge from childhood with the motivation to seek out any role beyond the one that our society dictates.

But even if there really were biological difference between the sexes along these lines, the biological argument would still be irrelevant. The reason can best be illustrated with an analogy.

Suppose that every black American boy were to be socialized to become a jazz musician on the assumption that he had a "natural" talent in that direction, or suppose that his parents should subtly discourage him from other pursuits because it is considered "inappropriate" for black men to become physicians or physicists. Most liberal Americans, we submit, would disapprove. But suppose that it *could* be demonstrated that black Americans, *on the average*, did possess an inborn better sense of rhythm than white Americans. Would *that* justify ignoring the unique characteristics of a *particular* black youngster from the very beginning and specifically socializing him to become a musician? We don't think so. Similarly, as long as a woman's socialization does not nurture her uniqueness, but treats her only as a member of a group on the basis of some assumed *average* characteristic, she will not be prepared to realize her own potential in the way that the values of individuality and self-fulfillment imply she should.

The irony of the biological argument is that it does not take biological differences seriously enough. That is, it fails to recognize the range of biological differences between individuals within the same sex. Thus, recent research has revealed that biological factors help determine many personality traits. Dominance and submissiveness, for example, have been found to have large inheritable components; in other words, biological factors *do* have the potential for partially determining how dominant or submissive an individual, male or female, will turn out to be. But the effects of this biological potential could be detected only in males (Gottesman, 1963). This implies that only the males in our culture are raised with sufficient flexibility, with sufficient latitude given to their biologial differences, for their "natural" or biologically determined potential to shine through. Females, on the other hand, are subjected to a socialization which so ignores their unique attributes that even the effects of biology seem to be swamped. In sum, the biological argument for continuing America's homogenization of its women gets hoist with its own petard.

3. Many people recognize that most women do end up as full-time homemakers because of their socialization and that these women do exemplify the failure of our society to raise girls as unique individuals. But, they point out, the role of the homemaker is not inferior to the role of the professional man: it is complementary but equal.

This argument is usually bolstered by pointing to the joys and importance of taking care of small children. Indeed, mothers *and* fathers find childrearing rewarding, and it is certainly important. But this argument becomes insufficient when one considers that the average American woman now lives to age 74 and has her *last* child at about age 26; thus, by the time the woman is 33 or so, her children all have more important things to do with their daytime hours than to spend them entertaining an adult woman who has nothing to do during the second half of her life span. As for the other "joys" of homemaking, many writers (e.g., Friedan, 1963) have persuasively argued that the role of the homemaker has been glamorized far beyond its intrinsic worth. This charge becomes plausible when one considers that the average American homemaker spends the equivalent of a man's working day, 7.1 hours, in preparing meals, cleaning house, laundering, mending, shopping, and doing other household tasks. In other words, 43% of her waking time is spent in activity that would command an hourly wage on the open market well below the federally-set minimum for menial industrial work.

The point is not how little she would earn if she did these things in someone else's home, but that this use of time is virtually the same for homemakers with college degrees and for those with less than a grade school education, for women married to professional men and for women married to blue-collar workers. Talent, education, ability, interests, motivations: all are irrelevant. In our society, being female uniquely qualifies an individual for domestic work.

It is true, of course, that the American homemaker has, on the average, 5.1 hours of leisure time per day, and it is here, we are told, that each woman can express her unique identity. Thus, politically interested women can join the League of Women Voters; women with humane interests can become part-time Gray Ladies; women who love music can raise money for the symphony. Protestant women play Canasta; Jewish women play Mah-Jongg; brighter women of all denominations and faculty wives play bridge; and so forth.

But politically interested *men* serve in legislatures; *men* with humane interests become physicians or clinical psychologists; *men* who love music play in the symphony; and so forth. In other words, why should a woman's unique identity determine only the periphery of her life rather than its central core?

Again, the important point is not that the role of homemaker is necessarily inferior, but that the woman's unique identity has been rendered irrelevant. Consider the following "predictability test." When a boy is born, it is difficult to predict what he will be doing 25 years later. We cannot say whether he will be an artist, a doctor, or a college professor because he will be permitted to develop and to fulfill his own unique potential, particularly if he is white and middle-class. But if the newborn child is a girl, we can usually predict with confidence how she will be spending her time 25 years later. Her individuality doesn't have to be considered; it is irrelevant.

The socialization of the American male has closed off certain options for him too. Men are discouraged from developing certain desirable traits such as tenderness and sensitivity just as surely as women are discouraged from being assertive and, alas, "too bright." Young boys are encouraged to be incompetent at cooking and child care just as surely as young girls are urged to be incompetent at mathematics and science.

Indeed, one of the errors of the early femininist movement in this country was that it assumed that men had all the goodies and that women could attain self-fulfillment merely by being like men. But that is hardly the utopia implied by the values of individuality and self-fulfillment. Rather, these values would require society to raise its children so flexibly and with sufficient respect for the integrity of individual uniqueness that some men might emerge with the motivation, the ability, and the opportunity to stay home and raise children without bearing the stigma of being peculiar. If homemaking is as glamorous as the women's magazines and television commercials portray it, then men, too, should have that option. Even if homemaking isn't all that glamorous, it would probably still be more fulfilling for some men than the jobs in which they now find themselves.

And if biological differences really do exist between men and women in "nurturance," in their inborn motivations to care for children, then this will show up automatically in the final distribution of men and women across the various roles: relatively fewer men will choose to stay at home. The values of individuality and self-fulfillment do not imply that there must be equality of outcome, an equal number of men and women in each role, but that there should be the widest possible variation in outcome consistent with the range of individual differences among people regardless of sex. At the very least, these values imply that society should raise its males so that they could freely engage in activities that might pay less than those being pursued by their wives without feeling that they were "living off their wives." One rarely hears it said of a woman that she is "living off her husband."

Thus, it is true that a man's options are limited by our society's sex-role ideology, but as the "predictability test" reveals, it is still the woman in our society whose identity is rendered irrelevant by America's socialization practices. In 1954, the United States Supreme Court declared that a fraud and a hoax lay behind the slogan "separate but equal." It is unlikely that any court will ever do the same for the more subtle motto that successfully keeps the women in her place: "complementary but equal."

Interpersonal equality

"Wives, submit yourselves unto your own husbands, as unto the Lord. For the husband is the head of the wife, even as Christ is the head of the church; and he is the savior of the body. Therefore, as the church is subject unto Christ, so let the wives be to their own husbands in everything." (Eph. 5)

As this passage reveals, the ideological rationalization that men and women hold complementary but equal positions is a recent invention of our modern "liberal" society, part of the equalitarian veneer which helps to keep today's version of the ideology nonconscious. Certainly those Americans who value open, honest, and equalitarian relationships generally are quick to reject this traditional view of the male-female relationship; and, an increasing number of young people even plan to enter "utopian" marriages very much like the following hypothetical example:

"Both my wife and I earned Ph.D. degrees in our respective disciplines. I turned down a superior academic post in Oregon and accepted a slightly less desirable position in New York where my wife could obtain a part-time teaching job and do research at one of the several other colleges in the area. Although I would have preferred to live in a suburb, we purchased a home near my wife's college so that she could have an office at home where she would be when the children returned from school. Because my wife earns a good salary, she can easily afford to pay a maid to do her major household chores. My wife and I share all others tasks around the house equally. For example, she cooks the meals, but I do the laundry for her and help her with many of her other household tasks."

Without questioning the basic happiness of such a marriage or its appropriateness for many couples, we can legitimately ask if such a marriage is, in fact, an instance of interpersonal equality. Have all the hidden assumptions about the woman's "natural" role really been eliminated? Has the traditional ideology really been exercised? There is a very simple test. If the marriage is truly equalitarian, then its description should retain the same flavor and tone even if the roles of the husband and wife were to be reversed:

"Both my husband and I earned Ph.D degrees in our respective disciplines. I turned down a superior academic post in Oregon and accepted a slightly less desirable position in New York where my husband could obtain a part-time teaching job and do research at one of the several other colleges in the area. Although I would have preferred to live in a suburb, we purchased a home near my husband's college so that he could have an office at home where he would be when the children returned from school. Because my husband earns a good salary, he can easily afford to pay a maid to do his major household chores. My husband and I share all other tasks around the house equally. For example, he cooks the meals, but I do the laundry for him and help him with many of his other household tasks."

It seems unlikely that many men or women in our society would mistake the marriage *just* described as either equalitarian or desirable, and thus it becomes apparent that the ideology about the woman's "natural" role nonconsciously permeates the entire fabric of such "utopian" marriages. It is true that the wife gains some measure of equality when her career can influence the final place of residence, but why is it the unquestioned assumption that the husband's career solely determines the initial set of alternatives that are to be considered? Why is it the wife who automatically seeks the part-time position? Why it it *her* maid instead of *their* maid? Why *her* laundry? Why her household tasks? And so forth throughout the entire relationship.

The important point here is not that such marriages are bad or that their basic assumptions of inequality produce unhappy, frustrated women. Quite the contrary. It is the very happiness of the wives in such marriages that reveals society's smashing success in socializing its women. It is a measure of the distance our society must yet traverse toward the goals of self-fulfillment and interpersonal equality that such marriages are widely characterized as utopian and fully equalitarian. It is a mark of how well the woman has been kept in her place that the husband in such a marriage is often idolized by women, including his wife, for "permitting" her to squeeze a career into the interstices of their marriage as long as his own career is not unduly inconvenienced. Thus is the white man blessed for exercising his power benignly while his "natural" right to that power forever remains unquestioned.

Such is the subtlety of a nonconscious ideology!

A truly equalitarian marriage would permit both partners to pursue careers or outside commitments which carry equal weight when all important decisions are to be made. It is here, of course, that the "problem" of children arises. People often assume that the woman who seeks a role beyond home and family would not care to have children. They assume that if she wants a career or serious outside commitment, then children must be unimportant to her. But of course no one makes this assumption about her husband. No one assumes that a father's interest in his career necessarily precludes a deep and abiding affection for his children or a vital interest in their development. Once again America applies a double standard of judgment. Suppose that a father of small children suddenly lost his wife. No matter how much he loved his children, no one would expect him to sacrifice his career in order to stay home with them on a full-time basis— *even if he had an independent source of income.* No one would charge him with selfishness or lack of parental feeling if he sought professional care for his children during the day. An equalitarian marriage simply abolishes this double standard and extends the same freedom to the mother, while also providing the framework for the father to enter more fully into the pleasures and responsibilities of child rearing. In fact, it is the equalitarian marriage which has the most potential for giving children the love and concern of two parents rather than one.

But few women are prepared to make use of this freedom. Even those women who have managed to finesse society's attempt to rob them of their career motivations are likely to find themselves blocked by society's trump card: the feeling that the raising of the children is their unique responsibility and—in time of crisis—ultimately theirs alone. Such is the emotional power of a nonconscious ideology.

In addition to providing this potential for equalized child care, a truly equalitarian marriage embraces a more general division of labor which satisfies what might be called "the roommate test." That is, the labor is divided just as it is when two men or two women room together in college or set up a bachelor apartment together. Errands and domestic chores are assigned by preference, agreement, flipping a coin, given to hired help, or—as is sometimes the case— left undone.

It is significant that today's young people, many of whom live this way prior to marriage, find this kind of arrangement within marriage so foreign to their thinking. Consider an analogy. Suppose that a white male college student decided to room or set up a bachelor apartment with a black male friend. Surely the typical white student would not blithely assume that his black roommate was to handle all the domestic chores. Nor would his conscience allow him to do so even in the unlikely event that his roommate would say: "No, that's okay. I like doing housework. I'd be happy to do it." We suspect that the typical white student would still not be comfortable if he took advantage of the fact that his roommate had been socialized to be "happy" with such an arrangement. But change this hypothetical black roommate to a female marriage partner, and somehow the student's conscience goes to sleep. At most it is quickly tranquilized by the thought that "she is happiest when she is ironing for her loved one." Such is the power of a nonconscious ideology.

Of course, it may well be that she *is* happiest when she is ironing for her loved one.

Such, indeed, is the power of a nonconscious ideology!

REFERENCES

Barry, H., III, Bacon, M. K., & Child, I. L. A cross-cultural survey of some sex differences in socialization. *Journal of Abnormal and Social Psychology*, 1957, *55*, 327–332.

Brown, R. *Social Psychology*. New York: Free Press, 1965.

Crandall, V. J., & Rabson, A. Children's repetition choices in an intellectual achievement situation following success and failure. *Journal of Genetic Psychology*, 1960, *97*, 161–168.

Dodge, N. D. *Women in the Soviet Economy*. Baltimore: The Johns Hopkins Press, 1966.

Flanagan, J. C. Project talent. Unpublished manuscript.

Friedan, B. *The feminine mystique*. New York: Norton, 1963.

Goldberg, P. Are women prejudiced against women? *Transaction*, April 1968, *5*, 28–30.

Goldberg, S. & Lewis, M. Play behavior in the year-old infant: early sex differences. *Child Development*, 1969, *40*, 21–31.

Gottesman, I. I. Heritability of personality: a demonstration. *Psychological Monographs*, 1963, *77*, (Whole No. 572).

Kagan, J. Acquisition and significance of sex typing and sex role identity. In M. L. Hoffman & L. W. Hoffman (Eds.) *Review of child development research*, *Vol. 1*. New York: Russell Sage Foundation, 1964. Pp. 137–167.

McDavid, J. W. Imitative behavior in preschool children. *Psyhological Monographs*, 1959, *73*, (Whole No. 486).

Milton, G. A. Five studies of the relation between sex role identification and achievement in problem solving. Technical Report No. 3, Department of Industrial Administration, Department of Psychology, Yale University, December, 1958.

Sears, R. R., Maccoby, E. E., & Levin, H. *Patterns of child rearing*. Evanston, Ill.: Row, Peterson, 1957.

Smith, M. E. The influence of age, sex, and situation on the frequency of form and functions of questions asked by preschool children. *Child Development*, 1933, *3*, 201–213.

Torrance, E. P. *Guiding creative talent*. Englewood Cliffs, N.J.: Prentice-Hall, 1962.

STATEMENT OF DR. PAULI MURRAY, PROFESSOR OF AMERICAN STUDIES BRANDEIS UNIVERSITY

Madam Chairman and members of the subcommittee: I am Pauli Murray,[1] professor of American Studies at Brandeis University. I teach legal studies,

[1] Biographical data: A.B., Hunter College: LL.B., Howard University; LL.M., University of California; J.S.D., Yale University. Former deputy, Office of Attorney General, Department of Justice, State of California; former associate: Paul, Weiss [Goldberg], Rifkind, Wharton & Garrison; member of Political and Civil Rights Committee of President's Commission on Status of Women (1962–63); former consultant, Equal Employment Opportunity Commission. Founder and member, National Organization for Women (NOW); member, Women's Equity Action League (WEAL); member, subcommittee on Women's Rights, American Bar Association; member, Commission on Women in Today's World. Church Women United; life member, National Council of Negro Women; life member, National Association for the Advancement of Colored People (NAACP). Compiler and editor, *States' Laws on Race and Color* (1951, 1955); author, *Human Rights U.S.A.: 1948–1966;* co-author: Murray and Eastwood, *Jane Crow and the Law: Sex Discrimination and Title VII*, 34 Geo. Washington Law Review 232 (1965).

civil rights, law and social change and a course on women in American society. My task in a college of liberal arts is to expose undergraduates to an understanding of the legal system in its various aspects—the judicial process, the legislative process and the administrative process, and my appearance before this committee is in the nature of "in-service-training." Many of my students are headed for law school; others plan careers in education, community organization, or social work. All of them, however, are asking themselves the question whether our legal system is flexible enough to acommodate necessary social change. What I have to say to this subcommittee is influenced by my own desperate need to answer this question in the affirmative coupled with the apprehension that in the area of women's rights as in other areas of human rights, our lawmakers will respond only when there is violence and disruption of nationwide proportions.

I appear before this Subcommittee, however, as a member of the National Board of the American Civil Liberties Union to testify in support of the provisions of Section H.R. 16098 which seek to extend protection against sex-based discrimination, particularly in education and employment.

The ACLU stands for the principle of equality of treatment under the law and equality of opportunity without regard to sex. It has been active in litigation to apply this principle for the purpose of eliminating sex-based discrimination in jury service, in the criminal law, employment, admission to state universities, and the like.[2]

In its most recent policy statement on academic freedom and academic due process, ACLU has declared: "A teacher should be appointed solely on the basis of teaching ability and competence in his professional field without regard to such factors as race, sex, nationality, creed, religious or political belief or affiliation, or behavior not demonstrably related to the teaching function." (ACLU Statement of Principles on Academic Freedom, etc., September 1966. p. 8.) On June 7, 1970, the Biennial Conference of ACLU overwhelmingly adopted a strong policy recommendation to its national board on the rights of women, including the principle that admission to colleges and universities should not be denied on the basis of ethnic origin, race, religion, political belief or affiliation, sex or other irrational basis. In ACLU's fifty years of experience seeking to protect individual rights, it has come to recognize that all human rights are indivisible and that the denial of these rights to any group threatens the rights of all. I am happy to espouse this principle here today.

Interrelation of race and sex discrimination

I have listened to the previous witnesses and wish to associate myself with their testimony which I wholeheartedly endorse, particularly the perceptive comments of Commissioner Wilma Scott Heide and her recognition of the urgency of effective legislative action to remove the barriers to the development of the talents of women in the United States. In view of the thoroughness with which my colleagues have documented widespread discrimination against women in the academic process, in the professions and in other employment, I shall attempt to highlight some areas for emphasis.

As a human rights attorney, I am concerned with individuals as whole human beings, being accorded the respect and dignity which is our common heritage. They are first and foremost *persons*, quite apart from any other identity they may possess, and as persons sharing our common humanity they are entitled to equal opportunity to fulfill their individual and unique potential. This is our starting point, for in my view it is only as we recognize and hold sacred the uiqueness of each individual that we come to see clearly the moral and social evil of locking this individual into a group stereotype, whether favorable or unfavorable. I have learned this lesson in part because I am both a Negro and a woman whose experience embodies the conjunction of race and sex discrimination. This experience also embodies the paradox of belonging simultaneously to an oppressed minority and an oppressed majority, and for good measure being left-handed in a right-handed world. As a self-supporting woman who has had the responsibility for elderly relatives, the opportunity for education and employment consonant with my potentialities and training has been a matter of personal survival.

[2] See. *e.g., Hoyt v. Florida*, 368 U.S. 57 (1961) ; *White v. Crook*, 251 F. Supp. 401 (N.D. Ala., 1966) (jury cases) ; *Kirstein v. The Rector and Visitors of the University of Virginia*, E.D. Va., Richmond Div. Civ. No. 220–69–R, Feb. 6, 1970, (admission of women to state university) ; *Phillips v. Martin Marietta*, 411 F. 2d 1 (CA 5, 1969) ; *cert.* granted U.S. Sup. Ct., No. 1058, October Term 1969 ; *Diaz v. Pan American Airways*, D.C. S.D., Fla. No. 69–206–Civ–CF, April 9, 1970, 62 LC. Par. 9432. (Title VII cases involving sex discrimination).

Moreover, in more than thirty years of intensive study of human rights and deep involvement in the civil rights movement I have observed the interrelationships between what is often referred to as *racism* and *sexism* (Jim Crow and Jane Crow), and have been unable to avoid the conclusion that discrimination because of one's sex is just as degrading, dehumanizing, immoral, unjust, indefensible, infuriating and capable of producing societal turmoil as discrimination because of one's race.[3]

The marked parallels in the status of women and of Negroes/Blacks have been documented by historians and social scientists. Whether the point of departure has been a study of women or of racial theories, contemporary scholars have been impressed by the interrelationship of these two issues in the United States. (Simone de Beauvoir, *The Second Sex;* Myrdal, *An American Dilemma,* Appendix V, 1944; Ashley Montagu, *Man's Most Dangerous Myth: The Fallacy of Race,* 4th ed.)[4]

The history of western culture and, more particularly, of ecclesiastical and common law strongly suggests that the subordinate status of women (in which they were not considered *persons* under the law) has provided the models for the subjugation of other oppressed groups. (See *e.g.* Myrdal, *op. cit.,* Daly, *The Church and the Second Sex* (1968)). In George Fitzhugh's famous defense of chattel slavery in the United States in 1850, he analogized it to the position of women and children.[5]

Dr. Montagu has noted that the pattern of antifeminist argument against equality is identical with that of the racist argument. He observed that in the matter of equal opportunities for scientific achievement women have had little chance to obtain employment in the science departments of our colleges as instructors—about 1 to 100. "Deny a particular group equality of opportunity," he says, "and then assert that because that group has not achieved as much as the groups enjoying complete freedom of opportunity it is obviously inferior and can never do as well." (*op. cit.,* p. 182). Moreover, he finds the same underlying motives at work in antifeminism as in race prejudice, "namely, fear, jealousy, feelings of insecurity, fear of economic competition, guilt feelings and the like." He reminds us that this interrelation has persisted right up to the present:

---

[3] "Race and sex are in every way comparable classes; and if exclusion in one case is a discrimination implying inferiority, it would seem that it must be in the other also . . .

"Not only are race and sex entirely comparable classes, but there are no others like them. They are large, permanent, unchangeable natural classes. No other kind of class is susceptible to implications of inferiority. Aliens, for instance, are essentially a temporary class, like an age class. Only permanent and natural classes are open to those deep, traditional implications which become attached to classes regardless of the actual qualities of the members of the class . . ." Blanche Crozier, *Constitutionality of Discrimination Based on Sex,* 15 B.U.L. Rev. 723, 727–728 (1935).

[4] "From the very beginning, the fight in America for the liberation of the Negro slaves was closely coordinated with the fight for women's emancipation. . . . The women's movement got much of its public support by reason of its affiliation with the Abolitionist movement." Myrdal, *op. cit.* Dr. Myrdal observed that the myths built up to perpetuate the inferior status of women and of Negroes were almost identical. "As in the Negro problem, most men have accepted as self-evident, until recently, the doctrine that women had inferior endowments in most of those respects which carry prestige, power, and advantages in society, but that they were, at the same time, superior in some other respects. The arguments, when arguments were used, have been about the same: smaller brains, scarcity of geniuses and so on. The study of women's intelligence and personality has had broadly the same history as the one we record for Negroes. As in the case of the Negro, women themselves have often been brought to believe in their inferiority of endowment. As the Negro was awarded his 'place' in society, so there was a 'woman's place'. In both cases the rationalization was strongly believed that men, in confining them to this place, did not act against the true interest of the subordinate groups. The myth of the 'contented woman', who did not want to have suffrage or other civil rights and equal opportunities, had the same social function as the myth of the 'contented Negro'." Myrdal, *op. cit.,* p. 1077.

"In connection with the modern form of race prejudice it is of interest to recall that almost every one of the arguments used by the racists to 'prove' the inferiority of one or another so-called 'race' was not so long ago used by the antifeminists to 'prove' the inferiority of the female as compared with the male. In the case of these sexual prejudices one generation has been sufficient in which to discover how completely spurious and erroneous virtually every one of these arguments and assertions are.

"In the 19th century it was fairly generally believed that women were inferior creatures * * * Was it not apparent to everyone that their intelligence was lower, that they were essentially creatures of emotion rather than reason—volatile swooning natures whose powers of concentration were severely limited entirely to knitting and childbirth? * * * Women had practically no executive ability, were quite unable to manage the domestic finances, and, as for competing with men in the business or professional world, such an idea was utterly preposterous, for women were held to possess neither the necessary intelligence nor the equally unattainable stamina. Man's place was out in the world earning a living; woman's place was definitely in the home." Montagu, *op. cit.,* p. 181.

[5] *Slavery Justified by a Southerner,* 1850, in McKittrick, ed., *Slavery Defended,* Prentice-Hall, 1963.

"We know that to gain even so much as a hearing women had to fight every inch of the way. Ridiculed, maligned, opposed at almost every turn, and even imprisoned, the leaders of the women's movement realized that they would actually be forced to fight—and fight they did. They pitched no battles, although there were a few clashes with the police, but they insisted on making themselves heard—until they succeeded.

"The leaders of groups upon whom the egregious epithet 'minority' has come to be visited would do well to take a leaf out of the suffragettes' book. In the year 1963 they [Negroes] finally did." (*op. cit.*, p. 184)

The implications of these findings, which are confirmed by my personal experiences and observations, are irresistible. In matters of discrimination, although it is true that manifestations of racial prejudice have often been more brutal than the subtler manifestations of sex bias—*e.g.* the use of ridicule of women as the psychic counterpart of violence against Negroes—it is also true that the rights of women and the rights of Negroes are only different phases of the fundamental and indivisible issue of human rights for all.

There are those who would have us believe that the struggle against racism is the Number 1 issue of human relations in the United States and must take priority over all other issues. I must respectfully dissent from this view. The struggle against sexism is equally urgent. More than half of all Negroes and other ethnic minorities are women. The costly lesson of our own history in the United States is that when the rights of one group are affirmed and those of another group are ignored, the consequences are tragic. Whenever political expediency has dictated that the recognition of basic human rights be postponed, the resulting dissension and conflict has been aggravated. This lesson has been driven home to us time after time—in the Civil War, the woman's suffrage movement, the violent upheavals of labor, and in the Negro Revolt of the 1960's.

The late Dr. Kyle Haselden, former editor of *The Christian Century*, once made the perceptive observation that we are all victims of the disease of prejudice. If it is true that, without exception, each of us carries the mote of prejudice in our eye, then it follows that prejudice manifested against one group through discriminatory action may well seek outlets against other groups when such action is prohibited. This theory is suggested in Dr. Montagu's sober comment on the racial crisis in 1964. He observed:

> It is a thought worth pondering whether there may not be some relation between the slackening of prejudice against women and the increase in the intensity of prejudices against ethnic and minority groups; that is, whether a certain amount of displaced aggression is not involved here. Man, it would seem, must have a scapegoat, and for his purposes any distinguishable group will do against which the exhibition of aggression or prejudice is socially sanctioned. It is a likely hypothesis that much of the deep-seated aggression which was at one time canalized in an antifeminist direction today serves to swell the tide of that which expresses itself in race prejudice. (*op. cit.*, p. 183)

The converse of this example is also worth pondering. It seems clear that we are witnessing a worldwide revolution in human rights in which traditionally excluded or alienated groups—blacks, women, youth, various ethnic minorities and social minorities, the handicapped, etc.—are all demanding the right to be accepted as *persons* and to share fully in making the decisions which shape their destinies. Negroes and women are the two largest groups of minority status in the United States. The racial problem has been more visible and periodically more acute because of the peculiar history of black slavery and racial caste which produced a Civil War and its bloody aftermath. The acuteness of racism has forced us to engage in national self-examination and the growing militancy of our black minority has compelled us as a nation to reverse our former racist policies, at least in a formal legal sense. In neglecting to appreciate fully the indivisibility of human rights, however, we have often reacted with the "squeaky-wheel-gets-the-grease" approach and not given sufficient attention to the legitimate claims of other disadvantaged groups—poor Whites, Women, American Indians, Americans of Puerto Rican, Mexican, and Oriental origin, and the like. In so doing, we have often set in motion conditions which have created a backlash and which, if developed to an intense degree, would threaten to destroy the gains which Negroes have made over the past few decades, meagre as these gains may have been for the masses of blacks.

The fact that women constitute more than 51% of the population, the very pervasiveness of sex discrimination which cuts across all racial, religious, ethnic, economic and social groups, and the fact that women have cause to believe they are not taken seriously—all these combine to make the revitalized movement for

Women's Liberation in the 1970's an instrument for potential widespread disruption if its legitimate claims are not honored. Given the tendency of privileged groups to retain their power and privilege and to play one disadvantaged group off against another, and given the accelerating militancy of Women's Liberation, there is a grave danger of a head-on collision of this movement with the movement for Black Liberation unless our decision-makers recognize and implement the rights of all. Dr. Ann Harris in her testimony before this Subcommittee has referred to attempts to satisfy the claims of black militants at the expense of women in institutions of higher learning. Her statement can be duplicated in incident after incident in government, private industry and in education.

The point I am trying to make here is that the United States cannot afford to repeat the costly errors of the nineteenth century in the shrunken world of twentieth century crises. One of these errors was the failure to grant universal suffrage at the end of the Civil War, a failure the political consequences of which are still being suffered today.

The enfranchisement of the Negro male while denying suffrage to all females—black and white—in 1870 delayed women's suffrage for a half century during which time Negro males were almost totally disfranchised in the South through legal and extra-legal measures—the "Grandfather clause," intimidation, terrorism and lynching. Viewing the aftermath of the Reconstruction in retrospect, one cannot help wondering if the history of that region might not have been vastly different if women had received the vote along with Negro males in 1870. The political emancipation of women in the South might well have eased the transition from a slave society to a society of free men and women. Political power in the hands of white women, in particular, could have reduced the fear of "Negro domination." Women, black and white, involving half of the population could have brought to bear their influence upon the difficult problems of reconstruction.

It is significant that, whatever other forces may have been at work in the South, a sharp drop in lynching followed the achievement of universal woman's suffrage in 1920 and the subsequent organization of white church women in the South against lynching. From 1919 to 1929, the number of recorded lynchings in which Negroes were victims dropped from 76 to 7, as the following table indicates:

| Year | Number of lynchings | | |
	White	Negro	Total
1919	7	76	83
1920	8	53	61
1921	5	59	64
1922	6	51	57
1923	4	29	33
1924	0	16	16
1925	0	17	17
1926	7	23	30
1927	0	16	16
1928	1	10	11
1929	3	7	10

Source: U.S. Commission on Civil Rights, Justice, 1961.

The humanizing effect of women's participation in the civil rights struggle in the South during the 1950's and 1960's has not been fully appreciated. Negro women led many of the most crucial demonstrations without loss of life and with superb discipline. I am thinking particularly of Mrs. Daisy Bates, the key adult figure and State Chairman of NAACP in the Little Rock crisis of 1957–1959, involving the integration of nine children in the Little Rock high school. White women took the initiation in organizing Save Our Schools campaigns when the local schools were closed in defiance of the Supreme Court mandate to desegregate Southern schools. When ACLU attorneys, including myself, were preparing the brief on behalf of the plaintiffs in *White* v. *Cook* (the landmark decision by a federal court that the Fourteenth Amendment prohibits sex discrimination as well as racial discrimination in jury service), we learned that the Department of Justice was persuaded to file an *amicus curiae* brief supporting our arguments because Mr. John Doar had discovered through his experience in the civil rights cases in the South that the Department was more likely to get a fair verdict when women were represented on Southern juries.

The emergent revitalized Women's Rights/Women's Liberation movement is no historical accident. It was born of the involvement of women in the civil rights movement of the 1940's, 1950's and 1960's. Because it affects a literal majority of the population it has a revolutionary potential even greater than the Black Revolt. It has the compelling force of an idea whose time has come, and neither ridicule nor verbal castigation can delay it. At present it has a controlled fury and a passion which is at times frightening when one realizes the depth of frustration from which it comes. I do not think the male members of this Subcommittee can fully appreciate the extent to which Women's Liberation has taken hold across the nation if you attempt to view it "objectively" merely through the facts and figures which have been presented here. Women are appealing, demanding, organizing for and determined to achieve acceptance as *persons*, as full and equal partners with men in every phase of our national life. They sense that we are in a deep national crisis of values, a crisis which makes us more vulnerable to internal disintegration than to destruction by external military attack. Transcending their cry for full equality is the apprehension that nothing less than our national survival is at stake, and they see this crisis in part as the result of our failure to utilize our human resources and release the creative energies which could bring about internal reconciliation and redeem our reputation as a genuine democracy in the eyes of the world.

We, as a nation, have lived through nearly three decades of racial turmoil which at times has approached civil war. I am convinced that one of the reasons we have not solved our racial problem is not so much that "all white people are racists" in the current rhetoric of black militancy, but rather, that we have not faced the more fundamental problem of the healthy relationship between the two sexes. Men have become enslaved by their dependency as well as their dominance. They pay a heavy price in shortened lives, military casualties, broken homes and the heartbreak of parents whose children are alienated from them. Many men find themselves unable to live up to the expectations of "masculinity" which men have defined for themselves, and many are now chagrinned to find that women are no longer willing to accept the role of "femininity" which men have defined for women.

Just as blacks have found it necessary to opt for self-definition, women are seeking their own image of themselves nurtured from within rather than imposed from without. I am led to the hypothesis that we will be unable to eradicate racism in the United States unless and until we simultaneously remove all sex barriers which inhibit the development of individual talents. I am further convinced that the price of our survival as a nation is the sharing of our power and wealth—or rather, the redistribution of this power and wealth—among black and white, rich and poor, men and women, old and young, red and brown and all the in-betweens.

This requires more than "objectivity." It demands a sensitivity, a recognition that individual human beings lie behind those depressing facts which have been assembled here. It demands that we women, who are the petitioners before Congress symbolized by this Subcommittee, keep before us the goal of liberating our own humanity and that of our male counterparts. It demands from those who hold formal power—predominantly white males—something closely akin to conversion, the imagination and vision to realize that an androgynous society is vastly superior to a patriarchal society—which we now are—and that the liberation of women through legislation, through a restructuring of our political and social institutions, and through a change of our cultural conditioning may well hold the key to many of the complex social issues for which we do not now have answers.

Discrimination against Negro/Black women

I earnestly hope that this Subcommittee will invite representative women from other minority groups and other economic and social sectors of American life to enrich this record with their views and social concerns. I listened to some of these women a few days ago at the Golden Jubilee Anniversary Conference of the Women's Bureau, U.S. Department of Labor and believe that they can provide the members of this Subcommittee with valuable insights with respect to the proposed legislation.

It is my special responsibility, however, to speak on behalf of Negro women who constitute about 93% of all nonwhite women, and I wish to call to your attention an article which appeared in the March 1970 *Crisis*, published by NAACP, "Job Discrimination and the Black Woman," by Miss Sonia Pressman, Senior Attorney in the Office of General Counsel of the Equal Employment Opportunity Commission and an expert in the law of race and sex discrimination. With your permission, Madam Chairman, I wish to submit a copy of this article for the record together with a "Fact Sheet on Nonwhite Women Workers," prepared by the Women's Bureau in October 1966. A more comprehensive document prepared by the Women's Bureau is the pamphlet *Negro Women in the Population and in the Labor Force,* issued December 1967.

These documents present the special problems of Negro/Black women because of their dual victimization by race and sex-based discrimination coupled with the disproportionate responsibilities they carry for the economc and social welfare of their families as compared with their white counterparts. All that has been reported here with respect to women generally applies with particular poignance to Negro women who, as Miss Pressman points out, are at the bottom of the economic totem pole. Consider the following latest figures from the U.S. Department of Labor:

April 1970

Number of women in work force (38.2 percent of total work force) __ 31, 293, 000
Median income full-time, year-round workers:

Men _____	$7, 664
Women _____	4, 457

Average income by race and sex:

White men_____	8, 014
Negro men (69.9 percent average earning for white men)_____	5, 603
White women (58.6 percent average earning for white men)____	4, 700
Negro women (45.9 percent average earning for white men)____	3, 677

In 1966 the median income of a nonwhite woman who had completed high school was less ($2,475) than that of a white man who had 8 years of education ($3,681) or that of a white man who had not completed the eighth grade ($2,945). (*1969 Handbook on Women Workers,* Women's Bureau Bulletin 294, p. 141)

Consider the fact that while women generally in the United States are the responsible heads of 11% (5.2 million) of all families, in March 1966, nonwhite women headed one-fourth of the 4.4 million nonwhite familes. Nearly 4 out of 10 or 1,871,000 nonwhite families were living in poverty in 1965. Of the 3,860,000 white families headed by a woman, 30 percent were poor. Of the 1,132,000 nonwhite families headed by a woman, 62 percent were poor. (*1969 Handbook on Women Workers,* pp. 130–131; *Negro Women,* p. 3)

Although on the average, Negro women have slightly more schooling than Negro men at the elementary and high school levels, their depressed wages stem from the fact they are concentrated in low-paying jobs as service workers and private household workers. Of the 2.9 million Negro women 18 years and over employed in March 1966, 58.5% held jobs as service workers including private household work. When the fact that the 1968 median wage of full-time year round household workers 14 years of age and older was only $1,523 is taken into account (See Labor D.C. (WB 70–193), p. 1) we can understand more clearly why protection against both race and sex discrimnation is crucial not merely for the Negro woman as an individual but also for millions of black youth in families headed by black women.

The Negro woman has a higher rate of unemployment, a higher incidence of poverty, a proportionately greater economic responsibility and less overall opportunity than white women or black or white men. If we are genuinely concerned about removing the causes of racial conflict, we must relate the statistics I have just described to the deep anger of black teenage girls and black women. The comparative unemployment rates by sex, color, and age, 1954–66 are depicted in Chart D. *Negro Women,* p. 10, which has been introduced as an exhibit. You will note the sharp rise in the unemployment rate of nonwhite teenage girls (14 to 19 years of age) coupled with a sharp drop in the unemployment rate for nonwhite teenage boys and a gradual sloping for white male and female teenagers. The rates of unemployment in 1966 are as follows: *Percent*

White males _____	2. 9
White females _____	4. 3
Nonwhite males _____	6. 6
Nonwhite females _____	8.8

The rate of unemployment among nonwhite female teenagers was highest of all:

14 to 19 Years of Age

Percent

White males _____	9. 9
White females _____	11. 0
Nonwhite males _____	21 .2
Nonwhite females _____	31. 1

In the face of these figures, is it any wonder that a black women college student at Brandeis University shortly before the Ford Hall crisis in January 1969 was overheard to say, "Black men get your guns!" I am also reminded of my beloved Grandmother's constant warning, "Idleness [i.e. unemployment] is the devil's workshop!"

It is important to recognize that while the appallingly low economic status of Negro women is related to lack of educational opportunity, it is integrally related to dual discrimination. A week ago, June 12, I listened to the Hon. Arthur A. Fletcher, Assistant Secretary of Labor, addressing the 50th Anniversary Conference of the Women's Bureau and telling the 1,000 women assembled there from every geographical and social sector of the nation the moving story of how his own mother carried the heavier economic load in rearing her children although her father worked hard to do his share. Mr. Fletcher explained that his mother held two college degrees but was forced to support her family by employment as a domestic worker. My own struggle for higher education through college and law school apart from scholarships for tuition was financed by working as a waitress, dishwasher, elevator operator, night switchboard clerk, and bus girl in a large hotel in Washington, D.C. during World War II. In this last job, the waiters whom we bus girls served were all Negro males, but they tipped us only 25¢ per night. Our salary of $1.50 per night plus a second-class meal supplemented by what we could steal from the kitchen constituted our weekly wage. If anyone should ask a Negro woman what is her greatest achievement, her honest answer would be: "I survived!"

Despite these depressing facts, there is a strong tendency throughout government and private industry to emphasize the "underemployment" of the Negro male in relation to the Negro female and to perpetuate the myth of the "matriarchal" Negro family. (See, e.g. the government report attributed to Daniel P. Moynihan, *The Negro Family*, 1965.) It is an open scandal that civil rights groups dominated by Negro male leaders have been instrumental in utilizing manpower programs and other programs of federal assistance to raise the status of Negro male youth while all but ignoring Negro female youth. I hope that this Subcommittee will inquire into the various programs financed by the Office of Economic Opportunity for a breakdown by race and sex. The results might be enlightening.

Let me offer an example of how this type of thinking has affected educational programs for the disadvantaged which are financed in whole or in part by Federal funds. Brandeis University is a coeducational private institution. During the decade 1961-70, it conferred degrees from its College of Arts and Sciences upon 3,583 candidates; of these 1,824 were men and 1,759 were women. These figures would suggest that Brandeis has a liberal admissions policy with respect to women, although there have been reports that women candidates for admission so far outclass male applicants in scholarship that higher standards for admission are required of women in order to keep a parity in numbers between the sexes. (This is not necessarily a reflection upon male applicants to Brandeis. It may well be that superior male students have options to attend such prestige schools as Harvard, Yale or Columbia which, traditionally, have been closed to female students.) The point being made here is that there is no patent evidence of blatant discrimination against women in Brandeis' admissions policies of regular undergraduates, if we look no further than the number of graduates it produces.

In 1968, however, Brandeis University instituted a program of compensatory education known as the Transitional Year Program (TYP), the purpose of which was to prepare disadvantaged students for the regular course of undergraduate study at Brandeis. Of the twenty-six students accepted for the school year 1968-1969, twenty-three were black and *all were male.* I do not know whether any women were recruited or applied. I do know that the report of a faculty committee evaluating the program [Brandeis Transitional Year Program, An Evaluation, May 15, 1969, p. 3] stated: *"Although the TYP was originally intended for a predominantly male and largely black group, the present proportions were not entirely the result of conscious effort. The complete absence of women in this year's program was dictated by the lack of women's dormitory space on campus.* (emphasis supplied).

It should be pointed out here that $40,000 of the $90,000 used to finance the TYP program for that school year came from Federal anti-poverty funds. Pressures primarily from women faculty members brought about some improvement in the TYP program of 1969–1970. Of the twenty-six students admitted to the program during the past year, 21 were men and 5 were women. (The ethnic division was: 5 White; 20 Black; 1 Spanish-surnamed.) Compare these rates of admission, however, with the Unemployment Rates, by Sex and Age, 1968 and 1969.

Age	1969	1968
Women:		
16 to 19 years	13.3	14.0
20 years and over	3.7	3.8
Total	4.7	4.8
Men:		
16 to 19 years	11.4	11.6
20 years and over	2.1	2.2
Total	2.8	2.9

Source: U.S. Department of Labor, Bureau of Labor Statistics: Employment and Earnings, January 1970, reported in "Background Facts on Women Workers in the United States," Women's Bureau, 1970, table 14.

Earlier, it was shown that the rate of unemployment among nonwhite male teenagers in 1966 was 21.2% as compared to 31.1% for nonwhite female teenagers. Thus, if Brandeis University or any other institution were addressing itself realistically to the need for compensatory education in order to make equal employment opportunity a reality, it would seem that the ratio of Black and White females admitted to the TYP program would be at least equivalent to if not greater than that of males. I do not believe that this "discrimination by oversight" or "discrimination by design" is peculiar to Brandeis University or that it is rooted in malice. I think it bears out my assertion that the continued emphasis upon the "underemployed Negro male" and upon the myth of the "matriarchal Negro family" has been a prime factor in the perpetuation of exclusion of disadvantaged Negro females from federally funded programs. Clearly, this situation can be remedied through the proposed amendment to Title VI of the Civil Rights Act of 1964, § 601 by adding "sex" as one of the prohibited grounds for discrimination, as HR 16098, Section 805(a) provides.

Prima facie evidence of discrimination against women on college faculties

At the hearing on Wednesday, June 17, Madam Chairman, you expressed the view that in cases of racial discrimination the legal principle has been developed that the absence of a particular racial or ethnic minority on juries or in employment is *prima facie* evidence of discrimination (in instances where the group in question is present in substantial numbers in the local population). You declared that the same principle should apply to sex discrimination and that the application of such principle would place the burden of overcoming the presumption of discrimination upon the employer institution. You also requested two types of documentation: (1) a comparative study of male and female honor graduates of a particular college or university over a period of years; and (2) a comparative study of male and female faculty members by rank of the same university. I assume that such data would reveal the potential academic resources compared by sex and the degree to which this potential is fulfilled at the faculty level.

I have obtained such information from my own institution, Brandeis University, and wish to introduce into the record three tables as follows:

TABLE 1.—BRANDEIS UNIVERSITY, COLLEGE OF ARTS AND SCIENCES—NUMBER OF MEN AND WOMEN GRADUATING WITH HONORS 1961-70

	Men	Women	Total
Number of degrees conferred	1,824	1,759	3,583
Cum laude without departmental honors	193	262	455
Magna cum laude without departmental honors	57	91	148
Departmental honors	76	54	130
Cum laude with departmental honors	185	152	337
Magna cum laude with departmental honors	119	131	250
Summa cum laude with departmental honors	43	29	72
Total	673	719	1,392

Note: Women represent: 49.1 percent of all degrees conferred (arts and sciences); 51.7 percent of all honors; 40.2 percent of highest honors; 11 percent of arts and sciences faculty (table 3); 6 percent of all full professors (table 3).

TABLE 2.—NUMBER OF WOMEN AND MEN GRADUATING WITH HONORS, 1961–70, BRANDEIS UNIVERSITY

Year	(1) Number of degrees conferred			(2) Cum laude with no departmental honors			(3) Magna cum laude with no departmental honors			(4) Departmental honors			(5) Cum laude, departmental honors			(6) Magna cum laude with departmental honors			(7) Summa cum laude with departmental honors		
	Male	Female	Total	Male	Female	Total	Male	Female	Total	Male	Female	Total	Male	Female	Total	Male	Female	Total	Male	Female	Total
1961	120	131	251	5	13	18	2	4	6	5	3	8	15	11	26	3	7	10	4	1	5
1962	126	143	269	7	22	29	2	2	4	4	2	6	9	12	21	12	9	21	2	1	3
1963	157	163	320	6	13	19	0	3	3	14	3	17	13	17	30	5	12	17	1	2	3
1964	156	154	310	14	24	38	1	6	7	7	5	12	21	10	31	12	12	24	3	2	5
1965	148	159	307	9	27	36	3	12	15	10	7	17	12	14	26	5	4	9	1	1	2
1966	173	155	328	13	20	33	3	5	8	11	8	19	21	17	38	10	6	16	1	3	4
1967	191	165	356	20	33	53	7	7	14	5	7	12	26	14	40	9	11	20	7	4	10
1968	219	201	420	17	28	45	7	14	21	8	7	15	15	19	34	14	16	30	8	6	12
1969	289	244	533	58	37	95	15	12	27	7	8	15	29	17	46	24	27	51	11	1	12
1970	245	244	489	44	45	89	17	26	43	5	4	9	24	21	45	25	27	52	8	8	16
Total	1,824	1,754	3,583	193	262	455	57	91	148	76	54	130	185	152	337	119	137	250	43	29	72

Source: This table was developed from the official Brandeis University Commencement Programs, 1961–70.

Note: Total graduating with honors, 1961–70: Males, 673; females, 719; total, 1,392.

Table 3.—BRANDEIS UNIVERSITY—MEN AND WOMEN FACULTY OF ARTS AND SCIENCES, 1969-70

Rank without regard to tenure	Total	Male	Female
Lecturer	36	26	10
Instructor	14	11	3
Assistant professor	98	85	13
Associate professor	66	62	4
Professor	122	114	8
Total, full-time faculty	336	298	38
Adjunct lecturer	1	1	0
Adjunct assistant professor	5	5	0
Adjunct associate professor	2	2	0
Adjunct professor	2	2	0
Consultant in music	3	3	0
Research assistant professor	1	0	1
Director of education prog	1	1	0
Total	15	14	1
Grand total	351	312	39

Proportion of faculty positions held by women:	Percent
Total	11. 0
Lecturer	27. 7
Instructor	21. 6
Assistant professor	13. 2
Associate professor	6. 0
Professor	6. 0

Source: Master catalog, Brandeis University, 1962–70.

These tables show that while women represent 49.1% of all degrees conferred by the College of Arts and Sciences during the ten year period 1961–1970, they took 51.7% of all honors and 40.2% of the highest honors. Yet they constitute only 11% of the Arts and Sciences faculty and only 6% of all full professors. Women obviously constitute a vast potential source of superior scholarship as well as models for oncoming women students to excel in the fields of their interest.

These figures, however, show that this potential is not being utilized at the faculty level and pose certain questions which apply not merely to Brandeis University but to all of the major institutions of higher learning in the United States. To what degree are promising women students encouraged to go on in graduate work? What percentage of them are offered scholarships and teaching fellowships in order to facilitate their graduate study? To what degree does a university like Brandeis, for example, try to place its women Ph. D's in other university settings if it wishes to avoid "in-breeding," and with what success? How many of its women graduates have won Alumni Awards? How many deans and other top-level administrators with special knowledge and insights into the problems of women students have been appointed? How aware are faculties and administrators of affirmative action programs which would accelerate policies of increased employment opportunities for women at all levels at the institution? These questions have a special relevance to an institution whose graduates are fairly evenly divided between the sexes and which depends heavily upon women supporters for fund-raising activities and potential financial support.

I have no figures for the number or percentage of women who hold tenured faculty positions at Brandeis, but would hazard a guess that it is lower than their ratio of full professors. Nor do I have any figures on the percentage and rank of women faculty members over a period of years, but it is my impression that Brandeis has increased the number of women on its faculty during the past two years.

In evaluating the data presented in Tables 1–3 above, we should bear in mind that Brandeis University is a comparatively young institution—barely 22 years old—compared to the more tradition-bound, male-oriented institutions such as Havard, Yale or Columbia. A co-educational, non-sectarian institution from its inception, Brandeis University was born in an international climate of opinion which produced the United Nations Universal Declaration of Human Rights, and indeed, the late Eleanor Roosevelt was on the Brandeis faculty for several years. It has been a pioneer in innovative programs, particularly with respect to foreign students and disadvantaged students. It has a capacity for flexibility and innovation not normally associated with larger, more moribund institutions, and therefore can be expected to institute a self-corrective process to overcome its underutilization of women as it has done in the case of Negro/ Black students and faculty.

Having said this, however, one must add that it is precisely because of Brandeis' outstanding reputation for excellence in scholarship and for liberal innovations that the Tables presented above underscore how pervasive is the face of male domination of institutions of higher education in the United States. For at Brandeis, women students have demonstrated unquestionably their ability on par with men. The wide gap between their performance and their employment opportunities is an indictment of a society which tolerates unjustifiable inequalities based upon sex.

A theory of educational and employment opportunity

In seeking to assert their rights to equal opportunities for education and employment, women have often been frustrated by narrow interpretations of federal policies which distinguish between educational opportunity and employment opportunity. I offer the theory that in the academic process, the opportunity for education, particularly at the graduate level, *may be considered as an integral part of the employment process*, since it represents *access* to academic employment in the universities. A graduate degree is in most instances an indispensable qualification for appointment to a university faculty. Protection against discrimination at the appointment level is meaningless unless such protection extends to every avenue of access to such appointment.

This principle has been applied in analogous situations. For example, the Supreme Court has held that the Constitution forbids racial discrimination in voting in primaries of political parties where the primary is an integral part of the electoral process. Similarly, the graduate program of a university which seeks to prepare scholars for academic employment is analogous to an apprenticeship training program in industrial crafts, and should be so interpreted. Further evidence of the recognition of need for protection of the right of *access* to employment opportunity is provided by legislation which extends the law of equal employment opportunity not merely to *employers* but also to labor unions and employment agencies, which are agents of *access* to employment opportunities. I respectfully urge this Subcommittee to consider this theory in developing the legislative history of proposed legislation in this area.

Inclusion of "sex" in all anti-discrimination legislation

In light of the overwhelming evidence of discrimination against women in many areas—housing, public accommodations, criminal law, education, employment, marital status, etc.—developed by the testimony in this hearing or by references to studies (see *e.g.* Kanowitz, *Women and the Law;* University of New Mexico Press, 1969), and in light of the need to protect all groups of minority status from actual or potential discrimination, as a rule of thumb all anti-discrimination laws and policies should automatically include "sex" as a prohibited ground of discrimination. The fact that in certain areas sex-based discrimination may not be widespread or may affect relatively few women is not a sufficient objection to this recommendation. The Constitution of the United States by its terms protects *individuals* in their civil rights and civil liberties. The Due Process Clause and Equal Protection Clause of the Fourteenth Amendment apply specifically to "any person." Similarly, the Fifth Amendment declares that "No *person* shall . . . be deprived of life, liberty, or property, without due process of law." Thus, *one* act of discrimination against *one* person because of his/her sex should be sufficient to invoke legislative protection.

I would therefore urge that this Subcommittee or an appropriate Committee of the House consider legislation to amend not only Title VI but also Titles II and IV of the Civil Rights Act of 1964 to include "sex" in every provision which now contains the words "race, color, religion and national origin." I would also urge that all housing anti-discrimination legislation be similarly amended as well as all legislation prohibiting discrimination in jury service.

Sec. 805(a).—Section 805(a) of H.R. 16098 (which proposes to amend Title VI, Sec. 601 of the Civil Rights Act of 1964 to include "sex" in prohibiting discrimination in federally assisted programs) would close a significant gap in the fair administration of these programs. The massiveness of federal financial aid and the variety of activities which receive federal assistance will perpetuate discrimination against women in a wide area of services and facilities unless sex discrimination is outlawed.

Moreover, the inclusion of "sex" in the provisions of Title VI would discourage the backward trend which is beginning to emerge in some areas of the South, as local school authorities develop plans for racial desegregation of public schools through the device of segregating schools on the basis of sex. Federal courts in Louisiana, Mississippi and Virginia have approved such plans despite the opposition of many of the boys and girls affected, and reportedly the Department of Justice has acquiesced. I submit that a public school segregated on the basis of sex in a male-dominated society contains seeds of psychological damage to the self-image of girls not unlike that condemned by the Supreme Court in *Brown* v. *Board of Education.* It would seem that segregation of the sexes when they are young ill prepares them for the close interaction they will experience in their adult relations and, indeed, may aggravate the tensions between the sexes in later life.

As presently written, Title VI excludes from coverage "any employment practice of any employer . . . except where a primary objective of the Federal financial assistance is to provide employment." The inclusion of "sex" in that title would not remedy discrimination against women seeking academic employment unless, as I have already suggested, the right to equal opportunity in employment can be interpreted to include the *right of access* to such employment. In other words, the qualification contained in Section 604 of Title VI should be held not to apply to those federal funds which provide for graduate scholarships and fellowships, particularly teaching fellowships or training programs, and which lead to degrees which are an indispensable qualification for academic employment.

Sec. 805(b): Amendment of Title VII to remove exemption of educational institutions.—Section 702, Title VII, of the Civil Rights Act of 1964, declares that Title VII shall not apply "to an educational institution with respect to the employment of individuals to perform work connected with the educational activities of such institution." The legislative history of Title VII indicates that this exemption was not in the bill as originally passed by the House but was inserted as part of the Dirksen compromise bill which was finally passed by the Senate and ultimately became law. A memorandum prepared by Kathryn G. Heath describing the legislative history of Section 702 which is appended to Dr. Bernice Sandler's testimony) indicates that there is no Congressional statement which seeks to justify the inclusion of this exemption. One can assume that it was inserted as a result of political pressures. Male members of the academic community do not differ essentially from industrial craftsmen who resist governmental interference with their seniority systems even though such systems have a built-in exclusion of disadvantaged groups suffering from past discrimination. The testimony adduced before this Subcommittee amply demonstrates that this exemption is an effective barrier to equal employment opportunity for women seeking professional or academic positions in educational institutions and therefore should be eliminated.

However, Section 805(b), standing alone would apply only to private educational institutions, since Section 701(b) of Title VII which defines the term "employer" expressly excludes from coverage "an agency of the United States, or an agency of a State or political subdivision of a State." In other words, publicly-supported institutions of learning, whether public schools or state colleges, would not be affected by the enactment of Sec. 805(b) and therefore the remedy for conditions at a state university which Dr. Ann Scott described on June 17 would not be effected as Sec. 805(a) now stands. An amendment is needed which will remove both public and private educational institutions of learning from exemptions, by providing an exception to Sec. 701(b) of Title VII in the case of educational institutions.

However, in view of the reports of the United States Civil Service Commission which indicate that in spite of an eight-year-old federal policy of equal employment opportunity without regard to sex, women have made few gains in the higher-paying grades, I would urge this Subcommittee to consider legislation which specifically forbids the United States or any agency thereof, or any State, State agency, or political subdivision thereof to discriminate in employment on grounds of race, color, sex, religion, national origin, age or any other non-merit factor.

Sec. 805(d): Removal of exemption of executive, administrative, professional, academic or administrative personnel or teachers in elementary or secondary schools from equal pay provisions of Fair Labor Standards Act.— The Equal Pay Act of 1963, as you know Madam Chairman, was adopted as an amendment to the Fair Labor Standards Act and consequently inherited the limitations and exemptions which were provided in that Act. One of these limitations was Sec. 13(a)(1) which declared that the Fair Labor Standards

Act should not apply to "(1) any employee employed in a bona fide executive, administrative, or professional capacity, including any employee employed in the capacity of academic administrative personnel or teacher in elementary or secondary schools." Whatever conditions justified this exemption with respect to wage and hours standards, if indeed it can be justified at all, these conditions have no reasonable relation to equal pay for equal work. Moreover, it is precisely in the areas included in this exemption that women suffer the most acute discrimination. The concentration of women in lower-paying jobs in industry, for example, offers no threat to male employees who hold professional and highly technical positions. Furthermore, professional workers on a salaried basis per annum do not customarily think of their earnings per hour or develop expectations of overtime compensation (perhaps they should). Equal pay for equal work, however, is a different story. It is in the professional fields and managerial occupations that women equally qualified by training and ability with men are paid less for jobs requiring substantially the same skills but which are often given different labels or downgraded by various subterfuges. The administration of the equal pay amendments to FLSA since 1963 provides numerous illustrations of inequalities in pay based upon sex and in which an employer attempts to justify such inequities by bringing himself within one of the exemptions of the Act. Sec. 805(d) would extend protection of women against sex bias to significant areas not presently covered by law.

Sec. 805(c): Addition of "sex" to jurisdiction of U.S. Commission on Civil Rights.—Although it it clearly indicated by previous testimony that there is an urgent need for studies and reports in the area of sex-based discrimination to be carried on by a continuing federal agency such as the United States Commission on Civil Rights (USCCR), I am not sure whether the addition of "sex" to the jurisdiction of the USCCR as provided by Sec. 805(c), as a practical matter, is the best answer to this need. Women constitute more than half of the total adult population, a group larger than the combined totals of all groups which conceivably might be covered by the Civil Rights Act of 1957(42 U.S.C.) which established the US Commission on Civil Rights and specified the jurisdiction of that agency with respect to denials of protection against discrimination because of race, color, religion or national origin. The functions of the Commission are investigative, information-gathering, appraisal of laws and policies, and acting as a national clearing house for information in the area of its competence. It well may be that institutional as well as individual discrimination against women is so pervasive and affects such a massive proportion of the total population that these functions could best be performed by a single agency equipped with the powers of the US Commisison on Civil Rights. Such an agency might have the independent status of a fact-finding, investigative or regulatory agency.

The one agency in the Federal Government which has traditionally had the responsibility for improvement of the status of women is the Women's Bureau now lodged in the Wage and Labor Standards Administration of the U.S. Department of Labor. I would strongly urge that an appropriate Committee of the House seriously consider whether the Women's Bureau might be the best qualified agency by tradition, experience, expertise and performance to undertake in the field of sex-based discrimination functions parallel to those of the U.S. Commission on Civil Rights. Obviously, to perform these functions adequately would require an enlargement of the powers of the Women's Bureau and vastly increased funding of its operations.

In closing, I wish to express my gratitude to you, Madam Chairman, and to the other members of the Subcommittee for inviting me to appear. I hope the views expressed will be helpful to your body in its further deliberations upon proposed legislation to eliminate discriminatory practices based upon sex. Thank you.

[Keynote speech, Barnard College Conference on Women, Apr. 17, 1970]

WOMEN IN THE SEVENTIES: PROBLEMS AND POSSIBILITIES

(By Alice S. Rossi)

For a sociologist to discuss the topic of *Women in the Seventies* is both a risky and presumptuous venture. It assumes an ability on the part of sociology to either predict the future course of events or to chart a desirable direction to take in the coming decade. Yet there is little precedence on which to build a case that sociology is particularly qualified or successful in predicting social change. Sociology predicted neither the sharp rise nor the fall of fertility rates in the past twenty-five years in the United States. It predicted neither the emergence nor the critical turning points in the civil rights movement during the 1960's. No urban sociologists warned us in the 1940's and 1950's of the consequences for our cities of heavy in-migration of poor southern blacks coupled with heavy out-migration of middle class whites to suburbia. We decried the political apathy of students in the 1950's and wrote of the "end of ideology" only to find our campuses alive with highly politicized students in the 1960's. In much the same way, the profession was taken by surprise last fall by the scope, persistence and political sting of the analysis and demands of the women's caucus I led at the annual sociology meetings, as I am sure other fields were by equally vigorous actions by women at their professional meetings in the course of the current academic year. I am also quite sure that at the moment, many of my male sociology colleagues are convinced that by merely waiting out the storm, the current upsurge of activism among professional women will die down and they can continue to operate departments, research institutes and the universities on a "business as usual" male basis.

I think they are profoundly mistaken in this expectation, at the same time I am deeply concerned by what I believe are difficult times ahead for the current women's rights movement. To say this is to admit that despite the poor record of my profession as predictors of future social and political events, I have entered the fray and shall discuss what I think the problems and possibilities are for significant change in the status of women during the 1970's. It should be clear from the outset, however, that I shall be speaking in more than my capacity as a sociologist. I shall draw on my own personal experiences as a woman in academia and private life, upon active participation in several reform movements in recent years, and upon a political commitment to fundamental change in American society.

To view personal experience, passion and politics as relevant ingredients to a sociological analysis is to take a radical departure from the scientific credo on which most sociologists of my generation have been reared. Since this is quite important to an assessment of what I have to say, let me expand on this point. To read contemporary sociological journals is to acquire a view of the field that is consistent with the value free scientific neutrality our textbooks urge upon young sociologists. I would submit, however, that a detached scientific neutrality is actually the exception rather than the rule in sociology, however much the passion and the politics are written out when sociologists commit themselves to paper and crowd our periodicals and bookshelves with their ounces of "truth." Politics is where research begins; it helps to select and define the problem to be studied; it is involved in procuring funds to support research; it is very much present in the way a sociologist sets up a study design and again when he or she attempts to get the results published. One of the glaring omissions in the graduate education of sociologists is a frank and open analysis of the political process within which research is conducted.

Passion is a second typically neglected component in sociology. To read the works of most sociologists of any generation, with such notable exceptions as C. Wright Mills, Lee Rainwater, Irving Horowitz or Lewis Coser, is to gain an image of bloodless insensates looking down at human behavior from some cognitive height of detachment. I am not sure in my own mind whether this is achieved by a purposeful suppression of a passionate component, or whether it derives from an absence of such passion in sociologists as an occupational specialty. Certainly our models of sociological excellence have prescribed the exclusion of passion and politics, but whether this operates as a self-selecting device in recruitment to the field, or as a consequence of rigorous socialization in graduate programs, is an unsettled question.

I have a theory about the direction sociology has taken in recent decades that is not unique to sociology, but characteristic of the work of the whole generation of men who are currently at the prestige pinnacles of our colleges and universities. I believe, too, that this thesis illuminates the basic generational confrontation taking place between faculty and students in higher education. Since it is relevant to any prediction of what lies ahead for women in academia, and I dare say in all large scale organizations today, it is perhaps legitimate to develop it briefly here. Power and prestige in academia are now in the hands of men in their 40's and 50's, a generation whose childhood and adolescence took place from the late 1920's through the early 1940's, years of depression and of war. Their careers were established during the post-war period of vast expansion in higher education, when there was room to spare for the sharp, ambitious and energetic survivalists of this generation. In any period in which professional, managerial and technical occupations undergo a vast expansion, the fields will attract a large proportion of socially mobile, self-made men. The GI Bill gave a boost to the upward mobility of the current generation of academic leaders, particularly in those fields which underwent the largest expansion in higher education: the natural and social sciences and engineering.

The men at the top of the prestige ladder in such fields in 1970 are the new intellectual elite in American society, the men whose ideas have given the major boost toward the technological transformation of our economy, contributed to the social and economic policies of the federal government, and to the growing dependence of academia on government and private industry. In my judgment, they are intellectual robber barons who dominate contemporary society in much the way the lumber, oil and land barons dominated the 19th century industrial expansion following the Civil War. They represent a highly competitive, ambitious generation of self-made men.

Most importantly, their theories of society and of human motivation mirror their own personalities and life experiences. An analogy can be drawn to the early 19th century spokesman of laissez faire economics, the utilitarian James Mill. He too was a self-made man, up from humble origins in Scotland, who cut his ethnic and religious ties in moving to London, and who forged a place for himself in English intellectual and political life as the spokesman for the new mercantile class pressing against the power and status of the English aristocracy. Bruce Mazlish[1] has given us a brilliant analysis of the congeniality of Mill's intellectual ideas to his own social mobility: the belief that one's past is irrelevant, that education can produce far better trained and knowledgeable men than a hereditary aristocracy ever can, that man is a rational being motivated by self-interest and that society can be organized to maximize that primarily rational motivation. If we examine contemporary social theories, I think we can detect echoes of this emphasis on rationality, from the conservative acceptance of the status quo in functionalist theory, to the shift to neo-classical economic theory in the work of such men as George Homans and Peter Blau, to the current fashionable emphasis on systems analysis and game theory of James Coleman. In psychology, I suspect there have been three dozen studies of achievement motivation to every one study on affiliation need. At first sight, game theory looks very new indeed, but a closer inspection suggests it is rooted in the same laissez-faire utilitarian economic model all over again: the postulate that an individual or a group is essentially and irrevocably motivated by the desire to maximize their own selfish interest, to take action based on rational assessment of what rewards will accrue to them.[2] I think it is the pervasive acceptance of this rational model that lies behind the inability of sociologists to predict many of the social and political events of the past twenty years. Self-gain goes no distance at all in explaining current middle class political protest among the young, or commitment to the expansion of human rights for groups other than one's own.

Furthermore, if we can not assume that human beings are motivated by more humane values and inner promptings than the narrow utilitarian base of self-interest, we are headed for enormous difficulty, if not outright failure, in many social and political struggles in the coming decade, whether the expansion of the rights of blacks and of women, or coping with the crises of population, environmental pollution, or international hostility. When young people decry the irrelevance and impersonality of their colleges and universities, they are attacking not only the complex bureaucratic structure of the modern university but the values of the men on faculties and in administrations who run these institutions. This is an extremely important point, for on it hinges whether change should be focused on a reformation of the organizational structure of higher education, or the personnel policies which determines the individuals who occupy the slots in that organizational structure. In other words, is it the organization or the men who run it that call for change?

What is the relevance of this analysis to the movement women have been forming in recent years? There are several points of importance: if you are a disadvantaged group, it is well to have a clear idea of the nature of your opposition as you engage in a political struggle to change an institution or to gain entry into it at significant levels. Secondly, women must be clear both individually and in terms of activist organizations, whether they want "in" on the value terms now current in government or corporations or universities, either because they

[1] Bruce Mazlish, "James Mill and the Utilitarians." *Daedalus*, Summer 1968, 1036–1061.
[2] I am indebted to Eugene Galanter, Professor of Psychology at Columbia University for this insight, at a recent (April 1970) conference on world crises at the American Academy of Arts and Sciences, Boston.

accept those terms or because they wish to work for change from within, and whether they should ally themselves with other groups which are pressing for changes in the structure of large scale organizations.

This analysis also serves as a warning concerning the women who have been able to find their way to significant status levels within organizations as they are presently structured. Unless and until the current women's movements are far stronger and more widely accepted as legitimate. I think a sizable propor- tion of women in high status positions will not be willing to join us, because they share the values of the high status men in their world. Thus, in organizing a program for the women's caucus in sociology, I had wanted to have a panel that included women from each phase of a sociological career line: I had no difficulty finding graduate student or young faculty women but not one of the five full professor women I approached would agree to join such a panel. Their reasons may interest you: one said women are looking for special privileges instead of working hard the way they did to reach the top; another admitted she simply didn't like working with women; another that we were either an ugly, or a frus- trated crowd that didn't know how or were not able to use our sex to get ahead in a man's world.

The question might well be raised of why and how it is that I am not in accord with my own generation of women in academia. I am, after all, a member of the generation that produced the intellectual robber barons that rule in academia today. I am not sure I can yet give a complete answer to that question, but in the belief that personal and intellectual biography may be of interest and is a legiti- mate component to a sociological analysis, let me override an impulse against such personal disclosure and describe at least those experiences which were in- fluential in my own life thus far. It may illustrate at least one attempt at blend- ing politics, passion and intellect that is closer to the life and work style of the emerging younger generation than it is to the predominant mode of members of my own generation. That done, you will perhaps have a better base from which to assess my predictions of what lies ahead for the women's movement during the 1970's.

PERSONAL-POLITICAL BACKGROUND

As an undergraduate and graduate student, I had no particular interest in the status of women, sex roles, or occupational choice. In fact, I entered college as an English major, pragmatism dictating an occupational choice of high school English teacher, but romanticism prompting an inner hope that I might become a famous writer. I was one of the tens of thousands of bright, eager New York students attending city colleges, in my case, Brooklyn College. As fate would have it, my first sociology instructor was Louis Schneider, and he began his introduction to sociology by reading a poem by Whitman and raising the ques- tion: who was this man? What does the poem tell about his time, his place on this globe? I found the sociological dimension of literature so fascinating, I fell in love with the field, and began a life long affair of the heart and mind that is second only to my own marriage and the three products of that marriage I am privileged to watch grow up. As a graduate student at Columbia, I was inter- ested in the microscopic analysis of social institutions; in family and kinship systems rather than the roles of women within family systems; in reference groups through work with Robert Merton; in studies of the professions. In fact, the occupational role I chose to study in Kingsley Davis' seminar was that of the politician. Not once during that seminar did I look into the sex-linked nature of occupational choice in American society. In the Columbia department, I was torn between attraction to the new research focus of the field symbolized by Paul Lazarsfeld, and the more familiar world of ideas and traditional scholarly investigation symbolized by Robert Merton. That the one was short on ideas and the other short on methods forced many of their students to forge their own competencies as sociologists, with varying styles in the balance between theory and research. My own bent, like that of Lipset, Blau and Coser, was toward Robert Merton, while others like my husband, Barton. Rosenberg and Coleman, were tipped toward Paul Lazarsfeld. Only a minority of the students in the department then were stimulated and drawn to the political and critical think- ing of C. Wright Mills and Robert Lynd. Even fewer of us, with very much a sense of being a traitor to the department, stole across campus to listen to Ruth Benedict in social anthropology or to Mirra Komarovsky in sociology.

But no woman in 1970, I hope, could be the total innocent I was in 1950 where the world of sex discrimination or sex inequality of rights and opportunities were concerned. I dreamed big dreams during those graduate student days of being one day the president of the American Sociological Society, and of writing a major opus that built on the twin strengths of my two theory and research mentors. I discounted as peevish envy, the claims of my male peers that I would not get a fellowship from the department "because I was a woman", and then when I was awarded one, the counter claim that "someone on the faculty must be trying to make you."

It would have been more congenial to my own intellectual bent to move from graduate training to a purely academic position as primarily a teacher, and secondarily a researcher. But this is a path difficult for a married woman in academia, particularly to one like myself, who is married to a sociologist. So I spent ten years as a research associate, following not the dictates of my own research interests so much as the availability of funds and research openings: intergroup relations in a Cornell research project; generational differences in the Soviet Union at the Russian Research Center at Harvard; ethnic and religious cleavage in community decision making in a project at the Harvard Graduate School of Education; kinship relations in the middle class in an anthropological project at the University of Chicago.

From these varied research undertakings, I developed an intellectual fascination with a problem that was seldom put in adequate terms within sociological theory itself: what are the connections, the strains, and accommodations between involvement in the institution of the family on the one hand, and the occupational system on the other. I was beginning to take a first step away from the confines of Parsonian claims that the family and occupational systems require "mechanisms of segregation" with only one member of a family participating significantly in the occupational system, a theory I now view as an intellectual put down providing a rationalized justification for men continuing to be the prime movers in work and politics.

The source of this growing interest was not only research and scholarship, however. It was also my own personal experience and observation as a faculty wife and mother of young children. As a faculty wife, I had ample opportunity to observe that some sociological theorists did a rather good job themselves of making sure that two members of a family did not hold significant jobs in the occupational system, by refusing to hire competent women whose husbands held appointments at the same universities. At Harvard and then again at Chicago, I saw numerous instances of women being dropped or kept off the male academic turf their husbands claimed as their own. I had offended one such theorist by negotiating an appointment at Harvard without first clearing such a horrendous step with him, as my husband's department chairman. The chairman happened to be Talcott Parsons. I watched women friends leave the university when they became pregnant and kept out when they tried to return after their children entered school. More importantly, I learned from personal experience of withdrawal during two years while I had my first two children, the truth of the existential thesis in psychology that "one becomes what one does," as I realized with horror that I was resenting my husband's freedom to continue his academic work despite the adventure of adding father to his roster of social roles, and even more that I was actually trying to prevent his playing an intimate and meaningful role in the care of the children, in order to have ascendancy in parenthood to complement his ascendancy in our shared profession.

But it took a return to academia, first by teaching undergraduate sociology at Chicago, and then in a research project on kinship, and a traumatic personal encounter with sex discrimination to jar me out of a romantic cocoon of political innocence, and to begin a long process of re-establishing connections back through my own life and to the Lynd-Mills exposure in graduate school, back through years in a variety of working class and white collar clerical jobs and to undergraduate radical politics, to begin to draw together and to focus the ideas, the personal experience, and the political commitment I now have. My own trial by fire involved a not untypical story of a bright woman Ph. D. accepting a research associateship to do a study the male principal investigator was not competent to do on his own, and had very little interest in. At least the interest was initially low, until the study was designed, by myself; fielded under my supervision, and partially analyzed by myself. At that point, he realized he had a good thing going, and simply announced, despite verbal agreements about coauthorship and professional autonomy, that my services were no longer needed. All this took place within a week of receiving assurance that the request for continuing funds from the National Science Foundation, based on a research proposal I drafted, would be forthcoming. I was a salaried Research Associate, he a full professor, and as the dean put it bluntly to me, "he is valuable university property; you, unfortunately, are expendable."

I date my own commitment—intellectually, personally, and politically—to concern for the status of women, the analysis of sex roles, the study of and active participation in such things as abortion law and divorce law reform, to the "slow burn" that began in that first major personal encounter with sex discrimination in academia. It was the immediate precipitant to the scholarship and writing that led me down the path of immodesty in writing the Daedalus essay on sex equality.

The response to that essay is an interesting illustration of the point I made in characterizing the current generation at the helm in academia. Several male colleagues accused me of breaking up their marriages. Young women wrote to say they decided to return to graduate school instead of having another baby. (By known count, the essay reduced the population by twelve 3rd or higher order births. I am sure Betty Friedan's book did even better in reducing the population. But this is a lesson our male experts on fertility have not yet learned: they think the population problem will be solved by technical gadgetry, when the real point is what women want and can do with their lives.) My husband received a sympathy bereavement card from a west coast sociologist as a condolence for having such an upstart wife that must surely embarrass him. A more recent example of this same sort, symptomatic of the current state of affairs in academia, was the reaction of male sociologists to the rather different roles my husband and I played at last fall's sociology convention. As secretary of the association, my husband was on the rostrum while I delivered a speech and submitted resolutions from the women's caucus. In the months since then, I have had offers for academic appointments on the west coast which are based on the premise that my husband and I are separated and about to be divorced. My husband has been asked how he felt when I delivered that speech, with his male colleagues not knowing how to take his response that he felt pride rather than embarrassment or anger as they expected. During earlier years, my colleagues at the University of Chicago criticized me for "not sticking to my last" as a research sociologist instead of writing analytic social criticism and ideology; others said it was inappropriate and would "ruin your career" to get involved in the "woman thing;" or to be publicly visible as an organizer for abortion law reform, or to write that "motherhood was not enough" in a woman's magazine. Writing outside the professional journals, I was told, should never be mentioned in a professional vita, and was something I could only do later in life should I become an elder statesmen in academia or need money to cover children's college education or save toward reduced income after retirement. Nowhere in that world did one hear anything about responsibility for writing out from academia to larger publics, nor any sense that there was a responsibility for a family sociologist to "do" something about fertility, contraception, abortion or women's rights, from the point of view of active attempts at social change to protect the health or defend the rights of women.

I was fortunate to have a supportive husband who possessed a delicious sense of humor and a social marginality to match my own. I purposely phrased that last sentence in a conventional way—how grateful, how lucky, to have a supportive husband! As you may know from reading Eli Ginsberg on life styles of educated women, that is an absolute rock bottom requirement for professional women—to have a supportive husband. Unfortunately, Mr. Ginsberg does not understand how a woman gets a supportive husband. It is not a "condition" she is fortunate to have as a base for being something more than homemaker, mother and husband-relaxer. It is something she looks for, and if she finds it, she marries him. I know what it is like to have an un-supportive husband, for I first married when I was politically and socially innocent. I divorced him. It didn't just happen, therefore, that my second husband was supportive. I chose him in part because he *was*.

Until this past fall, I had the unusual experience of being an independent academic person, under a five year research scientist award from the National Institute of Mental Health, which gave me an academic umbrella to legitimize my status within the university and provided the independence to work on whatever I wanted. The best education I ever had, I acquired on my own during the first year or so of that award: the luxury of getting lost in libraries again, to be free to re-acquire that delicious "itch to know", to tackle new fields, to turn down any lecture, paper, conference, that didn't interest me. With emotional roots secure in an exciting marriage and three young children, I carved out a professional life that centered on a major research undertaking on family and career roles of women college graduates, on the one hand, and growing absorption in active attempts at social, legal and political change that would benefit women. By last summer, it was clear to me that I felt increasingly out of rapport with my own generation and my graduate school colleagues, and shifted from research sociology at Hopkins to undergraduate teaching at Goucher. I wanted out from the research role and felt the need for a professional context closer to the younger generation, and one in which I could devote non-teaching time to writing. To sum up, a deviant from the "making it" generation has joined ranks with the "reforming generation" represented by my students and many in this audience.

WHERE WE ARE AT NOW

To attempt a preview of what lies ahead in the 1970s, a good starting place is an assessment of where we are at in the present. In some respects, the future is a continuation of trends rooted in the past and visible to us at the moment. One thing is clear: however significant we may consider the new emergence of the women's movement, its significance is not widely shared. The turn of a decade often triggers the publication of "looking ahead" books, but you will find no mention of protest and change in the status of women as a significant new note among those who participated in the crystal-gazing scholarship that produced *The Year 2000*, or even in the less ambitious new volume edited by Leonard Freedman, *Issues of the Seventies*. This latter volume divides neatly into two major sections, one on international issues, the other on national issues. Among the latter, are poverty, race, crime, distribution of power, alienation, and campus disorder in universities. Activist groups of women do not figure in any of the issues discussed where one might expect them in such a volume: women as poor, black, victims, disadvantaged, alienated, or protesters on campuses, do not appear. Not surprisingly, there is not a single woman author to any of the essays in the volume. Like the bulk of historical volumes, women are part of the climate and geography backdrop against which the human drama is acted out by men.

Most recent analyses that attempt to explain the renascence of the women's rights movement in the 1960's, after forty years of dormancy, have stressed the impact of participation in the civil rights movement upon younger women, who drew the same lessons their ancestors did from involvement in the abolitionist cause in the 19th century. Without detracting from the significance of this point at all, I would only point out that this holds for only one group within the younger generation of women now involved in women's liberation, and that the emergence of the liberation movement all told post-dates other significant signs of an awakening among American women much earlier in the decade. In fact, I would argue that it was the changed shape of the female labor force during the period beginning with 1940 that gradually provided the momentum that led to such events as the establishment of the Kennedy Commission on the Status of Women, and eventually to the formation of new women's rights organizations like the National Organization for Women. So long as women worked largely before marriage while they were single, or after marriage only until a first pregnancy, or lived within city limits where there was a diversity of activities to engage them, there were feeble grounds for any significant movement among women focussed on economic rights, since their motivation in employment was short-lived and their expectations were to withdraw when they became established in family roles. It was the gradual and dramatic change in the profile of the female labor force from unmarried young women to a majority of older married women that set in motion a vigorous women's rights movement. It is only among women who either expect or who find themselves relatively permanent members of the work force whose daily experience forced awareness of economic inequities on the grounds of their sex. This is changing now under the influence of women's liberation groups among the young, but this movement did not exist to trigger the larger movement early in the last decade. Knowledge and concern for this growing army of employed women facilitated the political recognition of problems concerning women's status by the formation of the Kennedy Commisison. It was these women, many in federal and state service, whose expectations were raised by involvement first with the national and then with the state commissions that were established during the Kennedy and Johnson administrations.

These were committed, knowledgeable, optimistic, and largely middle aged women who had high hopes as they filed their reports, that American society would finally put its own house in order where the status of women was concerned. The hopes of many of these women were dashed by the cold shoulder treatment they experienced at the spring 1966 conference of representatives from the state commissions brought together under Department of Labor sponsorship in Washington. From that frustrating and disappointing experience, when it seemed likely that their reports were to be politely filed in government drawers, a number of women concluded that little significant change could be expected until a strong political organization was built that had complete independence from the political establishment itself. This was the precipitant to the formation of the National Organization for Women in the fall of 1966. The scope of the areas of women's lives that NOW is concerned with has broadened greatly since its founding in 1966, but the core focus continues to be the expansion and firming up of the economic rights of women to equal treatment in hiring and promotion.

As an organization, NOW includes lively, dedicated women who are pressing hard and persistently against the barriers that restrict and confine women in American society. Except for its action in connection with the airline stewardess case, however, it has had relatively little public and media attention outside New York until this past year, when the extraordinary press coverage of the women's liberation groups set in. Why should this be the case? I would suggest that the answer lies in the social role arena that is the focus of discussion and action by these two streams within the women's movement. There are fundamental assumptions in our society as presently structured that men's primary social roles are in work and women's primary social roles are in the family. The conventional society assumes all men will want to work at a status level that challenges their abilities to the utmost; nothing is so threatening to conventional values as a man who does not want to work or to work at a challenging job, and most people are disturbed if a man in a presumably well-paying job indicates ambivalence or dislike toward it. The counterpart for women is any suggestion that they feel ambivalent toward maternity, marriage or homemaking, probably in that order. In more formal sociological terms, we might put this as follows: roles vary in the extent to which it is culturally permissible to express ambivalence or negative feelings toward them. Ambivalence can be admitted most readily toward those roles which are optional, least where they are considered to be primary. Thus men repress negative feelings toward work and more openly express negative feelings toward family and marriage responsibilities, while women are free to express negative feelings toward work, but tend to repress ambivalence or negative feelings toward family roles.

Applying these ideas to the issues that triggered public and media attention in the past decade helps to explain why reactions are more intense to women's liberation groups than to organizations like NOW. There was widespread concern in manpower, government and university circles during the past decade, when indications began to emerge that many middle class, bright young men were showing a departure from an unthinking acceptance of occupational aspirations similar to those of their fathers, either by showing a shift of occupational choice away from business, engineering and science toward teaching, social science and the humanities, or by indicating that their desire was for a life style that gave greater attention to the time spent away from the job. The movie *The Graduate* symbolized this generational contrast in its most dramatic form. Universities were concerned when men students, starting in Berkeley, expressed resentment to advanced training as a mouse race preparation for adult rat race lives. I doubt if anyone would have worried if it were women expressing such resentment. Incidentally, there are now beginning signs that young workers are showing much the same pattern as the university students earlier on. Older officials of the Steel Workers union in the auto industry report that young workers—40 per cent of 225,000 workers in the union are under 30 years of age—have different values than older workers; they take seriously the question of individual freedom, and consider compulsory overtime an infringement of this freedom. Douglas Frazer, a union director, suggests that in the big plants, efficiency has been "king" in the eyes of management and the older workers alike, but that in 1970, "we just have to tell these companies, in the spirit of our youth, that the king is dead and we are going to bury him in 1970." [3] As more wives work, and as the young move into the labor force, we can expect increasing numbers of workers to seek more from life than a pay-check and a high-pressure, exhausting work day.

The important point is that public airing of ambivalence or a shift of values toward the place of work in the lives of men, taps a vital nerve in American society. In light of the previous analysis of the generation currently in command, this is a violent rejection of all they have stood for and lived by. The counterpart for women is any airing of ambivalence or negative feelings toward what the culture has defined as their primary roles, in marriage and maternity. It is when even a minority of women begin to reject their role as sex object, postpone or reject marriage, stop smiling over a shiny waxed floor, or heaven forbid,

---

[3] New York Times, 10 March 1970.

question the desirability of having children or rearing them themselves as a full time job, that women tap the counterpart nerve in American society. So too, older suburban homemaker women may be expected to have extremely hostile responses to the challenge of the younger generation of women as the latter rejects the lives led by their mothers as shallow or parasitic.

Hence, it is when men question work, and women question family commitment, and both sexes question an uncritical commitment to nation-state, that we find responses among parents, teachers, employers and government officials ranging from a shiver of distaste to a convulsion of hate. The strange thing is that one hardly ever hears anyone point to precisely these emerging qualities among young people as healthy indicators that promise solutions to precisely the problems all would agree are reaching crisis proportions in the world at large : virulent nationalism and the consequence of international hostility will not be solved by upping nuclear deterrence but by the emergence of supra-national loyalties to the well being of all men and women on earth. The population explosion will not be solved unless more men and women remain unmarried, have fewer children, or none at all. Environmental pollution will not be solved unless we live simply and stop as a nation from rapaciously consuming more than half the world's raw materials. The technitronic future of increased leisure time will be meaningless unless men and women value that leisure time at least equally as much as their work time.

These are all examples of emerging values among the younger generation that are congenial and adaptive to the changed shape of society in the future. They also promise to be far better solutions than those currently recommended by the older generation : bigger sanitation systems to cope with the same level of waste of glass, metal and wood ; better contraceptive gadgetry ; more complex nuclear systems ; taller buildings and mass transit rather than out-migration from urban jungles, etc. More to the point of my present argument is the fact that it has been the implicit and explicit questioning of family roles among women's liberation groups that has triggered the current widespread public attention to the "woman issue." NOW's focus on employment issues, dealing as it does with what is culturally considered an optional role for women, can not compete with anti-marriage and anti-sexism compaigns and speeches from women's lib spokesmen.

EMPLOYMENT

What, now, are the problems and possibilities that lie ahead? Let me start with the bread and butter issue of women's employment. To gain a perspective on what lies ahead in the seventies in the employment area, requires that we step back a moment to examine what has been operating as a critical variable in the background of the changed profile of women's labor force participation. A lot of nonsense has been written in the past decade to account for the flow of older married women into the labor force. The emphasis has been on the impact of homemaking simplification via frozen foods and complex gadgetry on the one hand, and the search for self-fulfillment and a solution to the "problem without a name" on the other. This is to look for explanations on the supply side of the economic equation : what made women want to and able to move into the labor force.

In an economy as hard nosed as ours, however, such a stress is naive, for there must be powerful factors on the demand side of the equation that prompted employers to open their personnel doors and to hire older women. A significant factor underlying this willingness on the part of employers lies in the peculiarities of the demographic structure of the American population during the period 1940 to 1970. In an incisive demographic analysis, Valerie Oppenheimer [4] has shown that during the 1950's and early 1960's, several factors worked together to reduce the size of the traditional source of the female labor force, young unmarried women : young women were staying in school longer and marrying at an earlier age, thus shrinking the size of this traditional female labor pool. Even more important, the young women of the 1950's were born in the 1930's when the birth rate was very low, while at the same time there was a vast increase in the number of young children born during the baby boom of those post war years. As a result of the rippling effect of this low fertility cohort, the traditional pool of female labor shrunk during 1940 to 1960 from 6 million unmarried young

---

[4] Valerie Oppenheimer. *The Female Work Force in the United States: Factors Governing its Growth and Changing Composition,"* Unpublished Ph.D. dissertation, University of California (Berkeley), 1966.

women to only 3 million, while every other age cohort was increasing in size. Employers had to seek women workers from other sources than the young unmarried to fill their personnel ranks. Consequently the trigger was far more a matter of employer demand in the first place, than of assertive women pressing for entry into the labor force.

These were also years of vast expansion in precisely those segments of the occupational system that women have traditionally been prominent in: schools were flooded with the baby boom children come of school age, so college graduate women were assured a welcome despite age, marital and family status. Colleges and universities were expanding at a rapid rate and married women were taken on as part time instructors and full time research associates. Clerical, sales, and service occupations were expanding, and women with high school degrees were able to pick and choose among the available jobs.

This fortunate circumstance is now undergoing rapid change. There will be a reversal to this demographic pattern in the 1970's. The birth rate is now on the decline, the age at marriage is creeping upward. and the time interval between marriage and childbearing is widening. In the 1970's there will be more young unmarried women or childless married women seeking jobs, at the same time middle aged married women will be very numerous, for they will be the baby boom females grown to maturity. At the same time, as Allen Cartter [5] has shown, graduate schools will be producing large numbers of young people with advanced degrees, but these young people will face a very different job market than the doctorate-holding young people faced during the past twenty years. Up to 1970 the supply of Ph. D.s was far below the demand for them in institutions of higher education, but the reverse situation will hold from 1970 onward: the supply will exceed the demand in colleges and universities. This does not mean the society can not absorb or does not need highly trained people with advanced degrees. From one point of view, the excessive supply means an opportunity for reducing class size, providing students with more meaningful learning experiences, changing graduate curricula to prepare students for non-academic work, and for the non-academic institutions in business, government and welfare, to benefit from hiring highly trained young people. On the other hand, higher education is facing a financial crisis due to the cut-backs in government funding, corporations are pruning staffs of excessive frills, and government agencies are on an internal economy drive.

It is therefore of critical importance that women press hard during the next few years to secure equal protection of the law and to assure adequate representation of their sex in all segments of the economy. There is already a first sign of withdrawal of women from the labor force: in the last quarter of 1969, the Bureau of Labor Statistics showed a drop in the unemployment rate, but the drop was found to be due not to the happy event of people finding jobs, but because unemployed young people and women were withdrawing from actively seeking jobs, probably because they were not finding them.

What women must do in the next several years does not require new legislation, though most of us would agree that passage of an equal rights amendment to the constitution would cover a wide range of sex inequities in law and practice. Short of such passage, however, it is nonetheless the case that there has been a legal revolution during the 1960's where protection of women's economic rights are concerned.[6] Title VII of the Civil Rights Act of 1964 prohibits discrimination based on sex by all employers of 25 or more employees, employment agencies and unions with 25 or more members, with the exemption of educational institutions. The Equal Pay Act of 1963 requires equal wages and salaries for men and women doing equal work. Executive order 11246, as amended by 11375, prohibits discrimination based on sex by federal government contractors and subcontractors. The Age Discrimination In Employment Act of 1967 prohibits discrimination based on age between 40 and 65. While this act does not prohibit sex discrimination, it could play a significant role in enlarging employment opportunities for women over forty who wish to return to the labor market or change jobs. Municipal and state fair employment practice commissions and state agencies which administer state equal pay legislation also stand as available resources women can use to protect their employment rights. Women in colleges and universities are not covered by the Civil Rights Act, but women lawyers in activist

---

[5] Allan M. Cartter, "The Supply of and Demand for College Teachers." *Journal of Human Resources,* Summer 1966, 77–82.

[6] This brief summary relies heavily on Sonia Pressman's paper, "The Legal Revolution in Women's Employment Rights," (mi neo), a speech to a legal seminar presented by the Women's Equity Action League, Cleveland, Ohio, December 5, 1969.

groups are now working through the channels provided by Executive Order 11375 rather than pressing for congressional change in the educational institutions exemption in the 1964 act. WEAL, the Women's Equity Action League, has mounted an important campaign designed to apply pressure on colleges and universities to comply with this executive order, or face cancellation and future loss of government contracts, something no institution of higher education in these tight financial times would be willing to risk.

The mere existence of such laws on the statute books of the land does not itself solve anything unless and until women press for their implementation through concerted efforts to educate their sex and to develop test cases that will effect real changes in women's employment status. This is unglamorous hard work, rarely something that will make a flashy news story or gain coverage on TV or in the weekly magazines. But it is of far greater long range significance for the expansion of women's rights than any amount of bra-burning or anti-men speech making. Parenthetically, it is nothing short of outrageous that young women can graduate from an American high school, to say nothing of a women's college, without anywhere in the course of their education, being informed about existing laws that impinge on the freedom of women to live an autonomous life. Numerous women have informed themselves in recent years about the content of abortion law statutes and have been vigorous in working to repeal them, but I am shocked when I find that women college seniors do not know, to cite just a few examples, that there are states in which women are required by law to be given a maximum prison sentence for a given offense, or that in some states they are not legally able to retain their maiden name after marriage, or that many divorce courts will even reject a woman's plea for a change of name if she is the defendant in the divorce action rather than a successful complainant.[7] There is no professional field more appropriate for a young woman to enter who is concerned with women's rights or women's liberation than the law, and this is true regardless of your political ideology and of any political era that lies ahead, whether pre- or post-revolutionary.

At this juncture, it is not clear what national policies will emerge in the coming decade which impinge upon the lives of women. If one stands back from the immediacy of our time, it is ironic that national policies may undergo a shift that will be out of joint with changes among women themselves. In the post-Sputnik decade of national concern for scientific and technical manpower, there was a widespread campaign to interest women in entry into the labor force. From this perspective, government was serving as the spokesman for short-handed employers desperately trying to meet their personnel needs. The 1960's were a decade of womanpower, that "last major reservoir of manpower" as the specialists put it. But my own research on career choice of women college graduates finds little expansion of career aspirations among young women in the mid 1960's in the high status traditionally masculine fields, or any sharp upturn in aspirations for higher degrees. The roots of such choices lie in a women's childhood and adolescence, and young women in the 1960's were formed by the turned-inward and highly domestic suburban era of the late 1940's and 1950's. The laws we have reviewed which serve to strengthen women's economic rights were passed during this womanpower era. It is only in the past few years that Woman Power has emerged, younger women are showing all the signs of taking a skeptical view toward conventional women's roles anchored in domesticity and marriage, and beginning to search for more meaningful involvement in non-family roles. In other words, expectations are rising, but what may lie ahead in the early 1970's is a reversal of national policy, as a brake is put on military expenditure, conservative political elements are in the ascendancy with a new-old cry that women belong in the home, instead of taking jobs away from men or making "outrageous" demands for maternity benefits or child care facilities.

At the same time, however, there will be mounting pressure for a national population policy, as the nation comes to the realization that high fertility is no longer functional but a decided threat to human well-being in an urban, dense society. We are witnessing the advance wave of this emerging policy with the unprecedented shift in opinion toward abortion in the United States. Those of us who were working on this issue early in the 1960's are now both gratified and disturbed by the ease with which total repeal of abortion laws looms as a coming reality, gratified because this represents the fruition of long hard effort at expanding the rights of women to control their own reproductive lives, but disturbed by the quite mixed motivations behind many who now permit or en-

[7] A good review of the legal situation confronting American women is Leo Kanowitz, *Women and the Law: the Unfinished Revolution*, University of New Mexico Press, 1969.

courage the passage of such repeal legislation.

This concern stems not only from the fear that some political groups wish to curb the birth rate of the non-white population in the United States, but from quite another possibility: increased public dialogue on the undesirability of large families in the same period that there is shift in policy away from encouraging women to seek significant work in the economy, can have the effect of undercutting confidence in the choice of life goals of a significant proportion of the current younger generation of American women. It would be like putting them in a revolving door and spinning it madly, not permitting them easy entry or significant work *outside* the home, and not permitting them to fulfill themselves in a bountiful maternity *inside* the home. If our policies in the coming decade send out a message to young women that they should hold back on their fertility at the same time the economy cannot absorb their energies, the society may eventually pay a very heavy price indeed for such schizophrenic double bind message, in the form of a rise in alienation, escape into drugs, alcoholism or joyless sex, or an ever greater tendency to live vicariously through their few children than American women are now doing, and that is already excessive.

What I am saying, in effect, is that we have yet to acquire a broad enough context in which to make coordinated policy that affects the intimate lives of men and women. This is as true of government agencies as of radical liberation groups. I would like to think that women would themselves take the lead in calling attention to the human and humane dimensions of our lives in a broad context, rather than focusing on short-run, or merely politically expedient actions. The clamor for example, of women's liberation groups at recent congressional hearings on the birth control pill was, in my judgment, ill-advised and based on mis-information. This is in no way to say that women should not have completely safe contraceptives, nor that more emphasis should not be put on male contraceptives, sterilization and abortion as acceptable medical procedures to control unwanted births. The point is that we do not halt small pox vaccinations because a dozen children die from them each year, or stop using antibiotics because 500 users die a year, and by the same token, an element of risk in contraceptive pills is in and of itself, no basis for calling a halt to their manufacture and distribution. I am urging that we be more thoughtful and thorough in an analysis of a problem before rushing to the streets or into print with arguments that sound superficially analytic but are in actuality political posturing.

SEXUALITY

This discussion flows rather readily into a second problem area that I think merits and will receive increased attention as we move into the 1970's: research and education on the nature of human sexuality, and the implications of such research for the social roles of the sexes. Fifty years of acceptance of Freudian concepts of female sexuality will not be quickly undone by current research on the human sexual response, for psychoanalytic theories have penetrated deep into the modern scientific and artistic consciousness, and are reinforced a dozen times a day through commercial use in the attempt to sell everything from an Ohrbach's dress to deodorants and detergents. What concerns me equally is to be spared another fifty years of anti-Freudian polemics from the women's movement.

It may serve unstated political ends, but is historically false and analytically simplistic, to claim that women's sexual role reflects the bourgeois notion of man's natural desire to possess and amass private property, or to charge that the second class citizenship of women merely reflects capitalist society's need to make domestic slaves of women in one era or over-stimulated conspicuous consumers in another era.[8] Marxist analyses of women and capitalism have an element of truth only if you substitute urbanization and industrialization for capitalism. It is not capitalism per se but industrialization that replaced the ancient human communities that provided men and women and their children with a creative social environment. As the communist nations have industrialized, the same hard pinch of double jobs is detectable in the lives of their employed married women, and the same loss of humane values in the work place. In the area of sexuality, there is little evidence that the relations between the sexes are particularly different in communist new nations than in western Europe or the United States. The major difference is merely one of intensity, for no country

---

[8] A notable exception, marked by numerous incisive comments, is Juliet Mitchell, "Women: The Longest Revolution," *New Left Review*, Nov./Dec., 1969.

exceeds the United States in a media saturated with sex of an exploitative, male-dominant variety, typified so well by the infantile or cruel acts of physical rape that fill so many pages of Norman Mailer.[9]

A number of radical feminist analyses in recent years begin with a good critique of the Freudian fallacies concerning female sexuality, building on the physiological research by Masters and Johnson.[10] Let us assume it to be established now, that there is no differentiation between a clitoral and vaginal orgasm, that the myth of women's relative asexuality has been shown to be a biological absurdity, and further that women's sexuality has been suppressed through gender role socialization that urges passivity and submission to men. Liberation group discussions of those points can be enormously helpful to the psychological release of the submerged sexual selves of many women, as I have been witness to in Baltimore. But one must also reckon with the fact that the Masters-Johnson research only illuminates the physiological dimension of human sexuality. It tells us nothing about the non-sexual components of human sexual behavior. Despite the critiques of Freudian ideas of human psycho-sexual development, I have seen little as yet that suggests an alternative developmental theory, with the exception of recent work by John Gagnon and William Simon.[11] I would suggest, for example, that more critical attention should be paid to two factors which bear upon sexual behavior in our society. Despite the current critique of Freudian concepts of sexuality, we continue to view sex as an intense high pressure drive that constrains the individual to seek sexual gratification either directly or indirectly. This view is apparent not only in psychoanalytic literature, but sociological analysis as well. Kingsley Davis, for example, considers sex a high intensity, social constant that must be channeled lest it find expression in behavior which threatens the maintenance of collective life. We talk about our modern "liberation" of sex from a tabooed topic to an openly discussed and dramatically projected experience. Part of the Freudian legacy, however, is that we have become extremely adept at weeding out the sexual ingredient in many forms of non-sexual behavior and symbolism, but rarely engage in what I think might be an equally fruitful analytic investigation: an examination of sexual behavior for its capacity to express and serve non-sexual motives.

I would suggest that the sexual behavior of American men serves not merely sexual needs, but their needs for power and status as compensations for a lack of human gratification in other areas of life. This is further complicated by the pressure on American adults to remain pegged at an adolescent stage of development and of behavior. A man or woman of 45 is not the same person as a 20 year old, and to dress and perform sexually as if they were, is to require that men overperform sexually and that women persist in a coquettish young girlish sexual style that is equally inappropriate to her stage of sexual maturity. In the case of men, over-performance can be stoked by extra-marital or spouse swapping adventures or self-stimulation via pornographic literature or dramatic productions. Men are good at such detached self-stimulation since they learn sexuality via masturbation at an early age, an experience that paves the way for men's greater detachment in the sexual act itself than women tend to have. It may also be the case that marital satisfaction and happiness decline with duration of marriage in American society largely because American adults are expected to perform at 40 or 50 as they did at 20 or 25. This is in turn a reflection of what Henry Murray has described as the retarded adolescent stage of development of American society all told. If we as a culture could move in the direction of mature interdependence, between individuals, across social classes, religious, racial and sexual lines, to say nothing of across national boundaries, we might come to develop what Kenneth Boulding has described as "reconciling styles" in which we take primary pleasure in life from identifying with the process of change itself: watching and taking pleasure from our own individual growth and change, in the growth and change of our friends, spouses, children. In a mature cross-sex relationship, one might then welcome rather than resist the new elements in that relationship at 40 or 50 instead of trying to remain like 25 year old newlyweds or seeking new liaisons in a vain hope of recapturing the youthful quality of a fresh encounter or conquest.

But we must also analyze the dominant role of men in sexual behavior in the context of human sexual physiology. On a superficial level, one might claim that

[9] Mailer is thoroughly analyzed from this perspective by Kate Millett, *Sexual Politics*, Doubleday, 1970.
[10] William Simon and John H. Gagnon, "Psychosexual Development," in Gagnon & Simon. *The Sexual Scene*, Trans-Action Book 5, 1970, 23–42.
[11] Hiram Haydn, "Portrait: Henry A. Murray," *The American Scholar*, Winter 1969. 123–136.

the social pattern in which women are courted and men have the social initiative in sex is a social device that keeps women's sexual interest and capacity subjected to male control and male instruction. But it is a simple physiological fact that male sexual dominance can only be retained if he is the initiator, since his sexual performance is dependent on an erect penis. As long as he is the initiator, his periods of sexual disinterest or impotence are not known to women. This may be part of what lies behind the dislike reported by some married men to their wives' shift of contraception to birth control pills. With the fear of pregnancy gone, and a tendency at a steady level of sexual interest, some husbands report feelings of "humiliation" in their sexual lives, an oblique reference to periodic inability to perform sexually. But if sex were not serving non-sexual needs, if masculinity were not threatened in other areas of life, or if the cultural definition of male gender role was not premised on social and sexual dominance, it might be that occasional sexual impotence would be taken in stride, even become a source of amusement rather than humiliation to American men.

What has all this to do with the women's movement in the 1970's? I think we should be prepared for intense masculine backlash to the demands we make in personal and professional life that are rooted not merely in the specific area of work or home management or parental responsibility, but are displacements from a deeper level, as a threat to men's self-esteem or sense of sexual turf. Some feminists will say, fine and good: men have been our oppressors long enough, now they must give ground. But most women do not wish to live embattled and manless lives, and my impression is there are far more men in the younger generation than there were in my own who are eager to acquire a new life style, a gentler and more meaningful relationship with women. There is much need for research and sober analysis on the social correlates of varying styles of sexual behavior. Following that, a great need for a rather different conception of sex education than anything we have seen in school curricula or sex publications to date.

Some women who have been active this past year in women's caucuses in academic departments or professional associations have begun to put their heads together and to compare notes on the varying responses their demands are eliciting from their male faculty or colleagues. One of the more interesting hypotheses emerging from these early comparisons is that the men most resistant and in some cases almost hysterical about women's pressures for equal treatment in academia are men known to be sexually exploitative in their relations to women students. One such professor whose feathers were decidedly ruffled when the sociology women's caucus displaced a luncheon meeting he was to speak at, complained prettily, with an expectation that it would flatter rather than anger me, "but Alice, what is all the fuss about? There is always room in graduate departments for an extraordinary woman!" It was beyond his ability or willingness to understand my point that sex equality in academia would not be achieved until there was room for as many women of "average" ability as there clearly is now for "average" men holding down academic appointments. My west coast colleagues believe that beneath the surface, men such as this are not able to relate to a woman colleague at the same or higher status rank and feel comfortable only in superordinate positions from which they can dispense their professional and sexual favors to lower status women students and colleagues.

But the male backlash is bound to come, and there are beginning signs of it already. A male friend of mine sympathetic to the women's movement recently sent me a xeroxed copy of a letter of recommendation to the chairman of his department that illustrates this quite well. The applicant is an unmarried woman who had taught in the writer's department and taken graduate courses with him. He wrote:

"When Miss X arrived she was somewhat lacking in self-confidence, uncertain, whether there was a place for her in sociology. Now she recognizes that she can, as a female, contribute to the field without becoming a spinster or a swinger. I say this to emphasize that she is a mature person not swayed by the superficial values so evident on campuses today. In short, she is not a participant in the Woman's liberation movement but a competent sociologist . . . She is neither seductive nor emasculating and will be a useful colleague."

I am not citing such examples with any intention of dampening the ardor and the persistence of women's active pressure for equal treatment in their workaday lives, but to simply point out that we must be prepared to have thick skins at least equal to those of our grandmothers in the suffrage movement and the socialist movements of an earlier day. We shall need every bit of sex solidarity we can garner to withstand it. At the same time, I am making a plea that we be critical of easy and simplistic formulas that are now so widespread either in analyses of the position of women or in programs aimed to improve that position.

WOMEN'S RIGHTS ORGANIZATIONS

That brings me to another problem area that will confront the women's movement in the 1970's. It is apparent to all that there has already been a good deal of fractioning off of splinter groups within the larger movement. We have WITCH, WEAL, Radical Feminists, FEW, NOW, WRAP, and there are undoubtedly more to come. Listening to men, one senses some gleeful pleasure in seeing such sectarianism, with many people now viewing this as a dissipation of effort in a noisy fizzle that will soon dry up. This need not be the case at all, so long as those who form a new group do not then expend their efforts in fruitless attacks upon the group they left or in imitation of styles of protest and pressure that seem to get the most attention from the press. There is a sense in which diversity within a movement is a decided strength, for there is no one problem and no one solution to the kinds of changes necessary in American society to improve the status of women. Dialectic within the movement can benefit us all. Some women's liberation groups may be trying to recruit for a political revolutionary movement but find some of their members graduating from a consciousness-raising series of group sessions to affiliation with a local NOW chapter. Reciprocally, many NOW chapters have lost members to the liberation groups. Women lawyers have on occasion separated from the more diffuse organizations, the better to focus their efforts on campaigns that maximize their particular skills in seeking legal changes. Other groups may concentrate on guerrilla theatre or demonstrations protesting sex imagery in the media or beauty pageants. There is far more risk in frantically dissipating one's efforts by doing a great variety of things that go against the grain of an individual's own style or particular abilities than there is in organizational splitting and concentration on a particular target for legal, political or economic change.

From my own efforts in sociology, I think a good case can be made that a first confrontation in a national professional association of the factual situation facing graduate women students and women faculty is fine, coupled with general demands for a profession to live up to the norms of social equality. Beyond this, efforts should concentrate not on elaborate national organizational structure, but by breaking down to task forces on departmental levels to exert local pressure on departments and universities where policy decisions must be reviewed and changed to improve the academic situation facing women students and faculty. To elaborate cross-discipline national organizations can be helpful in increasing communication among women in various fields, but organization should be minimal, or we shall be swamped in pointless bureaucratic detail and kept from maximizing our efforts on the leverage points in the organizations that employ us where pressure can be most effective.

A few side comments are pertinent concerning the relationship between the women's rights movement on the one hand, and the civil rights movement of black Americans on the other. I think there is serious danger that the essentially middle class women's movement groups will be as guilty of misunderstanding the problems confronting black men and women today, as an earlier counterpart in the middle class suffrage movement in the 19th century misunderstood or was incapable of understanding the problems and political efforts of working class people. Our 19th century women's rights predecessors were also middle class, from the initial convention in Seneca Falls, New York in 1848 right down through the century to the passage of the 19th amendment in 1920. Along the way there were isolated women's rights spokesmen like Henrietta Rodman and Crystal Eastman and Margaret Sanger who understood and were able to affiliate with working class women, but this was the exception rather than the rule.

In recent years, many women in the women's rights movement seem to have taken up with great moral righteousness the task of informing black women that they should avoid the trap of moving through the same series of mistakes that middle class women feel they have been subjected to in the past. The conference on women last February at Cornell culminated in a dramatic session on the black woman in America, in which the largely white middle class audience moaned and hissed and booed black women and men on a panel who spoke of the need for black women to give attention to the status of the black man and his position in the community. Renee Neslett of the Boston Black Panthers defined the black woman as a strong person who can act independently and make decisions but most important of all, she was a woman with an ability to relate to men and who would do anything to help her man retain, or regain his manhood and insure the survival of her people.

In reading the transcript of this session of the conference, I felt a deep sense of anger and shame that the middle class women in the audience had not appreciated the difference in the relative position of the sexes among whites compared to blacks in American society. John Dollard's description of caste in a southern town is as relevant today as three decades ago, when he pointed out that within the white caste, it is the man who is in the superordinate position, and within the black caste, it is the woman who is in the superordinate position. If black women, largely poor but still more advantageously placed in society than black men, have the humanity and dignity to focus their energies in helping to raise the self-esteem of their men, to realize as one of my black students put it, that the black female is no better than her man despite a history of educational and economic superiority, then this is a very great tribute to black women in America, that is unfortunately not matched by a comparable dedication on the part of white men toward their women.

Another aspect of this problem is that we do not realize the continuing relevance of social class differences in the terms in which a problem is perceived and experienced as significant. Abraham Maslow's need hierarchy thesis is helpful here, for it suggests that middle class women, whose physical needs for food, clothing and shelter and sheer security of person are relatively assured, are free to concentrate on a higher level of need in terms of self-fulfillment. A working class person or group can not indulge in such luxury until the survival needs for essential life sustenance and social security have been met. I think, therefore, that the middle class women's rights movement can find a collaborative working arrangement with black women only on the bread and butter issues of protecting economic rights. Beyond this, the white women's movement should focus on trying to deepen its understanding of the differences in the situations they confront in relation to men compared to those black women face. In the interim, we should try to understand, before we try to give advice. Listen for example, to a black poet's phrasing of the issue :

> blackwoman
> is an
> in and out
> rightsideup
> action-image
> of her man . . .
> in other
> (blacker) words;
> She's together,
> if
> he
> bes.
>   (Don Lee)

Despite the optimists in our midst, or the pessimists who anticipate revolution in the streets followed by a magical transformation to a state of sex equality, I think we are in for a long, hard, cultural, legal and political battle before we reach any goal of sex equality for black or white in this nation. It will scarcely be won by will-of-the-wisp quickie-action skirmishes, but by the steady, persistent beat of the hearts and work of the minds of at least another generation. The vision I hope will be shared and the reality I hope will be lived by countless men and women in that future time, was well put by Elizabeth Barrett Browning in her poem *Aurora Leigh*, in which Aurora says :

> "The world waits
> For help. Beloved, let us work so well,
> Our work shall still be better for our love
> And still our love be sweeter for our work."

WOMEN AND WORK

[U.S. Department of Labor, Women's Bureau, April 1970]

PROFILE OF THE WOMAN WORKER: 50 YEARS OF PROGRESS

Now	*1920*

AGE

39 years old.	28 years old.

MARITAL STATUS

Married and living with her husband.	Single.

OCCUPATION

Most likely to be a clerical worker.

Many other women in service work outside the home, factory or other operative work, and professional or technical work.

About 500 individual occupations open to her.

Most likely to be a factory worker or other operative.

Other large numbers of women in clerical, private household, and farm work.

Occupational choice extremely limited.

EDUCATIONAL ATTAINMENT

High school graduate with some college or post-secondary-school education.

Only 1 out of 5 17-year-olds in the population a high school graduate.

LABOR FORCE PARTICIPATION

Almost half (49 percent) of all women 18 to 64 years of age in the labor force.

Most apt to be working at age 20 to 24 (57 percent).

Labor force participation rate dropping at age 25 and rising again at age 35 to a second peak of 54 percent at age 45 to 54.

Can expect to work 24 to 31 more years at age 35.

APRIL 1970.

Less than one-fourth (23 percent) of all women 20 to 64 years of age in the labor force.

Most apt to be working at age 20 to 24 (38 percent).

Participation rate dropping at age 25, decreasing steadily, and only 18 percent at age 45 to 54.

Less than 1 out of every 5 (18 percent) women 35 to 64 years of age in the labor force.

[U.S. Dept. of Labor, Women's Bureau, January 1970]

WHY WOMEN WORK

More than 30 million women are in the labor force today because their talents and skills are needed by the dynamic American economy. The development of new industries and expanded activities in other industries have opened new doors for women in business, the professions, and the production of goods and services.

Decisions of individual women to seek employment outside the home are usually based on economic reasons. Most women in the labor force work because they or their families need the money they can earn—some work to raise family living standards above the level of poverty or deprivation; others, to help meet rising costs of food, education for the children, medical care, and the like. Relatively few women have the option of working solely for personal fulfillment.

Millions of the women who were in the labor force in March 1968 worked to support themselves or others. This was true of the majority of the 6.4 million single women workers. Nearly all the 5.6 million women workers who were widowed, divorced, or separated from their husbands—particularly the women who were also raising children—were working for compelling economic reasons. In addition, the 2.3 million married women workers whose husbands had incomes of less than $3,000 in 1967 certainly worked because of economic need. If we take into account those women whose husbands had incomes between $3,000 and $5,000 (which is still below the $5,915 considered necessary even for a low standard of living for an urban family of four), about 2.2 million women are added. The marital status of women in the labor force in March 1968 follows:

Marital status	Women in the labor force in March 1968	
	Number	Percent distribution
Total	28,778,000	100.0
Single	6,357,000	22.1
Married (husband present)	16,821,000	58.5
With husband whose 1967 income was—		
Below $3,000	2,338,000	8.1
$3,000 to $4,999	2,153,000	7.5
$5,000 or over	12,313,000	42.8
Married (husband absent)	1,413,000	4.9
Widowed	2,483,000	8.6
Divorced	1,704,000	5.9

Mothers with husband present.—Of the 16.8 million married women (husband present) who were in the labor force in March 1968, 9.3 million had children under 18 years of age. About 2 million of these mothers—900,000 whose husbands had incomes in 1967 of less than $3,000 and 1.1 million whose husbands had incomes between $3,000 and $5,000—were helping to support their children. In fact, 24 percent of the 3.6 million working wives with children under 6 years of age and 20 percent of the 5.7 million working wives with children 6 to 17 years of age (none under 6) had husbands whose incomes were less than $5,000.

Nonwhite wives.—About 15.9 million married women (husband present) who were in the labor force in March 1968 were living in nonfarm areas. Of these nonfarm wives, 22 percent of the nonwhite (12 percent of the white) had husbands whose incomes were less than $3,000 in 1967. An additional 25 percent of the nonwhite wives (11 percent of the white) had husbands whose incomes were between $3,000 and $5,000.

Women heads of families.—Of the 49.8 million families in March 1968, 5.3 million were headed by a woman. Fifty-one percent of the women family heads were in the labor force, and more than three-fifths of these women were the sole support of their families. About a third of all families headed by a woman had incomes of less than $3,000 in 1967. Nearly a fourth of all families headed by a woman were Negro; their median family income in 1967 were $3,015, as compared with $4,879 for families headed by a white woman.

Wives whose husbands are unemployed or unable to work.—In the 43.3 million husband-wife families in March 1968, 732,000 husbands were unemployed and 5.6 million husbands were not in the labor force. About 320,000 wives of unemployed husbands and more than a million wives whose husbands were not in the labor force were working or seeking work. Many of these women were the sole support of their families.

Women whose husbands are employed in low-wage occupations.—There were 679,000 married women at work in March 1968 whose husbands were farmworkers; another 724,000 had husbands working as nonfarm laborers; and 915,000 had husbands employed in service occupations. The median wage or salary income of men in these three major occupation groups was low in 1967—it was below the poverty level among farmworkers and barely above the poverty level for nonfarm laborers.

Women's reasons for entering the labor force.—According to a special study, nearly half the women 18 to 64 years old who took jobs in 1963 went to work because of economic need. Particularly likely to have taken jobs for economic reasons were women who were widowed, divorced, or separated from their husbands (54 percent) and married women living with their husbands (48 percent). The proportion who indicated financial necessity, including husband's loss of job, as the reason for going to work was even higher among married women whose husbands earned less than $60 a week (73 percent) and those who had children under 6 years of age (56 percent).

Of married women who stopped working in 1963, only a small percentage did so because they no longer needed to work.

(NOTE.—Figures used are from the U.S. Department of Commerce, Bureau of the Census, and U.S. Department of Labor, Bureau of Labor Statistics.)

[U.S. Dept. of Labor, Women's Bureau, February 1970]

FACT SHEET ON THE EARNINGS GAP

A comparison of the median wage or salary incomes of women and men who work full time year round reveals not only that those of women are considerably less than those of men but also that the gap has widened in recent years. In 1955, for example, women's median wage or salary income of $2,719 was 64 percent of the $4,252 received by men. In 1968 women's median earnings of $4,457 were only 58 percent of the $7,664 received by men.

WAGE OR SALARY INCOME OF FULL-TIME YEAR-ROUND WORKERS,[1] BY SEX, 1955–68

Year	Median wage or salary income		Women's median wage or salary income as percent of men's
	Women	Men	
1955	$2,719	$4,252	63.9
1956	2,827	4,466	63.3
1957	3,008	4,713	63.8
1958	3,102	4,927	63.0
1959	3,193	5,209	61.3
1960	3,293	5,417	60.8
1961	3,351	5,644	59.4
1962	3,446	5,794	59.5
1963	3,561	5,978	59.6
1964	3,690	6,195	59.6
1965	3,823	6,375	60.0
1966	3,973	6,848	58.0
1967 [2]	4,150	7,182	57.8
1968 [2]	4,457	7,664	58.2

[1] Worked 35 hours or more a week for 50 to 52 weeks.
[2] Data for 1967 and 1968 are not strictly comparable with prior years, since earnings of self-employed are included.

Source: U.S. Department of Commerce, Bureau of the Census: Current Populations Reports, P–60.

This gap in earnings varies by major occupation group. It is largest for sales workers (women earn only 40 percent of what men earn) and smallest for professional and technical workers (women earn 66 percent of what men earn).

MEDIAN WAGE OR SALARY INCOME OF FULL–TIME YEAR–ROUND WORKERS, BY SEX AND SELECTED MAJOR OCCUPATION GROUP, 1968

Major occupation group	Median wage or salary income		Woman's median wage or salary income as percent of men's
	Women	Men	
Professional and technical workers	$6,691	$10,151	65.9
Nonfarm managers, officials, and proprietors	5,635	10,340	54.5
Clerical workers	4,789	7,351	65.1
Sales workers	3,461	8,549	40.5
Operatives	3,991	6,738	59.2
Service workers (except private household)	3,332	6,058	55.0

Source: U.S. Department of Commerce, Bureau of the Census; current population reports, p. 60, No. 66.

Another measure of the gap in the earnings of women and men full-time year-round workers is a distribution of these workers by earnings intervals. For example, 20 percent of the women but only 8 percent of the men earned less than $3,000. Moreover, 60 percent of the women but only 20 percent of the men earned less than $5,000. At the upper end of the scale, only 3 percent of the women but 28 percent of the men had earnings of $10,000 or more.

EARNINGS OF FULL-TIME YEAR-ROUND WORKERS, BY SEX, 1968

Earnings	Women	Men
Total	100.0	100.0
Less than $3,000	20.0	7.5
$3,000 to $4,999	40.0	12.6
$5,000 to $6,999	26.0	21.3
$7,000 to $9,999	10.9	30.9
$10,000 to $14,999	2.5	19.5
$15,000 and over	.4	8.2

Source: U.S. Department of Commerce, Bureau of the Census; Current Population Reports, P–60, No. 66.

The previous figures do not necessarily indicate that women are receiving unequal pay for equal work. For the most part, they reflect the fact that women are more likely than men to be employed in low-skilled, low-paying jobs. For example :

In institutions of higher education, women are much less likely than men to be associate or full professors.

In the technical field, women are usually in the lowest category of draftsman or engineering technician.

Among managers and proprietors, women frequently operate a small retail establishment, while the men may manage a manufacturing plant or a wholesale outlet.

In the clerical field, women are usually the class B and men the higher paid class A accounting clerks. Among tabulating machine operators, also, women are concentrated at the lower level.

In cotton textile manufacturing, women are usually the battery hands, spinners, and yarn winders (the lowest paying jobs), while men are loom fixers, maintenance machinists, and card grinders.

Nevertheless, within some of these detailed occupations, men usually are better paid. For example, in institutions of higher education in 1965–66, women full professors had a median salary of only $11,649 as compared with $12,768 for men. Comparable differences were found at the other three levels as shown in the following table.

MEDIAN ANNUAL SALARIES OF TEACHING STAFF IN COLLEGES AND UNIVERSITIES, BY SEX, 1965–66

	Number		Median annual salary	
Teaching staff	Women	Men	Women	Men
Total_____	26,734	118,641	$7,732	$9,275
Professors_____	3,149	32,873	11,649	12,768
Associate professors_____	5,148	28,892	9,322	10,064
Assistant professors_____	8,983	37,232	7,870	8,446
Instructors_____	9,454	19,644	6,454	6,864

Source: National Education Association: "Salaries in Higher Education, 1965–66," Research Report 1966–R 2, February 1966. (Copyright 1966, National Education Association. Reprinted by permission.)

Median salaries of women scientists in 1968 were from $1,700 to $4,500 a year less than those of all scientists in their respective fields. The greatest gap was in the field of chemistry, where the median annual salary of women was $9,000 as compared with $13,500 for all chemists. Additional details are given in the following table.

MEDIAN ANNUAL SALARIES OF FULL-TIME EMPLOYED CIVILIAN SCIENTISTS, BY FIELD, 1968

	Median annual salary			Median annual salary	
Field	Total	Women	Field	Total	Women
All fields_____	$13,200	$10,000	Biological sciences_____	13,000	9,900
			Psychology_____	13,200	11,500
Chemistry_____	13,500	9,000	Statistics_____	14,900	12,000
Earth and marine sciences_____	12,900	9,500	Economics_____	15,000	12,000
Atmospheric and space sciences____	13,400	11,300	Sociology_____	12,000	10,000
Physics_____	14,000	10,200	Anthropology_____	12,700	11,000
Mathematics_____	13,000	9,400	Political science_____	12,000	9,700
Computer sciences_____	14,100	11,800	Linguistics_____	11,500	9,600
Agricultural sciences_____	11,000	(¹)			

¹ Median not computed for groups with fewer than 25 registrants reporting salary.

Source: National Science Foundation: National Register of Scientific and Technical Personnel. 1968.

The jobs and salaries expected to be offered by 206 companies to June 1970 college graduates were reported in a survey conducted in November 1969. There was a substantial spread in the offers to be made to men and women with the same college majors as indicated in the following table.

EXPECTED SALARIES FOR JUNE 1970 COLLEGE GRADUATES, BY SEX AND SELECTED FIELD

	Average monthly salary	
Field	Women	Men
Accounting_____	$746	$832
Chemistry_____	765	806
Economics, finance_____	700	718
Engineering_____	844	872
Liberal arts_____	631	688
Mathematics, statistics_____	746	773

Source: Endicott, Frank S., Dr., "Trends in Employment of College and University Graduates in Business and Industry." Northwestern University (1970).

Surveys of average earnings for major office occupations made by the Bureau of Labor Statistics showed that in the period from July 1968 to June 1969 men's average weekly earnings were substantially higher than those of women among class A and class B accounting clerks and payroll clerks. For example, the weekly salary differential between the earnings of women and men class A accounting clerks ranged from $2.00 to $45.50 in the 88 important centers of business and industry surveyed regularly.

[U.S. Dept. of Labor, Women's Bureau, August 1969.]

FACTS ABOUT WOMEN'S ABSENTEEISM AND LABOR TURNOVER

FOREWORD

Interest in the comparative costs of employing men and women workers has been heightened by recent efforts to extend and enforce the principles of equal pay and equal opportunity in employment. Allegations of differences in costs are made to justify differential treatment.

This report summarizes the latest facts available about certain factors affecting labor costs; namely, absenteeism, labor turnover, job tenure, and labor mobility. The cost differentials are shown to be insignificant. The favorable findings for women workers emphasize the importance of judging work performance on the basis of individual achievement rather than of sex.

Jean A. Wells, Special Assistant to the Director, prepared the report, superseding "What About Women's Absenteeism and Labor Turnover?" published in 1965.

ELIZABETH DUNCAN KOONTZ,
Director, Women's Bureau.

Women workers have favorable records of attendance and labor turnover when compared with men employed at similar job levels and under similar circumstances. This conclusion is supported by a careful analysis of various impartially collected statistics on absenteeism and labor turnover which also indicates that the skill level of the job, the age of the worker, the worker's length of service with the employer, and the worker's record of job stability—all provide better clues to an understanding of differences in work performance than does the mere fact that the worker is a man or a woman.

These data contradict some generalizations about the comparative labor costs of men and women. However, such generalizations are based on studies which point to the sex of the worker as the major determining factor in situations where numerous other factors have much more influence.

Before examining details of studies that consider comparable characteristics of workers, however, it is pertinent to cite the overall averages of data compiled by official or independent agencies. Even these show smaller net differences in the work records of men and women than frequently are suggested.

NOTE 1.—This report provides the latest data available as of June 1969.
NOTE. 2.—Footnotes refer to sources listed on pages 8 and 9.

OVERALL AVERAGES OF ABSENTEEISM

A Public Health Service study [1] of worktime lost by persons 17 years of age and over because of illness or injury shows an average of 5.6 days lost by women and 5.3 days lost by men during the calendar year 1967. Significant differences were noted between men and women in the amount of time lost because of acute or chronic illness. Women lost an average of 3.7 workdays because of acute illness, whereas men averaged just 3.3 days away from work for this reason. On the other hand, men were more likely than women to be absent because of chronic conditions such as heart trouble, arthritis, rheumatism, and orthopedic impairment.

Another analysis also has indicated that women's illnesses usually keep them away from work for shorter periods than men's illnesses do. The Health Information Foundation of the University of Chicago [2] studied the total loss to the American economy from work absences that occurred because of illness or injury between July 1959 and June 1960. Since women lost more worktime because of acute conditions and men because of chronic conditions, the study found that the total financial loss caused by women's absences was about the same as that caused by men's.

The Bureau of Labor Statistics, in its monthly survey of the labor force, records the incidence of illness but not its duration. During an average week in 1968, 1.7 percent of women workers and 1.5 percent of men workers were absent from work because of illness. [3] In addition, an average of 1.2 percent of the women

[1] U.S. Department of Health, Education, and Welfare, Public Health Service. Vital and Health Statistics. Current Estimates From the Health Interview Survey. United States, 1967. PHS Publication No. 1000–Series 10–No. 52, tables 8 and 16. May 1969.
[2] The University of Chicago, Graduate School of Business. Health Information Foundation. The Economic Costs of Absenteeism. *In* Progress in Health Services, March–April 1963.
[3] U.S. Department of Labor, Bureau of Labor Statistics. Employment and Earnings, January 1969. Annual averages table A–19.

and 1 percent of the men did not report to work for other reasons, excluding vacations. This survey does not give the full story, of course, since women have, on the average, shorter periods of absences than men.

OVERALL AVERAGES OF LABOR TURNOVER

Available statistics on labor turnover also indicate that the net differences in job-leaving of men and women are generally small—even when considered on an overall basis.

Labor turnover rates, which refer to the movement of employees among firms, consist of both hiring and separation rates. The average turnover rates for men and women factory workers in 1968, collected by the Bureau of Labor Statistics on a quarterly basis,[4] are:

[Rate per 100 employees]

Type of labor turnover	Women	Men
Accessions (hires)	5.3	4.4
Separations (total)	5.2	4.4
Quits	2.6	2.2
Layoffs and other involuntary separations	2.6	2.2

Comparison of these quit rates with those analyzed in an earlier study[5] shows a narrowing of the gap between the rates of men and women. The fact that women have become relatively less inclined to quit their jobs than they were formerly is due probably to the higher proportion of older women in the work force and the increased interest of women in continuous employment.

A study of occupational mobility by the Bureau of Labor Statistics[6] indicates that men are more frequent occupation changers than women. According to that study, only 7 percent of the women but 10 percent of the men held a different occupation in January 1966 than in January 1965. Movement between occupations was greater among young workers than among mature ones. In the 18- and 19-year-old group, more than 1 out of 4 girls and almost 1 out of 3 boys had worked in more than one occupation in 1965. Among those workers 35 years or older, fewer than 4 percent of the women and 6 percent of the men had changed occupations.

The seeming inconsistency between the labor turnover rates and the occupational mobility percentages of the two studies made by the Bureau of Labor Statistics is explained by their different coverage. The study of turnover rates referred to job changes of factory workers only. The study of mobility rates, on the other hand, measured all occupational changes but not job changes within the same occupational classification. In addition, the latter figures exclude workers who left jobs in 1965 and had not obtained new ones by January 1966, either because they were unsuccessful in their jobhunting or had voluntarily left the labor force. Since there are relatively more women than men in this category, the figures for women's occupational mobility tend to be slightly understated.

Geographic labor mobility was also found to be somewhat less among women workers than men workers in a study made by the Social Security Administration.[7] Between 1957 and 1960, an average of 6.3 percent of women workers but 7.7 percent of men workers changed the region of their main job. The extent of regional movement among white women workers (6.4 percent) and Negro women workers (5.3 percent) was exceeded by both white men workers (7.8 percent) and Negro men workers (7.3 percent).

Another indication of women's increasing stability in the work force is revealed in trend figures on the worklife expectancy of women, as compiled by

[4] U.S. Department of Labor, Bureau of Labor Statistics. Employment and Earnings, May, August, and November 1968, and February 1969, table D–3.

[5] U.S. Department of Labor, Bureau of Labor Statistics. Labor Turnover of Women Factory Workers, 1950–55. In Monthly Labor Review, August 1955.

[6] U.S. Department of Labor, Bureau of Labor Statistics. Occupational Mobility of Employed Workers. Special Labor Force Report No. 84.

[7] U.S. Department of Health, Education, and Welfare. Social Security Administration. Geographic Labor Mobility in the United States, 1957 to 1960. Research Report No. 28. 1969.

the Department of Labor.[8] These figures show that the average number of years a woman works had more than tripled from 1900 to 1960 and had increased by almost one-third in the decade 1950–60. Worklife expectancy for those women born in 1900 averaged 6.3 years; in 1940, 12.1 years; in 1950, 15.2 years; and in 1960, 20.1 years. In each case, the percentage increase in women's average work-life expectancy far exceeded that of their average life expectancy.

The expected worklife of a woman is closely related to her marital status and the number of children she has.[9] In the large group of women who enter the labor force by age 20, the relatively small number who never marry have a worklife expectancy of 45 years. This is about 10 years longer than for those women in the group who marry but have no children and about 2 to 3 years longer than for those who become widowed or divorced. For the large number of married women with children, worklife expectancy declines with the higher number of children and the later timing of the last child. A woman marrying at age 20 has a worklife expectancy ranging from 25 years if she has just one child to 17 years if she has four or more children.

STUDIES OF COMPARABLE CHARACTERISTICS

Several studies provide insight into the job stability of men and women by comparing those who hold similar jobs or have similar employment character-istics. These studies present a much more favorable picture of women's work-life than frequently is realized and support the contention that hiring decisions of employers generally are based on factors other than the relative labor costs of men and women.

Job tenure.—In its study of the job tenure of American workers.[10] the Bureau of Labor Statistics found that continuous employment in the current job as of January 1966 averaged 2.8 years for women and 5.2 years for men. In comparable age groups, job stability was as great for single women as for all men. In fact, among those 45 years of age and over, single women averaged more time on the same job (15.5 years) than all men in the same age group (13.1 years).

Workers with the shortest job tenure were typically youth and married women. Young workers 14 to 19 years old—boys as well as girls—had spent an average of less than 1 year on their current job. The average job tenure of married women was generally shorter than that of single women in all age groups ex-cept the youngest (14–24 years). The job attachment of married women was greater for each age group, with the longest period (6.4 years) reported for those 45 years of age and over.

Illness absenteeism.—Detailed statistics of illness absenteeism were provided by the Bureau of Labor Statistics to the U.S. Public Health Service from the monthly survey of the labor force for the period July 1959 to June 1960. The analysis[11] compared men and women employed as civilian wage and salary workers by major occupational group, industry, type of employment, and type of manufacturing industry. On an average workday during that year, when illness rates were adjusted for age, relatively more women (1.6 percent) than men (1.3 percent) were absent from work because of illnesses lasting a work-week or more. However, among certain groups—for example, clerical workers and government workers—women had a lower rate of illness absence than men.

When sick absence days for the period July 1959 to June 1961 were analyzed by the U.S. Public Health Service[12] and adjusted to eliminate the effects of marital status as well as age on sickness absences, they showed fewer sick days per year for single women (3.9 days) than for single men (4.3 days). Within comparable age groups, single women used more sick leave than single men below 35 years of age but used less sick leave at 35 years and over.

Among "ever married persons," however, there were more days of sick ab-sence for women (6.1 days) than men (4.7 days) when compared by the total age-adjusted data as well as by individual age groups. It was thought that women's greater responsibility for childrearing and probably their lesser de-

[8] Wolfbein, Seymour L. Changing Patterns of Working Life. Paper prepared for the International Gerontological Seminar, Markaryd, Sweden, August 6–9, 1963. Issued by the U.S. Department of Labor, Manpower Administration.

[9] U.S. Department of Labor, Manpower Administration. Work Life Expectancy and Training Needs of Women. Manpower Report No. 12 May 1967.

[10] U.S. Department of Labor, Bureau of Labor Statistics. Job Tenure of Workers, Janu-ary 1966. Special Labor Force Report No. 77.

[11] Enterline, Philip E. Work Loss Due to Illness in Selected Occupations and Industries. *In* Journal of Occupational Medicine, September 1961.

[12] Enterline, Philip E. Sick Absence for Men and Women by Marital Status. *In* Archives of Environmental Health, March 1964.

pendency on their own jobs for economic support might explain the relatively higher sick absence of the "ever married women."

Labor turnover.—A private study [13] conducted among 65 large chemical and pharmaceutical laboratories revealed only moderate differences in the labor turnover of men and women chemists when they were grouped by type of degree required for the grade of work performed. A majority of the surveyed laboratories reported that in comparisons made on this basis. women's turnover rates were "about the same" as men's. No more than 10 percent of the laboratories reported them "much higher." The overall turnover rates were much less favorable for women than for men "mainly because women are disproportionately represented at the lowest level, where turnover is highest for both sexes." It is significant that directors of many of the largest laboratories said that differentials in turnover were not sufficiently great to be a deciding factor in employment of women.

Two studies have focused attention directly on factors which might explain the consistently high turnover rates of hospital nurses. One study, published by the Industrial Relations Center of Iowa State University,[14] surveyed staff registered nurses in several large general hospitals to learn specifically about their turnover, their propensity to leave, and their absenteeism. This investigation indicated that inadequate definitions of the nurses' role in the organization, poor communication and coordination. and unreasoable work pressures all had an adverse influence on the nurses' turnover and, to a lesser extent, on their absenteeism.

The second study of nurses also suggested that hospitals might look more closely at their methods of operation to learn some of the reasons for nurses' high turnover rates. Nurses leaving one sample hospital over a 15-month period were mailed exit questionnaires by three researchers at Western Reserve University.[15] The majority (69 percent) of reasons given for leaving were not related to job situations and in most cases were involuntary ones, such as pregnancy, illness. retirement, or moves to another city. The primary reasons cited for quitting voluntarily were: nature of work (10 percent). lack of promotion (7 percent), supervision and human relations (6 percent), to get new experience (4 percent), and other reasons (4 percent).

The survey report of the Western Reserve researchers contained these comments on the lack of job challenge felt by the nurses who had voluntarily quit their jobs:

> Some of the respondents, dissatisfied with what they were doing as a result of not using their experience and ability, left their jobs. Others left because their work was not appreciated or recognized, because of lack of advancement possibilities, or to get new experience somewhere else. These individuals did not find a chance to achieve what they expected. Their work did not satisfy their needs for what may be called self-actualization and psychological growth.

Federal employees' absenteeism.—A Public Health Service analysis [16] of the number of absences reported because of illness by a sample of employees in one large Federal agency corroborated the theory that employees in high-level jobs generally had fewer absences than those at lower levels, regardless of the sex of the worker. Thus, the generalization made in the report that women employees had more absences than men employees was based on the overall data, which did not take account of the fact that relatively more women than men were employed in the low grades. In addition, it was found that women employees with children generally had a greater number of absences than those without children. As a result, differences in the incidence of illness absenteeism varied much more among the women employees than among the men employees.

Since this report did not include statistical data concerning the length of each absence period—generally found to be longer, for men than women—it presented only a partial story of the illness absenteeism of Federal employees in one agency.

[13] Parrish. John B. Employment of Women Chemists in Industrial Laboratories. *In* Science, April 30, 1965.

[14] Lyons. Thomas Francis. Nursing Attitudes and Turnover: The Relation of Social-Psychological Variables to Turnover. Propensity to Leave. and Absenteeism Among Hospital Staff Nurses. Industrial Relations Center, Iowa State University, Ames, Iowa. 1968.

[15] Saleh, Shoukry D.. Robert J. Lee. *and* Erich P. Prien. Why Nurses Leave Their Jobs—An Analysis of Female Turnover. *In* Personnel Administration, January–February 1965.

[16] Backenheimer. Michael S. Demographic and Job Characteristics as Variables in Absences for I'lness. *In* Public Health Reports. December 1968.

A U.S. Civil Service Commission study [17] of sick leave records in 1961 showed relatively small difference in the total amount of sick leave averaged by women and men Federal workers—9.6 days for women and 7.9 days for men. But even this difference narrowed in most instances when comparisons were made of women and men with similar salaries, ages, or years of service.[18] For example, in 1961 among those earning $9,000 to $10,000 a year, 6.9 days of sick leave was the average for women and 6.3 days for men.

The highest average numbers of sick days occurred among those in the lowest salary levels—the levels where women workers are concentrated. Two groups of women had less sick leave, on the average, than their male counterparts: those 60 years of age and over (10.5 days for women, 11 days for men) and those with more than 30 years of Federal service (10.7 days for women and 11.3 days for men).

A study made by the Civil Service Commission [19] especially for the President's Commission on the Status of Women covered voluntary separations of full-time career employees between December 16, 1962, and February 2, 1963. On an overall basis, the relative separation (turnover) rate was about 2½ times greater for women than for men. The higher rate for women can be explained by the larger proportion of women than men who are under 25 years of age, who have lower grade clerical jobs, and who have fewer years of Federal service—all factors associated with high turnover. When the data for men and for women were compared separately by age group, by broad occupational group, and by length of service, differences in their relative turnover rates decreased.

French workers' absenteeism.—The importance of considering job levels and other factors in any study of absenteeism is further emphasized in an international report [20] on women industrial workers in Paris, France. The following quotation is from that report:

Detailed study of absentee figures for large numbers of employees of both sexes and at all levels of skill discloses that the comparatively high proportion of women at the lower levels of the occupational scale (even in countries where the employment of women is a long-standing tradition) goes a long way towards explaining their frequent irregularity at work. Highly trained women occupying responsible and skilled positions are seldom absent, even if they have several children to bring up.

Conclusion.—Meaningful comparisons of absenteeism and labor turnover of women and men workers must take into consideration similar job levels as well as other factors such as age and length of service. Many of the critical generalities frequently voiced not only exaggerate overall differences but also compare dissimilar groups of men and women.

[U.S. Dept. of Labor, Women's Bureau, April 1968]

WOMEN IN POVERTY—JOBS AND THE NEED FOR JOBS

About 11.2 million women and girls 16 years of age and over experienced the hardships of poverty in 1966. Of these, 1.8 million were heads of families, many of whom were employed but were unable to lift their families out of poverty. Others were members of husband-wife families in which both the husband and wife worked, and still the family was poor. In addition, in many impoverished families, women and girls needed and wanted work, but often could not find it. In some cases they lacked the essential education and training to qualify for a job even though job openings might have been available in the community. In other cases child care or other supportive services were lacking in the area in which they lived.

WOMEN HEADS OF FAMILY

About 5.2 million families in the United States were headed by a woman in March 1967. This means that in 1 out of every 10 families in our Nation, a widowed, divorced, separated, or single woman was responsible for raising children in a fatherless home or supporting aged parents or other relatives. The median (half above, half below) income of these 5.2 million families was $4,010

---

[17] U.S. Civil Service Commission. Draft Report on Government-Wide Sick Leave Study. 1961. March 1963.
[18] U.S. Civil Service Commission. Unpublished data.
[19] President's Commission on the Status of Women. Report of the Committee on Federal Employment. Appendix F. October 1963.
[20] Isambert-Jamati, Viviane. Absenteeism Among Women Workers in Industry. *In* International Labour Review, March 1962.

in 1966. About 1.9 million (37 percent) had annual incomes of less than $3,000 in 1966; 1.2 million (23 percent) had annual incomes of less than $2,000.

In more than half of the families headed by a woman, the head was in the labor force. In 3 out of 4 such families, she was the primary earner and the median family income was $4,450. If she worked full time year round, the median family income was $5,650 and if she worked part time year round, it was $3,450.

In additional, a great many female heads who were not in the labor force suffered severe deprivation. Many who had young children and who wished to work were unable to do so because of the absence of child care facilities. The median income of women who were heads of families and not in the labor force was $2,150 in 1966 for those who supported 1 or 2 children, and $2,700 for those who supported 3 or more children.

More than a fifth (1.2 million) of all families headed by a woman in March 1967 were nonwhite; their median family income in 1966 was only $2,825. Even when the family head worked full time year round, the median family income in 1966 was only $4,300.

Nonwhite women family heads who work are both occupationally and financially disadvantaged. About 1 out of 5 held white-collar jobs with median family income of $5,350 in 1966 as compared with more than 1 out of 2 white women family heads with median family income of $5,950. Even when the proportions in the broad occupational group were almost identical, as among women heads in blue-collar jobs—21 percent of white and 23 percent of nonwhite—the median income for nonwhite families ($3,600) was one-fourth lower than that of white families ($4,850). And among women family heads in private housework, an occupation in which 29 percent of the nonwhite and 5 percent of the white were employed, the median income for nonwhite and white families was $2,450 and $3,350, respectively, in 1966.

HUSBAND-WIFE FAMILIES

There were 42.6 million husband-wife families in the United States in March 1967. Of these, 4.8 million (11 percent) had incomes of less than $3,000 in 1966; 2.5 million had incomes of less than $2,000. The incidence of poverty was greater when the wife was not in the paid labor force than when she was—15 percent as compared with 5 percent.

Negro husband-wife families are the most disadvantaged. Of the 3.2 million such families as of March 1966, .9 million (28 percent) had incomes of less than $3,000 in 1965. Almost half a million had incomes of less than $2,000 in that year. As is true for all families, a working wife helps to lift Negro families out of poverty. The proportion of Negro husband-wife families who were poor in 1965 was about twice as high when the wife was not an earner as when she was—37 percent as compared with 18 percent.

In some husband-wife families, the husband is unemployed or not in the labor force. He may not be working or looking for work because he is unable to work, feels there are no jobs available, or does not have the education or skills to qualify for the job openings available in his locality. Many such families would be completely destitute if the wife did not seek and find a job. In March 1967 there were nearly 350,000 working wives who had unemployed husbands and more than a million working wives whose husbands were not in the labor force.

EMPLOYED WOMEN

There were 28.4 million women 16 years of age and over in the civilian labor force in 1967. Of these, 26.9 million were employed and 1.5 million were unemployed. Nearly half of all women between the ages of 18 and 64 were working or looking for work.

Having a job does not always prevent women or their families from living in poverty. A great many women work part time or part year because of family responsibilities or because they lack the skills and education necessary to qualify for the higher paying positions where employment is more stable. Others are in low-paying jobs and are unable to earn enough to bring family income above the poverty level even when they work full time year round. Among all women who worked 35 hours or more a week for 50 to 52 weeks in 1966, 26 percent had incomes from all sources of less than $3,000. Among those who worked full time for 40 to 49 weeks in 1966, 49 percent had incomes of less than $3,000.

Of the 26.9 million women who were employed in 1967, about one-third were sales workers, laborers, farm workers, service workers (except private household), or private household workers. These are the least rewarding and least rewarded occupations.

Almost 4.3 million women were employed in 1967 in service work outside the home as cooks, hospital attendants, kitchen helpers, maids, practical nurses, or waitresses, or in similar occupations. The median earnings of women in these types of jobs were only $2,815 in 1966 even when they worked full time year round.

Another 1.7 million women were employed as private household workers. This is the most disadvantaged group of all. The median earnings of those who worked full time year round in 1966 were only $1,297.

About 1.9 million women were employed in 1967 as sales workers, mainly in retail trade. Many of them worked in small retail establishments which are exempt from the minimum wage provisions of the Federal law. The median earnings in 1966 for this group of women workers were $3,103 when they worked full time year round.

Another 735,000 women were farm workers or nonfarm laborers. Some of the farm workers were unpaid family workers and the rest were poorly paid, as were the few women working as laborers in nonfarm industries.

UNEMPLOYED WOMEN

Unemployed women numbered 1.5 million in 1967. Slightly more than one-fourth were looking for part-time work only; the remainder wanted full-time jobs.

Unemployment has been more severe among women than among men almost consistently over the last decade. The unemployment rate for women in 1967 was 5.2 percent as compared with 3.1 percent for men.

Although nonwhite women were only 13 percent of all women workers in 1967, they constituted 23 percent of the unemployed. Unemployment is very high among all nonwhite women but is especially severe among nonwhite girls 16 to 19 years of age. The unemployment rate in 1967 for nonwhite women 20 years of age and over was 7.1 percent, but for nonwhite girls 16 to 19 years of age it was *29.5 percent*. Many of these girls are school dropouts; others are disadvantaged because of lack of vocational training, job guidance, and personal counseling.

ESPECIALLY DISADVANTAGED GIRLS AND WOMEN

Girl school dropouts and women living in urban slum areas are particularly disadvantaged, the more so when they are nonwhite. They have difficulty finding jobs; when they do, they rarely qualify for any but the most routine or menial.

According to the report of a special survey made by the Bureau of Labor Statistics of the U.S. Department of Labor in October 1966, almost one-fifth of the girl school dropouts 16 to 21 years of age in the labor force were actively looking for work but were unable to find it. Among those who were employed, only 15 percent were in white-collar jobs. The majority were service workers either inside or outside the home (45 percent) or blue-collar workers (36 percent). Nonwhite girl school dropouts had even less success in the job market. One-third of those who wanted jobs could not find them.

Many women who live in the slum areas of large cities are poor even though they are working. Others do not know how to find and seek jobs. Often transportation presents a problem. A recent survey of 10 slum areas in large cities in the United States showed that 35 percent of the women living in these areas were employed. More than a third of all unemployed persons were women 20 to 64 years of age and their number exceeded that of men of these ages. The unemployment rate for all women 20 to 64 years of age was 8.7 percent; among those married and living with their husbands it was 9.5 percent; and among those divorced, widowed, or separated it was 8.1 percent. (The unemployment rate for men 20 to 64 years of age was 5.4 percent; for boys and girls 16 to 19 years of age, 28.1 percent.)

Information is not available on the earnings of women in these areas. However, we do have some information on the incomes of families headed by a woman. Since more than one-third of the families in these 10 areas were headed by a woman, this group probably included many who were working. Among the families headed by a woman, 3 out of 5 had family incomes of less than $3,000 a year; 1 out of 5, less than $1,500.

WOMEN NOT IN THE LABOR FORCE

There are many women living in poverty who wish to work but cannot do so because of the lack of day care or other supportive services in the community or because they lack the education or training needed to qualify for or to find a job. Many of them lack confidence in their own ability; others need refresher training to update their skills. They need counseling and guidance.

Findings in the recent survey of the 10 urban slum areas referred to previously illustrate these problems. Persons living in the area who were not in the labor force were asked if they wanted a full-time job, and if so, why they hadn't been able to secure one. About 70,000 men and women who were not in the labor force indicated that they wanted a regular job. Of these, 12,500 or nearly one-fifth gave inability to arrange for child care as the reason for not working. Most of these respondents undoubtedly were women.

A previous survey of persons not in the labor force who wanted a regular job had been conducted by the Bureau of the Census for the Bureau of Labor Statistics in September 1966. Of the 5.3 million persons who fell into this category, 3.7 million were women. The primary reason for not being in the labor force given by 3 out of 10 of the women respondents was family responsibilities. Another 1 out of 10 women listed inability to arrange child care. More than 1 out of 10 women believed it would be impossible to find work due to age, racial discrimination, language difficulties, or the lack of skills, experience, transportation, education, or training. Of this discouraged group, 77 percent were 20 to 64 years of age, 24 percent were nonwhite, and 64 percent had not completed high school.

LIFTING WAGE STANDARDS

It is estimated that, as of February 1, 1968, almost 42.8 million non-supervisory employees are covered by the minimum wage provisions of the Fair Labor Standards Act. Included in this number are 9.7 million who were brought within the scope of the act by the 1966 amendments.

There are still 11.8 million nonsupervisory employees, however, who must rely on minimum wage protection at the State level. Only 3.5 million of these currently are covered by State minimum wage legislation. Moreover, in many States, the level at which the minimum wage is set is relatively low, and certain types of work are exempt altogether.

Of the 11.8 million workers exempt from the minimum wage provisions of the Federal law, 5.4 million are women—3.8 million white and 1.6 million nonwhite. Despite the fact that about 8 out of 10 white and nonwhite men and white women in nonsupervisory positions are covered by the Federal law, more than 5 out of 10 nonwhite women are still exempt.

Employees still exempt from the minimum wage provisions of the Fair Labor Standards Act include 2.2 million in domestic service. With very few exceptions, these workers also are exempt under State minimum wage regulations so that they are virtually without wage protection of any kind. Others are employed in small retail and service establishments.

It is clear that workers in those industries still exempt under the Federal law need the protection of good State minimum wage legislation. Fourteen States have no minimum wage legislation in effect, and in all to many of the States the minimums set are so low that even those employees who work full time year round cannot escape poverty.

NOTE.—The data in this report are from the U.S. Department of Commerce, Bureau of the Census; U.S. Department of Health, Education, and Welfare, Social Security Administration; and U.S. Department of Labor, Bureau of Labor Statistics, Office of the Secretary, and Wage and Hour and Public Contracts Divisons.

[U.S. Dept. of Labor, Women's Bureau, April 1968]

FACT SHEET ON THE AMERICAN FAMILY IN POVERTY

FAMILIES IN POVERTY [1]

About 6.1 million families, or 12 percent of the 48.9 million families in the United States, were poor in 1966. (This was 700,000 less than in 1964; 2.2 million less than in 1959.) Of the poor families, 5.6 million were nonfarm families and .5 million were farm families. An additional 3.6 million families were living in near poverty in 1966. Thus 9.7 million, or 20 percent of all families, were poor or near poor in 1966.

Of the 6.1 million poor families in 1966, 4.3 million were headed by a man and 1.8 million were headed by a woman. Although families headed by a

---

[1] The Social Security Administration poverty-income standard takes into account family size, composition, and place of residence. The index currently used classifies as poor those nonfarm households where total money income is less than $1,635 for the unrelated individual; $2,115 for a couple and $3,335 for a family of four. The near poverty index averages about one-third higher than the poverty index in dollar cost.

woman constituted only 11 percent of all families, they accounted for 30 percent of all poor families. The proportion of all poor nonwhite families that were headed by a woman was even greater—41 percent.

Type of family	All families			Poor families		
	Total	White	Nonwhite	Total	White	Nonwhite
Number (in millions)_____	48.9	44.0	4.9	6.1	4.4	1.7
Percent_____	100.0	100.0	100.0	100.0	100.0	100.0
Husband-wife_____	87.0	88.6	72.3	66.9	71.3	55.6
Male head (without wife)_____	2.4	2.3	4.0	3.4	3.3	3.5
Female head_____	10.6	9.1	23.7	29.7	25.4	40.9

The likelihood of poverty is greater among families headed by a woman than among husband-wife families. The likelihood is even greater if the families headed by a woman are nonwhite. In 1966, 60 percent of the nonwhite and 28 percent of the white families headed by a woman were poor. The comparable proportions for nonwhite and white husband-wife families were 27 and 8 percent, respectively.

Type of family	Poor families					
	Number (in millions)			As percent of all families		
	Total	White	Nonwhite	Total	White	Nonwhite
Total_____	6.1	4.4	1.7	12.4	9.9	34.9
Husband-wife_____	4.1	3.2	.9	9.6	8.0	26.8
Male head (without wife)_____	.2	.1	.1	17.3	14.6	30.8
Female head_____	1.8	1.1	.7	35.0	27.7	60.2

Poverty is less frequent in both white and nonwhite husband-wife families when the wife is in the paid labor force. Among white husband-wife families, 3 percent were poor in 1966 where the wife was a worker, 10 percent where she was not. The comparable proportions for nonwhite husband-wife families were 19 and 34 percent, respectively.

The employment of women family heads takes many such families out of poverty. Among white families headed by a woman in 1966, 19 percent were poor where she was in the labor force, 37 percent where she was not. The comparable proportions for nonwhite families headed by a woman were 50 and 72 percent, respectively.

The depth of poverty suffered by poor families can be measured by comparing the median income of a poor family of a certain size with the established poverty level for a family of similar composition. Thus the median income of poor families headed by a male with two children ($2,307) lacks by more than $1,000 the $3,335 required by a nonfarm family of four to escape poverty. In an even more serious plight are poor families headed by a woman with children in the home. If she has three children, her median income of $2,123 is more than $1,200 less than the minimum required to stay above the poverty line.

MEDIAN INCOME OF POOR FAMILIES

Number of children under 18	Male head			Female head		
	Total	White	Nonwhite	Total	White	Nonwhite
Total_____	$2,578	$2,554	$2,629	$1,823	$1,747	$1,954
1 child_____	1,663	1,623	1,777	1,360	1,413	1,284
2 children_____	2,307	2,348	2,174	1,595	1,635	1,493
3 children_____	2,727	2,723	2,694	2,123	2,041	2,306
4 children_____	3,308	3,400	3,190	2,306	2,161	2,397
5 children_____	3,590	3,868	3,234	2,614	(1)	(1)
6 or more children_____	3,440	3,733	3,164	2,867	(1)	(1)

1 Not shown for base less than 100,000.

CHILDREN IN POVERTY

There were 12.5 million children under 18 years of age living in poverty in 1966—7.5 million white and 5.0 million nonwhite. (This was 1.5 million less than in 1965 and 4.2 million less than in 1959.) About 13 percent of all white children were members of poor families in 1966 as compared with 49 percent of all nonwhite children. The incidence of poverty was highest (78 percent) among children in nonwhite families headed by a woman.

CHILDREN UNDER 18 YEARS LIVING IN POVERTY

Type of family	Number (in thousands)			As percent of all children under 18		
	Total	White	Nonwhite	Total	White	Nonwhite
Total_____	12,540	7,526	5,014	18.0	12.6	49.2
Male head_____	8,117	5,280	2,837	13.0	9.6	38.2
Female head_____	4,423	2,246	2,177	61.0	50.2	78

About 1 child out of 3 in both nonwhite and white poor families in 1966 was under 6 years of age.

NUMBER OF CHILDREN UNDER 18 YEARS LIVING IN POVERTY

[In thousands]

Age of children	Total	White	Nonwhite
Number_____	12,540	7,526.0	5,014
Percent_____	100.0	100.0	100.0
Under 6 years_____	35	34.1	34.6
6 to 17 years_____	65	65.9	63.6

Note: The figures in this fact sheet are from the U.S. Department of Health, Education, and Welfare, Social Security Administration: Research and Statistics Note No. 23—1967 (Dec. 6, 1967).

[U.S. Dept. of Labor, Women's Bureau, Oct. 1966]

FACT SHEET ON NONWHITE WOMEN WORKERS

Recent social, economic, and political developments have helped to improve the status of nonwhite women workers, but still there are substantial differences in the employment patterns of nonwhite and white women. A higher percentage of nonwhite than white women are in the labor force, are working wives, and are working mothers. In general, nonwhite women have higher unemployment rates, lower income, and less schooling than white women, and more of them are concentrated in low-skilled, low-wage occupations.

There were 3.5 million nonwhite women (about 93 percent of them Negro) in the labor force in 1965. Forty-six percent of all nonwhite women (37 percent of all white women) were workers. Nonwhite women were 13 percent of all women workers and 11 percent of all women in the population.

About 324,000 nonwhite women were seeking work in 1965; their unemployment rate was 9.3 percent (5.0 percent for white women). In 1965 almost every third nonwhite girl (every eighth white girl) 14 to 19 years old was looking for a job.

Nonwhite women were in all major occupational groups in 1965. More nonwhite women (30 percent) were in private-household work than in any other single occupation. In contrast, the most popular occupation for white women (34 percent) was clerical work. Another large occupational group for nonwhite women (25 percent) was service work (except private-household). Among white women, approximately the same number were employed in three major occupational groups—professional and technical workers, operatives, and service workers (except private-household). The percent distribution of white and nonwhite women workers in 1965 by major occupational group was as follows:

Major occupational group	Percent distribution of women workers	
	White	Nonwhite
Total	100. 0	100. 0
Professional and technical workers	13. 7	8.
Managers, officials, and proprietors (except farm)	4. 8	1. 5
Clerical workers	34. 1	11. 8
Salesworkers	8. 2	2. 0
Craftsmen and foremen	1. 1	. 7
Operatives	15. 1	14. 4
Nonfarm laborers	. 4	. 7
Private household workers	5. 6	30. 3
Service workers (except private household)	14. 0	24. 5
Farmworkers	2. 8	5. 6

About 30 percent of nonwhite women workers (25 percent of white) were on part-time schedules in 1965. More nonwhite than white women reported involuntary part-time work.

Almost 67 percent of nonwhite women (59 percent of white) reported some income in 1964. Their median income was $1,066 ($1,513 for white women). Income of less than $1,000 was reported by almost 48 percent of nonwhite women (39 percent of white). The median wage or salary income of nonwhite full-time year-round women workers ($2,674) in 1964 was 69 percent of that of white women ($3,859). This represented a substantial improvement since 1939, when it was only 38 percent.

Among women with children under 18 years of age, 46 percent of the nonwhite (34 percent of the white) were in the labor force in March 1965. Among women with children 6 to 17 years of age only, 58 percent of the nonwhite (44 percent of the white) were workers. The comparable percentage for nonwhite women with children under 6 years of age was 38 percent (23 percent for white).

The median number of school years completed by nonwhite women workers 18 years of age and over in March 1965 was 11.1 years (12.3 years for white women). Thirty-two percent of nonwhite women workers (17 percent of white) had completed 8 years or less of schooling : 29 percent of nonwhite (44 percent of white) had completed high school (no college) ; and 8 percent of nonwhite (10 percent of white) had graduated from college.

NOTE.—The sources of these data are the U.S. Department of Commerce, Bureau of the Census and the U.S. Department of Labor, Bureau of Labor Statistics.

[U.S. Dept. of Labor, Women's Bureau, May 1970]

WOMEN PRIVATE HOUSEHOLD WORKERS FACT SHEET*

In 1969 about 1.6 million women were employed as private household workers—including babysitters. Women constituted 98 percent of all workers in private household employment.

Annual wages in this occupation are very low :

In 1968 the median wage of even those women 14 years of age and over who were year-round full-time private household workers, including babysitters, was $1,523.[1]

The total cash income—which included wage and self-employment income as well as all forms of social insurance and public assistance payments—of almost all women in this field of employment in 1968 was still very low :

82 percent had total cash incomes under $2,000, and 57 percent, under $1,000.

Median total cash income of the women who were year-round full-time workers—about one-fifth the total—was $1,701.

Almost three-fifths of the women heads of families who reported private household work as the job held longest during 1968 had incomes below the poverty level.[2]

*The data in this fact sheet refer to women 16 years of age and over unless otherwise indicated.
[1] Median means half above, half below ; year round, 50 to 52 weeks ; and full time, 35 hours or more a week.
[2] The poverty level is based on the Social Security Administration's poverty thresholds, adjusted annually in accordance with changes in the Department of Labor's Consumer Price Index. Currently classified as poor are those nonfarm households where total money income is less than $1,748 for an unrelated individual, $2,262 for a couple, and $3,553 for a family of four.

The low annual wages of almost all women private household workers reflect the intermittent character of their employment as well as their low rates of pay when employed:

Part time/full time:
In 1969, 64 percent of the women private household workers worked part time (less than 35 hours a week).
Of the full-time workers, 64 percent worked between 35 and 40 hours a week. The remaining 36 percent worked longer hours.

Part year/full year:
Of women private household workers in 1968:
4 out of 10 worked 26 weeks or less;
2 out of 10 worked between 27 and 49 weeks; and
About 4 out of 10 worked 50 to 52 weeks.

Many women private household workers are heads of families:
Nearly 200,000 women in this occupation were heads of families in March 1969.
In 1960, two-thirds of the families headed by either men or women private household workers included children under 18 years of age. About one-fourth of the families with children under 18 had at least four children in the family.

Of the 1.4 million women 14 years of age and over who reported their occupations as dayworkers, housekeepers, maids, and laundresses, but excluding baby-sitters, in 1960:

More lived in the South than elsewhere:
About 54 percent were in the South;
Over 19 percent were in the Northeastern States;
About 18 percent were in the North Central States; and
More than 9 percent were in the West.

Negroes predominated:
Some 64 percent were Negro;
About 35 percent were white; and
Almost 1 percent were other nonwhites.

Relatively few were 'live-in" workers:
About 11 percent "lived in."

This was an urban occupation:
About 74 percent were in urban areas;
Some 21 percent were in rural nonfarm areas; and
About 5 percent were in rural farm areas.

The average private household worker was about 6 years older than the typical woman in the labor force:
The median age of all employed private household workers was 46 years. 53 percent were 45 years and over; 29 percent were over 55; and 10 percent were 65 and over.
The median age for white employed private household workers was 53 years, compared with 43 years for nonwhites.

In March 1949 less than 3 out of 10 private household workers were single:
27 percent were single;
37 percent were married and living with their husbands; and
36 percent were either widowed, divorced, or separated.

Educationally, the private household worker is disadvantaged:

Educational attainment March 1968	Women private household workers [1]		
	Total	White	Nonwhite
Years: Median years of school completed_____	8.8	9.5	8.4
Percent:			
Less than 8 years [2]_____	32.3	22.4	42.0
High school completed_____	19.3	25.3	13.5
Some college (1 to 4 years or more)_____	4.2	7.0	1.3

[1] 18 years of age and older.
[2] Includes persons reporting no school years completed.

Legislatively, the private household worker is disadvantaged:
Workers in this occupation receive credits toward an old-age, survivors, or disability pension only if they earn a maximum of $50 from any one employer in a calendar quarter. While private household workers are eligible for coverage under the Social Security Act, they are not covered by the

Federal minimum wage and hour law.

By and large, they are not afforded the protection of the major forms of labor legislation and social insurance from which most other workers benefit:

Wages.—Wisconsin is the only State with a minimum wage order which, effective July 1, 1970, covers domestic service workers (women and minors) without numerical or hourly exclusions. Private household workers are covered by the statutory rate in four States: Arkansas, where the law applies only to those private household employees who work for an employer of five or more persons in a regular employment relationship; Michigan, where the minimum wage law applies only to those private household workers who work for an employer of four or more persons at any one time in a calendar year; Nebraska, where the law covers private household workers but not babysitters and applies only to employers of four or more workers (except seasonal workers) ; and West Virginia, where the law applies only to those who work for an employer of at least six persons during a calendar week.

Hours.—Washington's maximum hours law establishes a 60-hour week for household workers; Montana's constitution establishes an 8-hour day for all employees, except those in agriculture.

Unemployment Compensation.—New York and Hawaii have limited coverage of domestic workers under their State unemployment compensation laws. In New York, coverage has been extended to all persons in personal domestic service in a private household where the householder pays $500 or more in a calendar quarter to all such employees. And in Hawaii, private household workers are covered only if they earn at least $225 from an employer in a calendar quarter.

Workmen's Compensation.—Coverage is compulsory for all regularly employed private household workers in Puerto Rico and for all but part-time workers in Alaska. Connecticut has compulsory coverage for all private household workers employed more than 26 hours a week by one employer; California, for those working more than 52 hours a week for one employer; Ohio, for those in households where the employer has three or more such employees; and New York, for those employed a minimum of 48 hours a week by one employer in cities of 40,000 or more. Massachusetts has compulsory coverage for private household workers other than those who are seasonal or casual, or who work less than 16 hours a week. For the latter group, coverage is elective. In Michigan, while coverage is compulsory in households employing three or more workers, the employer is not liable for any such employee unless the person worked 35 hours or more a week for at least 13 weeks during the preceding 52 weeks. Coverage is elective in New Jersey, but the employer is not required to insure. In jurisdictions that do not specifically cover private household workers under workmen's compensation laws, such workers may be brought under voluntary coverage, except in Alabama, the District of Columbia, Iowa, West Virginia, and Wyoming.

NOTE.—The statistical data in this report are from U.S. Department of Commerce, Bureau of the Census, and U.S. Department of Labor, Bureau of Labor Statistics. Legislative data are as of January 1970, except as otherwise noted.

[U.S. Dept. of Labor, Women's Bureau, June 1970]

LABOR LAWS AFFECTING PRIVATE HOUSEHOLD WORKERS

Private household work is one of the major fields of employment for women, who accounted for nearly all of the approximately 1.6 million household workers 16 years of age and older employed in March 1970. However, private household work is also one of the least attractive fields of employment, since the wages and working conditions often are substandard.

The 1968 median (half above, half below) wage of even those women private household workers 14 years of age and over who worked full time for 50 to 52 weeks a year was only $1,523. Since many workers in the occupation are employed only part time or part year, their earnings are clearly marginal. Moreover, surveys show that in this field of employment the fringe benefits and working conditions, including hours of work, have not kept pace with those in other fields.

One reason for substandard employment conditions in private household work is the exemption of the occupation from most laws providing labor standards protection. Legislation to improve existing working conditions and bring new status to the occupation would benefit workers now engaged in household employment and would attract new workers to meet the continuing demand for assistance in the home.

The National Committee on Household Employment, other private organizations, and a number of public agencies have expressed interest in developing standards for this occupation. The following information summarizes labor laws currently affecting private household workers and is an indication of areas where programs should be instituted or expanded.

Wages.—The Fair Labor Standards Act (FLSA), the Federal wage and hour law of most general application, applies to employees engaged in interstate or foreign commerce or in the production of goods for commerce, as well as certain large enterprises. As presently interpreted, this does not include private household workers who, as a result, are outside the protection of the standards in the act, including the requirement that most covered employees be paid at least $1.60 an hour and not less than 1½ times their regular rates for hours worked in excess of 40 a week.

In 29 States, the District of Columbia, and Puerto Rico, a minimum wage rate is set by law. Premium pay for overtime is required by law in 12 of these jurisdictions. However, it appears that the provisions in only four of these laws— those of Arkansas, Michigan, Nebraska, and West Virginia—are sufficiently broad to cover private household workers, and these laws contain numerical exemptions which almost eliminate household workers as a practical matter.

The Arkansas law, which requires the payment of at least $1.10 an hour, increasing to $1.20 on January 1, 1971, does not exclude private household workers from coverage. The law applies only to employers of five or more employees in a regular employment relationship.

The Michigan minimum wage requirement of $1.25 an hour applies to employers of four or more workers at any one time during a calendar year.

The Nebraska minimum wage law, which requires the payment of at least $1.00 an hour, specifically exempts babysitters employed in or about a private home, but not private household workers. However, the law applies only to employers of four or more persons at any one time except for certain specified seasonal employment.

The West Virginia minimum wage requirement of $1.00 an hour, plus 1½ times employees' regular rates for hours worked in excess of 48 a week, applies to employers of six or more workers in any week.

Twelve States have wage board programs under which regulations setting a minimum wage in an industry or occupation, or for a designated group of workers, can be issued pursuant to prescribed administrative procedures. It appears that under existing authority six of these States—California, Colorado, New Jersey, North Dakota, Utah, and Wisconsin—could issue orders covering private household workers, and that in most of these States the orders could include premium pay for overtime work. Only Wisconsin actually has issued a minimum wage order covering household workers. In California a wage board has recommended the issuance of a wage order covering women and minors who are domestic employees.

The Wisconsin order requires a minimum weekly wage of $58.50 for adult women and minors 18 years of age and over who are employed in domestic service in private homes for 45 hours or more a week if board and lodging are not furnished; $42.90 if board only is furnished; and $32.40 if board and lodging are furnished. For minors 17 years of age and under, the wage is $49.50 if board and lodging are not furnished, and lesser amounts if board and/or lodging are furnished. If employees are paid on an hourly basis, the rate is $1.30 an hour for adult women and minors 18 years of age and over and $1.10 an hour for minors 17 years of age and under. However, the order excludes from minimum wage coverage casual employment in or around a home in work usual to the home of the employer. "Casual" employment is defined as employment for not more than 15 hours per week for any one employer.

Wisconsin orders must be reviewed periodically and the rates revised, based on changes in the Consumer Price Index. A recent revision, effective July 1, 1970, provides that the minimum weekly wage for adult women and minors 18 years of age and over who are employed in domestic service in private homes for 45 hours or more a week will increase to $65.25 if board and lodging are not furnished; to $47.85 if board only is furnished; and to $36.25 if board and lodging are furnished. The hourly rate for adult women and minors 18 years of age and over will increase to $1.45. The hourly rate for minors 17 years of age and under will remain at $1.10. The definition of casual employment will change, so that the applicable rate will apply to domestic service in private homes regardless of the number of hours worked by the employee for any one employer.

Hours of Work.—There are no Federal laws of general application regulating hours of work, with the exception of the premium pay requirements in the FLSA, previously discussed. Laws or orders in 38 States and the District of Columbia specify that covered workers must not be employed more than a set number of hours a day and/or a set number of hours a week. Only three of these States—Kansas, Montana, and Washington—have laws which either could or do provide protection from excessive hours of work for private household workers.

Under the Kansas law, power exists to issue orders limiting the number of hours women household workers may be employed, but no such orders have been issued. The constitution of Montana appears to set an 8-hour limit on the workday of all workers in all employments except farming and stock-raising, thus covering workers in private homes. The State of Washington has provided by statute that private household workers, both male and female, shall not be employed more than 60 hours a week, except in emergency.

In addition, Industrial Welfare Order No. 33, issued by the State of Washington, recommends that female household workers not be employed in any week for more than 10 hours a day for 5 days, 4 hours a day for 1 day, and 6 hours on the remaining day. The order defines free hours as those hours when the employee is entirely free from any responsibility to the employer or the job; defines an emergency as an unforeseen condition calling for immediate action that is neither continuous nor regular; and states that overtime may be compensated for by extra time off during the same week to keep working time within the statutory 60-hour maximum.

Wage Payment and Collection.—There are no Federal laws of general application regarding wage payment and collection. Many States have comprehensive laws on this subject, and all States have laws relating to one or more of the following:

    (1) payment of wages in lawful money or medium redeemable in lawful money,

    (2) establishment of a regular payday, and

    (3) prompt payment when a worker is discharged or resigns.

    (1) *Medium of payment.*—These laws generally specify that employees must be paid for their labor in cash or check redeemable in cash. The medium of payment laws are sufficiently broad to cover private household workers in 33 jurisdictions—Alaska. Arizona, Arkansas, California, Colorado, Connecticut, Delaware, the District of Columbia, Florida, Georgia, Hawaii, Idaho, Illinois, Indiana, Louisiana, Massachusetts, Minnesota, Montana, Nevada, New Jersey, New Mexico, New York, North Carolina, North Dakota, Oklahoma, Oregon, Pennsylvania, Puerto Rico, South Carolina, Tennessee, Texas, Virginia, and West Virginia.

    (2) *Frequency of payments.*—These laws generally provide that the employer must pay his workers within the time specified in the law—for example, 1 week, 2 weeks, or 1 month—although usually he may pay more frequently if he chooses. The provisions for frequency of payment appear sufficiently broad to cover private household workers in 25 jurisdictions—Alaska, Arizona, California, Colorado, Connecticut, Delaware. the District of Columbia, Hawaii, Idaho, Indiana, Massachusetts, Montana, Nevada, New Jersey, New York, North Dakota, Ohio (if five or more employees), Oklahoma, Oregon, Pennsylvania, Puerto Rico, Tennessee (if five or more employees), Texas, Virginia, and West Virginia.

In addition to their regular frequency of payment laws, two States—California and Massachusetts—have special provisions relating to private household workers. The California law provides that employees who receive both board and lodging from the employer must be paid at least once each calendar month on a day designated in advance as a regular payday. A Massachusetts law provides that private household workers may be paid monthly.

    (3) *Termination payments.*—These laws provide that an employer must pay a worker at, or within a specified period of time after, termination of employment. The laws requiring termination payments immediately or within a specified time are of sufficiently general coverage to include private household workers in 28 jurisdictions—Alaska, Arizona, California, Colorado, Connecticut, Delaware, the District of Columbia, Hawaii, Idaho, Illinois, Indiana, Louisiana, Maine, Massachusetts, Minnesota, Montana, Nevada, New Jersey, New York, North Dakota, Oklahoma, Oregon, Pennsylvania, Puerto Rico, Texas, Virginia, West Virginia, and Wyoming.

Unemployment Compensation.—Under the unemployment insurance program, covered wage earners who lose their jobs are paid specified amounts for varying periods of time. The program is operated jointly by the Federal and State Governments, with the States establishing standards for the payment of benefits. Employers covered by the program are required to pay a payroll tax, and the tax revenues are put into a fund from which the unemployment benefits are paid. In most jurisdictions, employers who are not required by law to participate in the program may do so voluntarily.

Only two States—Hawaii and New York—have unemployment insurance laws with mandatory coverage of private household workers. Coverage in these States is limited, since the Hawaii law covers only those employers who pay $225 or more for household service in a calendar quarter, and the New York law covers only those who pay $500 or more to household employees in a calendar quarter.

Voluntary coverage of private household workers is permitted in all jurisdictions (including Hawaii and New York, regardless of the monetary test), except Alabama and Massachusetts.

Workmen's Compensation.—Workmen's compensation programs are established by State law (with some limited exceptions related to Federal employment or property). When covered employees suffer work-related injury or death, benefits are provided for the employees and/or their families. Private household workers generally are excluded from workmen's compensation coverage, although some steps have been taken toward coverage in eight States and Puerto Rico.

The Alaska law covers private household workers except for those employed part time. California covers those who work more than 52 hours a week for one employer. Connecticut covers those who work more than 26 hours a week for one employer. In Massachusetts all seasonal, casual, and parttime (less than 16 hours a week) workers are included in elective coverage, while all other come under compulsory coverage.

The Michigan law covers private household workers employed at least 35 hours a week for at least 13 weeks during the preceding 52 weeks. The New Jersey law covers all private household workers but does not require the employer to insure. The New York law applies to private household workers employed by the same employer at least 48 hours a week in cities of 40,000 or more; however, the law sets no penalty for failure to secure compensation. In Ohio workers are covered when the employer has three or more employees. Puerto Rico covers all workers regularly employed in private household service.

In those jurisdictions which do not cover private household workers, voluntary coverage is permitted in all except Alabama, the District of Columbia, Iowa, West Virginia, and Wyoming.

Social Security.—The Federal Social Security Act, which establishes the old-age survivors, disability, and health insurance program, provides compulsory coverage of private household workers who receive the same benefits as other workers covered by the program. For the purpose of determining the insured status of private household workers, a quarter of coverage is credited to a worker who receives at least $50 in cash wages from one employer in a calendar quarter. If the worker meets this test, wages received from all employers are credited for purposes of computing benefits.

It should be noted that some employers of private household workers fail to comply with the reporting requirements of the act. This practice has serious adverse effects on the protection available to those workers.

[U.S. Dept. of Labor, Bureau of Labor Statistics, Special Labor Force Report No. 120, *Monthly Labor Review,* May 1970]

MARITAL AND FAMILY CHARACTERISTICS OF THE U.S. LABOR FORCE

(By Elizabeth Waldman)

SPECIAL LABOR FORCE REPORT SHOWS THAT MARRIED WOMEN, MANY YOUNG AND CHILDLESS, ACCOUNT FOR NEARLY HALF OF THE INCREASE OF WORKERS IN 1968–69

As married women continued to respond to the demand for additional workers under the tight labor market conditions of the late 1960's, the multiworker family became more prevalent. In March 1969, the proportion of families in which both the husband and another family member worked was 52 percent (table 1), as compared with 43 percent in 1960. The other family member was far more likely to be the wife than a son or daughter. The proportion of multiworker families was 11 percentage points higher among Negroes than among whites, one indication of the apparently greater need for the earnings of more than one worker among the Negro families.

These facts and other information obtained from annual nationwide surveys of the marital and family characteristics of workers[1] provide the basis for the discussion in this article of the response of wives and other family members to the increased need for workers. The article also examines labor force activity, among mothers who are divorced, widowed, or separated from their husbands. Although this group is not a large proportion of the female labor force, their situation is of interest because current proposals for social welfare legislation concern them and the well-being of their children. Other topics include education, occupations, residence, and income. These national data provide an average measure which local officials may use to gage their own area situation.

OVER-THE-YEAR CHANGES

Between March 1968 and 1969, the additional jobs generated by booming business conditions reduced the number of unemployed husbands to about 620,000, of whom 85,000 were Negro.[2] The low unemployment rates of these family heads—4.5 percent of the whites in the labor force and 2.8 percent of the Negroes—indicated that large proportions of them were unemployed a relatively short time. About 75 percent of the unemployed husbands had been jobless for less than 15 weeks.

Of the 1.8-million increase in the labor force over the year ending in March 1969, wives supplied 775,000 and married men 400,000 (table 2). The contribution of single, widowed, divorced, and separated persons was comparatively more modest and mirrored their population growth. Most of the increase of married men in the labor force was among young husbands 25 to 29 years old, entering or reentering the labor force as they completed their schooling or military obligations. More than 300,000 of the additional married women were also young—between 20 and 24 years—representing an unprecedented yearly increase of 18 percent for wives in this age group in the labor force.

In part these increases are a function of more young persons in the population. The 20- to 24-year-olds among them represent the generation of post-World War II babies now reaching the ages when marriages most commonly occur, and their greater numbers will create an era of the young family in the early 1970's. In addition, the proportion of wives 20 to 24 years old with no children and, therefore, greater freedom to work has risen, undoubtedly reflecting such factors as increased birth control and the desire to take advantage of job opportunities. Moreover, there has been an increase in the proportion of young couples with or without children who prefer two paychecks during a period of rising prices.

Between March 1968 and March 1969, labor force participation rates for wives rose regardless of the presence of school-age or preschool-age children in the home, but young children continued to exert a major influence on the likelihood of a wife's working (chart 1). About a fourth of all wives with some children under 3 were in the labor force. The proportion rose to a third for the wives whose children were old enough to be in school. The labor force rate among wives with no children under 18 was lower than that of wives with school-age children, because of their age composition—half of them were at least 55 years old.

Negro wives, as a rule, have higher labor force participation rates than white wives, 51 percent compared with 39 percent in March 1969. Their rates tend to

---

[1] This article is based primarily on information from supplementary questions in the March 1969 monthly survey of the labor force, conducted for the Bureau of Labor Statistics by the Bureau of the Census through its Current Population Survey. Most of the monthly data presented here relate to the population 16 years old and over, including inmates of institutions and those members of the Armed Forces living off post or with their families on post (1,029,000 in March 1969). Sampling variability may be relatively large in cases where numbers are small. Therefore, small differences between estimates or percents based on them should be used and interpreted with caution.

This is the 11th in a series of reports on this subject. The most recent contained data for March 1967 and was published in the *Monthly Labor Review*, April 1968, pp. 14–22. It was reprinted with additional tabular data and an explanatory note as Special Labor Force Report No. 94.

Unless otherwise indicated, references to married persons relate to those living with their spouses. References to families and their heads are only to husband-wife families. (By definition, the husband is the head in these families.) A married couple or a parent-child group related to the head of the family and sharing his living quarters is treated as part of the head's family.

[2] Data for all persons other than white are used in this report to represent data for Negroes, since the latter constitute about 92 percent of all persons other than white in the United States.

fluctuate by the presence and age of children in much the same manner as for white wives. That is, Negro wives with preschool-age children had a smaller participation rate (44 percent) than those with school-age children (63 percent), and wives with school-age children had a rate greater than that for wives without children (48 percent).

MORE YOUNG WIVES WORK

Prior to the mid-1960's, the presence of young children was frequently cited as the principal factor responsible for the comparatively smaller labor force gains for younger married women. This was true because only a small proportion of mothers of young children were in the labor force. The proportion did not show much increase over the 1940's and 1950's. In the 1960's, however, the most significant increases in women's labor force participation took place among younger married women, while the number of workers over 35 and their participation rates climbed upward at a much slower pace than in the previous two decades. Thus, between 1960 and 1969 the number of wives under 35 in the labor force increased faster than the number of wives 35 and over, as shown below:

	Number of workers (in thousands)		Labor force rate	
	Less than 35 years	35 years or more	Less than 35 years	35 years or more
March 1969	6,179	11,416	40.1	39.3
March 1960	3,948	8,305	28.2	31.7
April 1950	3,618	4,932	25.0	23.0
March 1940	2,110	2,090	18.4	12.2

TABLE 1.—EMPLOYMENT STATUS OF FAMILY HEAD AND LABOR FORCE STATUS OF WIFE AND OTHER FAMILY MEMBERS, BY COLOR, MARCH 1969—HUSBAND-WIFE FAMILIES

Labor force status and relationship to head	Total	White	Negro and other races
Head employed:			
Number of families (in thousands)	37,523	34,588	2,935
Percent distribution	100.0	100.0	100.0
Wife or other member in labor force	51.8	50.9	61.7
Wife only in labor force	33.4	32.4	44.9
Wife and other member in labor force	8.9	8.9	8.9
Other member only in labor force	9.5	9.6	7.9
Neither wife nor other member in labor force	48.2	49.1	38.3
Head unemployed:			
Number of families (in thousands)	621	537	84
As percent of heads in the labor force	1.6	1.5	2.8
Percent distribution	100.0	100.0	100.0
Wife or other member in labor force	51.7	49.0	68.6
Wife only in labor force	36.2	34.1	49.4
Wife and other member in labor force	8.3	7.7	12.0
Other member only in labor force	7.2	7.2	7.2
Neither wife nor other member in labor force	48.3	50.9	31.3

Note: Due to rounding, sums of individual items may not equal totals.

Wives who were 20 to 24 years of age made the largest contribution to the labor force during the 1960's, and a major part of it occurred between 1968 and 1969. Since 1960, the population of wives in these ages had grown by about 29 percent, while their labor force had more than doubled to 2.2 million. Of this labor force increase, about 200,000 was due to changes in the composition of the population by presence and age of children, and some 600,000 occurred because of increases in labor force participation rates.

Over the decade, the labor force participation rate rose from 63 to 72 percent for childless wives 20 to 24 years old. Even more strikingly, the rate increased from 18 to 33 percent for wives with children under 6, with the most rapid changes occurring in the latter years of the decade (chart 2). Many young married women may simply have taken advantage of the tight labor market situation and the opportunity to earn money and bolster the income of their young husbands.

Some people are inclined to explain the increase in young childless wives in the population and work force solely in terms of the recent development of new contraceptive methods. However, this is a tenuous premise, since the two measures of the trend in births—the more popularly used birth rate (number of births per 1,000 population) and the more finely tuned fertility rate (number of births per 1,000 women of childbearing age, 15 to 44)—have similar historical patterns. Both rates have declined in periods of depression and prosperity, whatever the birth control methods available at the time. In the midst of the Great Depression, the birth rate had declined to 18.4 ; it rose to a peak of 26.6 in 1947, remained high (24.1 to 25.3) in the 1950's, and declined during our most recent period of prosperity to 18.4 in 1966, and about 17.7 in 1969.

A more relevant explanation of the increase in young childless wives and their increased labor force participation must include the reasons why married couples decide to use any form of birth control (abstinence, pills, etc.) at any point in time.

Today, as in the past, young couples may choose to delay having children so they may achieve greater mobility, either socially or at work, or they may not feel psychologically ready for childrearing. Also, young couples may prefer to postpone starting their families or to limit the number of children they have because they feel that children are liabilities in attaining a particular level of living. Working wives in younger families contribute proportionately more to family income than working wives in older families. Among wives with paid work experience during 1968, where husbands were under 25 years of age, median family income was $7,235 ; where husbands were over 25, it was $10,960. On the average, wives in the younger families contributed proportionately more (31 percent) to family income than wives in the older families (27 percent).

Childbirth patterns in the mid-1960's and later indicate that women under 30 have relatively low birth rates because they may choose to postpone having their first child.[3] On the other hand, women over 30 have been having low birth rates because most of them married early and completed their families. This is evident in the change in the married women's composition by child status. By 1969, proportionately fewer wives 25 to 34 years old had children under 6 and more had school-age children, but there was no change in the proportion with no children under 18. Over the decade, the number of wives 25 to 34 in the labor force grew by 38 percent, with the participation rate increasing considerably for the mothers of school- and preschool-age children (chart 2).

MARITAL COMPOSITION

Generally, the marital composition of the labor force was about the same at the end of the 1960's as it had been for many years. Married persons predominated, and, as indicated earlier, their share of the work force increased with the growth of the proportion of wives who worked. Next in rank came single persons (those who have never been married), for whom the effects of the "marriage squeeze"[4]—an excess of women over men in the ages at which marriage most often occurs—were evident in the population, but did not affect the proportion of women workers.

In March 1969, every ninth worker in the United States was divorced, separated,[5] or widowed, three marital categories dominated by women. Of the 50.4 million men in the labor force, only about 5 percent were divorced or separated, and relatively few (1 percent) were widowers. Of the nearly 30 million working women, 11 percent were divorced or separated and 8 percent were widows.

From March 1960 to March 1969, the number of women whose marriages had been disrupted by divorce or separation increased by about 30 percent to 5.3 million. Chances of finding these women in the work force are usually much greater than finding wives, widows, or even single women. As shown earlier (chart 1), the labor force participation rate of wives rose steadily through the 1960's from 31 to 40 percent. But the rate for divorcees, which is much higher (72 percent), showed no increase throughout the decade. Among separated women, the rate rose only from 52 to 54 percent.

[3] See "Women by Number of Own Children Under 5 Years Old, 1968 and 1967," *Current Population Reports,* Population Characteristics, Series P–20, No. 184, June 16, 1969 (U.S. Department of Commerce, Bureau of the Census).

[4] For a more detailed discussion of the "marriage squeeze" which is not expected to last beyond 1980, see *Current Population Reports,* Series P–25, No. 388, March 14, 1968 (U.S. Department of Commerce, Bureau of the Census), pp. 12 and 13.

[5] In this report, the term "separated" comprehends the broad marital category, "married, spouse absent." Persons in this category include those who are legally separated, and those whose spouses are away in the Armed Forces, in institutions, in regular employment elsewhere, or for other reasons.

TABLE 2.—EMPLOYMENT STATUS OF PERSONS 16 YEARS AND OVER, BY MARITAL STATUS, SEX, AND COLOR, MARCH 1968 AND 1969

[In thousands]

Marital status, sex, and color	1969						1968					
	Population	Total¹		Labor force			Population	Total¹		Labor force		
		Number	Percent of population	Employed	Unemployed Number	Unemployed Percent of labor force		Number	Percent of population	Employed	Unemployed Number	Unemployed Percent of labor force
ALL PERSONS												
Total, men	64,831	50,397	77.7	47,907	1,461	2.9	63,821	49,736	77.9	47,050	1,618	3.3
Married, wife present	44,440	38,623	86.9	37,065	662	1.7	43,947	38,225	87.0	36,552	787	2.1
Married, wife absent	1,689	1,122	66.4	1,058	61	5.4	1,566	980	62.6	921	54	5.5
Widowed	2,241	678	30.3	651	25	3.7	2,142	704	32.9	683	20	2.8
Divorced	1,571	1,177	74.9	1,133	38	3.2	1,570	1,132	72.1	1,078	50	4.4
Single	14,890	8,797	59.1	8,000	675	7.7	14,596	8,695	59.6	7,816	707	8.1
Total, women	71,919	29,898	41.6	28,613	1,285	4.3	70,679	28,778	40.7	27,468	1,310	4.6
Married, husband present	44,440	17,595	39.6	16,947	648	3.7	43,947	16,821	38.2	16,199	622	3.7
Married, husband absent	2,785	1,505	54.0	1,412	93	6.2	2,646	1,413	53.4	1,292	121	8.6
Widowed	9,500	2,504	26.4	2,427	77	3.1	9,305	2,483	26.7	2,401	82	3.3
Divorced	2,505	1,793	71.6	1,734	59	3.3	2,400	1,704	71.0	1,632	72	4.2
Single	12,689	6,501	51.2	6,093	408	6.3	12,381	6,357	51.3	5,944	413	6.5
IN NEGRO AND OTHER RACES												
Total, men	6,831	4,952	72.5	4,631	249	5.0	6,736	4,994	74.1	4,615	311	6.2
Married, wife present	3,607	3,126	86.7	2,965	95	3.0	3,604	3,160	87.7	2,976	129	4.1
Married, wife absent	542	380	70.1	360	20	5.3	570	411	72.1	391	20	4.9
Widowed	393	150	38.2	139	11	7.3	344	132	38.4	125	7	5.3
Divorced	193	153	79.3	148	5	3.3	195	149	76.4	147	2	1.3
Single	2,096	1,143	54.5	1,019	118	10.3	2,023	1,142	56.4	976	153	13.4
Total, women	7,880	3,797	48.2	3,517	280	7.4	7,694	3,691	48.0	3,385	306	8.3
Married, husband present	3,631	1,853	51.0	1,747	106	5.7	3,593	1,794	49.9	1,687	107	6.0
Married, husband absent	974	555	57.0	521	34	6.1	918	539	58.7	489	50	9.3
Widowed	1,145	345	30.1	334	11	3.2	1,160	351	30.3	333	18	5.1
Divorced	341	227	66.6	214	13	5.7	351	261	74.4	238	23	8.8
Single	1,789	817	45.7	701	116	14.2	1,672	746	44.6	638	108	14.5

¹ The male labor force includes members of the Armed Forces living off post or with their families on post, not shown separately.

Why this difference in labor force rates? The most obvious elements are the presence or absence of children, the ages of the women concerned, and their need for self-support. Divorcees in both the population and the labor force were older, on the average, than wives and separated women (table 3). Recent data show that of all divorces granted during 1967 in a 22-State area,[6] 39 percent of the couples had no children under 18 and 23 percent had only one child under 18. That year, the average age of women at the time of divorce was 30.1 years. The labor force rate for divorcees was 82 percent for those 25 to 34 years old, and not significantly lower until the ages of 55 and over; for divorcees 20 to 24 years old, the rate was 74 percent. In contrast, the labor force rate among wives 20 to 24 years old was 48 percent. At ages 25 to 34 it was down to 37 percent, rising to 48 percent between ages 45 and 54.

In March 1969, the proportion of divorcees with preschool-age children was less than half that of married or separated women. Even so, with children under 6 years of age, divorcees had much greater labor force participation rate than the other mothers of young children, suggesting that many have insufficient or no alimony and may have to work.

Separated women tend to be younger than other women who have ever been married. Their distribution in the population and labor force by presence of children resembles that of wives, and their labor force participation rate falls between those of wives and divorcees.

Not only were their participation rates higher, but divorced and separated women were more likely than wives to be employed in full-time jobs, about 90 and 83 percent, respectively, and the presence of children made little difference in the proportion. Among employed married women, 3 out of 4 worked at full-time jobs in March 1969. This proportion, which was constant throughout the 1960's, varied by the presence of children from 67 percent for wives with children under 6 to 70 percent with children 6 to 17, and 81 percent with no children under 18.

About 650,000 wives and 230,000 divorced, separated, and widowed women were unemployed in March 1969. The 3.7-percent unemployment rate for wives was somewhat above that for divorcees or widows, but well below the rate for separated women (6.2 percent). Unemployment rates among wives and separated women were especially high for those who were mothers of children under 6.

Three quarters of the 9.5 million widows in our country in 1969 did not work and had no young children at home. Widows who were in the labor force were considerably younger than the nonworkers, as indicated by the 17-year difference in their median ages—58 years for workers, 75 years for nonworkers. Like employed married women, 71 percent of the employed widows held full-time jobs. One out of eight of the employed widows had school-age children, and nearly all of these mothers headed their families.

White-Negro differences. The marital composition of Negro workers is strikingly different from that of white workers. In March 1969, 78 percent of the white men in the labor force were married, 17 percent were single, and 5 percent were widowed, divorced, or separated. For Negro men, these proportions were 65, 21, and 14 percent, respectively. About 60 percent of the white women in the labor force were married, and the proportion in the other ever-married group was 18 percent; the proportions for Negro women were 49 and 30 percent.

---

[6] *Monthly Vital Statistics Report*, Vol. 18, No. 1, Supplement, April 16, 1969 (U.S. Department of Health, Education, and Welfare, National Center for Health Statistics).

TABLE 3.—LABOR FORCE AND UNEMPLOYMENT STATUS OF WOMEN EVER MARRIED, BY COLOR AND BY PRESENCE AND AGE OF CHILDREN, MARCH 1969

Items	All women ever married					Women ever married, Negro and other races				
	Total	Married, husband present	Divorced	Husband absent	Widowed	Total	Married, husband present	Divorced	Husband absent	Widowed
Population:										
Number (in thousands)	59,230	44,440	2,505	2,785	9,500	6,091	3,631	341	974	1,145
Percent	100.0	100.0	100.0	100.0	100.0	100.0	100.0	100.0	100.0	100.0
No children under 18 years	52.0	43.1	61.8	47.5	92.3	48.2	38.3	50.1	41.8	84.2
With children 6 to 17 years only	24.5	28.5	24.7	24.4	6.2	24.5	27.6	31.1	27.3	10.3
With children under 6 years	23.4	28.4	13.5	28.1	1.5	27.4	34.1	18.8	30.9	5.5
Median age	46	42	46	38	70	43	39	42	39	65
Labor force:										
Number (in thousands)	23,397	17,595	1,793	1,505	2,504	2,980	1,853	227	555	345
Percent	100.0	100.0	100.0	100.0	100.0	100.0	100.0	100.0	100.0	100.0
No children under 18 years	50.4	44.6	59.4	49.2	85.5	44.1	36.2	49.3	46.5	78.8
With children 6 to 17 years only	31.5	34.9	27.7	27.8	12.5	30.3	34.2	32.6	28.8	14.2
With children under 6 years	18.0	20.4	12.9	23.0	2.0	25.2	29.6	18.1	24.7	7.0
Median age	43	41	43	37	58	41	39	39	39	55
Labor force participation rate	39.5	39.6	71.6	54.0	26.4	48.9	51.0	66.6	57.0	30.1
No children under 18 years	38.3	41.0	68.8	55.9	24.4	44.8	48.2	65.5	63.4	28.2
With children 6 to 17 years only	50.7	48.6	80.5	61.7	53.2	61.5	63.3	69.8	60.2	41.5
With children under 6 years	30.4	28.5	68.1	44.2	34.5	45.0	44.3	(¹)	45.5	(¹)
Unemployment rate	3.7	3.7	3.3	6.2	3.1	5.5	5.7	5.7	6.1	3.2
No children under 18 years	2.9	3.0	2.2	3.9	2.7	3.0	3.4	2.7	2.3	2.9
With children 6 to 17 years only	3.2	2.8	5.2	5.2	5.7	3.9	3.2	(¹)	4.4	(¹)
With children under 6 years	6.9	6.6	4.3	12.1	(¹)	11.7	11.5	(¹)	15.3	(¹)

¹ Percent not shown where base is less than 75,000.

CHILDREN AND THEIR FAMILIES

Over half of the 50.5 million families in the United States in March 1969 had children [7] under 18. At that time there were 67 million children below that age level, and most of them (85 percent) were in families where both parents were present and the father was employed. Another 10 percent of the children were in broken families headed by women; the mothers of half of this group were employed, and the mothers of almost the same proportion were not in the labor force. Relatively few were jobseekers, as shown below:

| | | Family with male head | | Family with female head |
	Total	Husband-wife family	Other	
Children:				
Number (in thousands)	66,979.0	59,447.0	655.0	6,877.0
Percent	100.0	100.0	100.0	100.0
Labor force status of head:				
Employed	90.6	95.4	87.8	49.2
Unemployed	1.8	1.6	1.7	3.3
Not in labor force	7.6	3.0	10.5	47.5

Almost a million children had jobless fathers, and another quarter million had unemployed mothers who were family heads. Families headed by jobless fathers tended to have more school and preschool-age children, on the average (2.64), than those in which the fathers were employed (2.37). The parallel situation among families headed by women was, on the average, 2.36 and 2.14 children, respectively. Families that averaged the largest number of children, 2.73, were those headed by nonworking mothers.

The consequences of income disparities between families headed by men and those headed by women are well known. Low family income may be translated into inadequate food, shelter, clothing, and educational opportunities for many school- and preschool-age children.

In 1968, mean income among husband-wife families with children under 18 was $10,760. Among fatherless families, this average was $4,550. The proportion of children in fatherless families whose income in 1968 did not reach $3,000 was about 10 times as large as that of children in families with both parents present which had a similar income that year; these proportions were 41 and 4 percent, respectively. This picture was better where the mothers who were family heads were labor force participants—relatively fewer children in such families were at the bottom of the income scale and more were at the top. In families headed by nonworking mothers, more than half the children were supported on less than $3,000 of money income a year (table 4). Money income is specified here because some of these broken families may be welfare recipients of goods and services in kind. Free clothing or medical care and surplus food commodities are not reflected in the income data.

Negro children, more than whites, were in low-income families, especially in fatherless families. Among children under 18 in husband-wife families, 9 percent of the Negroes and 3 percent of the whites were in families with less than $3,000 income in 1968. But of children in fatherless families, 51 percent of the Negro and 35 percent of the white children were in families with less than $3,000 income.

In March 1969, about 51 percent of the Negro children with working fathers, compared with 29 percent of those whose fathers were nonworkers, were in families with an annual income of $7,000 or more. Among Negro families headed by a woman the proportions of children in families with income that high were very much lower, 11 percent if their mothers worked and 3 percent if they did not.

CHILD CARE

The important labor force changes among married women in the 1960's triggered a national concern over the adequacy of child care in a working mother's absence. Many experimental programs were introduced to give low-income and nonworking mothers of young children occupational training and

---

[7] Refers to family head's "own" children, sons and daughters, including stepchildren and adopted children.

help in obtaining jobs and, at the same time, to provide for the care of their children. Today many Federal agencies are engaged in small-scale day care projects, and many State and local governments as well as private industry are experimenting in this field.

The labor force participation rate of wives is generally higher if female relatives, at least 18 years old, are available to look after their home and children. In March 1969, roughly 1 of 8 working wives had such relatives—a proportion that was about constant throughout the decade. The participation rate of wives with children under 6 and no adult female relative at home was 28 percent in 1969, compared with 35 percent if a female relative were present. This difference of 7 percentage points was also unchanged for 10 years. By encouraging public and private efforts in the day care field, society is responding to the pressure of other methods of child care than the availability of female relatives in the home.

TABLE 4.—CHILDREN [1] BY FAMILY TYPE, LABOR FORCE STATUS OF FAMILY HEAD, AND FAMILY INCOME IN 1968, MARCH 1969

[Percent distribution]

Labor force status of head and family income	Children by family type				Negro children by family type [2]			
		Male head				Male head		
	Total	Married, wife present	Other marital status [3]	Female head	Total	Married, wife present	Other marital status [3]	Female head
HEAD IN LABOR FORCE								
Children:								
Number (in thousands)	61,883	57,689	586	3,608	6,331	4,991	128	1,212
Percent	100.0	100.0	100.0	100.0	100.0	100.0	100.0	100.0
Under $3,000	4.6	3.0	3.6	29.9	22.6	8.1	8.6	45.4
$3,000 to $4,999	8.8	7.5	17.7	28.7	22.6	20.3	27.3	31.6
$5,000 to $6,999	14.4	14.0	25.4	19.9	19.1	20.4	37.5	11.7
$7,000 and over	72.2	75.6	53.3	21.5	43.1	51.2	26.6	11.3
HEAD NOT IN LABOR FORCE								
Children:								
Number (in thousands)	5,096	1,758	69	3,269	1,729	394	19	1,316
Percent	100.0	100.0	(4)	100.0	100.0	100.0	(4)	100.0
Under $3,000	42.2	20.3		53.5	49.0	26.9		55.5
$3,000 to $4,999	27.4	25.7		28.6	32.6	26.1		35.0
$5,000 to $6,999	13.6	22.4		9.1	9.2	17.5		6.8
$7,000 and over	16.8	31.6		8.8	9.2	29.4		2.7

[1] Includes only "own" children under 18 years old who are sons and daughters including stepchildren and adopted children of the family head.
[2] Excludes other races.
[3] Includes widowed, divorced, spouse absent and single men.
[4] Percent not shown where base is under 75,000.

EDUCATION AND INCOME

As a rule, educational attainment measured in years of schooling completed has a distinct influence on the labor force rate of wives. Generally, the more education the higher the rate of participation (table 5). For example, the overall rate for wives who were not high school graduates was 33 percent in March 1969, compared with 43 percent for graduates, and 45 percent for those with 1 year of college or more. Negro women, as might be expected, had much higher participation rates, but in the same pattern—44 percent for nonhigh school graduates, 58 percent for graduates, and 67 percent for those with some college education.

In family situations, considerations of child care and husband's income seem to rank high as determinants of a wife's labor force participation. Children are an extra financial responsibility to the family, and the lower the husband's income the greater the necessity for the wife to work. In families where wives were high school graduates with school-age children, wives in 1969 had a participation rate of 70 percent if the husband's annual income was less than $3,000. Compare this rate with those of wives with the same educational attainment and same type of family, whose husbands had an income of more than $10,000: these women had a participation rate of 49 percent.

Preschoolers present special problems of care which must certainly influence the participation rate of their mothers. This situation is particularly serious from the viewpoint of the family in which the husband's income is particularly low and the wife is not a high school graduate. In families where the husband earned less than $3,000 a year and there were children under 6, the wife had a labor force rate of 44 percent if she had at least a high school diploma, but of only 26 percent if she did not. From table 5, one can see that although this latter rate is somewhat higher than the rate for all women, it is still relatively low, considering the financial needs of these families.

TABLE 5.—LABOR FORCE PARTICIPATION RATES[1] OF MARRIED WOMEN, BY EDUCATION OF WIFE, PRESENCE AND AGE OF CHILDREN, AND INCOME OF HUSBAND, MARCH 1969

Income of husband and presence and age of children	All wives	Years of school completed				
		Less than 4 years of high school	4 years of high school	College		
				1 year or more	1 to 3 years	4 years or more
All income classes	39.6	33.0	43.1	45.3	40.9	51.0
No children under 18 years	41.0	28.9	50.2	54.0	47.9	61.6
Children 6 to 17 years only	48.6	46.7	49.5	49.7	44.5	56.5
Children under 6 years	28.5	26.6	29.0	30.1	28.7	31.9
Under $3,000	35.0	27.4	47.1	53.7	45.4	65.2
No children under 18 years	31.4	23.7	42.8	54.1	44.8	65.7
Children 6 to 17 years only	55.0	48.0	69.5	(2)	(2)	(2)
Children under 6 years	33.4	26.0	43.8	43.7	(2)	(2)
$3,000 to $4,999	40.6	33.9	49.3	49.1	45.7	54.8
No children under 18 years	38.5	28.8	50.8	52.4	47.7	61.7
Children 6 to 17 years only	55.0	52.4	60.4	49.5	(2)	(2)
Children under 6 years	34.1	29.3	39.0	41.0	40.6	41.5
$5,000 to $6,999	45.8	38.5	50.2	54.9	50.1	62.8
No children under 18 years	47.5	36.6	55.6	59.9	53.1	68.7
Children 6 to 17 years only	55.6	50.8	59.6	60.2	57.7	(2)
Children under 6 years	35.7	29.2	38.5	43.7	41.8	48.1
$7,000 to $9,999	42.9	34.0	45.3	52.5	45.3	63.7
No children under 18 years	48.2	30.9	57.5	60.9	52.8	72.6
Children 6 to 17 years only	52.4	44.8	54.1	64.0	54.2	79.0
Children under 6 years	28.3	25.3	27.1	36.0	32.6	42.0
$10,000 and over	33.3	30.4	32.4	36.2	32.4	40.0
No children under 18 years	40.8	29.8	42.0	47.0	43.0	50.9
Children 6 to 17 years only	38.4	37.7	36.5	41.8	36.4	47.9
Children under 6 years	18.3	18.3	17.4	19.6	16.8	22.2

[1] Labor force as percent of population.
[2] Rate not shown where base is less than 75,000.

Education seemed to have a great deal to do with the type of occupations in which women are employed. In March 1969, of all wives age 18 and over who were high school graduates and those who had some college training but no degree, over 70 percent were employed in white-collar occupations, whatever their age. Nearly 50 percent of the wives who were high school graduates and wives with less than 4 years of college were in clerical occupations. On the other hand, college graduates were concentrated almost exclusively (83 percent) in professional and technical occupations.

Among Negro wives, only about one-third of those with high school diplomas were in clerical positions and 47 percent were in operative and service occupations. Like whites, college graduates were highly concentrated in professional jobs.

RESIDENCE

Occupational distributions of women workers in each marital category were made for three types of areas related to where women live, but not where their jobs are located. The three categories are the central cities of the Nation's Standard Metropolitan Statistical Areas (SMSA's), the parts of the SMSA's outside the central cities, and the areas entirely outside the SMSA's. In March 1969, about 22 million women lived in central cities and 25 million each in SMSA's but outside the central cities and in areas entirely outside the SMSA's (table 6). In the central cities, 55 percent of the women were married, compared with two-thirds in the other two areas.

Generally, the labor force participation rate of all women living in central cities tended to be somewhat higher than in the rest of the SMSA's or in areas outside the SMSA's. Among women in and outside the central city within an

SMSA, there were differences in occupational distributions because of age as well as marital status. Among central city residents, for example, 17 percent of the married women 16 to 34 years old were in professional occupations as compared with 13 percent of the married women 35 and over. Younger women (16–34) tended more towards white-collar jobs than did their elders, whatever their marital status. Thus, about 70 percent of the younger women living in central cities were in white-collar jobs; 46 percent were in clerical jobs alone. Older women tended more towards blue-collar jobs than did the younger group.

TABLE 6.—LABOR FORCE PARTICIPATION RATES AND OCCUPATIONS OF WOMEN, BY RESIDENCE AND COLOR, MARCH 1969

[Numbers in thousands]

Residence and marital status	Popu- lation	Labor force, partici- pation rate	Employed					
			Num- ber	\- Percent distribution by occupation group				
				Total	White col- lar [1]	Blue col- lar [2]	Serv- ice	Farm
ALL WOMEN								
In SMSA,[3] total	47,036	42.2	19,034	100	64.4	14.9	20.4	0.3
Single	8,608	55.1	4,476	100	71.7	8.4	19.8	.1
Married, husband present	28,457	38.8	10,629	100	65.6	16.3	17.7	.4
Other marital status [4]	9,971	40.9	3,929	100	52.9	18.6	28.2	.4
In central city, total	22,431	43.8	9,417	100	62.0	16.4	21.6	([5])
Single	4,458	59.2	2,449	100	73.2	9.2	17.6	
Married, husband present	12,256	39.9	4,703	100	62.1	18.4	19.5	
Other marital status [4]	5,717	41.1	2,265	100	49.7	20.0	302	.1
Not in central city, total	24,605	40.7	9,617	100	66.7	13.4	19.2	.6
Single	4,150	51.8	2,027	100	70.0	7.4	22.3	.3
Married, husband present	16,201	37.9	5,926	100	68.3	14.6	16.4	.7
Other marital status [4]	4,254	40.5	1,664	100	57.3	16.6	25.4	.7
Not in SMSA, total	24,879	40.4	9,576	100	49.4	20.0	26.7	3.8
Single	4,083	43.1	1,618	100	55.7	13.8	28.8	1.7
Married, husband present	15,993	41.0	6,317	100	50.9	21.5	22.7	4.9
Other marital status [4]	4,803	35.9	1,641	100	37.8	20.6	39.7	1.9
NEGRO AND OTHER RACES								
In SMSA,[3] total	5,680	50.2	2,651	100	38.9	19.0	41.7	.4
Single	1,239	49.6	539	100	53.6	14.3	31.7	.4
Married, husband present	2,677	52.6	1,320	100	4.18	18.6	52.7	.3
Other marital status [4]	1,764	47.1	792	100	24.1	22.7	52.7	.5
In central city, total	4,429	50.3	2,067	100	39.4	19.5	41.0	([5])
Single	987	51.5	444	100	5.6	14.0	30.4	
Married, husband present	2,017	51.9	980	100	42.3	19.1	38.6	
Other marital status [4]	1,425	47.3	643	100	23.8	24.0	52.1	.2
Not in central city, total	1,251	49.9	584	100	37.2	17.1	44.2	1.5
Single	252	42.1	95	100	44.2	15.8	37.9	2.1
Married, husband present	660	54.7	340	100	40.3	17.4	41.2	1.7
Other marital status [4]	339	46.3	149	100	25.5	17.4	55.0	2.0
Not in SMSA, total	2,200	42.6	857	100	18.7	19.4	59.7	2.2
Single	549	36.4	158	100	24.0	24.0	48.7	3.2
Married, husband present	953	46.3	422	100	21.3	21.3	55.4	1.9
Other marital status [4]	698	42.6	277	100	11.6	13.7	72.6	2.2

[1] Professional, managerial, clerical, and sales workers.
[2] Craftsmen, operatives, and nonfarm laborers.
[3] SMSA refers to a Standard Metropolitan Statistical Area. Except in New England, this is a group of contiguous counties which contains at least one city of 50,000 inhabitants or more, or "twin cities" with a combined population of at least 50,000. The city in the title of an SMSA is the central city.
[4] Widowed, divorced, and husband absent.
[5] Less than 0.05 percent.

Women who lived outside the central city but within the SMSA tended to be employed in white-collar jobs more than those who lived inside the central city. the proportions were 68 and 62 percent, respectively. For blue-collar jobs, these proportions were 15 and 18 percent.

In contrast to the employment patterns in the metropolitan areas, women living outside the SMSA's tended less toward white-collar and more toward blue-collar and service occupations. This was probably due to the difference between job opportunities available within a reasonable commuting distance from their homes and those available in the suburbs or inner city.

Negro women tended to concentrate more heavily than whites in service occupations no matter where they lived. In central cities, 39 percent of married Negro women held these jobs; 14 percent were in private household work, and 25 percent in all other service occupations. However, younger Negro married women (16–34) were much less likely to be in service occupations. In central cities, only 28 percent of these women worked in service occupations, and a mere 6 percent were in private household jobs.

Strikingly, even over the short span of a year, occupational shifts among Negro women living in the central city have been noticeable. Compared with March 1968, data in 1969 show some of the improvements which have been in process during the latter half of the 1960's. These improvements include rising proportions of Negro women, particularly single women, in the better paying white-collar occupations and lower proportions in private household service jobs. This offers encouragement to the view that efforts aimed at the improvement of educational and vocational opportunities for minority groups are having a measure of success.

STATEMENT TO THE EQUAL EMPLOYMENT OPPORTUNITY COMMISSION FROM THE NATIONAL ORGANIZATION FOR WOMEN, HOUSTON AREA CHAPTER, JUNE 1970

(Dr. Sally Hacker, President, Houston chapter N.O.W.)

NOW is encouraged that the EEOC is holding hearings on the utilization of minority and women workers. There is a tendency to de-emphasize the problems of women workers, Anglo and minority; NOW would like to address these problems specifically.

1. MANNER OF PRESENTATION OF DATA AFFECTS POLICY; ANGLO AND MINORITY WOMEN

Average income figures for men and women show that women—white or nonwhite, regardless of education or region of the country—can expect to earn slightly more than *half* the salary men earn.

TABLE 1.—FIGURES FROM DEPARTMENT OF LABOR, REPORTS NOS. 82 AND 83—MEDIAN EARNINGS OF FULL-TIME YEAR-ROUND WORKERS, 1964

[BY SEX AND RACE]

	Men		Women	
	White	Nonwhite	White	Nonwhite
Median earnings of full-time year-round workers........	$6,497	$4,285	$3,859	$2,674
By education, 1965:				
Below 8th grade_____	2,571	1,988	909	824
8th grade_____	3,912	2,619	1,211	1,252
Below High School_____	4,365	2,804	1,238	1,018
High School_____	5,976	3,784	2,425	1,944
College_____	7,257	4,892	2,999	3,530
By region, 1965:				
United States_____	6,693	4,172	3,955	2,793
North East_____	6,807	4,931	4,048	3,359
North Central_____	6,892	5,277	4,012	3,341
South_____	5,873	3,100	3,573	1,828
West_____	7,478	5,933	4,590	4,182

Note: 1968 median earnings of year round full-time workers: Men, $7,664; Women, $4,457.

Source: Women's Bureau, O.O.L. "Fact Sheet on the Earnings Gap" February 1970.

There is no question concerning the deplorable conditions regarding racial and ethnic discrimination, as this table shows. But clearly there is also no question concerning the deplorable conditions nationwide, regarding discrimination against women. In the Houston area also, from 1960 census data, we see that regardless of occupational category, women—white or non-white—can expect to earn only slightly more than half the salary men earn. These figures are:

TABLE 2.—EARNINGS IN 1959 OF PERSONS IN THE EXPERIENCED CIVILIAN LABOR FORCE IN HOUSTON, BY OCCUPATION, COLOR, AND SEX, BASED ON 1960 CENSUS DATA

All occupations	Total, male	Nonwhite male	Total, female	Nonwhite female
1. Professional, technical, and kindred workers	$43,917	$2,865	$2,226	$1,147
	7,118	4,079	3,924	3,760
2. Managers, officials, and proprietors	7,118	3,265	3,354	1,407
3. Clerical, and kindred workers	4,871	4,035	3,225	1,816
4. Sales workers	5,504	3,012	1,900	1,293
5. Craftsmen, foremen	5,374	3,059	2,917	1,828
6. Operatives and kindred workers	4,376	3,127	1,886	1,341
7. Private household workers	1,400	1,493	831	858
8. Service workers	2,771	2,372	1,316	1,253
9. Laborers, except farm and mine	2,903	2,799	1,524	1,578
10. Occupation not reported	3,891	2,679	1,927	1,071

A common practice is to compare the status of minority men only with men in the majority group, and minority women only with women in the majority group. Comparisons are seldom made between the status of men and women. For some reason, it seems strangely difficult to convince people that this method of comparison—men with men, women with women—makes it *impossible* to explore sex discrimination. When people analyze or talk about the problems of sex discrimination, it is usually in terms of how difficult it is for a minority woman to get a job, or a promotion, compared to Anglo women. This method is a good one *only* for exploring racial or ethnic prejudice. It says *nothing* about prejudice against all women.

When *anyone*—a commission, a company, a union—presents statistics which *only* compare Anglo women with minority women, and do not compare women with men, they themselves are *at best guilty* of ignoring discrimination against women.

The very presentation of research findings often emphasizes differences between minority and majority women, ignoring *greater* sex differences. For example, we are told that, "the percent of majority women in the professions is twice as high as that of Negro women" (but we are not told that the percent of majority males in the professions is *3* times as high as that of majority females). We are told "the chances of an Anglo woman being a manager are about four times as high as those of her Negro counterpart", (but we are not told that the chances of an Anglo man being a manager are about *5* times as high as those of his female counterpart).[1]

Minority women will be cheated if they are led to expect only what Anglo women have; it's not that much. A good secretarial job pays only a fraction of a good managerial, official, or professional job, and only a fraction of many skilled labor jobs. In some instances minority women are better off than Anglo women already, and would have to take a step backward if all they are supposed to achieve is the status of the Anglo women. For example, from Table 1 again; with some college education non-white women already average more money per year than white women with some college education. Another example of the low status of Anglo women, from 1966 E.E.O.C. statistics, concerns the prestigious and lucrative occupational category of managers, officials and proprietors. Nation wide, Anglo women are as likely to hold this kind of job as are Spanish surname American men (2.64% vs 2.54%). The proportion of Anglo *males* holding these positions however, is 12.01%. In other words, Anglo men are about five times as likely to get these good jobs as are Anglo women or Chicano men. Another example, I have read that the oriental male has "little better than half as good a chance of becoming an official or manager as an Anglo; the American Indian's prospects are slightly lower than the oriental's; the chances of a man with a Spanish surname are only one-fifth as good as that of a member of the majority

---

[1] E.E.O.–1 Report, Part I, "Job Patterns for Minorities and Women in Private Industry—1966" page 9.

group; and for Negroes the figure is one-twelfth." [2] If we were to insert in this list the position of Anglo women—being held out as a standard for all minority women—Anglo women would fall just about even with Spanish surname men i.e., next to the bottom of the heap. Thus a comparison of minority women to Anglo women, in many cases, suggests to minority women that their aspirations should be equal to or below the status now held by minority men.

A further result of comparing Anglo with minority women, is the conclusion that minority women will achieve fairly full equality in employment opportunity if they are simply given as much access to secretarial and clerical jobs as the Anglo women are.[3] Minority women must be given this access; but *all* women should be given as much access to the really *good jobs* as Anglo men are. Who should be asked to support themselves or their families on the salary of an Anglo woman in secretarial or clerical work?

I hope no one represented at these hearings is guilty of presenting material which fails to compare men with women, not merely women with each other. The goal of equal employment opportunity cannot be met as long as discrimination against women in employment exists.

2. SHOULD WOMEN HAVE EQUAL EMPLOYMENT OPPORTUNITY?

One common assumption is that women have higher absentee rates and higher "quit" rates than men. Public Health Service Reports, according to an EEOC booklet, show that "in 3 of the last 4 years studied, men actually lost more days from work per year on the average because of disability than women (*including* days lost because of pregnancy and child birth). When an individual employer's statistics reflect significantly higher absenteeism for women, it may be because he restricts his employment of women to clerical and other low-paying jobs and employs predominantly young women who have had little working experience. Highly trained women occupying responsible and skilled positions are seldom absent more than men in similar positions." [4]

The same argument holds for "quit" rates; rates are highest among sales, service and unskilled workers, men or women.

Another common assumption is that women's salary is always secondary to the husband's; it is not that important for a woman to have equal employment opportunity. She only works to "bolster" the family income somewhat. If the assumed greater family-economic responsibility of men is the criterion for jobs and salaries, where should we stop applying this criterion? Should a single man get less than a married man? Should a man whose wife works get less money, fewer promotions, than a man whose wife doesn't work? Should a married man with no children get less than one with one child? A man with one child less than one with two children? In that case, welfare mothers probably deserve more opportunity than any of us.

Further, not all women are married. We know that at least 40% of all working women are single, divorced, widowed, separated or deserted and roughly 10% of all American households are headed by women. These women at least— if we wanted to pay people, or give them access to jobs on the basis of their needs or responsibilities—should get the same opportunity, training and pay as men.

But this isn't the way we say we do things; our ideal is to give equal opportunity to all. In practice, this means equal training, recruitment, hiring, pay, promotion—regardless of race, sex, creed or national origin. If women by nature, by inclination—all training and opportunity being equal—don't "prefer" or can't do men's work, why is it necessary to keep them out by law or practice? Let them make their own decisions. We need to start living up to our ideals. We need to stop accepting and justifying lower wages and poorly paid occupations as appropriate for women, not for men. The Commission must question closely to determine assumptions responsible for prejudice against women.

3. MOTIVATIONAL AND TRAINING PROGRAMS AND EDUCATION

We know that one problem of a disadvantaged group, such as minorities and women is motivation. Minority members who lack certain occupational skills, and who have been systematically excluded from higher paying occupations or positions, tend to lower their aspirations, or fail to raise them in the first place, according to a recent E. E. O. C. report.[5] We are apparently well aware of the

---

[2] E.E.O.–1, page 9.
[3] E.E.O.–1, page 11.
[4] *Toward Job Equality for Women,* an EEOC report, circa 1970, page 4.
[5] E.E.O.–1, page 21.

great need for special motivational and training programs for disadvantaged minorities. Who mentions the existence or even the *need* for such motivational and training programs for women? When companies and unions are questioned at these hearings about such programs, we urge that they be questioned extensively about programs to recruit, train, hire and promote women.

Another word about education, and its effect on income. Education is an important part of training. We encourage children to stay in school, get a better education. The educated man gets a better job, can achieve a better position in life. Is this true for women? Nationally, women with a college education can expect to earn about the same as a man with a high school education. One-sixth of working women with 4 years of college are working in clerical, sales, or service work, or as semi-skilled operatives.[6]

After much sophisticated analysis, researchers show that although Black people have not attained quite as much education, in general, as Anglos, that this lack of eduaction accounts for only a portion of the difference in income and job status. The rest is due largely to prejudice and its effects. The argument usually finishes by saying that although education is not a panacea, and won't erase all disparities between Black and Anglos, that it is "almost always a highly profitable investment for all workers."[7] What would be the interpretation if indeed the analysts discovered that Blacks were, on the average, *more* highly educated in every occupational category than Anglos? And getting poorer jobs and less money? This is the case for women, compared to men.

TABLE 3.—INDEXES OF OCCUPATIONAL POSITION FOR FEMALES BY INDUSTRY, 1966[1]

Sic	Industry	Median years of schooling[2]			
		Negro males	Negro females	Total females	Total males
10	Metal mining	7.2	8.9	12.5	10.3
11	Antimony mining	7.4	---	---	8.3
12	Bituminous mining	7.4	8.9	12.3	8.3
13	Petroleum	8.2	8.9	12.7	12.0
14	Quarry mining	5.9	8.9	12.4	8.9
19	Ordnance	9.0	10.9	12.0	11.2
20	Food	8.3	8.9	10.4	10.4
21	Tobacco	7.6	7.9	8.9	9.5
22	Textile	7.6	9.7	9.2	8.7
23	Apparel	---	10.5	9.2	---
24	Lumber	---	8.0	11.6	---
25	Furniture	8.7	10.1	10.9	9.4
26	Paper	8.2	10.2	11.1	10.8
27	Printing	---	12.1	12.3	---
28	Chemical	8.2	10.7	12.3	12.2
29	Petroleum	7.5	10.3	12.6	12.3
30	Rubber	9.3	10.8	11.0	11.2
31	Leather	9.2	10.7	9.5	9.1
32	Stone	7.6	10.6	11.8	9.9
33	Primary metals	8.4	9.2	12.2	10.1
34	Fabricating metal	9.0	10.9	12.0	11.2
35	Machinery	8.9	11.1	12.2	11.6
36	Electrical machinery	10.6	11.9	11.7	12.3
37	Transportation service	9.2	11.0	12.2	11.5
38	Instruments	10.9	11.4	11.9	12.3
39	Miscellaneous machinery	9.7	10.7	10.4	10.7
40	Railroad	8.0	8.5	12.3	10.2
42	Motor freight	8.3	9.4	12.3	9.8
44	Water	7.7	8.5	12.4	9.7
45	Air transportation	10.3	10.9	12.7	12.5
46	Pipeline	7.1	---	---	12.2
47	Service	9.3	12.1	12.6	11.8
48	Communications	10.6	12.4	12.4	12.5
49	Electric service	7.8	11.4	12.5	11.4
50	Wholesale	8.5	9.8	12.3	12.1
53	Retail	10.4	12.0	11.8	12.2
54	Food transportation	9.2	---	---	10.9
60	Banking	9.4	12.2	12.5	12.8
61	Credit	9.4	12.2	12.5	12.8
62	Broker	11.8	12.0	12.5	13.8
63	Insurance	12.4	12.5	12.5	13.0
64	Insurance	12.4	12.5	12.5	13.0
67	Holding	11.8	12.0	12.5	13.8
73	Miscellaneous business	9.9	11.5	12.4	12.4
		---	11.8	12.4	---

[1] Based on EEO-1 Reports.
[2] Taken from U.S. Census of Population, 1960, Final Report PC (2) — (pp. 98–101, 187–191).

[6] *Toward Job Equality for Women,* page 2.
[7] E.E.O.–1, page 21.

Women are on the average *better* educated than men in the same industries. Black women, in *every* industry, and all women in 23 out of 39 industries have an average educational level higher than that of men in the same industry. How "highly profitable" an investment is women's greater education compared to men?

Texas urban area figures, similar to national figures, show that at each level of education, women, regardless of race, are earning less than men.

TABLE 4.—INCOME IN 1959 OF PERSONS 25 YEARS OLD AND OVER BY YEARS OF SCHOOL COMPLETED, COLOR AND SEX FOR THE STATE (TEXAS), URBAN, 1960

	Total male	Total female	Nonwhite	
			Male	Female
Median education	10.9	11.1	8.1	8.8
Median income	$4,504	$1,382	$2,448	$867
Education:				
School year completed, elementary	1,465	647	1,161	598
1 to 4 years school	2,126	708	1,734	672
5 to 7 years school	3,136	835	2,369	770
8 years	3,735	931	2,498	844
High school:				
1 to 3 years	4,604	1,334	2,699	923
4 years	5,401	2,071	2,875	1,025
College:				
1 to 3 years	5,917	2,296	3,100	1,145
4 years or more	7,458	3,855	4,157	3,556

Unions, companies and the Commission have a great responsibility, not only to help motivate and train women, but to acknowledge and utilize the greater motivation and training among women, where it exists.

4. WOMEN WORKERS IN THE HOUSTON STANDARD METROPOLITAN STATISTICAL AREA

We have a serious question about the invitations to appear before this Commission at the Houston hearings. We have been told by Press Release that four major types of industry will be primarily concerned—petroleum, chemical, construction, and paper. From EEO–1 1966 data, these types of industries account for roughly 32% of the male labor force in the Houston area, for whom data could be presented. Unfortunately, they only account for 12% of the female labor force. Given the growth of female employment, particularly, in the medical and retail type industries, the four major types of industry focused on by EEOC probably represent less than 12% of Houston's female labor force today. We would have benefitted by the opportunity to hear from hospitals, retail stores and the like, who employ large numbers of Houston's working women. We might want to compare pay scales of men and women in professional and technical jobs, or to see if women in general merchandise stores are utilized primarily in sales and clerical positions, with little chance of promotion.

We will, however, compare the four major types of industries selected by EEOC with the average records for Houston industries as a whole. Considering all industries covered by the EEOC, report 1, for the Houston Standard Metropolitan Statistical Area, we have the following breakdown by sex, ethnicity and occupational category:

TABLE 5.—MINORITY AND MAJORITY GROUP EMPLOYMENT BY OCCUPATION AND SEX FOR THE, HOUSTON STANDARD METROPOLITAN STATISTICAL AREA

[Percent each group by occupational classification]

Group	Total	Officials, managers	Professionals	Technicians	Sales workers	Office clerical	Craftsmen	Operatives	Laborers	Service workers
Spanish surname, male	9,156	2.1	1.9	3.4	2.5	4.8	17.4	31.6	23.1	13.3
Spanish surname, female	3,039	.6	1.4	4.1	5.7	23.6	2.8	24.8	9.5	27.5
Negro male	23,741	.6	.2	.8	.9	1.6	6.7	32.9	38.0	18.3
Negro female	5,522	.6	5.1	10.0	2.8	7.2	1.5	14.1	10.1	48.5
Total male	191,502	10.9	10.0	5.9	6.2	7.3	20.9	21.2	11.6	6.0
Total female	56,931	2.1	4.4	5.5	10.2	50.6	1.6	8.2	3.0	14.4
Total	248,433	22,029,	21,548	14,428	17,614	42,796	41,024	45,385	23,915	19,694

Without much effort we can see that minorities and women are excluded from management. As on the national level, here in Houston too; Anglo [8] men are more than five times as likely as Anglo women and Spanish surname American men to be managers, officials, or proprietors. Anglo men are eighteen times as likely as Black people and SSA women to hold these prestigious and lucrative positions.

A finer analysis, Table 6, shows the paper and petroleum industries' record to be generally worse than that for the entire Houston SMSA, as far as all women workers in management are concerned. The construction industries are only worse for minority women; the chemical industries are worse only for Chicano and Anglo women, than Houston industries as a whole. Table 7 indicates the ratio of the percent of all men holding managerial, etc., jobs, compared to the percent of women holding such jobs, in 5 selected industries in the Houston SMSA.

As for professional work, all four industries again have poorer records than the city as a whole, concerning women.

Where do these important Houston area industries place the women workers? In petroleum and refining 93.2% of all female workers are in office and clerical work. Chemicals and allied products—90.6% of all female workers are in office and clerical work. Crude petroleum and natural gas—84.1% of all female workers are in office and clerical work. (The average for Houston SMSA is 50.6%). The paper industries do fall below this Houston figure. Only 41.8% of the female workers in the paper industries are limited to office and clerical jobs. But 42.5% of the women in these industries are used as operatives.

The figures for males in office and clerical work, in these industries range from 2.9% to 12.6%, near the Houston average of 7.3%. And even these men will earn higher incomes than the female secretaries and file clerks, on the average.

Another position women tend to be chosen for is service work—least prestigful, most poorly paid, and involving much more physical strength and labor than most office jobs, professional jobs and certainly than executive jobs. These four types of industries however, don't have that many service jobs available (though the construction industries manage to use 4 of their 6 Black women in service jobs), and the proportion of any group in service jobs is generally lower than the Houston SMSA averages.

What do we want from companies in these types of industries? Hire and promote more women—Anglo and minority—in professional, managerial, and craft level jobs.

So. That is the status of the few women employed by these 4 major types of industry. Perhaps the status of women in other industries, where many more women are employed, is better.

Most working women in Houston, in industries covered by the E.E.O.C. 1966 report, work in medical and other health services (8,169) 19,000 in 1969. The next largest number of women are employed in the general merchandise stores (7,558) 12,000 in 1969. The next largest in insurance type industries (3,209). Then comes petroleum and natural gas (2,660), banking (2,607), wholesale trade (2,276) and food stores (2,238).

The first three account for one-third of Houston's working women. Table 8 describes their status in these types of industry.

In the medical and health industries, discrimination still exists. Anglo and Chicano women came from 1/5 and 1/18 as likely as Anglo men to hold managerial job,—to 1/3 to 1/9, respectively. Black women remain at 1/18. Women in general are more likely to hold professional status here that they are in other Houston industries. But nursing no doubt accounts for many women in these professional jobs; and salaries for nurses are obviously nowhere near the income, in medical industries, of the male professionals.

In general merchandise stores, Anglo men are 5 times more likely to hold management positions than Anglo women, and 20 times more likely to hold such positions than minority women. Most women fill clerical or sales positions, except for Black women who are used in the low status service jobs. In the insurance companies, Anglo men are 20 times as likely as Anglo or Mexican American women to be managers, officials, etc.; no Black women hold such status. Thus the pattern of discrimination against women is replicated even in industries where on half to three fourths of the workers are women.

Women in some occupations—postal employees and school teachers for example—have no chance to be represented at these hearings. The Houston Post

---

[8] We use the figures for all men and for all women to approximate the situation for Anglos. These figures are from EEO–1, 1966 data.

Office employs over 5,000 people. November 1969 data reveal that roughly 25% of its employees are women. There are 16 levels of civil service classification. There are 302 people in supervisory positions, levels 8 through 16. No woman holds any of the 137 positions above level 8. Only 8 women (7 Anglo, 1 Mexican American) hold even the lowest supervisory classification of level 8. Why are women systematically excluded from supervisory (and better paid) positions?

Public school teaching is an occupation also exempt from these formal inquiries. It is, however, the occupation chosen by half of U.S. college educated women who plan for any type of career.[9] In Texas, as elsewhere, most elementary school teachers are women, many high school teachers are women, but only a small fraction of the administrators are women. Why are women systematically excluded from administrative (and better paid) positions?

This is the kind of questioning which must be directed to those Houston industries who employ large numbers of women.—hospitals, general merchandise stores, banks, insurance companies, phone companies. We turn to these types of industries later. If, indeed, at these hearings, however, we are limited to those industries who hire women hardly at all, then perhaps another approach is necessary. Why do industries discriminate against women, either by not hiring them or by using them only for office and clerical work? Though we understand that Houston's industries are growing rapidly, and that compared to the national levels, unemployment is not yet as serious in this area as nationally, the status of women compared to men has *decreased* within the last few years.

Some analysis by Jarolyn Lyle of the E.E.O.C. Research Department, for the Houston SMSA, apparently documents the loss of status of women here dramatically. There are several ways of keeping the employment status of women low. One. as we saw in the earlier tables, is to pay women less money for the same or similiar work. Another is to keep them in low-paying occupations. Her recent E.E.O.C. analysis assumes away discrimination in income for the same occupation. For example, it would assume a female engineer, technician, supervisor, office worker, craftsman, and so on, would get the same pay as a man in that type of work. That's quite an assumption. But this allows the researcher to see how much income a group loses, not on the basis of unequal pay, but on the basis of being kept out of the better jobs. In Houston SMSA, for 1966, using this kind of index, Anglo women earned 49% of the salaries earned by Anglo men; Mexican American women earned 42% of the salaries earned by Anglo men; black women earned 39% of the salaries earned by Anglo men. By 1969, the status of all women, compared to Anglo men, had fallen. Anglo women in 1969 earned 47% of that earned by Anglo men; Mexican American women earned 41% of that earned by Anglo men; black women earned 38% of the salaries earned by Anglo men. The status of minority women compared to Anglo women improved during the same time; black women had earned 81% of Anglo women's earnings, which rose to 82%. Mexican American women earned 85% of Anglo women's earnings, which rose to 87%.[10]

While the status of all women draws closer together, all women are increasingly losing ground in the occupational structure.

How, in the face of these dismal records, are we to continue calling this the land of equal opportunity, or to encourage women who want to work that they can or should, rather than choosing welfare, for example? One mother with several children and no day care service, calculated that her secretarial job cost her 65¢ a day. She quit. A mother on welfare wanted training in any one of several skilled jobs; she was told they were for men. The situation is the same on the management level. On Thursday we have a chance to hear from people with these experiences.

What is the company's responsibility, a store's responsibility, a medical center's responsibility for providing child care facilities for working parents? Can women take maternity leave without loss of position or seniority? Do women have as much access as men to training and retraining opportunities? Do they have a chance at promotion out of clerical and secretarial jobs, into technical, professional and management jobs? Do unions take seriously their responsibility to represent the needs and demands of women workers? Do men in personnel and management tend to judge all women by their own relatives—who may not have to work, or want to work?

---

9 1964 survey, of 1961 U.S. college and university graduates, NORC, University of Chicago.
10 Phone conversation, J. Lyle, 5/20/70.

TABLE 6.—MINORITY AND MAJORITY GROUP EMPLOYMENT BY OCCUPATION FOR SELECTED INDUSTRIES IN THE HOUSTON METROPOLITAN STATISTICAL AREA

Group	Total	Officials, managers	Professionals	Technicians	Sales workers	Office, clerical	Craftsmen	Operatives	Laborers	Service workers
CHEMICALS AND ALLIED PRODUCTS										
Spanish surname, male	235	4.7	7.2	7.2	3.0	5.5	8.1	35.7	24.3	4.3
Spanish surname, female	18	0	0	0	0	50.0	5.6	33.3	11.1	0
Negro, male	1,125	.4	.1	2.0	0	.8	7.1	39.0	39.8	10.8
Negro, female	35	2.9	0	0	0	40.0	8.6	40.0	0	8.6
Total, male	19,008	15.1	11.6	7.6	2.3	3.2	24.7	28.9	4.4	2.3
Total, female	1,483	1.1	2.4	2.8	.2	90.6	.4	1.5	.5	.5
Total	20,491	2,878.0	2,244.0	1,477.0	445.0	1,947.0	4,704.0	5,508.0	842.0	446.0
PAPER AND ALLIED PRODUCTS										
Spanish surname, male	50	2.0	0	0	0	0	22.0	48.0	26.0	2.0
Spanish surname, female	14	0	0	0	0	7.1	0	78.6	14.3	0
Negro, male	336	0	0	0	0	.3	16.1	53.6	23.2	6.8
Negro, female	15	0	0	0	0	6.7	0	46.7	33.3	13.3
Total, male	2,311	10.0	3.3	3.4	2.4	2.9	34.6	28.2	13.4	1.8
Total, female	395	.5	.3	1.3	0	41.8	6.1	42.5	6.8	.8
Total	2,706	234.0	77.0	83.0	55.0	233.0	823.0	819.0	337.0	45.0

Women are discriminated against in employment. They are beginning to act against such discrimination. Though the EEOC was set up primarily to help eliminate discrimination against minorities, roughly a fourth to a third of the cases brought to its attention are cases of sex discrimination.

Industry has many advantages. It enters into long range planning for this city, into redevelopment and development, it assumes and achieves many other positions of power and influence to which it is not elected. The theory is that what is good for the community is good for industry. We want to say to industry that it appears to be ignoring a sizable proportion of the work force, and of the city—women—in terms of equal employment opportunity. To deserve the leadership it assumes, industry must at least take primary responsibility for eradicating the discrimination which exists here against women in the occupational structure.

TABLE 7.—RATIO OF PERCENT ALL MEN, TO PERCENT ALL WOMEN, SPANISH-SURNAME WOMEN, AND NEGRO WOMEN HOLDING MANAGERIAL, OFFICIAL, OR PROPRIETOR OCCUPATIONS IN 5 SELECTED TYPES OF HOUSTON SMSA INDUSTRIES

	Ratio of all men, compared to (percent)—		
	All women	SSA women	Negro women
Houston	5 to 1	18 to 1	18 to 1.
Petroleum and refinery	48 to 1	X [1]	X.
Crude petroleum and natural gas	26 to 1	X	X.
Paper	20 to 1	X	X.
Construction	3 to 1	X	X.
Chemical	14 to 1	X	5 to 1.

[1] X equals no woman at all.

Source: EEO–1 1966 data.

APPENDIX: SUGGESTIONS TO THE EEOC

The EEOC was given the responsibility to investigate possible discrimination in employment against minorities and women, and to report its findings. EEO–1 is sub-titled "Job Patterns for Minorities and Women in Private Industry—1966". An examination of this 3 volume report indicates that data were collected, and presented in appendix tables, to allow a powerful analysis of the extent of discrimination against women. EEO–1 doesn't do it. Our specific recommendation here is this:

Contract new research to focus specifically on sex discrimination, based on the most recent data EEOC has, to parallel the extensive research done by Ashenfelter and others on racial and ethnic discrimination.

The following is a running commentary on the text of EEO–1.

On page viii of part I of EEOC–1, it is stated that "an independent analysis of the 1966 EEO–1 data was prepared by Orley Ashenfelter, now Assistant Professor of Economics of Princeton University, under an Equal Employment Opportunity Commission contract with the W. E. Upjohn Institute for employment. In his report, *Minority Employment Patterns,, 1966*, Mr. Ashenfelter states: 'the most important conclusion of this report is that the data collected through the EEO–1 Reporting System are generally accurate and highly useful body of material for the investigation of the employment patterns of minority groups in the United States.'" We would like to read the research proposal or contract for this independent analysis, to find out where women were excluded, and by whom.

On page 2, the Princeton study is cited for the source of Significant Findings, "among other sources". Under Significant Findings, 1-a, the report describes a rating system comparing minority males to majority males, and minority females to majority females. Why is it necessary to use two different rating scales? This method itself accepts and perpetuates the discrimination against women in employment, making it impossible to compare the status of women with that of men.

As pointed out in the statement read before the Houston hearings, it is also a gross disservice to minority women to compare them with majority women; if this is all they should expect, there are serious limits being placed on their aspirations and on their potential achievement of equal opportunity in employment. The report points out on p. 2 that "for example, Negro men average only three-fourths as much earning power as the majority group of men." Why aren't statistics presented on the proportion of majority group male earning power that all women have?

TABLE 8.—MINORITY AND MAJORITY GROUP EMPLOYMENT, BY OCCUPATION AND SEX, FOR SELECTED INDUSTRIES IN THE HOUSTON METROPOLITAN STATISTICAL AREA

	Total	Officials, managers	Professionals	Technicians	Sales workers	Office, clerical	Craftsmen	Operatives	Laborers	Service workers
GROUP MEDICAL AND HEALTH SERVICES										
Spanish-surname male	221	1.4	3.2	27.1	0	18.1	1.4	10.9	15.4	22.6
Spanish-surname female	650	1.1	4.9	16.2	0	15.2	0	20.0	8.2	34.5
Negro male	815	1.0	1.3	3.3	.1	1.6	3.1	11.0	16.2	62.3
Negro female	2,348	.5	11.8	18.3	0	4.3	.1	12.4	12.9	39.8
Total male	2,349	9.2	12.6	11.9	.2	4.9	7.5	14.4	9.2	30.1
Total female	8,169	3.1	19.1	25.3	0	16.3	.4	10.1	5.3	20.5
GENERAL MERCHANDISE STORES										
Spanish-surname male	301	6.3	.7	1.3	18.6	6.3	26.2	18.3	17.6	4.7
Spanish-surname female	313	1.3	0	.6	42.5	28.4	6.4	9.9	5.4	5.4
Negro male	792	.9	0	0	6.2	2.7	2.5	20.1	25.0	42.7
Negro female	490	0	0	0	24.5	9.4	1.4	4.5	5.3	54.9
Total male	4,714	19.6	.7	1.4	31.9	5.3	10.1	11.0	10.6	9.3
Total female	7,458	4.3	.3	.3	55.0	26.9	.9	2.9	1.2	8.2
INSURANCE										
Spanish-surname male	65	9.2	7.7	1.5	66.2	7.7	3.1	0	0	4.6
Spanish-surname female	92	1.1	0	1.1	0	96.7	0	0	0	1.1
Negro male	71	8.5	0	0	28.2	36.6	0	2.8	1.4	22.5
Negro female	64	0	0	0	7.8	54.7	0	.5	.1	37.5
Total male	3,400	20.6	22.6	8.3	32.4	13.1	1.4	0	0	1.0
Total female	3,209	1.1	1.1	4.4	1.3	90.2	.1	0	0	1.8

Point 3 indicates that a statistical analysis shows that lower level of education among minorities accounts for only about one-third of the difference in occupational ranking between Negro men and majority group men. How much does education account for in the different statuses between women and men? Comparing EEO-1 data in Tables 3 and 4 of Pt I, women appear to have *higher* average levels of education than men.

On page 6, there is a 5 paragraph statement on "Women Workers", which, to say the least, lacks punch.

On page 7 the report describes the construction of an index based on median earnings for each occupational category. The average income figure for men in the majority group is $5,016 compared to $3,883 for Negro men, or a difference of $1,133. Why weren't women compared to men, on the same kind of index? The report says "another set of indexes was constructed for females based on their median earnings in each occupational category."

The report describes in detail how minority males compare with Anglo males. About females, it says only that the "indexes for females showed a somewhat different, but nevertheless significant, pattern of underutilization of minority group workers as far as these three groups are concerned." These are racial and ethnic, not sex comparisons, again.

On page 8, Table 1 compares only minority women to Anglo women, minority men to Anglo men, and prevents comparing women to men. On page 9, we find further discussion of discrimination against minority men compared with Anglo men. The last paragraph: "For women workers, the distribution patterns are less obvious. The configuration of discrimination emerges once again although it is not as consistent, nor as pronounced as it appears in the male groupings." This again ignores sex discrimination.

Charts I and II of this report are given to us as visual aids that reflect the deviation of minority group male and female workers from Anglo occupational patterns. Again, these charts are set up to compare minorities with the majority group, only within sex, not between sex. There is no way to compare the status of women compared with men. It implies all minority women have to do to achieve equality in employment is greater access to clerical and secretarial jobs.

The Hammerman report is mentioned on page 4. It says, "The plight of minorities can be illustrated by using Negroes as a representative group since they comprise a large proportion of all minorities and are widely dispersed geographically. Herbert Hammerman, Chief of Reports for EEOC, employed this traditional method in a preliminary research report on EEOC data." Neither the Hammerman nor the Ashenfelter reports are set up to encourage, nor at times even allow, an investigation of discrimination on the basis of sex.

The only men who are actually as bad off as Anglo women in terms of the probability of holding managerial, official or proprietor occupations, are Black and Chicano men. Black, Chicano and American Indian males are also as poorly off as Anglo females when it comes to holding professional jobs. And this is the standard being held up for minority women to achieve.

Continuing on page 11, Section VIII is titled "The Job Picture by Industries." This analysis ignores sex discrimination also. Indices from the Princeton report are used to determine how "minority groups fare in various sectors of the economy."

Section IX—deals with education. And ignores sex discrimination.

Section X is titled "Characteristics of Job Discrimination", and again focuses only on the differences between Black and Anglo, based again on the Princeton report. They say, "In summary, Negro men can undoubtedly increase their earnings by obtaining more education, but the rate of gain and earnings is significantly less than that of Anglos." Again, as pointed out in the statement read at the hearings, EEOC should have done the same sort of analysis based on sex discrimination.

Section XI is a detailed study of specific industries indicating the deprived status of Negro males and Negro females, and some gains made in particular industries such as textile. Again, no mention or focus of analysis on sex discrimination.

Section XII—Concluding Comments. "The essence of a statement made at the beginning of this report should be repeated: job discrimination is a profound and pervasive condition in the American economies; it is a root cause of minority group problems because the lack of meaningful and purposeful employment that provides adequate earnings is one of the basic reasons for the tragic plight of minority groups in America." This statement is true. But this and the rest of the Concluding Comments completely ignore the status of women or the problems of women in employment. From the beginning of this report, only a few token comments were made toward sex discrimination.

The report says ". . . minorities must know their rights before they can exercise them, they must be aware of opportunities before they can take advantage of them. Some evidence indicates strongly that once rebuffed, minority groups do not persist in their effort to gain entry to a company or occupation even though there may have been a genuine change of, attitude. The rigid mores molded by centuries of practice persist on both sides." The same thing is true for women.

The last two paragraphs of the report discuss the need for conservation of human skill, intellect and creativity as the most important and natural resource. It argues that we can protect natural resources but we cannot store or reclaim labor or time. "If a man is unemployed or under employed for a week or a month that much production is lost; it is gone forever."

These are great thoughts. We hope the EEOC extends them soon to women.

The EEOC was given the task of exploring discrimination against minorities and women. It has ignored sex discrimination in this report, for all practical purposes. You owe the public at least another 21 pages of text, focusing on discrimination against women, based on sophisticated, EEOC-funded research.

Our next set of suggestions concern the questioning of companies and unions by the Commissioners. We have given some attention to the 700-page report of the Commission hearings held in Los Angeles, in 1969. The time we had available did not allow a thorough analysis of the share of time and questioning given to sex discrimination at the hearings. We hope however that the following commentary on this record will illustrate our point, and will encourage the Commission to give greater attention to sex discrimination at these Houston hearings.

In the opening remarks on page 3, Clifford Anderson reports full scale hearings on utilization of Blacks by the dominant employers of the textile industry in North and South Carolina. We need specific hearings on sex alone, as it seems too much for researchers and for hearings too, to do both at once. Our suggestion to the EEOC here is:

HOLD SEPARATE HEARINGS ON SEX DISCRIMINATION

Perhaps McDonnell-Douglas does not discriminate against women. But it is difficult to tell by either the oral testimony, questioning, or written reports. North American Rockwell, e.g., obviously does discriminate against women as well as minorities. Yet on page 4 the Chairman reports that everyone has copies of the background data on the aerospace industry in Los Angeles, which "spells out in graphic terms the reason we are here; to explore existing under-utilization of Mexican Americans and Blacks in that industry, and to stimulate action to change that under-utilization."

On page 6, Mr. Felker is testifying on behalf of McDonnell-Douglas Corporation. He says, "Consistent with the suggestions of the commission, I will direct my remarks to certain specific areas of minority effort and commitment." At the bottom of page 6 he says meetings with minority group representatives are held, schools are visited and personal examples of minority group members who have achieved a measure of success in a chosen field are provided to schools and community organizations. This is an important effort. There is a good deal of attention, throughout the report on recruitment, hiring and motivational programs directed toward minorities. Seldom if at all are such programs directed specifically toward women. By these methods, we will encourage minority groups to adopt or perpetuate the same discriminatory practices against women common among the majority group.

In communicating EEO policy to companies, Mr. Felker says, on p. 9, that after having communicated the policy, they found "that minority people with certain skills were applying for the first time, and from that time on we found that our percentages gradually increased in those skills." What about women?

On page 14, Commissioner Kuck does ask if they have a special recruitment program for women. He replies, "No, they do not." They find that the percentage of engineers across the country who are women is about .5%, and they recruit 1%, thus seeing no need for a special recruiting program. Commissioner Kuck asks later "And do you have minorities and women in that program (a supervisory training and management development program) at this time?" Mr. Felker's answer is, "Yes, the last time checked there were minorities in most all of the programs." What about women?

Talking about motivational programs on p. 18, Chairman Alexander asked "How do you motivate?" Mr. Felker replies that an industry-wide motivation task force has both Mexican American and Negro employees from various companies participating. What about women? Chairman Alexander asks, "Do you have a Black or Mexican-American vice-president?" He also asks, "Have you ever had any women, or Indians, or Orientals on your board of directors?" Good question.

Mr. Browne testifies for Lockheed Aircraft Corp. He says, on p. 25, that to insure continuing progress in equal employment opportunities they have regular top management reviews. He goes on to cite the number of persons of minority background and what percent they comprise and what the increase percent is at various levels of employment. He does not mention women.

Several following sections in the questioning deal specifically with minorities: Recruitment and Training of Minorities; Minority Recruitment Through Advertising, Minorities in Higher Job Levels, Minority Officials and Managers; Recruiting and Upgrading Mexican American Personnel; Mexican American Recruiting Techniques; Transportation Problems Facing Minorities.

On page 48 we find a section titled Employment of Women. Commissioner Kuck says "I appreciate your statements, Mr. Browne, but I felt that you neglected women in connection with it. I am just wondering what, if anything, you are doing in the way of employment of women? Mr. Browne says, "I don't know of my own knowledge. Commissioner Kuck asks 6 more questions about women in supervisory and management positions.

Questioning North American Rockwell Corporation, on p. 67, Commissioner Kuck asks if their targets include female employment. The response is, "We do not at this time have the same highly structured affirmative action program for our female employees as we do for minority groups." She asks 1 more question on opportunities for women, and notes the number in mgt. has decreased in the last 2 years.

This is good questioning. There is obviously not enough of it. We suggest that:

THE EQUAL EMPLOYMENT OPPORTUNITY COMMISSION NEEDS MORE WOMEN COMMISSIONERS

The rest of the report contains pages and pages of close questioning on opportunities and motivation efforts directed toward minorities, with relatively few questions on the status of women. Some tables in the written reports do present statistics allowing comparisons of men and women; some do not.

We attach a list of questions—some general, some specific—which the Commission might care to address to participating companies and unions.

Our suggestion overall, is that:

The Commission should, in the Houston hearings, question participating companies and unions as closely for discrimination against all women, Anglo and minority, as it does for discrimination on the basis of minority status.

A further suggestion concerns the types of industries invited to these hearings. As far as we can tell, they account for about a third of the male labor force in the Houston SMSA, but only about a tenth of the female labor force. We imagine that some industries employing large numbers of women—medical and health related, general merchandise stores—may not have been invited since their record of employing minorities and women is better than average. We would suggest that:

The Commission should also concern itself with industries employing high percentages of the female work force, and question the practice of these and other industries in using women primarily as sales, office and clerical workers, service workers, and operatives; it should question pay scales of female professionals and others, compared with men.

Our last suggestion is that:

The Commission should make a greater effort to locate, meet with, and provide hearing time for individuals and organizations active in the movement toward equal opportunity for women.

SUGGESTED QUESTIONS FOR PARTICIPATING COMPANIES AND UNIONS

What % and number of Anglo and minority women employees, compared with men, are:

(a) employed in the highest status, highest paying jobs? (management, executive, professional, official, or craft positions; or city as opposed to home and family news on Houston newspapers)

(b) are employed in low paying clerical, operative or service jobs?

(c) are included on legal staff on the Board of directors?
(d) are employed?
(e) were promoted last year?
(f) earn more than $10,000?

Are women applicants given the same aptitude tests as men applicants?

What investigation is undertaken in personnel offices to insure equal opportunities are given to women? What steps are taken if you discover someone there is discriminating against women?

How much money is spent on advertising high level, or relatively high paying jobs for women, compared with that spent on advertising good jobs for men?

Do you routinely place ads listing clerical jobs in female help wanted sections of the paper; and listing professional, managerial, craft jobs in male help wanted sections?

Do you use the services of employment agencies?

Do you specify sex on any jobs? (If so, what criteria do you use?)

Do you ever instruct the agency not to send women to you for any particular job opening?

Are incentive bonuses ever offered to women employees?

Are women in the same position as men as likely to be promoted?

What job does a secretary usually get promoted to, if she does win a promotion?

What is the average pay for clerical work in your company? Managerial, professional, technical, and skilled work?

Do you have "affirmative action programs" for women? Do you think you should?

In slack times, do women get laid off first, regardless of seniority?

Do you, or does your personnel office or the employment agency you work through, tend to make decisions for women, as whether or not they would travel, be willing to move to another city, work nights, or at an "un-romantic" laboring job?

Do you tend to make decisions for the public as to whether they would "accept" a woman in a responsible position? For workers, as to whether they would work for a woman?

SUGGESTIONS FOR QUESTIONS TO INDUSTRY REPRESENTATIVES

To be directed by Commissioners.

TRAINING

1. What formal programs, if any, does your company have to train women employees for management positions?
2. How long have these programs been in effect?
3. How many women in your company have participated in the management training? How are they now placed?
4. Are women actively recruited for management training?
5. What are the criteria for selection of trainees?
6. What is the average time spent in training positions before advancement and/or review?
7. Are women college graduates recruited for management Trainee programs— on college campuses?
8. What is the ratio of women compared to men in your current training programs?
9. Do you use women in paid (TV, newspaper, etc.) ads? If so, how are they portrayed? Do you have women recruiters?

WAGES AND BENEFITS

10. What is the highest wage and position of a woman (or women) in your company (on the payroll)?
11. Are pension trusts administered to permit women to participate fully? Are such plans including the surviving spouses and/or children of women employees?
12. Does your company allow leaves of absence for maternity? How long? Does the female employee return to work at same position & salary? If not, what arrangements are made to re-hire, train etc. when a woman returns to work after childbirth?

If the Commission has a chance to question Southwestern Bell, Atty. Sylvia Roberts suggests the following questions:

How many women switchmen are there opposed to how many men switchmen?

How do the pay scales of women workers compare with those of men workers?
How many women are in the plant department, compared with men?
How many toll test board men, framemen, installer repairmen, are women, compared to men?
How many men, compared to women, are in the traffic dept?
How many women are sent by the company to training in electricity and electronics schools compared to men?
How many women are in executive posts?
Are women paid the same pay differential for substituting on a man's job as a man would be (e.g., a woman outside plant clerk substitutes for toll test board man during lunch hours, but does not get paid what a total test board man does—but a man substituting would get this same rate of pay.)

UNIONS

1. Are women allowed, encouraged to join? What % members are women?
2. How many women are int'l or business representatives?
3. Do collective bargaining contracts contain the word "sex" in sections stating parties will not discriminate?
4. How do you go about motivating women to greater participation and to positions of greater responsibility?

SEX-SEGREGATED WANT ADS: DO THEY DISCOURAGE FEMALE JOB APPLICANTS?

(Testimony by Sandra L. Bem and Daryl J. Bem, Department of Psychology, Carnegie-Mellon University before the Pittsburgh Human Relations Commission, Feb. 1970)

Title VII of the 1964 Civil Rights Act forbids discrimination in employment on the basis of race, color, religion, national origin—and sex. Although the sex provision was treated as a joke at the time (and was introduced by a Southern Congressman in an attempt to defeat the bill), the Equal Employment Opportunities Commission—charged with enforcing the act—discovered in its first year of operation that 40% or more of the complaints warranting investigation charged discrimination on the basis of sex.

Title VII also forbids job advertisements from indicating a preference for one sex or the other unless sex is a bona fide occupational qualification for employment. In interpreting this provision, the EEOC issued the following guideline on August 9, 1968:

"It is a violation of Title VII for a help-wanted advertisement to indicate a preference, limitation, specification or discrimination based on sex unless sex is a bona fide occupational qualification for the particular job involved. The placement of an advertisement in columns classified by publishers on the basis of sex, such as columns headed 'Male' or 'Female,' will be considered an expression of a preference, limitation, specification, or discrimination based on sex."

On December 1, 1968, all of the New York City newspapers desegregated their want ads in compliance with a New York City Ordinance which paralleled Title VII. Several other newspapers—notably *The Christian Science Monitor* and *Newsday*—have voluntarily integrated their want ads in accord with EEOC guidelines.

Recently, the State Human Relations Act of Pennsylvania and the City Human Relations Ordinance of Pittsburgh were amended so that they, too, prohibit discrimination on the basis of sex. They, too, contain provisions covering employment and employment advertising parallel to those found in Title VII.

On September 10, 1969, the Greater Pittsburgh chapter of the National Organization for Women formally filed a complaint with the Mayor's Commission on Human Relations, charging that the sex-segregated want ad columns of *The Pittsburgh Press* were in violation of the Pittsburgh Human Relations Ordinance. *The Pittsburgh Press* classifies its job advertisements into columns labeled "Jobs-Male Interest" and "Jobs-Female Interest." In responding to the complaint, *The Press* maintained that its policy is not discriminatory because it prints a notice informing job applicants that such classifications are only for the convenience of its readers and that job seekers should assume that advertisers will consider applicants of either sex.

On January 15, 1970, the first author was asked to testify at the hearing on this complaint. As part of her testimony, she was asked to discuss the possibility that sex-segregated want ads, even of this modified form, might aid and abet sex discrimination in employment by discouraging female job seekers from applying for jobs listed in the "Male" column. The following study was conducted in order to provide information relevant to that question.

THE STUDY

Fifty-two women attending Carnegie-Mellon University in Pittsburgh were asked to rate each of thirty-two jobs which had been advertised in Sunday editions of *The Pittsburgh Press*. Sixteen of the ads had been drawn from the "Male Interest" column and sixteen had been drawn from the "Female Interest" column. Each woman was given a booklet containing all thirty-two ads. She was asked to read each ad and to rate it on the following scale: +3 if you would be definitely willing to apply for the job. +2 if you would be quite willing to apply for the job. +1 if you would be somewhat willing to apply for the job. −1 if you would be somewhat unwilling to apply for the job. −2 if you would be quite unwilling to apply for the job. −3 if you would be definitely unwilling to apply for the job.

The women were told to assume that they had the necessary prerequisites for each job: "We are only interested in your preferences, not your skills."

Segregated Want Ads.—Half of the booklets listed the ads in a sex-segregated format identical to that used by *The Pittsburgh Press*. The sixteen male jobs were listed in alphabetical order in a column labeled "Jobs—Male Interest." The sixteen female jobs were listed in alphabetical order in a column labeled "Jobs—Female interest." Of these, half listed the male jobs first and half listed the female jobs first.[1] In addition, the following disclaimer, quoted verbatim from *The Pittsburgh Press*, appeared on every other page of the booklet:

NOTICE TO JOB SEEKERS

"Jobs are arranged under Male and Female classifications for the convenience of our readers. This is done because most jobs generally appeal more to persons of one sex than the other .

"Various laws and ordinances—local, state and federal, prohibit discrimination in employment because of sex unless sex is a bona fide occupational requirement. Unless the advertisement itself specifies one sex or the other, job seekers should assume that the advertiser will consider applicants of either sex in compliance with the laws against discrimination."

Integrated Want Ads.—Half of the booklets listed the identical thirty-two ads in alphabetical order with no sex-labeling. The disclaimer again appeared on every other page of the booklet, but with its first paragraph deleted.

THE RESULTS

Do sex-segregated want ads discourage women from seriously considering those jobs which *The Press* classifies as "male interest"? Our results show this to be the case. When jobs were segregated and labeled on the basis of sex, as they are in *The Press*, only 46% of the women in this study were as likely to apply for "male interest" jobs as for "female interest" jobs. In other words, a majority of the women did prefer "female interest" jobs. But does this really reflect a true preference on the part of women for so-called "female interest" jobs? No, it does not. For when these same jobs appeared in an integrated alphabetical listing with no reference to sex, fully 81% of the women preferred the "male interest" jobs to the "female interest" jobs.[2][3]

For example, the job of newspaper reporter fell in popularity from 7th place when it appeared in the integrated listing to 19th place when it was segregated as a "male interest" job. It seems clear that the newspaper editor who wishes to hire only male reporters—in violation of the law—can place his ad in the "Male Interest" column, secure in the knowledge that this will effectively discourage female applicants. It is in this way that sex-segregated want ads can "aid and abet" discrimination in employment on the basis of sex.

WHAT ABOUT ACTUAL JOB SEEKERS?

What can we infer from this study about the effects of sex-segregated want ads on actual job applicants? Can we generalize these results to the actual job-seeking situation? It is our view that, if anything, this study probably *under-*

---

[1] A complete list of all the jobs can be found in the appendix at the end of this report.

[2] These results have been evaluated for statistical significance to insure that they did not occur by chance. They are significant at the .02 level of confidence by a X^2 test.

[3] Surveys have shown that jobs listed in "male interest" columns are also preferable in terms of objective features like salary. fringe benefits, opportunity for advancement, etc.

estimates the extent to which sex-segregated want ads discourage female applicants.

First, we required the women in our study to rate *every* ad regardless of how it was labeled. We suspect that many women never even bother to look at those ads which appear in the "Male Interest" column. Indeed, several of the women in our study explicitly stated that it had never previously occurred to them to look for jobs in the "Male Interest" column.

Second, we asked the women only to indicate whether or not they would be willing to apply for each job. They did not, in fact, have to expose themselves to the risk of encountering discrimination by actually applying for "Male Interest" jobs. Clearly it is easier for a woman to *say* she will apply than it is for her to actually apply.

Third, our study employed the modified form of sex-segregated want ads instituted by *The Pittsburgh Press*. But many newspapers contain no disclaimers and adhere to the more traditional headings of "Male Help Wanted" and "Female Help Wanted." We have obtained ratings from high school students which indicate that this more traditional format discourages female applicants from considering so-called "Male" jobs even more effectively than the relatively benign format employed in the present study.[4]

Finally, in our study, the disclaimers occupied 13% of the available space in the booklet. This rendered them far more prominent than they would be in any full page of classified ads in a newspaper. (For example, even if *The Pittsburgh Press* published the disclaimer on every page of classified advertising, which it does not, it would still occupy less than 3% of the page.) In sum, this study would seem to underestimate the extent to which sex-segregated want ads actually discourage women job-seekers from applying for "Male Interest" jobs.

In responding to the complaint lodged against it, *The Pittsburgh Press* stated that "there are fundamental differences between men and women . . . [which] manifest themselves in job preferences." But psychological research reveals no fundamental sex differences that would be relevant to the world of work in a modern technological society like ours. In fact, if "fundamental" sex differences were truly to be adopted as the criterion for a "bona fide occupational qualification," then we can think of only two jobs for which all members of one sex or the other would be disqualified: sperm donor and wet nurse! Indeed, an anthropologist visiting our culture would find it amusing that in the same society where the position of gynecologist is filled almost exclusively by men, modesty requires the position of lingerie salesperson to be filled by a woman.

APPENDIX

JOB TITLES OF CLASSIFIED ADVERTISEMENTS EMPLOYED IN THE STUDY [5]

Jobs from the "male interest" columns:	Jobs from the "female-interest" columns:
Advertising Assistant	Advertising Communications Co-ordinator
Assistant to Branch Manager	Assistant Manager
Bookkeeper	Bookkeeper
Buyer of Toy Department	Cosmetics Supervisor Beginner
Commercial Artist	Dietitian
Executive Secretary	Executive Secretary
Food Service Operations Director	Interior Decorator
Personnel Interviewer Trainee	Librarian
Pharmacist	Market Research Assistant
Programmers	Programmers
Public Relations	Radio Station Beginner
Real Estate Sales	Registered Nurses
Reporters	Social Worker
Teachers	Stewardess
Trainees, Airlines	Teachers
Writer	Travel Reservationist

[4] We are grateful to Mr John M Cipollini, Principal of Churchill Area High Schol, for permitting us to gather these data.

[5] The actual booklets contained not only job titles, but complete job descriptions as published by *The Pittsburgh Press*. In the integrated condition, jobs were simply arranged in strict alphabetical order with no reference to sex.

CONGRESS OF THE UNITED STATES,
HOUSE OF REPRESENTATIVES,
Washington, D.C., June 8, 1970.

Hon. CARL D. PERKINS,
House of Representatives,
Washington, D.C.

DEAR COLLEAGUE: It is ironic and tragic that a bill designed to strengthen the law against discrimination in employment should be perverted and distorted into a vehicle which, although initially designated to increase and perpetuate discrimination on the basis of sex, actually will authorize discrimination on the basis of race, color, religion and national origin, as well as sex.

Yet that is exactly what would happen under the amendment which Congressman Marvin L. Esch sponsored, and which the General Labor Subcommittee included, in the bill recommended to the House Education and Labor Committee—H.R. 17555, the "Equal Employment Opportunities Enforcement Act," to revise Title VII of the Civil Rights Act of 1964.

The Esch amendment would permit any employer to discriminate between employees in connection with pension and retirement plans, "notwithstanding any other provisions" of Title VII, and thus to do so on the basis of "race, color, religion, sex. or national origin."

The effect of his amendment is so startling that it is hard to believe it. Yet that is precisely what the Esch amendment says. It thus simply repeals Title VII so far as concerns pension and retirement plans.

This matter I call to your attention in the hope that you, as a member of the Education and Labor Committee, will vote against the Esch amendment when the Committee considers H.R. 17555, which I understand will be in the next few days.

Title VII of the 1964 Civil Rights Act was a great milestone in the national effort to eliminate irrational bias in employment. It makes it unlawful for any employer "to discriminate against any individual" on the basis of race, color, religion, sex or national origin with respect to "compensation, terms, conditions, or privileges of employment." The employee's option to retire at a certain age is clearly a "privilege" of employment, and the terms and benefits of a retirement plan are certainly derived from the employment relationship. Therefore, Title VII plainly prohibits discrimination with regard to pension and retirement plans on the basis of race, color, religion, sex, or national origin. Since the same language of Title VII applies to race discrimination as to sex discrimination, it is clear that both race and sex discrimination are not permissible with respect to pensions and retirement plans.

The Esch amendment stems from the fact that the Equal Employment Opportunity Commission, acting pursuant to the historic mandate of Title VII, issued Guidelines on sex discrimination in February 1968 (33 F.R. 3344; 29 C.F.R. 1604.31) stating that a "difference in optional or compulsory retirement ages based on sex violates Title VII." These Guidelines were issued after extensive consideration by EEOC for over two years, plus comprehensive public hearings held in May 1967. The Commission also said that it would later rule (but it is still studying) whether other sex differences in pension and retirement plans, such as differences in annuity computations, benefits to survivors, etc., are valid under the equality mandate of Title VII.

The Bell Telephone companies, the principal lobbyists for the Esch amendment, have persistently sought to obtain legislative repeal of the EEOC ruling. They seek the amendment in order to retain their present pension and retirement systems, which discriminate in different aspects, against not only their women employees but also their male employees. This is but another example of sex discrimination by the telephone companies which have long relegated women to the lesser paid jobs in the communications industry. Telephone companies are defendants in some of the most significant court suits by their women employees protesting employment discrimination based on sex. Both the courts and the EEOC have repeatedly ruled against the telephone companies in sex discrimination cases. For example, Weeks v. Southern Bell Tel. & Tel. Co., 408 F. 2nd 228 (CA 5, 1969) ; Cheatwood v. South Central Bell Tel. & Tel. Co., 303 F. Supp. 754 (N.D. Ala. 1969) ; Tuten v. Southern Bell Tel. Co., 2 FEP Cases 299 (M.D. Fla 1969).

The Esch amendment is copied from the language proposed by the Bell Telephone companies which would legislatively sanction many types of sex discrimination, including such matters as optional retirement age, the age and employment tenure required for participation in pension plans, survivorship benefits, computation of amount of the pension, the date and conditions under which rights to annuities become vested, and other aspects of pension and retirement plans. However, the Esch amendment inexplicably omits the words "male" and "female", perhaps in order to obfuscate and veil its effect, and thus broadens it from a vehicle of sex discrimination to one which permits discrimination on the basis of race, color, religion, and national origin, as well as sex.

It is inconceivable to me that the Congress would adopt a provision which would sanction race discrimination in pension and retirement plans. Indeed, I am astonished that the Esch amendment is drafted so broadly, since the Bell Telephone companies lobbyists for this amendment have heretofore explicitly requested legislation to permit such discrimination only on the basis of sex. But even if the Committee amends the Esch amendment to restrict it to sex discrimination, it would still be contrary to our national policy of nondiscrimination and should not be adopted.

For your convenience I have prepared the attached analysis detailing some of the specific defects of the Esch amendment, with particular emphasis on its sex discrimination features. I hope you will read it before you vote on H.R. 17555, and that it will persuade you to vote against the amendment, in its entirety.

With warm regards.

Sincerely yours,

MARTHA W. GRIFFITHS,
Member of Congress.

ANALYSIS BY MARTHA W. GRIFFITHS CONCERNING THE ESCH AMENDMENT TO H.R. 17555 (91ST CONG.)—THE "EQUAL EMPLOYMENT OPPORTUNITIES ENFORCEMENT ACT"—TO PERMIT RACIAL AND SEX DISCRIMINATION IN PENSION AND RETIREMENT PLANS

The amendment sponsored by Congressman Marvin L. Esch to H.R. 17555, now pending in the House Committee on Education and Labor, would add the following new subsection to section 703 of Title VII of the Civil Rights Act of 1964:

"(k) Notwithstanding any other provision of this title, it shall not be an unlawful employment practice to observe a pension or retirement plan, the terms or conditions of which permit but do not require certain employees to retire at earlier ages than other employees, or provide for other reasonable differentiation between employees, provided that such pension or retirement plan is not merely a subterfuge to evade the purposes of this title."

Title VII prohibits discrimination concerning "compensation, terms, conditions, or privileges of employment" on the basis of "race, color, religion, sex, or national origin." The Esch amendment permits discrimination "notwithstanding any other provision" of Title VII. Hence, the Esch amendment would permit discrimination, in pension and retirement plans, on the basis which Title VII prohibits, namely, race, color, religion, sex, or national origin.

Although the Esch amendment would apparently not sanction such discrimination in connection with compulsory retirement age, it would permit such discrimination in many other aspects of pension and retirement plans, including optional retirement age, the age required for participation in pension plans, survivorship benefits, computation of the amount of pension payments, the date and conditions under which rights to annuities become vested, and any other aspect which might be deemed a "reasonable differentiation between employees". However, the Esch amendment contains no definition as to what is a "reasonable differentiation" besides optional retirement age, and does not state any criteria by which to judge what discrimination is "reasonable". Hence, that phrase does not really limit the scope of the Esch amendment. Nor does the proviso that the pension plan should not be "merely a subterfuge to evade" Title VII provide any real protection against such discrimination. If the plan contains any element besides that which is a "subterfuge," the plan would then no longer be "merely" a subterfuge, even though it blatantly discriminates on a basis by Title VII. This is not an idle fear, in view of the recent decision by the U.S. Court of Appeals for the Fifth Circuit that sex discrimination in employment is permissible if it is associated with another element not prohibited by Title VII. *Phillips* v. *Martin Marietta Corp.*, 411 F. 2d 1; rehearing den., 416 F. 2d 1257 (C.A. 1969). The Supreme Court granted certiorari on March 2, 1970 (No. 1058, Oct. Term, 1969), and will hear, and I hope reverse, that decision next fall.

Sometimes I hear the argument made that sex distinctions in retirement ages are reasonable because of sex differences in actuarial mortality tables. Yes, women do live longer than men. When a man retires at 65, he will receive approximately 10 years of pension payments, while a woman who retires at 62 will receive approximately 20 years of such payments. If any sex is entitled to an earlier optional retirement age privilege, it should be the male. Frankly, no sex differential is reasonable for retirement age, and the Esch amendment would simply permit unwarranted discrimination based on sex.

There is no valid national need for the Esch amendment. Over 95 percent of all pension plans under collective bargaining reported pursuant to the Welfare and Pension Plans Disclosure Act contain no distinction between men and women workers. The other 5 percent contained sex differentials only as to the age required for participation in the pension plan or for retirement. (Incidentally, the pension plans of the Bell Telephone companies, the principal lobbyists for the Esch amendment, affect the most employees.) Furthermore, industry at present rarely makes sex the basis for differences in the pensions paid to the retired employee, or in the amount of credited service and earnings necessary to receive such benefits. Yet the Esch amendment would sanction and encourage sex discrimination in all of these aspects, and others, of pension and retirement plans, "notwithstanding any provision of Title VII." In trust, the Esch amendment is so broad as to constitute virtually a blank check for sex discrimination in pension and retirement plans.

Neither the Federal Civil Service nor the Social Security retirement systems provide for different retirement ages as between men and women, whether for compulsory retirement or for optional retirement. Both systems are totally devoid of sex discrimination, except for two aspects. One aspect, which will be abolished by the Social Security Amendments of 1970 passed by the House on May 21, 1970 (H.R. 17550), concerns the difference in computing benefits for Social Security retirees under which men retiring between ages 62 and 65 receive lower pensions than women retiring at such ages. The other aspect concerns survivorship benefits, which are granted to a male employee's widow without requiring her to show that she was the employee's dependent, but are not granted to a female employee's widower unless he shows he was the employee's dependent. This distinction is based on a concept of welfare, rather than compensation for work performed, and I have introduced bills to end this distinction and to put widowers and widows on the same footing for survivorship benefits based on their spouse's employment. I believe the dependency distinction between widows and widowers will eventually be abolished. In any event, it does not justify the broad and virtually unlimited sex discrimination which the Esch amendment would permit and encourage in all non-Federal pension and retirement plans.

Since the Federal Civil Service and Social Security retirement systems operate effectively without broad scale sex discrimination, I see no reason why non-Federal pension and retirement plans cannot also operate effectively without sex discrimination.

There may be some women who would want to take advantage of an earlier optional retirement age than is available to their male colleagues. But their concern must be balanced against the fact that the disadvantages of sex differentials in pension and retirement plans far outweigh that particular benefit. Permitting sex discrimination in relation to optional retirement will foster the continuation of discrimination now practiced against women who are able and desire to work beyond the optional retirement age. Experience has shown that where such earlier option exists, many employers deny promotion to qualified women on the ground that they may be retiring at an earlier age. In addition, many employers also exert pressure on women to retire at the earlier age in order to replace them with younger women or men. The earlier optional retirement age privilege is not an unalloyed benefit to women. Finally, with respect to the small group of women who are now near retirement age and who might have planned to retire under the optional privilege, it should be noted that the Equal Employment Opportunity Commission announced, on September 16, 1968, that it would construe the Guidelines on sex discrimination as permitting women workers, who were then within 10 years of retirement age under existing retirement plans permitting optional retirement, to retain their right to exercise that option. That E.E.O.C. ruling certainly destroys any possible argument that the equality mandate of Title VII is unfair to any women having a sex discriminatory preference under an existing retirement plan.

We should also consider the source of the argument that sex differentials in optional retirement ages favor women and, therefore, should not be abandoned. That argument is not supported by the almost 200,000 member National Federation of Business and Professional Women's Clubs, a traditional protector of the rights of the working woman, or by the Citizen's Advisory Council on the Status of Women, or by the National Organization for Women whose goal is "full equality for women in truly equal partnership with men," or by the National Woman's Party which has fought for women's rights since the early 1900's. On the contrary, the principal lobbyists for the Esch amendment are the Bell Telephone companies who have long relegated women to the lesser paid jobs in the communications industry, and who fear that the elimination of sex differences in retirement age may result in earlier retirement for men, or longer service and increased credits for women, and thereby increase the companies' pension costs. I don't know why the Bell Telephone companies are worried about this, since the hearings before the Joint Economic Committee's Subcommittee on Fiscal Policy, of which I am chairman, revealed that in 1966 those companies had over $5 billion in their pension trust funds and had never paid out one cent of the principal—all pensions are paid entirely from the interest earned by the trust funds. Hearings on Private Pension Plans, 89th Congress, Part One (May 2, 1966), pp. 228, 235.

Furthermore, I find it difficult to understand the reasoning that a system which discriminates in some ways against men rather than against women should, therefore, be continued. We in the Congress are elected by all the people, men and women, and it ill behooves us to discriminate against either men or women solely on the basis of sex. Indeed, I resent the implication that women should be favored over men on the assumption that women are incapable of withstanding unprotected the rigors of economic life and hence must be especially protected and favored by the law. Whatever validity that concept had five or six decades ago, it has none today. According to the 1969 Handbook on Women Workers published by the Department of Labor (Women's Bureau Bulletin 294), women head 11 percent of all families (page 28), and comprise 37 percent of our total labor force 16 years of age and over (pages 9, 10, 22). Women are now certainly entitled to be rid of the "adult children" myth which brands them as incapable of equal participation in our present economy. They are willing to take their chances with equal privileges if society will but grant them equal opportunities.

Moreover, while the direct effect of an earlier retirement age for women primarily discriminates against men, its indirect effect also discriminates against women,—namely, the wives and families of male employees who are denied retirement age privileges available to female employees. Discrimination is a seamless web. If we permit it to exist against the interests of one group, it will inevitably work against the interests of the other.

The Esch amendment has no place in a country dedicated to the proposition of equality of opportunity regardless of race, color, religion, sex, or national origin. It should be roundly rejected.

Thank you for permitting me to express my views on Section 805 of your bill, H.R. 16098. I fully support that section and will work with you to obtain its enactment.

WOMEN AND THE LAW

ARE WOMEN EQUAL UNDER THE LAW?

(Gene Boyer, May 1970)

IN BASIC CIVIL AND POLITICAL RIGHTS

1. Are men and women treated equally under the law?
In several states, the punishments for some crimes are not only different, but of greater or lesser degree, depending on the sex of the criminal. Until as recently as 1968, two states (Pennsylvania and Connecticut) had laws which decreed that any woman convicted of a crime must be given the maximum penalty.

A prostitute is treated as a far worse criminal than the man caught consorting with her. He is, in fact, charged with a lesser crime and receives a lighter punishment for participating equally in the same illegal act.

2. Do men and women have the same freedoms to use public places?
Among other inequities sanctioned by the law, women are discriminated against in places of public accommodation. Many restaurants, clubs and cocktail lounges refuse to serve women, or restrict them to certain rooms and times, or require their being escorted by a male.

Golf courses have "men only" days and hours. Airlines encourage wives to accompany husbands on business trips by offering a bargain rate of one-half the regular fare for the wife . . . but a husband is not allowed to travel half-fare on his wife's business-trip ticket.

3. Do men and women have the same obligations as citizens?
One state (Mississippi) still prohibits women from serving on juries. Almost half the states permit women to be excused from serving on juries solely by reason of being a woman. In Louisiana, a woman must pre-register in order to be considered eligible for *jury service.*

Many women consider non-conscription during periods of compulsory *military service* an abrogation of their rights as citizens.

Women are still held to "handmaidenry" in our political system, rarely achieve appointments to policy-making bodies in *public life.* In Wisconsin, for example, the governor-appointed Council on Home and Family is composed of 16 men to 1 woman; the Council on Highway Safety has a ratio of 9 men to 1 woman; the Higher Educational Aids Board has 14 men, 1 woman. No woman serves on the parole board that decides the fate of women offenders in the prisons.

4. Does the United States subscribe to the principles expressed in the United Nations Declaration on the Political Rights of Women?
The United States has so far failed to ratify any of the 20 Human Rights Conventions of the United Nations, including the Declaration on the Elimination of Discrimination Against Women, but with the exception of the one against slavery.

5. Are both men and women guaranteed equal protection of the law under the United States Constitution?
The Supreme Court has never decreed that women are persons under the law and entitled to its equal protections under the 14th amendment to the Constitution.

6. Do men and women have the same rights to legal residence?
The domicile of a married woman automatically follows that of her husband. If he has moved to a separate domicile, or deserted her, this can seriously affect

385

her rights to vote, to run for public office, serve on juries, have her estate properly administered, etc.

In 5 states (Alaska, Arkansas, Delaware, Hawaii and Wisconsin), a wife may take legal steps to establish separate domicile for all purposes.

In 13 additional states (California, Connecticut, Florida, Illinois, Indiana, Iowa, Maine, Massachusetts, Michigan, New Jersey, New York, North Dakota and Wyoming), she may do so for voting purposes. In 3 of these (Maine, New York and New Jersey) she may do so for the purpose of holding public office also.

In every case, the burden of special effort is upon the woman, while the man's legal residence follows him automatically.

7. *Are men and women equally free to change their name?*

In those cases where women have petitioned to legally retain their maiden names after marriage, the courts have uniformly rejected the effort.

Many states have statutes expressly denying to married women the right to change their surname to one other than their husband's. No comparable restriction is imposed on married men.

When a married man changes his surname, his wife's surname is automatically changed regardless of her wishes.

8. *Do married women have equal rights to married men—or to single women—under the law?*

Based in common law, many states have laws which cause a woman to forfeit rights when she marries, such as restricting married women from executing contracts, managing their own property, engaging in business without the consent of their husbands, etc.

Under common law, a man and wife become a single legal entity and the husband is the symbol and representative person for that entity. (The word "women" means "wife-of-man.")

IN MATTERS OF FAMILY LAW AND POLICY

9. *Do divorce laws favor women in the division of property?*

Except in the 9 community property states (Arizona, California, Hawaii, Idaho, Louisiana, New Mexico, Nevada, Texas and Washington), the wife is financially at the husband's mercy upon divorce.

In the 41 common law states, all monies earned by a husband during marriage belong exclusively to him and no monetary value is attached to the wife's domestic services in helping to produce the family income or acquire property.

10. *Do divorce laws favor women in the awarding of alimony and custody of children?*

More than one-third of the states permit alimony to be awarded to either spouse at the discretion of the court.

Often child support payments are camouflaged as alimony because taxes on alimony payments to an ex-wife are payable by her, not the ex-husband, while the total amount of alimony is subtracted from the ex-husband's income (child support is deductible only up to the $600 exemption allowed). As a result of lumping child support payments together with alimony, the husband enjoys a tax advantage.

In only a very few states is the mother given automatic preference in custody of children, and then only if they are very young. The general rule today is to award custody in accordance with the child's best interests.

11. *Do divorce laws favor women in establishing grounds for divorce?*

The only grounds for divorce common to all 50 states and the District of Columbia is adultery. Cruelty is recognized as grounds for divorce in 45 states, but the definitions of cruelty differ widely. Incompatability is recognized as a ground for divorce in only 4 states.

A woman who has been deserted by her husband must wait from 1 to 5 years before she can begin to sue him for divorce. The only state where a woman can begin suit after 6 months is Hawaii.

At present it is necessary to establish fault with the husband in order for the wife to receive alimony, a legal manipulation which adversely affects any possibilities for reconciliation between the parties or future amiable relationship.

It would not be necessary to establish fault in a divorce if alimony were viewed as recognition of the contribution made by a spouse to the family which is otherwise uncompensated; to reimburse for loss of earning capacity suffered by either spouse because of the marriage; and to continue the responsibility of a self-supporting spouse toward a financially dependent one until such time as the need is no longer acute (a form of "workmen's compensation" upon loss of job).

12. Do married men and women have the same rights to their earnings?

In the community property states (except Texas), all of an employed woman's earnings belong to a common fund which is legally under the control of the husband, the wife having no "say" as to how her income is spent.

A man need not pay wages to his wife who works in his business. This exemption, which is permitted in most states, does NOT apply to a husband employed by his wife, or children employed by their parents.

In no state does the law give the woman the right to tell her husband how to spend his earnings or to claim his labors without recompense.

13. Do married men and women have the same rights to property purchased by them from their individual earnings?

Unless there is a title or a record establishing otherwise, property purchased by the wife—such as a car or television set—is generally considered to be the property of the husband, even if the purchase was made entirely from her individual earnings.

A wife owns none of the property accumulated during marriage in her husband's name in the common law states. In some states, like Wisconsin, she has a "dower right" to only one-third of his estate when he dies.

14. Are married men and women equally responsible for each other?

In all states, a husband is liable for support of his wife regardless of her ability to support herself. This is based in the legal concept of "the perpetual tutelage of women."

A wife is not obliged to support a husband who is unable to support himself in 19 states, a denial of the mature woman's abilities to care for dependents. (Alabama, Colorado, Florida, Georgia, Hawaii, Indiana, Iowa, Kentucky, Maryland, Massachusetts, Mississippi, Missouri, Rhode Island, South Carolina, Tennessee, Texas, Virginia, Washington and Wyoming.)

15. Are parents equally responsible for their children?

In 4 states (Colorado, Montana, Ohio and Rhode Island), the father alone is required to support legitimate children. In 6 states (Alaska, Colorado, Minnesota, Mississippi, Ohio and Rhode Island) the father alone is required to support illegimate children.

Differential responsibility shows up in laws governing matters other than support. In Wisconsin, only the father's signature is acceptable on the driver's license application of a minor.

IN MATTERS OF EMPLOYMENT

16. Do the same labor standards apply to men and women? Are they equally protected in such matters as minimum wages, overtime pay, maximum hours, safety and health?

In 11 states there are no minimum wage laws at all. (Alabama, Florida, Georgia, Iowa, Mississippi, Missouri, Montana, South Carolina, Tennessee, Texas and Virginia.)

In 39 states, the District of Columbia and Puerto Rico there are minimum wage laws, but in 7 of these the laws apply to women and minors only. (Arizona, California, Colorado, Minnesota, Ohio, Utah and Wisconsin.)

When coupled with other restrictions—such as maximum hours, weight-lifting or night-work prohibitions—these so-called "protective" labor laws serve to bar women from equal opportunities in employment, in promotion and training for advancement.

Weight-lifting restrictions for women exist in 10 states (Alaska, California, Maryland, Massachusetts, New York, Oregon, Ohio, Utah, Washington, and in Puerto Rico). In California, for example, a woman who regularly carries growing children off to bed is prohibited from carrying as little as 10 pounds on the job!

Recently, decisions on test cases in state courts have declared these restrictive laws in conflict with, and overridden by, the federal laws providing equality of opportunity in employment.

17. Are women entitled to the same pay as men for the same work?

Only 31 states have equal pay laws guaranteeing women the same wage for the same work done by men on the same or similar job.

Only 15 states, including Wisconsin, have Fair Employment Practices laws which include prohibitions against discrimination in employment on the basis of sex. Equal pay is not always specified as a requirement in these laws.

Many employment contracts are written—including those for professionals, such as teachers—which pay premiums for head-of-household or additional dependents, and which serve to defeat the principle of equal pay for equal work.

18. Are women entitled to equal opportunities in hiring, training and promotion under Title VII of the Civil Rights Act of 1964?

This major piece of legislation, perhaps second only to women's suffrage in 1920 in securing equal rights for women, has shortcomings: women employed in government service or in the field of education are not covered; the Equal Employment Opportunity Commission, the enforcing agency, lacks effective powers.

While the law specifically prohibits the advertisement of jobs under sex-designated column headings, only a few major newspapers (such as the New York Times) are voluntarily complying.

Current practices in the professions, education, labor unions, among employers in business and industry, operate to prevent women from achieving promotions to supervisory and executive positions. Among these practices are: excluding women from conferences, from training courses, from membership in professional organizations, from quasi-social meetings, groups or facilities which are, in reality, arenas of business negotiations.

Women are often prevented from acquiring franchises, dealerships, distributorships and other opportunities for going into business as entrepreneurs by such "subtle" practices as requiring excessive financial resources or extra guarantors on loans from the female investor.

19. Are women in control of most of the wealth of our country?

Women own approximately 51% of the stock and securities issued in this country, which is not surprising in view of the fact that they constitute 53% of the adult population.

Less than 3% of women with income from any source earn over $10,000 per year, as compared to 24% of men.

Women are conspicuous by their absence from the ranks of stockbrokers, financiers, corporation and bank presidents, boards of directors of major corporations, insurance companies, high government officials and other elements of control over the economics and wealth of our country.

IN MATTERS OF HEALTH, EDUCATION, AND WELFARE

20. Do boys and girls have the same rights to parental support?

In 7 states, boys have a right to parental support up to age 21 while girls have that right only to age 18. (Arkansas, Idaho, Nevada, North Dakota, Oklahoma, South Dakota, Utah)

21. Are boys and girls equally entitled to a high school education?

High schools are permitted to refuse attendance to girls who are married or pregnant: married boys and unwed fathers are usually allowed to attend.

22. Do boys and girls have the same opportunity to enter college, if they qualify academically?

Quotas limiting registration of girls in certain classes and colleges are common; such quotas are invoked even at coeducational, tax-supported state institutions of higher learning.

Many more scholarships and other financial aids are available to male students.

Prejudice and discouraging counseling practices are responsible in large part for the continuing low enrollments of women in schools of medicine, law, engineering, business administration, and other "traditional" male fields.

23. Are men and women equally entitled to control their own reproductive processes?

The men who make the laws which control contraception and abortion have, in effect, control over the reproductive processes of women.

While the idea of legally required prevention of conception to mitigate the population explosion is regarded as an intolerable intervention in individual liberties, the woman who is victim of an accidental conception is forced by law to go through a pregnancy against her will and, in many cases, bear an unwanted child.

Since it is comparatively easier for the affluent woman to obtain an illegal abortion, it is the low-income woman whose liberty and freedom of choice is most often abrogated, and who frequently becomes the hapless victim of fatal quackery.

24. Are men and women living in poverty given equal opportunities toward a better life?

The latest available data shows that, among the poor, women outnumber men 8 to 5. Women and children together constitute over ⅔ of all persons living in poverty.

Many Federal programs designed to relieve poverty conditions fail to include women proportionately. Manpower Development and Training, Job Corps, etc., concentrate on skills for males, while the unemployment rate among females is higher.

Adequate housing is also extremely difficult to find for the woman who is head-of-household, has dependents to support, is seasonally employed, unemployed, marginally or under-employed. Of the better than 5 million women heading a family, 35% are counted among the poor.

25. Are women, as well as men, on Aid to Families with Dependent Children (AFDC) entitled to retain some human dignity and pride?

In Wisconsin, and other states, the law requires a woman applicant for AFDC to declare her willingness to file criminal non-support charges against the father in order to be eligible for benefits.

In many cases, rather than jeopardize the possibility of a reconciliation with her deserting husband, a woman will refuse to file charges and will, instead, risk starvation for herself and children. The state does not need her charges to pursue a deserting father.

IN MATTERS OF SOCIAL INSURANCE AND TAXES

26. Do men and women enjoy equal unemployment compensation benefits?

Several categories of employment are excluded from coverage in most states: employment by state and local governments, non-profit organizations, agricultural workers and domestic workers in private homes. Except for agricultural workers, women represent a substantial part of the labor force in excluded categories.

In addition, women are disqualified for benefits under unemployment compensation if they leave work due to pregnancy and maternity, or because of domestic or marital obligations. In 7 states, a man may leave the job because of domestic or marital obligations and still receive benefits (Alaska, Arkansas, Idaho, Maine, Minnesota, Montana and Utah).

27. Do men and women have the same protections against unemployment, loss of seniority and enforced retirement due to circumstances beyond their control?

An employer can discharge an employee for pregnancy any time he chooses, regardless of her state of health or willingness to work. In Wisconsin she cannot collect unemployment compensation under any circumstances for 10 weeks before the birth of the child and 4 weeks thereafter.

An employer has no obligation to grant a woman employee a leave of absence for maternity with or without loss of seniority upon her return. Ailing men and those in military service are frequently granted long leaves of absence with continuing benefits, sometimes over a period of years.

An employer is within legal rights in insisting that a woman employee retire at an earlier age than a man and receive smaller benefits under a company-sponsored retirement plan.

Domestic workers in private homes, most of whom are women, are not protected under unemployment compensation and may miss out on social security benefits due to laxness on the part of their employers in failing to file appropriate forms and contributions for the employee's social security account.

28. Do income tax laws allow equitable deductions for workers' out-of-pocket expenses necessitated by employment?

Deductible items for income tax purposes for the employed person include secretarial expense, automobile expense, on-the-job, educational expense to obtain promotion, expense of entertaining customers, etc., etc., . . . but *not* home and child-care expense during working hours!

29. Do social security laws treat men and women equitably?

A woman who has been employed most of her life and contributed regularly to her social security account may (1) receive nothing from her account if she elects instead to receive benefits from her husband's account; (2) receive lesser retirement benefits than the never-employed wife or widow of a man who happened to earn more as a worker than the employed woman.

A woman who has been married to an employed man for anything less than 20 years, if divorced, is not eligible to receive any retirement benefits from his account in her old age!

30. Is an aged woman entitled to live at least as comfortably as an aged man of comparable life-long economic means?

At present, a widow who becomes entitled to benefits at age 62 or after receives only 82½% of the retirement benefit her husband would have received had he lived.

The law tacitly expects an aged widow to live on less than a surviving widower or a retired single male.

*31. All other things being equal, should a couple's retirement benefits be greater
if they were both employed outside the home and both contributed to the social
security system?*

Under present law, an aged couple may receive less in total monthly benefits
if both husband and wife worked than a couple whose benefits are based on the
same total earnings derived from the husband's employment alone.

Example: If only the husband worked and had average earnings of $7800
per year, benefits paid to the couple at age 65 would be $323 monthly ($218 to
the husband and $105 to the wife). If both worked and had average earnings
of $3900 a year each—combined annual earnings of $7800—their benefits would
be $134.30 each, or a total of $268.60 . . . $54 per month less than the one-earner
family!

In effect, it is the contributions of working wives which support a system
whose benefits accrue in large measure to non-contributing dependents.

STATEMENT IN SUPPORT

(By Miss Marguerite Rawalt, Attorney,[1] member of bar of District of Columbia,
Texas, Virginia, U.S. Supreme Court)

Madam Chairman and members of the Subcommittee on Education:

My appearance here today is to express support of Sec. 805 (a), (b), and (c)
of H.R. 16098, as urgently needed measures to eliminate sex discrimination in
employment by Federal government contractors and by educational institutions,
and to extend the jurisdiction of the U.S. Civil Rights Commission to research
of existing laws and policies relating to discrimination on the basis of sex in
addition to its present jurisdiction of race discrimination.

Proposals such as these serve to point out the present lack of constitutional
protection of the women of this country, whose one constitutional guarantee is
that of the right to vote. Meanwhile, unless and until our nation's women can
have the same protection. the same rights as men citizens under the constitution,
they must continue to expend energies in seeking statutory changes, piece by
piece, bit by bit, just as herein proposed. Today it is timely to make a plea to
members of the House of Representatives to submit the Equal Rights Amendment
to the states by signing the pending discharge petition, and by voting for the
measure without crippling amendments of any kind.

It is the focus of this statement to treat of the legal status of women under the
present constitution, as authoritatively interpreted by the highest court of the
land, and thus to demonstrate the need of a specific constitutional declaration
against discrimination on account of sex. The proposed Equal Rights Amendment
reads:

"Equality of rights under the law shall not be denied or abridged by the
United States or by any State on account of sex."

If such amendment were in the constitution at this time, it would be the legal
test and yardstick to insure the very purposes which Sec. 805 proposes. This is
my advocacy and the views of thousands of women organized in many business
and social welfare groups, seeking favorable action by the Congress to submit
the proposed amendment for ratification, at the same time enacting the specific
steps of Sec. 805 toward legal equality.

Women of America, black and white, are the real underprivileged half of the
population under the laws on our statute books and the controlling decisions of
the Supreme Court. As the spotlight is belatedly turned upon discrimination
under archaic laws, and upon tolerated and unfounded prejudice and stereotyping of women, women are moving out of the ranks of the silent and submissive
majority into a knowledgeable and growing feminist movement reaching into
every city and town, university campus, and business establishment.

---

[1] Miss Rawalt served as member of the President's Commission on the Status of Women
(1961–3) and of the first Citizens' Advisory Council on the Status of Women (1963–8);
as Co-Chairman with Congresswoman Edith Green of the Committee on Civil and Political
Rights of Women, and Chairman of the Task Force on Family Law and Policy. She was
National President of the Federal Bar Association, and of the National Association of
Women Lawyers; National President of the National Federation of Business and Professional Women's Clubs; Chairman of Legal Committee and General Counsel of the
National Organization for Women (1966–1969) during which time it prosecuted first
appeals in Title VII cases.

As an attorney and organization worker, I have come into first-hand knowledge of the lack of constitutional inclusion of women under the 14th and 5th amendments. The U.S. Supreme Court is the final and definitive interpreter of the constitution. Yet, to this date, one fails to find that our high court has ruled that a woman is a "person" or a citizen entitled to "equal protection of law" under the 14th amendment, although a scant few lesser ranking courts have so held. This was recognized by President Kennedy's Commission on the Status of Women, composed of 11 men and 15 women, in their *1963* report, *American Women* [1] which recommended that:

"Early and definitive court pronouncement, particularly by the U.S. Supreme Court, is urgently needed with regard to the validity under the 5th and 14th amendments of laws and official practices discriminating against women, to the end that the principle of equality become firmly established in constitutional doctrine."

The Commission continued by calling upon: "interested groups to give high priority to bringing under court review cases involving laws and practices which discriminate against women; appropriate Federal, State and local officials to scrutinize carefully those laws, regulations, and practices which distinguish on the basis of sex to determine whether they are justifiable in the light of contemporary conditions to the end of removing archaic standards which today operate as discriminatory; and encouraging efforts on the part of all interested groups in educating the public and urging private action, and action within the *judicial, executive,* and *legislative branches* of government, to the end that *full equality of rights may become a reality.*"

Seven years have passed since this declaration of need of Supreme Court pronouncement without such constitutional issue being passed upon by the Court. In that time, it has been petitioned two times to accept such cases, one case involving maximum hours laws applicable only to women.[2] Certiorari was denied in the other case styled Bynacker v McMichael, at the same term of Court.[3] The issue was whether the divorcing wife was entitled to a court order for an accounting from her husband, of the community property assets which he was concealing. The Court denied certiorari over the contention of her attorneys that she was being denied her property without due process of law and being denied equal protection of law, under the 14th Amendment.

The 14th Amendment, ratified in 1868, forbids any State to "deprive *any person* of life, liberty or property without due process of law; or to deny *any person* the equal protection of the laws." The 5th Amendment, applicable to the Federal Government, forbids depriving "any person or life, liberty or property without due process of law."

As interpreted by our courts, the 5th and 14th Amendments to the Constitution uphold a whole network of State discriminatory laws not only limiting women in the right to work, limiting the rights of married women in ownership and management of property, precluding them from choosing their domicile, and restricting other civil and political rights. For example:

1. The lack of constitutional protections for women of the U.S. has supported the failure of our Congress to ratify the United Nations Convention on Political Rights of Women, thus creating a cloud upon our international image as a democracy.

2. The 14th Amendment did not give women the right to vote (before 19th Amendment).

3. The 14th Amendment has never yet been applied by the Supreme Court to guarantee to an individual female citizen, the right to work at any lawful occupation of her choice, although the Court has applied its "equal protection" clause to insure the right to work to Chinese laundrymen, Japanese fishermen, a train conductor, and an Austrian cook. The Court as early as 1872 denied the application of the amendment to give a woman the right to practice law.

4. The Supreme Court, on the other hand, has applied the 14th Amendment to limit, restrain, and deny freedom to work to women by upholding maximum hours limitations, upholding exclusion from certain occupations. Its 1908 decision in *Muller* v. *Oregon* excluded women from "equal protection" by the rationale that "sex is a valid classification" for imposing restrictions which barred women from jobs. This precedent stands today, 62 years later, and has been the bulwark of the existing multitude of State laws enacted under the euphonious label of "protective labor laws".[1]

5. Title VII of the Civil Rights Act of 1964, forbidding discrimination in employment, after 5 years of operation, has not received consideration by the Su-

preme Court. One case which the Court accepted on March 2, 1970 does not involve the constitutional issue.

6. The 14th Amendment does not insure equitable property rights to married women.

7. The 14th Amendment has not fully opened doors to jury service by women.

8. Through the decades, the 14th Amendment failed to abrogate laws imposing longer prison terms on women criminals than for men. It was not until 1968 that the Pennsylvania Supreme Court struck down such a law in that State.

1. *Our country's international image.* The legal status of women of the United States is one of the greatest hypocrisies of our nation. The United States solemnly signed the United Nations Charter whose preamble asserts that "We the peoples of the United Nations, determined to reaffirm faith in the equal rights of men and women and of nations large and small . . ." and whose purposes declare "fundamental freedoms for all without distinction as to race, sex, language, or religion". Yet the United States has refused to ratify the U.N. Convention on the Political Rights of Women, which merely affirms that "women shall be entitled to vote in all elections, be eligible to hold public office, on equal terms with men." The Assistant Secretary of State in 1947, explained that "if the Equal Rights Amendment were added to the Constitution there would be nothing of a constitutional nature to prevent signing." [4]

The American Law Institute's "Statement of Essential Human Rights" declares that "*Every one* has the right to protection against arbitrary discrimination in the provisions of the law because of race, religion, sex . . ." and that "Barring an individual or group from the exercise of any right on the grounds of WHO they are (e.g. women, Negroes, Catholics) as distinguished from WHAT they have done (e.g. criminals or mental incompetents) would constitute arbitrary discrimination."

2. *The 14th Amendment did not give women the right to vote.* In 1873 Susan B. Anthony and other women were indicted and fined by the Federal Court of New York for having cast ballots in the 1872 presidential election. The Court ruled that "equal protection of law" did not apply to give them voting rights.

It required 50 years of pleading and persuasion before the U.S. Congress and before the State legislatures before the (19th) amendment was ratified to declare that the right to vote "shall not be denied or abridged by the U.S. or any State on account of sex."

In 1963 a court decision states that a Negro's vote and a woman's vote are an equal vote, whatever their race or sex.[5]

3. *The 14th Amendment did not give women the right to practice a lawful profession.* In 1872, the U.S. Supreme Court upheld the denial to a woman of the right to practice law in Illinois. The 14th Amendment was held inapplicable. The Court thus affirmed the decision of the Illinois Supreme Court which had said:

"That God designed the sexes to occupy different spheres of action . . . that it belonged to men to make, apply and execute the laws, was regarded at common law as an almost axiomatic truth." [6]

Ultimately, all States extended the right to practice law to women.

4. *The 14th Amendment has not been held to extend to women the right to work at any lawful occupation of an individual's choice.* In a line of decisions from 1884 to 1963, the U.S. Supreme Court has made it clear that the equal protection clause of the 14th Amendment guarantees the right to follow any of the common legitimate occupations of life—If you are a male citizen or a male alien.

The Court struck down a San Francisco ordinance which denied licenses to operate laundries to Chineses.[7] In 1914 it outlawed a Texas statute which operated to deny the job of freight train conductor to a fireman-engineer.[8] In 1915, the Supreme Court voided an Arizona statute which restricted an alien Austrian cook from working in a restaurant. Said the Court:

"It requires no argument to show that the right to work for a living in the common occupations of the country is the very essence of the personal freedom and opportunity that it was the purpose of the amendment (14th) to secure." [9]

To this writing, research has failed to disclose a single case in which our high court has upheld the right of an individual female to work at any lawful occupation of her choice. To the contrary,—

4(a). *The 14th Amendment has been applied to limit and restrict women in the right to work at any occupation of their choice.*

Sex discrimination exists under the labor laws of every State, the District of Columbia and Puerto Rico, with the single exception of the State of Delaware which repealed all such laws effective in 1966.

Beginning with the Massachusetts statute of 1874 limiting hours of work for women, an expanding deluge of laws limiting not only hours of work, but over-time pay (reserved to the men), exclusion from certain occupations altogether, weight that might be lifted on certain jobs, varying from a low 12-pound maxi-mum to a 35-pound one. exclusion from night work when pay was highest, etc. These laws were in truth enacted for the men, and by the men at a time when no woman had a voice or a vote. And at a time when relatively few women worked outside the home. Today, the women's workforce is more than 30 million. Under the beneficent-sounding and deceptive banner of "protection" of the "weaker sex" these limitations continue to this day, solidified into union contracts which pre-clude most of the 3½ million women right out of promotions, overtime pay, and even seniority rights. These laws reach nationwide to impose limitations upon non-union women numbering in millions. Because of "exceptions" they offer no "protection" against long hours to the semi-professional thousands in offices, nor to the scrub-women who work into the night cleaning offices and business establishments.

Today, 41 States and the District of Columbia have maximum hours limitations on women workers. This precludes employers from promoting them to supervisory jobs where overtime may be required and must be available, and precludes them from opportunities to earn the attractive double pay for overtime. Weight-lifting limitations (varying from 12 to 35 pound maximums) imposed by state law or by company policy are a basis for keeping women out of jobs they are qualified to fill.

These restrictive laws for women, under the guise of "protection" came under early review by the U.S. Supreme Court. In 1905, that Court held that a New York law limiting the hours of labor for male and female workers in a bakery was a violation of the 14th Amendment and invalid.[10] But, just three years later, the Supreme Court upheld the Oregon statute imposing maximum hours for women only which likewise was challenged under the 14th Amendment as a denial of equal protection of law. In a 1908 landmark decision titled *Muller* v. *Oregon*, the Court upheld the hours limitation for women workers by declaring the principle *"Sex is a valid basis for classification"*. Women, *as a class*, could be denied equal protection under the 14th Amendment. This decision has supported and undergirded the whole structure of restrictive labor laws on women workers, and stood unchallenged until Congressional action of 1964.[25]

This doctrine of placing all females in a "class" as a ground for denying 14th Amendment protection, has mushroomed through the years. In the field of educa-tion, a Supreme Court decision of 1938 established that a state university cannot refuse to admit a person to study, solely on the ground of his race. *Missouri ex rel Gaines* v. *Canada*. The University of Missouri was ordered to admit Mr. Gaines to its law school, his preference over the school he was attending. But 20 years later, Miss Allred was refused admission to the Texas State University's Agricultural and Mechanical College, solely on the ground of her sex, notwith-standing the fact that she could not major in floriculture in any other school in the state. *Allred* v. *Heaton* (1960) "Sex is a reasonable classification" repeated the State Court. The U.S. Supreme Court denied certiorari.[11]

5. *Title VII, Civil Rights Act of 1964 has not opened wide the doors of employ-ment opportunity for women.*

Hopes leaped high among women when Congress enacted the Civil Rights Act of 1964 which, after amendment, makes it unlawful to discriminate in employ-ment on account of race, color, religion, sex, or national origin.[12]

The prohibition against discrimination on account of "sex" was added on the floor of the House, by amendment. The Chairman of the House Judiciary Com-mittee, a distinguished lawyer, argued heatedly against this amendment, on the ground, "it would put in question the protective labor laws for women".[13] Con-gresswoman Martha Griffiths presented realistic examples of the situation supporting inclusion of women, else the "white woman would be last at the hiring gate".

Title VII created the Equal Employment Opportunity Commission (EEOC) to administer these provisions but without giving to the Commission any enforce-ment powers. Its role is conciliation. The Commission's rulings today require that virtually all jobs must be open to men and women, based upon qualifications only.

FEDERAL COURTS AND TITLE VII—AND STATE "PROTECTIVE" LAWS

Women themselves, in industry, have courageously filed complaints with the EEOC and have followed up by bringing suits in Federal courts to remove dis-crimination against them. The first three cases to be decided all ruled against the women plaintiffs. Two upheld weight-lifting limitations by State law and company policy. The third refused to find a "substantial constitutional question" in the conflict between an 8-hour maximum hours law of the State and the 14th Amendment. The U.S. Supreme Court refused to take appeal from the three-judge constitutional ruling and remanded the case for appeal through the U.S. Court of Appeals. These decisions were in June and August, 1967, and May 1968. At this point, Title VII stood not only meaningless so far as discrimination against women was concerned—it stood with two adverse decisions against it. What Congress had seemingly given, the courts had taken away.

The National Orgaization for Women, a newly formed civil-rights-for-women organization, came immediately to the fore, offering legal and financial assistance to the women in all three cases. Women attorneys of NOW's Legal Committee volunteered their professional time and talents, filed appeals, battled delaying tactics, and prepared and filed briefs in two U.S. Courts of Appeals, as well as the appeal to the Supreme Court. I was Chairman of that legal committee and General Counsel for NOW until a few months ago.

As a result, two landmark decisions came out of two Appellate Courts, turning the losses into wins. The U.S. Court of Appeals, 5th Circuit, in March 1969 handed down the first authoritative and final decision, reversing the District Court of Georgia, in *Weeks* v. *Southern Bell Telephone and Telegraph Co.*[14] The Court rejected a 35-pound weight limitation as a valid exception to the statute where the applicant had seniority and qualifications for the job.

The second landmark decision was handed down in September 1967 by the U.S. Court of Appeals for the 7th Circuit, Chicago. Its decision voided sex discrimination based on weight-lifting limits, separate seniority lists for men and women, and job classifications serving to exclude women from the better paying posts. *Bowe et al* v *Colgate-Palmolive Co. et al.*[15] Two cases which involve the 14th Amendment issue and whether State hours laws are constitutional, are pending decision in the U.S. Court of Appeals, 9th Circuit, San Francisco. *Mengelkoch v N. American Aviation Co.,*[2] *Rosenfeld* v. *Southern Pacific RR.*[15 16]

The Supreme Court agreed on March 2, 1970 to accept for decision a case involving the question whether a large industrial employer may legally deny a job to a woman applicant on the ground that she is mother of pre-school-age children. *Phillips* v *Martin-Marietta.*[17] No constitutional conflict is involved.

Employment discrimination reality. Within the past month an authentic survey was published by the Bureau of National Affairs, a first survey of 150 executives, about 60% representing larger companies employing 1,000 or more, and 40% executives from smaller companies. The survey revealed that today—

59% (nearly ⅗ths) of employers still disqualify women on the basis of sex.

51% of employers still apply the state "protective" laws, notwithstanding EEOC rulings, and even recent rulings of State Attorneys General that Federal law supersedes.

49% apply weight-lifting limitations.

44% apply State maximum hours laws for women.

Thus, the only avenue open to women in industry to be free from the shackles of hours limitations, occupational shut-outs, weight-lifting limitations and other restrictions on their employment, is to incur the cost and delay, risk to their jobs, of bringing individual or class suits in Federal Courts, case by case, employer by employer, State law by State law, to seek the right to employment at any lawful occupation of their choice—even the right to be considered for promotion to better paying positions. A constitutional amendment banning sex inequality would provide the unassailable yardstick for elimination of State laws binding women only. It would overrule "sex as a valid classification" foundation of present State restrictive laws.

6. *The 14th Amendment does not insure fair and equitable property rights to married women.*

In every State in the Union, one or another kind of legal disabiilty or restriction limits the property rights of married women, as reported by the President's Commission on the Status of Women.[18]

Property rights are fixed by State statutes. The 1944 opinion of the Florida Supreme Court summarized the situation:

". . . a woman's responsibilities and faculties remain intact from age of maturity until she finds her mate; whereupon, incompetency seizes her and she needs protection in an extreme degree. Upon the advent of widowhood she is reinvested with all her capabilities which had been dormant during her marriage, only to lose them again upon remarriage. Intermittently, she is protected and benefited accordingly as she is married or single."[19]

There are 42 common law States, and 8 community property States. Under common law principle, each spouse owns whatever property he or she earns. Where the husband was the sole wage-earner or businessman, ALL the property acquired during the marriage was therefore HIS property. State statutes have variously modified the common law principle, yet some limitation remains in every jurisdiction.

In the community property states, husband and wife each owns an outright one-half of real property acquired during marriage, even though the wife has no outside earnings. But in most jurisdictions, the husband and not the wife, has sole management rights, enabling him to create debts and dissipate the property without knowledge or consent of his wife. Texas revised such law in 1968. Compare the action of the courts in the *Hynacker* case.[20]

An equitable division of property upon termination of marriage which follows a formula "that there first be deducted from each spouse's property the debts of that spouse. Inherited or separate property would then be excluded. The remaining properties, the marital property, would then be divided equally 50–50, between husband and wife." Such a formula appears in a recent draft uniform law on Dissolution of Marriage proposed by the National Conference of Commissioners on Uniform State Law.

The Presidential Commission on the Status of Women stated its considered conclusions that

"Marriage as a partnership in which each spouse makes a different but equally important contribution is increasingly recognized in this country.

"During marriage, each spouse should have a *legally defined* substantial right in the earnings of the other, in the real and personal property acquired through those earnings and in their management." [21]

It seems clear that the proposed constitutional amendment would crystallize the 50–50 marriage partnership principle and set up a controlling legal test for eliminating remaining inequities.

7. *The 14th Amendment has not opened doors to jury service for women.*

The Civil Rights Act of 1957 provided that women were entitled to sit on all Federal juries. "Entitled" on the one hand, but subject to a whole variety of conditions and practices applicable only to women, which still serve to limit State jury service.

Until 1966, three States totally excluded women from serving on juries. Indicative of the fact that State statutes still control, the Supreme Court in January 1970 upheld Alabama and Georgia statutes on jury selection, although holding that the particular jury commissions had abused their discretion in the exclusion to large degree of Negroes from the jury rolls.[22]

There are still not less than 20 States and the District of Columbia which provide different treatment for men and women as jurors, such as the requirement that any woman must affirmatively request to be listed.

A constitutional amendment is needed which cannot be twisted into a ruling that "sex is a reasonable classification."

8. *The 14th Amendment, through the decades, was not applied to abrogate longer prison sentences for women criminals than for men.*

It was not until 1968 that the Supreme Court of Pennsylvania voided that State's Muncy Act in a case in which a woman convicted of robbery was sentenced to prison for a term of up to 10 years, instead of the 1-to-4-year term which would have been the maximum sentence for a man for the same offense.[23]

The legislative rationale when such laws were enacted was that "it required longer to rehabilitate a female criminal than a male."

[1] *American Women* (1963) Report of President's Commission on the Status of Women, obtainable Govt. Printing Office, Washington, D.C. 20402. $1.25.
[2] Mengelkoch v. Industrial Welfare Comm. and N. American Aviation Co. (C.D. Calif., 1968) 284 F. Supp. 950 ; appeal refused by USSC, 1968, 393 U.S. 83.
[3] Ethelyn Bynacker v. Bernard E. McMichael, U.S. Sup. Ct. No. 112, Misc. O.T. 1968, pet. cert. denied.
[4] Cong. Rec. July 19, 1956, p. 12349.
[5] Gray v. Sanders (1963) 372 U.S. 368.
[7] Yick Wo v. Hopkins (1886) 118 U.S. 356.
[6] Bradwell v. Illinois (1872) 83 U.S. 130 ; in re Lockwood (1894) 154 U.S. 116.
[8] Smith v. Texas (1914) 233 U.S. 630.
[9] Truax v. Raich (1915) 239 U.S. 33.
[10] Lochner v. New York (1905) 198 U.S. 95.
[11] Missouri ex rel Gaines v. Canada (1938) 305 U.S. 337 ; Allred v. Heaton (1960) Tex. Civ. App. 336 S.W. 2d 251 ; cert. den. 364 U.S. 517.
[12] Civil Rights Act 1964, effective July 1, 1965 ; 78 Stat. 241–352 ; Title VII 78 Stat. 254–6, 42 U.S.C. 2000.
[13] Cong. Rec. House 110 Cong. Rec. 88th Cong. 2578 ; 2580 ; 3732 ; also H. Rep. 914, Part 2, to H.R. 7152, 88th Cong.

[14] Weeks v. Southern Bell Tel. & Tel. Co. (CA–5, 3–4–69) 408 F. 2d 228, rev. and rem. S.D. Ga. 277 F. Supp. 117.

[15] Bowe et al 1. Colgate-Palmolive Co. (CA–7, 9–26–69) 416 F. 2d 711 rev. S.D. Ind. 272 F. Supp. 332.

[16] Leah Rosenfeld v. Southern Pacific Co. (C.D. Calif. 11–22–68) 293 F. Supp. 1219, pending appeal in CA–9.

[17] Phillips v. Martin-Marietta (CA–5, 10–13–69) 416 F. 2d 1257, pet. reh. den.; Cert. granted March 2, 1970.

[17-a] Bureau Natl. Affairs, Bull. No. 1047, pt. 2, 3–5–1970, ASPA-BNA Survey on Employment of Women.

[18] American Women (1963) p. 47.

[19] Taylor v. Dorsey (1944 Fla. Sup. Ct.) 19 S. 2d 876.

[20] Task Force Report on Family Law & Policy—to Citizens Advisory Council on Status of Women. Obtainable from Council Room 4211, U.S. Dept. Labor Bldg., Washington, D.C. 20210.

[21] American Women supra p. 47.

[22] White v. Crook (M.D. Ala. 1966) 251 F. Supp. 401; Hoyt v. Florida (1961) 368 U.S. 57; Carter v. Jury Commission (1970) 396 U.S. 320; Turner v. Fouche (1970) 396 U.S. 346.

[23] Commonwealth v. Jane Daniel (Pa. Sup. Ct. 1958) 243 A 2d 400.

[24] States of New York, N. Dakota, Minnesota, Maryland, Connecticut, Pennsylvania, Delaware, Massachusetts, Louisiana, California.

[25] Muller v. Oregon (1908) 208 U.S. 412.

WOMEN AND EDUCATION

STATEMENT OF ANN SUTHERLAND HARRIS, ASSISTANT PROFESSOR OF ART HISTORY, COLUMBIA UNIVERSITY

I am Professor Ann Sutherland Harris, Assistant Professor of Art History in the Graduate Faculties at Columbia University. I am also active in Columbia Women's Liberation and I am a member of N.O.W. I do not represent Columbia University in an official capacity, but I am a spokeswoman for Columbia Women's Liberation, which supports this testimony and helped to prepare the report presented here today.

Mrs. Chairwoman and members of the Committee, I am here today to testify to the need to extend the protection of the Civil Rights Act of 1964 and the Fair Labor Practices Act of 1938 to women in institutions of higher education by means of several amendments in Section 805 of H.R. 16098.

Much of my evidence concerning discriminatory practices against women will be drawn from my knowledge of the situation at Columbia University, but my research merely confirms my long-held suspicion that the situation at Columbia is typical of comparable high-endowment, high-prestige private universities in the United States. Research into this problem is handicapped at present, however, by the lack of precise studies of particular colleges and universities. That the overall distribution of women in institutions of higher education is highly suggestive of discriminatory attitudes and practices prejudicial to women no one can deny. My testimony therefore will concentrate on Columbia and other institutions for which I have been able to obtain statistical data and evidence of discriminatory practices. Women's groups at the University of Maryland, of Chicago, at Harvard and at Columbia have prepared their own studies of the faculties (and some other areas) of those institutions. University Committees are preparing or have prepared studies of women at Berkeley, Pittsburgh, Stanford, Oregon and Minnesota. Chicago has just published a useful study of women students and faculty (*Women in the University of Chicago*, Report of the Committee on University Women, May 1, 1970). The study that Columbia Women's Liberation prepared of women faculty at Columbia University will be read into the record as an example of the kind of statistical study now being prepared in order to document discrimination against women in higher education.

I am only one of thousands of women who believe that Congress will be increasingly occupied in the 1970s with the legislation necessary to insure that women have equal rights and equal opportunities in the United States. Women are organizing now as they have not since fighting to win the right to vote fifty years ago, for more and more women are realizing that they are treated as second-class citizens. The word "sex" was added to Section 702 of Title VII of the Civil Rights Act of a joke, and women will not forget that insult. Equality for women is not a joke. It is a serious issue, although many otherwise fair-minded individuals still refuse to believe that discrimination against women is a serious problem, or is a problem that should be taken seriously.

I will begin my testimony with some quotations made by men famous in the academic world, quotes that reveal all too clearly how women are regarded by academic men. When President Nathan Pusey of Harvard realized that the draft was going to reduce the number of men applying to Harvard's graduate school, his reaction was, "We shall be left with the blind, the lame and the women".

Harvard has no tenured women professors, and its excuse for limiting its female undergraduate enrollment to 25% of the total is that there is insufficient accommodation for more women. What they really mean is that they are reluctant to give a man's place to a woman. At Yale, when the new women undergraduates recently protested the quota on female undergraduates and made the modest demand for an additional fifty women at an Alumni dinner, one of the male alumni was cheered when he said, "We are all for women, but Yale must produce a thousand male leaders every year". Yale clearly does not think that women have similar leadership potential, or, as Kingman Brewster put it, "Much of· the quality that exists at Yale depends on the support of people who don't believe strongly in co-education". But Yale is slowly learning that women are fed up with vicarious participation in aspects of human activity outside the home. Charles de Carlo recently succeeded Esther Rauschenbusch as President of Sarah Lawrence, one of many recent examples of women presidents being succeeded by male presidents (virtually no woman has ever been president of a co-educational or male institution of higher education). He said, shortly after his appointment, that "Feminine instincts are characterized by caring qualities, concern for beauty and form, reverence for life, empathy in human relations, and a demand that men be better than they are". What is a man who does not think that women are people doing as President of a woman's college? Charles de Carlo thinks that women are myths—muses, madonnas, but not people with the potential and full range of characteristics ascribed to men.

Other academic men think that women are chickens. The following statement appeared in the education newsletter of the American Sociology Association this winter in an article headed, "Have you ever considered a Doctorate in the Sociology of Education, my Dear?"

"Some years ago, a colleague and I shared an office with a great view of the campus. When we were not consumed by teaching, research and/or community service, we would on occasion observe SOME OF THE COMELY GIRLS PASSING BENEATH OUR WINDOW. While male scholars will dispute most generalizations, they will readily agree that THERE JUST AREN'T ENOUGH CHICKS IN THEIR AREA OF SPECIALIZATION, to put it in professional sociological language (sic). Hence, my friend and I determined to print some handbills or perhaps put up a sign inviting SOME OF THE SWEET YOUNG THINGS to consider doing advanced work in our field. Alas, we never followed through, and many a PRETTY GIRL WHO STILL WALKS THE STREET who could have been saved. This clear-cut case of creativity (sic) followed by indecision was duly noted by our professors, however, and we both were awarded doctorates shortly thereafter". (Capital letters and sics mine.)

It is not my impression that those men were primarily interested in the intellectual capacities of the women they idly thought of attracting into their profession, nor do I think that they would have written a similar piece suggesting that blacks be recruited because of their soft voices and sexy sense of rhythm as they walked past their windows. Sexual discrimination is, as has been remarked before by others, the last socially acceptable form of discrimination.

Sometimes the statements are not couched in such obviously insulting terms. Sometimes what may to the uninitiated seem to be a perfectly reasonable objection to giving women the same opportunities as men appears in serious publications. For example:

"Too many young women are casually enrolling in graduate schools across the country without having seriously considered the obligation which they are assuming by requesting that such expenditures be made for them. And they are not alone to blame. Equally at fault are two groups of faculty—undergraduate instructors who encourage their women students to apply to graduate school without also helping them consider the commitment that such an act implies, and graduate admissions counsellors who blithely admit girls with impressive academic records without looking for other evidence that the applicant has made a sincere commitment to graduate study." (Edwin C. Lewis, assistant to the vice-president for academic affairs and a Professor of Psychology at Iowa State University, quoted in *The Chronicle of Higher Education*, Feb. 9, 1970).

That women who go to graduate school do make a serious commitment is proved by all studies of working women that have taken degree of education into account. All such studies show that the amount of education a woman has received is a more important factor than either marriage or children with respect to her decision to work. The higher her level of education, the more likely she is to be working full-time. Helen Astin found that of the almost 2,000 women doctorates that she surveyed ten years after they completed their Ph.D., 91% were working. 81% of them full-time. The percentage of men who work full-time is not, incidentally, 100%, as most of us think, but was in 1968, 69.4% of all men of working age.

The attitudes of mind behind Professor Lewis' quote and the other quotes given above are not uncommon. A recent questionnaire published by the AAUW (American Association of University Women) in their January *Journal* showed that the majority of the over 3,000 men who replied believed that "women's first responsibility is to be the feminine companion of men and a mother, that women have less need to achieve in the working world, that they have adequate opportunity to develop their potential, that the job turnover rate and sick-leave rate of women is higher than that of men (and) that women have difficulty dealing with males in subordinate positions." (*AAUW Journal*, May 1970, pp. 203-4). The majority of the women did not agree with those statements, however, and they were right not to. With women now comprising over a third of the work force. more women of working age are working than are staying at home. It's working women, and not the suburban housewife, who comprise the silent majority. For some time. women have voted with their feet to get out of the home, even though the jobs that they are offered are for the most part menial and poorly paid. Those women, however, who wish to become professors, lawyers and doctors can hardly have less need to achieve in the working world than men, for they will need far more determination than men to reach the same status and enjoy the same opportunities and compensations. The sick-leave rate and turn-over rates for women are in fact slightly lower than those of men, when those rates are standardized, as they must be, for occupation and income, according to the latest figures from the Women's Bureau of the Department of Labor.

As the author of the AAUW article reporting on the questionnaire remarked, "If males bring this mind set to employment situations, it undoubtedly affects their behavior towards females." That is an understatement. That men's notions of women's "place" and women's "roles" do affect the way men treat women in employment situations in academe is made abundantly clear by the statistics showing the distribution of women in the academic world, as it was also by Lawrence Simpson's recent study (see below). The rule is a simple one: the higher, the fewer. Although more women than men finish high school (and this has been true since 1920), fewer women than men go on to college, largely because it is harder for a woman to gain entrance to college with the necessary financial support. Fewer women than men go on to get higher degrees, again largely because graduate departments discriminate against women in admissions policies and in the distribution of fellowships. Once they qualify, the higher-the-fewer rule continues to apply: the higher in terms of rank, salary, prestige or responsibility, the fewer the number of women to be found. Moreover, their numbers have been declining since 1946, despite the increase in the numbers of MAs and PhDs going to women in the 1960's. The number of women presidents of colleges can be counted on two hands and is declining still.

STUDENTS

My testimony regarding discrimination against women students at under-graduate and graduate level will discuss both covert and overt discrimination. I shall begin with a collection of quotations given to me by women students at Columbia and elsewhere this year.

"I know you're competent and your thesis advisor knows you're competent. The question in our minds is are you *really serious* about what you're doing."

"The admissions committee didn't do their job. There is not one good-looking girl in the entering class."

"Have you ever thought about journalism? (to a student planning to get a PhD in political science). I know a lot of women journalists who do very well."

"No pretty girls ever come to talk to me."

"A pretty girl like you will certainly get married; why don't you stop with an MA?"

"You're so cute. I can't see you as a Professor of anything."

Professor to student looking for a job: "You've no business looking for work with a child that age."

"We expect women who come here to be competent, good students, but we don't expect them to be brilliant or original."

"Women are intrinsically inferior."

"Any woman who has got this far has got to be a kook."

"There are already too many women in this Department."

"How old are you anyway? Do you think that a girl like you could handle a job like this? You don't look like the academic type."

"Why don't you find a rich husband and give all this up."

"Our general admissions policy has been, if the body is warm and male, take it; if it's female, make sure it's an A— from Bryn Mawr."

To a young widow with a five-year-old child who needed a fellowship to continue at graduate school: "You're very attractive. You'll get married again. We have to give fellowships to people who really need them."

"Somehow I can never take women in this field seriously."

Women graduate students at the University of Chicago were so angered by these and similar statements that they collected a page of them and appended to it a page addressed to their professors explaining why such comments are offensive and harmful. I quote part of their excellent analysis:

"Comments such as these can hardly be taken as encouragement for women students to develop an image of themselves as scholars. They indicate that some of our professors have different expectations about our performance than about the performance of male graduate students—expectations based not on our ability as individuals but on the fact that we are women. Comments like these indicate that we are expected to be decorative objects in the classroom, that we're not likely to finish a PhD, and if we do, there must be something "wrong" with us. Single women will get married and drop out. Married women will have children and drop out. And a woman with children ought to stay at home and take care of them rather than study and teach.

"Expectations have a great effect on performance. Rosenthal and Jacobson (1968) have shown that when teachers expected randomly selected students to "bloom" during the year, those students' IQs increased significantly above those of a control group. Rosenthal and Jacobson (1966) had already shown that experimenter expectation made significant differences in the performance of the subjects—even when verbally identical instructions were read to the groups of subjects. The teachers and the experimenters stated that they had treated all subjects or students exactly alike. They were, however, giving both verbal and nonverbal cues about what was to be the appropriate behavior (R. Rosenthal and L. Jacobson, *Pygmalion in the Classroom: Teacher Expectation and Pupil's Intellectual Development*, New York, 1968). It would be surprising to find that graduate schools are immune to this phenomenon. When professors expect less of certain students, those students are likely to respond by producing less."

Rosenthal and Jacobson also found that experimenters who were told that one group of white rats was more intelligent than another identical group of white rats found in the tests they ran that the supposedly brighter rats did in fact perform better than the supposedly dumb rats. If male scholars believe that women are intellectually inferior to men—less likely to have original contributions to make, less likely to be logical, and so on—will they not also find the evidence to support their beliefs in the work of the women students in their classes, evidence of a far more sophisticated nature than the speed at which one rat finds its way through a maze? Rosenthal and Jacobson's experiments are extremely important to all scholars of human subjectivity and prejudice, for they show that it works both ways. Not only will those people who believe a certain human being or animal to be less intelligent innately find the evidence to support that belief in the behavior of the human being or animal, but they will respond to human beings that they believe are good or intelligent in different ways from those they use when responding to human beings that they believe are bad or less intelligent. Their behavior will be subconscious. Indeed, they will firmly believe that their judgment is rational and objective.

One remark above all is repeatedly made to women students. Although, you will recall, that one professor noted that he found it difficult to take women in his field "seriously," women students are asked again and again, "Are you really serious?" Since the vast majority of women students are as serious as the men students, the women start questioning themselves. Are they supposed to be more serious than men are? Are male students more serious than women students? How serious do you have to be? It is even asked of women who have completed PhDs at great personal and financial cost when they apply for their first jobs, which in my field were being openly advertised at last year's convention as "man preferred." (And the women investigating jobs not so labelled in interviews learned that men were generally preferred when the employer could afford to discriminate against women.) The study just completed by the Women's Committee at the University of Chicago confirmed what most of us have known from personal experience for a long time, namely, that women receive significantly less perceived support for career plans than men do, and that a large number of women had met or had heard of discriminatory experiences with respect to women. Moreover, the women students felt that men students were often preferred by the faculty.

Accurate statistics documenting the attrition rates of either male or female students are difficult to come by. The statistics that I have seen indicate that the attrition rate for both sexes is higher in the humanities and social sciences than in the physical sciences and professional schools. Since women are more often found in the former two fields, their overall attrition rate is higher than that of men, but when the figures are compared by field, the differences are small. The Chicago study provides that first published break-down of drop-out rates for selected departments that I have seen. A cohort analysis for students in various fields who entered in 1962, 1963 and 1964 showed the following:

26% of the men and 33% of the women in the Biological Sciences left before completing a higher degree.

16% of the men and 20% of the women in the physical sciences left before complting a higher degree.

40% of the men and 51% of the women in the Social Sciences left before completing a higher degree.

24% of the men and 19% of the women in the Humanities left before completing a higher degree.

The average difference in attrition rates of men and women graduate students was in fact only 5%, with women actually having a lower attrition rate than men in the Humanities. The College of Physicians and Surgeons at Columbia told Columbia Women's Liberation that the attrition rate of men students was equal to or higher than that of the women students. The proper study of attrition rates is, however, in its infancy. Other factors such as the greater availability of fellowship support in the physical and biological sciences than in the social sciences and humanities almost certainly contributes to the lower attrition rates in the two former fields. Women are more likely to be studying in fields where there are fewer fellowships available. This should make it more difficult for them to complete their graduate studies. However, I know from conversations with an Associate Dean at Columbia that women have a higher completion rate without fellowship support than men do, a discovery that I fear will be used to justify once more discrimination against women when awarding fellowships. I regard it as additional evidence that women who go to graduate school are more highly motivated than men who do.

Columbia University has statistics on the numbers of men and women applying to graduate school for admission and for financial aid, on the numbers of each sex awarded places and fellowships and on their relative attrition rates, but it has refused to release them, either to the new University Senate Subcommittee on Women or to Columbia Women's Liberation, because, the administration says, the figures will be "misinterpreted." I think however that if the picture was rosy for women, they would be delighted to prove that women are not discriminated against. In private conservation, one Dean told me that he was certain women were discriminated against when fellowships were handed out, and moreover that such discrimination was fair because women were less likely to finish than men were. He was unmoved by my argument that denying women fellowships support will almost certainly increase their attrition rate, thus making the prophecy self-fulfilling. He also either did not know or would not tell me the comparative attrition rates. Incidentally, when Columbia Women's Liberation first asked for such statistics, the Dean responsible for compiling them denied they existed, but as one of his former assistants said, "That's nonsense. X is a chart man from the word go. And I helped to compile them last year."

In my opinion, and in the opinion of others who have thought about this problem, the slightly higher attrition rates of women than of men graduate students (and at Chicago the overall difference was 5%, a figure that is statistically insignificant) are largely explained by the lack of encouragement and by the actual discouragement experienced by women graduate students for their career plans. They are continually told that they will not finish, that women's minds are not as good as men's minds, that the "difficulties of combining the career (sic) of marriage and motherhood with a career as a scholar and teacher" will be beyond the physical and mental energies of all but the "exceptional woman" (but never, of course, of men, who are presumed to spend no time at all being husbands and fathers). Women are told that they are welcome first and foremost as decoration for the male academic turf. Even in academe, women are sex objects.

Dr. Benjamin Spock, who is no friend of women outside the home, made an observation about juvenile delinquents that is relevant here. He said:

"To admit to a child that you don't trust his morals, his character, is definitely unwise. In a sense it gives him permission to be bad. He can say, 'If that's all they think of me, there is no point in trying to be good.' Child guidance workers have learnt how often an adolescent's bad behavior began in response to a parent's accusation or implication that he was seriously misbehaving when he really wasn't." (London *Observer* Sunday Magazine, Nov. 16, 1969, p. 45).

That, in effect, is what happens to women graduate students. They are repeatedly accused of being intellectual delinquents, overtly and covertly. As a result, they are more anxious than are men students about their work and futures, and this anxiety helps to stifle a great deal of the pleasure many of those women felt for the subjects that they had chosen to pursue. It is not surprising that some women decide that they are not cut out to be scholars and teachers. Rather, it is surprising that the drop-out rates of women are not far higher than they are. That they are not I take to be evidence of women graduate students' higher degree of commitment, produced as a natural defense mechanism in response to the sexual discrimination that they meet in their daily lives.

At four hours of open hearings on the status of women at Columbia, held by the University Senate in March this year, many women graduate students testified to the misogynist atmosphere of the University. Other women have spoken to me privately, but were reluctant to testify publicly for fear of reprisals. One woman, when she discovered that the one professor in her special area of interest disliked women, had to switch to another university in the city where, she hoped, the faculty would be less prejudiced. Another woman told of her discovery that all the men in her department had summer fellowships, and of how they teased her for not getting one. She had a straight A record. Another woman told me how her professor gave her A— after A—, but reluctantly, until a visiting scholar and old friend of the professor in question gave her an A+ and praised her to her professor. Now the Columbia professor gives her As, but he still conveys to her his resentment of her obvious talents. A Polish woman, who grew up in Poland where a third of the engineers are women, enrolled in the engineering program at Columbia, expecting her decision to be accepted as a normal and unremarkable one by the faculty and her fellow students. After two years of misogynist hassle, she gave up her plans. "I can't stand it anymore," she said, "I'm switching to liberal arts."

It is generally assumed that it is more difficult for a woman than for a man to get into college, let alone into graduate school. Dr. Sandler has cited evidence in support of our allegation that women are discriminated against at college-entry level. My first acquaintance with the problem of discrimination against women in academe came in conversations with older faculty women who were complaining about the fact that their women undergraduates needed A or A— records to gain admission while their men undergraduates could obtain places with B averages. I found more substantial evidence that this was indeed the case during meetings with students and faculty following the upheavals at Columbia during the spring of 1968. The students in my department drafted a bill of rights for students and included the word "sex" in the discrimination clause. The senior faculty were puzzled because our department has more women than men graduate students and awards more than 50% of its PhDs to women. A senior faculty member told the following story to try and allay the students' fears. He said that faculty dealing with graduate admissions in our department had noticed that the worst women applicants were considerably better than the worst men applicants. All the women applicants were, in fact, highly qualified.

Suspecting that the administration, which does a preliminary sifting of all graduate admissions applications, were holding back the folders of qualified women in order to keep up the numbers of men in a subject that attracts a majority of women students, the faculty called for all the folders in order to do the preliminary sifting themselves. As a result, a number of women were admitted who would not otherwise have been offered places. The moral of the story was, "We don't discriminate against women but the administration does." I not only found the element of buck-passing of responsibility on this serious issue disturbing, I found the wider implications of that incident shocking. It meant that quite possibly the admissions folders of all graduate applications to Columbia, as presifted by the administration, reached all the departments concerned with fewer women than would have been the case if the applicants were judged on ability alone. Nor should it be assumed that the administration of universities are worse than faculty with regard to sexual discrimination. Lawrence Simpson found that there was no difference between the attitudes of administrators and faculty in his study of employment practices with regard to women in his recent study (a convenient summary can be found in *College and University Business*, Feb. 1970, p. 72f).

Despite that presifting and despite the discouraging comments addressed to women graduate students, Columbia now awards more doctorates to women than any other American university. In 1956–7, when the national percentage of PhDs going to women was 11%, Columbia awarded only 4.6% of its PhDs to women. In the last two years, almost 25% of its PhDs have been awarded to women, a figure considerably above the national average of 14% (in 1968). There has been, however, no comparable change in the numbers of women employed by Columbia. The percentage of women with tenure in the graduate faculties has remained steady at just over 2%. And although in theory Columbia could draw its faculty from all the graduate schools in the country, and does in the case of male faculty, it is also significant that the small number of women with tenure are almost all Columbia products.

The Chicago report also contains evidence that it is easier for a man than for a woman to get into graduate school. The most conclusive evidence is the grade average of the women, which is significantly higher than that of the men (p. 93). 9.1% of the women reported straight A averages compared with 6.8% of the men; 24.9% of the women reported A—averages compared with 20.1% of the men; and 32.2% of the women had B+ averages compared with 31.6% of the men. Only 30% of the women compared with 41% of the men had grade averages of B or lower. My own experience and that of colleagues suggests that such results are to be expected, for women students who request letters of recommendation for graduate school have, on the average, much better records than do the men students. And they all know that they will need better grade averages to get in; they expect to be discriminated against, in fact, a sad state of affairs.

Analysis of published admissions figures provides additional evidence in support of the widely-held assumption that you have to be better on the average to get a place in graduate school if you are a woman than if you are a man. Before examining the statistics, it is worth remembering that women candidates for graduate school are the survivors of a long, sifting process. Although more women than men finish high school, socially approved lower self-aspirations for women insure that fewer women than men will even think of going on to college. Those women who do have to jump over another hurdle of double standards, and even then they are either denied places at or are allowed only a small number of places at America's most prestigious undergraduate colleges—Harvard, Yale, Princeton, Columbia, Notre Dame and Dartmouth. Moreover, the range of subjects offered, the facilities (libraries, laboratories), the endowments and the faculties of the supposedly-equivalent women's colleges do not measure up to those of their male counterparts (see Kate Millett, *Token Learning: A Study of Women's Higher Education in America*, published by the Education Committee of New York N.O.W. in 1968 and out-of-print). About 43% of the BAs awarded in the United States go to women. Again, the lack of societal approval for careers for women will insure that many able and capable women will stop their professional training with a BA, which will, as is well known, entitle them to become the secretary of the male college graduate who has just collected his BA. Women who have definite career plans and consequently choose to go on to graduate school are, therefore, a very special group of women. With all this, it is not surprising that Bernard commented that "only the very best of the good women students" go to graduate school (Jessie Bernard, *Academic Women*, Pennsylvania State University, 1964, p. 80). Out of these, only the hardiest survive. As a group, women PhDs have higher IQs, higher G.P.A.s, and higher class rank, than their male counterparts. How ironic that women who have demonstrated such promise and such dedication to their chosen fields should continually be treated as though their work is and should be peripheral and of secondary importance to society. Like all women, even this select group is treated as second-class human beings.

Women majoring in fields traditionally attractive to women (education, languages, English, social work) may apply to graduate programs even though they do not have A undergraduate records. Women who want to enter traditionally male-dominated fields such as medicine, mathematics, physics and economics will be doing so only because they have demonstrated exceptional ability (and have straight A records in their special field to prove it). Thus, while women graduate students are, to start with, a much more highly preselected group than are men graduate students, the women entering male-dominated fields will be a very highly preselected group indeed. All things being equal, we should expect to see a higher proportion of female applicants than of male applicants accepted for graduate school, above all in those areas where women applicants are in a minority. I have only seen the explanation that the minority group of candidates were more highly qualified and therefore that a higher proportion of them should be accepted in the case of men applicants to graduate school. I am willing to accept that as long as the reverse situation is also conceded. Thus, the professor in my department explained that the higher proportion of male to female graduate applicants accepted was due to the fact that few men considered becoming art historians unless·they showed special aptitude in college. When women are accepted in a higher proportion than are men, the tendency is to say that women are being discriminated for. I would argue that when either sex are in the minority, that a higher proportion of the minority applicants will be accepted if their applications are judged for ability and not for sex, and furthermore that the proportional differences favoring the minority group will increase in proportion to their minority status.

Thus, if only 10% of the applications to a particular program are from women, then I would anticipate that a higher proportion of them will be accepted than a field attracting—say—40% of its applications from women.

As stated above, Columbia's administration has not released its statistics on admissions applications and acceptances. Three departments, however, kindly responded to a letter of enquiry from Columbia Women's Liberation and provided the following information. The College of Physicians and Surgeons reported that "approximately 10% of all applications come from women and give-or-take the same percentage have been accepted (i.e., the ratio of women applying to accepted equals the ratio of men applying to accepted)." They do not state, however, what proportion of their male applicants are accepted. Clearly they think that they treat women fairly. We suspect that they discriminate against women. Professor Barbara Low, the only woman Professor of Biochemistry at Columbia, who testified at the Senate Hearings and is now a member of the Columbia Senate Subcommittee on Women, also thought so, and her work brings her into daily contact with the College of Physicians and Surgeons. The School of Journalism reported in a jaunty letter that 25% of its applications came from women and that 20% of its places were offered to women. That drop in percentages needs explanation. The Chemistry Department provided more elaborate statistics. In all three years reported (1968–9, 1969–70 and 1970–1), women applicants were in the minority (respectively 17.2%, 26.6% and 14.1%). In two years (1968–9 and 1970–1), a smaller proportion of women applicants than of men applicants were offered places (respectively 35% of the women and 50% of the men; 61% of the women and 68% of the men).

In 1969–70, 55% of the women and 53% of the men were offered places, a fairer result but not as high a differential in favor of women as is to be expected when only one in four applicants is female. Women law students also testified to discriminatory standards in the admissions practices of the Columbia Law School at the University Senate Hearings in March. In anonymous testimony, another woman told of her discovery that the School of Architecture operated a quota, allotting some 10–15% of its places to women. Now that students are on the admissions committee and the female quota has been dropped, the School of Architecture will next year admit more women than men students, an astonishing reversal of numbers which reveals all too clearly how many potential women architects and city planners, not to speak of lawyers and doctors, have been or are being denied access to the education and training necessary for them to gain entry into these rewarding professions. Moreover, it seems to us that whenever a certain graduate or professional program regularly admits only a small and uniform percentage of women students (as Columbia's College of Physicians and Surgeons with its regular 10% of women), that a quota system may be presumed to be operating. It may even be used not only to limit the number of women doctors but also the number of doctors from minority groups. Thus a Barnard senior has told a friend of mine in Barnard's Placement Office of her discovery that this year it is even more difficult than usual for women to get into medical school because medical schools are trying to raise their black enrollment figures. She is on the waiting list of a couple of schools that are waiting to fill places with blacks before accepting more women applicants. That quotas of any kind exist is reprehensible. That all groups that are discriminated against should have to divide that quota between them, thus making black equality possible only at the expense of female equality, is even more reprehensible.

The University of Chicago report gives the numbers and percentages of male and female applicants and male and female accepted applicants to graduate programs in forty-two departments (p. 33f). In the seven departments comprising the Physical Sciences, the percentage of applicants who were women varied from 6 to 22%, that is, a clear minority in all cases. In four fields, the percentage of women accepted was higher than that of the men accepted (59 vs. 60%; 77 vs.

86% ; 61 vs. 84% ; 42 vs. 59%—an average difference of 13.5%). The authors of the report argue that these percentages indicate that women applicants received, if anything, preferential treatment. We would argue that percentage differences favoring women are to be expected in those fields that attract few women. In three of the physical science departments at Chicago, however, (astronomy, mathematics, and physics), the percentages of women accepted was well below that of the men accepted (respectively 62 vs. 40% ; 41 vs. 20% ; 70 vs. 51% ; an average difference of 20.6%). Women applicants to those three departments were clearly discriminated against.

In only one of the seven departments of Biological Sciences at Chicago, in all of which women applicants were in the minority (13 to 44%), was the ratio of women accepted below that of the men accepted (Biophysics). 14% of the men but only 11% of the women who applied to Chicago's Medical School were accepted. Seven of the twelve departments in the social sciences accepted a higher proportion of their male than of their female applicants. Women were in a minority again in all twelve departments (13 to 44%). The Dean in charge of Columbia's statistics on graduate admissions has assured representatives of Columbia Women's Liberation that his figures will "look good" when they are finally released. The Chicago Committee on Women actually thought that the statistics on graduate admissions at Chicago favored women. A more thoughtful analysis of their figures proves otherwise. The degree of discrimination against women varies at Chicago from school to school and from department to department, but the higher grade averages alone of the women graduate students at Chicago is proof of their higher calibre.

I am aware of one other blatant example of discriminatory practices with regard to women applicants to graduate school. The chairman of one famous east-coast graduate department of art history, who shall be nameless, sent out letters to the chairmen of his respective departments at the Seven Sisters colleges, instructing them to discourage women from applying at all on the grounds that women who applied to graduate school directly from college had a higher attrition rate than those who waited for a few years to "make up their minds," a statement for which no proof was forthcoming. (The women who waited would no doubt be told when they applied that they were "too old.") When our department became aware of this practice, since confirmed by women students at Columbia who had applied to the other department and had been rejected on the same grounds, the professor in charge of our graduate admissions did not know whether he wanted to charge his friend with sexual discrimination or not, for the policy clearly helped our department by increasing the number of highly-qualified women applicants. It is significant that the professor responsible recently thanked his wife in the preface of a book for reading all the dull articles in connection with the subject concerned, thus enabling him to concentrate on the interesting and significant material, a new variation on the theme of the scholar who uses his wife as a secretary-typist. Needless to say, his department has no full-time female faculty, a significant omission in a field that has for ten or fifteen years attracted more women than men graduate students.

I have become aware in the last few years of significant differences in the prestige of schools or subjects dominated by women. It seems that the presence of a majority of women lowers, so to speak, the "property value" of the profession concerned. Thus, PhDs in Education at Columbia are scorned by those in male-dominated fields, quite wrongly in my experience. Librarians are so conscious of the fact that it is a woman-identified profession that they are currently trying to attract men in order to improve the status and salaries of librarians. The University of Chicago report uncovered a similar phenomenon. Six of the eleven female full professors at Chicago (there are 475 male full professors) were in the department of Social Service Administration. At the Assistant Professor rank, the ratio was reversed sharply—15 men but only two women, although women comprised 68% of the students in that traditionally female-dominated field. I quote the report (p. 5) :

"Another matter of concern to the Committee in connection with recruitment was the statement of women in the School of Social Service Administration that men had in recent years been given preferential treatment.* The vastly different ratios in that school between men and women in tenured and nontenured positions seems to support this allegation. . . . The Committee recognizes the argument that it may be desirable to provide male models in a traditionally women's field (just as it recognizes the parallel argument of the desirability of providing female models in traditionally men's fields). More important, however, we ques-

---

*NOTE.—Here also is an example of the preselection theory favoring men.

tion a second assumption—that the influx of a large number of men raises the level of professionalization, or even that, rightly or wrongly, it raises the prestige of the field and should therefore be encouraged."

I have been informed by other women that small colleges in a large east coast state system have become identified as schools producing women planning to become high school teachers and consequently have trouble attracting male undergraduates. Their administrations are busy changing the image of these schools to "truly co-educational liberal arts colleges" in order to keep up the numbers of men and in order to avoid being typed as an inferior kind of school. Harvard persists in calling itself a male undergraduate college even though Radcliffe has no faculty of its own and is in fact little more than a hotel for women. I find these cases particularly significant proof of society's basically discriminatory attitude towards women and their intellectual capacities.

FACULTY

My main body of evidence in support of my contention that women faculty are systematically discriminated against with regard to hiring practices, promotion and salaries is in the report that Columbia Women's Liberation prepared on the faculties of Columbia University and Barnard College. Nothing that I have learned since helping to prepare that report last year changes my conviction that institutions such as Columbia are among the worst offenders. Dissertations by Lawrence A. Simpson ("A Study of Employing Agent's Attitudes Toward Women in Higher Education", Pennsylvania State University; abstract available from *Dissertation Abstracts*, vol. 29, no. 12,196, order 69–9810, University Microfilms) and Helen Berward ("Attitudes Toward Women College Teachers in Institutions of Higher Education Accredited by the North Central Association", University of Minnesota, Minneapolis, 1962) came to the conclusion that women are discriminated against when seeking employment as faculty by all kinds of institutions of higher education. Dr. Simpson summarized Berwald's research as follows: "When all variables were equal except sex, the male candidate was typically chosen for employment". And to quote Simpson's summary of his own more recent study:

"Prospective academic women must recognize that they should, in effect, be more highly qualified than their male competitors for higher education positions. Additionally, women should be aware of the attitudes that may be expected from employing agents in the academic fields which typically employ few females. Perhaps the most important application of the study is that employing agents in higher education must seriously re-examine their own attitudes regarding academic women and be keenly aware of any prejudices or rationalizations which cause academic women to be treated in any other way than as productive human beings. In a period when higher education faces a shortage of qualified teachers, the denial of a teaching position to a qualified female applicant, based solely on the negative attitudes toward women of an employing agent, is open to serious question". (*College and University Business*, February, 1970, pp. 72–73.)

Women earned about 13% of all the PhDs awarded in the 1960s (and now earn just under 40% of the MAs) and comprised about 22% of the faculty in all institutions of higher education. In all kinds of institutions, however, women are distributed unevenly, clustered in the lower ranks, in part-time positions, and in institutions considered to be low-prestige (e.g., junior colleges, educational schools, undergraduate rather than graduate departments and so on). This uneven distribution is discussed elsewhere in other testimony. I will concentrate on the "elite" schools, from which women are most systematically excluded, and on the "elite" of the women's schools, where we would at least expect to find women in the majority of the controlling positions.

Men may, and are, encouraged to teach at women's schools. It is rare indeed to find women in full-time teaching positions in men's undergraduate colleges. Only Wellesley, in fact, of the Seven Sisters colleges has more female than male faculty in tenured ranks and in chairmanships. In the rest, male faculty dominate the upper levels and in some cases the lower levels as well. At Vassar women have dropped from 55.6% of the faculty in 1958–9 to 40.5% in 1969–70. The number of women with full professorships has dropped during the same period from 35 to 16. At Vassar it was thought that a co-educational facility provided a healthier atmosphere for women students. The reverse does not apparently apply to Harvard, Princeton, Yale or Brown. Barnard has two more female than male full-time faculty but the men have 78% of the full professorships and chairmanships. To quote the Columbia Faculty Report, "even the one group of educational institutions founded to give women access to professional careers do not, after more than fifty years of activity, serve as models demonstrating to the community the ability of women to manage demanding careers". The consistent exclusion of women from positions on the faculties of the Seven Brothers schools is probably the most blatant example of sexual discrimination to be found in academe. Women learn to confine their job applications to co-educational institutions and to women's schools. Men may work anywhere, on the other hand, and can even expect to receive preferential treatment at the best women's colleges.

When John Parrish reported on the distribution of women faculty at ten high endowment (Chicago, Columbia, Cornell, Harvard, Johns Hopkins, M.I.T., Northwestern, Princeton, Stanford and Yale) and ten high enrollment (Berkeley, C.C.N.Y., Indiana, Illinois, Michigan, Michigan State, Minnesota, N.Y.U., Ohio and Pennsylvania State) institutions of higher education in 1960 (in the AAUW *Journal*, 1962), he reported the following statistics. At the eight reporting high endowment institutions, women as percent of total faculty were 2.6 of the full professors, 7.5 of the associate professors, 8.5 of the assistant professors and 9.8 of the instructors. At the ten high enrollment institutions, women were 4.3% of all full professors, 10.1% of all associate professors, 12.7% of all assistant professors and 20.4% of all instructors. I have not seen the same statistics computed for 1970, but the statistics that I have seen from individual institutions in those two groups indicate that the overall percentages of women have remained level or have declined. The decline is particularly marked at the upper levels. Princeton gave tenure to a woman for the first time last year. Yale has three women professors with tenure. Harvard has no full or associate professors that are women, and even at assistant professor level can muster only a paltry 4.6% of women (*Preliminary Report on the Status of Women at Harvard*, prepared by the Women's Faculty Group, released April 15, 1970). Women at Stanford comprise a mere 5% of ALL the full-time teaching faculty. At U.C.L.A. and Chicago, the same group comprises only 7%. At Stanford, 1.6% of the full professors are women (8 of a total of 498) ; at U.C.L.A. they are 3.6%. 4.4% of the associate professors at Stanford are women : at U.C.L.A. the figure is 7%. 2.2% of the full professors at Chicago are women; the figure for women associate professors is 7.8%. All things being equal, one would have expected that the women who were associate professors in 1960 would be full professors in 1970 raising those average percentage figures to the 7.5% reported by Parrish. The assistant professors and instructors should also have moved up proportionally. A glance at the figures shows that they did not. Nor will they move up in this decade unless academic men learn to recognize their own and institutional sexual discrimination and learn to accept women at the top as well as the bottom.

Most students of this problem are reluctant to compute relative rates of promotion for women and men faculty. At Columbia, we tried the crude but we think useful procedure of simply counting the numbers of men and women on the faculty in full-time positions who received their PhDs in the 1960s and then studying their distribution by rank. There are 195 male faculty at Columbia who received doctorates in the 1960s. 47% are assistant professors, 38% are associate professors and 15% are full professors. There are 25 women full-time faculty at Columbia in the same category. 96% (24) are assistant professors, one is an associate professor (tenure granted this year, PhD 1961) ; there are no female full professors who obtained their PhD in the 1960s at Columbia. Well over 50% of the men who earned their PhDs in 1963 and 1964 have been given tenure. None of the women in that group has been promoted to the rank of associate professor with tenure, although one woman is an assistant professor with tenure, an anomaly brought about by the extreme reluctance of her department to promote her. These differences in promotion rates are too great for discrimination against women not to be a large part of the story.

The lower median salaries of women in academe than of men (and the gap is widening, not decreasing) is partly explained by their exclusion from the better-paying jobs and higher ranks, but even with such factors standardized, women in academe still earn less than men with comparable qualifications. When the faster promotion rates of male faculty are also taken into account, then the differences are even greater. The idea that women, married or single, don't really· need jobs or don't need them as much as men do is a hard one to kill. A friend of mine at Columbia, also, like me, an assistant professor married to an assistant professor, has a daughter. By the time that she and her husband have paid for a trained nurse to look after their daughter five days a week, and for a house cleaner, and by the time they have paid the higher taxes to which their double income entitles them, she has $1,000 left of her $11,000 salary with which to pay for books, fees for professional periodicals and for memberships in professional associations, taxis, clothes and all the other overheads of a career. Wives are worth a good deal of untaxed income, but the male professors who distribute departmental budgets generally think that they alone bring money into the home and that double-income couples are rich. They forget that working couples have to buy on the open market the services many wives perform in return for their keep. If, as happens frequently, the wife is denied full-time employment on account of *de facto* or *de jure* nepotism rules, it will actually cost that couple money for her to work, for the money she brings into the home will not cover the cost of her replacements.

Considering what kinds of things business men may deduct from their taxes, working couples are unfairly penalized at present, and these unfair tax laws undoubtedly prevent some highly trained women from working, simply because they know that it would not pay their family for them to do so. Other women work for small financial rewards simply because their work is a pleasure for them. Single academic women are penalized financially but for different reasons. It is always assumed that they are only supporting themselves, although the same financial penalities do not apply to bachelors. The idea that money should be distributed equitably is nearly always raised when women's salaries are discussed. A man may earn as much as he likes. Here, as in so many areas affecting men and women, double standards apply.

One area of academic employment where the percent of women employed regularly tops the 22% average of women employed at all levels is part-time teaching and/or research. These positions do not have the status or fringe benefits of full-time positions and are thus comparatively poorly paid. They also are often not tenured. When men hold such positions, it is nearly always because they have another full-time job. Such arrangements permit the university to invite men who may have unusual expertise in some relevant area to teach one or two courses a year in that specialty. Women in part-time positions, however, often do not have other full-time jobs, although some have other part-time jobs. In my experience, women with part-time positions carry heavier loads than men do. Some teach as many or more hours than full-time faculty. The administrations and faculties of universities know, in fact, that academic men often marry academic women, and that faculty wives provide a good captive labor market, seldom in a position to demand the full-time position that they deserve because they cannot threaten to leave and go elsewhere. In New York City, there are a sufficient number of institutions of higher education for most couples who wish two full-time jobs to find them, but few cities in the United States offer such a range of choices within a small, geographical area. Apart from women working in the administration, part-time women faculty are, I believe, the most financially exploited group of women in academe. The women at the University of Pittsburgh worked out that by working for lower salaries than those men with their qualifications would receive, they were saving the University $2,500,000 a year. It is not difficult to see how they could have arrived at that figure.

A regular complaint of women in academe are the punitive effects of nepotism rules, for these almost always mean that the wife, not the husband, is denied employment. The advisability of hiring huband and wife in one, small department may be debated. All other forms of nepotism rules (husband and wife may not both have tenure; may not both have full-time jobs; may not both work at the same institution, period) should be declared null and void by Section 805 when it is applied, for nepotism rules constitute *de facto*, if not *de jure*, discrimination against women. (Harvard, incidentally, will and has employed father and son but not husband and wife in full-time tenured posts.) Application of nepotism rules leads to farcical situations. The most famous is that of Dr. Maria Goeppert Mayer, the first woman to win the Nobel Prize for physics since Marie Curie. Her husband is also a physicist. Department after Department hired him, while graciously allowing her to use the laboratory facilities free (Carolyn Bird, *Born Female, The High Cost of Keeping Women Down*, Pocket Books, 1969, p. 58). I was told last month about a psychology department in Pennsylvania that is using a college junior to teach freshmen and sophomores rather than use the wife of a faculty member who has a M.A.

One recent case at Columbia illustrates both sexual discrimination and covert nepotism rules (many institutions claim not have them and do not print them in official literature). A brilliant European couple were invited to teach in one Department, for they specialize in different areas. He did not have a PhD; she did. He had not published a book; she had. He was hired as a visiting Associate Professor; she, after considerable hassle, as a visiting Assistant Professor. Throughout the negotiations, they were told that the nepotism rule would prevent Columbia's offering her a full-time position in the same Department as her husband, although in reply to a questionnaire circulated by the AAUW a few years ago, Columbia declared that it did not have any nepotism rules. Clearly

Columbia does not think that it should have nepotism rules. The couple concerned have since returned to Europe where she has just been given a distinguished appointment to a rank above that of her husband, an appointment to which her academic achievements clearly entitle her. She has told me that she does not think a married woman will receive such fair treatment in America for many years.

ADMINISTRATION

I regret that I do not have more substantial evidence with which to document my suspicions about women working in the administration of colleges and universities. I suspect that these women are the most financially exploited group of all and are also the women whose abilities and leadership potential are most completely ignored by their male employers. We were not able to do a study of women in the administration at Columbia because published catalogues and directories do not provide an accurate list of all male and female administrative staff. We could not get more accurate statistics from the management. Women's groups at Pittsburgh and Harvard have included material about administration women in their studies, and these show very clearly that the higher-the-fewer rule applies even more rigorously in this area. It is a commonplace at Columbia that men with BAs are hired as Directors of Admissions while women with BAs are hired as assistants to the Director of Admissions. The work is the same but the salaries and fringe benefits are not. The employee handbook declares that only a high school diploma and typing skills are required for secretarial positions, requirements that justify offering low salaries for these jobs. The majority are held by women with BAs, many of them from excellent schools. The highest category that women are regularly permitted to hold is that of Administrative Assistant. Many of them run the offices of individual departments, hiring and firing all the other supporting staff, supervising the budget, keeping track of all confidential matters that concern the chairman and senior faculty, and managing the day-to-day operations of the department, especially its liaison with the central administration. It is a challenging job with many responsibilities. None of them earn over $8,000 a year, and some have held these jobs for ten or twenty years. Columbia last year made one woman an Assistant Dean, but one such appointment is, by definition, tokenism.

At the Open Hearings held by the University Senate in March, one woman administrative assistant dared to testify. Since almost no administrative women have tenure, they are all most reluctant to make themselves visible by complaining about the treatment of women, but many of them attended the Hearings and assured our group of their support. The woman who did testify reported on the results of her own survey of the rank of administrative assistant. She found that there were only two men with such positions, both of them in the Department of Physical Education. "The only high-paying independent positions open to women", she stated, "are in such traditionally 'female' areas as artistic properties, public ceremonies, placement, interior decorating and nursing." A former employee, who also testified at the Hearings, noted that in one of the departmental libraries, two of the three female clerks had BAs, the other an MA. Their supervisors, both male, did not have any higher degrees. And when a young man applied for a job as a typist, the personnel office offered to train him in computer programming. (Both testimonies were included in Minda Rickman's *Village Voice* article, "Women at Columbia: A Supporting Role", June 4, 1970). The almost total exclusion of women from visible responsible positions in the administration of Columbia and all other institutions of higher education (with the possible exception of some women's schools) is clear evidence of discriminatory policies with regard to women. As Dr. Rita W. Cooley, professor of political science at New York University said, "The universities tend to think automatically in terms of men when filling a new position. In a sense it's like racism. This discrimination exists at an unconscious level. There is no opportunity for women in administration. We are up against a strong cultural phenomenon, mass male chauvinism. If a woman wants to be an administrator, the field is very narrow" (*College and University Business*, February, 1970, p. 60).

In March I attended the 25th annual conference on Higher Education as a panelist to discuss the impact of the new feminism on higher education. There too I found women administrators a particularly vociferous group, who felt particularly vulnerable because of their small numbers and low positions. The most heartfelt complaint of all came, of course, from a black woman. In academic world, as outside, black women are discriminated against on two counts, race and sex. It is no accident that the lowest salaries at Columbia are those of the maids who clean the men's dormitories (women clean their own).

410

Those responsible for investigating charges of sexual discrimination should also look at the following areas faculty honors and awards; sex of commencement speakers and recipients of honorary degrees; by-laws of alumni associations (the Graduate Alumni Association of Columbia has many women members but women may not hold office in that organization) ; composition of committees appointed to study special problems; the composition of the Pulitzer Prize Committee, administered by Columbia University; sex of trustees, etc. The Chicago report (p. 63 f.) has an interesting appendix with data of this kind. As is to be anticipated, there are few women represented in any of these categories. I wonder how long it will take for women to achieve 50/50 representation at this level?

UNIVERSITIES AND THE EMPLOYMENT GRAPEVINE

An important area where prejudice against women now flourishes in academe is the informal grapevine of job openings that grows from department to department across the country. The cliché opening, "Do you know a good man for the job", results in continuous but largely unconscious discrimination against women. Most of the men who use this phrase would deny vigorously that they are discriminating and would not also consider a "good woman", but the "good man" is an effective subconscious roadblock because the image we all tend to carry in our minds of a scholar is a masculine one. Many women's groups have been calling for advertising of all job openings in order to insure to all women who believe themselves to be qualified the right to apply for the jobs they wish to have. The semi-secret grapevine also tends to discriminate against women just because there are fewer women in academe, and those few are as prone to discriminate against women unconsciously as are their male colleagues. Also, it is generally true that women who have "made it" in a man's world tend to deny the existence of or minimize the importance of discrimination against women. At all events, women play a minor part in the grapevine communications system, and it is there that word of the best jobs passes, from chairman to chairman across the country.

All graduate departments as well as placement offices dealing with undergraduates seeking employment come into daily contact with employers who discriminate against women. Mrs. Jane Schwartz Gould, who runs the Barnard Placement Office, gave a long and amply-documented account of the experiences she has in her job at the University Senate Hearings in March (see her own account in the latest issue of the *Barnard Alumnae Magazine*, spring, 1970, p. 29 f.). Our faculty receive regular requests for graduate students with all but their PhDs completed, man preferred, but as more of our graduate students are female than male, our faculty have to try and talk other faculty into having women. The professional schools also touch the outside employment world in the same way and receive daily evidence of discriminatory attitudes. The School of International Affairs, for example, held a careers conference this winter. The following quotation comes from their student newspaper, *The Communique* (Dec. 1969, p. 2) :

"A second truth which emerged from the career conference was the fact that the Master in International Affairs was of no use at all to women for job placement in international business. One representative suggested that women interested in business would be wisest to take courses in stenography and to realize their interests vicariously by marrying businessmen. . . . The problem is less of inappropriate training and selling techniques, apparently, than of the sex of the product."

Those in charge of enforcing laws forbidding sexual discrimination must pay particular attention to this area. If all colleges and universities refused to recommend students to potential employers with a record of sexual discrimination, they would have enormous impact on the outside world. I cannot think of any single action that would have more beneficial effect for women than for all institutions of higher education to refuse to cooperate with sexist employers. Guidelines for eliminating sexual discrimination on the campus by means of these amendments should, in my opinion, contain a firm directive to this effect. It will be especially important if the current recession continues. PhDs are already a glut on the market in some fields. When that happens, the women will find it even more difficult than usual to find suitable employment.

DE FACTO AND DE JURE SEXUAL DISCRIMINATION

These amendments, if Congress will give the Civil Rights Commission the funds necessary to insure that the law is enforced, will be no doubt regarded primarily as applicable to the kinds of problems discussed above. I predict that women will find these amendments applicable to other situations. I should like to discuss some brieflly, both because I think the Committee should know the way the femininst wind is blowing these days, and because I think they should be aware, if they are not already, that sexual discrimination is a tricky thing to define.

Some women are arguing, and I support them, that the almost complete absence of serious academic study of women by academics constitutes *de facto* sexual discrimination. Women are seen as part of the social background against which the main events of human (women would say masculine) history are played out. They are seen from a male perspective, and their roles are distorted or misunderstood or undervalued. Like black studies at its inception, the faculty and administration of most schools will regard "women's studies" as a pseudo-intellectual fad at first. Cornell ran a full and varied program this year that was enormously popular with undergraduates of both sexes. If institutions refuse to inaugurate women's studies and if women students claim that they are being discriminated against, what will the courts decide?

Another area where male-oriented attitudes are harmful to women are the student health services. The male body is the norm. Gynecological services are regarded as abnormal and are rarely provided. Men students can buy contraceptives without seeing a doctor. Women's contraceptives are more complicated and require the presence of a doctor and/or trained para-medical personnel. It is common knowledge that most student health services will not provide any students with contraception, although some make an exception for married students (and require the husband attend the surgery as well). Since private doctors also chose to enforce their moral codes upon their women patients, some women students have been unable to obtain adequate contraception. It is she, and not he, who must take the consequences, of course, and with so few states' abortion laws repealed or at least modified, these women students find themselves forced to drop out of school during the forced pregnancy. The same situation applies outside academe, of course, but women outside academe are using the same arguments when opposing abortion laws or laws that forbid the sale or advertising of contraceptives. I predict that test cases concerning sexual discrimination in the dispensing of health care will follow the passing this amendment.

Is lack of paid maternity leave for women staff and faculty *de facto* discrimination against women? I think so. Society is pleased to honor the men who leave their jobs to serve in the armed forces. Their jobs are guaranteed for their return. They are given free education to enable them to return to the job market at a higher level than that at which they left it. They are paid for their services in times of war, and honored if they give their lives in the course of that service. There are no memorials to the millions of women who have died in childbirth, and when a working woman becomes pregnant, she must take leave of absence. Often she will lose her job and accumulated seniority. This applies to academic employment as it does elsewhere. How different are the services that men and women perform for society at large, the men because of their greater physical strength, the women because their bodies are designed to bear children. Again, I predict test cases from women using these arguments when these amendments become law. The lack of child care facilities, on campuses as elsewhere, also tends to discriminate against women rather than against men, even though some young fathers take their share of parental responsibilities more seriously than did their fathers. Moreover, the lack of child care facilities penalizes a woman who wants to work for a far longer period of time than does pregnancy. America is the only industrialized nation in the west that does not have a government-supported system of child care centers available to women of all income groups. Until child care centers are universally available, all talk of equality for women is hollow, on campus as elsewhere. Now that we know that children of working mothers who are looked after by other adults for part of the day do not grow up to be societal misfits, as the folk mythology would have us believe, there is no excuse for society in general not to provide care for children before the age of five as well as after. The Committee may think that the discussion of these issues is irrelevant, but if they do think so, then I think they will have seriously underestimated the strength and universal appeal of the new feminism.

I would like to conclude this section with a quotation from a woman I believe to be the most brilliant of the new, young feminists. It is one of many thoughtful, dissenting comments of Jo Freeman, a graduate student of political science and a member of the committee that prepared the much-cited Chicago report.

"As long as the University does not concern itself with the variety of life styles prevalent among academic women and the many needs they have that differ from those of men, it will inevitably discriminate against otherwise qualified women. The life styles of the population of intelligent, highly-educated women is much more heterogenous than those of intelligent, highly-educated men. The University is geared to serve the needs of the latter and those of the former group who most closely resemble these men or who can organize their lives, however uncomfortably, into the environment created for intelligent, highly-educated men. Failure to realize that women as a group have a wider diversity of life styles than men as a group will result in an exclusion of those women whose life styles least resemble those of men."

CO-EDUCATION

It will not be possible to do more than consider briefly here some of the issues concerning co-education that the passing of Section 805 will raise. Section 805 will call into question the existence of any educational institution that limits its enrollment to members of one sex, whether male or female, as well as the nature of the "co-education" that exists at institutions now calling themselves co-educational. Thus, I assume, that all quotas limiting the percent of women to men in co-educational institutions will no longer apply. Men's colleges that have "gone co-ed" will not, in theory, be permitted to make that change a gradual one, aiming at—say—33% female and 67% male enrollment. They will be required to choose applicants on the grounds of ability, and accept whatever the resulting sexual proportions are. There will be great reluctance on the part of some traditionally-male colleges to admit women on an equal basis. They will plead lack of dormitory space, but they will mean that they do not wish to deny a place to a man in order to accommodate a woman. They will prefer to accept a small number of women who will be accommodated in new buildings as soon as they can be provided. That will not, in my opinion, constitute true co-education. Dormitories are not built for men or women; they are built for people and can be used by people of either sex. Lack of accommodation must be recognized as a false defense against equality with women. At present 92% of all women attend co-educational institutions of higher education. The majority of sex-segregated schools are run by religious foundations, a fact that explains why only 28% of Roman Catholic women attend co-educational institutions. Thus it will be seen that we are dealing with a minority group of institutions within the broader spectrum of higher education, but a highly visible one. The Seven Sisters and Seven Brothers are among the most famous educational institutions in the world.

A first painful point must be made. Sex-segregated education does not benefit women. The Gourman Institute ratings for all women's schools are at least two hundred points (on a scale of 800) below those of their supposedly-equivalent men's school, with the Catholic schools collecting the lowest ratings of all, some of them below the 400 needed for accreditation. The kind of courses offered and the philosophies behind the majority of these schools are dissected effectively in Kate Millett's study, *Token Learning* (cited above). Even at the best known of the women's schools, the smaller endowment, more limited facilities and similar range of courses, especially in male-oriented fields, will affect all the women students. Our society does not value the education of women as highly as it values the education of men. Therefore, we do not invest as much money in female as we do in male education. As with racially segregated education, sexually-segregated education works to the disadvantage of the group which is discriminated against. I am therefore certain that it will benefit women to make all kinds of educational institutions accessible to them.

Lifting the barriers will not, as some fear, empty the Seven Sisters or fill them with the male and female dregs of the race to get into the Seven Brothers. As now, all educational institutions will have and preserve their own particular character and identity, to which size, location, faculty interests and available facilities will contribute. Some women's colleges are already planning to become radical women's schools. At first, few men will wish to attend them, although I believe that they should be permitted to apply on an equal basis. I predict, however, that when the word gets round about the intellectual excitement being generated in the new feminist women's colleges, that men will apply and harmonious co-education will result. The feminist heritage of the women's schools should provide an excellent foundation for the new coeducation, although the alumni and alumnae of these schools will resist the idea strongly to start with. Yale has already discovered that if you limit female enrollment severely, the few women admitted are more intelligent on average than the men (this was proved when their grade averages were published) and this situation still makes men distinctly uncomfortable. The same phenomenon has been observed at Oxford and Cambridge for years for the same reason (12% of the Cambridge undergraduates are women, a slightly higher proportion at Oxford).

The main argument, and it is a good one, for retaining the women's schools is that they provide women with a supportive atmosphere as long as our society is male-dominated and male-oriented. Few, if any, of the women's colleges now take their responsibilities in this area very seriously, and most are male-dominated, if not male-oriented, as we have seen. I am not sure why the best women's colleges abandoned active support of the feminist cause. They seem to prefer a neutral stance, and as a result give their women students little or no preparation for the discriminatory world outside. Only when they take themselves seriously, I fear, will the rest of society take them seriously also.

I am certain that true co-education will not only benefit the women, but will also contribute to better understanding between the sexes in academe. If I have concentrated my attack on the "elite" male-dominated schools, it is only because the most conclusive evidence of sexual discrimination comes from them. They will have the biggest changes to make, and will see little advantage in conceding fair shares to the opposite sex. Without the amendments in Section 805, true co-education will take far longer to achieve in the United States.

CONCLUSION

My testimony this morning has shown the widespread existence of discrimination against women in all strata of higher education. As students, staff and faculty and as concerned women, we have a keen interest in changing negative institutional values and policies. However, we do not think that the provisions of this bill designed to correct discrimination against women and designed to emphasize the importance of education (Title VI) can offset the detrimental nature of Title VII of H.R. 16098.

The "disruptive acts" which Title VII deals with are so broadly defined as potentially to stifle expression of justifiable grievances by powerless groups: minority groups such as Black and Brown people, majority groups such as women. Section 701 places the power to define "disruptive acts" with "trustees, administrators, and other duly appointed officials"; the last named group is not at all defined and could be interpreted as officials of any level of government. This set of people may not be responsive to claims for equitable treatment made by unrepresented groups: racial minorities—for most of these officials are white; and women—for most of these officials are men. For example, we spoke earlier about the lack of adequate gynecological services available to women students. Columbia Women's Liberation undertook to remedy this situation at Columbia and found the administration willing to deal with the issues. However, an administration that did not wish to concern itself with the needs of their own women students might define as disruptive actions taken in the pursuit of fair treatment in this area.

The harsh provisions for punishment in Title VII give a person deemed guilty by any court of record a "double punishment": she or he is given a sentence by the courts and then a further sentence by the Federal Government. He or she is blacklisted at all universities by virtue of being unable to receive any federal money for five years, not even a loan. The effect would be to purge universities of all dissident voices, of those who have given, and will continue to give universities and societies the impetus to change. We believe that women like ourselves are one such group. Our dissent at Columbia has not only been tolerated but has been welcomed by many of those at whom it is directed. At other educational institutions, women who have criticized their faculties for sexual discrimination have been "censured for conduct unbecoming", a rare procedure in academe, normally reserved for actions such as outright plagiarism. As women who may in the future find our problems turned aside by those who refuse to recognize the existence of sexual discrimination, we cannot turn our backs on the grievances of the oppressed, the powerless and the dissident, for women are among those people.

You may ask if we are not concerned with disruptive acts. We would answer yes. We are saddened and horrified by the disruption by the powerful, not by the dissidence of the powerless. The war in Indochina, racism and sexism in America, the punitive repression of groups such as the Black Panthers, these are all examples of the use of disruption, unconstitutional acts, inhumane treatment, brutalization—all acts by the powerful, not the powerless. The exploitation of black and white women in the labor market is the "public order" upheld by the powerful, just as putting students in front of a de facto firing squad is violence by the powerful. Because women's liberation is a movement to end all human oppression and exploitation, we do not advocate violence. We therefore find it inexcusable that violence is visited upon the powerless by the powerful.

We urge members of Congress to recognize that the true problems in our society are war, militarism, exploitation, racism and sexism, and to work for the elimination of these problems, rather than to attack those who protest these cancers on the public order. We urge Congress to investigate and cure the causes of militarism, racism and sexism, rather than repress the dissidence which is merely the symptom of the just grievances of oppressed groups.

The advancement of women through this bill would come at the cost of the repression of all progressive groups working for change, including women's liberation groups. Because of the repressive aspects of this bill as it stands with the inclusion of Title VII, we of Columbia Women's Liberation and I as an individual cannot give it the whole-hearted support that we would wish to give it at this time.

STATEMENT OF DR. BERNICE SANDLER, CHAIRMAN, ACTION COMMITTEE FOR FEDERAL CONTRACT COMPLIANCE IN EDUCATION, WEAL

I am Dr. Bernice Sandler of the Women's Equity Action League* (WEAL), where I am Chairman of the Action Committee for Federal Contract Compliance in Education. I am also a psychologist with the Department of Health, Education and Welfare, and a former Visiting Lecturer in the Department of Counseling and Personnel Services at the University of Maryland. However, I am not speaking as a representative of H.E.W., but as an individual and as a member of the Women's Equity Action League.

I come before this distinguished committee on behalf of Section 805 of H.R. 16098. You will be hearing from several witnesses who will address themselves to various aspects of this bill. I will limit my testimony to the crucial area of sex discrimination in our universities and colleges, and to how Section 805 will begin to alleviate some of the dreadful injustices and inequities suffered by American women on the campus.

The Women's Equity Action League (WEAL) has initiated since January 31, 1970 formal charges of sex discrimination under Executive Order 11246 as amended, against more than 100 universities and colleges. This Executive Order forbids Federal contractors from discriminating against race, creed, color, national origin, and sex. According to the National Science Foundation report entitled "Federal Support to Universities and Colleges, Fiscal Year 1968," universities and colleges receive about 3.3 billion dollars of Federal contracts per year. As Federal contractors, universities and colleges are subject to the provisions of the Order.

In its initial complaint, WEAL charged an industry-wide pattern of sex discrimination and asked for a class action and compliance review of all universities and colleges holding Federal contracts. At that time WEAL submitted to the Secretary of Labor, George P. Shultz, more than 80 pages of documents substantiating its charges of sex discrimination in the academic community.

Half of the brightest people in our country—half of the most talented people with the potential for the highest intellectual endeavor are women. Yet these gifted women will find it very difficult to obtain the same kind of quality education that is so readily available to their brothers. These women will encounter discrimination after discrimination—not once, not twice but time after time in the very academic institutions which claim to preach the tenets of democracy and fair play. The women will face discrimination in admission where they will encounter both official and unofficial quotas; they will face discrimination when they apply for scholarships and financial assistance. When they graduate, their own university will discriminate against them in helping them find jobs. They will be discriminated against in hiring for the faculty. If hired at all, they will be promoted far more slowly than their male counterparts, and they will most likely receive far less money than their colleagues of the other sex.

In a speech on the floor of the House of Representatives on March 9, 1970, Congresswoman Martha W. Griffiths stated:

"Yet most of these institutions discriminate outrageously against half of our citizens—women. They neglect and disregard their potential talent. They place

---

*The Women's Equity Action League was incorporated in 1968 in Ohio to promote greater economic progress on the part of American women and to seek solutions to economic, educational, tax, and employment problems affecting women. There are members in more than 34 states. National headquarters are at 22414 Fairlawn Circle, Fairview Park, Ohio 44126. Information regarding Federal contract compliance should be addressed to Dr. B. Sandler, 10700 Lockridge Drive, Silver Spring, Md. 20901.

innumerable obstacles and hurdles in the way of academic women. Is our nation so rich in talent that we can afford to have our universities penalize the aspirations of half of our population? Should the Federal Government close its eyes to such unjust discrimination and continue to provide the billions of dollars that help to support those unjust practices?"

The position of women in higher education has been worsening; women are slowly being pushed out of the university world. For example, in 1870, women were one-third of the faculty in our nation's institutions of higher learning. A hundred years later, women hold less than one-fourth of the positions. In the prestigious Big Ten universities, they hold 10% or less of the faculty positions. The proportion of women graduate students *is less now* than it was in 1930. The University of Chicago, for example, has a *lower* proportion of women on its faculty *now* than it did *in 1899*.

Women are 22% of the graduate students in the Graduate School of Arts and Sciences at Harvard University. But of the 411 tenured professors at the Graduate School of Arts and Sciences at Harvard University, *not one* is a woman. Let me repeat that. Of the 411 tenured professors at the Graduate School of Arts and Sciences at Harvard University, the number of women is: ZERO. At the University of Connecticut, a state-supported institution, women are 33% of the instructors but only 4.8% of the full professors. On the University of Massachusetts campus at Boston, also a state-supported institution, there are 65 women faculty, but only two of these have tenure. Even in academic areas where women would be expected to be found in substantial numbers, women are conspicuously absent. For example, out of 105 professors in the School of Education at the University of Michigan, only 6 are women. Again, at the University of Michigan, out of 58 professors in social work, only 12 are women; in library science, out of 14 professors, only 3 are women.

Even when women are hired they generally remain at the bottom of the academic hierarchy. The higher the rank, the lower the percentage of women. In a typical study of 188 major departments of sociology, Dr. Alice Rossi, a noted sociologist at Goucher College found that women accounted for—

    30% of the doctoral candidates,
    27% of the full-time instructors,
    14% of the assistance professors,
    9% of the associate professors,
    4% of the full professors, and
    less than 1% of the departmental chairmen.

Figures like these cross my desk almost daily; they are by no means unusual. They can be duplicated readily in practically all departments and universities throughout the country merely by reading the college catalogue. In many places, the figures are worse, for in some departments and institutions women are simply not hired at all.

One typical rationale—excuse, if you will—for justification of figures such as these, appears as: "Isn't it the simple truth that there just aren't enough qualified women to fill these posts?" The so-called "shortage of qualified women" is an academic myth. A higher percentage of women with doctorates go into college teaching than do men with doctorates. Let me give you some examples of the so-called "shortage" of qualified women. Columbia University awards 24% of its doctorates to women, but only 2% of its tenured graduate faculty are women. Using a particular academic field as an example, nationally women earn 23% of the doctorates in psychology. At Rutgers, the State University of New Jersey, only 9% of the graduate faculty in psychology are women. At the University of Maryland Department of Psychology, there are only 2 women on a faculty of 35—less than 6%. At the University of Wisconsin Department of Psychology, only 1 out of 34 faculty is a woman—less than 3%. At the University of California at Berkeley, the percentage of women in the Department of Psychology is *zero*; not one of the 42 faculty members is female. The same is true at Columbia University; there are simply no women "qualified" to teach there, despite the fact that the Department of Psychology at Columbia grants 36% of its doctorates to women. Apparently women are somehow qualified to earn doctoral degrees but are not considered "qualified" to teach once they have earned these degrees. How does one explain such large discrepancies? Indeed, it would be more accurate to ask how the universities and colleges of the United States can explain these discrepancies.

Where do these qualified women go, for it is clear that very few of them will teach in the major universities and colleges. Do they marry and give up their careers? This is another academic myth: 90% of the women with doctorates are working. Many end up teaching on the faculty of junior colleges and community colleges where they comprise about 40% of the faculty, and where the pay, status, and research opportunities are substantially less than in the major universities. I have appended to this report a selected list of various academic disciplines and the percentages of doctorates awarded to women. In virtually every major institution the percentage of women on the faculty is far below the percentage expected on the basis of the number of doctorates awarded in particular fields.

Undoubtedly the percentage of degrees awarded to women would still be higher if the discriminations based on sex were eliminated. Official and unofficial quota systems for women are widespread. Just a few weeks ago WEAL filed against the University of North Carolina—a publicly supported institution—which states quite openly in a publication by the Office of Undergraduate Admissions: "Admission of women on the freshmen level will be restricted to those who are especially well-qualified." And indeed, in the freshman class at the General College at the University of North Carolina, for this current year, there were 1893 men and only 426 women. For the last decade at the University of Michigan, according to G. C. Wilson, Executive Associate Director of Admissions, the Office of Admissions has "adjusted" requirements to insure that an "over-balance"—that is, a majority—of women would not occur in the freshmen class. Thus at the University of Michigan, women have comprised about 45% of the entering freshman class for a number of years, despite the fact that in terms of grades and test scores, there are *more* qualified female applicants than males. Girls need higher grades for admission to many colleges and universities. Unofficial quotas exist in many graduate and professional schools. The percentage of women with M.D. degrees *is approximately the same today as it was 50 years ago* when women first won the right to vote. In the Soviet Union 75% of the physicians are women; in our country it is barely 7%.

Women are denied admission to graduate and professional training programs because of the rather odd and illogical reasoning on the part of university decisionmakers: "If a woman is not married, she'll get married. If she is married, she'll probably have children. If she has children, she can't possibly be committed to a profession. If she has older children, she is too old to begin training." Now it is true that she may very well marry. Many of her fellow male students will do likewise. She may very well have children. Men also become parents, but we do not as a society punish them by limiting their professional development and professional opportunities.

Essentially *our universities punish women for being women.* They punish women for not only having children, but even for having the potential to bear children. Such blatant discrimination against women has gone virtually unchecked for years. In every sector of university life, women are losing ground.

Women who are actually hired to teach have not crossed over the last barriers of discrimination. They will be promoted far more slowly than their male counterparts. 90% of the men with doctorates and 20 years of academic experience will be full professors; for women with the same qualifications barely half will be full professors. In other words, women have about half the chance that men have to become a full professor. And this is after 20 years of full-time dedicated service. The figures at specific universities tell the story. At Stanford University, for example, 50% of the men have the rank of associate or full professor. Only 10% of the women are at these ranks. Somehow, many of the women who are "qualified" enough to be hired, are not "qualified" enough to be promoted.

Salary discrepancies abound. Deans of men make more money than deans of women, even in the same institution. Numerous national studies have documented the pay differences between men and women with the same academic position and qualifications. Women instructors make less than men instructors; women assistant professors make less than men assistant professors; women associate professors earn less than men associate professors; and women full professors earn less than men full professors. Indicative of the widening gap between salaries of men and women is the extreme difficulty in getting salary information from practically all institutions, including the publicly supported ones.

At the administrative level, women are most conspicuous by their absence. The number of women college presidents is decreasing, even at women's colleges. Women rarely head departments. Even in the fields where one would expect women to be, such as in education, they simply do not move to the top. At the University of Maryland, for example, in the College of Education, only one department—Special Education—is headed by a woman. Even in women's colleges there has been a decline in the number of high administrative posts held by women. At Smith College, for example, (and Smith was a noted pioneer in the education of women) the percentage of women in high administrative posts has declined from nearly 70% in 1962 to less than 50% in 1969.

Many of the best scholarships are limited to men only. It took a highly active and sophisticated group of New York University Law School students earlier this year to get women to be considered eligible for some highly coveted $10,000 law scholarships. Practically all Federal scholarship and loan aid is for full-time study—a practice that works to virtually eliminate married women with families from receiving such aid, since they may need a part-time schedule. Indeed, many schools forbid or discourage part-time study, particularly at the graduate level, thus punishing women who attempt to combine professional training and home responsibilities simultaneously.

When I first started exploring sex discrimination in higher education I naively thought that there were merely isolated individual instances of discrimination, and that where such discrimination existed, it was merely a matter of a particular department or a particular individual chairman or administrator. Certainly every professional woman has anecdotes about discrimination, but there has been little that has been written or documented in terms of the total picture within the university community. As WEAL's activities and filings have become known, women and men from all over the country, from small and large colleges and universities, from public and private institutions, from institutions of all sorts, have contacted me, sending me statistical data and asking WEAL to file on their behalf against their college or university. Let me add here that none of WEAL's filings have been based on anecdotal material; about twenty have been based on discriminatory advertising; the remainder and majority of the complaints have been based on hard statistical data. As more and more information has been collected, there is no question whatsoever that there is a *massive, consistent and vicious pattern* of sex discrimination in our universities and colleges. On campus after campus, women are almost always restricted to the lower academic ranks, and in some instances not hired at all. Departments that hire women in any numbers equal to the amount of qualified women available (based on the number and percentage of doctorates awarded to women in each field) are indeed a rarity, and truly an exception to the general overall discriminatory pattern.

Even in the placement of its own graduates, universities discriminate. The College Placement Council, to which over 1000 major colleges and universities belong, publishes a thick *College Placement Annual*, listing corporate and governmental employers who recruit college graduates. This *Annual* is used by college placement offices throughout the country as well as by the Department of Defense, despite the blatant discriminatory ads contained within it, such as "sales personnel, male only," "personnel for executive development program, male only," "engineer, male only," "social worker, male only," "geologist, male only," and of course, "secretary, women only."

Such advertising is a violation of Title VII of the Civil Rights Act of 1964 and of Executive Order 11246, as amended. Nevertheless it is used on practically all campuses. University administrators, who would be horrified if a placement bulletin for their students listed job openings for "whites only," apparently see little or nothing wrong with job openings that read "male only."

Whether by design or accident women are *second class citizens on the campus.* As students they are often excluded and often actively discouraged from entering professional fields. (One member of my own department at the Univeristy of Maryland feels strongly that "women shouldn't be professionals" and tells this to his women students.) As faculty, women can look forward to low pay, low status, and little or no opportunity for promotion, and even difficulty in finding employment. With the beginning of a surplus of Ph.D.'s in some academic areas we expect to see the position of women continue to worsen, for indeed women are often "the last ones hired" and "the first ones to let go" in the academic community.

Why has this massive discrimination gone virtually unchecked, unnoticed and unchallenged for so long? The reasons are many. Sex prejudice is so ingrained in our society that many who practice it are simply unaware that they are hurting women. *It is the last socially acceptable prejudice.* The Chairman of a department sees nothing wrong in paying a woman less because "she is married and therefore doesn't need as much," or pay her less because "she is *not* married and therefore doesn't need as much." Many of the most ardent supporters of civil rights for blacks, Indians, Spanish-speaking Americans and other minority groups simply do not view sex discrimination as discrimination. No university would today advertise for a *"white* assistant professor"; yet these same concerned humanitarians see nothing wrong with advertising for a *"male* assistant professor." These same humanitarians fail to notice that half of each minority group are women. Both Congresswoman Shirley Chisholm and Pauli Murray, a noted Negro lawyer, have both stated that they suffered far more from being a woman than from being a Negro.

It is also very dangerous for women students or women faculty to openly complain of sex discrimination on their campus. Each day, in my role as Chairman of the Action Committee for Federal Contract Compliance in Education, my mail includes letters from women who want WEAL to file a formal complaint of sex discrimination against their university. With practically no exceptions these women plead for anonymity. Even the Head of a department in one major state-supported university, as well as numerous other women with tenure, ask that their names be kept confidential. And well they might. I know of two women who protested against sex discrimination recently in a large publicly supported university system, and they were promptly and officially censured by the university for their actions. In effect, they stand to lose their tenure if not their jobs. At a recent meeting of professional women I counted at least four women whose contracts were not renewed after it became known that they were active in fighting sex discrimination at their respective institutions. Moreover, most grievance procedures within universities have no procedures concerning grievances about sex discrimination. Unless women band together and protest as a group it is virtual academic suicide to protest sex discrimination on practically all campuses.

Madam Chairman, believe it or not, it is completely within the law to discriminate against women in universities and colleges. Section 702 of Title VII of the Civil Rights Act of 1964 exempts every "educational institution with respect to the employment of individuals to perform work connected with the educational activities of such institution." Title VI of the same Civil Rights Act forbids discrimination in programs or activities which receive Federal assistance, but it only applies to discrimination based on race, religion or national origin. It does not forbid sex discrimination. The Equal Pay Act of 1963 specifically excludes "executive, administrative, or professional employees." Even the U.S. Commission on Civil Rights has no jurisdiction whatsoever concerning sex discrimination; it is limited by law to matters pertaining to race, color, religion or national origin.

Executive Order 11246 as amended, under which WEAL is filing its charges of sex discrimination, is at best an administrative remedy for such discrimination. Unfortunately, the actual rules and regulations adopted by the Department of Labor to implement the Order, arbitrarily restrict the effectiveness and activities of the Office of Federal Contract Compliance by requiring far less in the way of affirmative action from state-supported institutions than that required of privately supported institutions. There is nothing in the Executive Order as amended that says that state-supported institutions need to conform less than private schools; indeed no distinction is made whatsoever between private and state institutions in the Executive Order itself. Yet the Department of Labor regulations dated May 28, 1968 (F.R. Volume 33, No. 104) *exclude* state agencies from having affirmative action plans. It is incredible that the Department of Labor arbitrarily requires less from our public institutions than from our private ones. This distinction between standards for public and private institutions must be changed immediately.

Let us not forget that the Executive Order does not have the status of law. It can be amended or suspended at the pleasure of a particular administration. Furthermore, any institution that wanted to continue discrimination is legally free to do so if it gives up its government contracts. There are simply no laws whatsoever that forbid universities and colleges from continuing their vicious patterns of sex discrimination and their violation of the human rights of women. The Executive Order is the *only* weapon that women now have in legally fighting sex discrimination in education, and the enforcement of this Order by the Department of Labor (which has the policy responsibility for the Executive Order) and the Department of Health, Education, and Welfare (which conducts the actual compliance reviews) has been far from satisfactory.

For example, Order No. 4, which I mentioned earlier, sets forth goals and timetables for plans for affirmative action for minority groups under the Executive Order as amended. The Executive Order and Order No. 4 itself make no distinction whatsoever between different minority groups. Yet as of this date, no statement has come from the Secretary of Labor that Order No. 4 *does* apply to women, as indeed it should if the Department of Labor follows the Executive Order. We assume that Order No. 4 *does* apply to women, but our own well-placed sources within government tell us that some Federal agencies are interpreting Order No. 4 as *not* applying to women. We need a strong statement from the Secretary of

Labor confirming the applicability of Order No. 4 to women. Anything less than such a statement must be construed as disregarding the mandate of the Executive Order. If the Labor Department means to enforce the Executive Order they will have no difficulty in issuing a clear and strong statement of policy on the applicability of Order No. 4 to women, and to do so without further delay.

Moreover, WEAL's *class action* charges of an industry-wide pattern of sex discrimination throughout the academic community have basically been ignored, despite our well-documented charges and our subsequent filing of charges against more than 100 institutions of higher learning within a few short months. Only *three* compliance reviews have been started by the Office for Civil Rights of the Department of Health, Education, and Welfare: Howard University, Borough of Manhattan Community College (of the City University of New York), and the University of Maryland. At this rate it will easily be a generation before attention is paid to the remainder of our existing formal complaints, let alone the countless others already in preparation.

In fact, until WEAL filed its complaints, the Department of Labor and the Office of Federal Contract Compliance and all other compliance agencies of the U.S. government shamelessly ignored all aspects of the Executive Order that pertained to sex discrimination. Sex was simply not included in any of the compliance reviews undertaken by the Office for Civil Rights of H.E.W., which handles all contract compliance for all universities and colleges.

WEAL recently submitted a comprehensive plan of affirmative action to Secretary Shultz for use with universities and colleges that have Federal contracts. (This affirmative active plan is in *The Half Eaten Apple: A Look at Sex Discrimination in the University*, which is appended to Dr. Scott's testimony.) This plan was developed by Dr. Ann Scott of the University of Buffalo and follows the policy guidelines of Order No. 4. There is no reason why this kind of plan cannot be implemented by *all* institutions of higher education that hold Federal contracts. Again, if the Department of Labor is serious about enforcing Executive Order 11246 as amended in universities and colleges, particularly with respect to sex discrimination, they should use this plan as a model plan of affirmative action. We need a clear statement from the Department of Labor as to whether this plan is acceptable, and if not, *why not*. So far there has been silence.

In a recent letter I received from Assistant Secretary of Labor Arthur A. Fletcher, he referred to the lack of resources to handle our complaints. It may well be that as a result of our charges additional personnel will be needed. If that is the case then it is the responsibility of the Department of Labor to come before the appropriate committees of Congress and ask for the necessary supplemental funding to enforce the Executive Order. This assumes, of course, that they are serious when they say they intend to enforce the Executive Order. The next move is up to the Department of Labor.

THE NEED FOR NEW LEGISLATION

New legislation is vitally needed if women are to be accorded the fair treatment that is the birthright of their brothers. Existing legislation, including the 14th Amendment, has been woefully inadequate, particularly in the area of education. It is perhaps instructive to compare race discrimination and sex discrimination at this point. Racial segregation of our educational system was outlawed by the Supreme Court in 1954, yet as recently as 10 years ago the Supreme Court declined to hear a case in which the Texas Court of Civil Appeals upheld the exclusion of women from a state college, Texas A and M. In another court case, under the 14th Amendment, in February 1970 a three judge Federal court dismissed as "moot" a class action in which women sought to desegregate all male and female public institutions in Virginia. The Court had previously ordered the University to consider without regard to sex the women's plaintiffs' applications for admission to the University of Virginia at Charlottesville, and to submit a three year plan for desegregating the University of Virginia at Charlottesville. To give you an idea of the results of a sex segregated university and college system,* let me quote from the Report of the Virginia Commission for the Study of Educational Facilities in the State of Virginia, 1964: "21,000 women were turned down for college entrance in the State of Virginia; during the same period of time, NOT ONE application of a male student was rejected."

---

*Sex segregated colleges, particularly when operated by the same governing body are particularly reminiscent of race segregated facilities: they are separate, but hardly equal. Dr. Kate Millett of Barnard College recently analyzed a series of coordinate "brother-and-sister" colleges, and demonstrated that the women students were given a vastly inferior education compared to that of their "brothers." The course offerings are less varied, facilities are inferior, faculty are paid less, etc.

In general the 14th Amendment has not been applied in any meaningful fashion concerning women's rights. No case has ever reached the Supreme Court where the Court ruled that a woman was a "person" within the meaning of the Equal Protection clause of the 14th Amendment. Corporations have been declared as "persons." Negroes are considered "persons." But *not women*. As long as there is no Equal Rights Amendment, women can only rely on the possibility of enlightened court interpretations of the 14th Améndment, and history has shown that this is clearly insufficient. Even if the Equal Rights Amendment were passed, new legislation such as that encompassed in Section 805 would be needed if we are to begin to correct many of the inequities that women face, particularly in the area of education. It would forbid laws and official practices that currently exclude women from public and private colleges and universities (including higher admission standards for women, and in the administration of scholarship programs). It would end many of the discriminatory practices now legally engaged in by universities and colleges today, such as in the hiring and promotion of women, and it would correct salary inequities.

EXTENSION OF THE EQUAL PAY ACT (FAIR LABOR STANDARDS ACT OF 1938)

Women in education have not been covered by the Equal Pay Act because of the exemption of executive, administrative and professional employees. Figures concerning salary differences between men and women are notoriously difficult to obtain even in publicly supported institutions. U.S. Office of Education figures reveal consistent differences in salary at every academic level from instructor to full professor; women are simply paid less than their male counterparts. In fact, in *every* study that I know of, whether it be limited to a single campus or a single profession or a large segment of the educational community, women earn less than men, and the gap is widening.

I know of one full professor who is earning less than a newly hired male assistant professor in her department who is fresh out of graduate school. I know of another woman, an associate professor for more than 10 years who discovered she was earning more than $1000 below the *bottom* of her university's scale for associate professors. I know of a third woman, at what must surely be the world's wealthiest and most prestigious university, who is teaching *without any pay* because there "is not enough money" to pay her. In fact, within the last two weeks I have heard of two more women—highly qualified and respected professionals—who have worked *without pay* at their respective institutions. I do not know how widespread this pattern of work without pay is. But I do know that the Equal Pay Act as it currently stands does not apply to these women, or any other academic women. Make no mistake, without an extension of the Equal Pay Act, university *women will continue to earn less for equal work.*

ELIMINATION OF THE EDUCATIONAL EXEMPTION OF SECTION 702 OF THE CIVIL RIGHTS ACT

The educational exemption of Section 702 of the Civil Rights Act of 1964 must be eliminated if sex discrimination on the campus is to be ended. Practically all universities and colleges receive Federal monies from a variety of sources as well as having tax exempt status. These institutions are prohibited from discriminating against *students* in order to receive certain grants and monies, but there is nothing that forbids universities and colleges from discriminating against women or other minority groups on their faculties. Only the Executive Order applies, and only to those institutions that hold Federal contracts. As I mentioned earlier the enforcement of this Order leaves much to be desired. Deprived of legal recourse, women in education are clearly second class citizens on the campus.

It is not clear what the rationale was for adopting the educational exclusion of Title VII, Section 702 when the Civil Rights Act of 1964 was passed. There is no explanation printed in the legislative history. The Section was adopted without any discussion and no reasons are given as to why so wide an area of employment was excluded from coverage.

It is ludicrous to exclude from coverage those very institutions whose conduct should be a model of freedom and respect for human dignity. Our educational institutions, unfortunately, are fallible; they, like all others, cannot stand above or outside the law, but must have a strong legal and moral commitment to treat citizens fairly and without regard to their sex. As long as educational institutions are permitted to discriminate they cannot possibly serve as adequate models of democracy in action to their students.

I am concerned, however, about the elimination of Section 702 as contained within this bill, since it would leave Section 701(b) intact. Section 701(b) defines "employer" as *not* including the United States, a corporation wholly owned by the Government of the United States, an Indian tribe, or a State or political subdivision thereof. If Section 701(b) remains intact and the educational exclusion of Section 702 is repealed, it is possible that public institutions such as state universities might well be construed as being government units and as such would still be exempt from the provisions of the Civil Rights Act. If this is so, then the aim of eliminating the educational exemption would be severely undermined unless Section 701(b) was also amended. Nearly 7 million people are employed at the State and local level, with school teachers forming the largest group of employees. It would be tragic to leave the States free to discriminate in their educational employment practices while requiring private institutions to have higher standards of non-discrimination. I urge this Committee to amend Section 701(b) by eliminating the words "or a State or political subdivision thereof."

EXTENDING TITLE VI OF THE CIVIL RIGHTS ACT OF 1964 TO FORBID SEX DISCRIMINATION

Title VI currently forbids discrimination on the grounds of race, color and national origin in Federally assisted programs. In fiscal 1969 Federal aid to State and local governments alone exceeded 20 billion dollars. In all of these programs sex discrimination is completely legal. It is legal for a Federally assisted medical school to discriminate against women students, although the school is forbidden by Title VI to discriminate against other minorities. It is legal for vocational employment and training programs to be restricted to one sex only. It is legal for universities and colleges which receive Federal aid to discriminate against their women students in any way they desire. Quota systems which limit the number of women in admission to higher education will continue to be legal unless Title VI is amended to include sex. Discrimination in scholarships and other forms of financial aid will continue to be legal unless Title VI is amended to include sex.

I want to point out that on moral grounds alone, Federally assisted programs should be administered so that *all* citizens enjoy equal participation and equal benefits from these programs. Yet half of our citizens—women, be they black, Spanish-speaking, white, Indian or whatever—can be denied this basic right of equal participation on the basis of their sex alone, unless Title VI is amended to include sex.

EXTENDING THE JURISDICTION OF THE CIVIL RIGHTS COMMISSION TO INCLUDE SEX

One of the major problems in obtaining civil rights for women in education as well as in other areas is that there is no special governmental agency charged with women's rights. While the Women's Bureau within the Department of Labor is charged with the welfare of women in industry, and does collect a good deal of data regarding the economic status of women, the main concern of the Bureau, by law, is focused on employment, not civil or human rights. Similarly, the U.S. Office of Education collects data on women, but by law the focus is on education, not on women and their civil and human rights.

In contrast, the U.S. Civil Rights Commission is specifically empowered by law to deal with civil rights and human rights of citizens deprived of these rights by reason of color, race, religion or national origin. But sex is not included in their mandate. As long as sex is omitted from legislation pertaining to discrimination, it is quite possible for an employer to refuse to hire a black woman, supposedly not because she is black but because she is a woman. Civil rights, particularly in educational employment, can be denied to half of each minority group on the basis of sex.

There is no single clearing house for information concerning legal developments regarding the civil rights of women. For example, in a recent opinion, the Wisconsin Attorney General stated that nepotism regulations in Wisconsin would be regarded as sex discrimination for the purposes of Wisconsin's equal employment statute. At roughly the same time, five University of Arizona faculty wives brought suit to end nepotism rules at the University of Arizona. In California, State Senator Mervyn K. Dymally has introduced bills in the State legislature that would require all State College Trustees and all University of California Regents to use compensatory hiring to integrate women into faculty, administrative and support staff. In a few universities, women have discovered that Title VII of the Civil Rights Act applied to the placement services of a university and they have filed legal charges based on discriminatory ads and practices. All of these events are of enormous significance in ending inequities for women. Had events of the same magnitude occurred in relation to other minorities, the Civil Rights Commission might well have held hearings; they might have studied these issues further and collected additional information; they might well have submitted reports to the Congress; they might well have conferred with representatives of State governments and with universities and colleges; they might have issued materials and acted as a clearinghouse to disseminate this information. There is no way to get word of these activities out to women all over the country in other universities and colleges; no single governmental agency has this as one of its basic responsibilities.

The critical need for such information dissemination can best be illustrated perhaps by WEAL's activities under Executive Order 11246. This Order was amended to cover sex discrimination in October 1967, effective October 1968, but was unknown to most women leaders simply because there is no agency with the responsibility to disseminate this kind of information. Because of lack of knowledge, the Executive Order lay dormant and unused until January 1970. Indeed, the Civil Rights Commission's own publication "Equal Employment Opportunity Under Federal Law: A Guide to Federal Law Prohibiting Discrimination on Account of Race, Religion, or National Origin in Private and Public Employment," Clearinghouse Publication No. 17, published some 10 months after the Order went into effect (and some 22 months after it first was issued) *fails* to mention that the Executive Order applies to sex discrimination. And the Commission cannot be faulted for this omission, since, by law, sex discrimination is not one of their concerns.

I cannot stress enough the critical necessity for the Civil Rights Commission to collect and disseminate information relevant to sex discrimination. There is a crucial need for such an agency to raise questions and issues, to hold hearings, and to perform a "watchdog" function in the same manner that it does so admirably for other minorities. Under current legislation, such functions at best are fragmented, isolated, uncoordinated, and therefore completely ineffective.

ADDITIONAL COMMENTS

If Section 805 is passed, the psychological effect of such legislation on women would be enormous. Women need moral and legal support if they are to have the courage to fight for their rights in the academic community. We need to undo the wrongs that have been done. Too many women already have had their academic careers stunted by the effects of sex discrimination. Such legislation would state loudly and clearly that the time has come for sex discrimination to end in America's colleges and universities.

Women on campuses all over the country have begun to form groups, across departmental and professional lines. They are beginning to do more than complain; they are examining their own university's commitment and treatment of women. Women faculty, women staff, and women students are all participating. Women's rights are being included in a variety of student protest activities. In January, 1969, at the University of Chicago, the first demonstration concerning equal rights for women took place. In February, 1970, a group of women students from Yale University seized the microphone at a Yale Alumni dinner and made several complaints and demands concerning the treatment of women at Yale. We need to give women alternate and better ways of combating sex discrimination than seizing a microphone or taking over a building. It is within the power and responsibility of this Committee and of the Congress to make such change possible by passing legislation, such as that in Section 805, that will alleviate sex discrimination on our campuses.

Women in the professions are becoming highly sensitive to the need for the recognition of the inequities within their professions. At the Fall 1969 meeting of the American Psychological Association, women psychologists charged that organization with accepting "male" job openings. (WEAL has since filed formal charges against the American Psychological Association and the American Personnel and Guidance Association for this very reason.) The women proceeded to form a new group, the Association for Women Psychologists. In other professional organizations such as the American Sociological Association, the Modern Language Association, the American Historical Association, the American Political Science Association, the American Society for Microbiology, and the American Association for the Advancement of Science, women have begun to form caucuses and organize as pressure groups to end discrimination within their respective professions. In April 1970, a Professional Women's Caucus emerged which will represent all professional women. These are but a few examples of activity by women in the academic and professional worlds. They will not accept second class citizenship any longer.

We live in a rapidly changing world. The roles and responsibilities of both women and men are changing. No longer do women need to choose between a career *or* marriage; now the choice for most women is: what is the best way to combine work *and* marriage? If we are to come to grips with the problem of population growth it is vital that women have alternate life styles other than extensive child bearing. There is little reason for a woman to limit her family if the only realistic alternative is a job far below her capabilities, coupled with extensive educational and occupational discrimination. The abolition of our abortion laws and the dissemination of the Pill and other birth control information will not have much impact if there is no other style of life for a woman to pursue. Dr. Roger Revelle, Director of the Center for Population Studies at Harvard University recently testified in hearings before a Subcommittee of the Committee on Government Operations, House of Representatives, 91st Congress:

"One way to influence them [individual families] is to make alternative careers available for women, careers other than parenthood, other than the domestic pattern which is the norm of American life. If you look at our college and university enrollment, I think it is nothing short of disgraceful that there are about twice as many men as women in our colleges and universities. We will never persuade women to play their full role in society, let alone to have fewer children, unless we give them opportunities for something else to do—something meaningful and important to do. This means, among other things, a much greater opportunity for higher education than they have at the present time."

Women have been discriminated against in the past in many areas of life, of which the university is but one. We need to begin to redress these wrongs. Passage of Section 805 is a symbolic and actual beginning. It will give hope and dignity to women, the second class citizens of the nation. As a member of the Women's Equity Action League, as an educator of counselors and as a psychologist, as a teacher, as a woman, a wife and a mother, and above all, as a human being, I urge you to support Section 805 of H.R. 16098.

(The 80 page WEAL Sex Discrimination Report submitted to the Secretary of Labor, George P. Shultz, has been made available to Representative Edith Green, Chairman of the Special Subcommittee on Education.)

WOMEN'S EQUITY ACTION LEAGUE.—UNIVERSITIES AND COLLEGES CHARGED WITH SEX DISCRIMINATION UNDER EXECUTIVE ORDER 11246 AS AMENDED [1]

January 31, 1970:
Class action filed against all universities and colleges holding Federal contracts.
University of Maryland, College Park, Md.

March 16, 1970:
City University of New York, New York, N.Y.
University of North Carolina, Chapel Hill, N.C.

March 25, 1970: Harvard University, Cambridge, Mass. (National Organization for Women—N.O.W.).

March 26, 1970: University of Pittsburgh (University Committee for Women's Rights).

April 14, 1970: Western Carolina University, Cullowhee, N.C.

April 22, 1970:
American Psychological Association.
University of Tennessee, Knoxville, Tenn.
American Personnel & Guidance Association.
Northeastern Illinois State College, Illinois.
De Pauw University, Greencastle, Indiana.
Marymount College, Tarrytown, New York.
Hartwick College, Oneonta, New York.
Frostburg State College, Frostburg, Maryland.
Clarion State College, Clarion, Penna.
Lincoln University, Lincoln University, Penna.
George Washington University, Washington, D.C.
Susquehanna University, Selingsgrove, Penna.
Univ. of North Carolina at Wilmington, N.C.
Virginia Commonwealth University, Richmond, Va.

---

[1] Charges filed by WEAL unless otherwise indicated.

Southern Illinois University, Carbondale, Ill.
Michigan Technological University, Houghton, Mich.
Pacific Lutheran University, Tacoma, Wash.
Mercer County Community College, Trenton, New Jersey.
Rutgers University at New Brunswick, N.J.
    Douglass College in Rutgers, New Brunswick, **N.J.**
    Rutgers at Camden, N.J.
    Rutgers at Newark, N.J.
    Livingston College, New Brunswick, N.J.
Chesapeake Community College, Wye Mills, Maryland.

April 26, 1970:
Boston College, Boston, Mass.
Northeastern University, Boston, Mass.
University of Massachusetts at Amherst, Mass.
University of Massachusetts at Boston, Mass.
Radcliffe College, Cambridge, Mass.
University of Rhode Island, Kingston, R.I.
University of New Hampshire, Durham, N.H.
Massachusetts Institute of Technology, Cambridge, Mass.
Tufts University, Medford, Mass.
Brandeis University, Waltham, Mass.
Salem State College, Salem, Mass.
Clark University, Worcester, Mass.
Brown University, Providence, R.I.
Amherst College, Amherst, Mass.
Assumption College, Worcester, Mass.
Holy Cross College, Worcester, Mass.
Smith College, Northampton, Mass.
University of Connecticut, Storrs, Conn.
University of Miami, Coral Gables, Fla.

May 11, 1970:
Columbia University, New York, N.Y.
University of Georgia, Athens, Ga.
Western Washington State College, Bellingham, Wash.

May 25, 1970:
Entire State University system of the State of Florida:
    Florida International University, Miami, Florida.
    Florida Technological University, Orlando, Florida.
    University of South Florida, Tampa, Florida.
    University of West Florida, Pensacola, Florida.
    Florida Atlantic University, Boca Raton, Florida.
    Florida State University, Tallahassee, Florida.
    Florida A & M University, Tallahassee, Florida.
    University of Northern Florida, Jacksonville, Florida.
    University of Florida, Gainesville, Florida.
All two year colleges under the Division of Community Colleges administered
    by the Florida State Dept. of Education.
Eastern Illinois University, Charleston, Illinois.
Winthrop College, Rock Hill, South Carolina.

June 1, 1970: *Entire State University* and *State College system of California:*
University of California at Berkeley.
University of California at Davis.
University of California at Irvine.
University of California at Los Angeles.
University of California at Riverside.
University of California at San Diego.
University of California at Santa Cruz.
University of California at San Francisco.
University of California at Santa Barbara.
California State College at Dominguez Hills.
California State College at Fullerton.
California State College at Hayward.
California State College at San Bernadino.
California State College at Long Beach.
California State College at Los Angeles.
California State Polytechnic College.
Chico State College.

Fresno State College.
Humboldt State College.
Sacramento State College.
San Diego State College.
San Fernando Valley State College
San Francisco State College.
San Jose State College.
Sonoma State College.
Stanislaus State College.

May 28, 1970: University of Michigan, Ann Arbor, Mich. (FOCUS on Equal Employment for Women).

Additional filings by Women's Equity Action League (WEAL), July 1970
  University of Minnesota
  Carnegie-Mellon (Pittsburgh)
  Wayne State University (Detroit)
  University of Wisconsin
  Brooklyn College
  Phi Delta Kappa (honorary education society, for men only).

WEAL Fact Sheet on percentages of doctorates awarded to women in selected fields in 1967–68

	Percent		Percent
General biology	29. 0	English and literature	27. 4
General zoology	14. 8	Journalism	15. 6
Bacteriology, virology, mycology, parisitology, and microbiology	18. 0	General arts	25. 0
		Music	14. 5
Biochemistry	22. 3	Speech and dramatic arts	18. 5
Pharmacology	14. 1	Fine and applied arts	34. 0
Education of mentally retarded	44. 4	Linguistics	20. 6
Education of deaf, speech, and hearing	23. 8	French	38. 1
		Italian	18. 0
Art education	34. 0	Spanish	31. 7
Music education	11. 0	Philology and literature of romance languages	35. 8
Early childhood education	100. 0		
Elementary education	42. 4	German	23. 9
Secondary education	17. 0	Pharmacy	10. 0
Adult education	21. 4	Library science	31. 8
Education administration, supervision and finance	8. 2	Mathematics	6. 0
		Philosophy	9. 1
Counseling and guidance	20. 9	Chemistry	8. 0
Rehabilitation counselor training	23. 0	Psychology	22. 5
		Anthropology	23. 9
History and philosophy of education	19. 2	History	13. 0
		Political science	11. 3
Curriculum and instruction	24. 5	Sociology	18. 5
General education	18. 7	Social work	22. 0

Source: Earned Degrees Conferred: Part A—Summary Data, Office of Education, OE–54013–68–A.

WEAL FACT SHEET ON SEX DISCRIMINATION IN UNIVERSITIES AND COLLEGES

"21,000 women were turned down for college entrance in the State of Virginia; during the same period of time not one application of a male student was rejected."—Report of the Virginia Commission for The Study of Educational Facilities in the State of Virginia, 1964. Cited in the Feb. 6–8 debate in the U.S. House of Representatives on Title VII of the Civil Rights Act.

"A girl needs higher marks to enter college than a boy."—Caroline Bird, *Born Female: The High Cost of Keeping Women Down.* Pocket Books, 1969.

"In 1940 28% of college faculties were women. In 1960, the percentage was down to 22%. 40% of teacher's colleges faculties are women; only 10% of the faculties of prestigious private universities are women."—Dr. Edwin C. Lewis, Professor, University of Iowa, *Developing Women's Potential.* Iowa State University Press, 1968.

"The percentage of M.D. degrees awarded [to women] in accredited medical schools has not increased since 1920. A similar situation prevails in the field of law . . . Even in college teaching, the proportion of women has declined from a peak of 30% in 1930 to about 22% today—a ratio just about equal to what it was fifty years ago. The loss of proportion of women in college teaching applies to all types of institutions—and to all kinds of curriculums—the arts and humanities as well as the sciences. The women who do teach in college tend to predominate at the lower professional ranks."—Dr. Lindley J. Stiles, Dean, School of Education, University of Wisconsin, "Women, Wisdom and Education," in *Women in College and University Teaching*, University of Wisconsin, 1963.

"In the United States, the situation for women university faculty members is not generally as favorable as for men in these positions.—Dr. Gladys L. Borchers, Professor Emeritus, University of Wisconsin, "Some Investigations Concerning the Status of Faculty Women in American Colleges and Universites,"—*Women in College and University Teaching*, University of Wisconsin, 1963.

". . . the shortage of college teachers is one of the critical labor problems of the present decade, and the next. The shortage has been apparent for some time; yet the proportion of new college teachers who are women [has not increased] for more than a decade."—Dr. Esther Westervelt, Associate Professor, Columbia University, "Counseling Today's Girls for Tomorrow's Womanhood," in *New Approaches to Counseling Girls in the 1960's.* (Midwest Regional Pilot Conference cosponsored by the Women's Bureau and the U.S. Office of Education, 1965).

"In 1879, women held more than a third of the faculty positions in colleges and universities. By the 1960's, that ratio had dropped to less than a fourth. The proportion of women will probably dwindle even further.—*Time*, November 21, 1969 (p. 54).

"Since the 1930's, women have actually received a decreasing proportion of master's degrees, doctorates and faculty appointments."—Richard E. Farson, "The Rage of Women," *Look*, December 16, 1969.

"Recent analysis by Harmon of the careers of men and women holding Ph.D.s further underlines that sharp sex difference in ascending the academic ladder to a full professorship: confining attention to men and women who have spent twenty years in academia and who hold Ph. D.s in the social sciences, Harmon shows that 90% of the men had reached a full professorship, something achieved by only 53% of the single women and 41% of the married women. It is also clear from these data that it is sex and not the special situation or responsibilities of married women that makes the greatest difference in career advancement."—Dr. Alice S. Rossi, Associate Professor, Goucher College. "Cradles, Jobs or Rocks", to appear in the *Atlantic Monthly*, March 1970.

"It is well known that the professional schools have consistently discriminated against the qualified woman on the assumption, among other things, that she would marry early, and be irrevocably lost to the profession. It is a fallacy to assume that she would marry at all, and more than likely marry early, and that she could not remain professionally active, if she should marry."—Dr. Donald W. Fletcher, Dean of the Graduate School, San Francisco State College, "The Female Mind, A Wasted Natural Resource," *Women's Education*, Vol. VI, no. 4, December 1967.

"Professor Jo Tice Bloom of Bowie State College . . . did point out that only 18% of all college teachers in the United States are women and that the majority of women college professors teach in state colleges, not the major universities. . . . She also noted that 88 percent of women college teachers earn less than $10,000 a year, 55 percent of the male professors earn the same salary."—*The Evening Star*, December 30, 1969, reporting on a panel discussion on discrimination against women historians and history professors at the American Historical Association.

"Across all work settings, fields, and ranks, women experience a significantly lower academic income than do men in the academic teaching labor force for the same amount of time . . . Within each work setting, field and rank category, women also have lower salaries . . .

". . . in the social sciences, women tend to be promoted less rapidly than do their male counterparts. This suggests that in fields in which women compromise a larger component of the total labor force, more discrimination in promotions may be expected."—Dr. Helen Astin, Bureau of Social Science Research, "Sex Differences in Academic Rank and Salary among Science Doctorates in Teaching," *Journal of Human Resources*, Vol. III, no. 2, Spring 1968.

"The barriers which certain colleges and universities and professional schools and certain employers place in the way of girls' career plans have been so often discussed that I need not dwell on them here. . . . I wish we might be more free to publish some of our experiences but I realize how unwise it would be to jeopardize future openings. Let me, just for the record, air two stories which concern two different schools at the same university. One concerns a girl who, while still 15, was admitted to the school of engineering. On the first day of her laboratory course the students were told that lockers for their laboratory equipment and clothes would be assigned later that week. But two weeks passed and she received no locker assignment. Finally she took the problem to her professor who referred her to an assistant who referred her to another assistant who told her he would be glad to assign her a locker if she wanted one, but they were in the men's lavatory. Last year this university's school of medicine was surveyed by a State commission regarding its policies on women students; the flat response was that they admitted very few and did not expect to increase the proportion because women got married and did not persist in the profession."—Dr. Esther Westervelt, in a paper given at the Midwest Regional Pilot Conference cosponsored by the Women's Bureau and the U.S. Office of Education, 1965.

"Women with doctorates are less likely than men to be teaching advanced courses. Women hold lower ranks than men with comparable qualifications in all kinds of institutions."—Dr. Jessie Bernard, Penn. State University, *Academic Women*. Penn. State University Press, 1964.

". . . . women tend to be concentrated at the lower levels of academic rank and to make less money than their male counterparts. Those in the higher ranks are found primarily in departments of education, home economics, and library science, and are more often in women's colleges than in coeducational schools . . . "As in public school teaching, administrative positions in the colleges go mostly to men and there is no indication of change in the near future. In fact the proportion of women in college educational leadership positions was lower in the mid-1960's than it was 25 or even 10 years before. In this respect, women seem to be advancing to the rear."—Dr. Edwin C. Lewis, *Developing Women's Potential*, Iowa State University Press, 1968.

". . . there are 1,043 persons with faculty status at Stanford [University]. Of these, 49 are women, or less than 5%. . . . The majority of these faculty women, 31 of the 49, are placed at the lowest of the three ranks—assistant professor. Women comprise nearly 10 percent of Stanford's assistant professors, but less than 2 percent of the professors . . ." Of the non-professional faculty at Stanford, women account for 30.5% of the Instructors, 25.2% of the Lecturers, 23.4% of the Research Associates, and only 13.3% of the Senior Research Associates, and only 13.3% of the Senior Research Associates. ". . . As is the case with the various professorial ranks, women tend to be appointed more commonly at the lower ranks of the non-professorial faculty . . . In summary, women comprise a small minority of the Stanford faculty. Most hold appointments at the lower ranks, at which tenure is not often available."—Dr. Alberta E. Siegel, Associate Professor, Stanford University, "Education of Women at Stanford University," *The Study of Education at Stanford*, Vol. VII, March 1969.

"[the findings] suggest that women who report experiences with employer discrimination are professionally active and scholarly productive. Therefore one cannot interpret their complaints as a form of rationalization or as an excuse for their failure to achieve recognition."—Dr. Helen Astin, *The Woman Doctorate*, Basic Books, February 1970, chapter 8.

"The traditional bias against women in law, medicine, and business—and its frustrating effect on female grads—is evident in women's choice of graduate degree programs. About 2 out of 5 (40.1%) of the female '68 grads surveyed are enrolled in graduate schools. . . . only 4.5% are in law school; 2.2% are in medical school; 2.1% are studying for the MBA's."—"Why Doesn't Business Hire More College Trained Women?" *Personnel Management—Policies and Practices*. Prentice Hall, Inc. April 15, 1969.

"We are aware of discriminatory practices towards girls in college admissions . . . and the discriminatory practices are usually reflective of the attitudes of a culture, but we have not yet used all the resources available to effect . . . changes."—"Implications for the Future," summary of Midwest Regional Pilot Conference cosponsored by the Women's Bureau and the U.S. Office of Education, 1965.

WOMEN'S EQUITY ACTION LEAGUE,
January 31, 1970.

Hon. GEORGE P. SHULTZ,
Secretary, Department of Labor,
Washington, D.C.

DEAR MR. SECRETARY: Please consider this letter as a formal complaint under Executive Order 11246, as amended by Executive Order 11375.

The Women's Equity Action League (WEAL) hereby requests that you instruct the Office of Federal Contract Compliance to insist that *all* Federal agencies doing business with universities and colleges enforce the Executive Orders which have been completely ignored. We know of no meaningful compliance efforts that have been undertaken. We ask that the Office of Federal Contract Compliance institute an immediate *"class"* action and *compliance review* for *all* universities and colleges receiving Federal contracts. We ask that as stated in the Executive Orders, *universities end discrimination* and *take affirmative action* "to ensure that applicants are employed, and that employees are treated during employment, without regard to . . . sex."

Each year millions of dollars in Federal contracts are disbursed to universities and colleges. And each year, these same universities and colleges discriminate against women in a variety of ways. They discriminate by having quotas for women in admission to undergraduate and graduate programs; they discriminate in scholarships and financial assistance; they discriminate in the hiring of women for their faculties; they discriminate by paying their women faculty members less than their male counterparts, and they discriminate by promoting women far more slowly than men. Whether by design or accident, the effect is the same: women are second class citizens on many a campus.

For example, the proportion of women studying in college is not increasing; it is tending to remain fairly constant. At the advanced levels, the proportion of women is *less now* than it was in 1930. The proportion of M.D. degrees awarded to women has not increased since 1920, and a similar situation exists in Law and Engineering schools. Such *consistent* percentages of women students can only be a result of quotas whether openly admitted or not. (Why are 85% of Finland's dentists and 75% of Russia's physicians women? In our country only 7% of our physicians are women?)

In the last century, women held more than one-third of the faculty positions in colleges and universities; today the proportion of women is less than one-fourth. (At most of the "Big Ten" universities it is about one-tenth.) In study after study, women are now found mainly in the lower reaches of academia. For example, of 183 graduate departments of Sociology across the country, women are 30% of the doctoral candidates, 14% of the Assistant Professors, 9% of the Associate Professors, and only 4% of the Full Professors. At the University of Maryland in the College of Arts and Sciences nine out of the 15 departments examined had no women who were Full Professors, although all had women in the lower academic ranks. The figures can be duplicated, department by department, university by university, in practically all areas of higher education.

Moreover, numerous studies reveal consistent pay differences between men and women with the same academic rank, with the same length of service, and with the same academic qualifications. Deans of Women make less money than Deans of Men, even in the same institution. In the same departments, women instructors usually make less than male instructors, women Assistant Professors make less than male Assistant Professors, Women Associate Professors make less than male Associate Professors, and women Full Professors make less than male Full Professors. Some studies indicate that the size of these differences in salary may be *increasing*.

Administrative positions in higher education rarely go to women. Women are rarely heads of departments. (In the School of Education at the University of Maryland only *one* department—Special Education—is headed by a woman; in the College of Arts and Sciences only the Department of Dance is headed by a woman.) In fact, the *proportion* of women in college and university leadership positions is *lower now* than it was 25 or even 10 years ago.

Executive Order 11246 as amended by Executive Order 11375 specifically *forbids discrimination by Federal Contractors because of Sex*. Universities often get as much as one-third of their total funds from government contracts. Yet the universities have been allowed to continue discriminating against women at all levels. The Federal government, despite the applicability of the Executive Orders, has done nothing to change this. This is shocking and outrageous. Remedial steps need to be taken at once to bring the universities and colleges in line with the Executive Orders referring to Federal contractors and sex discrimination.

Specifically, these areas of discrimiation must be examined and remedied:

1. *Admission quotas to undergraduate and graduate schools.*—Admission to college is analogous to being admitted to the "apprenticeship" programs of industry. Without open admissions, there can be no fair treatment. Quotas must be abolished; admission must be based on ability, not sex.

2. *Discrimination in financial help for graduate study (scholarships, fellow-*

ships, research grants, teaching assistantships, etc.).—Financial help must be extended purely on the basis of ability and/or need, and not on the basis of sex.

3. *Hiring practices.*—Discrimination against hiring women in academic positions must end.

4. *Promotions.*—Criteria for upgrading should be irrespective of sex.

5. *Salary differentials.*—Women and men at the same academic level and with similar qualifications should receive similar salaries.

WEAL asks that the OFCC act immediately in these areas to end discrimination against women by all universities and colleges receiving Federal contracts.

I have appended to this letter some background materials showing clearly the pattern of sex discrimination in higher education. WEAL will be glad to confer with the OFCC in implementing the Executive Orders and in developing plans for affirmative actions on the part of the institutions involved.

This complaint is grounded also in a specific charge of discrimination in faculty hiring and promotion at the University of Maryland. The investigator should contact me for the names of persons who will discuss this case in support of the complaint.

Sincerely yours,

NANCY E. DOWDING, Ph. D., *President.*

WEAL FACT SHEET ON SOME REASONS WHY IT IS DIFFICULT FOR GIRLS TO GET GOOD COUNSELING

Almost any discussion concerning the role of women in American society sooner or later focusses on the need for better counseling of girls. Recommendations are made, and much is said as to how counseling can be improved. Yet little changes: girls who aspire to be physicians are "counseled" into becoming nurses; still worse, girls who aspire careers are told they will probably get married and therefore shouldn't consider a career; etc.

I recently did a rough tabulation of some 343 departments of counselor education, using data from the *Directory of Counselor Educators, 1967-68* (OE–25036–B). These figures represent virtually *all* of the institutions that train counselors in the United States.

Of the 343 departments:

209 have *no* women at all (61%).

82 have one woman (25%).

52 have two or more women (15%).

In other words, 85% of the departments have only one woman or no women on their faculty. According to U.S. Office of Education figures, women account for 20.9% of the doctorates in Counseling and Guidance.

Moreover, those women who were teaching in counselor education programs had significantly lower ranks than their male counterparts. About one-half (49%) of the women were at the lowest academic rank, that of Assistant Professor. In contrast, only 31% of the male educators were at that rank.

Few, if any, counselor educator programs offer courses concerning the counseling of women, although courses concerned with other minority groups are being instituted in several universities.

Leadership from the counselors' own professional organization, the American Personnel and Guidance Association (APGA) has been sadly lacking. The APGA still has ads in its *Placement Bulletin* that list the sex of an applicant as a job qualification, and I quote several from the March 1970 issue:

Assistant or Associate Professor, male preferred (Northeastern Illinois State College, Chicago, Illinois).

Counselor, . . . man (Mercer County Community College, Trenton, New Jersey).

Counselor, male preferred, (Virginia Commonwealth University, Richmond, Va.).

Psychometrist, male preferred (Southern Illinois University, Carbondale, Ill.).

Despite a series of letters between Dr. Willis Dugan, the Executive Director and the Women's Equity Action League, in which Dr. Dugan promised that the offending policy would be eliminated, the ads continue to list sex as a qualification.

Such ads, of course, are a violation of both the letter and spirit of Title VII of the Civil Rights Act and Executive Order 11246 as amended. In April,

WEAL filed against the APGA under Title VII and the Executive Order. I might add here, that as a member in good standing I asked that news of the filings be given to the membership; as of this date, no mention of WEAL's action has appeared in any of the numerous APGA publications.

I would not want to give the impression that the APGA is unconcerned with human rights, the dignity of individuals, or discrimination. Just this year, the APGA created a new office within its administrative structure to deal with human relations. It is called the "Office of Non-White Affairs."

[U.S. Dept. of Labor, Women's Bureau, August 1968]

FACT SHEET ON EDUCATIONAL ATTAINMENT OF NONWHITE WOMEN

Nonwhite women and men have made significant progress in raising their level of educational attainment over the last several decades. The median [1] years of school completed by nonwhite women and men 25 years of age and over in March 1967 were 9.8 years and 8.9 years, respectively. The comparable medians in April 1940 were 6.1 years and 5.4 years.

The rise in educational attainment has been even more pronounced among nonwhite women and men 25 to 29 years of age. In March 1967 the median years of school completed by nonwhite women in this age group was 12.1 years; by nonwhite men, 12.2 years. In contrast, the median years of school completed by nonwhite women and men 25 to 29 years of age in April 1940 were 7.5 years and 6.5 years, respectively.

Another measure of the continuing increase in the level of education achieved by the nonwhite population is the rising proportion of the population 5 to 19 years of age enrolled in school. In 1966, 87 out of 100 nonwhite girls in this age group were enrolled in school. The comparable ratio for nonwhite boys was 90 out of 100. These ratios have increased significantly since the turn of the century.

Year	Nonwhite enrollment rates (per hundred)	
	Girls	Boys
1960	86	87
1950	75	75
1940	69	68
1900	33	29

A further illustration of the rise in educational attainment of the nonwhite population is a comparison of the proportions who had completed the various levels of schooling in March 1967 with those in October 1952. About 56 percent of nonwhite women 25 years of age and over had gone beyond elementary school in March 1967 compared with about 31 percent in October 1952. Among nonwhite men the percentages were 49 and 27.

At the upper end of the educational scale, 11 percent of nonwhite women and 10 percent of the men had had some college training in March 1967 compared with only 6 and 5 percent, respectively, in October 1952. Furthermore, a higher proportion of both nonwhite women and men were college graduates in March 1967 than in October 1952. Among women the proportion increased from less than 3 to almost 5 percent. Nonwhite men made even better progress—from 2 to 5 percent.

There is a direct relationship between educational attainment and income. The median income in 1966 of nonwhite women and men 25 years of age and over was higher at each level of education attained.

Years of school completed	Median income in 1966	
	Nonwhite women	Nonwhite men
Less than 8 years	$932	$2,376
8 years	1,303	3,681
1 to 3 years of high school	1,698	4,278
4 years of high school	2,475	5,188
Some college	3,964	5,928

---

[1] Half above, half below.

The median income of nonwhite women was lower than that of nonwhite men at every level of educational attainment. The gap was narrower between those with some college, but even at this educational level the median income of the women was only 67 percent of that of the men.

Among year-round full-time workers, the 1966 median wage or salary income of nonwhite women was only 65 percent of that of nonwhite men.

NOTE.—The figures in this fact sheet are from the U.S. Department of Commerce, Bureau of the Census.

[AAUW Journal, Jan. 1970]

CAN CONTINUING EDUCATION ADAPT?

(By Kathryn F. Clarenbach)

Dr. Clarenbach is a specialist in women's education, at the University of Wisconsin. She is also chairman of the Governor's Commission on Status of Women, Wisconsin.

During the decade just ended, the proliferation of programs directed toward continuing education for women has exceeded almost all expectations. From coast to coast, scarcely an institution of higher learning has not responded in one way or another to the tidal wave of women seeking to resume or begin advanced studies.

Just as the women themselves come in all ages, levels of education and motivations, so the programs represent a vast range of content, structure, philosophy and approach. Where one college may emphasize professional preparation in a given discipline, another will concentrate on refresher courses. Vocational workshops, research, public education via conferences and symposia receive varying attention. Some programs believe in separating the mature students from the young while others advocate homogenized situations. The rather elaborate centers on certain campuses contrast sharply with virtually no separately identifiable staff or facilities elsewhere.

Staff come to continuing education for women from a wide range of academic backgrounds, none specifically trained for this new and wide-ranging responsibility, and a large number themselves returnees to the professional world. Interinstitutional program cooperation has been accentuated as has the participation of growing numbers of voluntary organizations with a concern for adult education. A steady trickle of foreign visitors from every continent to observe and exchange ideas is a reminder of the world-wide dimensions of continuing education for women.

Whatever the primary emphasis or the degree of institutional commitment, all of the hundreds of programs share the common goals of developing and utilizing the potential of women, expanding educational opportunities, and thus helping to fill the enormous social need of our time for educated brainpower. Inspired in part by the American *rigor mortis* which Sputnik engendered, their creation was more specifically urged by the 1957 manpower study, "Woman Power." Early programs such as the Minnesota Plan and the Radcliffe Institute for Independent Studies were viewed at first by many skeptics and traditionalists as just another fad to amuse the women. By 1970, however, there is no longer any question among informed people that continuing education of women, and of men, must be built into our educational system, not as an afterthought or a special frill, but as a serious responsibility every bit as essential as the education of the young.

What has been accomplished during the 1960's *via* continuing education for women? What are the serious omissions? What have we learned? Where do we go from here?

Obviously accomplishment number one is the official opening of educational doors to adults—especially women—and confirmation of their academic ability. In any estimate of women beyond traditional college age enrolled in university and vocational classes, conservative figures must reach several hundred thousand per year.

The opening of the most select academic door on my campus is represented by the 1965–69 Carnegie-financed E. B. Fred Fellowship for mature women. This five-year program provided scholarships to 49 women, all of whom were candidates for doctoral and advanced professional degrees. Their success in degree completion and moving into faculty positions in higher education has been phenomenal. Grandmothers on campus are now no longer oddities. Faculties have learned to respect the classroom achievement of adult women, sometimes over their own bodies.

On many campuses the attainment of continuing education programs has involved long and sometimes incredibly stubborn tasks of persuading administrators that flexibility is not synonymous with lowering standards. As far back as 1963 the President's Commission on the Status of Women spelled out some essentials if we were to provide adequate education for women; in light of women's discontinuities, social mobility and other facts of life, they advised that provision must be made for ready transfer of credits, increased uses of testing for credit combined with substitution of relevant life experience for course work, permitting part-time study, innovative opportunity to tailor-made interdepartmental courses of study, re-assessment of age limits and timing requirements, plus the very basic provision of financial assistance in significant dimensions.

Some inroads have been made in these recommendations for flexibility, from the elimination of required physical education for adults, and modification of application forms appropriate to self-supporting adults, to removing age limits for admission to professional schools, permitting part-time study and giving some modest attention to easing credit transfer. Equivalency testing, however, remains in its infancy, and financial assistance to the mature women is virtually still a dream.

Both of these failures reflect a refusal on the part of trustees and college administrators to acknowledge the real value of the potential contribution of women. Foundation support, notably from the Carnegie Corporation of New York, Rockefeller Brothers, AAUW, Danforth and the Kellogg Foundation, made possible the initial large-scale movement for continuing education for women. Subsequent modest fellowship provisions, often of pathetic proportions ($30 to $100 book and/or fee allotments), have been made available by community voluntary groups. NDEA loans are finally granted to students carrying half-time loads, but are still not available to the many adults who must earn fewer than half-load credits. Beyond these several sources of funds, very little advance has been made to meet this enormous need. It would be interesting to calculate the actual financial investment, less tuition and fees of enrollees and less foundation and federal funds, made by colleges and universities in continuing education for women.

It is true that critical shortages in several professions and occupations are being met by federal and state training funds. All too often, however, the limited occupational range, the small scope of the investment, the glaring shortage of trained personnel which motivated the programs are all grim reminders that women are still marginal workers. Thus many women have been induced to enter or re-enter areas of acute shortages in traditionally "women's" fields (e.g., social work, health fields, teaching) at both professional and subprofessional levels by these financial aids. Non-credit and liberal studies unfortunately continue to be virtually ignored.

The need which continuing educators have seen from the outset, and have constantly re-affirmed, for a full-scale nation-wide provision of measures comparable to a G.I. Bill has had almost no serious attention. The basic discontinuity in the educational and professional lives of American women is time out for childbearing and rearing. When these enterprises are considered to be as socially useful as military service, perhaps women will be accorded educational opportunity somewhat equivalent to the military veteran.

The absence of adequate financial support is also one reason the bulk of continuing education clientele continues to be middle or upper-class women, the majority of whom have had some previous college-level education. Even as traditional education is moving belatedly and with hesitant steps in the direction of education for racial minorities and the economically deprived, so too with continuing education. What began as a white, middle-class, and often middle-aged enterprise (staff as well as clientele) is all too slowly extending its techniques and opportunities to those whose need is greatest.

Another unfulfilled objective of the 60's has been in the area of child care. Directors of continuing education for women have universally acknowledged the need for establishment of child care facilities on campus as a nonacademic service for the mature woman student. Just as housing, food service, recreation, counseling, cultural events, health service, have gradually won their place as bona fide responsibilities of educational institutions, so too should child care. But progress in this area is no faster than in financial support.

Continuing educators especially have been dismayed at the sizable population of wives of graduate and undergraduate students who themselves must delay or forego their own studies for want of child care and/or financial aid.

At a time when a young family is already on campus, when the household is geared to the rigors and arrangements of study, it is a criminal social waste to prevent those wives who would like to proceed with their own intellectual development from doing so. The high rate of divorce among this group might be lowered if both partners were enabled to pursue their interests and attain equivalent levels.

By now it is abundantly clear that the shorter the role discontinuity for women, the more realistic the chances for academic success and job placement. This means no necessarily prolonged span of years at home or child rearing and, indeed, increasing numbers of young women and their husbands are opting for no discontinuity at all just as industry, unions, hospitals and other institutions are beginning to provide day care for young children of working parents, so too should college and vocational schools.

It has become the path of least resistance to accept the life-in-stages pattern as *the* acceptable life style for women (especially affluent women), rather than as simply *one* of *many* equally valid patterns. This acceptance is being re-assessed. How to counsel and educate the young in the realities of life ahead, how to keep women current with a field when not totally engaged in it (now-adays a major problem even for men and women who *are* totally engaged), how to help assure that those women who do qualify will be equally welcome in graduate or professional school and have equal access to subsequent suitable employment, are universal problems of increasing urgency.

These problems confront continuing educators and form much of the agenda of the recent national gatherings of program directors. Such meetings are called by the Adult Education Association and the National Association of Deans and Women's Counselors as well as the U.S. Office of Education and the Women's Bureau of the U.S. Dept. of Labor.

While leaders have met together over a six or seven-year period, they have considered and to date rejected the establishment of a separate formal asso-ciation of continuing educators. When AAUW's *Women's Education* ceased its quarterly publication last year, it left a real gap in program and research interchange which has not yet been filled. The lack of funding for this function is a sad commentary in itself; the absence of the function is a step backward.

After a decade of efforts to modify institutional procedures, encourage women to raise their own sights and self-evaluation, assist in the placement of women in socially useful and individually rewarding enterprise, persistent roadblocks recur. They are rooted deeply in tenacious attitudes reminiscent of nineteenth century opposition to women in higher education.

There are still departments in colleges and universities of good repute (in-cluding my own) which pride themselves on never having had a woman among their tenured faculty. In other departments individual faculty members, having had an "unfortunate" experience with a female advisee who forsook her graduate work for marriage or motherhood, are no longer willing to invest their time with any of the high risk sex. Many women, young or not-so-young, have difficulty finding university employment at a level of responsibility or income commen-surate with their education and ability. Policies of nepotism and no-maternity leave have scarcely been challenged. Unless the women for whose education these vast efforts are being put forth have equal (or even reasonable) opportunity for both study and employment, continuing education for women may be guilty of compounding the frustrations.

So long as women settle for sub-professional status, project associate or lec-turer rather than tenured faculty, part-time hourly wage without fringe bene-fits rather than the going salary, they can quietly and safely go about their busi-ness of self-fulfillment and readiness for emergency and/or secondary employ-ment. No boats are being rocked, no male preserves are being threatened with in-vasion. But the growing demands of women for full and equal participation run headlong into institutional resistance supported by age-old myths of womens' place and stereotypes of women's potential.

In my observation the self-expectation of American women is rising perceptibly and passive acceptance of second best is dwindling rapidly. Campus ferment among women students, graduate and undergraduate, demanding their rightful opportunity, has begun to erupt, and this is only the beginning. Continued educa-tion directors are increasingly aware that they must work with these students in pressing for necessary social and institutional change.

From the vantage point of continuing education for women, with our unpre-cedented life-span view of women's education, and with our constant nagging question of "Education for what?" certain imperatives for the 1970's seem inescapable. Here are some of the top priorities for every continuing education program:

1. Participate in the growing movement to amend the Civil Rights Act of 1964 to remove the exclusion of educational institutions (teaching and administrative staff) from the prohibitions of sex-based discrimination. With a legal basis for prohibiting discrimination in higher education, the Equal Employment Opportunity Commission could be involved in compliance, and formal complaints and even court action could be instituted.

2. Take affirmative action to encourage employment of women in both faculty and administrative positions. The decrease in the past 35 years in percent of women on faculties is likely to accelerate during periods of campus unrest and tension; already we hear that the weaker sex can't deal even with elementary schools. Very special concerted, systematic counteraction to the undercutting of women is called for. As a starting point, conduct surveys on your campus to learn and highlight the facts of the relative standing of women on the faculty.

3. To educate both faculty and students, make every effort to inaugurate within the various disciplines courses dealing with woman as subject. Well stocked libraries and up-dated bibliographies widely available are part of this responsibility.

4. Extend as broadly as possible the techniques and services developed over the past decade. The very young, the poor, the non-high school graduate have special needs to which continuing education for women can contribute. Counseling the counselors and training the trainers is sometimes the most effective route to breaking down the traditional concepts of "women's fields" and "women's levels of responsibility."

5. Accelerate efforts toward institutional flexibility, significant financial aids and child care. As with racial minorities and the poor, women continue to require special attention in higher education.

STATEMENT OF HON. MARTHA W. GRIFFITHS, A REPRESENTATIVE IN CONGRESS FROM THE STATE OF MICHIGAN

Madam Chairman and members of the House Special Subcommittee on Education, the enactment of the four paragraphs of Section 805 of Congresswoman Green's bill (H.R. 16098) would constitute another milestone of progress on the road toward ending some of the large discriminations and injustices which are perpetrated against women, particularly working women. I fully support every provision of the four paragraphs in Section 805, and I hope that the committee and the Congess will adopt these provisions without any weakening amendments.

It is indeed astounding that in the 1970's American women still continue to be subjected to pervasive discrimination. Women do not seek special privileges. They ask only to be treated as persons under the law, entitled to the full protection of the law. In this day and age when women are increasingly involved in all phases of the economy and as supporters of families, it is irrational and unjust that our country continues to deny to them the equality of legal right and opportunity, which is due to every person.

Our country has made significant progress in eliminating legal discrimination against racial and ethnic minorites. We must do the same for women also. Women as well as men must be allowed and enabled to hold jobs for which their intelligence, training, and experience have prepared them. The woman who performs work equal to that of a man should receive equal pay. The woman who pays part of her earnings into pension plans should have the same benefits, and the same rights to protect her husband and family, as a man has to protect his wife and family by the the money he pays into the pension plan.

Indeed, I put it categorically: the law must provide the same rights and benefits to women as to men. That is why I and so many of our colleagues in the Congress are sponsoring the Equal Rights Amendment. I hope that this amendment will be approved by the Congress and ratified by the states. That amendment will eliminate many of the irrational sex distinctions now in the law including some of those which would be affected by Section 805 of H.R. 16098. However, the imminent adoption of the Equal Rights Amendment should not be viewed as an excuse to delay congressional action in adopting Section 805. The times demand that we strike down laws which discriminate against, or fail to assist, any person solely because of his or her sex.

Madam Chairman, let me here emphasize that my struggle against sex discrimination and my constant efforts to obtain the enactment of the Equal Rights Amendment and laws to eliminate sex discrimination are not merely to aid women. I am against sex discrimination whether it hurts the man or the woman. I believe that sex discrimination is as evil as race discrimination. The laws of our country, both federal and state, are full of all sorts of irrational discrimination, sometimes against men, more often against women, which are based only on the irrelevant factor of sex.

SUBPARAGRAPH (A)

When we enacted the Civil Rights Act of 1964, we established in Title VI of that act, the national policy that federal funds be spent without discrimination on account of race, color, or national origin. Paragraph (a) of Section 805 would simply add the word "sex". Our government is a government of all the people. It is the government of women, as well as men, and the principle of non-discrimination in connection with federally-assisted programs is just as relevant—is just as important—for women and for men, as it is for blacks and whites, for Christians and Jews, and for every racial or ethnic group.

Subparagraph (a) would simply say that any person or institution that wants to get the benefit of the federal dollar must comply with the fundamental principle that there be no discrimination based on race or sex or national origin. That principle is right and just; it is good for our country; and I fully support it.

SUBPARAGRAPH (B)

The second paragraph of Section 805 of your bill will delete the exemption concerning educational activities, which is now present in Section 702 of Title VII of the Civil Rights Act of 1964. That particular exemption has operated to sanction racial, religious and sex discrimination against teachers, professors, and instructors in all educational institutions from kindergarten to the post graduate schools. It constitutes a glaring and invidious loophole in the policy of non-discrimination in employment which we enacted in Title VII of the Civil Rights Act of 1964.

The extent of discrimination against women in the educational institutions of our country constitutes virtually a national calamity. Recently, I spoke on the floor of the House of Representatives about this matter. My speech of March 9, 1970 particularly emphasizes that the federal government itself is violating both national policy as well as the President's Executive Orders 11246 and 11375, by providing billions of dollars in federal contracts to universities which discriminate against women. My speech detailed some of the patterns of gross discrimination against women in the universities and colleges of our country. I respectfully request that my speech, a copy of which is here attached, be included as part of the record of this hearing.

THE FEDERAL GOVERNMENT VIOLATES NATIONAL POLICY, AS WELL AS THE PRESIDENT'S EXECUTIVE ORDERS, BY PROVIDING BILLIONS OF DOLLARS OF FEDERAL CONTRACTS TO UNIVERSITIES WHICH DISCRIMINATE AGAINST WOMEN

(Mrs. GRIFFITHS asked and was given permission to address the House for 1 minute and to revise and extend her remarks and include extraneous matter.)

Mrs. GRIFFITHS. Mr. Speaker, it is a national calamity that agencies of the Federal Government are violating our national policy, as well as the President's Executive orders, by providing billions of dollars of Federal contracts to universities and colleges which discriminate against women both as teachers and as students.

Our national policy, as expressed by Congress in 5 United States Code section 7151, plainly states:

"It is the policy of the United States to insure equal employment opportunities for employees without discrimination because of race, color, religion, sex or national origin. The President shall use his existing authority to carry out this policy."

The President's Executive Order 11246, as amended by Executive Order 11375, specifically forbids sex discrimination by Federal contractors. These orders are administered by the Office of Federal Contract Compliance of the Department of Labor. The Department of Health, Education, and Welfare has been designated as the compliance agency to obtain compliance with the Executive orders by colleges and universities with Federal contracts. However, billions of dollars in Federal contracts continue to go every year to colleges and universities which perpetrate vicious patterns of discrimination against women, despite the Executive orders to the contrary. And neither the Labor Department nor HEW does anything to stop or mitigate such discrimination.

Half of our brightest people, the people with talent and the capacity for the highest intellectual and fruitful endeavors, are women. They encounter pervasive discrimination when they try to enter college—when they apply for graduate and advanced training—when they attempt to join the faculties of our most esteemed universities and colleges—and if they finally succeed in becoming teachers, they get less pay and fewer promotions than their male colleagues.

Many universities and colleges with Federal contracts, although forbidden by Executive order from discriminating against women, nevertheless do so by applying quotas for women in admission to both undergraduate and graduate training programs. They discriminate against them in awarding scholarships and providing financial assistance. They discriminate against them in hiring their faculty members. They discriminate by paying their women faculty members less than their male colleagues with similar qualifications. They discriminate by promoting women far more slowly than men.

Although these institutions of higher learning like to view themselves as bastions of democracy, yet they penalize fully half of their potential students by requiring women to meet higher admission standards for admission than men. For example, at the University of North Carolina, admission of women on the freshman level is "restricted to those who are especially well-qualified." There is no similar restriction for male students. In the State of Virginia, 21,000 women were turned down for college entrance, while not one male student was rejected. What has the Federal Government done to change inequities such as these? Nothing—indeed, the Federal Government has not even made a murmur of protest.

Quota systems exist at many universities and colleges, whether openly admitted or not. In fact, the consistent low percentages of women students in medicine, law, engineering, and other professional fields, as well as in many undergraduate schools, can be the result only of quotas. They are the principal reasons why the percentage of women with M.D. degrees has not increased since 1920, the year that women first got the right to vote. It is sex discrimination in the universities which accounts for the fact that only 7 percent of U.S. physicians are women.

The undergraduate and graduate programs in universities are analogous to the training and apprenticeship programs of industry. Open admission policies, free of discrimination against women, are essential if women are to have the same employment opportunities as other citizens. Unless the universities open their training programs to women on equal basis, women will continue to get the short end of the stick in employment opportunities.

The tragic fact today is that women are losing ground in every segment of university life. Their proportion as students in college is not increasing. Their proportion as students at the graduate level is less now than in 1930. Whereas they held more than one-third of university faculty positions in the 1870's, they now hold less than one-fourth, and at the prestigious Big Ten universities they hold only about one-tenth, of the university faculty positions.

Moreover, women on the faculty generally are at the bottom of the academic hierarchy. Often they lack tenure. The higher the academic rank, the less is the percentage of women. For example, a recent study of 188 sociology departments in universities across the country showed that women are 30 percent of the doctoral candidates, but only 14 percent of the assistant professors, only 9 percent of the associate professors, and only 4 percent of the full professors.

For years there has been a shortage of college teachers, yet there have been little serious efforts to recruit women for college faculties. The excuse often given that there is a shortage of qualified women is ridiculous. For example, at Columbia University women receive about 25 percent of its doctoral degrees, but comprise only 2 percent of the tenured faculty in its graduate schools. Furthermore, contrary to academic mythology, a higher percentage of women with doctorates go into college teaching than do men with doctorates. The argument that women are lost to the academic world when they marry is also a myth, since over 90 percent of the women with doctorates are in the labor force. Women comprise 40 percent of the faculties in teachers' colleges, and about the same in junior colleges. But in the prestigious private and State universities the percentage of women teachers is much less.

Is it discrimination against women, or mere coincidence, that the great University of Chicago has a lower percentage of women on its faculty now than it did in 1899? Can anyone seriously argue that there are less qualified women now than in 1899?

Even in the field of education, where one might expect women to predominate, they are generally conspicuously absent in the upper ranks. A recent study shows that the University of Maryland's Department of Early Childhood Education, where women professors are 47 percent of the faculty, has almost all of these women—13 out of 15—at the lowest rank of assistant professor.

Women college teachers simply do not get promoted as often or as quickly as their male colleagues with similar qualifications. Ninety percent of the men with Ph. D.'s and at least 20 years of academic experience are full professors, whereas barely half of the women with the same qualifications have that rank. At Stanford University, 50 percent of the men, but only 10 percent of the women, on the faculty are associate or full professors. Somehow, women who are qualified enough to be hired are not "qualified" enough to be promoted. In some places they simply are not hired at all. The University of Pennsylvania, for example, has only four departments with more than two women, and 26 departments with no women at all. Similar incredible examples exist in many universities and departments in practically all areas of higher education.

Even when the universities hire women, they do not get the same salaries as men on the campus. Numerous studies document the pay differences between men and women with the same academic rank and qualifications; deans of women make far less than deans of men, even at the same institutions.

I heard of one woman who had been an associate professor for more than 10 years, discovered that she was earning at least $1,000 less than the bottom salary which that university paid to its men associate professors. In the academic world, women instructors earn less than male instructors; women assistant professors earn less than male assistant professors; women associate professors earn less than male associate professors; and women full professors earn less than male full professors; and there is every indication that the gap between the salaries of men and women faculty members is growing wider.

The picture is even more dismal at the administrative level. The number of women college presidents is decreasing. Women rarely head departments. At the University of Maryland, for example, in the College of Education, only one department—Special Education—is headed by a woman. At Columbia College, the undergraduate men's college of Columbia University, only one woman—the librarian—is on the administrative staff. The proportion of women in college and university leadership positions is lower than it was 25 or even 10 years ago.

The vast extent of Federal moneys received by universities and colleges is documented in the recent report by the National Science Foundation entitled "Federal Support to Universities and Colleges, Fiscal Year 1968," report No. NSF 69–32, dated September 1969. That report reveals that 2,174 universities and colleges received $3,367 million from the Federal Government in fiscal year 1968. Of this amount, $2,340 million went to support academic science, and $1,027 million to support nonscience activities, at those institutions. Virtually all of those funds came from the following Government agencies.

[In millions of dollars]

Department of Agriculture	144
Department of Commerce	10
Department of Defense	243
Department of Health, Education and Welfare	2, 212
Department of Interior	28
Atomic Energy Commission	110
National Aeronautics and Space Administration	130
National Science Foundation	423
Department of Labor, Housing and Urban Development, Transportation and Office of Economic Opportunity	67
Total	3, 367

These funds, received by these universities and colleges under contracts with the Federal Government, are a major source of their total operating budget. Yet most of these institutions discriminate outrageously against half of our citizens—women. They neglect and disregard their potential talent. They place innumerable obstacles and hurdles in the way of academic women. Is our Nation so rich in talent that we can afford to have our universities penalize the aspirations of half of our population? Should the Federal Government close its eyes to such unjust discrimination and continue to provide the billions of dol-

438

lars that help to support those unjust practices?

Our national policy mandates equal treatment and opportunity for all citizens, including women. The Labor Department has recently shown much concern about racial discrimination in the construction industry, and the Department of Health, Education, and Welfare is heavily involved in eliminating racial discrimination in elementary and secondary schools. I applaud their concerns about such discrimination; but I also ask: Where is their concern about discrimination against women in our universities and colleges?

Let me emphasize again that Executive Orders 11246 and 11375 specifically forbid Federal contractors from discriminating against women in employment. Many of our universities and colleges have Federal contracts and receive substantial amounts of Federal funds. But neither the Department of Labor, which is responsible for enforcing these Executive orders, nor the Department of Health, Education, and Welfare, which is the compliance agency for universities, has made any effort whatsoever to invoke these Executive orders to prevent sex discrimination in employment or training by institutions of higher learning. Under the Labor Department's own guidelines, Federal contractors with 50 or more employees and a contract of $50,000 or more, must develop a written plan of affirmative action to prevent discrimination based on race, color, religion, sex, or national origin. I know of no university or college that has done so.

Worse yet, no university or college has been asked to do so. Under the same guidelines, all Federal contractors, including universities, are required to make an analysis of problems and an evaluation of opportunities for the use of minority employees, as well as specific goals and timetables for correcting existing discrimination. Again, I know of no university or college that has been asked to do so. Moreover, under these guidelines, universities and colleges with Federal contracts are required to state that there will be no discrimination in advertising for employees. I know of no instance where any Government agency has required, or requested, them to do so. Women in various professional organizations have been trying, largely without success, to get university departments to eliminate sex preference in advertisements placed for new faculty. Yet in column after column of job ads in professional journals, there are many advertisements which specify "male" or "prefer male, but will consider female." Both the Departments of Labor and Health, Education, and Welfare have been equally remiss and derelict in carrying out their responsibilities under the Executive orders.

Furthermore, Federal agency compliance programs are supposed to include a determination of nondiscrimination for each contractor prior to the award of any contract over $1 million. I know of no instance where this has been done, in terms of sex discrimination, in awarding contracts to universities and colleges, despite the requirements of the Executive orders. Nor do I know of any onsite compliance review concerning sex discrimination at any institution of higher learning.

Thus, despite the existence of Executive orders that specifically forbid such flagrant discrimination against women, the Federal Government has done absolutely nothing to enforce the orders in universities and colleges. Women in academic life are particularly vulnerable and unprotected from the ravages of sex discrimination. They are not protected by title VII of the Civil Rights Act of 1964 because section 702, for no rational or ascertainable reason, exempts every "educational institution with respect to the employment of individuals to perform work connected with the educational activities of such institution"—42 U.S.C. 2000e–1. They are not protected by the Equal Pay Act of 1963—Public Law 88–38. 29 U.S.C. 206(d)—which is a part of the Fair Labor Standards Act, because the latter act does not apply with respect to "executive. administrative or professional employees" 29 U.S.C. 213. The callous disregard which the Departments of Labor and Health. Education, and Welfare have demonstrated toward the requirements of Executive Orders 11246 and 11375. so far as it concerns discrimination against women by universities and colleges with Federal contracts. has made the Executive orders. for women, "only a promise to the ear to be broken to the hope. a teasing illusion like a munificent bequest in a pauper's will."

It is shocking and outrageous that universities and colleges, using Federal moneys, are allowed to continue treating women as second-class citizens, while the Government hypocritically closes its eyes. Remedial action must be taken, at once, to bring the universities and colleges in line with the requirements of the Executive orders. I am now assembling a list of all universities and colleges with Federal contracts. As a first step, I call upon the Secretary of Labor and the Secretary of Health, Education, and Welfare to contact all of these institutions to obtain from them full and detailed information, with respect to men and women, concerning: First, admission policies, including quotas; second, financial aid; third, hiring practices; fourth, promotions; and fifth, salary differentials for those with similar qualifications. I also call upon the Secretary of Labor to take prompt action on the complaint filed with him on January 31, 1970, by the Women's Equity Action League—WEAL—concerning the pattern of blatant discrimination against women in our universities and colleges with Federal contracts. WEAL's complaint strongly indicts the pervasive patterns of sex discrimination perpetrated by many universities. I believe it will interest every Member of Congress, and the general public, and I therefore include it as part of my remarks at this point in the Record.

[Submitted by Women's Equity Action League (WEAL) to the Department of Labor, May 25, 1970.]

DISCRIMINATION AGAINST WOMEN TEACHERS AT EASTERN ILLINOIS UNIVERSITY

Administration and enrollment.—Eastern Illinois University, a state-supported institution of higher education, is located in Charleston, Illinois, established as a teachers college in 1895, and was given the status of university in 1957. Despite being structured as a university, it is mainly devoted to preparing people to teach in grade schools and high schools. The University is governed by the Board of Governors of State Colleges and Universities, consisting of nine appointed members, none of whom are women. This Board is also responsible for three other state universities. In the fall of 1969, EIU enrolled 7,277 students, of whom 3,476 were men and 3,801 were women, according to the EASTERN UNIVERSITY CATALOG of April 1970. The president of Eastern is a male Ph.D., who has held his position since 1956. The University has 23 officers of instruction (the vice president for instruction, the deans, and the directors of divisions), all of whom are male except for the dean of the school of home economics, a woman.

The instructional staff.—According to the official EASTERN ILLINOIS UNIVERSITY CATALOG for 1970, the instructional staff of the University has 593 teachers on it. Of these, 443 are men and 150 are women. However, 32 of the total number are part-time teachers, of whom 25 are women. Therefore, the full-time teaching staff contains 561 persons, of whom men comprise 78% of the total and women comprise 22% of the total.

Patterns of hiring in all departments, 1969–70.—According to New Faculty at Eastern, 1969–70, a booklet containing names and pictures of new appointees to the teaching staff, approximately 101 persons were hired, 25 women (25+ per cent of this total) and 76 men (75+ per cent of this total). Admittedly, this booklet omits a few names because of the "dictates to a printing deadline." However, it appears on examination to be nearly complete. Of all teachers listed, 1 full professor was a woman; 6 full professors were men. Of the associate professors hired, 2 were women; 8 were men. Of the assistant professors hired, 5 were women; 37 were men. Thus, of 101 teachers hired, only 8 women (8%) were hired at professorial ranks, whereas 51 (51%) men were hired at professorial ranks. However, 7 women hired into the professorial ranks (or 7% of all teachers hired) were in fields traditionally open to women: women's physical education, home economics, music education, business education, or education. Consequently, only 1 of the professorial appointees was a woman, and she was hired as an assistant professor, the lowest professorial rank. Thus, a woman with a Ph.D. in the humanities or the sciences had, apparently, little or no chance of being hired at EIU in 1969.

Patterns of hiring in selected departments of Eastern Illinois University.—At least 4 departments at Eastern have no women on their teaching rosters: history (23 men), philosophy (6 men), physics (9 men), and chemistry (13 men). At least 5 departments have only one woman apiece: economics (10 men and 1 woman), botany (15 men and 1 woman), political science (7 men and 1 woman), geography (6 men and 1 woman), and zoology (24 men and 1 woman). At least one department has only 2 women: sociology (9 men and 2 women). At least 1 department has only 4 women: speech (13 men and 4 women). At least one department has only 5 women: foreign language (13 men and 5 women).

Distribution of women teachers by rank.—The history, philosophy, physics, and chemistry departments have no women at any rank. The speech department has only 1 woman in the professorial ranks (full professor); the rest of the women in it are at the lowest ranks—2 instructors and 1 faculty assistant. Except for a few administrators' favorites, the exceptions who prove the rule,

440

women tend to fall into the junior ranks.

Promotions.—New faculty at Eastern, 1969–70 shows that no women were promoted to full professor in 1969, though 11 men were. Of 16 people promoted to associate professor in 1969, only 3 were women. Of 6 people promoted to assistant professor, none was a woman. One person, a man, was promoted to instructor. Thus, only 8.8 per cent of those promoted were women. Of the full-time faculty, women promoted formed .5%, whereas men promoted formed 5% of the total. The booklet of new faculty for 1968 shows that 6 of 21 promotions (28%) went to women. The booklet for 1967 shows that 3 of 21 promotions (14%) went to women. The book'et for 1966 shows that 5 of 17 promotions (29%) went to women. The booklet for 1965 shows that 4 of 18 promotions (22%) went to women.

Salaries.—The University administration has made it virtually impossible for a faculty member to view the salaries of its employees for the years after 1967. The latest salary figures on file in the University Library are for 1966–67. Later figures can be obtained only by asking for them in the President's Office (and the President of EIU has clearly implied that he does not want faculty members prying into salary figures) or by going to the state capital, 100 miles away. However, one does not need to look at salary figures to see that the men in the history, philosophy, physics, and chemistry departments are making 100 per cent more than the women in those departments; women have 0 per cent of the jobs in those departments. Very likely, analysis of the EIU salary statistics for 1969 will show inequities in the salaries of women as contrasted with the salaries of men. A supplement to the present report will supply this analysis.

The English department.—In the fall of 1969 the English department had 51 teachers: 35 men and 16 women. It is dominated by extremely misogynistic males who are obviously eager to reduce the women Ph.D.'s in the senior ranks to insignificance in number or power. The head of the department, a covert misogynist, was helped into power by an overt, frank misogynist, a male senior professor with long service in the Department and great influence in the University. Between them they have managed to harrass and humiliate all the women senior professors except for one highly privileged female, the head's Pearl Mesta, denying them the right to teach advanced courses which they have earned, making them divide their advanced courses with males of lesser (sometimes dubious) qualifications, making them teach more than their share of underclass courses, giving them teaching schedules prejudicial to their health and/or professional advancement, deriding them to students, denying them the opportunity to lecture at English department colloquia (an all-male privilege), and so forth. Enclosed is evidence of one instance of the overt misogynist's efforts to prevent women from having the same opportunity as men in the Department. Four of the 5 women who are currently senior professors would like to testify confidentially about the unjust treatment which they have received as employees in the English department and/or the University in general. This treatment is supposed to be illegal under Executive Orders 11246 and 11375.

REPORT ON THE UNIVERSITY OF ILLINOIS, URBANA-CHAMPAIGN, ILL..

(By Jane Loeb, Ph. D., Chairman, Urbana AAUP Committee on the Status of Women, and Assistant Professor of Educational Psychology, University of Illinois, Urbana)

The number of men and women holding academic appointments during 1969–70 with the University of Illinois at Urbana-Champaign, as listed in the University of Illinois Undergraduate Courses Bulletin for 1969–70, is summarized in Table 1. These figures reveal that at no rank does the proportion of women employed approach their proportion in the population, and that as rank increases the proportion of women employed decreases. For example, at the lowest rank, that of Instructor, nearly 25% of those employed are women; at the highest rank, Full Professor, 4.2% are female. Thus, women are employed less frequently than men, and when employed they tend to hold relatively low ranks.

Comparison of the salaries of male and female academicians at the University is possible, based on responses to a questionnaire distributed by the Committee on the Status of Women of the Urbana chapter of the American Association of University Professors. Approximately 400 questionnaires were sent to all known female academicians and a sample of males who matched them on department membership and rank. For all 84 matched pairs of respondents, the mean salaries reported for 1969–70 were $11,880.38 for men and $10,461.05 for women.

These data strongly suggest that men and women within the same departments, holding the same rank, tend not to be paid the same salaries: women on the average earn less than men.

TABLE 1.—NUMBER OF MEN AND WOMEN HOLDING ACADEMIC APPOINTMENTS AT THE UNIVERSITY OF ILLINOIS, URBANA-CHAMPAIGN, 1969–70

	Full professor		Associate professor		Assistant professor		Instructor	
	Number	Percent	Number	Percent	Number	Percent	Number	Percent
Men	1,157	95.8	564	85.5	616	83.8	259	75.3
Women	51	4.2	96	14.5	119	16.2	85	24.7

PRELIMINARY REPORT ON THE STATUS OF WOMEN AT HARVARD

From: The Women's Faculty Group
Date: March 9, 1970

Our purpose in this memo is, first, to propose the creation of a committee of the Faculty to study the status of women at Harvard and, second, to formulate questions that such a committee might study. Section I describes the participation of women in the Faculty, the Administration, and the Graduate School of Arts and Sciences. Section II summarizes reasons for reviewing this situation. Section III suggests the composition of the proposed faculty committee and enumerates the policy questions to be raised.

I. PARTICIPATION OF WOMEN IN THE FACULTY OF ARTS AND SCIENCES

A. *Faculty*

Women are underrepresented at the highest and most visible levels of the Faculty, at least in comparison with their representation in the student body. Women constitute roughly 20 percent of the graduate and of the undergraduate students taught under the Faculty of Arts and Sciences. Table I shows the numbers of women holding selected teaching and research appointments during the academic year 1969–70. Although women occupy 13.5 percent of the positions covered in Table I, their appointments are concentrated at the lower levels—in Teaching Fellowships, in Lectureships, and in research.

TABLE I.—WOMEN IN SELECTED CORPORATION APPOINTMENTS UNDER THE FACULTY OF ARTS AND SCIENCES,[1] 1969–70

Title	Total	Women	Percent women
Regular faculty:			
Full professors	444	0	0.
Associate professors	39	0	0.
Assistant professors	194	9	4.6
Instructors	18	3	16.7
Teaching fellows	1,104	226	20.5
Other faculty lecturers	233	36	15.5
Research:			
Senior research associates	3	1	33.3
Research associates	63	11	17.5
Research fellows	397	51	12.9
Total	2,495	337	13.5

[1] Students in GSAS as of Oct. 1, 1969: Men, 2,480; women, 600.

Beginning on July 1, 1970, one woman Full Professor will hold the Zemurray-Stone Radcliffe Professorship, established specifically for women. There are two Professors emeritae, one of whom is a former incumbent of the Zemurray-Stone chair.

The high percentage of women Lecturers requires comment. Our interviews of 26 of the 36 female Lecturers revealed that the Lecturer category includes the part-time teaching appointments of administrative officers of Radcliffe and of research appointees as well as full- and part-time tutorial leaders and language teachers. Of the 26 Lecturers interviewed, 13 are full-time teachers. Most of these teach foreign languages and carry exceptionally heavy course loads. Nine of the female Lecturers hold administrative or research posts. The Lectureship is, for men as well as women, an exceptional appointment, outside the "real" system.

The high percentage of female Research Associates and Fellows is also significant. Like the Lectureship, these positions are outside the "real" system. Such research appointments may be valuable professional experience when used for a one-, two-, or three-year period of post-doctoral training. A problem arises, however, when limited appointments become career positions for lack of alternative possibilities. The fact that the percentage of women holding these positions rises as the categories become more senior (women are 12.9 percent of Research Fellows, 17.5 percent of Research Associates, 33.3 percent of Senior Research Associates) suggests that women are more likely to become career research personnel than men.

Table I pertains to the Faculty of Arts and Sciences only. Appendix I cites comparative statistics for Harvard University as a whole for 1959–60 and 1968–69. In other parts of the University, in contrast to the Faculty of Arts and Sciences, women hold a small number (10) of Associate and Full Professorships. Appendix I also shows that in the University as a whole the percentage of faculty positions (Instructorships and Assistant, Associate, and Full Professorships) held by women declined slightly between 1959–60, when it was 5.06 percent, and 1968–69, when it was 4.68 percent.

B. Administration

There are four problems that concern women who hold Corporation Appointments in the Administration at Harvard.

1. Although 111 of Harvard's 447 administrative employees with Corporation Appointments are women, only nine, or 8.1 percent, of the women are in the highest ranks (Deans, Associate Deans, Assistant Deans, Directors, Associate Directors, Assistant Directors). Of 336 male administrative employees, 96, or 28.4 percent, are in the highest ranks.

2. There are no women Assistant Directors (see Table II below). Women holding this position (roughly defined as assisting the Director and having one or more secretaries under her) are given lesser titles such as Administrative Assistant.

3. A greater percentage of male than of female administrators are eligible to attend faculty meetings. In certain senior categories, there are no women who are eligible to attend. Except in special cases (*e.g.*, University Librarian), the right to attend does not seem to be granted because of title. For example, 25 male Directors may attend faculty meetings although only nine are Lecturers; two female Directors are also Lecturers but only one is eligible to attend. The line of separation seems to be one of sex (see Table II).

TABLE II. —ADMINISTRATORS ELIGIBLE TO ATTEND FACULTY MEETINGS, 1969–70 [1]

Title	Men			Women		
	Number	Also lecture	Eligible to attend	Number	Also lecturer	Eligible to attend
Director	45	9	25	4	2	1
Associate director	16	5	5	1	1	0
Assistant director	18	1	1	0	0	0

[1] Figures as of fall 1969. Source: Directory of Officers and Students.

4. A general impression exists among women that they are paid less than men at the same administration level. It may be that this results in part from the fact that they have accepted titles that disparage their responsibilities. But the feeling persists even where the titles are equivalent. This is not the place to prove or disprove this allegation; perhaps it is enough to say that the impression is so widespread that it should either be proved or disproved.

C. Graduate School of Arts and Sciences

The percentage of women graduate students has increased slightly over the past ten years. Moreover, there seems to have been an increase in the number of women receiving scholarships and Teaching Fellowships.

TABLE III.—HARVARD GRADUATE SCHOOL OF ARTS AND SCIENCES

| | 1959–60 | | | | 1968–69 | | | |
	Number of men	Number of women (Rad-cliffe)	Total	Percent women	Number of men	Number of women	Total	Percent women
Applications	2,818	872	3,690	23.6	4,653	1,679	6,332	26.5
Admitted	1,267	365	1,632	22.3	1,408.	460	1,868	24.6
Registered (new students)	685	174	859	20.3	597	226	823	27.5
Registered (all resident students)	1,749	394	2,143	18.4	2,237	653	2,890	22.6
Holders of scholarships [1]	597	143	740	19.3	756	219	975	22.5
Holders of teaching fellowships	486	69	555	12.4	898	213	1,111	19.2
Total receiving Ph.D	303	32	335	9.6	372	87	459	19.0

[1] These figures exclude staff tuition scholarships and outside fellowships, governmental and nongovernmental.

The percentage of applicants accepted is similar for men and women. In 1968–69, 29.7 percent of men applicants were accepted, and 26.7 percent of women applicants. In 1967–68, 26.6 percent of men applicants were accepted and 26.9 percent of women applicants. This situation has been described approvingly by the Dean of the Graduate School as an "equitable harmony" (Dean's Report on the GSAS, 1967–68, p. 5). Given, however, the comparatively smaller numbers of women applying to the Graduate School, one might ask whether accepting equal percentages of men and women actually constitutes equal treatment. If women applicants are a more highly pre-selected group, they may be a more able and more highly motivated group. Equal treatment of such a group would result in the acceptance of a higher percentage of them.

Conventional wisdom holds that "the drop-out rate is markedly greater for female students that for males" (*Report of the Committee on the Future of the Graduate School*, March 1969, p. 5) and that female students progress toward the Ph.D. at a slower rate than their male counterparts (Dean's Report on GSAS, 1964–65, p. 2). It seems clear, however, not only that the reasons for these phenomena have not been examined by the University in recent years, either in the Wolff report on the Graduate School or in other studies, but also that the phenomena themselves are insufficiently documented. Dr. Humphrey Doermann's study "Baccalaureate Origins and the Performance of Students in the Harvard Graduate School of Arts and Sciences" contains an appendix that seems to be the only study in recent years documenting the female attrition rate (see Appendix II). But the Doermann report does not prove that women are currently dropping out at a greater rate than men, or that, in the past, they dropped out at a greater rate *if given equal scholarship opportunities.*

II. REASONS FOR REVIEWING THE SITUATION

Many explanations might be given for the lack of female participation described in the preceding section: overt discrimination, stereotyped conceptions of the woman's role held by both men and women, sociological and psychological factors. But, whatever the causes, a change in the situation would benefit the Harvard community.

A woman who has sucessfully earned a graduate degree has demonstrated sufficient professional commitment to warrant consideration for employment on equal terms with men. Moreover, women faculty members and administrators, both as professionally trained scholars and as women, have worthwhile contributions to make to the University.

The scarcity of outstanding women scholars in the senior ranks at Harvard tends to discourage the professional aspirations of women students and junior faculty. Graduate women are in fact being trained professionally in an institution that barely recognizes members of their sex as professionals. At present women are regarded as exceptional in the Faculty, not as a normal and permanent component of the Harvard scene. The fact that women do not reach the highest positions in the Administration contributes further to the impression that at Harvard women cannot expect to attain rewards commensurate with their abilities and training. The scarcity of women at all levels deprives students and faculty of both sexes of the intellectual stimulation that comes with a more heterogeneous community.

It cannot be to Harvard's advantage to have women virtually excluded from policy-making, especially in a *de facto* coeducational institution. The University has begun to recognize that it is appropriate to have people participating in the decisions that affect them; as a result, students have been appointed to a number of committees. Women have been consulted by faculty committees as expert witnesses on the problems of women; they should now take a more active and visible role in committees and other policy-making bodies.

In the past few years, the economic and social status of women has been changing. Attitudes and practices in industry, in government, and in the community at large are being challenged and reevaluated; as a result, women are beginning to have greater areas of choice and increased opportunities to contribute to the world outside the home. Harvard should not lag behind in an important area of social change.

III. COMPOSITION OF THE COMMITTEE AND POLICY QUESTIONS TO BE RAISED

We propose that a committee of the Faculty be formed to study the status of women in the Faculty, the Graduate School and the Administration. We suggest that the committee be composed of the following:
2 female faculty members
2 male faculty members
1 female Research Associate or Fellow
2 administrators (1 male, 1 female)
1 female graduate student
1 Radcliffe undergraduate
1 Harvard undergraduate
The following sections raise policy questions that the committee should consider.

A. *Faculty*

We recognize that any attempt to increase the participation of women in the Faculty is necessarily limited by the absolute size of the pool of qualified candidates from which to draw. It may be, however, (1.) that our mechanisms of recruitment, established many years ago for the recruitment of male academics, prevent us from identifying all possible members of that pool; (2.) that stereotyped opinions of the female role prevent us from recognizing that changing career/family patterns now make it possible for more women to engage in full-time academic careers; (3.) that institutional changes such as part-time appointments would further increase the number of qualified women who could pursue academic careers.

The committee should therefore ask the following questions:

Do departmental search, recruitment and promotion policies give adequate attention to female candidates?

Are the present criteria for hiring and promoting men and women the same? Should these criteria be the same?

How are qualified women to be recruited and retained, especially at the higher levels?

Do hiring and search committees take the marital and family status of women into account in making job offers and recommendations for promotion? Should the marital/family status of a woman be a consideration in hiring and promotion?

Should academic positions be made more flexible for both men and women with respect to age guidelines and part-time employment?

Should the University establish or support day-care centers for the children of faculty and employees?

The problem of recruitment requires additional comment. It may be that search committees which fill senior faculty positions fail to seek distinguished women candidates. It also seems likely that conventional opinions about the incompatibility of family responsibilities and an academic career are applied rigidly and inappropriately by search and hiring committees, and that talented and qualified women are thus needlessly eliminated from job consideration. Some female graduate students and academics feel that job interviewers, here and elsewhere, overreach themselves in inquiring about a woman's plans for a family, her husband's job future, and so on.

The question of part-time appointments also requires comment. Some members of the Harvard community have expressed a desire to see the academic structure made more flexible for both sexes, because of the needs of some female academics and because of changing male career patterns. There seems to be a need to regularize and institutionalize the flexibility that now exists in the form of *ad hoc* and exceptional amendments to the regular structure, notably the Lectureship, while avoiding the second-class status of the present part-time appointments. It must be emphasized, however, that women should not be assigned automatically to part-time positions.[1]

B. *Administration*

In contrast to the situation in the Faculty, there are large numbers of women in the Administration. Although the great majority of these women are concentrated in the lower ranks, a number of them seem to be performing work comparable to that of male administrators at higher ranks.

The committee should therefore ask the following questions:

Is sex a factor in the hiring, promotion, or salary scale of administrators?

What criteria determine whether an administrator is eligible to attend faculty meetings? Is sex a factor?

C. *Graduate school of arts and sciences*

Women are a minority of the graduate students enrolled at Harvard. Moreover, female graduate students feel that, because of their sex, every stage of graduate education is more difficult for them: admission to graduate school, competition for financial aid and Teaching Fellowships, and especially job placement. Women students experience what has been called a "climate of unexpectation": fear of discrimination, awareness of their real difficulties in working out career patterns, and the assumption on the part of some faculty members that "women don't pan out."

The committee should therefore address itself to the following groups of questions:

Are women admitted to the Graduate School on equal terms with men? Should "equal terms" be defined as equal percentages?

Do admissions policies regarding women vary by department?

Do admissions committees consider marital status and family plans when assessing female candidates?

Are women discriminated against in the awarding of financial aid, Teaching Fellowships, and postdoctoral grants? Are married women discriminated against more than single women?

Are female Teaching Fellows discriminated against in appointments as non-resident or resident Tutors in the Houses?

Should the possibilities for part-time graduate work be increased for both men and women?

What sort of advisory facilities are available for graduate women? Should these facilities be improved?

Has the University made adequate provision for low-cost housing for graduate women?

Do departmental advisors use the sex of candidates as an eliminating factor in recommending students for interviews or for jobs?

How can departments help students to counter discrimination they face on the national job market

Are there channels within Harvard departments for female job candidates to register complaints if they feel that they are encountering prejudice?

---

[1] For a recent decision by Princeton concerning part-time professorial appointments, see Appendix III.

APPENDIX I.—HARVARD UNIVERSITY OFFICERS, 1959-60 AND 1968-69

Title	1959-60				1968-69			
	Total	Male	Female	Percent female of total	Total	Male	Female	Percent female of total
Corporation	7	7	0	0	5	5	0	0
Board of overseers	32	32	0	0	30	30	0	0
Officers of instruction:								
University professors	5	5	0	0	5	5	0	0
Professors	424	420	4	0.94	580	577	3	0.5
Associate professors	126	118	8	6.3	151	143	8	5.3
Assistant professors	207	199	8	3.9	401	384	17	4.2
Research professors and assistant research professors	2	2	0	0	3	3	0	0
Clinical professors, associate and assistant clinical professors, and clinical associates	236	228	8	3.4	357	340	17	4.8
President and professors emeriti	157	155	2	1.3	184	175	9	4.9
Lecturers	224	196	28	12.5	406	356	50	12.3
Visiting professors and associate professors, visiting lecturers, and visiting associates, consultants, critics, and fellows	107	104	3	2.8	158	149	9	5.7
Associates	117	112	5	4.3	235	211	24	10.2
Instructors	571	519	52	9.1	791	722	69	8.7
Tutors	57	56	1	1.6	75	71	4	5.3
Teaching fellows	673	597	76	11.3	1,296	1,091	205	15.8
Research associates, research fellows and assistants, and members of research staffs	876	796	107	12.2	1,530	1,286	244	15.9
Assistants	332	288	44	13.3	385	317	68	17.7
Miscellaneous academic appointees	232	221	11	4.7	371	326	45	12.1
Officers of administration:								
Deans, executive officers, syndics, and masters	141	123	18	12.8	167	126	41	24.6
Directors, library officers, and curators	298	230	68	22.8	469	327	142	30.3
Health services	84	79	5	6.0	137	126	11	8.0
Athletic administration and coaches	32	32	0	0	33	33	0	0
Proctors and freshman advisers	166	166	0	0	98	96	2	2.0
Board of preachers	7	7	0	0	6	6	0	0
Business officers	31	30	1	3.2	91	79	12	13.2
Miscellaneous administrative appointees	13	8	5	38.5	103	83	20	19.4
Radcliffe trustees and administrative appointees					118	30	88	74.6

APPENDIX II

The Doermann report "Baccalaureate Origins and the Performance of Students in the Harvard Graduate School of Arts and Sciences" documents the female attrition rate as follows:

In 1962, women comprised 25% of the entering student group which enrolled for the first time in the Harvard Graduate School of Arts and Sciences; in 1967 women comprised 26% of the entering group of students. Women comprised about 13% of the Ph.D. recipients in 1965 and 1966 combined. Taken alone, this information might seem to suggest that the general endurance and quality of women's performance in doctoral study is weaker for women than for men [sic]. However, if one examines the performance of the women who did complete the Ph.D. in 1965 and 1966, it appears that the number of registered semesters taken to complete the degree is not significantly different than for male degree recipients, and that in the Natural Sciences and Social Sciences a slightly larger proportion of women graduates completed their work in ten semesters or less (and also in 14 semesters or less) than did the men. Also, women who were married when they received the degree in all three areas tended to have completed the degree slightly more rapidly than had women who were unmarried at the time of completion. (Doermann Report, Appendix A)

But, as Dr. Doermann points out, "the actual performance which generated the results for the 1965 and 1966 Ph.D. recipients occurred 5 to 10 years ago," and "the patterns may have changed since then." He also points out that "the number of Ph.D.'s awarded to women has shown a higher percentage increase in each of the 3 major areas [Natural Sciences, Social Sciences and Humanities] than for men between 1955-and-1956 and 1965-and-1966."

A fuller study of the question, based on statistics and individual case studies, is clearly needed. But the following *caveats* must be borne in mind. (1.) If it is true that women work at a slower rate or have special financial difficulties or tend to move away from Boston, a study of female drop-outs is more difficult, because the very definition of "drop-out" becomes problematic. A number of female graduate students discontinue registration in the Graduate School, frequently because their husbands move away, but continue to work on their theses. They then receive the Ph.D. several years after the records show them as having "dropped-out." (2.) A comparison of the male and female attrition rates is meaningful only if women are actually competing on equal terms with men for scholarship funds and Teaching Fellowships. (3.) The significance for the academic profession of female attrition may be different from the significance of male attrition. A male who "drops-out" presumably moves to another profession; a female who "drops-out" may be more likely to return at a later date either to graduate school (not necessarily Harvard) or to a job, such as secondary school or junior college teaching, that uses her original professional training. (4.) As long as highly trained women experience difficulty in gaining employment commensurate with their skills, women will face pressures for dropping-out greater than those faced by men. Consequently, statistical evidence on attrition will be a dangerous basis for any arguments about the relative motivation of men and women.

APPENDIX III

PART-TIME PROFESSIONAL APPOINTMENTS AT PRINCETON

The Dean of the Faculty of Princeton University sent the following memorandum to departmental chairmen on February 20, 1970:

For some time Princeton University has had a limited number of professors and associate professors on part-time appointment—two-thirds, one-half time, or less. Those on part-time appointment have wished less than full-time duty for such reasons as special research or writing, other professional activities, or particular personal pursuits. Occasionally professor [sic] as they approach retirement prefer less than full-time during a period of transition to emeritus status.

It now appears to be advantageous to consider part time appointments in the professorial ranks on a somewhat more regular, though still limited, basis. Part-time appointments will be permitted both for personal reasons and as a means of building distinction and strength in ways that may not be possible on a full-time basis. It may be of advantage to the University to make a part-time appointment because of a priority need in a specialized area that does not require a full-time person, or because a person of considerable distinction is only available on a part-time basis, or because two persons on half-time would bring more strength and distinction to the department than a single full-time appointment.

Another important advantage of part-time appointments is they [*sic*] may facilitate the appointment of more women scholars to the Princeton Faculty.

This matter has been discussed with the Committee on Appointments and Advancements. The Committee, generally speaking, sees no objection to a larger number of new part-time appointments or to internal shifts to a part-time basis within the professorial ranks. This does not mean, however, that we anticipate situations in which more than a small proportion of the total membership of any department would be appointed on a part-time basis. Thus, all proposals for part-time appointments will be evaluated on the basis of number of full-time and part-time faculty members in the department as well as in terms of circumstances of the individual in question. Similarly, proposals to shift from part-time to full-time service must be viewed in the light of individual circumstances and the departmental situation.

For persons on continuing tenure a voluntary shift to a part-time basis presents no special problems of Faculty rights and privileges. At the present assistant professor level, part-time employment would seem to require no adjustment in the rule that requires notification by December 1st of their sixth year whether or not the department intends to recommend promotion to associate professor. In cases where scholarly progress is interrupted by pregnancy and maternity some special modification of this six-year rule should perhaps be made. This matter is now being studied.

Part-time appointments may also raise complications with respect to eligibility for leave. In the tenure ranks, such appointments have been handled in the past on an *ad hoc* basis, apparently with satisfaction. At the assistant professor level, the equivalent of 1-in-6 could be worked out in departments where that policy applies by dealing in terms of full-time equivalents.

WOMEN AND THE PROFESSIONS

[From the Russell Sage Foundation, 1969]

THE WOMAN DOCTORATE IN AMERICA

(By Helen S. Astin)

OBSTACLES IN THE CAREER DEVELOPMENT OF PROFESSIONAL WOMEN

It is obvious that women doctorates represent a dedicated and committed group so far as their work patterns and professional achievements are concerned. Their deep interest and scholarly involvement in their specialized fields persist over time, and their career patterns (which are characterized by only a few short interruptions for the bearing and rearing of their children) attest to their valuable contributions to American society. Although over half the women in the sample were married and had families, 9 out of every 10 were working—an impressive proportion indeed.

But despite their noteworthy record of participation in the labor force and the abundant evidence that their talent and training are put to good use, women doctorates often find themselves unhappy and frustrated because of the barriers they encounter in their career development. Sometimes, the problems that confront them are inherent in their family situation (for example, when they are unable to find adequate domestic help or when their husbands object to their working outside the home) and sometimes the problems result from overt or subtle forms of discrimination. This chapter discusses both kind of obstacles and in addition, examines the characteristics of those women doctorates in the sample who reported experiences with sex discrimination.

Domestic obstacles

Although half of the women in the sample reported that they utilized some sort of outside help, they still felt that the difficulty of finding dependable, interested, and competent help (whether a part-time or full-time housekeeper or a baby-sitter) constituted a major obstacle to their career development. Many of the academic women in the sample spoke of the problems that had sometimes arisen during examination periods when housekeepers had failed to report for work or when one of their children had become sick and the baby-sitter could not come. One woman reported that she had had to change housekeepers so frequently during one year that she was forced to resign from her academic appointment. Finally, she decided to remain at home until her youngest child was ready to start first grade.

The professional woman not only faces the problem of finding the right kind of help but also is confronted with a number of additional problems relating to employing assistants for housework and child care. For instance, the law makes no provisions for deducting housekeeper costs as business expenses. One woman in the sample wrote a long letter describing the costs involved in her being employed outside the home. Her salary raised the family's combined income to a bracket that increased their income tax considerably. These higher taxes, in combination with the housekeeper's wages and her own transportation costs, resulted in a situation where her outside employment represented an actual financial loss to the family.

Immigration laws, too, work indirectly to penalize the woman who wishes to take outside employment. Previously, the shortage of domestic help in this country could be alleviated somewhat by importing domestic workers from other countries. Recent legislation that makes it much more difficult for domestic workers to immigrate here, however, has made this solution no longer tenable.

Besides the problem of finding domestic help, which seems to be the greatest obstacle that professional women encounter, a small proportion of the women (12 per cent) considered their husbands' negative attitudes a major block to their career development. (Another 6 per cent cited the negative attitudes of other relatives.) There are a number of reasons why a husband may look with disfavor on his wife's working outside the home. The wife's professional involvement and achievement may threaten the husband who does not feel adequate or successful in his own work. Moreover, a man may feel that his wife's work will be interpreted as a financial necessity resulting from his own failure to be a good provider. Thus, to the insecure husband, the wife's employment is a threat to self-esteem, and his attitude toward it is negative. Disagreements regarding child-rearing practices may also explain a husband's negative attitudes. The husband may feel very strongly that a mother should always be available to her young children and thus may object to his wife's working on the grounds that it will cause her to be absent from the home. Negative attitudes may also be based primarily on the realistic recognition that the wife's being employed will constitute a financial drain on the family rather than a contribution.

About one-fourth of the married women in the sample considered their husband's job mobility a hindrance to their own career development. When the husband moves from one location to another to take a new job, the wife must move too, of course, but often the timing of such a move is unfortunate with respect to her own career development. In such circumstances, the woman may not be able to find a new job that will allow her to continue working in her own area of research; she may be forced to take a job that is simply not commensurate with her skills and training.

A number of the women described some of the dilemmas that confront them when their husbands decide to move. Frequently, the hardships created by such moves are so severe that the wife must terminate her career temporarily. Of those women who were unemployed at the time of the survey, 30 percent cited the lack of challenging jobs in their community as the reason. It is understandable that the husband's taking a job at an academic institution in a small town may create problems in the wife's career development, particularly if the institution has antinepotism rules that prevent her being employed by the same institution. Antinepotism rules and the lack of challenging jobs may not be the only factors that adversely affect the woman who has to relocate as a result of her husband's job mobility. Employer discriminatory practices may also create problems. Since the woman must find a new job by her own initiative rather than by being sought out, she often encounters subtle discrimination on the part of prospective employers.

Forms of employer discrimination

Discrimination in selection for employment or in the reward system refers to differentiation on a categorical rather than on an individual basis. Thus, an employer may differentiate his employees entirely on the basis of sex rather than on the basis of merit. It has often been suggested that prejudiced discrimination is a major deterrent to the educational and vocational development of women in general. For example, women's lower rates of educational attainment, particularly at the postgraduate level, are frequently alleged to result from a systematic bias that operates against women, manifesting itself in reluctance to grant them admission to graduate and professional schools and to award them scholarships and other kinds of financial aid.

Because of the lack of systematic data, it is difficult to ascertain the validity of the charge that prejudiced discrimination against women exists with respect to graduate school admissions, but the evidence that is available indicates that such is not the case. For instance, a recent publication of the Association of American Medical Colleges (*Datagrams*, 1965) reveals that women applicants to medical school fare about as well as men applicants. During the academic year 1964–1965, 47.6 percent of the women applicants were accepted, as compared with the 47.1 percent of the male applicants. With respect to financial assistance during graduate study, it appears that women receive about as much financial aid as men: 57 percent of all the women doctorates of 1957 and 1958 had held either assistantships or fellowships during graduate training, as compared with 53 percent of the men doctorates of 1955 (Harmon, 1965). The differences in years studied (1955 and 1957–1958) may obscure a difference favoring men, since such funds were probably more available in the later years.

However, it should be remembered that the fields typically studied by women (humanities and education) are in general not as well subsidized as the natural sciences are. Regarding other types of awards, Bernard (1964; p. 50) report that ". . . the National Science Foundation Awards in 1959 were given to women in about the same ratio as to men; 12 percent of the applicants were women, and 12 percent of the awards went to women."

Nevertheless, the attrition rates of women students seem to be much higher than those of male doctoral and medical students. For instance, the attrition rate in medical school is twice as great among the women medical students as it is among the men (that is, 16 percent and 8 percent, respectively). Moreover, a greater proportion of women graduate students with Woodrow Wilson Fellowships interrupt or discontinue their graduate training; a recent study of Woodrow Wilson Fellows showed that only 17 percent of the women Fellows had received their Ph.D. six to eight years after they entered graduate training, as compared with 42 percent of the male Fellows (Mooney, 1957).

In short, though women may be less likely than men to complete their graduate training, there is little evidence of prejudiced discrimination against women at the graduate or medical school level. With respect to employment practices, and particularly to salary scales, the situation is rather different, however. White (1967; p. 1087) reported that women lawyers at full-time paying jobs earned considerably less money than men lawyers. His thorough investigation of the reasons that may account for this differential in income forces him to conclude that "discrimination against women lawyers by their potential employers is at least a substantial cause and probably the principal cause for the income differential which we have observed between men and women." A recent study of sex differences in academic ranks and salaries revealed that, when field and type of institution are controlled, ". . . the beginning academic rank of new scientists in college and university teaching positions is unrelated to sex. Over time, women in the natural sciences continue to receive promotions comparable to those of their male cohorts. However, women in the social sciences tend to be promoted less rapidly than do men. Salary differentials, on the other hand, exist in both beginning and later academic positions, regardless of major field specialty, work setting, or academic rank." (See Bayer and Astin, 1968; p. 191.)

Moreover, certain policies relating to tenure and promotions tend to affect the careers of women negatively. For example, one of the women in the sample reported that the state university where she is employed has an administrative policy that forces pregnant faculty members to leave their position for a period of six months without pay. Such forced interruptions in the careers of professional women create even further problems such as denial of tenure on the grounds that their appointment has not been uninterrupted for the specified period of time.

Although one can investigate some of the policies and practices that discriminate against women, there remains a subtle type of discrimination that is hard to assess. It is very difficult, for example, to prove that the polite rejection of a professional woman's inquiry into a position is motivated by sex discrimination. For example, one woman in the sample wrote as follows: "There was an opening in an agency in an area of research that was directly germane to my interests and skills. Thus I wrote to the appropriate person enclosing vita and research reprints. The answer was negative and not very encouraging. It read: 'I appreciate your expression of interest in the position I posted. . . . Although your professional experience and interests are clearly germane to many program areas in our agency, I am less certain about their applicability to the type of research activities I am now planning. . . .'" Even if this reply is accepted at its face value, it is still puzzling that the prospective employer, who was recruiting publicly, did not pursue the woman's inquiry further, perhaps by finding out whether she had considered branching out into some of the new aspects of research that he was planning, especially in view of the great expenditure of time and energy often involved in the recruiting process. Research, academic, and other high-level positions often remain unfilled for long periods of time, primarily, it would seem, because the employer ignores women applicants and continues to search for a man on the assumption that he will attract good students or outstanding colleagues.

Though they may be difficult to investigate adequately, these subtler forms of prejudice are frequently most distressing to professional women. For example, the woman may express feelings of loneliness because she cannot find someone with whom she can share a coffee break, chew over an idea, or pursue a research interest (Bernard, 1968).

In the present study, an attempt was made not only to obtain an estimate of the proportion of women who had experienced employer discrimination during their career development but also to gather information about the prevalence of different types of discriminatory practices. Therefore, respondents were asked whether they had experienced employer discrimination in general and what particular discriminatory practices had affected them. One-third indicated that employer discrimination had been a problem in their career development. The proportions of the total sample of respondents citing experiences with each of the different types of discrimination were as follows: prejudices against hiring a woman, 25 per cent; differential salaries for men and women with the same training and experience, 40 per cent; differential sex policies regarding tenure, seniority, and promotions, 33 per cent; unwillingness on the part of the employer to delegate administrative responsibility and authority to professional women employees, 33 per cent; and other forms of sex discrimination, 12 per cent. The finding that differential salaries for men and women was the most freqently encountered type of sex discrimination is consistent with the results of other studies (White, 1967 ; Bayer and Astin, 1968).

Characteristics of the women who report experiences with sex discrimination

Frequently, people try to refute reports of sex discrimination by claiming that the women who say that such discrimination has affected their careers adversely are those who have been unsuccessful professionally and who are merely trying to rationalize their own incompetence. Or, they argue, such women are perennially dissatisfied and would complain whatever their situation of status.

In order to test the possible truth of such assertions, an investigation was made of just what type of woman reports experiences with employer discrimination. Are the women who say that they have had such experiences the ones who have been less successful professionally and who use such claims as a way of justifying their lack of achievement? Also of interest was the question of where these women had been employed and any other characteristics that might distinguish them from women who did not report experiences with discrimination.

A few rather small but statistically significant zero-order correlations emerged from these analyses. For example, with respect to field of specialization women in the biological sciences were most likely to report experiences with sex discrimination ($r=.06$) ; whereas women research psychologists were least likely to do so ($r=-.06$). Moreover, women in research jobs tended more often to claim such experiences ($r=.07$). Closely related to this finding was the finding that the women who reported experiences with employer discrimination were also the ones who had more publications to their credit ($r=.08$) and who had received more honors and awards for professional achievement ($r=.11$). The last two correlations suggest that women who report experiences with employer discriminations are active professionally and publish frequently. Therefore, their complaints cannot be interpreted as a form of rationalization or as an excuse for their failure to achieve recognition. Furthermore, their comments are not based on hearsay, but reflect their own experiences as professionally active women. The relationship between scientific or scholarly productivity and experience to employer discrimination may also be interpreted on the basis of some personality dimension (such as aggressiveness, candor, or competitiveness) that would account not only for their greater productivity but also for their readiness to voice their opinions and express their disapproval of discriminatory practices.

Both the women's own occupational mobility and that of her husband were related to her having had experience with sex discrimination ($r=.11$ and $r=.15$, respectively). The explanation for these relationships is obvious : the more often a woman changes jobs, either on her own initiative or because her husband's job mobility necessitates the family's moving to a new location, the greater her opportunity to experience employer prejudices in, for example, hiring practices. The two mobility variables and the productivity and recognition variables continued to correlate significantly with the discrimination variable, even after the job variables (type of employer and type of position or work performed) were controlled statistically.

The job variables themselves were related in some ways to experience with employer discrimination : women in administrative, teaching, or service positions were less likely to say that they had had experiences with discrimination than women in research positions. The negative relationship between holding an administrative position and having experience with employer discrimination seems easy enough to account for : the very fact that a woman has risen to an administrative post suggests that her employment situation is a favorable one in that she does not face severe competition with men for salaries, promotions, and so forth. With respect to the findings for women in teaching and service positions, however, the explanation is probably to be sought in the personal characteristics that distinguish these women from women in research jobs. It seems likely that the women in teaching and services are less productive (in terms of scholarly publication) by choice; they recognize and passively accept their lower status and are thus not so apt to complain about discrimination as the woman in research who has been productive and who cannot explain her lower salary or failure to receive deserved recognition except on the basis of sex discrimination on the part of colleagues and employers.

After the effect of the job variables was controlled, the following additional variables yielded significant relationships with the criterion of experience with employer discrimination (see Table 32): being a nun ($r=-.16$), job mobility ($r=.12$), publications other than ones related to field of specialization ($r=.10$), honors and awards received ($r=.12$), writing a book or monograph at home ($r=.10$), husband's mobility ($r=.14$), husband is a university professor ($r=.06$), sincere interest in field as the major reason for pursuing the doctoral degree ($r=.06$).

Table 32.—*Personal characteristics of the women who report experiences of employment discrimination, after control of the job variables*

Variable	Partial
Nun	−.16
Job mobility	.12
Publications other than in field of specialization	.10
Honors received	.12
Writing book or monograph	.10
Husband's mobility	.14
Relatives' negative attitudes	.09
Husband is university professor	.06
Interest in field (reason for pursuing doctorate)	.06

Note: Teaching ($F=-5.83$), administration ($F=-4.87$), and services ($F=-4.93$) carried significant weights in the final solution between job characteristics and employer discrimination.

The negative relationship between being a nun and having had experiences with employer discrimination is easy to understand. Most nuns are nonsalaried employees of their church or religious order, and their placement in different jobs is determined primarily by the needs of that religious community. Moreover, they are not in competition with the opposite sex for jobs. Examining the remaining variables, it is found that the woman who has the deepest professional commitment (as indicated by her having published more and received more awards and honors) is the one who feels that discrimination has been a significant obstacle to her career development. The relation between the husband's having an academic position (that is, university professor) and the wife's reporting employer discrimination may reflect the existence of antinepotism regulations or the lack of available and challenging jobs in a small university community.

The last variable that was significantly related to experiences with discrimination involves the woman doctorate's report of her major reason for pursuing the doctoral degree. That the woman who entered doctoral training primarily because of a sincere interest in her field tends to feel that she has been discriminated against probably reflects her great dedication and commitment. Because of her high aspirations and achievements, she is probably less able than other women doctorates to accept the fact that she may be judged on the basis of an irrelevant criterion such as her sex rather than on her merit and scholarly abilities.

Summary

The professional women in the sample, in the seven- to eight-year period following receipt of the degree, have encountered a number of obstacles to their career development. Their biggest problem centers on the difficulties of finding and keeping competent domestic help. Not only is such help hard to find, but also it is costly, especially since the expenses incurred are not tax-deductible. In some cases, the wife's being employed represents such a drain on finances that it is more sensible if she does not work. The loss to society that results from this paradoxical situation may be a serious one.

There are other factors inherent in the family situation that may interfere with the woman doctorate's career development, though they probably play a minor role in comparison with the difficulties connected with using household help. For instance, the husband may (for good or poor reasons) object to his wife's working outside the home. Moreover, his change of jobs may necessitate his wife's giving up a position suitable to her abilities and either becoming unemployed or taking a job that is beneath her talents and training.

The other major hindrance to the career development of professional women is conscious and unconscious discriminatory behavior on the part of male colleagues and employers. Over one-third of the women in this sample believed that discriminatory practices had adversely affected their careers. The forms of discrimination most often experienced were lower salary scales for women and differential treatment with regard to promotions, tenure, and seniority.

RELATED SURVEY QUESTIONS TO CAREER OBSTACLES

30. Problems that you encounter developing your career fully:	Major problem	Minor problem
Finding adequate help at home	18	22
Husband's job mobility	6	8
Husband's negative attitudes toward my working	2	4
Relatives' negative attitudes toward my working	1	5
Employer discrimination	12	24

31. If you have experienced any employer discrimination practices, indicate what kind:	
Employer prejudices against hiring a woman	25
Differential salaries for men and women with the same training and experience	40
Differential sex policies regarding tenure, seniority, and promotions	33
Unwillingness and reservations on the part of employer to delegate administrative responsibility and authority to professional women employees	33
Other	12

32. If you are not currently employed, indicate below the importance of each of the following factors in your decision not to work at this time:	Major factor	Minor factor
No challenging professional jobs available in my community	22	8
Pregnancy	10	1
Taking care of my children	56	9
Other domestic responsibilities	24	28
Poor (physical) health	7	7
Mental or emotional illness	1	0
Other	29	4

33. If you are not working at present (or working part time), when do you plan to return to work:	
This year	17
Later	68
Probably never again	15
34. If you are not employed at present would you now consider entering the labor market?	
Yes	52
No	48
35. If yes, what type of job would you consider?	
Part time	84
Full time with flexible hours	58
Full time with defined work hours	40

36. Indicate the extent to which the following factors might facilitate your return to the labor market:	Greatly	Somewhat
More flexible working hours	42	30
Change in husband's attitude	5	10
More adequate domestic help	39	21
More readily available day care centers for children	16	16

[*College and University Business,* McGraw-Hill, Feb. 1970]

DISCRIMINATION AND DEMOGRAPHY RESTRICT OPPORTUNITIES FOR ACADEMIC WOMEN

(By Alice S. Rossi)

Women faculty members have always posed some perplexing questions for the administrators of colleges and universities. In this study on assessing the female contribution to higher education, I will review the status of women in our institutions during the past three decades, placing particular emphasis on the future trends as I see them, and, on the basis of my research with 15,000 women college graduates, evaluate how the twin factors of motivation and discrimination bear upon the role of women in both higher education and the job world.

The greatest change since the turn of the century has been the narrowing of the gap between the sexes in obtaining the first degree: Women obtained only 19 per cent of the bachelor's degrees at the turn of the century, 40 per cent by the early 1960s, and about 43 per cent during the last five years. At the master's level, the increase has been from 19 per cent at the turn of the century, to a high of 38 per cent in 1940, then down to 32 per cent by the early 1960s. At the doctorate level, the number of women graduates increased from 6 percent at the turn of the century to peak at 16 per cent in the early 1930s, then slip to 13 per cent in 1940, then down to a low of 11 per cent in the early 1960s, where it has remained.

Women faculty members must be recruited from bachelor's and higher degree holders. What is interesting to note is that at the turn of the century, when women made up only 19 per cent of the bachelor's degree holders, they represented 20 per cent of the teachers at the college and university level. This suggests that a much larger proportion of women college students had college teaching as a career goal than is true in our own era. By the early 1960s, women represented 22 percent of these teaching faculties, down slightly from a peak of 28 per cent in 1940. While the national figures are higher than those from the very large and most prestigious universities, it is clear that teaching at the college level has not kept pace with the increasing rate of college attendance and graduation of American women.

There has been a noticeable expansion of part-time faculty over the last 25 years, as colleges and universities responded to the growing demand for their services. Early in the 1960s, of all the teaching and professional personnel in institut.ions of higher education, 44 per cent were full time faculty, but a hefty 37 percent were part-time faculty. It is among the part-time faculty that women are heavily represented, and this is clearly an insecure hold on positions in higher education—an expendable labor supply for colleges and universities to add or drop from their staffs in response to variations in the size of the student body and budgetary appropriations.

Many women in the 1960s owe even their small and insecure foothold in academia to the fact that Ph.D.s have enjoyed a long period of a sellers' market. For 25 years, the institutional need and desire for Ph.D. holding faculty has been in excess of the number available, hence there was need for non-Ph.D. women teachers to fill out the faculty staff. But this situation is expected to undergo rapid change in the 1970s; after 1970, there will be a buyers' market in which the number of academic teaching posts to be filled will be lower than the number of Ph.D.s available. This does not mean Ph.D.s will go unemployed, since there are many spheres away from the college and university where their skills are badly needed. From this perspective, the future looks dim indeed for academic women since academic employers will have an ample market of male Ph.D.s to fill new positions. Unless a woman has a Ph.D., and perhaps even then, she may find an even more competitive situation facing her in academia in the next decade than she has had during the last few decades of great expansion in institutions of higher education.

Taking all teachers—elementary, secondary and college—as the educational pool, statistics show there has been an increase in their number between 1930 and 1960 of some 87 per cent. But, between the respective educational levels, much variation is apparent. There has only been a 36 per cent increase in the number of elementary school teachers, while the number of secondary school teachers has grown 146 per cent, and the number at the college and university level has increased 360 per cent. Furthermore, sex differences appear at each educational level: Women high school teachers increased only 83 per cent during the 30 year period, but men high school teachers increased by 260 per cent, shifting the field from predominantly female to one in which men are now a slight majority. At the college level, the two percentages are a 265 per cent increase for women, but a 395 per cent increase for men.

Any rapidly expanding occupation must draw from those in the labor force with the necessary educational qualifications. This is typically white males, and it is this tendency that leads to the decline of the representation of women at the secondary and college level of teaching. Education below the college level is exerting increased pressure for higher levels of knowledge and skill: Many high school biology teachers today are equivalent in knowledge and skill to college science teachers in the past. Any field which undergoes such knowledge expansion is most likely to draw more heavily from men than from women as long as women aim their aspirations for schooling and working at a lower level than men do. The crisis that may lie ahead for women aspiring to college teaching in the 1970s is not peculiar to this segment of the female labor force. Much of the great increase in the numbers of older married women in the labor force over the last 20 years is rooted in the peculiarities of the demographic structure of the American population during these particular years. Up to 1940, the traditional source of the female labor force had been young unmarried women. During the 1950s and early 1960s, a pattern of earlier marriages developed and schooling was extended, thus shrinking the size of the available labor pool of unmarried women. Even more important, the young women of the 1950s were born in the 1930s, when the birth rate was very low, while at the same time there was a vast increase in the numbers of young children being born during the baby boom of those post war years. As a result, the traditional pool of female labor shrunk during those 20 years from 6 million to 3 million while every other age category was increasing in size.

It would be comforting to believe that the shift in women's employment over the past 25 years, with an increasingly large proportion of married older women in the work force, was essentially due to changes on the supply side of the economic equation, with women pressing for entry and seeking wider horizons than those provided by the home and family. In an economy as hard-nosed as ours, this is a highly unrealistic economic assumption. The shift had as much if not more to do with employer demand as with women assertively seeking jobs. Employers flung doors open, beckoning women in.

Looking ahead to the 1970s, there will be a reverse in this demographic pattern: The birth rate is now on the decline, age at marriage is creeping upward, and the time interval between marriage and childbearing is widening. In the 1970s there will be more young unmarried women or childless married women seeking jobs; at the same time middle-aged married women will also be very numerous, for the baby boom females will have grown to maturity. Some expanding service occupations may well be able to absorb large numbers of both categories of women, but it is less clear what the situation will be in academic circles.

Ambitious women who aspire to careers on what has been masculine turf must have thick skins and the utmost inner security to withstand what they so often experience, subtle and overt forms of punishment rather than encouragement and support. Yet highly committed career women are in even greater need than men of such support and encouragement during the early years of their careers. My analysis of the background of the highly committed career graduate women shows them to differ from women who enter traditional feminine fields in ways that depress their confidence in themselves in early adulthood. Indeed, my major hypothesis was that deviant choices in adult roles are rooted in other kinds of deviance earlier in the life line. (By deviance I mean merely departure from a cultural expectation of appropriateness for one's sex, age, class and so forth.) The message derived from my study seems to be that young American women with serious professional goals have a special need to obtain compensatory rewards through adult socialization that can build up their confidence and stoke their motivation to reach the goals they set for themselves. Yet the qualitative quotes are full of ego-depressing rather than ego-building experiences. It is little wonder that so many women learn to hide their ambition, to redirect their energies into nonoccupational activities or lower their sights and try patiently to accept positions below their ability. In the words of one such woman:

"We take jobs far below the salary and title we deserve, just to get a foot in the door. All too often, that's all we get in—a foot."

Looking at this situation from the point of view of the employer, what are the factors involved that make so many men prejudiced against ambitious professional women or simply insensitive to the fact that they are discriminatory toward women? A major figure in this situation in academia is the department chairman, and a perspective on his attitudes toward women colleagues can be gleaned from a review of what it has taken him to reach the position he now enjoys. Typically, his success comes after long years of hard work: struggling to finish a degree; getting a promising teaching post, and writing and publishing while his wife carried most of the responsibilities for home management and child rearing.

As an academic researcher myself, and also as the wife of a department chairman, I have been in a position to observe some of the more subtle processes that cause such men to look unfavorably and with erroneous assumptions on young aspiring women in academia. For example, a mutual friend had recently been made chairman of his department at a Midwestern university, some seven years after he first entered that department. This is the complaint he brought out in the course of a conversation:

"I have worked damned hard for seven years to become a tenured professor at this place and chairman of the department. Now I earn $20,000 and along comes a fresh new Ph.D. with a brand new appointment in the department as an assistant professor at $12,000. But his wife has the same appointment at another college nearby. Why between them they now earn $4,000 more than I do after seven years of hard work!"

When pressed to explain what bothered him about this, he explained:

"They are now building a better house than I'll ever be able to afford. They serve vintage wines, take off for ski trips, week-ends while we are at home with the kids. . . . I don't think he'll amount to much though. It's not good to start off so well. He'll drift I'm sure, postpone writing, because there's no pressure on him to publish in order to live well or better."

Sensing a tortured rationalization, my husband laughed, and the man finally blurted out: "Well, it's just not fair!" Underneath his protestation about his young colleague's probable low productivity was merely a peevish personal gripe. It is much the same pattern that often lies behind the refusal to increase the salary of an academic woman. Since most academic women, if married, have husbands in academic or professional fields with more than adequate incomes of their own, department chairmen are sometimes motivated not by a woman's performance on the job, but personal resentment of the higher style of life a joint household of career people can enjoy.

There is also another element in employers' handling of professional women on their staffs: their inability to distinguish between these women and their own homemaker wives. They overlook the fact that these professional women have no psychic need to make a fuss about their home duties as their own wives do in order to match the busyness of their ambitious husbands, and they overlook the fact that the professional women's husbands are often ideologically committed to helping in home maintenance and child care.

One more example will serve to underscore the special situation of the young academic woman. This case comes not from my research files, but from personal correspondence with a friend and former research assistant of mine, who is now a young faculty member at a California university. This woman worked for me for two years while she had one small child and through her second pregnancy. She did all her graduate work in record time while her two children were preschoolers. During the spring and summer prior to her move to California, she completed all the analysis of data for her dissertation, which she planned to write the next summer. When she arrived in California, she was able to set up a household, settle her two children in school, arrange household help, and prepare her lectures during a few weeks before the beginning of the fall term. She has been teaching full time and loving it. Yet, she has been told by her department chairman that she is not being kept on next year because he doubts that her dissertation will really be completed.

This young woman has several young male colleagues who will be kept on, even though their dissertations are still far from complete. Had her chairman taken the trouble to review her pattern over the last five years—her ability to hold down a full-time job through a pregnancy, to move from a job to graduate training and maintain a normal pace along with family responsibilities—he might have realized that she was the one young faculty person who was *most* rather than *least* apt to complete her dissertation and receive the doctorate during that year.

This also illustrates one way in which college administrators can help their women faculty: by getting to know each new woman who joins their faculty, keeping well enough informed of her progress to raise hard direct questions if she is not retained or promoted by her department.

The question of academic productivity is often raised when women faculty members are discussed: How adequate are our criteria of productivity in comparing men with women, and what is it in men's productivity that we want more women to emulate?

Academic productivity has been traditionally measured by the number of published articles and books completed by the academic man or woman. But, if there is any institution in modern society that should place quality above quantity, it should be the university. Many of us share Jacques Barzun's charge that what we have been witnessing in recent years is not so much a knowledge explosion as a publication explosion. I suggest the university should push and push hard to assess quality, not merely quantity. One fine article can often equal a dozen mediocre ones, or one book surpass three. Married academic women may indeed write and publish less often than their male colleagues. Since many women are supplementary rather than exclusive breadwinners, they have had the luxury of avoiding the trap of publish-or-perish thinking. Before we push women into such a competitive race, we should be sure it is a race either sex should be in.

Universities should depart from a narrow time perspective in judging faculty productivity. The contemporary college is no longer a local, parochial, social community turned in upon itself, but a cosmopolitan national community of talented professionals. In making this transition from a local to a cosmopolitan institution, we should not lose sight of the teaching goal of the enterprise by merely valuing teaching equally with research. We should show a willingness to value the delayed impact on the younger generation of women students that may flow from having young married women on the teaching staff. For college students to have such a woman as a teacher and model may influence them to persist in their own professional careers rather than withdraw from them, and raise their goals to more demanding positions than they have considered for themselves. To truly value this mission and the potential influence of women faculty upon women students, a university must depart from the parochial concern for immediate status pay-off in the form of current faculty productivity by sharing a societywide goal of encouraging greater social contributions from young women a generation hence.

In brief, concern for productivity must make room for the role of the teacher as model to the young, for charisma and style of teaching, for the quality and not merely the quantity of research and scholarship produced by faculty members. Until these factors are taken into account, it is too early to judge women faculty as less productive than men.

What of the price paid for high productivity among faculty members following the conventional focus on publications, honorary awards, national commission participation, and all the other high prestige activities our jet age professors engage in outside the office and classroom? To be productive in this modern sense exacts a great price: a lopsided life of almost all work, little play, and little family or community life.

The important point is this: Many women do not want such a life, and the woman student watching her professor juggle frequent flying trips with class and research schedules may conclude that college teaching is not for her. More than men, women may seek a better-rounded life style that permits significant but not excessive commitment to work, with time and energy for the pleasures of sociability with friends and their own children, time and energy for cultivating a garden, walking or swimming, and doing what they can in political and community affairs.

The men and women who manage our academic institutions should answer this question: Isn't it time the university, as the most far-seeing of our social institutions, prepared itself for life in the postindustrial world? I hope that world is not merely "post" something, but "for" something—a compassionate world with the time, room and flexibility to create a style of living that permits both men and women to live deeply and meaningfully at play and at home, as well as at work.

[The Journal of Human Resources, Spring 1968]

SEX DIFFERENCES IN ACADEMIC RANK AND SALARY AMONG SCIENCE DOCTORATES IN TEACHING*

(By Alan E. Bayer and Helen S. Astin**)

ABSTRACT

Employment information, reported by approximately 2,700 recent science doctorates to the 1964 National Register of Scientific and Technical Personnel, indicates that the

---

*This paper was sponsored by the Commission on Human Resources and Advanced Education and was supported by grants from the Carnegie Corporation and the Russell Sage Foundation. The authors are indebted to Milton Levine of the National Science Foundation for providing the necessary data and to Herbert Soldz of the National Academy of Sciences—National Research Council for his assistance in developing the tabulations.

**Dr. Bayer is a Research Scientist and Director of Sociological Studies, Project TALENT, Institute for Research in Education, American Institutes for Research, Palo Alto, California. Dr. Astin is a Research Associate, Institute for the Study of Human Problems, Stanford University, Stanford, California.

beginning academic rank of new scientists in college and university teaching positions is unrelated to sex. Over time, women in the natural sciences continue to receive promotions comparable to those of their male cohorts. However, women in the social sciences tend to be promoted less rapidly than men. Salary differentials, on the other hand, exist in both beginning and later academic positions, regardless of major field specialty, work setting, or academic rank. These data support the contentions of women doctorates that salary discrimination is practiced more severely than is discrimination regarding tenure or promotions.

While women comprise about 10 percent of the annual output of doctorates in the United States,[1] little is known about the sex differentials in the reward system for this highly trained female sector of the labor force. In lower occupational ranks and at lower levels of educational attainment, however, several studies have demonstrated sex discrimination.[2] Among doctorates, discrimination against women has also been reported. In a recent follow-up study of women doctorates seven to eight years after graduation, Astin notes that one-third of the women report discrimination regarding tenure and promotions and two-fifths report salary differentials.[3]

Several general sex comparisons on income and rank of doctorates have been undertaken recently, but the lack of control for a number of relevant contingencies related to rank and salary differentials has resulted in an inability to assess adequately the presence or amount of discrimination experienced by women doctorates. Salary and rank are usually related to length of time in the labor force, field of specialization, type of employer, and type of work activity. Each of these factors is also related to sex: i.e., women doctorates tend to have had less experience in the labor force than male graduates of the same period, primarily because of career interruptions for child bearing and rearing; women tend to specialize in the field of education, the social sciences, or the humanities, while men more often select the biological and physical sciences; women are more concentrated than men in academic institutions; and male doctorates are more likely to be engaged in nonteaching tasks, such as administration and research, than are women doctorates.[4]

In a recent National Education Association report on salaries in higher education, the median nine-month 1965–66 salary of women is reported at $7,732, 16.6 percent lower than that of men, at $9,275.[5] While women are shown to be at lower academic ranks, with one full professor in 12 a woman and one instructor in three a woman, these salary differentials persist within academic ranks. At the full professor level, women's salary is 91.2 percent of the men's. At each lower rank level, women's relative salary increases, reaching 94.0 percent of the men's at the instructor level. Women are also concentrated in the smaller universities and colleges, where salaries tend to be lower for both sexes. Within each institutional type, however, female salary levels remain below those of the males. These differentials are most marked in large universities, with women receiving less than 80 percent of the salary of the men in the same institutions and least marked in the state colleges where women receive almost 91 percent of the salary of the men.

In a recent report by Jessie Bernard it is also noted that women are found to have consistently lower salaries than men and to be in the lower academic ranks. She suggests that this is in part because they teach the less controversial, more standard, aspects of their subjects, usually elementary courses.[6] While in virtually every field a greater proportion of women than of men teachers do not hold the doctorate degree, even those women with doctorates are less likely than men to be teaching advanced courses.[7] Furthermore, the academic rank of women is inferior to that of men with comparable qualifications in all kinds of academic institutions.[8]

[1] Lindsey R. Harmon and Herbert Soldz, compilers, *Doctorate Production in the United States, 1920–1962*, Publication No. 1142 (Washington: National Academy of Sciences—National Research Council, 1963), p. 53.

[2] See, for example, U.S. Department of Labor: Women's Bureau, *Economic Indicators Relating to Equal Pay*, 1963 (Washington: U.S. Government Printing Office, 1963).

[3] Helen S. Astin, "The Woman Doctorate in America: Demographic and Career Characteristics of Professional Women," unpublished report of the Commission on Human Resources and Advanced Education, 1966.

[4] For a further discussion of these sex differences, see Harmon and Soldz, *Doctorate Production . . .*; Astin, "The Woman Doctorate . . ."; and Lindsey R. Harmon, *Profiles of Ph.D.'s in the Sciences*, Career Patterns Report No. 1, Publication No. 1293 (Washington: National Academy of Sciences—National Research Council, 1965).

[5] National Education Association, Research Division, "Salaries in Higher Education Continue to Grow," *NEA Research Bulletin*, 44 (May 1966), pp. 50–57.

[6] Jessie Bernard, *Academic Women* (University Park, Pa.: Pennsylvania State University Press, 1964), pp. 120–26.

[7] Bernard, *Academic Women*.

[8] Bernard, *Academic Women*, pp. 180, 189–91.

Although these reports are highly suggestive of sex discrimination, such a conclusion is not justified without controlling other relevant variables that affect academic rank and salary. The present paper further specifies the sex differentials in rank and salary through introducing control, by selection of the sampling frame and the methodological technique of elaboration of partials, for a number of other factors affecting income and rank. These variables include level of education, field, length of time in the labor force, work activity, and work setting.

The Sample

In 1964 the National Science Foundation, through the National Register of Scientific and Technical Personnel, made the sixth regular biennial survey of the background, education, specialization, and employment of U.S. scientists. Selected from this basic file were natural science (mathematics, physics, chemistry, earth sciences, biological sciences) and social science (psychology, sociology, economics) doctorates of 1957 through 1962 who were employed full-time in academic settings and reported that their primary work activity was teaching.[9]

Two time lapse periods since the doctorate are employed in the analysis of sex differentials. The first offers an appraisal of sex differentials from five to six years after the doctorate, employing male doctorates of 1958–59 and female doctorates of 1957–58.[10] The second time period, employing doctorate recipients of 1962, offers a comparative appraisal of sex differentials in beginning positions. The resulting sample is 1,662 male and 103 female teaching scientists who have been in the labor force five to six years since the doctorate and are presently working, and 1,112 male and 92 female teaching scientists who have only recently completed the doctorate and have recently entered academic teaching.[11]

In addition to control for level of education, length of time in the labor force, and work activity through the selection of the sample, homogeneity of the sample for analyses of rank and salary differentials is further guaranteed through holding "constant" the categories of major field area and type of employer.[12]

Academic rank is treated as a dichotomized variable due to the small number of females in the sample. High rank includes those at the level of associate or full professor and low rank includes those who are designated as assistant professors, instructors, or lecturers.

All salary data are based on the academic year (9–10 month basis), adjusted where necessary for those on 12-month appointments.[13] These data represent basic salary before deductions for income tax, social security, retirement, etc., but do not include bonuses, subsistence allowances, royalties, or other payment for professional work not a usual part of the principal professional employment.

---

[9] For a further discussion of sampling and the specialized fields included in the study, see the paper by Alan E. Bayer and John K. Folger, "Estimated Coverage of Science Doctorates in the National Register," unpublished report of the Commission on Human Resources and Advanced Education, 1966.

[10] Women doctorates who graduated an average of one year earlier than the males are utilized in this analysis to correct partially for the fact that women doctorates who were graduates of these years have often interrupted their careers and have been out of the labor force a total of approximately nine months since receipt of the doctorate (see Astin, "The Woman Doctorate . . ."). Thus, in the comparison of these two groups, an approximate control for length of time in the active labor force is introduced.

[11] The number of employed in the analyses is less than these totals as only 1,634 (92.6 percent) of those in the older group and 1,117 (92.8 percent) of those in the younger group reported academic rank. Salary reports were made by 1,604 (90.9 percent) of the older group and 1,088 (90.4 percent) of the younger group.

[12] A large number of field and employer categories were initially analyzed, but similarity in outcomes justified collapsing categories into those herein reported in order to increase the N in each category. Nevertheless, the small number of cases, particularly of women, requires that the data reported herein be interpreted with caution. The reported statistics are indicative of sex differences but should not be employed as highly precise measures of the actual population differences in rank and salary.

[13] If the academic appointment is for a calendar year rather than an academic year, the salary is adjusted to five-sixths of the reported annual salary. Inasmuch as those on calendar year appointments may often be paid for their additional services at a lower rate than during the academic year (15 percent rather than two-ninths of the academic year salary, for example), this adjustment tends to underestimate the equivalent salary for an academic year. As men are probably more likely to hold full year contracts, this adjustment would tend to understate the equivalent academic salary for the aggregate of males and thereby yield a conservative estimate in the reported salary differentials of the sexes.

TABLE 1.—ACADEMIC RANK OF MALE AND FEMALE DOCTORATES, BY FIELD, LENGTH OF EMPLOYMENT, AND TYPE OF ACADEMIC EMPLOYER [1]

Length of employment and type of academic setting	Natural sciences				Social sciences				Total			
	Male		Female		Male		Female		Male		Female	
	Total number	Percent high rank	Total number	Percent high rank	Total number	Percent high rank	Total number	Percent high rank	Total number	Percent high rank	Total number	Percent high rank
5-6 years in employment:												
College	419	60.6	35	62.8	208	74.5	23	60.9	627	65.2	58	62.1
University	602	47.3	17	52.9	311	63.7	19	52.6	913	52.9	36	52.8
Total	1,021	52.8	52	59.6	519	68.0	42	57.1	1,540	57.9	94	58.5
2 years in employment:												
College	289	28.4	26	34.6	143	34.3	17	35.3	432	30.3	43	34.9
University	355	7.3	17	0.0	249	16.1	21	23.8	604	10.9	38	13.2
Total	644	16.8	43	20.9	392	22.7	38	28.9	1,036	19.0	81	24.7

[1] Two by two (sex × rank) chi-square tests of significance of sex differences are not statistically significant for any of the 18 comparisons in this table.

Statistical note: The reader is cautioned against precise conclusions from these data as the relative academic position of women doctorates in the various subcategories is based on a small sample. See text and footnote 12.

TABLE 2.—MEAN ACADEMIC INCOME OF MALE AND FEMALE DOCTORATES, BY FIELD, LENGTH OF EMPLOYMENT, TYPE OF EMPLOYER, AND ACADEMIC RANK

Length of employment, type of employer, and academic rank	Natural sciences			Social sciences			Total		
	Male mean salary	Female mean salary	Women's mean salary as percent of men's mean salary	Male mean salary	Female mean salary	Women's mean salary as percent of men's mean salary	Male mean salary	Female mean salary	Women's mean salary as percent of men's mean salary
5 to 6 years in employment:									
College:									
High rank	$9,126	$8,113	89.0	$8,952	$8,485	95.5	$9,060	$8,279	91.4
Low rank	8,067	7,682	92.2	8,351	7,963	95.3	8,138	7,800	95.8
University:									
High rank	9,949	9,138	91.9	10,148	9,070	90.1	10,031	9,100	90.7
Low rank	8,373	8,288	98.8	8,314	8,222	98.8	8,358	8,253	98.8
Total	8,954	8,226	91.8	9,203	8,468	[1]92.1	9,038	8,342	[2]92.2
	(N=1,007)	(N=43)		(N=514)	(N=40)		(N=1,521)	(N=83)	
2 years in employment:									
College:									
High rank	8,584	[3]	[3]	8,481	[3]	[3]	8,547	7,170	[1]83.8
Low rank	7,571	7,231	95.5	7,622	7,130	93.6	7,587	7,187	[2]94.7
University:									
High rank	9,077	[3]	[3]	9,285	[3]	[3]	9,203	[3]	[3]
Low rank	8,139	7,547	92.7	8,076	7,756	96.0	8,114	7,648	94.3
Total	8,057	[2]7,241	[2]89.8	8,142	7,779	[2]95.6	8,089	7,494	[2]92.6
	(N=631)	(N=37)		(N=387)	(N=33)		(N=1,018)	(N=70)	

[1] t-test (one-tail) of difference between mean income of male and of female significant at 0.01 level.
[2] t-test (one-tail) of difference between mean income of male and of female significant at 0.05 level.
[3] Statistic not computed, N<8.

Statistical Note.—The reader is cautioned against drawing precise conclusions from these data as reported income has been adjusted for gross comparability and means in the various subcategories are based on a small number of women. See text and footnotes 12 and 13.

FINDINGS

Within each major field area, academic setting, and career length category, no significant sex differences in academic rank emerge (Table 1). However, although none of these differences are statistically significant, suggestive relationships are observed over time within fields and academic settings. With the exception of women natural scientists in universities, of which there are few, women tend to hold starting positions (two years after the doctorate) which are of comparable or higher rank than those of the men. At the later point in the career (five to six years in the labor force), major field differences appear. In the natural sciences those women who persist in academic teaching tend toward an aggregated higher rank than do their male colleagues. On the other hand, in the social sciences, wherein there is a greater proportion of women, the aggregate of men emerge as obtaining higher rank than women over time.[14]

Across all work settings, fields, and ranks, women experience a significantly lower average academic income than do men in the academic teaching labor force for the same amount of time (Table 2).[15] Within each work setting, field, and rank category, women also have lower salaries. Their mean salaries are as low as 83.8 percent of the mean salary reported by men and as high as 98.8 percent of the male mean salary.[16] No large or consistent increases or decreases in sex differences in salary emerge over time. However, the salary differences observed follow a uniquely different pattern than the one we would expect on the basis of rank differentials within academic fields. The salaries of women social scientists are not generally as discrepant from those reported by men as are the salaries of the female natural scientists, in spite of the finding that the female social scientists are not as often represented in proportion to their numbers in the high ranks as the women natural scientists are.

DISCUSSION AND CONCLUSIONS

The small sample size employed in this study generally yields statistically insignificant sex differences in academic rank and salary and permits only tentative conclusions. Nevertheless, the data are suggestive of sex differentials in the academic reward system even when a number of sex- and salary-related contingencies are taken into account.

In starting positions, women tend to hold academic ranks which are higher than or comparable to those of men within the same work setting and field.[17] This may be partially a function of the greater amount of pre-doctoral work experience by women since they tend to start and complete their graduate training on the average of two years later than do the men.[18] Over time, women in the natural sciences emerge as receiving promotions on par with men, while in the social sciences women tend to be promoted less rapidly than do their male counterparts. This suggests that in fields in which women comprise a larger component of the total labor force, more discrimination in promotions may be experienced.

The data on salary differentials do not appear to relate directly to the practices regarding academic promotions when they are expressed in terms of differential proportions in high versus low academic ranks. Academic salary practices and raises do not appear to be completely dependent on academic scholarship and

---

[14] A similar finding for a limited group of social scientists is reported by Blaine E. Mercer and Judson B. Pearson, "Personal and Institutional Characteristics of Academic Scientists," *Sociology and Social Research*, 46 (April 1962), p. 266. "It was hypothesized that female sociologists will have experienced greater promotional difficulties than male sociologists. Academic folklore seems to support such an hypothesis. However, the chi square yield for the contingency distribution, in which the sex of the respondents is cross-classified against rapidity of occupational ascent, is not significant at the .05 level, nor even at the .20 level of significance. The cell weightings are in the hypothesized direction, but only slightly so."

[15] For this select group of relatively recent teaching doctorates in the sciences, academic salary distributions approach normality within sex categories. Thus, means rather than medians are employed in this analysis.

[16] Within each academic setting, field, and rank category, the variance in male salary is also observed to be larger than that of the women, indicating that male salary is less consistent than female salary for similar academic positions.

[17] The sameness of the work setting and field are for gross categories in this report. One may argue, therefore, that the differences in salary are a mere artifact of the type of institution at which women tend to be employed: i.e., in small private colleges or small private universities which pay lower salaries in general. However, a pilot check on the distribution of all the women in this sample with more detailed category break-outs does not completely justify the above assumption. See footnote 12.

[18] Astin, "The Woman Doctorate . . ."

merit, as reflected in promotions to higher rank. Rather, it may be that institutions often operate on differential pay scales for women and men whereby they justify the greater salaries for men on the basis of greater economic need on the part of these who are the primary family bread winners. It appears that academic women are more apt to receive recognition equal to that received by men when the rewards are academic title or position than when the reward system is based on monetary acknowledgements. These data tend to support the contentions of women doctorates, studied by Astin, who more often report incidences of salary discrimination than occurrence of discrimination regarding tenure and promotion.[19]

[19] Astin, "The Woman Doctorate . . . ."

[Exhibit A, U.S. Department of Labor, Women's Bureau, 1968]

FACTS ON PROSPECTIVE AND PRACTICING WOMEN IN MEDICINE

The need for larger numbers of well trained and able men and women in the health professions is of great national concern. The increasing longevity of the population as well as its continuing growth, new benefits under medicare and medicaid, the health problems of the socially and economically disadvantaged all underscore the estimated manpower requirement for 3.7 to 4.0 million health workers by 1975.

In addition to the need for professional nurses, technicians, subprofessionals, aides or attendants there will be a rising demand for physicians to man our hospitals, to handle out-patient work loads, to provide professional care to our aged and needy, and to serve the general public as a whole. This is an area in which we need to make maximum use of all our human resources, to urge that an increasing number of boys and girls with the ability to qualify as physicians be encouraged to pursue such a career, to make it possible both educationally and financially for those with the potential to qualify in this demanding profession, so that all our people may have the professional services they seek.

The problem is acute. In June 1967, fewer than 8,000 physicians were graduated from our 89 United States medical schools. This is far below the needs of our society. According to recent estimates, there is one doctor for every 720 Americans, a ratio which has remained unchanged for more than three decades.[1] At the same time patients have at least doubled their number of doctor's visits, on the average. Moreover, the number of family physicians (internists, pedi,-atricians, part-time specialists in private practice, and general practitioners) per 100,000 in the population dropped from 94 in 1931 to 50 in 1965.

Estimates published by the U.S. Public Health Service indicate that we will need 400,000 physicians by 1975—over 100,000 more than are active today. This would amount to an annual net increase of at least 10,000 a year. These needs can be met only as we meet the Nation's training facility requirements, and encourage larger numbers of our qualified young people to seek and obtain medical training.

To further the understanding of past and present trends in the training, characteristics, and utilization of women physicians, this book of facts on prospective and practicing women in medicine has been compiled.

WOMEN AS PERCENT OF ALL STUDENTS AND GRADUATES, U.S. MEDICAL SCHOOLS,
SELECTED YEARS, 1905–67

The market influence of World War I and World War II on the number of women enrolling in and graduating from U.S. medical schools is evident in a chart based on information from the education numbers of the Journal of American Medical Association.

Since the middle of the 1950's, however, the increase has been relatively steady and not associated with any wartime activities. In fact in the last 10 years, the proportion of women among all students and among all graduates has increased by nearly one-half.

[1] Rashi Fein, *The Doctor Shortage: an Economic Analysis.*

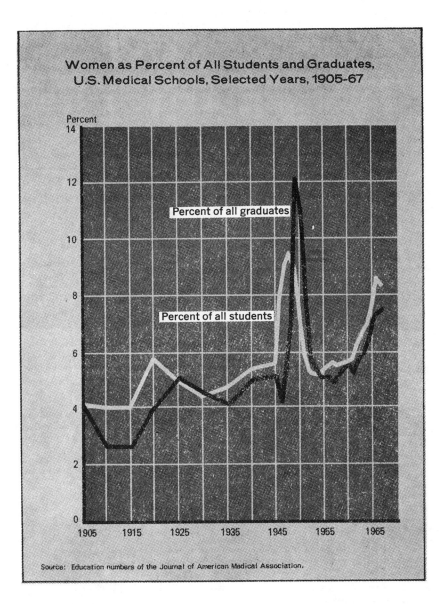

Women as Percent of All Students and Graduates, U.S. Medical Schools, Selected Years, 1905-67

Percent

Percent of all graduates

Percent of all students

1905 1915 1925 1935 1945 1955 1965

Source: Education numbers of the Journal of American Medical Association.

ADMISSION OF WOMEN TO U.S. MEDICAL SCHOOLS

The number of women applying for admission to U.S. medical schools more than tripled between 1929–30 and 1965–66, while the number of men applicants increased by 29 percent. But the percentage of women applicants accepted by these medical schools was less in 1965–66 (48 percent) than in 1929–30 (66 percent) after dropping to a low of 31 percent in 1950–51 following World War II.

Women accounted for a larger proportion of the acceptances in recent school years than back in 1929–30 and 1935–36. But the percentage of women accepted into medical schools has tended to relate consistently to the proportion of total applicants who are women. Thus women comprised 3.5 percent of the applicants and 4.5 percent of the acceptances in 1929–30. Similarly they comprised 9 percent of the applicants and 8.9 percent of the acceptances in 1965–66.

ACCEPTANCE DATA ON MEN AND WOMEN APPLICANTS TO U.S. MEDICAL SCHOOLS FOR SELECTED SCHOOL YEARS 1929–30 TO 1965–66

School year	Women				Men		
	Number of applicants	Number accepted	Percent accepted	As percent of total acceptances	Number of applicants	Number accepted	Percent accepted
1965–66	1,676	799	47.7	8.9	17,027	8,213	48.2
1964–65	1,731	824	47.6	9.1	17,437	8,219	47.1
1960–61	1,044	600	57.5	7.0	13,353	7,960	59.6
1955–56	1,002	504	50.3	6.3	13,935	7,465	53.6
1950–51	1,231	385	31.3	5.3	21,049	6,869	32.6
1940–41	585	303	51.8	4.8	11,269	6,025	53.5
1935–36	689	379	55.0	5.5	12,051	6,521	54.1
1929–30	481	315	65.5	4.5	13,174	6,720	51.0

Source: The Journal of Medical Education, vol. 42 No. 1, January 1967, Association of American Medical Colleges, Datagram. vol. 7, No. 8, February 1966.

WOMEN STUDENTS AND GRADUATES OF U.S. MEDICAL SCHOOLS

The number of women students in medical schools almost tripled between 1930 and 1967. During the same period there was a similar increase in the number of women graduates. A comparison of women as percent of all students and as percent of all graduates in one year shows, for the most part, only a slightly smaller percent of women graduates. The outstanding exception to this general rule was in 1949 and 1950 when the percentage of women graduates was unusually high reflecting the increased enrollments of women in medical school immediately following World War II.

WOMEN STUDENTS AND GRADUATES OF U.S. MEDICAL SCHOOLS, 1930–67

Year	Women students	Percentage of all students	Women graduates	Percentage of all graduates	Year	Women students	Percentage of all students	Women graduates	Percentage of all graduates
1930	955	4.4	204	4.5	1953	1,463	5.3	363	5.5
1935	1,077	4.7	207	4.1	1954	1,502	5.3	360	5.2
1940	1,145	5.4	253	5.0	1955	1,537	5.4	345	4.9
1945	1,352	5.6	262	5.1	1960	1,710	5.7	405	5.5
1946	1,868	8.0	242	4.2	1961	1,745	5.8	354	5.3
1947	2,183	9.1	342	5.4	1962	1,955	6.3	391	5.8
1948	2,159	9.5	392	7.1	1963	2,081	6.7	405	5.9
1949	2,100	8.9	612	12.1	1964	2,244	7.0	449	6.5
1950	1,806	7.2	595	10.7	1965	2,503	7.7	503	7.3
1951	1,564	5.9	468	7.6	1966	2,589	8.6	524	7.4
1952	1,471	5.4	351	5.7	1967	2,771	8.3	583	7.5

Source: Association of American Medical Colleges.

NUMBER OF U.S. MEDICAL SCHOOLS HAVING 10 PERCENT OR MORE WOMEN ENROLLEES OR GRADUATES

At the beginning of World War II, women comprised 10 percent or more of all students in 4 U.S. medical schools. At the end of World War II and for the next three school years a considerably larger number of schools had this high a proportion of women among its students—ranging from 18 in 1945–46 to 31 in 1947–48. With the return of veterans to school, the number of U.S. medical schools in which women were 10 percent or more of the students dropped to 2 in 1951–52 and 1952–53. It was not until the 1960's that more than 4 schools had this high a proportion of women among its students. In 1966–67, women made up 10 percent or more of the student body in 18 U.S. medical schools.

The trend is similar in relation to number of U.S. 4–year medical schools where women made up 10 percent or more of the graduates. The peak number was 42 in 1948–49. There has also been an acceleration in the 1960's. In 1966–67, women constituted 10 percent or more of the graduates in 18 4-year U.S. medical schools.

NUMBER OF U.S. MEDICAL SCHOOLS HAVING 10 PERCENT OR MORE WOMEN ENROLLEES OR GRADUATES

Year	Number of schools		Number of 4-year schools		Year	Number of schools		Number of 4-year schools	
	Total	With 10 percent or more women students	Total	With 10 percent or more women graduates		Total	With 10 percent or more women students	Total	With 10 percent or more women graduates
1941–42	77	4	67	6	1954–55	81	3	75	6
1942–43	76	4	66	4	1955–56	82	3	76	7
1943–44	77	5	69	8	1956–57	85	4	78	8
1944–45	77	3	69	4	1957–58	85	4	78	5
1945–46	77	18	69	2	1958–59	85	(1)	79	6
1946–47	77	28	70	5	1959–60	85	4	81	6
1947–48	77	31	70	13	1960–61	86	5	81	2
1948–49	78	23	71	42	1961–62	87	10	83	8
1949–50	79	10	72	38	1962–63	87	9	83	7
1950–51	79	4	72	16	1963–64	87	11	84	8
1951–52	79	2	72	5	1964–65	87	14	84	10
1952–53	79	2	72	4	1965–66	88	16	84	10
1953–54	80	4	74	7	1966–67	89	18	84	18

1 Data not published.

Source: Education numbers of the Journal of the American Medical Association.

WOMEN AS PERCENT OF ALL STUDENTS IN U.S. MEDICAL SCHOOLS, 1966–67 AND 1956–57

In 1966–67 there were 89 medical schools in operation in the United States. All but 5 of these schools had a full 4-year approved program. The total enrollment was 30,652 with 2,771, or 8.3 percent, women. All of the schools admitted women but one school, Woman's Medical College, admitted no men.

In three coeducational schools women were about one-fifth of the total students—University of Puerto Rico, Howard University, and Rutgers State University. [The latter school had less than a 4-year program in 1966–67.] In 14 other schools, women constituted between 10 and 15 percent of the students. At the other end of the scale, women were less than 5 percent of the total in 17 schools.

The largest number of women students outside of Woman's Medical College was at State University of New York, Downstate, with 102 enrolled. Women numbered 50 or more at 8 other coeducational schools. In fact, more than half of all the women students were in 23 medical schools.

Ten years previously, women students numbered 1,646 and were 5.7 percent of the total. They were found in 83 of the 85 medical schools in operation. No women students were enrolled in Dartmouth Medical School (less than a 4-year approved program) or Jefferson Medical College.

Women were 10 percent or more of the students in only 3 coeducational schools—University of Puerto Rico, Howard University, and Seton Hall University (less than a 4-year approved program). They were between 8 and 10 percent of the students in three other coeducational schools. They were less than 5 percent of the students in 39 of the schools.

The proportion of women students had more than doubled between 1956–57 and 1966–67 at 12 coeducational medical schools. On the other hand the proportion of women among all students had dropped in another 12 schools with the largest decrease in the Medical College of Alabama—2.2 percent in 1966–67 as compared with 7.4 percent in 1956–57.

U.S. MEDICAL SCHOOLS RANKED IN ORDER OF PERCENTAGE OF WOMEN STUDENTS ENROLLED IN 1966–67, AND NUMBERS OF MEN AND WOMEN, AND WOMEN AS PERCENT OF TOTALS, 1966–67 AND 1956–57

Rank (1966–67)—Medical school	1966–67			1956–57		
		Women			Women	
	Men	Number	As percent of total	Men	Number	As percent of total
Total	30,652	2,771	8.3	27,494	1,646	5.7
1. Woman's Medical College	0	204	100.0	0	182	100.0
2. University of Puerto Rico	166	49	22.8	159	25	13.6
3. Howard University	322	79	19.7	261	36	12.1
4. Rutgers State University [1]	13	3	18.8			
5. Boston University	244	42	14.7	265	21	7.7
6. State University of New York, Downstate	652	102	13.5	545	42	7.2
7. University of California, San Francisco	428	61	12.5	290	22	7.1
8. University of New Mexico [1]	58	8	12.1			
9. Case Western Reserve University	310	41	11.7	295	29	8.9
10. New York University	423	55	11.5	473	49	9.4
11. University of Chicago	250	30	10.7	265	22	7.6
12. Loma Linda University	303	36	10.6	360	16	4.3
13. University of Wisconsin	353	42	10.6	300	18	5.7
14. Columbia University	422	50	10.6	427	45	9.5
15. Temple University	493	58	10.5	465	26	5.3
16. Stanford University	275	32	10.5	217	15	6.5
17. University of Kentucky	248	28	10.1			
18. Albert Einstein College of Medicine [2]	349	39	10.1	144	7	4.6
19. Albany Medical College	225	24	9.6	221	9	3.9
20. New York Medical College	447	47	9.5	459	27	5.6
21. Meharry Medical College	212	22	9.4	239	19	7.4
22. Yale University	290	30	9.4	301	21	6.5
23. University of Illinois	695	70	9.2	606	38	5.9
24. California College of Medicine	289	29	9.1			
25. Wayne State University	469	47	9.1	268	17	6.0
26. West Virginia University [2]	210	21	9.1	54	4	6.9
27. Harvard Medical School	488	48	9.0	484	31	6.0
28. University of Colorado	310	30	8.8	299	23	7.1
29. State University of New York at Buffalo	353	34	8.8	288	12	4.0
30. Louisiana State University	471	45	8.7	407	21	4.9
31. State University of New York, Upstate	357	34	8.7	273	15	5.2
32. University of Pittsburgh	348	33	8.7	349	13	3.6
33. University of Michigan	713	67	8.6	727	35	4.6
34. Northwestern University	490	46	8.6	496	24	4.6
35. Dartmouth Medical School [2]	86	8	8.5	48	0	0
36. Indiana University	750	68	8.3	562	21	3.6
37. University of Southern California	256	23	8.2	255	11	4.1
38. Johns Hopkins University	336	30	8.2	272	21	7.2
39. University of Miami	287	25	8.0	222	14	6.0
40. St. Louis University	404	35	8.0	469	12	2.5
41. Washington University	303	26	7.9	335	12	3.3
42. George Washington University	373	32	7.9	353	19	5.1
43. Duke University	298	25	7.7	304	15	4.7
44. University of Mississippi	275	23	7.7	208	6	2.8
45. University of Texas, Southwestern	371	30	7.5	373	17	4.4
46. University of Iowa	451	36	7.4	418	15	3.5
47. University of Florida [2]	219	17	7.2	44	3	6.4
48. University of Texas, medical branch	549	42	7.1	565	36	6.0
49. University of Maryland	452	34	7.0	351	12	3.4
50. New Jersey College of Medicine, Seton Hall University [2]	282	21	6.9	71	9	11.3
51. Hahnemann Medical College	398	29	6.8	377	21	5.3
52. University of North Dakota [1][2]	85	6	6.6	75	5	6.3
53. University of Oregon	314	22	6.5	278	15	5.1
54. Ohio State University	543	38	6.5	552	15	2.6
55. University of Minnesota	601	42	6.5	454	20	4.2

U.S. MEDICAL SCHOOLS RANKED IN ORDER OF PERCENTAGE OF WOMEN STUDENTS ENROLLED IN 1966–67, AND NUMBERS OF MEN AND WOMEN, AND WOMEN AS PERCENT OF TOTALS, 1966–67 AND 1956–57—Continued

Rank (1966–67)—Medical school	1966–67			1956–57		
		Women			Women	
	Men	Number	As per-cent of total	Men	Number	As per-cent of total
56. Tufts University School of Medicine	416	29	6.5	416	25	5.7
57. University of Missouri	305	21	6.4	164	6	3.5
58. University of Tennessee	629	43	6.4	753	34	4.3
59. University of California, Los Angeles	280	19	6.4	170	10	5.6
60. Jefferson Medical College	621	42	6.3	682	0	0
61. Vanderbilt University	193	13	6.3	193	9	4.5
62. University of Vermont	183	12	6.2	168	11	6.1
63. Cornell University	317	21	6.0	314	21	6.3
64. University of Oklahoma	375	24	6.0	354	19	5.1
65. University of North Carolina	267	17	6.0	244	8	3.2
66. State University of South Dakota[1][2]	83	5	5.7	74	3	3.9
67. Medical College of Virginia	354	21	5.6	337	27	7.4
68. Bowman-Gray School of Medicine	202	12	5.6	194	15	7.2
69. University of Louisville	343	20	5.5	360	19	5.0
70. University of Kansas	422	24	5.4	398	17	4.1
71. University of Arkansas	351	19	5.1	323	18	5.3
72. University of Washington	299	16	5.1	276	14	4.8
73. Georgetown University	427	22	4.9	402	22	5.2
74. Loyola University Stritch School of Medicine	322	16	4.7	318	12	3.6
75. Emory University	267	13	4.6	278	8	2.8
76. Marquette University	376	18	4.6	379	18	4.5
77. University of Nebraska	324	15	4.4	309	9	2.8
78. University of Pennsylvania	480	22	4.4	483	20	4.0
79. University of Rochester	263	12	4.4	268	11	4.0
80. Tulane University	489	21	4.1	493	13	2.6
81. Baylor University	330	14	4.1	321	15	4.5
82. Medical College of Georgia	369	14	3.7	356	20	5.3
83. University of Virginia	286	9	3.1	282	15	5.1
84. Medical College of South Carolina	299	9	2.9	294	11	3.6
85. University of Cincinnati	377	11	2.8	320	16	4.8
86. University of Utah	231	6	2.5	207	5	2.4
87. Medical College of Alabama	305	7	2.2	277	22	7.4
88. Chicago Medical School	279	3	1.1	276	1	.4
89. Creighton University	280	3	1.1	278	9	3.1

[1] Basic sicences only, 1966–67 (less han a full 4-year approved program).
[2] Basic sciences only, 1956–57 (less than a full 4-year approved program).

Source: Education numbers of the JAMA for appropriate years.

WOMEN AS PERCENT OF ALL GRADUATES OF U.S. MEDICAL SCHOOLS, 1966–67 AND 1956–57

A total of 583 women graduated from 83 U.S. medical schools in 1967. They constituted 7.5 percent of all graduates.

Women were one-fifth or more of all graduates of three coeducational medical schools—University of Puerto Rico, Howard University, and Boston University. In 14 other schools, they were between 10 and 20 percent of the graduates. At the other end of the scale, women were less than 5 percent of all graduates in 27 schools.

Ten years previously, women graduates numbered 330 and were 4.8 percent of the total graduating. They had graduated from 74 medical schools.

Women accounted for between 10 and 20 percent of the graduates in only 6 coeducational school in 1956–57. They were less than 5 percent in 48 schools.

The proportion of women graduates had more than doubled between 1956–57 and 1966–67 at 25 coeducational medical schools which had women graduates both years. On the other hand, the proportion of women among all graduates had dropped at 17 schools. Moreover at one of these 17, Creighton, no women were graduated in 1966–67 although women had comprised 4.3 percent of their 1956–57 graduating class.

UNITED STATES MEDICAL SCHOOLS RANKED IN ORDER OF PERCENTAGE OF WOMEN IN 1967 GRADUATING CLASS, AND NUMBERS OF MEN AND WOMEN GRADUATES, AND WOMEN AS PERCENT OF TOTAL, 1967 AND 1957

	1967			1957		
		Women			Women	
Rank 1967—Medical school	Men	Number	As percent of total	Men	Number	As percent of total
Total	7,160	583	7.5	6,466	330	4.8
1. Woman's Medical College	0	37	100.0	0	40	100.0
2. University of Puerto Rico	34	10	22.7	34	7	17.1
3. Howard University	76	22	22.4	64	8	11.1
4. Boston University	49	13	21.0	67	2	2.9
5. West Virginia University	43	10	18.9			
6. Stanford University	41	7	14.5	52	5	8.8
7. State University of New York, Downstate	140	20	12.5	143	2	1.4
8. George Washington University	84	12	12.5	83	5	5.7
9. Temple University	113	16	12.4	111	3	2.6
10. Loma Linda University	78	10	11.4	93	5	5.1
11. New York Medical College	104	13	11.1	104	5	4.6
12. Case Western Reserve University	73	9	11.0	68	5	6.8
13. Yale University	65	8	11.0	76	4	5.0
14. University of Vermont	41	5	10.9	39	1	2.5
15. University of Wisconsin	82	10	10.9	75	2	2.6
16. Columbia University	104	12	10.2	101	13	11.4
17. University of Florida	53	6	10 2			
18. Meharry Medical College	45	5	10.0	52	1	1.9
19. University of California, San Francisco	90	11	10.0	71	3	4.1
20. Albert Einstein College of Medicine	82	9	9.9			
21. University of Illinois	163	16	8.9	139	7	4.8
22. State University of New York, Upstate	85	8	8.6	61	2	3.2
23. University of Pittsburgh	75	7	8.5	88	3	3.3
24. University of Minnesota	143	13	8.3	107	2	1.8
25. Tufts University School of Medicine	99	9	8.3	108	5	4.4
26. Northwestern University	125	11	8.1	122	4	3.2
27. Louisiana State University	115	10	8.0	93	3	3.1
28. Johns Hopkins University	82	7	7.9	62	5	7.5
29. University of Missouri	70	6	7.9	21	0	0
30. New York Univeristy	108	9	7.7	121	6	4.7
31. University of Utah	48	4	7.7	55	2	3.5
32. Harvard Medical School	139	11	7.3	140	5	3.4
33. University of Tennessee	139	11	7.3	182	3	1.6
34. St. Louis University	90	7	7.2	112	0	0
35. Wayne State University	91	7	7.1	63	2	3.1
36. University of Chicago	66	5	7.0	65	4	5.8
37. California College of Medicine	81	6	6.9			
38. University of Kansas	96	7	6.8	102	5	4.7
39. University of Oklahoma	83	6	6.7	85	3	3.4
40. Ohio State University	127	9	6.6	129	4	3.0
41. Medical College of Georgia	86	6	6.5	73	5	6.4
42. University of Maryland	100	7	6.5	89	5	5.3
43. State University of New York at Buffalo	89	6	6.3	62	3	4.6
44. Emory University	60	4	6.3	72	2	2.7
45. University of Oregon	75	5	6.3	63	2	3.1
46. University of Washington	74	5	6.3	69	3	4.2
47. University of Iowa	107	7	6.1	95	2	2.1
48. University of Rochester	62	4	6.1	60	5	7.7
49. University of Texas Medical Branch	141	9	6.0	119	10	7.8
50. University of Southern California	67	4	5.6	66	2	2.9
51. University of Michigan	172	10	5.6	177	9	4.8
52. Indiana University	172	10	5.5	132	7	5.0

UNITED STATES MEDICAL SCHOOLS RANKED IN ORDER OF PERCENTAGE OF WOMEN IN 1967 GRADUATING CLASS, AND NUMBERS OF MEN AND WOMEN GRADUATES, AND WOMEN AS PERCENT OF TOTAL, 1967 AND 1957—Con.

	1966–67			1956–57		
		Women			Women	
Rank 1967—Medical school	Men	Number	As per-cent of total	Men	Number	As per-cent of total
53. Loyola University Stritch School of Medicine	72	4	5.3	80	2	2.4
54. Washington University	72	4	5.3	89	4	4.3
55. Duke University	76	4	5.0	76	4	5.0
56. University of Kentucky	57	3	5.0			
57. Medical College of South Carolina	76	4	5.0	71	3	4.1
58. University of Colorado	80	4	4.8	68	2	2.9
59. University of Arkansas	83	4	4.6	74	3	3.9
60. New Jersey College of Medicine	63	3	4.5			
61. University of Mississippi	65	3	4.4	23	1	4.2
62. University of Miami	66	3	4.3	30	4	11.8
63. University of Louisville	80	4	4.3	88	2	2.2
64. Marquette University	94	4	4.2	96	4	4.0
65. Vanderbilt University	46	2	4.2	51	2	3.8
66. University of Texas, Southwestern	92	4	4.2	88	3	3.3
67. University of North Carolina	71	3	4.1	56	2	3.4
68. University of Nebraska	72	3	4.0	77	0	0
69. Bowman-Gray School of Medicine	49	2	3.9	49	6	10.9
70. Hahnemann Medical College	100	4	3.8	94	3	3.1
71. Baylor University	76	3	3.8	86	4	4.4
72. Jefferson Medical College	155	6	3.7	165	0	0
73. Albany Medical College	54	2	3.6	46	3	6.1
74. Cornell University	80	3	3.6	80	6	7.0
75. University of California, Los Angeles	66	2	2.9	33	3	8.3
76. Georgetown University	103	3	2.8	102	12	10.5
77. University of Alabama	72	2	2.7	69	2	2.8
78. University of Pennsylvania	119	3	2.5	119	7	5.6
79. University of Cincinnati	88	2	2.2	76	3	3.8
80. Chicago Medical School	65	1	1.5	66	0	0
81. University of Virginia	68	1	1.4	73	2	2.7
82. Medical College of Virginia	77	1	1.3	87	8	8.4
83. Tulane University	127	1	.8	123	1	.8
84. Creighton University	69	0	0	66	3	4.3

Source: Education numbers of the JAMA for appropriate years..

LOCATION OF PHYSICIANS, 1965

About 19,526 women physicians were located in the United States and outlying areas as of December 31, 1965, according to data provided by the American Medical Association. Thus, women account for 6.7 percent of the total number of physicians.

More than one thousand women physicians were located in each of the following four States: California, Illinois, New York, and Pennsylvania. In contrast, fewer than one hundred reside in each of 21 States.

In relation to population, New York leads all States with 21.7 women physicians per 100,000 civilian persons. In that State 10.1 percent of all physicians are female. Only Alaska has a larger proportion on the distaff side—12.9 percent. The District of Columbia has a strikingly large number of women physicians per 100,000 civilian persons—45.6 in 1965. In this area, women also comprise 12.3 percent of all physicians—a higher percentage than in all the States except Alaska.

States that have relatively few women—as a share of the total number and in proportion to population—include Idaho, Nebraska, Nevada, North Dakota, and Wyoming.

LOCATION OF NON-FEDERAL PHYSICIANS, 1965

Location	Number of M.D.'s		Percent women of total M.D.'s	M.D.'s per 100,000 population [1]	
	Total	Women		Total	Women
All locations	292,088	19,526	6.7		
Federal	22,814	698	3.1		
Non-Federal	269,274	18,828	7.0	138.2	9.7
United States	266,045	18,421	6.9	138.6	9.6
Alabama	2,733	104	3.8	79.5	3.0
Alaska	155	20	12.9	70.1	9.0
Arizona	1,941	99	5.1	122.3	6.2
Arkansas	1,691	55	3.3	86.7	2.8
California	32,441	2,433	7.5	177.3	13.3
Colorado	3,274	181	5.5	169.4	9.3
Connecticut	5,063	376	7.4	179.5	13.3
Delaware	651	50	7.7	131.0	10.1
District of Columbia	2,920	359	12.3	371.0	45.6
Florida	8,027	372	4.6	140.5	6.5
Georgia	4,285	220	5.1	100.5	5.2
Hawaii	901	77	8.5	139.0	11.9
Idaho	615	16	2.6	89.7	2.3
Illinois	14,306	1,134	7.9	135.0	10.7
Indiana	4,932	219	4.4	101.1	4.5
Iowa	2,883	130	4.5	104.5	4.7
Kansas	2,427	134	5.5	110.6	6.1
Kentucky	3,054	148	4.8	97.3	4.7
Louisiana	3,973	237	6.0	113.5	6.8
Maine	999	59	5.9	102.5	6.1
Maryland	5,760	522	9.1	166.3	15.1
Massachusetts	10,544	841	8.0	198.6	15.8
Michigan	10,050	633	6.3	122.6	7.7
Minnesota	5,289	252	4.8	149.0	7.1
Mississippi	1,713	60	3.5	74.4	2.6
Missouri	5,522	282	5.1	123.5	6.3
Montana	671	22	3.3	96.4	3.2
Nebraska	1,643	36	2.2	112.6	2.5
Nevada	412	12	2.9	95.4	2.8
New Hampshire	867	70	8.1	130.8	10.6
New Jersey	9,081	667	7.3	134.8	9.9
New Mexico	894	58	6.5	88.7	5.8
New York	38,601	3,911	10.1	214.1	21.7
North Carolina	4,946	251	5.1	102.6	5.2
North Dakota	565	15	2.7	88.3	2.3
Ohio	13,293	889	6.7	130.0	8.7
Oklahoma	2,399	110	4.6	98.0	4.5
Oregon	2,673	139	5.2	141.1	7.3
Pennsylvania	16,602	1,324	8.0	144.3	11.5
Rhode Island	1,299	88	6.8	149.8	10.1
South Carolina	2,002	66	3.3	80.4	2.7
South Dakota	534	22	4.1	76.7	3.2
Tennessee	4,267	203	4.8	111.8	5.3
Texas	11,218	578	5.2	108.0	5.6
Utah	1,303	47	3.6	132.2	4.8
Vermont	676	50	7.4	170.3	12.6
Virginia	4,850	280	5.8	112.9	6.5
Washington	4,266	246	5.8	145.6	8.4
West Virginia	1,745	76	4.4	96.4	4.2
Wisconsin	4,789	242	5.1	115.7	5.8
Wyoming	300	6	2.0	89.6	1.8
Puerto Rico and outlying areas	1,995	190	9.5	69.1	6.6
Address unknown	1,234	217	17.6		

[1] Civilian population as of July 1; see U.S. Bureau of the Census, Current Population Reports, Population Estimates, series P–25, No. 324.

AGE DISTRIBUTION OF PHYSICIANS, 1965

Women comprised 6.7 percent of the total number of physicians in 1965 and 17.7 percent of all inactive physicians according to data provided by the American Medical Association. But there were some variations within the different age groups. Thus women under age 30 were 9.3 percent of all physicians due to the fact that they are graduating from medical schools in increasing numbers. Women were the smallest proportion of all physicians at age 55 to 59—5.0 percent in 1965.

Women between 30 and 49 years of age made up nearly half of the inactive physicians in these age groups. After age 50, the proportion of women among all inactive physicians declined as the age increased. Thus women were only 11.5 percent of the inactive physicians 60 years of age and over.

Among the 2,572 inactive women physicians in 1965, 3.3 percent were under 30, 27.6 percent were between 30 and 45, 18.3 percent were between 45 and 60, and 50.8 percent were age 60 and over. Among the inactive men physicians, the corresponding percentages were 1.6, 6.1, 7.7, and 84.6.

AGE DISTRIBUTION OF PHYSICIANS, 1965

Age group	Number of M.D.'s		Number of women M.D.'s		Women as percent of total M.D.'s	
	Active and inactive	Inactive	Active and inactive	Inactive	Active and inactive	Inactive
All ages_____	292,088	14,513	19,526	2,572	6.7	17.7
Under 30 years_____	32,586	272	3,020	84	9.3	30.9
30 to 34_____	40,604	456	2,555	209	6.3	45.8
35 to 39_____	39,054	468	2,554	222	6.5	47.4
40 to 44_____	40,556	520	2,816	280	6.9	53.8
45 to 49_____	31,100	378	1,968	186	6.3	49.2
50 to 54_____	28,748	428	1,698	154	5.9	36.0
55 to 59_____	25,464	588	1,284	131	5.0	22.3
60 to 64_____	18,383	980	} 3,631	} 1,306	} 6.7	} 11.5
65 to 69_____	13,583	1,868				
70 and over_____	22,010	8,555				
Under 40_____	112,244	1,196	8,129	515	7.2	43.1
40 to 59_____	125,868	1,914	7,766	751	6.2	39.2
60 and over_____	53,976	11,403	3,631	1,306	6.7	11.5

TYPE OF PRACTICE OF PHYSICIANS, 1965

According to data provided by the American Medical Association, 698 of the 16,954 active women physicians in 1965 were employed by the Federal Government: 59 in the Department of Defense (15 Air Force, 34 Army, and 10 Navy), 128 in the Public Health Service, 451 in the Veterans' Administration, and 60 in other Federal agencies. About 3.1 percent of all Federal physicians were female.

The active women physicians (Federal and non-Federal combined) may be classified into five categories of practice, as shown below:

Type of practice	Women physicians	
	Number	As percent of total
Total active_____	16,954	6.1
Private practice_____	8,119	4.5
Training programs_____	4,036	9.3
Full-time hospital service_____	2,236	8.0
Full-time medical school faculty_____	699	7.8
Preventive medicine, administration, and research_____	1,864	11.5

Women were less likely than men to engage in private practice. They indicated a preference for such forms of practice as hospital service, teaching, preventive medicine, administration, and research.

TYPE OF PRACTICE OF PHYSICIANS: UNITED STATES AND OUTLYING AREAS, 1965

Type of practice	Number of M.D.'s		Percent of M.D.'s		Percent women of total M.D.'s
	Total	Women	Total	Women	
All types of practice	292,088	19,526	100.0	100.0	6.7
Federal physicians	22,814	698	7.8	3.6	3.1
Training programs [1]	3,902	121	1.3	.6	3.1
Full-time hospital service	15,373	410	5.3	2.1	2.7
Preventive medicine [2]	3,539	167	1.2	.9	4.7
Non-Federal physicians	254,761	16,256	87.2	83.2	6.4
Private practice	180,752	8,119	61.9	41.6	4.5
Training programs [1]	39,606	3,915	13.6	20.0	9.9
Full-time hospital service	12,722	1,826	4.3	9.3	14.4
Full-time medical school faculty	9,001	699	3.1	3.6	7.8
Preventive medicine [2]	12,680	1,697	4.3	8.7	13.4
Inactive physicians	14,513	2,572	5.0	13.2	17.7
Retired	10,328	1,157	3.6	5.9	11.2
Not in practice	4,185	1,415	1.4	7.3	33.8

[1] Interns, residents, and fellows.
[2] Includes administrative medicine, laboratory medicine, and research.

SPECIALIZATION OF ACTIVE PHYSICIANS, 1965

Specialists outnumbered general practitioners about three to one among the active women M.D.'s in 1965 according to data provided by the American Medical Association. Specialists numbered 12,644 or 74.6 percent of the women.

There are more than 30 specialties recognized by the profession. Women accounted for at least 10 percent of all physicians engaged in the specialities of anesthesiology, pediatrics, physical medicine and rehabilitation, preventive medicine, psychiatry (child and other), public health, and pulmonary diseases.

When the detailed specialities have been grouped into five major categories, the proportion of physicians in each category who were women is as follows: general practice 5.2 percent, medical specialties 8.6 percent, surgical specialties 3.5 percent, psychiatry and neurology 11.5 percent, and other specialties 7.4 percent.

SPECIALTY OF ACTIVE PHYSICIANS, 1965

Specialty	Number of M.D.'s		Percent of M.D.'s		Percent women of total M.D.'s
	Total [1]	Women	Total	Women	
Total	277,575	16,954	100.0	100.0	6. 1
General practice [2]	83,309	4,310	30.0	25.4	5.2
Medical specialties	61,860	5,304	22.3	31.3	8.6
Allergy	907	70	.3	11.	7.7
Cardiovascular disease	1,867	50	.7	.3	2.7
Dermatology	3,511	231	1.3	1.3	6.6
Gastroenterology	626	10	.2	.1	1.6
Internal medicine	38,115	1,798	13.7	10.6	4.7
Pediatrics [3]	15,179	3,033	5.7	17.9	19.3
Pulmonary diseases	1,115	112	.4	.7	10.0
Surgical specialties	84,351	2,948	30.4	17.4	3.5
Anesthesiology	8,621	1,223	3.1	7.2	14.2
Colon and rectal surgery	647	2	.2	*	.3
General surgery	27,466	257	9.9	1.5	.9
Neurological surgery	2,038	7	.8	*	.3
Obstetrics and gynecology	16,766	1,043	6.1	6.2	6.2
Ophthalmology	8,380	278	3.0	1.7	3.3
Orthopedic surgery	7,507	38	2.7	.2	.5
Otolaryngology	5,307	57	1.9	.3	1.1
Plastic surgery	1,129	30	.4	.2	2.7
Thoracic surgery	1,463	5	.5	*	.3
Urology	5,027	8	1.8	.1	.2
Psychiatry and neurology	20,254	2,330	7.3	13.7	11.5
Child psychiatry	795	169	.3	1.0	21.3
Neurology	2,152	138	.8	.8	6.4
Psychiatry	17,307	2,023	6.2	11.9	11.7
Other specialties	27,801	2,062	10.0	12.2	7.4
Administrative medicine	4,057	243	1.5	1.4	6.0
Aviation medicine	682	1	.2	(4)	.1
General preventive medicine	826	124	.3	.7	15.0
Occupational medicine	1,644	61	.6	.4	3.7
Pathology [5]	8,458	837	3.0	5.0	9.9
Physical medicine and rehabilitation	1,053	144	.4	.9	13.7
Public health	1,461	257	.5	1.5	17.6
Radiology [6]	9,620	395	3.5	2.3	4.1

1 Excludes 1,786 temporarily foreign and 1,234 whose addresses are temporarily unknown to the AMA.
2 Includes no specialty and other specialties not recognized.
3 Includes pediatric allergy and cardiology.
4 Less than 0.05 percent.
5 Includes forensic pathology.
6 Includes diagnostic roentgenology and therapeutic radiology.

SPECIALIZATION WITHIN TYPE OF PRACTICE OF ACTIVE PHYSICIANS, 1965

A tabulation of specialization within type of practice from data provided by the American Medical Association shows how many women physicians are taking training programs in certain specialities as well as their concentration in certain specialties in private practice, hospital service, and in teaching, research, and preventive medicine.

Of the 4,036 women physicians in training programs, 1,414, or more than one-third, were in medical specialties, mainly pediatrics and internal medicine. About 950 were training for general practice and another 675 were in surgical specialties.

Among the 8,119 women in private practice, 5,470, or about two-thirds, indicated a specialty other than general practice. Among women in hospital service, the largest numbers were in medical specialties, and psychiatry and neurology. Among those in teaching, research, and preventive medicine, the two largest groups were in pediatrics and preventive medicine and other specialties.

In relation to all active physicians, women were 13.9 percent of the pediatricians and 11.9 percent of the anesthesiologists in private practice. Moreover, they were 13 percent or more of those in training programs in pediatrics, anesthesiology, pathology, and preventive medicine and other specialties. Similarly, women were well represented among pediatricians, psychiatrists, and anesthesiologists in hospital service.

SPECIALTY WITHIN TYPE OF PRACTICE OF ACTIVE PHYSICIANS, 1965

Specialty	Total	Type of practice			
		Private practice	Training programs [1]	Hospital service	Teaching, research, preventive medicine
TOTAL NUMBER OF M.D.'S					
Total	277,575	180,752	43,508	28,095	25,220
General practice	83,309	65,951	8,633	5,775	2,950
Medical specialties	61,860	37,408	11,277	7,240	5,935
Internal medicine	38,115	22,432	7,595	4,590	3,498
Pediatrics	15,719	9,726	2,777	1,563	1,653
Other medical specialties	8,026	5,250	905	1,087	784
Surgical specialties	84,351	59,850	15,146	6,622	2,733
Anesthesiology	8,621	6,050	1,167	988	416
Obstetrics and gynecology	16,766	12,566	2,623	1,048	529
General surgery and other surgical specialties	58,964	41,234	11,356	4,586	1,788
Psychiatry and neurology	20,254	9,291	4,316	4,719	1,928
Other specialties	27,801	8,252	4,136	3,739	11,674
Pathology	8,458	1,896	2,116	899	3,547
Radiology	9,620	5,609	1,657	1,816	538
Preventive medicine and other specialties	9,723	747	363	1,024	7,589
NUMBER OF WOMEN M.D.'S					
Total	16,954	8,119	4,036	2,236	2,563
General practice	4,310	2,649	957	328	376
Medical specialties	5,304	2,279	1,414	750	861
Internal medicine	1,798	677	568	321	232
Pediatrics	3,033	1,354	775	348	556
Other medical specialties	473	248	71	81	73
Surgical specialties	2,948	1,828	675	320	125
Anesthesiology	1,223	721	269	187	46
Obstetrics and gynecology	1,043	676	250	67	50
General surgery and other surgical specialties	682	431	156	66	29
Psychiatry and neurology	2,330	1,033	546	573	178
Other specialties	2,062	330	444	265	1,023
Pathology	837	133	290	99	315
Radiology	395	158	104	101	32
Preventive medicine and other specialties	830	39	50	65	676
PERCENT WOMEN OF TOTAL M.D.'S					
Total	6.1	4.5	9.3	8.0	10.2
General practice	5.2	4.0	11.1	5.7	12.7
Medical specialties	8.6	6.1	12.5	10.4	14.5
Internal medicine	4.7	3.0	7.5	7.0	6.6
Pediatrics	19.3	13.9	27.9	22.3	33.6
Other medical specialties	5.9	4.7	7.8	7.5	9.3
Surgical specialties	3.5	3.1	4.5	4.8	4.6
Anesthesiology	14.2	11.9	23.1	18.9	11.1
Obstetrics and gynecology	6.2	5.4	9.5	6.4	9.5
General surgery and other surgical specialties	1.2	1.0	1.4	1.4	1.6
Psychiatry and neurology	11.5	11.1	12.7	12.1	9.2
Other specialties	7.4	4.0	10.7	7.1	8.8
Pathology	9.9	7.0	13.7	11.0	8.9
Radiology	4.1	2.8	6.3	5.6	5.9
Preventive medicine and other specialties	8.5	5.2	13.8	6.3	8.9

[1] Federal and non-Federal programs.

According to the American Medical Association, more than 44,000 graduates of medical schools outside the United States were practicing medicine or taking advanced training in this country in 1966. About 13 percent of these graduates were women. The fact that the proportion of women among these foreign physicians exceeds the proportion of women among graduates of U.S. medical schools may be due in part to the availability of advanced or specialty training in this country or to the lack of it in other countries. It may also reflect the fact that women comprise a larger share of the graduates of medical schools in certain foreign countries.

Women accounted for a fifth or more of the foreign physicians from 10 countries, located mainly in the Far East or Eastern Europe. They comprised between 10 and 20 percent in 11 countries, 5 to 10 percent in 17 countries, and less than 5 percent in the remaining 6 countries.

GRADUATES OF MEDICAL SCHOOLS OUTSIDE THE UNITED STATES, PRACTICING IN THE UNITED STATES, 1966 [1]

Country	Number	Women as percent of total	Country	Number	Women as percent of total
Total	[2] 44,178	[2] 12.6	Brazil	203	9.9
			Greece	624	9.8
Union of Soviet Socialist			Puerto Rico	178	9.0
Republics	194	33.5	South Africa	256	8.6
Latvia	177	29.9	Belgium	387	8.5
Philippines	5,056	29.9	Turkey	591	8.3
China	485	27.6	Netherlands	664	8.3
Thailand	602	25.9	Cuba	1,979	8.0
Lithuania	192	22.4	Dominican Republic	328	7.9
Poland	542	21.8	Switzerland	2,313	7.3
Yugoslavia	258	20.5	Japan	514	7.2
Rumania	227	20.3	Haiti	174	6.3
Korea	1,060	19.6	Spain	694	6.1
Israel	128	18.8	Canada	5,722	5.9
Austria	1,571	17.9	Scotland	1,024	5.6
Germany	4,150	16.9	Pakistan	358	5.3
England	1,062	13.2	Iran	1,000	5.1
Hungary	822	13.0	Italy	2,811	4.8
Argentina	909	12.2	Lebanon	451	4.4
Iraq	141	12.1	Egypt	315	4.1
Formosa	440	11.8	Mexico	1,201	3.5
Australia	177	10.7	Peru	340	3.2
Czechoslovakia	501	10.6	Colombia	596	1.8
Ireland	814	10.3			

[1] Persons serving as interns and residents are included.
[2] Includes graduates from countries reporting less than 100 graduates in this country, not listed separately.

Source: American Medical Association.

WOMEN GRADUATES OF MEDICAL SCHOOLS IN OTHER COUNTRIES, 1965

According to questionnaires returned by member organizations and presented at the 10th Congress of the Medical Women's International Association, the Republic of Germany had the highest proportion of women among its medical school graduates—36 percent in 1965. In four other countries and the combined group of England, Wales, and Scotland, women accounted for about one-fourth or more of the medical school graduates. In 10 additional countries which reported the proportion of women among medical school graduates, they constituted between 10 and 20 percent of the total. Only 2 of the reporting countries had a smaller proportion of women among their graduates than the United States where the figure in 1965 was 7.3 percent.

Further details on the individual countries may be obtained from the Women's Bureau.

WOMEN GRADUATES OF MEDICAL SCHOOLS IN OTHER COUNTRIES, 1965

Country	Total graduates	Women graduates	
		Number	As percent of total
Germany	2,575	921	35.8
Austria	[1] 196	[1] 59	[1] 30.1
Thailand	262	69	26.4
England, Wales, and Scotland	2,042	535	26.1
India	7,000	1,700	24.3
Sweden	315	76	24.1
Denmark	247	48	19.4
Israel	88	17	19.3
Finland	216	40	18.5
Norway	217	37	17.1
Switzerland	302	45	14.9
Australia	658	81	12.3
Brazil	[2] 1,596	[2] 185	[2] 11.6
Italy	2,519	274	10.9
Canada	922	94	10.2
South Korea	700	70	10.0
Hong Kong	72	7	9.7
Spain	1,768	148	8.4
Madagascar	36	3	8.3
Japan	2,996	239	8.0
New Zealand	106	6	5.7
Republic of China	277	13	4.7

[1] Data are for 1963.
[2] Data are for 1964.

Source: Data compiled from questionnaires returned by member organizations and presented at the 10th Congress of Medical Women's International Association, Rochester, N.Y., July 9–15, 1966.

WOMEN PHYSICIANS IN OTHER COUNTRIES, 1965

According to questionnaires returned by member organizations and presented at the 10th Congress of the Medical Women's International Association, women were about one-fourth of all physicians in 4 countries—Finland, Israel, Philippines, and Thailand. Moreover, they were between 10 and 20 percent of the physicians in 17 other reporting countries. In only three reporting countries were women a smaller proportion of all physicians than in the United States—6.7 percent in 1965.

A chart based on the same information plus information on the United States shows that in 9 out of the 29 countries, or nearly one-third, women were between 10 and 15 percent of all physicians. In five countries, women were between 20 and 25 percent of all physicians; in two countries, they were less than 5 percent.

Further details on the individual countries may be obtained from the Women's Bureau.

WOMEN PHYSICIANS IN OTHER COUNTRIES, 1965

Country	Total physicians	Women physicians	
		Number	As percent of total
Philippines	18,611	4,602	24.7
Finland	[1] 3,384	[1] 818	[1] 24.2
Israel	5,573	1,338	24.0
Thailand	4,268	1,017	23.8
Germany	86,752	17,320	20.0
Italy	88,560	16,650	18.8
Austria	13,514	2,349	17.4
Scotland	7,146	1,217	17.0
Denmark	6,801	1,113	16.4
South Korea	9,000	1,450	16.1
England and Wales	[2] 48,806	[2] 7,852	[2] 16.0
Sweden	8,163	1,259	15.4
Hong Kong	1,270	184	—14.5
Switzerland	8,369	1,137	13.6
France	54,764	7,021	12.8
Australia	14,024	1,767	12.6
Netherlands	13,636	1,700	—12.5
India	80,200	9,600	12.0
Norway	4,659	558	12.0
New Zealand	3,464	350	10.1
Republic of South Africa	7,651	766	10.0
Japan	110,859	10,282	9.3
Canada	23,205	1,753	7.6
Brazil	42,176	2,998	7.1
Republic of China	7,904	550	7.0
South Vietnam	1,061	65	6.1
Madagascar	629	29	4.6
Spain	37,743	925	—2.5

[1] Excludes those abroad.
[2] Totals represent total of posts rather than total of medical personnel.

Source: Data compiled from questionnaires returned by member organizations and presented at the 10th Congress of Medical Women's International Association, Rochester, N.Y. July 9–15, 1966.

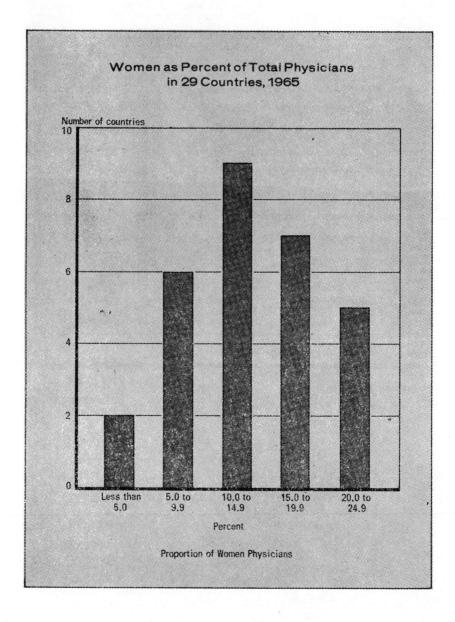

Women as Percent of Total Physicians
in 29 Countries, 1965

Number of countries

Less than 5.0 · 5.0 to 9.9 · 10.0 to 14.9 · 15.0 to 19.9 · 20.0 to 24.9

Percent

Proportion of Women Physicians

DEGREES EARNED IN SELECTED FIELDS OF STUDY, 1956, 1960, AND 1965

A comparison of the increase in the number of degrees earned by women at all levels and in selected health professions between 1956 and 1965, according to figures from the Office of Education, shows that almost the smallest growth has been in medical degrees. Although the number of doctoral degrees awarded to women doubled over the period, the number of degrees in medicine and osteopathy earned by women rose by only about one-third. In fact the proportionate rise in degrees earned by women was greater in nearly all the other health professions. The only exceptions were first-level degrees in public health, degrees in occupational therapy, and a decline in number of degrees awarded women as doctors of dental surgery.

Between 1956 and 1965, the number of medical degrees earned by women per year rose by 126. The comparable numerical increase per year among men was 296 or more than twice as much. Proportionately, however, the rise in the number of medical degrees earned was greater among women than among men, 35 percent as compared with 4 percent.

DEGREES EARNED IN SELECTED FIELDS OF STUDY, BY SEX 1956, 1960, AND 1965

Level of degree and fields of study	Women				Men			
	1965	1960	1956	Percent change [1] 1956–65	1965	1960	1956	Percent change [1] 1956–65
All bachelor's and 1st professional	219,260	139,385	111,727	96.2	319,670	255,504	199,571	60.2
All master's	35,984	23,560	20,027	79.7	76,211	50,937	39,413	93.4
All doctor's [2]	1,775	1,028	885	100.6	14,692	8,801	8,018	83.2
Doctors: [2]								
Education	529	309	282	87.6	2,179	1,281	1,301	67.5
Engineering	10	3			2,114	783	610	246.6
Health professions	16	8	7	128.6	157	99	137	14.6
Biological sciences	230	119	117	96.6	1,698	1,086	908	87.6
Physical sciences	127	62	68	86.8	2,702	1,776	1,599	69.0
Social sciences	185	120	109	69.7	1,806	1,117	1,015	77.9
All others	678	407	302	124.5	4,036	2,659	2,448	64.9
Doctor of medicine and osteopathy [2]	488	402	362	34.8	7,253	7,095	6,957	4.3
Doctor of dental surgery [2]	23	26	34	−32.4	3,112	3,221	2,975	4.6
Doctor of veterinary medicine [2]	35	18	14	150.0	861	807	896	−3.9
Nursing:								
Bachelor's and 1st professional	7,831	6,580	5,265	48.7	77	81	50	54.0
Master's	792	585	239	231.4	17	14	1	1,600.0
Doctor's	7				1			
Public health:								
Bachelor's and 1st professional	60	78	51	17.6	76	90	101	−24.8
Master's	231	133	123	87.8	542	394	354	53.1
Doctor's	2	5	2		22	19	21	4.8
Other health professions, all levels:								
Hospital administration	44	38	15	193.3	230	182	113	103.5
Social work, social administration	2,893	1,587	1,268	128.2	1,557	934	661	135.6
Pharmacy	520	428	377	37.9	3,163	3,246	3,157	0.2
Optometry	8	4	8		381	338	345	10.4
Physical therapy	567	372	328	72.9	87	93	92	−5.4
Occupational therapy	430	343	362	18.8	20	10	27	−25.9

[1] A percent increase unless otherwise indicated.
[2] Doctor's degrees cover only doctoral degrees in philosophy, education, engineering, etc. Doctoral degrees in the medical professions are first professional degrees.

Source: U.S. Department of Health, Education and Welfare, Office of Education: Earned Degrees Conferred, 1955–56 1959–60 and 1964–65.

STUDYING ATTITUDES OF THE MEDICAL PROFESSION TOWARD WOMEN PHYSICIANS: A SURVEY

EXCERPTS FROM: WOMEN PHYSICIANS: THE MORE EFFECTIVE RECRUITMENT AND UTILIZATION OF THEIR TALENTS AND THE RESISTANCE TO IT—A SEVEN YEAR STUDY, BY HAROLD I. KAPLAN, PROFESSOR OF PSYCHIATRY AND DIRECTOR OF PSYCHIATRIC TRAINING, NEW YORK MEDICAL COLLEGE; SPONSORED BY THE NATIONAL INSTITUTE OF MENTAL HEALTH

The author was the Principal Investigator of the National Institute of Mental Health Special Residency Training Program. . . . The questions posed in the survey were as follows:

(1) Do you make any special provision in the medical schooling of women with children in the area of special time off, less night work, extra vacations, etc.?

(2) Do you make any special provision in the professional assignment of women doctors with children in the area of special time off, less night work, extra vacations, etc.?

(3) Do you make special provision in the work schedule of women medical students and/or physicians when they are pregnant and when they are post-partum?

(4) Do you make any special provisions for the children of women medical students and/or women physicians in reference to nurseries, etc.?

(5) Can you offer any explanation for the increasing percentage of women doctors in your country and throughout the world?

There follows a summary of the results of the aforementioned survey. Although much of this survey was carried out several years ago (it has taken several years to complete it), the author recently spot checked the accuracy of some of the answers that had been given. This spot check confirmed the fact that most of these answers are currently valid and topical. While some responses are directly quoted, others are not, for obvious reasons, identified by direct quotation. Most medical school respondents were Deans, Associate or Assistant Deans, and on occasion a Chairman of the Admissions Committee. Well over 95% of all the medical schools in the United States and Canada cooperated magnificently and responded to the survey.

CONCLUSIONS OF THE SURVEY OF AMERICAN AND CANADIAN MEDICAL SCHOOLS STUDYING WOMEN PHYSICIANS

I. There were a significant number of schools which were very negative about single or married women in medicine

(A Western medical school) : "In this school we have not been overly impressed with the women that have been admitted to medicine even though academically they are entirely satisfactory. I think they ordinarily have so many emotional problems that we have not been particularly happy with their performance. In this medical school we screen all women applicants as carefully as possible. In order to be as certain as we can concerning their motivation for studying medicine."

(A Western medical school) : "We have admitted a few married women without children, but our experience with them has been almost uniformly poor. At the present we would not admit one unless she were an outstanding student. Up to the present we have refused to admit married women with children.

(A Western medical school) : Over a period of years it has been the practice of the Dean and the admissions committee to scrutinize carefully applicants who are married women and even to discourage them. *Author's comment: Thus while no school in the United States overtly or officially refuses to accept women, prejudice does seem to manifest itself by refusing medical school admission to married women with or without children, schools being very unimpressed with single women as medical students, or simply by an administration of a school being disinterested in adapting to the unique problems women have.*

II. How are pregnant medical students treated in American medical schools?
This is another measure of attitude to women; some schools simply deny
that there is any unique problem or avoid facing it in reference to pregnancy

(From the State University of Iowa School of Medicine) : "In our experience, female medical students who become pregnant during the school year have not been adversely affected insofar as educational progress is concerned. One year we had three senior women give birth to children during the academic year. Each of them had cleverly arranged to be on the obstetrics service at the time of delivery and thus they claimed they did not miss a single day of school. We do not make any programmatic modification for women medical students with children in our medical school program. However, most of these students deposit their newborn in the metabolism research center where studies are being conducted on the metabolism of newborn infants."

(An Eastern medical school) : "I have enough understanding my wife and daughters without attempting to explain the questions in this paragraph." *Authors comment: The respondent is avoiding, for personal reasons, facing the problem of women in medicine.*

III. Some schools are ambivalent in their attitude toward women, pregnancy, and medicine; while they deny any problem exists or avoid facing it, they make special provisions for this "non-existent" problem when it occurs

(From the University of Florida at Gainesville) : "We have made no particular concessions to a medical student who becomes pregnant. In general, the educational performance declines when they become pregnant. We have arranged the rotations in the clinical years to substitute a vacation at the time of delivery."

(A Midwestern medical school) : "If a married medical student becomes pregnant, she must discontinue her training until after the birth of her child. Then if her physical condition permits her to resume work, she is usually allowed to continue." *Author's comment: Although they are somewhat punitive in their attitude, they attempt some sort of restitution.*

(University of Washington School of Medicine) : "We do not have specific policies as to the admission of women to the School of Medicine. We, however, on the basis of our own experience, are reluctant to accept married women with children because of the obligations that they may have in tending to the problems of their children." *Author's comment: Although reluctant to admit women, on the other hand, this school is very flexible once a woman becomes pregnant.*

"If a female medical student becomes pregnant during her medical school year, she is allowed to carry on as long as she can and then arrangements are made for the completion of her work at a later time. These arrangements will depend upon the state of her medical career and we more often than not make whatever arrangements appear to be most suitable to her."

(University of Texas Medical Branch at Galveston) : "I have no doubt that unofficially married women with children would tend to be discouraged on an individual basis by the Admissions Committee. If the student becomes pregnant "the typical" course of events is for the student to lose as little as three days and as much as ten days from classes as a result of childbirth. If this period coincides with scheduled quizzes or examinations, the faculty is invariably considerate in setting up an alternative schedule. We have found it almost inevitable that we have a visit to the Student Loan Office for an additional loan or a scholarship, generally a few months before the baby comes, occasionally immediately afterwards. Again we have been so far fairly liberal on this if the student is in good standing; although I suppose in making such awards we sentimentally subserve the notion that conception is an Act of God." *Author's comment: Act of God?*

(Baylor University College of Medicine) : "Inasmuch as the M.D. degree is not granted in gender, all who are granted it must qualify for its requirements. If necessary, the woman with children is given as much flexibility as is practical in the arrangement of courses of study, but pregnancy in this faculty is no substitute for academic achievement and ultimate qualifications." *Author's comment: While critical of women physicians, they make an effort to adapt to them!*

(University of British Columbia) : "No discrimination against applicants on the basis of race, sex, color, creed, or place of geographic origin . . . We will not admit students who do not have adequate prospects of financial backing, further we would not admit students where there is likely to be conflict between two jobs. That is the academic pursuit and the responsibility of looking after a family. If these two were in conflict, we would likely not accept the student since even though as I have noted above there is no discrimination against women students, there is certainly no special privileges for them. We have several women medical students who have children but they get treated the same as any other medical student." *Authors comment: This is a classical example of avoiding facing the conflict they themselves describe.*

(University of Colorado) : "While programmatic modifications are difficult to make the first 2 years, more flexibility is afforded to women with children the second 2 years. Programmatic modifications have been made in many instances for married women with children at the residency level. This, again, would be individualized by service and for the individual. The type of modification would depend in part on the overall needs of the service and on the requirement of the various specialty boards . . . special arrangements have been made in Pediatrics for a number of women residents with children. In some instances this amounted to their participation on a half-time basis as a resident during a fairly large part of their residency program. To my knowledge, exceptions have not been made, however, during the internship." *Authors comments: While doing it reluctantly they do try to correct the situation.*

(University of Missouri) : In answer to the question about pregnancy : "We had a student in this category . . . already having two children at home, delivered her third in the spring of her freshman year. She missed a week to ten days of active classroom work and laboratory participation, but was able to keep herself fairly abreast of what was going on during this interval due to the fine cooperation of her classmates." (Meharry) : "All students have to meet the time requirements for advancement and graduation. So far our women students, by plan or good fortune, have had to repeat no work on account of undue absences associated with pregnancy."

Authors comment: In summary, while all schools in the United States had an official policy of accepting male or female students based upon merit and equality of the sexes, a small number clearly are prejudiced against women in medicine and a larger number are opposed to women students with children.

Once a female medical student becomes pregnant, most schools are flexible in allowing her to continue so long as she does not miss too much time. The most startling and frequent observation from many schools, among which are some of the most progressive and highly regarded ones in the world, is that most pergnant medical students, after bearing a child, return to a full academic schedule in from 3 days to two weeks; this observation, taken for granted by the medical schools, skirts the issue that such a post-partum recovery period is inadequate for a woman and potentially dangerous to her health. Furthermore, the unstated reason for the students returning to work after such an inadequately short recovery period is usually because there has been no provision made for their absence and they fear that they will lose the academic year's credit if they stay out longer.

Not only should this not be the case—provision for a longer post-partum period should and must be made—but almost every foreign country provides a safer and longer post-partum recovery period for women . . . The fact is that educational conditions and climate appear to be considerably more humane, intelligent and flexible outside the United States for the woman medical student or doctor with or without children. Since America is the leader in so many other areas of education, its "backwardness" in this area becomes all the more startling, disturbing, and troublesome. The fact that the Eastern European nations appear to have taken the leadership in this more flexible approach is well known; but by no means is such liberality limited to the Eastern bloc, for many countries of the West also have most enlightened policies, as for example, Sweden. There follows examples of different foreign countries policies in the aforementioned area.

Russia. (Department of Public Health of the U.S.S.R.) : "according to article 122 of the U.S.S.R. Constitution, the woman in U.S.S.R. enjoys equal rights with men in all fields of economic, cultural and socio-political life, i.e. equal rights with men in labor, education, social security, etc. The woman in the U.S.S.R., including physician mothers, and also the women-medical students have the right to have a paid leave for pregnancy and delivery—56 days before delivery and 56 days after delivery. And in case of complications during delivery, 72 days after delivery. *The students preserve their scholastic standing during this period and proceed with their studies as if they missed no time.* Women having a child until it is one year of age may not have night-duty and women doctors or women medical students are not required to serve night duty in hospitals. Working physician mothers and medical students have first preference in placing their children in nurseries and kindergartens."

Hungary (Hungarian Consul General) : "Women doctors and medical students receive the special leave and allowance offered to all women who are pregnant."

Sweden (Swedish Committee on International Health Relations) : "In some some hospitals there are joint day-nurseries for children of all women working in the hospsitals: doctors, nurses and auxiliary personnel. They are flexibly treated as to schedules."

FINDINGS AND RECOMMENDATIONS ABOUT TRAINING WOMEN PHYSICIANS IN THE
UNITED STATES

Findings: The percentage and number of women physicians is increasing slowly in the United States, now making up about 9% of the medical profession. Compared with the rest of the world, however—in Russia it is 65%, in England 24%—the United States has been slow to utilize the talents of women interested in medicine.

Many reasons may be given for the disparity between America's utilization of women in medicine compared with that of the rest of the world. The author explored the area of prejudice against women physicians on the part of medical educators and has concluded that it is a significant factor manifesting itself in: resistance in some schools to simply admitting women (whether single and/or married with or without children; resistance to making adequate provisions for women once they are in school (e.g. if they marry and have children) and encounter problems unique to women (e.g. childbirth and the care of children). Schools may refuse to provide any time off for childbirth, or insist upon rigid adherence to work or night schedules—whereas minor modifications in these areas might allow a student who is a mother to successfully perform both. In fact, many medical schools have observed that women students usually return to school a few days post-partum; this observation is used as a justification for the conclusion that women are capable of adhering to our rigid educational system, if motivated, and to confirm the absence of a need for special programming for physician mothers. Rather, in the authors view, the aforementioned represents a criticism of the American Medical educational training available to women physicians, the enforcement of such a rigid system appearing to seriously limit the recruitment of women into medicine. Using foreign countries, as an example where flexible provisions are made for women, the author concludes that such programming is a major factor in encouraging more women to seek medicine as a career.

[Florence Howe, Modern Language Association, Dec. 1969]

A REPORT FROM THE COMMISSION ON THE STATUS OF WOMEN IN THE
PROFESSION

The Commission on the Status of Women exists not because of the Modern Language Association and not because of the New University Conference, but rather because, after a pause of more than forty years, women are once again involved in open struggles for freedom, independence, dignity, and power. Whether we in this room know it or not and whether we like it or not, we in MLA, along with our sisters in the American Sociological Association, the American Psychological Association, and other associations, are part of the professional wing of a national movement of women. The movement is just that: Largely unconsolidated, and mostly without clear channels of communications, there are hundreds of women's liberation groups in cities and on campuses across the country, and there are larger organizations of professional women like NOW (National Organization of Women) or of welfare mothers, like the National Welfare Rights Organization. There has also been a response to the womens' movement: a new Presidential Commission has been appointed, for example, and the American Association of University Women, which twelve years ago abandoned its standing committee on the status of women on the theory that all problems had been solved, has recently reorganized itself to focus once again on issues of discrimination. With all this, we are only at the very beginning of a long and difficult series of tasks. I know also that, as teachers of language and literature, our role is crucial.

It is not simply that discrimination against women in all but a few professions is a fact of life; it is not simply that women in educational institutions do not have the national legislative protection afforded to Blacks and women in the Civil Rights Act of 1964; it is not even that women's legal rights with regard to their bodies still have to be won; it is rather that our social institutions—chiefly marriage and the family—have codified, and our economic institutions have incorporated, a particular role for women based on certain underlying assumptions about their alleged "nature."

Men have written in the myths we call the Old Testament, in the religion we call Christianity, and in the poetry and prose we call the classics that woman is man's inferior not simply biologically and intellectually but morally and emotionally. What is worse, women have believed it all, and still believe it. Teachers of language and literature have helped, as much as any other group, to propagate and proselytize these beliefs as stereotypes that keep women in their place. We share that guilt, men and women alike. We are awakening only slowly to our responsibility and power.

Let me put aside for a moment our own self-interest, the interest of women in the profession, to talk briefly about a larger and related problem, one that bears directly on the fact that the proportion of women choosing professions of any sort has been generally declining, in spite of the fact that proportion of women going to college has been increasing. In the 1940's women earned an average of 15% of all doctorates; in the 50's, 10%; in the sixties, 11%. Even more startling, the proportion of women teaching in colleges and universities has declined from 28% in 1940 to 22% in 1966, a figure very close to that of 1900—when the statistic was 19.7%. Even the proportion of women who are high school teachers has declined from 68% in the 1920's to 46% in 1966. But it is not only a question of statistics.

Why, for example, were fifth grade girls in a year-long study conducted by Paul Torrance, already convinced that girls can't solve scientific problems, even after they had solved such problems as well as boys? Why is it that in the early school years, girls learn more readily than boys and then tend to drop behind after adolescence? Why do our brightest female students suffer in college from what sociologists call "goal depression," the disease that tells them it's all too difficult, there's no use trying? When I went to graduate school twenty years ago, I did so at the urging of my college professors, but even then, and for a good portion of my professional life since, I believed it preferable and certainly more proper that I become the wife of a professor than the professor herself. A long-term sociological study of some 8,000 recent woman college graduates confirms my early view as not only still current but widespread. From college, as well as from the general environment, most women learn that family relationships will be "the primary source of satisfaction in their lives." Most women who are career-minded after marriage willingly put their careers in second-place to their husbands'. They have been taught by their culture and their teachers to keep their place. Our responsibility, as members of the Commission and as members of the educational establishment, is to undertake seriously the education of women.

The larger problem I have sketched is also relevant to those relatively few women who have altogether different aspirations, who are passionate about their work, and who can share that work with a personal life. For none of them, at least in my experience and study, ever escapes wholly the cultural net. As it has for Black people, the struggle for independence both scars and strengthens women. Thus, some professionals take the position that the rest of womankind is merely shiftless, lazy, and unintelligent. Others find it impossible to speak publicly. Many of us find it extraordinarily difficult to push in where we are not welcome. For these reasons and others, the question of discrimination is complex: who can charge department chairmen if no women have, indeed, applied?

The Commission was asked to investigate "discriminatory practices" in order to *assure* "equitable standards." While it is evident that establishing standards or legislation, especially with the possibility of enforcement will be useful, such procedures alone won't change consciousness. And until consciousness about the nature of women is altered, until we destroy the idea that woman must be, as John Stuart Mill so aptly described her one hundred years ago, a "willing slave," we—and this is a much larger we than the Commission or the people in this room—won't have done our job.

The Commission considers that its responsibility is broadly educational and that it has at least a dual task, one for the immediate months ahead, and one for later. First, to uncover all there is to know about women in our profession so that we can, next December, recommend further action to improve that condition. We will be building on work that others have done: a recent study of women sociologists, a recent Yale study, and one sponsored in part by the MLA of women in some English departments. From these and others, we know several rough outlines: although the proportion of Ph.D.'s granted to women in particular graduate departments is well over 20%, and in some cases, well over 50%, the proportion of tenured women faculty in those departments is at best 2%. We know that where women are teaching in undergraduate institutions, it is at disproportionately lower ranks and at generally non-prestigious institutions. We know also that there has been a sharp decline in the number of women on faculties of women's colleges—at my own, for example, a decline of 27% in twenty-nine years. The best single statistic to demonstrate the place of women in our profession is that while 22% of all those who teach English in four year institutions are women, the comparable figure for two year junior and community colleges is twice that—44%. In short, we know enough to be concerned or alarmed—and this year's job maket can only make things worse for women.

But we know that there is a lot more to learn. Our study will include *all* modern language departments of colleges and universities in the MLA Directory, including two year colleges and graduate departments. We will ask questions about such matters as salary, rate of promotion, graduate students, nepotism practices, and perhaps the most unexplored subject of all, the use of part-time faculty. To ease our task, we should like one woman (or man, especially where there is no woman) in each department in as many institutions as possible to volunteer to help us with this study. We ask you to send us your names.

As a final part of this preliminary report, the Commission wishes to propose two motions to the Executive Council and to offer several guidelines to departments and members. We do this at the specific urging of a number of department chairmen.

THE GUIDELINES TO EQUITY

We recommend the following reforms to departments and institutions for discussion and adoption as policy. We should appreciate hearing from department chairmen, deans, and others who have discussed, adopted or dismissed our recommendations. These begin from a principle of equity between men and women: specifically, from the principle that in the case of a professional husband and wife, it is better that both careers be somewhat slowed through years of child-rearing than for the woman's to halt altogether. The principle assumes that it is not equitable to reward men and to punish women for marrying. To effect equity, we are, with one exception, proposing new forms of flexibility within existing institutional apparatus.

1. An easy transfer of graduate credits and fellowships from one school to another would facilitate the completion of studies interrupted by geographical necessity.

2. Half-time teaching or research appointments, with real half-time salaries, accumulation of tenure, etc., would allow men and women to rear children without an interruption in their professional lives.

3. An anti-nepotism rule would allow husbands and wives to share a single appointment and concomitant child-rearing responsibilities.

4. For women graduate students or faculty, who are raising children, we recommend extra stipends for child care.

5. For graduate students and faculty we recommend the establishment of university supported, parent-controlled day care centers.

TWO FINAL RECOMMENDATIONS

We recommend a conscious and continuing review of curriculum and texts by individuals and departments in order to establish criteria for the education of men and women with special regard to breaking down crippling sexual stereotypes. There is much to be done in this area, most of it still undiscovered. We recommend both that traditional courses be taught with new consciousness; and that new courses be attempted experimentally—in woman as archetype, for example. We should be glad to act as a clearing house and will publish reports of activities in this regard.

Finally, the MLA itself. Let it not be said that we omit the hand that feeds us. Anyone may calculate, with a little patience and arithmetic, the proportion of women who belong to the association—upwards of 25% and the proportion who have served on the Executive Council, for example since 1945—less than 1% And anyone may see that women answer MLA phones and men hold MLA press conferences. We recommend, therefore, that the MLA review its own councils, committees, editorial boards, and staff positions to achieve move equitable representation of its women members.

I wish to conclude by thanking the Commission members for their support, the NUC women for theirs, as well as the hand that feeds us. Many Council members have been supportive both with advice and funds to do the work we have cut out for ourselves. But 7 of us—5 women and 2 men—cannot do much without your help. I hope that many of you will come to the Implementation Workshop tomorrow morning to offer specific recommendations and to join us in our work. (And that those of you who read this will volunteer your services as well.)

First the motions: 1) Because we believe that salary scales of men and women ought to be equitable, we recommend that the MLA request that the American Association of University Professors include as a fixed item in their annual survey of academic salaries the salaries of men as compared to women. 2) Because we believe that laws are a useful means of beginning to effect change, we recommend that the MLA and individual members pressure the Congress for two amendments to Title VII of the Civil Rights Act. First, an end to the exemption of educational institutions from the law. Second, we recommend that to Title VII be added an amendment prohibiting discrimination based on marital status. Obviously women suffer more than men in this regard, both because of nepotism policies and the prejudice against both marriageable and married women of child-bearing age.

Departmental statistics won't tell us what we need to know about the patterns of individual careers and about the suffering and humiliation endured by scholars and teachers who happen to be women. And so the Commission is also going to write for publication a series of "case studies." Thus far, we have been collecting material only as it has come to us by chance: we have received, for example, a copy of a letter from the Dean of an important graduate school to a woman applying for a fellowship. I quote the essential sentence: "Though I do not doubt the sincerity of your intellectual aspirations, I do very much doubt the likelihood that the ordinary wife of a graduate student will go ahead and pursue a scholarly career after her husband achieves his degree and enters into a regular position." In the few days of this meeting, I have been told about several chairmen refusing quite openly to hire women. Many women have asked the Commission to organize itself as a "grievance committee." At its next meeting, the Commission needs to discuss that and other questions coming out of this Convention. In the meantime, we will be glad to accept letters and biographical accounts that document "discriminatory practices."

I mentioned a second educational task, one for the slightly more distant future, and one that the Commission has discussed only briefly thus far. We are drafting a proposal to the National Endowment for the Humanities for a study focussed on the relationship between the teaching of literature and the American woman's understanding of herself. Since such a study would involve the special areas of the MLA's professional competence, which extends not only to our students but to those who go on to teach our children, it might provide an exceptional opportunity to contribute to that broader problem of consciousness about which I spoke earlier. We should be glad to hear from you about this study.

[P.S. Fall 1969]

Women in Political Science: Some Preliminary Observations[1]

Victoria Schuck

A systematic study of the role of women academics in political science waits to be done. Evidence compiled from documentary sources, the results of a recent questionnaire sent to political science department chairmen, and statistics provided by biographical information in the 1968 Directory of the APSA suggest a certain patterning in the educational and academic life. But the gross statistics also raise questions which deserve further research.

Women have always been a part of the profession of political science. One present member of the APSA reports having received her Ph.D. in 1910, seven years after the Association was founded. Data on dissertations reveal that the first generation of female political scientists constituted a rather exclusive band who sought graduate work and

1 The writer is indebted to James M. Bruce and Marjorie S. Childers of the Sociology Department at Mount Holyoke College for their suggestions on the presentation of the data; to Mae C. King, Staff Associate of the APSA for obtaining statistics on women members of the Association from the 1968 Biographical Directory; and to Nan W. Bauer, Sandra K. Borys, Susan A. Shapiro, Holly Sidford, and Gill B. Singer, Mount Holyoke undergraduates for assisting in the processing of the questionnaire.

published along with their male fellow scholars. Between 1912 and 1920 women wrote seven of the 125 dissertations in political science which were published. From one or two·a year published in that period, the number increased to four or five, or a total of 11.7 percent, in the decade of the '20s and early '30s (1920-1933).[2]

The first generation of women political scientists came of age with the successful drive for women's suffrage and the flourishing of women's colleges. Having achieved doctoral degrees and gained academic positions, they concluded that a woman henceforth need only qualify herself professionally to win recognition commensurate with her qualifications and abilities. They believed by the end of the '20s that sex discrimination was buried; what counted were the qualifications of the individual.[3]

Two developments in the '30s and '40s coupled with a changed view of woman's role in the society in the late '40s and throughout the '50s, led to "the great withdrawal" of professional women from academic pursuits generally and political science specifically. First there was the depression when resources for graduate financing were scarce, and when career expectations for women were often nonexistent because of the one-job-per-family rule and that normally for the male. Secondly there were the distractions of the war, and finally in its aftermath developed the attitude that the role of women should be to return to "real values" and "real femininity" — that women were greater powers for good when exerting their influence on children and the home rather than competing with men.[4]

The proportion of women receiving doctorates in political science from the mid '30s through the '50s would seem to corroborate these conclusions. It is true that in terms of absolute numbers — and they are always small — no diminution has taken place in the total number of women awarded Ph.D.'s in political science in any decade.[5] Indeed, except for the twenty-year period 1930-1949, when numbers barely increased, the total number of women awarded degrees in political science doubled and redoubled in each ten-year period. At the same time, the ratio of women to men receiving doctorates fell from the peaks of 9.7 percent in the second half of the '20s and 10.0 in the first half of the '30s to 5.8 in the '50s and remained substantially below the proportion of women awarded Ph.D.'s in all fields, political science and other.[6] (See Table 1.)

The arresting in the '60s of the decline in political science degrees awarded to women is attributable to the number of women receiving doctorates in 1967 and 1968, which is within a percentage point of the total proportion of Ph.D.'s awarded to women in all fields.[7] The increasing numbers have come at a time of resurgence in radical politics coincidentally supporting a stronger role for women. A result has been greatly increased pressures for women to act as a group. Unlike the women of the '20s, the women of the '60s do not wish to leave the role definition of women in political science solely to individuals.[8] They wish to define the role collectively.

---

2   The total includes theses listed in political science, international law and relations, and public administration. Institutions awarding Ph.D.'s customarily required publication until the early '30s when the practice began to wane. The Library of Congress list of printed doctoral dissertations began in 1912 and is used as a source through 1933.

3   The testimony of several faculty women, American and European, who received their Ph.D.'s in the 1920's.

4   See Jessie Bernard, *Academic Women*, Pennsylvania Park, Pennsylvania, The Pennsylvania State University Press, 1964.

5   The median number of Ph.D.'s won by women 1940-1949 was 5, minimum 1 and maximum 14. For 1950-1959, median 11.5, maximum 15 and minimum 7. For 1960-1968, median 21, maximum 65, and minimum 12.

6   Figures for Ph.D.'s completed do not always agree. In the '20s, '30s, and '40s, when reports were biennial, the annual figures were arrived at by interpolation. See "Earned Doctorates in the Social Sciences . . . by Subject and Institution," *American Universities and Colleges* 8th-10th ed., 1966-1968, pp. 1692-1693; U. S. Library of Congress, Catalog Division, *A List of Doctoral Dissertations. . . .* Washington, D.C., U.S. Government Printing Office, 1921 ff.; *Index to American Doctoral Dissertations, Combined with Dissertation Abstracts. . . .* Compiled for the Association of Research Libraries, University Microfilms, Inc., Ann Arbor, Michigan, 1958 ff.; U.S. Office of Education, *Earned Degrees Conferred by Higher Educational Institutions*, 1955-56, Washington, D.C., U.S. Government Printing Office, 1957; U.S. Bureau of the Census, *Statistical Abstract of the United States*, Washington, D.C., U.S. Government Printing Office, 1956 ff. If these sources were used, the percent of Ph.D.'s received by females in political science would look like this:

1912-1920	5.9 (7)	1940-1949	6.4 (52)
1921-1929	10.1 (19)	1950-1959	5.8 (113)
1930-1939	8.8 (45)	1960-1968	8.6 (234)

    The percent of females receiving Ph.D.'s in the entire country would look like this:

1912-1920	12.6 (647)	1940-1949	14.1 (4450)
1921-1929	14.6 (1607)	1950-1959	9.8 (8239)
1930-1939	14.7 (4035)	1960-1968	11.3 (15.550)

    For Table 1, the National Academy of Sciences tables were selected as the most consistent through 1961.

7   The proportion of women in political science was 9.7 percent in 1967; for the country at large 11.3 in 1967; 11.4 percent for political science in 1968; and 12.5 for the country in 1968.

8   The rejection of the "feminine mystique" and the ingesting of the middle aged woman into the labor force, both phenomena being forerunners of the present professional movements, began in the early '60's. Women in professional groups have sought and been sought by the radical left groups. A petition at the fall meeting of the Association in 1968 urged the APSA Council to establish a special commission for the study of the status of women within the profession. The Caucus for a New Political Science elected a woman to its governing offices in 1968. The Caucus submitted a resolution of the status of women for consideration of the APSA Council in the spring of 1969. A representative of the Caucus in consultation with the APSA Committee on the Status of Women in the Profession worked out a modification of the resolution, and this was approved with some additions at the business meeting of the Association in New York in September 1969. See as typical of popular discussion "Woman's Changing Role in America," in U.S. News and World Report, September 8, 1969, pp. 44-46; Sherry Petchul, "Woman's Liberation, the Longest Revolution?" in Christian Science Monitor, October 7, 1969.

Questionnaire

The APSA Committee on the Status of Women in the Profession, appointed in March 1969, sent a questionnaire to chairmen of political science departments and graduate schools last May. The Committee asked four questions: the number of faculty in political science and the distribution by rank and sex; the number of undergraduate majors by sex; the number of M. A. and Ph.D. candidates by sex; and the number of students applying for admission to graduate school for the fall term 1969-70 and the number accepted, by sex.

Replies to one round of mailing came from 473 chairmen or 51.4 percent of the total mailing list of the Association. In some geographic areas fewer colleges and universities responded than in others. The greatest proportion of nonreplies came from the South and so called border states (59.1 and 54.7 percent respectively). Next in descending order of response were institutions located in New England (48.7 percent), the Middle Atlantic states (46.3), the Midwest (44.1), Southwest (43.7) and Mountain states (38.0). The Northwest produced the fewest nonreplies (36 percent).

In terms of size and character of departments, 59 percent of the nonreplies are from institutions with no faculty in political science (31.9 percent) or from institutions with faculty in combined departments (history and political science or social sciences, 27.3 percent). Although institutions with no political science or combined departments are

statistically overrepresented, the no-department replies do not affect results of the present investigation. Those with combined departments are difficult to separate for analysis and have little effect on results. The only other category which is overrepresented comprises small institutions with faculty from one to five members, including especially the private women's college and private coeducational institutions. This group, representing 25.4 percent of the nonrespondents, might affect the sample if institutions not replying have no women faculty. But no evidence of this effect has appeared, nor is there reason to believe that the nonrespondents differ substantially from the sample.[9]

Replies have been classified by size of department and type of institution — whether private or public, coeducational, women's or men's, and whether offering undergraduate work only or both undergraduate and graduate degrees. Undergraduate and graduate enrollments for 1968-69 and admission figures for the fall of 1969 are also tabulated. The purpose is to determine whether these variables are related to the presence or absence of women faculty and women students.

The survey covers 473 departments of political science ranging from 0 faculty to 63, with a total of 4,401 members. (See Table 2.) Seven colleges report no faculty in political science. Public coeducational institutions make up 44 percent of the sample; private coeducational, 36; and private women's and men's institutions, about 16 percent. The "other" category includes public institutions for men when these are not specifically noted. If one looks first at the table indicating the number of departments with and without women members, one sees that more than half report none. As Table 3 indicates, women are by no means evenly distributed among institutions which do have female faculty (49.5 percent). The distribution depends on the type and size of college or university. Some 76 percent of the institutions having women are in the "small department" categories (0-15). There appears to be no significant difference between the percentages provided by public and private coeducational colleges in the "small department" categories. But the larger the department, the more likely it is to have women. The largest public coeducational institutions — state universities and city universities — all report

---

Data on Women in the Profession from the National Register Survey*

Total Political Responses	5176
Women Responses	474

Degrees Held

Ph.D.	207
M.A.	251
B.A.	14
No Report	2

Type of Employer

Educational Institution	333
Federal Government	25
Other Government	14
Non-Profit	26
Business and Industry	7
Self-Employed	5
Military	1
Other	3
Not employed	51
No Report	9

Years of Employment and Salary

Years		Median Salary
1 or less	54	$8200
2-4	130	8800
5-9	100	9500
10-14	39	11900
15-19	27	
20-24	22	
25-29	12	
30-34	16	
35-39	6	
40+	7	
No Report	61	

Salary		$9700

Overall Women

Ph.D. Median	11000
M.A. Median	8500

*As part of the continuing series of reports of data from the APSA-NSF Register Project, the following information is provided to political scientists. An extensive article on the subject follows.

---

9   The writer wishes to express appreciation to the Committee on the Status of Women in the Profession for use of the data which are available with the permission of the Committee.

The nonresponse from institutions in the 6-10 faculty group was 8.3 percent; in the 11-15 group, 2.5 percent; in the 16-25; 3.7 percent; and in the 26+, 92 percent. The faculty members in the nonresponding combined departments total 921 and in other nonresponding departments 1,101, making a grand total of 2,022. Faculty data on nonresponding departments, compiled from American Universities and Colleges, 10th edition, Washington, D.C., American Council on Education, 1968. Seventy-five women's colleges, many of which are church related, did not respond. Some 47 of them have no political science faculty or have a combined department. Eighteen in the 1-5 faculty range did not respond.

having women on the faculty. The major difference however is not one of size but type of institution; more all-women's colleges have women faculty than do all other kinds of institutions. On faculties of institutions exclusively for men, women are clearly underrepresented.

If one examines the table (see 4a) showing the ratio of women to men faculty members in all kinds of institutions, it is equally clear that the small departments have the highest proportion of women. The 1969 questionnaire shows women's colleges having two women faculty for every one elsewhere. In the same year the private men's college would seem to be almost impossible of access for a woman faculty member. Moreover the larger the department, the smaller the proportion of women in political science would seem to be. Table 4b reveals proportionately more women than men teaching in institutions which offer undergraduate work only. The table implies 44.4 percent of women in strictly undergraduate institutions, and 29.0 men faculty teaching undergraduates only.

What about the rank of women on college faculties? Tables 5 and 6 indicate that if most institutions do not have women to begin with, those that do usually have no more than one or two. The size of the institution makes little difference to the proportion. One might think that the larger the department, the more women in each rank, but with few exceptions this is not so. Most women, in all institutions, are concentrated in the lower ranks. Although the rank of instructor is disappearing, the ratio of women to men on this level is two to one. As numbers of all faculty in all ranks increase, it is still less and less likely that there will be more than one woman in each except in that of assistant professor. A woman who is a full professor is almost an exception; tenured positions at all levels appear to be a masculine preserve. In short, tokenism is the prevailing pattern, other than in the women's colleges, and in few of them do women constitute a majority in a department.[10]

The "differential access" to scholarship and teaching which the above paragraphs and tables bring out might be indicated by another measurement. If one takes the twenty departments de-

scribed as "distinguished" or the ten producing the greatest number of doctorates, and compares the proportion of women by rank at these institutions with all others in the sample, the smaller proportion of women in the prestigious ten or twenty becomes apparent. (See Table 7.)

But before one labels all of this discrimination by sex, it should be noted that the "withdrawal" of the '40s and '50s meant almost a couple of generations of women lost to research and teaching in political science. Then too the greater proportion of jobs in the small colleges means that women have heavier teaching schedules and less and less time as well as facilities for research.

Several explanations may account for the higher ratio of women in the lower untenured ranks: the recency of their appointments, their possession of fewer advanced degrees, and their youth. About as many have received doctorates in the present decade as in all the years from 1910 to 1959 (246 to 257).[11] Information presented in the *Biographical Directory* suggests the youthfulness of the women in the Association holding Ph.D.'s:[12]

Number and Years in Which Women Received Doctorates

Year	Number	%
1967-1960	117	56.0
1959-1950	52	24.9
1949-1940	16	7.7
1939-1930	17	8.1
1929-1920	7	3.3
(1910)	(1)	
	209	100.0

The total number of women in teaching, according to the 1968 *Directory*, is 404, or five percent of the entire professional membership — men and women. There is no knowing at this time how the Committee's sample, the membership data from the *Directory*, and the totals of women receiving graduate degrees as given in the Statistical Abstracts can be reconciled.

The pattern of appointments to academic positions may also be a reflection of the problem of meeting the requirements of a particular field. According to

---

10 It should be noted that the maximum number of women reported was seven at San Fernando Valley State College in California, which is in the 26+ grouping. Two institutions have six women: San Jose State College and Brooklyn College, each in the 26+ faculty category. Three institutions report five women each: Michigan State University in the 26+ category; California State College at Fullerton and the University of Minnesota School of Public Administration in the 16-25 group. Eleven institutions report 4 faculty women each: Georgetown, Florida State, American, University of Maryland, Indiana University, UC at Berkeley, and the City University of New York, in the 26+ group; Montana State College of Mineral Science and Technology in the 11-15 group; and Barnard, Trinity College, and Tennessee State University at Nashville in the 6-10

group. Six women's colleges indicate a majority of women in their departments.

11 The National Science Foundation, National Register Survey for 1968 gives the number of women holders of Ph.D.'s as 207 and M.A.'s as 251 (474 responses).

12 Almost 39 percent of the women listed in the *Directory* gave no information about themselves. The data were compiled by Mae C. King, staff associate, APSA. Also see "Women in the Political Science Profession," Washington, D.C., APSA, October 1968 (mimeograph) and "Women in the Political Science Profession — 1969 Addition to the October 1968 Report," APSA, October 1969 (mimeograph).

the *Directory,* the first fields of women in 1967 were:[13]

	Number	%
Public Administration	20	2.4
Political Theory — normative and historical	95	11.4
International Politics, Organization, Administration and Foreign Policy	113	13.6
American Government, Voting Behavior, Legislatures, Metropolitan Government, State and Local, Administration, Constitutional Law, etc.	113	13.6
Comparative Government and Political Development	490	59.0
	831	100.0

Whatever the reason — for example, the availability of foundation support and scholarships — which may have lured them into comparative governments and development, it has not always been easy to find the right women for teaching positions.

It is likely that the absolute numbers of professional women in political science, if not the proportion, will grow. The questionnaire produced the following totals of undergraduate majors which are indicative:[14]

Undergraduate Political Science Majors — Spring 1969

Number Females	Number Males	% Females	No Breakdown Given	Total Enrollment
11,670	38,661	23.2	8,051	58,381

The number of women in graduate school is considerably less — 17.5 percent of the over-all graduate enrollment. (See Tables 8, 9.) Not all institutions gave a breakdown of their figures, but it is clear that there are more candidates for the M.A. (20.6 percent) than for the doctorate (14.7 percent).

The proportion of women admitted to graduate work for the fall of 1969 seems to have increased, for returns to the questionnaire indicate that they were 22.9 percent of the acceptances (they were 20.8 percent of the applicants). Put another way, 43.2 percent of the male applicants were accepted and 48.9 percent of the female. The most likely explanation for this ratio of women to men is that it represents a hedge against the draft — an assurance that graduate departments will maintain full programs throughout the year. (See Table 10.)

Increasingly the question is being asked, why the great disparity in the proportion of men and women in graduate work? A recent HEW study points to marriage, work begun immediately after graduation, and competing fields such as law and urban studies as partial answers.[15] It may well be inferred that many large graduate departments in political science have found women poor risks for limited fellowship money, because of the high drop-out rate for marriage. The very best women receive awards. But in the middle ranks, most departments place their bets on men.

There is the further question as to how much the socialization of the eventual graduate student in political science is dependent upon his having models among his undergraduate and graduate instructors in the field. Typically 50 percent of the graduate students in any field are drawn from undergraduate non-majors, and there is no information to indicate that graduate students in political science are any different.[16] And yet it is often argued that a woman needs role models to cite women as a reference group. Young women, it is contended, find incentives to study and scholarship in joining faculty women as well as men at the undergraduate and graduate level. The evidence provided by the questionnaire suggests that in small departments more women on the faculty will lead to more undergraduate majors, but as departments become larger, this pattern does not hold. Data on graduate enrollment show certain inconsistencies, although it may be possible to say that there are slightly more women candidates in departments where women are faculty members. (See Table 9.)

If the distribution suggests discrimination, this inference cannot be proved until more is learned from individual faculty members at every kind of institution about their experience in undergraduate and graduate school, and in teaching and research. More information is also necessary from graduate students about their backgrounds, characteristics, and education generally. Meanwhile, it may be remarked that the almost instinctive movement of women to form a Women's Caucus in the Association in the past year is a reaction to a minority position in the Association and also in the teaching ranks. But this minority status has a history and can be related to the age of women political scientists, their traditional minority status, and the kinds of institutions that appoint them. Over the years, the proportionate numbers of women in political science have dipped and then risen, so that they are now more in line with the proportion of doctorates granted over-all in the United States. The appointment of more than one or two women by some state colleges (albeit often converted teachers colleges) and by large state and city universities and the increased numbers admitted to candidacy for advanced degrees may well be more than straws in the wind. They may definitely presage alteration of the minority status for women. Only after further accumulation and study of all evidence and factors can the complexities of the whole question of women's role and prospects in political science be defined and met.

13 *Ibid.* The category "American Govrnment . . ." is an ad hoc catch-all one, because the members in specific fields are too small to be meaningful otherwise. For comparisons with holders of doctorates in all fields see *P.S.* Winter 1969, vol. 2, pp. 12-13 and Summer 1969, vol. 2, p. 54. In 1963 Somit and Tanenhaus listed the proportion of political scientists in each field American Government, 48 percent; International Relations, 20 percent; Comparative Government and Political Theory, each 12 percent. See Albert Somit and Joseph Tanenhaus, *American Political Science,* New York,

New York, The Atherton Press, 1967, p. 54.

14 Eleven percent (53) of the institutions in the sample either listed "no major" (35) or omitted the number (18).

15 U.S. Department of Health, Education and Welfare, *Special Report on Women and Graduate Study, Resources for Medical Research,* Report No. 13, June 1968, Washington, D.C., U.S. Government Printing Office.

16 *Ibid.*

Table 1. Number of Women Receiving Ph.D.'s — 1912-1968

Ph.D.'s in Political Science

Years	Female	Male and Female	% of Female
1912-19	7	118	5.9
1920-29	25	299	8.4
1930-39	53	568	9.3
1940-49	59	687	8.6
1950-59	113	1,953	5.8
1960-68	246	2,821	8.7

Total Ph.D.'s in U.S.

Female	Male and Female	% of Female
4,525	554	12.2
1,816	11,889	15.3
3,763	25,586	14.7
4,092	30,555	13.4
8,208	82,814	9.9
15,680	138,153	11.4

Source: National Academy of Science — National Research Council, *Doctorate Production in the United States Universities 1920-1962* . . . compiled by Lindsey R. Harmon and Herbert Soldz, Washington, D.C., Publication No. 1142, National Academy of Sciences; U.S. Bureau of the Census. *Statistical Abstract of the United States,* Washington, D.C., U.S. Government Printing Office, 1964 ff.

Source: Office of Scientific Personnel, *Summary Report 1968 Doctorate Recipients from U.S. Universities,* prepared in the Education Employment Section, Manpower Studies Branch, OSP-MS-Z, Ap. 1969, Washington, D.C.

Table 2. Number and Percent of Departments of Political Science by Size Responding to Questionnaire

Size of Department	Number of Departments	% of Sample	Number of Faculty Members	% of Faculty Members	Faculty Average Size
0 - 5	230	48.6	685	15.6	3.0
6 - 10	102	21.6	749	17.0	7.3
11 - 15	65	13.7	827	18.8	12.7
16 - 25	39	8.3	786	17.8	20.2
26+	37	7.8	1,354	30.8	36.6
Total	473	100.0	4,401	100.0	9.3

Number of Institutions by Size of Department and Type of Institution

Size of Department	Public Coeducational Number	%	Private Coeducational Number	%	Private Women's College Number	%	Private Men's College Number	%	Other Number	%	Total
0 - 5	63	27.4	108	47.0	31	13.5	16	6.9	12	5.2	230
6 - 10	46	45.1	30	29.4	8	7.8	14	13.7	4	3.9	102
11 - 15	43	66.2	16	24.6	1	1.5	5	7.7	0	—	65
16 - 25	29	74.4	10	25.6	0	—	0	—	0	—	39
26+	27	73.0	6	16.2	0	—	3	8.1	1	2.7	37
Total	208	44.0	170	35.9	40	8.5	38	8.0	17	3.6	473

Table 3. Number and Percentage of Departments With Women on the Faculty

Size of Department	Public Coeducational With Females	%	Private Coeducational With Females	%	Private Women's College With Females	%	Private Men's College With Females	%	Other With Females	%	Total With Females	%
0 - 5	22	34.9	35	32.4	18	58.1	4	25.0	2	16.7	81	35.2
6 - 10	24	52.2	17	56.7	6	75.0	2	14.3	1	25.0	50	49.0
11 - 15	34	79.1	11	68.8	1	100.0	1	20.0	0	—	47	72.3
16 - 25	19	65.5	5	50.0	0	—	0	—	0	—	24	61.5
26+	27	100.0	4	66.7	0	—	1	33.3	0	—	32	86.5
Total	126	60.6	72	42.4	25	62.5	8	21.1	3	17.6	234	49.5

Table 4a. Number of Faculty Members by Size of Department and by Type of Institution

Size of Department		Public Coeducational		Private Coeducational		Private Women's College		Private Men's College		Public Men's College		Other		Total	
		Male	Female	Male	Female	Male	Female	Male	Female	Male	Female	Male	Female	Male	Female
0 - 5	Number	183	29	267	38	51	21	47	5	13	0	29	2	590	95
	Percent	86.3	13.7	87.5	12.5	70.8	29.2	90.4	9.6	100.0	—	93.5	6.5	86.1	13.9
6 - 10	Number	315	37	193	19	49	17	93	2	6	0	17	1	673	76
	Percent	89.5	10.5	91.0	9.0	74.2	25.8	97.9	2.1	100.0	—	94.4	5.6	89.9	10.1
11 - 15	Number	494	55	183	16	12	2	65	0	0	0	0	0	754	73
	Percent	90.0	10.0	92.0	8.0	85.7	14.3	100.0	—	—	—	—	—	91.2	8.8
16 - 25	Number	570	34	175	7	0	0	0	0	0	0	0	0	745	41
	Percent	94.4	5.6	96.1	3.9	—	—	—	—	—	—	—	—	94.8	5.2
26+	Number	909	72	191	11	0	0	114	3	54	0	0	0	1,268	86
	Percent	92.7	7.3	94.6	5.4	—	—	97.4	2.6	100.0	—	—	—	93.6	6.4
Total	Number	2,471	227	1,009	91	112	40	319	10	73	0	46	3	4,030	371
	Percent	91.6	8.4	91.7	8.3	73.7	26.3	97.0	3.0	100.0	—	93.9	6.1	91.6	8.4

Table 4b. Distribution of Faculty by Department Size, Type of Institutions, and Undergraduate and Graduate Offerings

Size of Department		Public Coeducational			Private Coeducational			Private Women			Private Men			Public Men			Other			Total Faculty
		Undergraduate	Undergraduate and Graduate	Total	Undergraduate	Undergraduate and Graduate	Total	Undergraduate	Undergraduate and Graduate	Total	Undergraduate	Undergraduate and Graduate	Total	Undergraduate	Undergraduate and Graduate	Total	Undergraduate	Undergraduate and Graduate	Total	
0-5	Male Number	155	28	183	243	24	267	47	4	51	43	4	47	13	0	13	29	0	29	590
	Percent	84.7	15.3	100.0	91.9	8.9	100.0	92.2	7.8	100.0	91.5	8.5	100.0	100.0	—	100.0	100.0	—	100.0	
	Female Number	26	3	29	36	2	38	20	1	21	4	1	5	0	0	0	2	0	2	95
	Percent	89.7	10.3	100.0	94.7	5.3	100.0	95.2	4.8	100.0	80.0	20.0	100.0	—	—	—	100.0	—	100.0	
6-10	Male Number	164	151	315	134	59	193	44	5	49	74	19	93	6	0	6	11	6	17	673
	Percent	52.1	47.9	100.0	69.4	30.6	100.0	89.8	10.2	100.0	79.6	20.4	100.0	100.0	—	100.0	64.7	35.3	100.0	
	Female Number	25	12	37	14	5	19	14	3	17	1	1	2	0	0	0	1	0	1	76
	Percent	67.6	32.4	100.0	73.7	26.3	100.0	82.4	17.6	100.0	50.0	50.0	100.0	—	—	—	100.0	—	100.0	
11-15	Male Number	93	401	494	23	160	183	12	0	12	22	43	65	0	0	0	0	0	0	754
	Percent	18.8	81.2	100.0	12.6	87.4	100.0	100.0	—	100.0	33.8	66.2	100.0	—	—	—	—	—	—	
	Female Number	17	38	55	3	13	16	2	0	2	0	0	0	0	0	0	0	0	0	73
	Percent	30.9	69.1	100.0	18.8	81.2	100.0	100.0	—	100.0	—	—	—	—	—	—	—	—	—	
16-25	Male Number	0	570	570	0	175	175	0	0	0	0	0	0	0	0	0	0	0	0	745
	Percent	—	100.0	100.0	—	100.0	100.0	—	—	—	—	—	—	—	—	—	—	—	—	
	Female Number	0	34	34	0	7	7	0	0	0	0	0	0	0	0	0	0	0	0	41
	Percent	—	100.0	100.0	—	100.0	100.0	—	—	—	—	—	—	—	—	—	—	—	—	
26+	Male Number	0	909	909	0	191	191	0	0	0	0	114	114	54	0	54*	0	0	0	1,268
	Percent	—	100.0	100.0	—	100.0	100.0	—	—	—	—	100.0	100.0	100.0	—	100.0	—	—	—	
	Female Number	0	72	72	0	11	11	0	0	0	0	3	3	0	0	0	0	0	0	86
	Percent	—	100.0	100.0	—	100.0	100.0	—	—	—	—	100.0	100.0	—	—	—	—	—	—	
Total	Male Number	412	2,059	2,471	400	609	1,009	103	9	112	139	180	319	73	0	73	40	6	46	4,030
	Percent	16.7	83.3	100.0	39.6	60.4	100.0	92.0	8.0	100.0	43.6	56.4	100.0	100.0	—	100.0	87.0	13.0	100.0	
	Female Number	68	159	227	53	38	91	36	4	40	5	5	10	0	0	0	3	0	3	371
	Percent	30.0	70.0	100.0	58.2	41.8	100.0	90.0	10.0	100.0	50.0	50.0	100.0	—	—	—	100.0	—	100.0	

* U.S. Military Academy

Table 5. Number of Departments and Number of Faculty Women by Rank

Number of Females on Faculty	Instructor		Assistant Professor		Associate Professor		Full Professor		Other	
	Number of Departments	% of Total	Number of Departments	% of Total	Number of Departments	% of Total	Number of Departments	% of Total	Number of Departments	% of Total
0	393	83.1	373	78.9	417	88.2	426	90.1	445	94.1
1	69	14.6	83	17.5	54	11.4	43	9.1	19	4.0
2	9	1.9	15	3.2	2	.4	3	.6	3	.6
3+	2	.4	2	.4	0	0.0	1	.2	6	1.3
Total	473	100.0	473	100.0	473	100.0	473	100.0	473	100.0

Table 6. Distribution of Male and Female Faculty by Rank and Size of Department

Male

Size of Department	Instructor		Assistant Professor		Associate Professor		Full Professor		Other		Not Specified		Total
	Number	%	Number	%	Number	%	Number	%	Number	%	Number	%	
0 - 5	91	15.4	223	37.8	122	20.7	137	23.2	15	2.5	2	.4	590
6 - 10	105	15.6	222	33.0	151	22.4	160	23.8	29	4.3	6	.9	673
11 - 15	105	13.9	247	32.8	154	20.4	214	28.4	34	4.5	0	—	754
16 - 25	55	7.4	245	32.9	165	22.1	261	35.0	19	2.6	0	—	745
26+	101	8.0	350	27.5	222	17.5	261	36.0	139	11.0	0	.2	1268
Total	457	11.3	1287	31.9	814	20.2	1228	30.5	236	5.9	8	.2	4030

Female

Size of Department	Instructor		Assistant Professor		Associate Professor		Full Professor		Other		Not Specified		Total
	Number	%	Number	%	Number	%	Number	%	Number	%	Number	%	
0 - 5	25	26.3	31	32.6	21	22.1	12	12.6	4	4.2	2	2.2	95
6 - 10	23	30.3	20	26.3	9	11.8	13	17.1	5	6.6	6	7.9	76
11 - 15	24	32.9	21	28.8	11	15.1	10	13.7	7	9.5	0	—	73
16 - 25	8	19.5	19	46.3	5	12.2	5	12.2	4	9.8	0	—	41
26+	13	15.1	30	34.9	12	14.0	13	15.1	18	20.9	0	—	86
Total	93	25.1	121	32.6	58	15.6	53	14.3	38	10.2	8	2.2	371

Table 7a. Male and Female Faculty by Rank in "Distinguished" Departments Compared With all Other Departments in the Sample

Rank																		
	Instructor			Assistant Professor			Associate Professor			Full Professor			Other			Total		
Departments	M	F	% Females	M	F	% Females	M	F	% Females	M	F	% Females	M	F	% Females	M	F	% Females
Distinguished*	19	1	5.0	156	11	6.6	107	5	4.5	255	3	1.2	80	7	8.0	606	27	4.3
Other**	438	92	17.4	1131	110	8.8	707	53	7.0	973	50	4.9	156	31	16.6	3424	344	9.1

*18 institutions: Yale, Harvard, California (Berkeley), Chicago, Columbia, Princeton, Wisconsin, Stanford, Michigan, Cornell, Northwestern, California (UCLA), Indiana, North Carolina, Minnesota, Illinois, Johns Hopkins, Duke. (Syracuse and MIT omitted — did not respond to questionnaire.) For classifications see Albert Somit and Joseph Tanenhaus, *The Development of Political Science from Burgess to Behavioralism*, Boston, Allyn & Bacon, Inc., 1967, p. 164.

**455 institutions.

Table 7b. Male and Female Faculty by Rank in "Largest Producers of Doctorates" Compared With all Other Departments in the Sample

Rank																		
	Instructor			Assistant Professor			Associate Professor			Full Professor			Other			Total		
Departments	M	F	% Females	M	F	% Females	M	F	% Females	M	F	% Females	M	F	% Females	M	F	% Females
Largest Producers*	21	1	4.5	86	5	5.5	60	4	6.3	160	3	1.8	31	4	11.4	358	17	4.5
Other**	436	92	17.4	1201	116	8.8	754	54	6.7	1068	50	4.5	205	34	14.2	3672	354	8.8

*institutions: Columbia, Chicago, Harvard, NYU, American, Yale, California (Berkeley), Princeton, Michigan. (Syracuse omitted — did not respond to questionnaire.) For classifications see Somit and Tanenhaus, *op. cit.*, p. 159.

**464 institutions.

Table 8. Graduate Enrollment in Political Science Classified by Size of Departments — Spring 1969

Total Graduate Enrollment*

Size of Department	Female	Percent	Male	Percent	Total
0 - 5	17	23.0	57	77.0	74
6 - 10	110	19.4	456	80.6	566
11 - 15	278	20.3	1,093	79.7	1,371
16 - 25	340	13.4	2,197	86.6	2,537
26+	879	18.6	3,851	81.4	4,730
Totals	1,624	17.5	7,654	82.5	9,278
No Breakdown					1,016 (9.9%)
Grand Total			(11 institutions)		10,294

M. A. Candidates

Size of Department	Female	Percent	Male	Percent	Total
0 - 5	11	19.3	46	80.7	57
6 - 10	105	22.1	370	77.9	475
11 - 15	235	23.5	766	76.5	1,001
16 - 25	248	17.2	1,191	82.8	1,439
26+	532	21.2	1,982	78.8	2,514
Totals	1,131	20.6	4,355	79.4	5,486
No Breakdown					556 (9.2%)
Grand Total			(13 institutions)		6,042

PH. D. Candidates

Size of Department	Female	Percent	Male	Percent	Total
0 - 5	1	25.0	3	75.0	4
6 - 10	3	7.5	37	92.5	40
11 - 15	43	12.3	307	87.7	350
16 - 25	140	13.7	882	86.3	1,022
26+	352	15.7	1,887	84.3	2,239
Totals	539	14.7	3,116	85.3	3,655
No Breakdown					579 (13.7%)
Grand Total			(13 institutions)		4,234

*Total Graduate Enrollment includes persons not in a degree program.

Table 9. Graduate Enrollment in Political Science and Departments by Number of Females on The Faculty — Spring 1969

Number of Female Faculty	Graduates 462 Institutions				M.A. 460 Institutions				Ph.D. 460 Institutions			
	Male	Female	Total	% Female	Male	Female	Total	% Female	Male	Female	Total	% Female
0	2,301	383	2,684	14.3	1,218	296	1,514	19.6	984	149	1,133	13.2
1	2,029	468	2,497	18.7	1,173	338	1,511	22.4	750	109	859	12.7
2	897	150	1,047	14.3	623	94	717	13.1	268	55	323	17.0
3+	2,427	623	3,050	20.4	1,341	403	1,744	23.1	1,114	226	1,340	16.9
Total	7,654	1,624	9,278	17.5	4,355	1,131	5,486	20.6	3,116	539	3,655	14.7

Table 10. Number of Male and Female Applicants Admitted to Graduate Study — Fall 1969

Size of Department	Number Male Applicants	Number Male Accepted	% Male	Number Female Applicants	Number Female Accepted	% Female	Total Applicants	Total Accepted	Total
0 - 5	238	45	18.9	21	8	38.1	259	53	20.5
6 - 10	423	323	76.4	184	143	77.7	607	507	76.8
11 - 15	738	393	53.3	228	114	50.0	966	466	52.5
16 - 25	1,875	905	48.3	387	187	48.3	2,262	1,092	48.3
26+	4,728	1,787	37.8	1,280	575	44.9	6,008	2,362	39.3
Total	8,002	3,453	43.2	2,100	1,027	48.9	10,102	4,480	44.3

STATEMENT OF WOMEN'S RIGHTS COMMITTEE OF NEW YORK UNIVERSITY
SCHOOL OF LAW

LAW SCHOOL DISCRIMINATION AS A NATIONAL PROBLEM

At the first National Conference of Women Law Students held at NYU this Spring, women testified at length about discrimination. These women came from law schools across the country—from Hastings and Berkeley in California, from Duke in North Carolina, from Michigan and Minnesota, from Yale and Harvard, and many other schools. It would fill several weeks of testimony to describe and detail all of the examples of discrimination which were discussed and related at that Conference. The very fact that there was such an over-whelming response to our Committee's invitation to spend a weekend discussing discrimination against women, by so many women law students from so many different schools, is a sign of how serious and pervasive the problem of dis-crimination is.

The catalogue of discriminatory policies and practices and incidents which we have experienced at NYU and which we have described today, is virtually duplicated at every law school which was represented in the Conference. It

TABLE I.—DISTRIBUTION OF WOMEN FACULTY AT LEADING AMERICAN LAW SCHOOLS

School	Number of women	Total number of faculty
Boston University	1	50
Columbia University	1	63
Cornell University	0	23
Duke University	0	19
Fordham University	0	31
Georgetown University	1	70
George Washington University	2	88
Harvard	1	82
Indiana University:		
Bloomington	1	25
Indianapolis	1	21
Loyola University (California)	1	34
Marquette University	1	21
New York University	2	149
Ohio State	1	39
Rutgers (Camden and Newark)	4	43
St. John's University	0	37
Stanford University	0	36
Temple University	1	48
University of California, Berkeley	1	45
University of Chicago	1	39
University of Connecticut	0	41
University of Florida	2	37
University of Iowa	0	34
University of Maine	0	12
University of Maryland	0	30
University of Michigan	1	62
University of Minnesota	0	38
University of Missouri:		
Columbia	1	17
Kansas	2	23
University of North Carolina	0	26
University of Oregon	0	16
University of Pennsylvania	0	38
University of Southern California	3	53
University of Texas	1	52
University of Virginia	1	52
University of Wisconsin	1	40
Wayne State	1	31
Yale	2	60
Total	35	1,625

Note: The following table is a breakdown of the number of women faculty (35) according to professorial title:

Assistant or associate professor	8
Instructor or lecturer	6
Librarian or librarian-assistant professor	9
Professor	7
Research assistant professor	1
Visiting associate professor	4
Total	35

Source: All of the above statistics have been compiled from the Association of American Law Schools Directory of Law Teachers, 1968–70.

is not too difficult to infer that the discrimination is duplicated on *every* law school campus.

The Association of American Law Schools is another illustration of the national scope of the problem of discrimination against women. The Articles of the AALS, which set forth policies and guidelines binding upon member law schools, contain, to date, not a single reference to or admonition against discrimination against women. This year the AALS created the Committee on Women in Legal Education to suggest some amendments to the Articles to deal with sex-based discrimination. While the Committee is now preparing certain proposals to present to the AALS Convention this Winter, Committee members have already expressed fears that policy positions barring discrimination against women will cause some member law schools to threaten to disaffiliate from the AALS, rather than to submit to such anti-discrimination pressures. This deepseated resistance to breaking down the barriers against women further points up the need for federal legislation and enforcement. AALS guidelines and arguments of moral suasion will not prevent law schools which resent and resist the influx of women into law from using their institutional power to continue to discriminate against women.

TABLE II.—FEMALE LAW SCHOOL ENROLLMENT AS OF FALL, 1969

School	Total enrollment	Female enrollment	Percent female students
Boston University	965	138	14
Brooklyn	1,048	75	7
University of California (Berkeley)	792	95	12
University of California (Hastings)	1,171	82	7
University of California (Los Angeles)	765	73	9
University of Chicago	459	71	15
Columbia University	989	99	10
Cornell University	400	17	4
Duke University	307	22	7
Fordham University	760	53	7
Georgetown University	1,300	110	8
George Washington University	1,659	145	8
Harvard University	1,649	124	7
Howard University	364	68	19
University of Illinois	637	35	5
Indiana University (Bloomington)	422	26	6
Indiana University (Indianapolis)	654	41	6
University of Iowa	429	23	5
University of Kansas	279	9	3
Loyola University (Chicago)	403	27	7
University of Maryland	535	43	8
University of Maine	138	8	6
University of Michigan	1,052	71	7
University of Minnesota	591	49	8
University of Mississippi	332	23	7
University of Missouri (Columbia)	362	11	3
University of Montana	122	2	2
University of Nebraska	330	8	2
University of New Mexico	182	16	9
New York University	2,094	239	11
State University of New York (Buffalo)	485	20	4
University of North Carolina	545	25	5
University of North Dakota	120	2	2
Northwestern University	516	53	10
University of Notre Dame	344	20	6
Ohio State University	450	22	5
University of Oregon	293	16	5
University of Pennsylvania	528	54	10
Rutgers (Camden)	223	10	5
Rutgers (Newark)	422	54	13
St. John's University	806	31	4
University of South Carolina	496	9	2
University of South Dakota	159	7	4
University of Southern California (Gould)	1,143	79	7
Stanford University	426	59	14
Syracuse University	388	14	4
University of Tennessee	357	16	4
University of Texas	1,468	106	7
Vanderbilt University	363	12	3
University of Virginia	806	49	6
Wake Forest University	189	3	2
Washington & Lee University	178	0	0
University of Wisconsin	729	51	7
Yale University	588	74	13

Note: The above statistics are taken from Law Schools and Bar Admission Requirements in the United States, published by the section of Legal Education and Admissions to the Bar, fall 1969.

STATEMENT SUBMITTED BY THE NATIONAL ASSOCIATION OF WOMEN LAWYERS

By Margaret Laurance

My name is Margaret Laurance and I am an attorney practicing here in Washington.

I am here as a representative of the National Association of Women Lawyers (NAWL) and am Chairman of their Status of Women Committee. This organization, founded at the turn of the century, is the prominent women's organization for attorneys. It undertakes through a membership of over 1,200 to promote the interests and welfare of women lawyers through aiding in the enactment of legislation for the common good and in the administration of justice.

Bill, H.R. 16098 (in particular Section 805), is quite relevant to women lawyers and to the continued discriminatory and discouraging treatment from the legal profession, both in industry and government.

NAWL being keenly aware of discrimination against women in law schools, the existant double-standards of pay, responsibility, advancement, hiring and recruitment of women lawyers passed the following resolution February 21, 1970.

"On August 8, 1968, the NAWL conference resolved to take immediate action in support of pending legislation . . . to amend the civil rights act which would charge the U.S. Civil Rights Commission to putting forth efforts to eliminate sex discrimination in all areas of civil rights in addition to its current responsibilities in regard to race discrimination. Such discrimination is recognized and admitted to by Deans of various law schools including Dean Murray Schwartz of UCLA."

The *Muller* v. *Oregon* [1] Supreme Court decision enunciated the principle that sex is a basis for classification and thus women as a *class* could be denied equal protection under the 14th Amendment. Through the Civil Rights Act of 1964 [2] addition of the word "sex", the enacting of some legislation protecting rights of women in the labor area has developed, and changed the impetus and direction which the 1908 decision had wealed.

There is a wedge, offered by Title VII to the Civil Rights Act, for a prohibition to discrimination based on race, color, religion, sex and national origin in all terms, privileges and conditions of employment in private industry. The Equal Pay for Equal Work in the Fair Labor Standards Act [3] requires equal salaries for equal governmental work without regard to sex, yet it does not apply to executive, administrative or professional employees.

If there can be a legislative addition by the banning of sex discrimination in federal financial programs, the extension of Civil Rights benefits to the education area, including the hiring of law school professors, and the equal pay of a woman lawyer doing comparable work to her counterpart, this will inevitably have a positive effect on the discriminatory and professional problems noted herein.

NUMBERS OF LAWYERS AND PROFESSIONALS

Although women are entering what used to be the "man's world" in more and more areas, the liberal sixties do not even equal the roaring twenties in the ratio of women to men entering the legal profession. (2.5% as compared to 4.5%). There are over 8,000 women lawyers in the United States today. This is approximately 3% of the total in the legal profession. The ratio in 1957 of men to women was 2.7%, a figure which was to be status quo for at least the next half-dozen years. [4]

Only one percent of the federal judges appointed by the President of the United States are women. This equals the one percent of engineers that are women which is the smallest percent of women in any professional group. Women physicians amount to 7% of their field while 9% of scientists are women. These figures help make up the disparity in the professional working women totals, supplied by the Department of Labor. More than 40% of all white collar workers are women but only one out of every ten is a management position, and one out of every seven professional jobs is filled by women. This resulted in an

[1] *Muller* v. *Oregon* (1908) 208 U.S. 412.
[2] Civil Rights Act of 1964, effective July 1, 1965, 78 Stat. 241–352, Title VII, 70 Stat. 254–6, 42 USC 2000.
[3] 29 USCA, Section 206(d)(1) (1938, as amended 1963), also see 5 USC Section 5301 (1967).
[4] White, "Women in the Law", 65 *Mich. L. Rev.* 1052 (1967), at 1052.

earning gap whereby only 3% of the women, but 28% of the men, had incomes of $10,000 or more in 1968.[5]

In the thirty years since prior to World War II, women professional and technical workers have increased by 2½ million from 1.5 million to 4 million.[6] However the number of women lawyers amongst that group moved upward only from 4,500 to 8,000.

In the matter of finding a carrer in the law, these 8,000 women may see it as an interesting and challenging area, yet they are faced with the problem of limited job opportunities. Whether the area of employment is government service, law firm, corporative or higher positions, the hiring and retaining policies including salary and advancement opportunities are curtailed usually for a woman.

GOVERNMENT SERVICE

Government general attorneys (federal) are sometimes considered the ideal non-discriminatory area for a woman attorney applicant.

In 1959 women attorneys numbered 424 and composed 7% of the total of general attorneys in the federal government. Subsequently the number of women lawyers employed in the federal service increased, but the percentage of the total went down.[7]

Year	Total general attorneys	Women attorneys	Percent women
1966	9,086	501	5.5
1967	9,447	581	6.2
1968	10,044	611	6.1
1969	10,172	634	6.2

1969 showed a grade distribution difference between men and women attorneys that would indicate about one grade difference basically for all the levels. Thus, a woman attorney could expect to be hired at a lower grade and/or raised at a slower rate.[8]

Grade	11	12	13	14	15	16	17	18	Above 18
Women	99	171	147	126	60	5	5		5
Men	60	2,217	2,305	1,952	1,636	319	149	51	73

On August 8, 1969, President Nixon issued Executive Order No. 11478, similar to an Order issued two years previously by President Johnson, one part of which prohibits sex discrimination in the executive branch of the Federal Government, and in competitive positions in the legislative and judicial branches. To enact that order the Civil Service Commission established the Federal Women's Program. This program entails the appointment of a representative in each agency to help promote and carry out the goals which include increased hirings and advancement of women employees.

What has been the reaction of agencies in their hiring of attorneys under the directives of these Executive Orders?[9]

---

[5] U.S. Dept. of Commerce, Bureau of the Census, *Current Population Changes*, p. 60, No. 66, quoted in "Fact Sheet on the Earnings Gap". Women's Bureau, Wage and Labor Stds. Administration, U.S. Dept. of Labor (Washington, D.C., 1970) p. 2.

[6] Women's Bureau, Wage & Labor Stds. Administration, U.S. Dept. of Labor *Fact Sheet on Women in Professional & Technical Positions* (Washington, D.C., 1969) p. 1.

[7] Figures supplied by the Civil Service Commission, Bureau of Policies and Standards.

[8] *Ibid,* Figures as of October 1, 1969.

[9] U.S. Civil Service Commission, Bureau of Management Services, *Study of Employment in the Federal Government*, 1968 : Note—the percentages indicated by *agencies* are approximate since the Civil Service Commission breakdown for the agency listing by sex of the category "Legal & Kindred" into further separate listings, including attorneys, did not occur until this past year.

Large agencies or branches showing a lowering of, or low ratio of men to women in the legal area which are particularly significant include:

	Percent of women	
	1968	1966
Judicial branch (clerkships, etc.)	40.0	59.0
State Department (AID and Peace Corps)	30.0	34.0
Treasury (IRS, Customs)	22.0	23.5
HUD	38.6	44.0
Federal Trade Commission	8.0	8.0
NLRB	9.3	9.3
SEC	9.0	5.5

Some agencies indicated some or significant accord with the Presidential orders:

	Percent of women	
	1968	1966
OEO	16.0	10
Justice	25.5	21
Interior	48.0	48
Commerce	48.0	33
EEOC	43.0	20
FCC	38.0	37

Certain agencies with over ten on the legal staff hired none or only one woman. The Federal Maritime Commission lists only one woman attorney while the Export-Import Bank has had no female on their staff in either 1966 or 1968.

Another section of an agency, the FBI, actively recruits attorneys for its positions as agents. Yet Civil Service Commission Regulations permit the exclusion of women attorneys from being hired by the Bureau on the ground that the positions require the bearing of firearms.[10]

HIGHER POSITIONS FOR ATTORNEYS—IN GOVERNMENT

Information that women composed 13% of the federal employees in grades 8 to 12, less than 1% at grade 13, .3% in grade 14, and .1% in grade 15 is demeaning but it is frequently stated that women attorneys hold the highest percentage of positions in each of those grades. Yet there are no women general counsel. The number of hearing examiners in 1969 was 572 of which 7 are women. This position requires seven years minimum of legal experience and the admittance to a Bar of a State. Between 1966 and 1968 there were 23 new positions created but none of these went to a woman. In 1966, as in 1969, there were only 7 women attorney hearing examiners.[11]

JUDICIAL BENCH—WOMEN'S IMPACT

Indications that the federal government service does not fill very many higher positions with women attorneys also exists for the judicial branch. According to one source, the *Directory of American Judges* shows only 200 women of 9,700 judges on the bench in 1967.[12] Fifty years ago the first woman judge ascended the bench.[13] However, today on the federal courts there is one woman on the Court of Appeals [14] and four women serving on the District Court level.[15] Currently there is

---

[10] S. Pressman, Speech Before the Boston, Massachusetts Chapter of FEW (unpublished) April 29, 1970. (EEOC attorney in the Office of General Counsel).

[11] Figures obtained from the Civil Service Commission, Bureau of Policies and Standards, Washington, D.C.

[12] Sassower, Doris' What's Wrong With Women Lawyers?" *TRIAL*, Oct.–Nov., 1968, pp. 37–8.

[13] Judge Genevieve Cline of Ohio appointed to the U.S. Customs Court.

[14] Judge Shirley M. Hufstidler of California on the 9th Circuit. She is the second woman to ever be appointed to the Court of Appeals, the first being Judge Florence E. Allen of Ohio.

[15] See: Abernathy, Maurine H. "Women Judges in the United States Courts", 55 *Women Lawyers Journal* 2, Spring 1969, at 57.

one woman judge serving on the U.S. Tax Court and one still active on the U.S. Customs Court. Yet no woman has sat on the bench of the U.S. Court of Claims, the U.S. Court of Customs and Patent Appeals, nor the U.S. Supreme Court. Why has there been so few women appointed over the years and a percentage of only one percent of the federal judgeships currently filled by women? The New York legislature in 1968 created 125 new judicial positions in that State, yet only two of these were filled by women attorneys. Those responsible for such a poor showing can be not only the State's governor and party leaders for lack of "endorsement", but also such as Mayor John Lindsay who appointed no woman to the positions created for New York City.

LAW FIRMS AND CORPORATIONS ATTITUDE—HIRING POLICIES

Law firms and corporations express attitudes at best no less discriminatory. On one's just job the prospective employer is inclined to doubt everything from a woman's ability to her dedication or willingness to "behave" in a male setting.

A recent survey [16] taken of Harvard Law School Alumnae showed that 72% of the men went into law firms while only 52% of the women found positions there. This survey indicated definite tendencies on the part of the business and legal firms not to expect women to become partners, nor think they would make good litigators, or a belief that clients would prefer male attorneys.

A recent report [17] shows that of the group of three large law firms in San Francisco there were 178 attorneys employed, but no minority lawyers and only 14 women. Chicago held a similar showing with 287 professional of which only ten were women. In New York the 25 largest firms hiring a total of 1,833 lawyers had 136 women and 10 minority group members. Two of the larger Washington, D.C., firms list 107 professionals, only 10 of which are women and one is a minority member. Under Title VII of the Civil Rights Act, a law firm is included amongst those businesses employing over 25 people which must file annual reports with the EEOC.

A survey from six major cities indicates that on 40 of the largest law firms employing a total of 2,708 lawyers, there were only 186 women and 11 non-white. These figures are even more striking when it is realized that women constitute over 50% of the total population of these cities. This emphasizes the great under utilization of women in the legal profession.

A recent testimony before a Senate Judiciary sub-committee [18] indicates one Harvard law school graduate's experiences with law firm interviews.

"Of the law firms which I approached for jobs, four told me they simply would not hire women; two firms would not hire a woman because 'their senior partners' would object (a standard excuse); several firms stated that women were hired only to do probate, trusts and estate work (the traditional domain of 'lady lawyers') ; and almost everyone I spoke to felt that women were suited— perhaps— to legal research, but less suited to work involving negotiations such as labor law."

This experience is not unique, for even in this city of Washington, D.C., there are situations very comparable. A women applicant using the services of the local bar associations placement office might find herself rebutted by the comment that "women attorneys' placement applications are not forwarded to law firms as they do not wish to hire women." In a city which holds the highest number and percentage of women lawyers in the United States, due to the government employment, this is a rash comment to be made. Certainly these law firms could hire the women attorneys to work solely with local female government attorneys, or be relegated to the vast amounts of governmental research which are existant in a political metropolis of this size !

What of the attitude of these law firms toward a woman once she is hired? Of 3,000 leading law firms in 1957 only 32 firms reported a woman partner.[19]

[16] *Harvard Law Review*, "Miss Glancy Surveys HLS Alumnae", April 30, 1970 at 3.
[17] Brown, William H. III. Chairman EEOC, unpublished address presented before the August 1969 meeting of the American Bar Association at pgs. 8 and 9.
[18] Testimony of Mrs. Brenda Feigan Fasteau, on behalf of the National Organization for Women, before the sub-committee on Constitutional Amendments, Senate Judiciary Committee, May 5, 1970, in support of the Equal Rights Amendment to the U.S. Constitution.
[19] Sassower, D. "What's Wrong With Women Lawyers?", *Trial*, Oct.–Nov., 1968 at 37–8. The author, a New York attorney, comments currently that the figures have changed little in the years since the survey.

A recent article in the New York Times [20] profiled three women law partners in New York City prominent firms, but it is enunciated that these particular women are the only ones who have achieved partner status in these large law firms.

A large law firm may not find itself in the same bind as a business corporation in its discriminatory hirings of attorneys. An Executive Order 11246 [21] mended by 11375, prohibits discrimination based on various factors, including sex, by federal government contractors and in federal assisted projects. The Department of Labor's Office of Federal Contract Compliance (OFCC) recently issued interpretations of these orders. Whether the OFCC's affirmative action requirement to counter sex discrimination will apply to women attorneys that are (or should be) hired by these corporations has yet to be tested by the EEOC.

LAW FIRMS AND CORPORATIONS ATTITUDES—PAYMENT AND WORK SELECTION

Yet once an attorney is employed by a law firm or business corporation what are the differences in pay or work selection? A ten year study was conducted of women law school graduates by James J. White.[22] He determined that the proportion of females engaged in trusts and estates (60%), domestic relations (50%) and tax (31%) were higher than those properties of men in these areas.[23] Only 30% of the women stated they engaged in "general practice" while 50% of the male control group so characterized their work.

This study revealed that the woman was likely to increase her earnings by moving out of "general practice". By exhibits the article reveals [24] that "the males make a lot more money than do the females. The differential in present income is approximately $1,500 for those in their first year after graduation, and with the passage of each year the males increase their lead over the females until ... the class of 1957 [shows] a $7,300 to $9,000 lead and with no substantial appearance of abatement in their rate of gain. In 1964, 9% of the males earned more than $20.000, but only 1% of the females reached that level; 21% of the males exceeded $14,000, as compared with only 4.1% of the females. The converse is true at the levels below $8,000, where one finds 56.3% of the females but only 33.6% of the males. These figures are not distorted by the inclusion of housewives or others who are not employed full time at a paying job because only those employed full time at a paying job were included."

LAW SCHOOLS CONSIDERATION OF WOMEN—TEACHERS

Any pay differential based on sex in the employment of law school faculty could not be included in such a survey for usually the salary figures here are more secretive. However, discriminatory hiring policies of the law schools may be revealed by the number of faculty members. The White study showed in 1966 that of approximately 2,335 teaching faculty members in 134 accredited law schools there were but 51 full-time teaching women faculty in 38 law schools, or about 2% of the total.[25] From the 1969–70 Directory of Law Teachers it can be shown that there are now 53 of such full-time teaching women faculty in 45 law schools out of a total of 144 accredited law schools.

LAW SCHOOLS—ADMISSION AND PLACEMENT OF WOMEN STUDENTS

If law schools discriminate in hiring, what type of admission or recruitment policy can be expected towards women?

Law schools do not actively recruit at women's colleges. In a recent American Bar Association Journal article [26] it was noted that "although no law school uses either a formal or informal quota system to limit the number of females enrolled, they do admit to scrutinizing female applicants more closely for ability and motivation."

---

[20] *New York Times*, Monday, June 22. 1970.
[21] *Executive Order No. 11246, 30 Fed. Reg.* 12319 (Sept. 24, 1965), as amended by *Executive Order No.* 11375, *32 Fed. Reg.* 14303; also see 42 USC Section 2000(e) note (1970).
[22] White, "Women in the Law", *Mich. L. Rev.* 1052 (1967).
[23] *Ibid* at 1062.
[24] *Ibid* at 1057.
[25] *Ibid* at 1112 (Footnote 107).
[26] Dinerman, Beatrice, "Sex Discrimination in the Legal Profession", 55 American Bar Association Journal 951 (Oct. 1969). (The author is not a lawyer but a University research associate preparing a book on sex discrimination in various male-dominated professions).

All law schools are now opened to women.[27] Harvard University did not admit women until 1950, nor were all Washington, D.C. law schools open until 1951. Even in the last decade some law schools were closed to women. The World War II era brought about an opportunity for women to enter the law schools in increased numbers but that trend abated and turned downward when the 1950's found fewer women in the law schools.

Figures supplied by the White study indicate no more than 2,600 women graduates in the ten-year span through 1965 compared to slightly over 100,000 male graduates. Currently law school enrollment figures are up for women.[28]

Year	Women	Total	Percent total
1962	1,800	49,000	3.8
1969	5,000	72,000	6.9

At the last annual meeting of the Association of American Law Schools two resolutions were accepted for study to be presented as amendments to the Association's Articles at the next annual meeting. They are:[29]

"The Association urges that members of the legal profession provide equal employment opportunities to female applicants for legal positions.

"The Association urges that member schools take steps within their power to eradicate sex-based discrimination within law schools and particularly in the placement process."

Additionally, this organization appointed a committee office to make a study of women in legal education.[30] It has met once and is expected to complete a report in about six months.

The fact that such a committee is currently needed has already been brought out by information from others here before you today. Placement bias exists even before a graduate has a diploma in her hands. From a questionnaire submitted to Deans and placement offices of law schools, the response of 63 who answered indicated that 43 believed sex discrimination to be significant, 14 stated it to be extensive and only 6 found it to be insignificant.[31] A recent article in the Washington Post[32] reported that at the University of Michigan Law School one large New York-Washington firm was barred by unanimous faculty vote from using job recruiting facilities because of charges that it discriminates against women. This firm, Royall, Koegel and Wells, which is the firm Secretary of State Rogers was a partner in until his recent cabinet role, made statements in October 1969 indicating that the firm would hire fewer female law graduates than men and that those hired would need higher qualifications.

While most women graduates practice full time after leaving law school, they vary considerably from men in the type of job they may undertake.

About 25% of both men and women found their first jobs with firms of 4 or under and only slight differences in the percentage of men and women being employed initially by the federal government or law firms of over 30. However, men far exceeded women in obtaining a position with a firm in the 5 to 30 man category and conversely women were the predominant employee percentagewise in state and local government positions.[33] Many times a large firm will hire a woman attorney to do research, work in the library or do various specialized roles.[34] Law schools are in their own realm basic employment agencies and have an obligation to eliminate discrimination by firms using their facilities

---

[27] Asso. Amer. Law Schools, 1969–70 *Pre-Law Handbook* (Washington, D.C., 1970). (This edition notes the discrimination briefly—see pgs. 8 and 18).

[28] Figures obtained from Association of American Law Schools, Washington D.C., Office, Washington. D.C.

[29] Asso. American Law Schools, *1969 Proceedings Annual Meeting,* (Washington, D.C., 1970) at 142–3.

[30] Included amongst the committee members are Daniel G. Collins, New York University, Chm., Frederica K. Lombard, Wayne State, Ellen A. Peters, Yale, Frank T. Read, Duke, James J. White, University of Michigan.

[31] White study at 1085.

[32] Washington Post, April 17, 1970.

[33] White study at 1057.

[34] *Ibid* at 1060.

MYTHS AS REASONS FOR DISCRIMINATION

Why does a firm consider it imperative to discriminate based on sex? Some of the myths offered in response are that women will marry (they do—approximately 70%) and have children and thus cease working. Professor White states that "marriage alone does not usually cause a woman who is working to cease working, and our data is consistant with these findings." [35] Only 6% of those in the ten-year sample indicated that they had left to get married.

Another fallacy is that based on intelligence. Samples have shown that neither the total of female graduates nor the full-time employed females considered separately differed significantly from their counterparts in class rank or law review participation. [36] In job length of service the women and men both changed jobs quite frequently. As time out of law school extends (7 years or more), the woman is the one who remains at a job for a longer period of time. [37]

LOCATIONS OF MOST AND LEAST DISCRIMINATION

Where do these female attorneys locate? Do some parts of the country or types of living present more of a discrimination problem to her? It was concluded that of the Harvard Law Alumnae [38] more than 80% started work in the East—mainly in New York, Boston and Washington, D.C. Men tended to be more widely located. The reason, the surveyor suggested, was that women are not as aggressive to go out into new places.

Statistics compiled from the American Bar Association's *1967 Lawyer Statistical Report* indicate that of the 8,000 women attorneys in 1966 these States or areas [39] had the highest concentration, at least above the then national average of 2.8%.

[Answers in percent]

Washington, D.C.	4.8	Georgia	3.3
California	3.7	Maryland	3.1
Vermont	3.7	Hawaii	3.0
Oklahoma	3.5	New York	3.0
Massachusetts	3.4		

In contrast to these areas of the country certain states had less than 2% of the country's women attorneys.

[Answers in percent]

Kentucky	1.9	Minnesota	1.8
South Carolina	1.9	North Dakota	1.5
Delaware	1.8	West Virginia	1.5
North Carolina	1.8	Rhode Island	1.0

Of these states with extreme discriminatory practices, Minnesota has the highest number of attorneys (over 5,000) in the State, followed by North Carolina; thus these areas might be considered the most discriminatory in the United States.

Based on city size the women attorneys tend to gravitate to the areas of over 500,000 (50%). One-fourth of the women are employed in areas of under 50,000 population. This has remained the same for over 20 years. Over 1,000 female lawyers are employed in the New York City area. By the percentage of attorneys in cities of over 500,000 population there are the areas of the highest employers of women. [40]

[Answers in percent]

Washington, D.C.	4.8	New Orleans	3.2
San Francisco	4.2	Seattle	3.2
Los Angeles	3.8	Boston	3.0
Brooklyn-N.Y. City	3.3	Detroit	3.0
Cincinnati	3.3		

[35] *Ibid* at 1066.
[36] *Ibid* at 1072.
[37] White at 1090.
[38] Strandridge and Scott, "Miss Glancey Surveys HLS Alumnae", *Harvard Law Record*, April 30, 1970.
[39] Amer. Bar Foundation, *The 1967 Lawyer Statistical Report* (Chicago, 1968).
[40] *Ibid* at page 80.

Other California cities and Tulsa and Oklahoma City, Oklahoma, as well as Tucson, Arizona and Atlanta, Georgia, rank high in percentage of female attorneys in cities of over 200,000 population.

Some cities of over 200,000 population have less than 1.75% women attorneys. El Paso, Texas, Mobile, Alabama, and Grand Rapids, Michigan with 0.7% (2 attorneys), 0.9% (3 attorneys) and 1.2% (5 attorneys), respectively, are on the bottom. Norfolk, Virginia, Richmond, Virginia, and Rochester, New York, each had only 1.6% women lawyers with Norfolk having 9 attorneys, Richmond having 16 attorneys, and Rochester 19 attorneys. Minneapolis, Minnesota has a 1.7% female attorney population which numbers 36 women in 1966.

COMPARISONS TO OTHER "MINORITY" ATTORNEYS

In comparison to world-wide or even black and other minority groups in the United States, these figures could not be more depressing. Of the nation's 320,000 lawyers, 8,000 are women and approximately 3,000 are Negroes. The United States population as a whole may be considered at 22 million Negroes and 101 million women. This means that one of every 7,300 Negroes is an attorney and only one of every 12,500 women is an attorney. A United Nations Commission [41] report ten years ago shows that in Denmark where women comprise approximately the same proportion of the population as they do in the U.S., 50% of the lawyers are women. In the Soviet Union 36 percent of the attorneys are women, and in Germany women are 33 percent of the lawyers. France has 14 percent women attorneys and Hungary claims 9 percent of its public prosecutors are women, while Poland indicates that 25 percent of its judges are women.

COURT DECISIONS AFFECTING EMPLOYMENT OF WOMEN ATTORNEYS

What has this country's court system done to aid the proportion of women in the professions which are lower here than in most developed countries in the world?

A fairly recent case brought under Title VII of the Civil Rights Act was brought by a woman attorney employee of a bank urging that the bank discriminated against her in her professional capacity.[42] The underlying charge was filed by a woman attorney, formerly employed in the bank's law division, who alleged that male lawyers at the bank were paid higher salaries than she for comparable work, and held corporate titles which were denied to her. Herein the court action involved the obtainment by discovery of some particular bank records. The decision was adverse to the EEOC, which acts in these cases as a conciliator.

EEOC rulings under the Civil Rights Act have stated that an employer cannot refuse to employ married women or women with children unless he has a similar policy for men.[43] When the EEOC is unable to achieve conciliation of a case, it is up to the alleged victim of discrimination to secure an attorney and institute suit in the federal district court.

The Commissioner's view that sex is rarely a bona fide qualification for a job was adopted in *Weeks* v. *Southern Bell Telephone & Telegraph Co.*, 408 F.2d 228 (1969) and subsequent court decisions have adopted this approach.[44]

In contrast, a 5th Circuit Court of Appeals ruling in *Phillips* v. *Martin Marietta Corp.*[45] found that an employer could lawfully refuse to hire women with preschool age children although it hired men with such children. A petition of certiorari was filed and granted. In support of this petition the Department of Justice filed an *amicus curiae* brief, marking the first time such a brief has been filed in a case on sex discrimination.

FURTHER NEEDS AND RECOMMENDATIONS

What are the opportunities for the woman law graduate today?

As enunciated throughout this report, Title VII is only partially applicable to a woman attorney. It covers no government or education hirings nor does it

[41] 1959 U.N. Commission on Status of Women.
[42] *Union Bank* v. *EEOC* (USDC C.D. Calif., May 1967) 296 F. Supp. 313.
[43] Pressman, S. Unpublished speech before the Seminar for Women Executives, U.S. Dept. of Agriculture, Washington, D.C. (September 1969).
[44] *Cheatwood* v. *South Central Bell Telephone & Telegraph Co.*, — F. Supp. — (M.D. Ala., July 31 and Aug. 5, 1969) ; *Bowe* v. *Colgate-Palmolive Co.*, (C.A. 7 Sept. 26, 1969) rev'g. in part 272 F. Supp. 332.
[45] *Phillips* v. *Martin Marietta Corp.*, 411 F. 2d 1 (MD, Fla. 1968–69) cert. granted March 2, 1970, 25 L. Ed. 2d. 252.

apply to law firms or businesses of less than 25 employees. Perhaps, initially, this mass of exclusion area could be covered under an amended act.

Additionally, thus, to consider a law school placement office as an "employment office" under the act would increase the opportunity to restrict firms and businesses from recruiting which have anything *but* an open non-discriminatory policy toward woman. A law school funded with any form of federal financial aid or at a land grant college should be *required* to recruit female students, even from the women's colleges. Additionally, it should be encouraged to use greater effort to offer financial assistance to any woman law student.

Further, the government could be under a strict requirement to actively recruit women for the U.S. District Attorneys offices and in each agency. To counter a negative view towards such a requirement policy perhaps an agency could be required to show by annual report why it had *not* hired women in proportion to men for its positions. The same type of report could apply to the problem of federal attorneys' promotions.

The current surveys being conducted by interested groups and associations can perhaps tend to eliminate some of the myths and negative assumptions found towards the female legal profession. At least if more publicity were given, more facts known, more fallacies uncovered, any real basis for discriminatory pay or hiring practices would be revealed.

The time has come to open the profession to all who are able to make a contribution to it.

———

WOMEN AND GOVERNMENT ACTION

[National Organization for Women, June 1970]

BACKGROUND ON FEDERAL ACTION TOWARD EQUAL EMPLOYMENT OPPORTUNITY
FOR WOMEN

The First Executive Order.—On September 24, 1965, President Johnson signed
Executive Order 11246 which barred discrimination on the basis of race, creed,
color or national origin in companies with Federal contracts or subcontracts and
said those contracts would be suspended or cancelled and the contractor declared ineligible for further government contracts if it did not comply with
the order.

It also called for the issuance of Certificates of Merit to employees and unions
which satisfied the Order's requirements for employment or affirmative action,
and provided that such companies would not have to file the reports called for
in the Order and future regulations.

The Second Executive Order.—On October 13, 1967, President Johnson amended
that order with Executive Order 11375 which said:

"It is desirable that the equal employment opportunity programs provided for
in Executive Order No. 11246 expressly embrace discrimination on account of
sex."

He revised the first order to include sex discrimination in a paragraph which
concluded: "The policy of equal opportunity applies to every aspect of Federal
employment policy and practice."

In a section that took effect in October, 1968, the Order said: "The contractor
will take affirmative action to ensure that applicants are employed, and that employees are treated during employment, without regard to their race, color,
religion, sex or national origin."

"The contracting agency or the Secretary of Labor may direct that any bidder
or prospective contractor or subcontractor shall submit, as part of his Compliance Report, a statement in writing . . . with supporting information, to the
effect that the signer's practices and policies do not discriminate on the grounds
of race, color, religion, sex or national origin, and that the signer either will affirmatively cooperate in the implementation of the policy and provisions of
this order or that it consents and agrees that recruitment, employment and the
terms and conditions of employment under the proposed contract shall be in
accordance with the purposes and provisions of the order."

Obligations of Construction Contractors.—On May 28, 1968, the Labor Dept.
Office of Federal Contract Compliance (OFCC) which was to enforce these
Orders, published in the Federal Register a detailed statement of the obligations of contractors and subcontractors under Order 11246. It talked only about
construction contracts, but included all areas relating to construction such as
research, insurance, transportation, utilities and fund depositories as well as
supervision, inspection and other on-site activities.

The regulation called for contractors to file compliance reports within 30 days
after receiving awards unless reports had been made within the past year. Contracts of $1 million or more could not be granted without previous compliance
reviews unless reviews had been made within the past six months.

It also called for investigation of complaints with reports to the OFCC Director
within 60 days and said that if the Director had reasonable cause to believe there
had been an equal opportunity violation, he could issue notice requiring the

contractor to show cause within 30 days why action should not be taken.

"Minority" Is Defined to Include Females.—On January 17, 1969, the same day the OFCC published its proposed guidelines on sex discrimination, it published amendments to the May 28th regulations. Those amendments added "sex" to all places where the previous statement had read "race, creed, color or national origin," and it declared :

"The term 'minority group' as used herein, shall include, where appropriate, female employees and prospective female employees."

Originally Proposed Guidelines on Sex Discrimination.—The guidelines said—

"Recruiters must include in the itineraries of their recruiting trips, women's colleges, and the female students of coeducational colleges, technical institutes and high schools."

"Written advertisements should be designed to attract women by specifically inviting them to apply for those jobs where they are not typically represented."

"Women workers should be sought for part-time work. Many women with valuable skills are excluded from the job market because of the rigidity of the conventional hours of work. Affirmative action should include a careful examination of the company's work needs so that these women may not be excluded from job opportunities. In some cases a resdesign of the hours of work may be a useful means of more fully utilizing this important labor source."

"Advertisements in newspapers and other publications for employment should not express a sex preference either by placing the ad in a column headed 'Male' or 'Female' * * *."

"An employer should not deny employment to women with children or to married women unless it has similar exclusionary policies for men."

"Where State laws provide special minimum wages, overtime pay, or brief rest periods for women, the benefits of these statutory provisions must also be given to men."

"The employer should make all jobs available to both sexes unless he is precluded from doing so by a justifiable occupational qualification or by a valid State law. * * * If there is such a State law and it contains provisions for employees' exemptions, the employer's application for exemptions must have been denied. * * * In the absence of a valid State law, no employer's policies or practices should exclude women from specific jobs, from working certain hours, or from jobs requiring ability to lift and carry weights."

Bona fide Occupational Qualifications (BFOQ)– "* * * there are a few instances where there can be a valid reason to exclude all men or all women from any given job. If asserted, the contractor would have the burden of proving the justification for this exceptional condition."

"Seniority lines and lists should not be based upon sex."

"One of the increasingly important ladders to middle and top management is the management trainee program. Few, if any, women ever get into these programs in most companies. An important element of affirmative action would be a commitment to develop women managers through these programs, with the goals and timetables required" in the May 28th regulation.

"Women are not actively recruited for training for a number of jobs, such as those involving skilled crafts and outdoor work. * * * Both sexes should be represented in all training programs and affirmative action programs should include this goal."

Employers "must take affirmative action" to eliminate "ghetto departments" where women doing work similar to that performed by men in all-male departments are paid less money.

"There should be no difference for male and female employees in either mandatory or optional retirement age."

"Employers should allow a pregnant employee to take a leave of absence for a reasonable time, and be reinstated in her original job or to a position of like status and pay."

Comparison of "employees' education, training, experience and skills * * * has often revealed substantial underutilization of some employees. It is quite clear from aggregate data that this must be the situation with respect to women also in many companies and that such a self analysis could be of similar value there, too."

Compliance Reviews Ordered.—On October 24, 1969, OFCC Director John L. Wilks issued Order No. 1 to heads of all government agencies stating that—"By the beginning of fiscal year 1971, each agency shall take all steps necessary to be able to perform compliance reviews on at least 50% of the facilities assigned, and to revisit such facilities as may be necessary."

Order No. 4 on Affirmative Action Programs.—On February 5, 1970, Order No. 4 was published in the Federal Register (It had been signed on January 30). This detailed what would be required in an affirmative action program for non-construction contractors and outlined the procedures for compliance.

First, it noted that many construction contractors had not complied with the law and declared that companies that did not have affirmative action programs and did not appear able to comply with the law would not receive awards. It said that the compliance agency would issue notices giving contractors 30 days to show why the government should not institute enforcement proceedings under Executive Order 11246 *as amended.* (my emphasis) There are some 30 show cause orders in existence as of this date (June 24).

Then it discussed the contents of affirmative action programs required for non-construction companies: "An acceptable affirmative action program must include an analysis of areas within which the contractor is deficient in the utilization of minority groups and, further, goals and timetables to which the contractor's good faith efforts must be directed to correct the deficiencies and thus to increase materially the utilization of minorities at all levels and in all segments of his work force where deficiencies exist."

It called for: "An analysis of all major job categories at the facility, with explanations if minorities are currently being underutilized in any one or more job categories."

It noted that the most likely areas of underutilization are officials and managers, professionals, technicians, sales workers, office and clerical and skilled craftsmen.

It called for: "Establishment of goals and objectives by organization units and job category, including timetables for completion."

"Development and execution of action-oriented programs designed to eliminate problems and further designed to attain established goals and objectives."

It said that the employer should adopt a policy to: "Recruit, hire and promote all job classifications without regard to race, color, religion, *sex* or national origin, except where sex is a bona fide occupational qualification." (my emphasis) and

"Insure that all other personnel actions such as compensation, benefits, transfers, layoffs, return from layoff, company sponsored training, education, tuition assistance, social and recreational programs will be administered without regard to race, color, religion, *sex* or national origin, except where sex is a bona fide occupational qualification." (my emphasis)

"Where employees are featured in product or consumer advertising, both minority and non-minority employees should be pictured."

"When employees are pictured in consumer or help wanted advertising, both minorities and non-minority employees should be shown."

The Order called for analysis of the racial composition of the work force and applicant flow, but made no mention of the need for an analysis by sex. It called for analysis of the processes of selection, transfer and promotion; of seniority practices and provisions of union contracts; of apprenticeship programs and of all formal and informal company training programs.

It called for corrective action if the studies found:

"Lateral and/or vertical movement of minority employees occurring at a lesser rate (compared to work force mix) than that of non-minority employees;

"The selection process eliminates a higher percentage of minorities than non-minorities;

"Position descriptions inaccurate in relation to actual functions and duties;

"Man (sic) specifications not validated in relation to position requirements and job performance;

"Minorities underutilized or underrepresented in apprenticeship programs or other training or career improvement programs."

* * * Order No. 4 specifies that: "Goals should be specific for planned results, with timetables for completion."

The Order suggests an inventory of minority employees to determine their academic, skill and experience level and the initiation of formal career counseling and remedial job-training and work-study programs.

Order No. 4 became effective on January 30, 1970.

Adopted Guidelines on Sex Discrimination.—On June 9, 1970, nearly 17 months after the proposed guidelines were first issued, the Labor Dept. issued its guidelines on enforcement of Order 11375. They provided that:

"The placement of an advertisement in columns headed "Male" or "Female" will be considered an expression of a preference, limitation, specification or discrimination based on sex."

"Employees of both sexes shall have an equal opportunity to any available job that he or she is qualified to perform, unless sex is a bona fide occupational qualification. In most Government contract work there are only limited instances where valid reasons can be expected to exist which would justify the exclusion of all men or all women from any given job."

"The employer must not make any distinction based upon sex in employment opportunities, wages, hours or other conditions of employment. In the area of employer contributions for insurance, pensions, welfare programs and other similar "fringe benefits" the employer will not be considered to have violated these guidelines if his contributions are the same for men and women or if the resulting benefits are equal."

"An employer must not deny employment to women with young children unless it has the same exclusionary policies for men ; or terminate an employee of one sex in a particular job classification upon reaching a certain age unless the same rule is applicable to members of the opposite sex."

"The employer may not refuse to hire men or women, or deny men or women a particular job because there are no restroom or associated facilities, unless the employer is able to show that the construction of the facilities would be unreasonable for such reasons as excessive expense or lack of space."

"An employer must not deny a female employee the right to any job that she is qualified to perform in reliance upon State 'protective' law."

"When, under the employer's leave policy, the female employee would qualify for leave, then childbearing must be considered by the employer to be a justification for leave or absence for female employees for a reasonable period of time. * * * If the employer has no leave policy, childbearing must be considered by the employer to be a justification for a leave of absence, for a female employee for a reasonable period of time. Following childbirth, and upon signifying her intent to return within a reasonable time, such female employee shall be reinstated to her original job or to a position of like status and pay, without loss of service credits."

"Seniority lines and lists must not be based *solely* upon sex." (my emphasis)

"The employer shall take affirmative action to recruit women to apply for those jobs where they have been previously excluded. This can be done by various methods. Examples include 1. including in itineraries of recruiting trips women's colleges where graduates with skills desired by the employer can be found, and female students of co-educational institutions and 2. designing advertisements to indicate that women will be considered equally with men for jobs."

"In many companies management trainee programs are one of the ladders to management positions. Traditionally, few, if any, women hve been admitted into these programs. An important element of affirmative action shall be a commitment to include women candidates in such programs."

"Distinctions based on sex may not be made in other training programs. Both sexes should have equal access to all training programs and *affirmative action programs* should require a demonstration by the employer that such access has been provided." (my emphasis)

Comparison of Proposed and Adopted Guidelines.—Comparison shows how the guidelines were weakened—

Recruitment at women's schools and colleges and advertising inviting women to apply for jobs are no longer required, just suggested. The reference to creating part-time jobs is totally eliminated.

The new guidelines do not require that the benefits of protective laws be extended to men. And they create a huge loop-hole by allowing employers to refuse to hire women if they don't have space to build new restrooms—a ludricous excuse.

The section dealing with bona fide occupational qualifications is much weaker than the original, no longer requiring the contractor to prove his justification for refusing to hire women, and the new section on fringe benefits makes it possible for employers to continue or establish reduced benefits for women.

There is no mention of the need to eliminate "ghetto departments" and the guidelines say that seniority lines must not be based *solely* on sex, leaving the door open for more "sex-plus" decisions.

There was an improvement—the section on protective legislation wipes it out as an excuse for denying women jobs. This could be attributed to the Equal Employment Opportunity Commission ruling that protective laws are invalid when they discriminate against women.

One would assume, based on the language in all the orders and regulations detailed here, that the sex guidelines were issued as an additional aid to deal with questions that apply particularly to women: male/female help-wanted columns, maternity leave, protective legislation, etc., and to focus on areas where women face particular discrimination.

However, the National Organization for Women is very concerned that the OFCC is accepting Federal contractors' Affirmative Action Programs that do not contain equal opportunity for women. The OFCC is not requiring that Federal contractors analyze job categories to determine if underutilization of women exists. Consequently, no goals and timetables are being set to correct deficiencies on the basis of sex.

A few contract compliance officers, because of their own concern for equal opportunity for women, have on their own initiative been asking that contractors analyze job categories for underutilization of women and that they set goals and timetables for the correction of these deficiencies. The majority of contract compliance officers do not even ask for an analysis of the easily identifiable underutilization of women. The official policy of the OFCC and the Compliance Agencies is evident: sex discrimination is to be de-emphasized in contract compliance. Recent statements and actions by government officials and agencies make this all too clear.

After holding up some $7.7 billion in contracts from the McDonnell Douglas Corporation of St. Louis, the Defense Dept. announced that the Pentagon and company officials had reached agreement on goals and quotas for the hiring of Negroes in categories that included professional, supervisory, management and technical positions. The company has 33,000 workers, including 8,500 professional and technical employees and 6,390 office and clerical workers. There was no mention of women in the plan.

Contracts for some 30 other companies are being held up, including a $700 million award for the Newport News Shipbuilding and Dry Dock Company (which has about $7 billion in Defense Dept. contracts) and North American Rockwell Corporation in California must submit a satisfactory plan to obtain a $20 billion contract on which it is bidding. Will these Affirmative Action Programs be accepted if they do not deal with equal opportunity for women?

On June 18, 1970, two N.O.W. members, including the author of this paper, attended a workshop conducted by the Defense Dept.'s Contract Compliance Office for some 200 representatives of major Federal contractors. The N.O.W. representatives were not invited to the meeting but learned about it through an employee of one of the participants and believed it would be instructive to hear how Defense Dept. officials viewed corporate responsibility in carrying out the Executive Orders.

The workshop was conducted by Seymour Maisel, Chief of the New York Regional Office of Contract Compliance for the Defense Dept.; Benjamin Collier, his Deputy; and Irving Matlott, Director of Personnel and Industrial Relations for the Bulova Watch Company. It was sponsored by the New York Chamber of Commerce and was held in the Chamber's "Great Hall" at 65 Liberty Street.

Mr. Maisel told the assembly that the Department of Defense had the major compliance office among all government agencies—it has jurisdiction over most primary industries. He noted that written affirmative action plans had been required since July 1, 1968.

Mr. Collier went through each section of Order No. 4, explaining and elaborating on its provisions. He mentioned the word "female" several times in referring to the obligations of contractors; however, most of his discussion—and the visual material used—referred only to racial and ethnic minorities.

After the talk, in answer to questions from N.O.W. members, Mr. Maisel stated that: 1. Order No. 4 does not address itself to the "female problem"; 2. The definition of women as "minority" as specified in the Federal Register January 17, 1969 has not been "reaffirmed"; minorities are defined as Negro, Spanish-surnamed, American Indian and Oriental; 3. Companies should look at the utilization of females, but they do not have to set goals: the requirement for setting goals "does not apply" to females; 4. The guidelines do not speak of affirmative action *programs* in regard to sex, just of affirmative action: therefore, the exclusion of women from affirmative action programs under Order No. 4 would not make a bid "unawardable."

In effect, minority group women are counted as statistics in setting goal *standards*, but they can be totally excluded from employment, upgrading or training programs without this showing up in compliance reports.

This outrageous interpretation is a deliberate distortion of the original intent of the Executive Order banning sex discrimination and of subsequent Labor

Dept. regulations which have made it clear that discrimination against women is to be considered on a par with discrimination against racial and ethnic minorities.

However, the Defense Dept.'s own history in regard to contract compliance indicates that it has pursued its duties without much enthusiasm. Its compliance agency had been an independent department headed by Gerard Clark until 1967 when it was put under the Defense Supply Agency. Clark quit, believing that it was a conflict of interest for a compliance agency to be a part of an office whose chief mission was to move supplies with as little difficulty or delay as possible.

On September 15, 1969, the first OFCC order on compliance was issued to agencies directing them to begin to enforce the Executive Orders. Although the Dept. of Health, Education and Welfare sent copies of it to its staff with order for enforcement, the Defense Dept. turned it over to its General Counsel and said it would not enforce it until it was published in the Federal Register.

On April 1, 1970, the Defense Dept.'s compliance office issued an Equal Opportunity Evaluation Report form for staff use. It instructs staff to provide: "Information as to the number or percentage of unemployed minorities; the availability in terms of skill levels of minorities and females; the underemployment of minorities and females."

It inquires: "Does the Affirmative Action Plan or did the Contract Relations Officer's review reveal underutilization of minorities and/or females?"

It orders: "Explain whether the Affirmative Action Plan contains acceptable numerical or precentage goals to correct the deficiencies and to increase materially the utilization of minorities and females."

N.O.W. has learned that a revised form, dated May 11, 1970, does not include "female" in any of these instances (or any other instances).

N.O.W. Board member Dr. Ann Scott, who is coordinating our OFCC enforcement project for universities and corporations, has sent a letter to Secretary of Labor James D. Hodgson detailing our objections to the weakened sex discrimination guidelines and asking for a statement that Order No. 4 be applied to sex discrimination. N.O.W. President Aileen Hernandez is sending a similar letter along with the complaint that we are filing June 25th. Rep. Edith Green has sent a letter to Secretary Hodgson requesting him to issue a statement to the effect that the prohibition against sex discrimination must be enforced according to Order No. 4, with goals and timetables, and asking for an explanation of the rationale for every change from the proposed guidelines to the adopted version. She also asked if the Labor Dept. plans to have a woman on every OFCC compliance team (the Defense Dept. has one woman out of a total of 110 compliance officers) and whether every compliance review will include investigation of sex discrimination as a matter of course.

N.O.W. calls upon all members of Congress who are concerned about equal employment opportunity for women to contact the Secretary of Labor and the President asking for a return of the more stringent guidelines and for the application of every aspect of Order No. 4 to women, with no Affirmative Action Program accepted unless equal opportunity for women is an integral part of its goal.

The complaint filed with the Secretary includes the 100 largest defense contractors (most of which are among the 500 largest U.S. industrial corporations) the remaining 100 largest industrials, the 10 largest retail companies all of which have Federal contracts, and asks for compliance reviews of Federal contractors among the next 900 largest industrials, 50 commercial banks, 50 life insurance companies, 40 retail companies, 50 transportation companies, 50 utilities and 60 largest non-industrials. These companies employ over 22 million people. Since the OFCC has authority over companies employing over 14 million, N.O.W. is confident that this complaint covers virtually all contractors affected by the Executive Order.

While N.O.W. continues to seek blanket compliance enforcement of Order No. 4 with respect to women, it will file individual complaints against companies if needed.

ON THE EQUAL EMPLOYMENT OPPORTUNITY COMMISSION (EEOC)

N.O.W. President Aileen Hernandez resigned from the Equal Employment Opportunity Commission in 1966 in dissatisfaction at the way complaints against sex discrimination were being handled. The EEOC continues to display its lack of concern for the rights of women.

In 1968, the EEOC held hearings in New York City on discrimination in white collar employment. Though categories of male and female appeared in staff studies, the transcripts show that the Commissioners hardly asked a question relating to discrimination against women.

In 1969, the EEOC held hearings in Los Angeles. Clifford Alexander, then EEOC Chairman, declared: "Any company that takes equal employment seriously is able to hire qualified blacks and Spanish surnamed Americans from this area's rich resources." The EEOC recommended that the Justice Dept. file a suit against virtually the entire motion picture and TV film industry and its craft unions. The press release detailing the Commission's findings provided numerous statistics on the lack of blacks and Mexican-Americans in industry employment, but said not one word about women.

It is not surprising that when the case was settled out of court, the agreement provided for a 20% employment quota for blacks and Mexican-Americans in industry crafts, including make-up artists, costumers, film editors, cameramen, sound technicians, etc. The Los Angeles Times labor reporter called the case "a major test of the Nixon Administration's handling of alleged job discrimination." It was a test that augurs ill for women.

On February 18, 1970, the new Commission Chairman William H. Brown III condemned the utility industry for not improving minority employment, and he gave statistics to back up his case. There was no mention of women. On May 19, 1970, he released nationwide figures on minority group membership in construction and non-construction unions with hiring hall or other referral arrangements. They included bakery & confectionary workers, bookbinders, hotel & restaurant employees, lithographers & photoengravers, musicians, office employees, printing pressmen—there was no breakdown by male and female.

There is little reason to expect that the Houston hearings would have been different. The announcement for the hearings, issued March 30, made only one reference to women: that "Black females, compared to white females, had the lowest relative occupational standing in 46 urban labor markets studied by the commission."

It is an outrage and an insult to black women to expect that they should be satisfied with the status of white women in this society. Yet, this is a common practice of the EEOC. The Report of the President's Task Force on Women's Rights and Responsibilities includes the statement that:

"The Equal Employment Opportunity Commission, the agency charged with enforcement of legislation forbidding discrimination in employment, has published a three-volume report. (Job Patterns for Minorities and Women, 1968) based on a survey of numbers of persons employed in the private sector by industry, occupation, sex and race. One can examine this whole report and never find a table or narrative statement that compares the employment situation for white men, Negro men, white women, Negro women. There are not even any tables comparing white women with white men or Negro women with Negro men."

"The tables are all based on comparison of minority men with white men, minority women with white women. The underlying assumption of this appears to be that sex differences in industry and occupational distribution of white men and white women are insignificant or perhaps that these differences do not result from discrimination."

The study, in fact, made it impossible to compare men and women since it was based on an index that represented different values for men and women. White men were assigned the value of 100 and minority men were compared to that value. White women were also assigned the value of 100 and minority women compared to that standard.

Dr. Sally Hacker, President of Houston N.O.W. and a sociologist, re-analyzed all the data to compare the status of white and minority women with white and minority men—the job the EEOC should have done itself. Her figures showed for example, that in Texas urban areas, women at each level of education, regardless of race, earn less than white and minority men. Other charts included analyses of the percentages of men and women, white and minority, employed as office managers, professionals, technicians, sales workers, clericals, craftsmen, operatives, laborers and service workers in each of the industries under investigation.

She also provided the Commissioners with a set of suggested questions for company and union officials—such as inquiry into the number of white and minority women, compared with men, in management, professional and craft positions and in clerical, operative and service jobs; the numbers in management training programs and the numbers in unions. None of the questions were asked.

The lack of concern for statistical information about women is not limited to the EEOC. Herbert Bienstock, Regional Director for the Labor Dept's. Bureau of Labor Statistics in New York told a N.O.W. member attending a Labor Dept. Conference June 17 that statistical studies often do not include sex breakdowns because it is an added cost and the question of discrimination against women "is not a priority." Not surprisingly, running unemployment and income figures provided to the media by the BLS give figures in terms of black and white but not in terms of male and female.

The full statistics would reveal, for example, that the median income of white and Negro women in 1968 was less than that of white and Negro men.

From census data :

White men	$7, 870
Negro men	5, 314
White women	4, 580
Negro women	3, 487

This holds true for professionals, managers, clerical and sales workers, operatives and service workers :

CENSUS DATA FOR 1967

	White men	Negro men	White women	Negro women
Professional and managerial	$9, 545	$6, 208	$5, 910	$6, 209
Clerical and sales	6, 875	5, 515	4, 312	4, 425
Operatives	6, 475	5, 414	3, 590	3, 296
Service workers (excluding household)	5, 536	4, 159	3, 061	2, 905

The unemployment rates in 1969 were (BLS) :

	Percent
White men	1. 9
Negro men	3. 7
White women	3. 4
Negro women	6. 0

The true unemployment rate for women is probably much higher than those figures since many the Census Bureau chooses to count as "housewives" are women who have despaired at finding decent jobs, and they are not included in unemployment statistics.

In 1966, there were 6.9 million men over 16 and 11.2 million women over 16 living in poverty. (Census data.) It is outrageous for the various branches of the U.S. Government to declare by their actions and their statements that sex discrimination is not a top priority question for this country.

The Government, in fact, discriminates in its own hiring policies. There is no woman OFCC Regional Director in any of the 11 regions ; there is one woman EEOC Regional Director out of 13. There is only one woman out of five EEOC Commissioners. In general Federal employment, nearly 80% of women workers are concentrated in the lowest 6 grades. Nearly 20% are in grades 7 to 12 and little more than 1% are in grades 13 and above, earning $16,700 or more. There are 181,229 individuals in 13 and above—only 6,556 are women. (Civil Service Commission report for 1968.)

All Federal agencies have been instructed to set up Federal Women's Programs to improve employment opportunities for women. Little has been done in this area—some agencies have not even hired the necessary personnel to manage the program. (One exception is the Maritime Agency run by Helen Bentley.) In its five years of operation, the EEOC has provided assistance funding to only one local fair employment commission investigating sex discrimination— and that one is more the result of an activist female human rights official than the urgings or interest of the Federal agency.

N.O.W. Demands.—N.O.W. demands that the Secretary of Labor, James D. Hodgson, immediately issue a statement to the effect that Order No. 4 applies to women and that Affirmative Action Programs that do not provide equal opportunity for women will be rejected. N.O.W. demands that the strong elements in the original sex discrimination guidelines be returned.

N.O.W. demands that the Federal Government begin its own Affirmative Action Program by bringing women into top positions of compliance agencies and all departments of government equal to their representation in the population. The next three appointments to the EEOC should be women with substantial experience and commitment in the area of women's rights. Another six of the EEOC Regional Directors should be women. In the regional agency assistance offices now being set up by the OFCC, at least six of the directors, deputy directors and community relations officers should be women. Half of the government's compliance officers should be women, and all compliance teams should have female representation.

N.O.W. demands that the EEOC hold public hearings on sex discrimination in public and private employment in Washington, D.C.

N.O.W. demands that all government statistics that are coded on the basis of race also be coded on the basis of sex and that public statements and literature that provide information about the status of ethnic and racial minorities also provide information about the status of women.

We shall not be satisfied until every vestige of sexism in this country is abolished.—Lucy Komisar, National Vice President for Public Relations.

A LEGISLATIVE HISTORY OF EQUAL EMPLOYMENT OPPORTUNITY PROVISIONS DIRECTLY RELATED TO EDUCATION OR TRAINING UNDER PUBLIC LAW 88–352 (CIVIL RIGHTS ACT OF 1964), JULY 2, 1964, TITLE VII (EQUAL EMPLOYMENT OPPORTUNITY), AT 78 STAT. 253 (42 U.S.C. 200E–2000E–15)

(Dr. Kathryn Heath, USOE)

I. PROVISIONS IN TITLE VII WITH PORTIONS DIRECTLY RELATED TO EDUCATION OR TRAINING

Sec. 702. (Exemption)

This title shall not apply to an employer, with respect to the employment of aliens outside any State, or to a religious corporation, association, or society with respect to the employment of individuals of a particular religion to perform work connected with the carrying on by such corporation, association, or society of its religious activities or to an educational institution with respect to the employment of individuals to perform work connected with the educational activities of such institution.

Sec. 703 (Discrimination because of race, color, religion, sex, or national origin)

*   *   *   *   *   *   *

(d) It shall be an unlawful employment practice for any employer, labor organization, or joint labor-management committee controlling apprenticeship or other training or retraining, including on-the-job training programs to discriminate against any individual because of his race, color, religion, sex, or national origin in admission to, or employment in, any program established to provide apprenticeship or other training.

(e) Notwithstanding any other provision of this title, (1) it shall not be an unlawful employment practice for an employer to hire and employ employees, for an employment agency to classify, or refer for employment any individual, for a labor organization to classify its membership or to classify or refer for employment any individual, or for an employer, labor organization, or joint labor-management committee controlling apprenticeship or other training or retraining programs to admit or employ any individual in any such program, on the basis of his religion, sex, or national origin in those certain instances where religion, sex, or national origin is a bona fide occupational qualification reasonably necessary to the normal operation of that particular business or enterprise, and (2) it shall not be an unlawful employment practice for a school, college, university, or other educational institution or institution of learning to hire and employ employees of a particular religion if such school, college, university, or other educational institution or institution of learning is, in whole or in substantial part, owned, supported, controlled, or managed by a particular religion or by a particular religious corporation, association, or society, or if the curriculum of such school, college, university, or other educational institution or institution of learning is directed toward the propagation of a particular religion.

*   *   *   *   *   *   *

Sec. 705 (Equal Employment Opportunity Commission)

*   *   *   *   *   *   *

(4) The Commission shall, in any of its educational or promotional activities, cooperate with other departments and agencies in the performance of such educational and promotional activities.

*   *   *   *   *   *   *

520

A. Kennedy Administration Omnibus Civil Rights Proposal.—President Kennedy's February 28, 1963 message on civil rights to the 88th Congress during its 1st Session focuses on problems of Negroes and on achieving first-class citizenship for citizens regardless of color.[1] The draft *Civil Rights Act of 1963* in his civil rights message to the Congress the following June 19 focuses on problems of Negroes among minority groups and also broadens the ground for nondiscrimination to include race, religion, or national origin as well as color. Title VII in this draft is on "Commission on Equal Employment Opportunity." This title contains no exemption for an educational institution, "sex" is not identified as a factor in the nondiscrimination "ground," there is no provision on apprenticeship or other training or retraining, and there is no provision on educational activities of the Commission.[2] Chairman Celler (D., N.Y.) of the Committee on the Judiciary, introduced the Administration's draft as a House bill. It was referred to the Committee on the Judiciary and became *H.R. 7152.*[3]

B. Substitute Reported by Subcommittee 5.—An amendment to *H.R. 7152* in the nature of a substitute was reported on October 2, 1963 by Subcommittee 5 to the full Committee on the Judiciary.[4] Insertion of a new title in this draft results in *title VIII* rather than *VII* providing for an Equal Employment Opportunity Commission. Enlarged content results in title VIII being on "Equal Employment Opportunity" rather than solely on the Commission. Title VIII contains no general exemption for educational institutions and "sex" is not identified as a factor in the nondiscrimination "ground." Provisions are included relating to apprenticeship or other training. In addition, there is a provision on educational activities of the Administrator of the Commission as distinct from the Commission itself. Though section numbers differ, pertinent provisions enacted into law appear in this draft in the following initial form:

Sec. 803 (Exemption)—Later to be revised into Sec. 702

This title shall not apply to an employer with respect to the employment of aliens outside any State, or to a religious corporation, association, or society.[5]

Sec. 804 (Discrimination Because of Race, Religion, Color, National Origin, or Ancestry)—Later to be revised into Sec. 703

*   *   *   *   *   *   *

(d) It shall be an unlawful employment practice for any employer, labor organization, or joint labor-management committee controlling apprenticeship or other training programs to discriminate against any individual because of his race, religion, color, national origin, or ancestry in admission to, or employment in, any program established to provide apprenticeship or other training.[6]

(e) Notwithstanding any other provision of this title, it shall not be an unlawful employment practice for an employer to hire and employ employees of a particular religion or national origin in those certain instances where religion or national origin is a bona fide occupational qualification reasonably necessary to the normal operation of that particular business or enterprise.[6]

Sec. 808 (Administrator of the Equal Employment Opportunity Commission)— Later to be revised with portions included in Sec. 705

*   *   *   *   *   *   *

(d) The Administrator shall, in any of his educational or promotional activities, cooperate with other departments and agencies in the performance of such educational and promotional activities.[7]

---

[1] House of Representatives. *Civil Rights.* (Message From the President of the United States Relative to Civil Rights) 88th Congress, 1st Session. Document No. 75. February 28, 1963. 11 p.

[2] P. 14–24 *in* House of Representatives. *Civil Rights.* (Message From the President of the United States Relative to Civil Rights, and a Draft of a Bill to Enforce the Constitutional Right to Vote, to Confer Jurisdiction Upon the District Courts of the United States to Provide Injunctive Relief Against Discrimination in Public Accommodations, to Authorize the Attorney General to Institute Suits to Protect Constitutional Rights to Education, to Establish a Community Relations Service, to Extend for Four Years the Commission on Civil Rights, to Prevent Discrimination in Federally Assisted Programs, to Establish a Commission on Equal Employment Opportunity, and for Other Purposes; 88th Congress, 1st Session. Document No. 124. June 19, 1963. 24 p.

[3] June 20, 1963. 38 p.

[4] H.R. 7152, October 2, 1963. 99 p.

[5] *Ibid.* p. 74.

[6] *Ibid.* p. 76.

[7] *Ibid.* p. 82.

C. Substitute Reported by the Committee on the Judiciary.—An amendment to *H.R. 7152* in the nature of a substitute was reported on November 20, 1963 to the House by the Committee on the Judiciary and was committed to the Committee of the Whole House on the State of the Union.[8] *Title VII* (rather than

VIII) is on "Equal Employment Opportunity" in this text.

Sec. 703 (Exemption)—Later to be revised into Sec. 702

The exemption to the title appears in the same language as that in section 803 of the earlier substitute bill as quoted in paragraph B above.[9]

Sec. 704 (Discrimination because of race, color, religion, or national origin)— Later to be revised into Sec. 703

The word *Ancestry* is deleted from the section heading.[10] Subsection (d) now reflects this deletion also:

(*d*) It shall be an unlawful employment practice for any employer, labor organization, or joint labor-management committee controlling apprenticeship or other training programs to discriminate against any individual because of his race, color, religion, or national origin in admission to, or employment in, any program established to provide apprenticeship or other training.[11] Subsection (*e*) remains the same as in section 804(e) of the earlier substitute bill quoted in paragraph B above.[12] The Committee report states:

Section 704(e) provides for a very limited exception to the provisions of this title. Notwithstanding any other provisions, it shall not be an unlawful employment practice for an employer to employ persons of a particular religion or national origin in those rare situations where religion or national origin is a bona fide occupational qualification.[13]

[Report No. 914, *Part 2*, December 2, 1963, 32 p., gives additional views. P. 26–30 on *title VII* focuses on discrimination in employment of Negroes. The employment situation for *females* as well as Negroes is reflected in *Table 1* on "Unemployment rates by color, age, sex, and by selected major occupational group, 1962" on p. 27, and in *Table 3* on "Median annual wage and salary incomes of white and nonwhite persons, 1939, 1947, 1957, 1960" on p. 28.]

Sec. 706 (Equal Employment Opportunity Commission)—Later to be revised into Sec. 705

Educational or promotional activities of the Administrator identified in section 808(d) of the earlier text shown in paragraph B above now are vested in the Commission by section 705(i) as follows:

(i) The Commission shall, in any of its educational or promotional activities, cooperate with other departments and agencies in the performance of such educational and promotional activities.[14]

D. House Action on H.R. 7152.—Debate on *H.R. 7152* in the House of Representatives extended from January 31 through February 10, 1964.[15] Of the 18 amendments to title VII adopted by the House, four are pertinent. Three of the four were offered, debated, and adopted on February 8, 1964. Mr. Smith (D., Va.) made the proposal adding *sex* to the prohibited bases of discrimination and it was adopted by teller *vote* of 168 to 133.[16] Mr. Reid (R., N.Y.) offered the amendment, adopted by voice vote, which makes it clear that discrimination is prohibited in *retraining* as well as training programs.[17] Mr. Purcell (D., Tex.) proposed the amendment, also adopted by voice vote, which retains the exemption in section 704(e) as section 704(e)(1) and adds a new exception as section 704(e)(2).[18] The fourth pertinent amendment was offered two days later by Mrs.

---

8 H.R. 7152, November 20, 1963. 87 p.
9 *Ibid.* p. 68.
10 *Ibid.*
11 *Ibid.* p. 69–70.
12 *Ibid.* p. 70.
13 P. 27 *in* House of Representatives. *Civil Rights Act of 1963.* 88th Congress, 1st Session. Report No. 914. November 20, 1963. 121 p.
14 H.R. 7152, November 20, 1963. p. 74.
15 *Congressional Record* 110 (Part 2) : 1511–2804 ; January 31–February 10, 1964.
16 *Ibid.* p. 2577–84 ; February 8, 1964. This amendment inserts the word *sex* after the word *religion* in section 704 subsections (a)(2), (c)(1), (c)(2) and (d) and in section 705(b) of H.R. 7152, November 20, 1963, p. 68–71.
17 *Ibid.* p. 2584–85 ; February 8, 1964. This amendment inserts the words *or retraining, including on-the-job training* before the word *programs* in section 704(d) of H.R. 7152, November 20, 1963. p. 69.
18 *Ibid.* p. 2585–93 ; February 8, 1964.

Bolton (R., Ohio) as a correction to the Smith amendment. It was adopted without objection on February 10, 1964.[19] That same day, *H.R. 7152* of November 20, 1963, as amended during debate in the House of Representatives, passed the House by *vote* of 290 yeas, 130 nays, and 11 not voting.[20] Pertinent sections now are as follows:

Sec. 703 (Exemption)—Later to be revised into Sec. 702

The exemption is the same as that appearing in section 803 of the bill as reported by Subcommittee 5 and in section 703 of the bill as reported by the Committee on the Judiciary; namely:

Sec. 703. This title shall not apply to an employer with respect to the employment of aliens outside any State, or to a religious corporation, association, or society.[21]

Sec. 704 (Discrimination because of race, color, religion, or national origin)— Later to be revised into Sec 703

(*d*) It shall be an unlawful employment practice for any employer, labor organization, or joint labor-management committee controlling apprenticeship or other training *or retraining, including on-the-job training* programs to discriminate against any individual because of his race, color, religion, *sex*, or national origin in admission to, or employment in, any program established to provide apprenticeship or other training. [Italics supplied on additions.][22]

(*e*) Notwithstanding any other provision of this title, (*1*) it shall not be an unlawful employment practice for an employer to hire and employ employees of a particular religion, *sex*, or national origin in those certain instances where religion, *sex*, or national origin is a bona fide occupational qualification reasonably necessary to the normal operation of that particular business or enterprise, *and (2) it shall not be an unlawful employment practice for a school, college, university, or other educational institution or institution of learning to hire and employ employees of a particular religion if such school, college, university, or other educational institution or institution of learning is, in whole or in substantial part, owned, supported, controlled, or managed by a particular religion or by a particular religious corporation, association, or society, or if the curriculum of such school, college, university, or other educational institution or institution of learning is directed toward the propagation of a particular religion.* [Italics supplied to show additions.][23]

Sec. 706 (Equal Employment Opportunity Commission)—Later to be revised into Sec. 705

Subsection (i) is the same as that appearing in the bill as reported by the Committee on the Judiciary; namely:

(*i*) The Commission shall, in any of its educational or promotional activities, cooperate with other departments and agencies in the performance of such educational and promotional activities.[24]

E. Senate Action on H.R. 7152 as Passed by the House.—House-passed *H.R. 7152* was read by title in the Senate on February 17, 1964. Announcement was made that the leadership "will propose to the Senate that the measure be placed on the calendar, without referral to Committee, and that, subsequently, the Senate as a body proceed to its consideration."[25] On February 26, 1964, the bill was read by title and put on the Calendar.[26] On March 26, 1964, the Senate agreed to consider the bill, tabled a motion to refer it to the Committee on the Judiciary, and began substantive debate.[27] Thirty of the many proposed amendments to

---

[19] *Ibid.* p. 2718–21; February 10, 1964. This amendment inserts the word *sex* in section 704, subsection (a)(1), twice in subsection (b), and twice in subsection (e), and three times in section 705, subsection (b). The latter makes *sex* as well as *religion* and *national origin* subject to the bona fide occupational qualification exception to what constitutes "an unlawful employment practice."

[20] *Ibid.* p. 2805; February 10, 1964.

[21] H.R. 7152, February 10, 1964, p. 32.

[22] *Ibid.* p. 34.

[23] *Ibid.* p. 34–35.

[24] *Ibid.* p. 39.

[25] *Congressional Record* 110 (Part 3) : 2882; February 17, 1964. Supporters of H.R. 7152 considered the Senate Committee on the Judiciary to be hostile to the bill.

[26] *Ibid.* p. 3692 and 3719; February 26, 1964, and H.R. 7152, February 26, 1964, Senate Calendar No. 854. 55 p.

[27] *Congressional Record* 110 (Part 5) : 6417; March 26, 1964, for *vote* to consider H.R. 7152 adopted by 67 yeas and 17 nays, with 16 not voting. *See* p. 6455 for *vote* of 50 in favor and 34 against with 16 not voting which tabled the motion of Senator Morse (D., Ore.) to refer the bill to the Committee on the Judiciary, and for start of substantive debate.

H.R. 7152 related in whole or in part to *title VII* and seven were adopted.[28] Of the seven, *Amendment No. 656* of May 26, 1964 is of direct interest here. This proposal, drafted as the *Civil Rights Act of 1964* (instead of 1963) in informal bipartisan conferences, in the nature of a substitute *H.R. 7152*. It is the first of two drafts known as the Dirksen-Mansfield compromise introduced by Senator Dirksen (R., Ill.) for himself and Senators Mansfield (D., Mont.), Humphrey (D., Minn.) and Kuchel (R., Calif.).[29] On June 8, 1964, a bipartisan group of 38 Senators moved to bring the debate on *H.R. 7152* to a close.[30] With certain changes not pertinent in this paper, *Amendment No. 1052* in the nature of a substitute *H.R. 7152* was submitted on June 10, 1964, as the Dirksen-Mansfield compromise in place of the earlier draft.[31] That same day, the Senate adopted cloture on *H.R. 7152*.[32] After disposing of other amendatory proposals, *Amendment No. 1052*, as amended, passed the Senate on June 17, 1964 by a *vote* of 76 yeas and 18 nays, with 6 not voting.[33] Exactly a year after the President sent his draft *Civil Rights Act of 1963* to the Congress, the Senate acted on its version, known as the *Civil Rights Act of 1964*, by a *vote* of 73 in favor and 27 against *H.R. 7152*.[34]

F. House Action on Senate-passed H.R. 7152.—Instead of the usual Conference procedure to resolve differences between *H.R. 7152* as passed by the House and by the Senate, *House Resolution 789* was adopted by the House calling for acceptance of the bill as amended by the Senate.[35]

G. Enactment of Senate-passed H.R. 7152 into Public Law 88–352.—The President signed the House-accepted Senate version of *H.R. 7152* into *Public Law 88–352* (Civil Rights Act of 1964) on July 2, 1964.[36]

H. Differences in Perintent Sections Between the House-passed Version of H.R. 7152 and the one Passed by the Senate, Adopted by the House, and Enacted into Public Law 88–352.—The House-passed version of title VII includes an introductory section on "Findings and Declaration of Policy." [37] This section does not appear in the Senate-passed version with the result that provisions in the title which are directly related to education appear in sections 702, 703 (d) and (e), and 705(i) instead of 703, 704 (d) and (e) and 706(i) Each of these provisions appears otherwise in exactly the same way in *Amendment No. 656*, its successor *Amendment No. 1052*, and—as shown in Part I herein—in *Public Law 88–352*.[38] Except for the numbering, sections 703(d) and 705(i) in the Senate version also are the same as in the House-passed version of *H.R. 7152*. Italics added in the other pertinent provisions quoted as follows reflect the additions which constitute the changes made by the Senate :

Sec. 702 (Exemption)

This title shall not apply to an employer with respect to the employment of aliens outside any State, or to a religious corporation, association, or society *with respect to the employment of individuals of a particular religion to perform work connected with the carrying on by such corporation, association, or society of its religious activities or to an educational institution with respect to the employment of individuals to perform work connected with the educational activities of such institution.*[39]

Sec. 703 (Discrimination because of race, color, religion, sex, or national origin)

---

[28] For ready reference, *see* Appendixes 7–9 in United States Equal Employment Opportunity Commission. *Legislative History of Titles VII and XI of Civil Rights Act of 1964.* Washington : Government Printing Office, n.d. vii p., Parts I through IV, and Appendixes 1–11.

[29] H.R. 7152 Amendment No. 656, May 26, 1964, Senate Calendar No. 854. 74 p.

[30] *Congressional Record* 110 (Part 10) : 12922 ; June 8, 1964.

[31] *Ibid.* p. 13310–13319 ; June 10, 1964, and H.R. Amendment No. 1052, June 10, 1964, Senate Calendar No. 854. 74 p.

[32] *Congressional Record* 110 (Part 10) : 13327 ; June 10, 1964. The *vote* was 71 yeas and 29 nays.

[33] *Ibid.* (Part 11) : 14239 ; June 17, 1964. Senator Humphrey (D., Minn.) reported there were more than 360 proposed amendments to the bill as of June 4, 1964. On June 18, 1964, Senator Hruska (R., Nebr.) reported more than 500 had been submitted and more than 100 votes had been taken "not to mention quorum calls which occurred." *Congressional Record* 110 (Part 10) : 12702 ; June 4, 1964, and (Part 11) : 14326 ; June 18, 1964.

[34] *Ibid.* (Part 11) : 14511 ; June 19, 1964, and H.R. 7152, June 19, 1964, 126 p.

[35] *Congressional Record* 110 (Part 12) : 15869 ; July 12, 1964, for House Resolution 789, and p. 15897 for *vote* recorded as 289 yeas, 126 nays, 1 answering "Present," and 15 not voting.

[36] 78 Stat. 241 (42 U.S.C. 2000a–2000h–6).

[37] H.R. 7152, February 10, 1964. p. 27–28.

[38] H.R. 7152 Amendment No. 656, May 26, 1964, Senate Calendar No. 854, p. 39–40 ; H.R. 7152 Amendment No. 1052, June 10, 1964, Senate Calendar No. 854, p. 39–40 ; and Public Law 88–352 (Civil Rights Act of 1964) July 2, 1964 at 78 Stat. 255 (42 U.S.C. 2000e–1).

[39] H.R. 7152, June 19, 1964. p. 91–92.

(e) Notwithstanding any other provision of this title (1) it shall not be an unlawful employment practice for an employer to hire and employ employees, *for an employment agency to classify, or refer for employment any individual, for a labor organization to classify its membership or to classify or refer for employment any individual, or for an employer, labor organization, or joint labor-management committee controlling apprenticeship or other training or retraining programs to admit or employ any individual in any such program, on the basis of his* [instead of "of a particular"] religion, sex, or national origin in those certain instances where religion, sex, or national origin is a bona fide occupational qualification reasonably necessary to the normal operation of that particular business or enterprise, and (2) it shall not be an unlawful employment practice for a school, college, university, or other educational institution or institution of learning to hire and employ employees of a particular religion if such school, college, university, or other educational institution or institution of learning is, in whole or in substantial part, owned, supported, controlled, or managed by a particular religion or by a particular religious corporation, association, or society, or if the curriculum of such school, college, university, or other educational institution or institution of learning is directed toward the propagation of a particular religion.[40]

I. Intent of Changes Made by the Senate to House-passed Sections 702 and 703(e) of H.R. 7152.—Senator Dirksen (R., Ill.) obtained unanimous consent on June 5, 1964, to have printed in the *Congressional Record* "an annotated copy" of the House-passed *H.R. 7152* "showing by black brackets and italics, matter deleted and matter inserted" by Senate changes.[41] Chairman Celler (D., N.Y.) of the House Committee on the Judiciary, outlined the substance of many of the Senate changes when the House considered the Senate-passed version of *H.R. 7152.*[42] Then, shortly after the House vote on *House Resolution 789*, Senator Dirksen also obtained unanimous consent to have a June 29, 1964 analysis of the House-and Senate-passed versions of the proposed Civil Rights Act printed in the *Congressional Record* "in parallel columns, in order to show in every case the difference in the sections and in the titles." [43] None of the three explains the intent of the changes directly related to education. Without a Senate Committee report, a published record of the informal discussions during which the Dirksen-Mansfield compromise was hammered out, or a House-Senate Conference report, clues are limited under title VII to inferences from the definition of "employer" and the few pertinent comments on education under the title in the long and complicated debate on the bill.[44]

a. Sec. 701 (Definitions) and related inferences.—Under the definition of "employer" in section 701(b), "a State or political subdivision thereof" is excluded from coverage under *title VII* of the *Civil Rights Act of 1964.* Under the definition of "person" in section 701(a), the title applies to "one or more individuals" and to such organizations as labor unions, partnerships, associations, corporations. legal representatives, and unincorporated organizations. Under the definition of "employment agency" in section 701(c), "the United States Employment Service and the system of State and local employment services receiving Federal assistance" specifically are included in coverage.[45] Accordingly, under *title VII*, schools, colleges, universities, or other educational institutions or institutions of learning are excluded from coverage to the extent that they are State or local *public* institutions. Included, by contrast, are such in-school as well as on-the-job training and retraining programs as those under the *Manpower Development and Training Act of 1962* and related amendments.[46]

b. Sec. 702 (Exemption) and related inference.—Senator Humphrey (D., Minn.) stated in his explanation of *Amendment No. 656* that section 702 "has been amended to limit the general exemption of religious groups to those practices relating to the employment of individuals of a particular religion to perform work connected with the employer's religious activities, and to extend the exemption

---

[40] H.R. 7152, June 19, 1964. p. 94.
[41] *Congressional Record* 110 (Part 10) : 12807–12820 ; June 5, 1964.
[42] *Ibid.* (Part 12) : 15895–15896 ; July 2, 1964.
[43] *Ibid.* p. 15998–16004 ; July 2, 1964. This analysis was prepared at the request and under the supervision of Mr. McCulloch (R., Ohio).
[44] Before the House vote was taken on July 2, 1964, Chairman Madden (D., Ind.) of the House Rules Committee, reported "This bill has been considered by both bodies a total of approximately 114 days." *See* the *Congressional Record* 110 (Part 12) : 15869 ; July 2, 1964.
[45] Public Law 88–352, July 2, 1964 at 78 Stat. 253–55.
[46] Public Law 87–415, March 15, 1962 (76 Stat. 23) as amended (42 U.S.C. 2571–2628).

to private educational institutions with respect to the employment of individuals to perform work connected with the educational activities of such institutions." [47] Senator Dirksen (R., Ill.) had this to say : "The general exemption of a religious corporation, association or society from this title of the bill is limited by the amendment to the employment of individuals of a particular religion to perform work connected with its religious activities. A similar exemption is provided for an educational institution with respect to the employment of individuals to perform work connected with the educational activities of the institution." [48] By not modifying the term "educational institution," section 702 expands the exclusion from title VII coverage to a private as well as a public educational institution "with respect to the employment of individuals to perform work connected with the educational activities of such institution"—not just the public institutions excluded under definition of "employer" in section 701.

c. *Sec. 703(e)*.—Senator Humphrey (D., Minn.) states : "In section 703(e) the exemption where religion, sex, or national origin is a bona fide occupational qualification, which in the House bill is available only to employers, is extended to employment agencies, labor organizations, and joint labor-management committees." [49] Senator Dirksen (R., Ill.) states : "The amendment broadens the coverage and extends the same treatment to (1) employment agencies when classifying or referring individuals for employment, (2) to labor organizations when classifying its membership or classifying individuals for employment, (3) to employers, labor organizations or joint labor-management committees controlling apprenticeship or other training programs." [50]

Hon. JAMES EASTLAND,
Chairman, Senate Judiciary Committee,
Washington, D.C.

DEAR MR. CHAIRMAN : The Senate Judiciary Committee now has H.R. 10805, which passed the House on July 11, 1967. This bill would extend the life of the U.S. Commission on Civil Rights for an additional five years until January 31, 1973. I voted for the bill and I continue to support it.

I am writing to you to request that you, as Chairman of the Senate Judiciary Committee, introduce an amendment to the bill to extend the Commission's authority (which now primarily concerns discrimination based on race, color, religion or national origin), to include discrimination based on *sex*. I suggest the following text of such amendment :

"Sec. 2. Section 104(a) of the Civil Rights Act of 1957 (71 Stat. 635, as amended, 42 U.S.C. 1975c(a)) is further amended by adding the word 'sex' after the word 'religion' in subparagraphs (1), (2), (3) and (4) of Sec. 104(a)."

The Commission on Civil Rights is not a law-enforcing or prosecuting agency. Rather, it is an independent bipartisan agency which engages solely in fact-finding and research. It was created in 1957 to investigate allegations of denial of voting rights, to study and collect information concerning legal developments constituting denial of equal protection of the laws, and to appraise the laws and policies of the Federal Government involving denial of equal protection of the laws. In each of these aspects, the Commission's duties were related to discriminations and denials of equal protection because of "race, color, religion or national origin".

The Civil Rights Act of 1964 expanded the Commission's duties to include studying denials of equal protection in the administration of justice, investigating allegations of fraud or discrimination in Federal elections which result in denial of voting rights, and serving as a national clearinghouse for information concerning denial of equal protection of the laws. Its clearinghouse function was still, however, tied to "race, color, religion, or national origin".

Women throughout this country are still being subjected to substantial discrimination on the basis of sex in many activities, including employment, jury service, property rights, etc. The Congress took a major step against such sex discrimination in enacting Title VII of the Civil Rights Act of 1964 to prohibit employment discrimination based on race, color, religion, *sex* or national origin. As you know, I supported the amendment on the House floor which added the word "sex" to Title VII.

I regret that we did not also try to include the word "sex" in Title V of the

---

[47] *Congressional Record* 110 (Part 10) : 12722 ; June 4, 1964.
[48] *Ibid.*, p. 12818 ; June 5, 1964.
[49] *Congressional Record* 110 (Part 10) : 12722 ; June 4, 1964.
[50] *Ibid.* p. 12818 ; June 5, 1964.

1964 Civil Liberties Act when we extended the life of the Commission and broadened its functions.

The Commission has performed a very useful service. It is the only independent agency which can examine the impact of various Federal programs and activities affecting civil rights. Its reports have been widely published and circulated, and have greatly assisted the Congress, the Federal Executive agencies, State and local governments, and the people throughout the country, in acquiring information needed to deal with problems of civil rights. I am convinced that the Commission can perform a most useful service to the people of the nation by engaging in study and research, and disseminating information, concerning discrimination based on sex.

Civil Rights are rights that belong to every American. They are not limited solely to those of Negroes. The Commission on Civil Rights has recognized the breadth of this concept by recently undertaking examinations of the problems faced by American Indians and Mexican Americans. The recent three-Judge court decision in *White* v. *Crook*, 251 F. Supp. 401 (D.C. Ala., 1966), which invalidated Alabama's law excluding women from jury service, squarely recognized that women, too, are persons entitled to equal protection of the laws under the 14th Amendment to the United States Constitution. Nevertheless, many states will continue sex discrimination in jury service, and in many other fields, particularly employment. I think the expansion of the Commission's functions to include study and reporting on the problems of sex discriminations would be a substantial step toward the elimination of such discriminations from American life.

I hope that you will introduce and support the above amendment to H.R. 10805.

With warmest regards.

Sincerely yours,

MARTHA W. GRIFFITHS,
Member of Congress.

My present bill on this subject (H.R. 837) was vigorously endorsed in the report of, The President's Task Force on Women's Rights and Responsibilities, entitled: "A Matter of Simple Justice," page 9. April, 1970, which pointed out: "Perhaps the greatest deterrent to securing improvement in the legal status of women is the lack of public knowledge of the facts and the lack of a central information bank." The Task Force report cited the fact that as recently as 1968, Connecticut and Pennsylvania were enforcing laws which required judges to impose longer prison sentences on women than on men for the same offense. These laws were declared unconstitutional in *Daniels* vs *Commonwealth of Pa.* 243 A. 2nd 400 (1968) and *U.S. ex rel Robinson* vs *York*, 281 F Supp. 8 (D.C. D. Conn., 1968). There are other states, however, such as New York and Arkansas, with similar discriminatory statutes, which are still imposing longer prison terms on women than on men for the same crime. Most of these discriminations could be eliminated if the Civil Rights Commission conducted vigorous programs of research and publicity on sex discrimination with the same energy that the Commission displayed in studying and reporting on race discrimination. Indeed, such a program by the Commission also would help to eliminate race discrimination because half of the racial and ethnic minorities are composed of women.

SUBPARAGRAPH (D)

Paragraph (d) of Section 805 would correct the grave injustice which now exists in the Equal Pay Act of 1963. That act guarantees that men and women performing equal work must receive equal pay. However, the Equal Pay Act was enacted as part of the Fair Labor Standards Act which regulates maximum hours and minimum wages. The Fair Labor Standards Act, unfortunately, contains a provision which makes the Act inapplicable to persons working in executive, administrative, or professional capacities or as outside salesmen. Thus, that exemption also applies to the Equal Pay Act. The net result is that women who work in executive, administrative, or professional capacities do not receive the benefits of the Equal Pay Act. This is utterly unjust. There is no rational justification for saying that the principle of equal pay for equal work should not apply to persons in executive, administrative, or professional work. Although Title VII of the Civil Rights Act of 1964 does protect some executive, administrative, and professional employees against sex discrimination in connection with their pay, that Title is itself limited and, therefore, does not provide the same measure of protection as could be obtained under the Equal Pay Act. Millions of teachers and professors are now excluded from Title VII because of the educational activities exemption. Furthermore, the Equal Employment Opportunity Commission has no enforcement powers under Title VII as it now stands. It is, therefore, important that the Equal Pay Act be liberated from the handicap of the executive—administrative—professional exemption. The Equal Pay Act provides an enforcement mechanism under which the Secretary of Labor can institute suits on behalf of the aggrieved employee. It also provides for criminal penalties in aggravated cases of willful violations. We must use every available tool and mechanism to combat sex discrimination which irrationally and unjustly deprives millions of people of equal employment opportunities simply because of their sex. We must root out such discrimination in every level and in every area irrespective of whether the discrimination strikes initially at a man or at a woman. I particularly applaud the House Committee on Education and Labor which recently rejected a proposal to pervert Title VII of the Civil Rights Act of 1964 into an engine of discrimination in pension and retirement plans. Here are copies of my letter of June 8, 1970 to Committee Chairman Carl D. Perkins with an accompanying analysis, and I respectfully request that they be included as part of the record of this hearing.

U.S. CIVIL SERVICE COMMISSION—FEDERAL PERSONNEL MANUAL SYSTEM

LETTER

WASHINGTON, D.C., *January 15, 1969.*

FPM Letter No. 332–12.
Subject: Restriction of Consideration to One Sex.

To Heads of Departments and Independent Establishments:

It has been a longstanding policy of the Commission that consideration of eligibles or employees for competitive appointment or appointment by noncompetitive action to positions in the competitive services shall not be restricted to one sex, except in unusual circumstances when the Commission finds the action justified.

Questions have been raised about whether the Commission has departed from this policy in view of the fact that material has been removed from the Federal Personnel Manual which contained a description of that policy and the procedure for reviewing unusual circumstances to determine whether restriction of consideration to one sex is warranted. The Commission has not departed from the policy described above. The material in question was removed from FPM chapter 713 with the understanding that it would be reissued at a later date when changes in that chapter were made. Because those changes have not yet been made, we are reissuing the material in question by means of this letter in advance of reincorporation in the Federal Personnel Manual.

The Commission has provided exceptions to the basic employment policy that no position shall be restricted to one sex for the following: (1) Law-enforcement positions requiring the bearing of firearms; and (2) Institutional or custodial positions where the duties may be properly performed only by a member of the same sex as the persons under his or her care or for whom the services are rendered.

Certification of eligibles will be made by the Commission without regard to sex except where the position falls in one of the categories covered by the exception descibed above. An appointing officer who asks for certification of one sex only for appointment to a position in one of these categories must provide a statement to the certifying office of the Commission indicating the employment circumstances which, in his opinion, bring the position under one or the other of the exceptions. This statement should appear on the request for certification (Standard Form 39).

A certifying office of the Commission may sustain objections to an eligible in unusual circumstances where it can be clearly and logically concluded from the facts at hand that the *particular male or female eligible* cannot reasonably be expected to perform effectively the duties of the position. Objections of this kind, if based on the physical requirements of a particular job, will not be sustained unless it can be shown that the person is not physically able to perform the duties of that particular job. For example, work of an arduous nature will have to be evaluated in the light of the actual physical demands of the job and the physical capacities of the eligible. Determinations with respect to the physical inability of a particular person to perform the duties of a position effectively will be made in accordance with the instructions in FPM chapter 339, Qualification Requirements (Medical).

The following are examples of the kinds of employment conditions which by themselves, will not warrant sustaining objections because of the sex of an eligible:

(1) Travel, including extensive travel, travel in remote areas, or travel with a person or persons of the opposite sex.

(2) Rotating assignments or other shift work.

(3) Geographical location, neighborhood environment, or outdoor work.

(4) Contact with public or a particular group or groups.

(5) Exposure to weather.

(6) Living or working facilities, except where the sharing of common living quarters with members of the opposite sex would be required.

(7) Working with teams or units of the opposite sex.

(8) Monotonous, detailed, or repetitious duties.

(9) Limited advancement opportunities.

In making selections other than from certificates (i.e., selections for appointments outside registers and for noncompetitive actions), each agency is responsible for ensuring that it implements the basic employment policy described above in the same way that it is implemented by the Commission in certifying eligibles for competitive appointment.

FPM Letter No. 332–11, dated September 30, 1968, provides that a Federal agency may place a job advertisement under a separate male or female column heading only when the position being filled is one for which the Commission has found that restriction of consideration to one sex is justified. The policy described above is for application in making these recruitment advertising judgments.

NICHOLAS J. OGANOVIC,
Executive Director.

U.S. CIVIL SERVICE COMMISSION,
Washington, D.C., August 7, 1970.

Hon. EDITH GREEN,
Chairman, Special Subcommittee on Education, Committee on Education and Labor, U.S. House of Representatives, Washington, D.C.

DEAR MADAM CHAIRMAN: This letter provides the additional information you requested during our presentation of testimony on July 31, 1970.

Your questions on Federal employment concerned the following points:

AVERAGE GRADE LEVELS FOR MALE/FEMALE

	Male	Female
1961 [1] (GS only)	GS–9.0	GS–4.0.
1969 (GS only)	GS–9.6	GS–5.2.

[1] (1960 data not available)

EEO TRAINING AT THE FEDERAL EXECUTIVE INSTITUTES (BERKELEY AND KINGS POINT)

As you requested, I checked with our Executive Seminar Centers at Kings Point and Berkeley to determine the coverage given the matter of equal opportunity for women. As I indicated at the hearing, this topic is given coverage at the sessions. During the first 6 months of this year, the center at Kings Point covered equal opportunity for women to some extent at each one of its sessions. It is covered under the topic of "Current Trends in Personnel Management" which is a component of each one of the sessions. In addition to presentations on the subject itself, there are living examples presented to the students. For example, Dr. Martha Peterson, President of Barnard College, and Dr. Nina Reese, who leads the graduate studies program of the City College of New York, have both participated in the Kings Point sessions during the first 6 months of this year. While their topics have not been equal opportunity for women, they have demonstrated to the class the ability of women to handle top level assignments and this is one of the reasons for their selection to appear at the Center.

The Berkeley Center has also been cognizant of the need to provide coverage on the question of equality for women. For example, on Friday, August 7, 1970,

Aileen Hernandez, President of the National Organization of Women and a former member of the Equal Employment Opportunity Commission, will lead a session on civil rights and public policy.

A frequent speaker at the Berkeley Center is Mrs. Dorothy Jongeward who is a consultant on education and family life and discusses men's attitudes towards women in the work force. Another frequent session, entitled "Focus on American Women", is presented at the Center by a panel of women from the San Francisco Bay Area. The focus is on discrimination against women in American life. Our Center Director in Berkeley is working closely with the Director of the Women's Bureau in determining additional appropriate speakers on the subject of equality of women.

VACANCY ANNOUNCEMENTS FOR CIVIL SERVICE POSITIONS

Civil Service Commission policy precludes limiting vacancies to one sex except in unusual circumstances when the agency has obtained CSC approval. These exceptions are:

Law-enforcement positions requiring the bearing of firearms; and

Institutional or custodial positions where the duties may be properly performed only by a member of the same sex as the persons under his or her care or for whom the services are rendered.

A copy of our directive spelling out this procedure is provided as an attachment. You will note that this directive also precludes paid advertising under a separate column with male or female headings.

MINORITY GROUP (NEGRO ONLY) STATISTICS FOR 1967 AND 1969
(GS–9 AND ABOVE)

NEGRO PERCENT OF GRADE LEVEL

	1969	1967
GS–9	6.2	5.3
GS–10	3.5	3.0
GS–11	4.1	3.3
GS–12	2.7	2.3
GS–13	2.2	1.7
GS–14	1.6	1.3
GS–15	1.4	1.0
GS–16	1.1	1.1
GS–17	1.4	1.5
GS–18	1.4	.8

As stated in our testimony on record, minority group statistics have not been collected by sex. The Negro employment figures noted above include both male and female Negroes.

I believe this supplies the information requested. Miss Markoff and I appreciated the opportunity to testify before your Subcommittee. If we can supply any additional information, please let me know. We have already returned the corrected testimony.

Sincerely yours,

IRVING KATOR,
Assistant Executive Director.

U.S. CIVIL SERVICE COMMISSION,
Washington, D.C., October 12, 1970.

Hon. EDITH GREEN,
Chairman, Special Subcommittee on Education of the Committee on Education and Labor, U.S. House of Representatives, Washington, D.C.

DEAR MRS. GREEN: This is in further response to your letter of September 8, 1970, concerning participants in the Executive Training Centers and our interim reply of September 11, 1970.

During Fiscal Year 1970, the participants at the Executive Training Centers were as follows:

	Total	Female	Male
Kings Point, N.Y.	622	23	599
Berkeley, Calif.	642	8	634
The total persons trained at the centers to date is as follows:			
Kings Point (opened 1963)	4,076	129	3,947
Berkeley (opened 1967)	2,500	39	2,461

In my previous letter to you, I forwarded a copy of the Civil Service Commission Executive Director's memorandum to Directors of Personnel, Directors of Equal Employment Opportunity and Federal Women's Program Coordinators which urged once again that their personal attention be directed to inclusion of women at the Executive Training Centers, as well as in all types of training classes. In addition to written directives and memoranda,, we encourage participation of women employees through meetings and conferences with agency personnel. In a recent series of presentations throughout various agencies in the D.C. Metropolitan area and throughout the nation, the Director of the Federal Women's Program has stressed, to a variety of audiences ranging from employee level through top management, that improvement in women's participation in training programs is a major objective of the Federal Women's Program and one that will be closely observed by agency headquarters, the Civil Service Commission and Congressional committees.

We are hopeful that the above will show marked improvements in agency enrollment in future seminars.

Sincerely yours,

IRVING KATOR,
Assistant Executive Director.

EQUAL EMPLOYMENT OPPORTUNITIES ENFORCEMENT ACT—HEARINGS BEFORE THE SUBCOMMITTEE ON LABOR OF THE COMMITTEE ON LABOR AND PUBLIC WELFARE, U.S. SENATE 91ST CONGRESS, FIRST SESSION ON S. 2453—TO FURTHER PROMOTE EQUAL EMPLOYMENT OPPORTUNITIES FOR AMERICAN WORKERS, AUG. 11, 12, SEPT. 10 AND 16, 1969

PREPARED STATEMENT OF WILMA SCOTT HEIDE, MEMBER, PENNSYLVANIA HUMAN RELATIONS COMMISSION

I am Wilma Scott Heide, a Behavioral Research Scientist, a member of the Pennsylvania Human Relations Commission, and of the Pennsylvania Boards of Directors of the American Civil Liberties Union (ACLU), vice-chairman of the Allegheny County Council on Civil Rights and a leader of the National Organization for Women, Inc. (NOW). However, I am here today as a citizen to briefly share some observations, raise some fundamental questions and make specific recommendations to this Senate Subcommittee so you may truly act to legislate effectively and thus not only promote but unequivocally *advocate* equal employment opportunity for American workers.

First, thank you for this opportunity. I had no intention of taking a day away from my other citizen commitments, my family and my employment to personally address this subcommittee. However, the quality and equality of life to which I am committed within and outside my home compel me to be here and be heard. If the federal legislation under question is *at all* equivocal, ineffective, incomplete, or uncommitted to human equity, then our more local, regional efforts are diminished by just that much absence of national leadership and/or action. I do detect a need for fuller commitment of this nation to human equity as variously evident in the approach and content of both bills S. 2453 and S. 2806 and in the serious omission from both of necessary provisions. So much for my reasons for being here.

Now, for some observations and fundamental questions vis-a-vis S. 2453 and S. 2806. It may be revealing to note that : S. 2453 . . . "may be cited as the 'Equal Employment Opportunities Enforcement Act' " (lines 3 and 4, page 1 of Bill; S. 2806 . . . "may be cited as the 'Equal Employment Opportunity Act of 1969.' " I have 3 observations/questions: (1) is the omission of the word enforcement from the administration bill S. 2806 significant and indeed reflect the real intent? Its proponents claim it is designed for enforcement not mere administration of the law. (2) Why does S. 2806 state "Act of 1969?" Why must the date be included in the title of the law? Will the administration have some other laws to introduce in 1970 or 1971, depending on the political climate then? If the commitment to equity is present, the Act will be independent of the year or the climate and will in title, approach, and content reflect the ongoing commitment to Law, Order, and Justice, so frequently proclaimed. However, neither S. 2453 nor S. 2806 maintains active advocacy as purposes of the bills.

"To further promote equal . . . opportunities . . ." is weak, weasel language that communicates little more than platitudinous niceties. Measure that language, I urge you, against the unequivocal language and force of bills designed to repress and punish citizen unrest often arising from unequal opportunities and other fundamental inequities.

In studying bills S. 2806 from the administration and S. 2453, the former places reliance on the courts via the Justice Department to enforce equal employment opportunity under Title VII of the 1964 Civil Rights Act. This may be *one* important option needed by the EEOC in its resources to fully implement equal employment opportunity. To depend on this method alone for EEOC enforcement power might be utter folly and an outrageous insult to the intelligence particularly of those citizens still excluded from equal opportunity and for the following reasons:

1. Approximately only 1% (not 5–10–50) of the U.S. Justice Department's *total* budget is allocated to its Civil Rights Division although this division represents one of seven (not 1 of 100) major divisions of Justice. The Civil Rights Division itself has jurisdiction in eight principal areas, only one of which deals with employment cases under Title VII. Thus, it is conceivable that only ⅛th of 1%, and certainly *less than* 1%, of its funds are available for employment justice. Who can honestly claim satisfaction with putting all one's enforcement eggs in *that* basket?

2. Forty of the Justice Department's own 76 Civil Rights Attorneys have been meeting secretly to draw up grievances that reflect concern about this Administration's back-tracking on civil rights in the instance of school desegregation. This action has been mandated since 1954. One shudders at the inactivity of the Justice Department since 1964 on employment and indeed that inactivity is confirmed by the report of Richard Nathan of the Brookings Institution for the U.S. Commission on Civil Rights, dated April, 1969 and on page 76.

3. There are several other reasons for favoring S. 2453 over S. 2806, the most fundamental of which is: Bringing suit against recalcitrant employers is a time-consuming, costly and awkward enforcement method that requires the EEOC to assemble witnesses and assume all the burden of proof even after probable cause has been established. No wonder aggrieved persons and groups feel little hope of redress. A cease and desist order, while not enough (as I shall detail shortly), does put an immediate stop to discrimination and puts the onus of litigation on the offending employer or contractor. I leave to your sense of real justice which has demonstrated more effective practice in producing equity.

4. In those instances where the Justice Department has acted for employment equity, not a single one of the 33 cases to date has been initiated in cases of sex discrimination, although sex discrimination has made up from ¼ to ⅓ of EEOC cases at any one time. While the symbol of justice may appear as a woman, the practice and concept of justice in the U.S. has seldom involved women themselves, women's real needs as persons, let alone their real definitions as persons entitled to full protection under all laws guaranteed to other U.S. citizens. In short, by systematic sexual inequity in law and practice, women have been and are today denied sexual equality so that gross and outrageous legislation without representation even seems natural and inevitable.

In brief, I am truly grieved that the EEOC Chairman was somehow persuaded to accept S. 2806 and that the protest of other EEOC members has not been more forceful and illuminating of S. 2806's real and present dangers.

S. 2453 is the more desirable of the bills for reasons I will detail and yet it, itself, is inadequate in the absence of necessary provisions which I will recommend. S. 2453 is desirable for the following reasons and I would urge retention of these provisions with extensions as noted:

1. Removal of the burden of enforcement from the complainant by providing authority to the EEOC to issue cease and desist orders and to enforce them through the courts. The EEOC needs, additionally, the authority to prosecute appeals to or from the Circuit Court of Appeals and discretion to proceed on its own or through the Justice Department. I recommend that S. 2453 be so amended.

2. Deletion of the exception for state and local governments from coverage of Federal Civil Rights Acts is good. The exemption of educational institutions from employment coverage is unthinkable, if we value at all the critical role of education in social change to promote human equality. In fact, I would specifically advocate inclusion of educational institutions and public employees in general and teachers and administrators in particular, in coverage under all civil rights legislation.

3. The expansion of coverage to employers of eight (as against the present 25) is desirable.

4. The transfers to the EEOC of enforcement of nondiscrimination in employment by government contractors and subcontractors from the U.S. Department of Labor, Office of Federal Contract Compliance and from the Civil Service Commission authority to enforce nondiscrimination in Federal employment are

important steps in the direction of better coordination and commitment to employment equity. I would additionally advocate transfer of administration of the Federal Women's Program to the EEOC. Steps to eliminate Social Security laws and practices that disadvantage working women should come under the jurisdiction of the EEOC.

Neither bill addresses itself to some serious situations I would like to see corrected by specific amendment to S. 2453. While S. 2453 represents some improvements, I would suggest that lines 11–22 on page 3 of this bill raise serious value questions. This part deals with violating confidentiality of EEOC information in processing complaints (after probable cause is established) and effecting conciliation. Now, as a State Commissioner, I am not unfamiliar with the rationale and value of confidentiality and do not oppose practical implementation of the same. I do protest the relative sanction of a fine of not more than $1,000.00, or imprisonment for not more than one year or both for revealing information *about* a violation and yet can only say (even if S. 2453 becomes law) to those who violate the law: "You must cease and desist." Does this mean that revealing data about a violation is indeed more serious than the act of violation?

This Subcommittee might be well advised to reverse the negative sanctions for the respective behaviors from that now proposed. In fact, this raises the whole question of the serious commitment of this nation to equal opportunity in employment or elsewhere and is but one of numerous examples of laws which protect "the haves" as against "the have nots." Is it more serious if someone robs $50.00 (or whatever) from my purse or your wallet or, if others deprive whole groups of people of employment opportunity to even acquire and retain the discretionary $50.00? The negative sanctions applied for robbing or already acquired possessions contrasted with the slap on the wrist (if that) for systematically still excluding blacks and women (especially) from the chance to acquire equity must suggest we are a long distance from justice in social concept and the law.

This brings me to my final recommendations: The EEOC has issued guidelines that state that: (1) Title VII supersedes state protective (so-called) laws and that (2) classified employment advertising segregated by sex without a proven bona fide occupational qualification (BFOQ) violates Title VII of the 1964 Civil Rights Act. I urge amendment of S. 2453 to make both of these guidelines specific sections of the law in unequivocal language so that newspapers be specifically named as subject to the jurisdiction of the law. The present typical sex segregated want ads represent a flagrant frustration of equal employment opportunity especially for women at their point of entry; it seriously blunts the aspirations of the young and irresponsibly denies employers the full range of pools from which to draw human resources. As women and men, we're perfectly able to define our own interests and preferences. In a day when overpopulation is of increasingly critical concern, we cannot encourage, and dare not countenance, parenthood as the chief occupation of one half the population and so sex stereotype roles as to absolve the other half from all but economic responsibility for that.

The recommendations for coverage to strengthen the EEOC and for programs to be shifted to the EEOC require the priorities, funds and quality of commitment to guarantee effective results. The legislation you recommend must include specific attention to effective fiscal and other behaviors.

Now, I note that my Senators: Hugh Scott and Richard Schweiker have both sponsored both Bills—S. 2806 and S. 2453. Since these bills are different in intent and probable effect, I would like to ask Senator Scott, who is not here, and Senator Schweiker of this Labor Subcommittee precisely and pointedly where they stand on Equal Employment Opportunity. Are they for both bills? Are they covering all options? Is this dual sponsorship window-dressing? More important than what they, or anyone else, sponsor is what they advocate regardless of political consequences. I have stated that S. 2453, with certain specific amendments and additions, is clearly preferable with provisions of S. 2806 to be available for discretionary use at the option of the EEOC.

As a constituent of Senators Scott and Schweiker with several different constituencies of my own relevant to social issues, I am frankly worried. Laws and practices in this achievement-oriented culture are still primarily decided by white men. Most of these white men have as their birthright the opportunities and facilitating social system that still effectively excludes most blacks and most women from significant roles. Until middle-aged affluent white male-dominated America sees the outrageous incompatibility of a democracy with still present need of people like me to plead for my birthright along with my black brothers and sisters, citizen unrest will increase and multiply. Women's violence will be redirected from self-hate, husband-pressuring, and child-battering to changing the present inequitable system. Just as Black is Beautiful: Women are People. Please take Civil Rights *Laws* more seriously if you want order and justice in this land.

JOB EQUALITY FOR WOMEN—SPEECH BY SONIA PRESSMAN, SENIOR ATTORNEY, OFFICE OF THE GENERAL COUNSEL, EQUAL EMPLOYMENT OPPORTUNITY COMMISSION, APRIL 29, 1970

I'd like to discuss with you developments in the law of sex discrimination in employment under Title VII of the Civil Rights Act of 1964. Title VII, which is administered by the Equal Employment Opportunity Commission—the EEOC, became effective on July 2, 1965. It prohibits discrimination based on race, color, religion, sex, and national origin by covered employers, employment agencies, and unions. We receive about 12,000 charges of discrimination a year, about 25% of which involve sex discrimination. Charges of sex discrimination represent our second largest category of cases, after charges of race discrimination.

I should like to briefly review for you the highlights of our rulings in processing these charges.

JOB CLASSIFICATION AND BONA FIDE OCCUPATIONAL QUALIFICATION (BFOQ)

The Commission has held that, as a general rule, employers may not maintain job classifications based on sex. Title VII does, however, permit the hiring of members of one sex only when that is reasonably necessary to the normal operation of a particular business or enterprise. In such instances, sex is termed a "bona fide occupational qualification," or BFOQ. It is obvious, for example, that an employer need hire only a woman as a ladies' restroom attendant, fitter in a ladies' dress shop, actress, model for women's clothes, and for jobs in the entertainment industry where *sex appeal* is an essential qualification. Beyond such examples, however, all jobs must be open without regard to sex.

Thus, an employer cannot refuse to hire women because of his own preferences, or those of his employees, customers, or clients. Women cannot be denied employment because of assumptions or stereotypes about women as a class, or because the job requires supervision over men, late-night work, lifting of heavy weights or other strenuous physical activity, and so on.

In the area of BFOQ, publicity focussed on charges of sex discrimination in the employment of flight cabin attendants, commonly referred to as stewards and stewardesses. The EEOC found reasonable cause to believe that airlines discriminated on the basis of sex when they refused to hire males as stewards,[1] and when they required stewardesses to resign on marriage or on reaching their early thirties.[2]

There have been a number of court decisions, some of which are pending on appeal, dealing with a male's right to be a steward,[3] and a stewardess's right to remain on the job after marriage.[4] It appears that these questions will ultimately be resolved at the appellate court level.

The Commission's view that sex is rarely a BFOQ for a job was not adopted in several early District Court cases.[5] However, the first appellate court decision

---

[1] 33 Fed. Reg. 3361 (Feb. 24, 1968).
Similarly, on May 21. 1969. the Commission found that women cannot be denied positions as pursers aboard United States merchant marine vessels. EEOC Decision in Case No. YNY 9–047.
In re *Kusner* v. *Maryland Racing Commission*, Law No. 37,044 (Circuit Court. Prince George's County, Maryland, 1968), involves bfoq, although it was not a Title VII proceeding. In that case. the Court ordered the Maryland Racing Commission to issue a jockey's license to Kathy Kusner, after indicating that the prior denial of such a license had been based on sex.
[2] EEOC Decisions (issued Aug. 1968), CCH Employment Practices Guide, Transfer Binder, New Developments, Aug. 1968–April 1969, ¶¶ 8001–8003; Pressman, *Airline Stewardes and Pilot Cases* (Speech of Apr. 14, 1969), CCH Employment Practices Guide, New Developments, ¶ 8007.
[3] *Diaz* v. *Pan American World Airways, Inc.*, — F. Supp. — (S.D. Fla., Memorandum Opinion Apr. 9, 1970).
[4] *Evenson* v. *Northwest Airlines, Inc.*, 268 F. Supp. 29 (S.D. Va., 1967); *Cooper* v. *Delta Airlines, Inc.*, 66 LRRM 2489 (E.D. La., 1967); *Lansdale* v. *United Airlines*, 62 LC ¶¶ 9416 and 9417 (D.C. Fla., 1969), pending on appeal in the Fifth Circuit; *Sprogis* v. *United Airlines*, 62 LC ¶ 9399 (D.C. Ill., 1969).
[5] *Ward* v. *Firestone Tire and Rubber Co.*, 260 F. Supp. 579 (W.D. Tenn.. 1966) (*not appealed*); *Bowe* v. *Colgate-Palmolive Co.*. 272 F. Supp. 332 (S.D. Ind.. 1967). *rev'd in part in* 416 F. 2d 711 (C.A. 7, 1969); and *Gudbrandson* v. *Genuine Parts Co.*, 59 LC ¶ 9225 (D.C. Minn., 1968) (*not appealed*).

issued in March of 1969 adopted the Commission's approach,[6] as have all subsequent court decisions,[7] except for a recent case dealing with the flight cabin attendant's job.[8] With that exception, the courts have indicated that sex would be a BFOQ for a job only where the employer proved that all of substantially all members of one sex were unable to perform it.

TERMS, CONDITIONS, AND PRIVILEGES OF EMPLOYMENT

As a general rule, equal terms, conditions, and privileges of employment must be made available for men and women. Thus, employees are entitled to equality with regard to wages and salaries. Title VII covers both the obvious types of discrimination where men and women in the same job classification are receiving disparate wages or salaries, and the more subtle type where only women are employed in a job classification and the wage rate is discriminatorily depressed because only women have traditionally been employed in that classification.[9]

Title VII prohibits the establishment or maintenance of seniority lists or lines of progression based on sex. The problems of correcting discriminatory seniority lines based on sex are similar to those involved in correcting racially-discriminatory seniority systems.[10] In both cases, it is necessary to ensure that the new system does not carry forward and incorporate the effects of past discrimination. Otherwise, blacks and women with long years of plant service will still find themselves excluded from jobs and departments that were formerly closed to them. In these situations, employers and unions have a unique opportunity to utilize the collective bargaining relationship in a creative manner. At the request of the parties, the EEOC will, wherever possible, supply experienced staff to assist in developing seniority systems untainted by discrimination.

The EEOC has said that an employer may not refuse to hire married women or women with children, legitimate or illegitimate, and may not discharge female employees because of marriage or parenthood, unless it has a similar policy for men. Contrary to these views, the Fifth Circuit Court of Appeals, in the case of *Phillips* v. *Martin Marietta Corporation* found that an employer could lawfully refuse to hire women with pre-school age children although it hired men with such children.[11]

At Senate Judiciary Committee hearings this past January, spokesmen for women testified in opposition to the nomination of Judge G. Harrold Carswell to the Supreme Court because he had joined with the majority of the appellate court in denying the petition for rehearing in the *Phillips* case.[12]

On March 2, the Supreme Court granted the petition for certiorari in *Phillips*, after an *amicus curiae* brief in support of the petition had been filed by the EEOC and the Department of Justice. This was the first time that the Department of Justice had filed a brief on a matter of substance in a case involving sex discrimination. *Phillips* will be the first Title VII case argued before the Supreme Court.

With regard to insurance coverage, the Commission has stated that an employer may not discriminate on the basis of sex with regard to medical, hospital,

---

[6] *Weeks* v. *Southern Bell Telephone and Telegraph Co.*, 408 F. 2d 228 (C.A. 5, 1969), *rev'g in part* 56 LC ¶ 9084 (S.D. Ga., 1967).

[7] *Cheatwood* v. *South Central Bell Telephone and Telegraph Co.*, — F. Supp. —, 60 LC ¶ 9299 (M.D. Ala., 1969) : *Bowe* v. *Colgate-Palmolive Co.*, 416 F. 2d 711 (C.A. 7, 1969), *rev'g in part* 272 F. Supp. 332 (S.D. Ind. 1967).

[8] *Diaz* v. *Pan American World Airways, Inc.*, — F. Supp. — (S.D. Fla., Memorandum Opinion Apr. 9, 1970).

[9] Such discrimination can be ascertained by comparing the wages of these women with the wages of men doing comparable work in the company involved, or men doing the same work at other plants in the industry.

[10] The applicability of Title VII to racially discriminatory seniority systems was involved in *United States* v. *Hayes International Corporation*, 514 F. 2d 1038 (C.A. 5, 1969), *rev'g* 295 F. Supp. 803 (N.D. Ala., 1968) ; *Local 189. United Papermakers and Paperworkers, AFL–CIO. CLC* v. *United States (Crown Zellerbach Corporation)*, 416 F. 2d 980 (C.A. 5, 1969), *aff'g* 282 F. Supp. 39 (E.D. La., 1968), *cert. being sought ; Quarles* v. *Philip Morris, Incorporated*, 279 F. Supp. 505 (E.D. Va., 1968).

[11] 411 F. 2d 1, *aff'g* 58 LC ¶ 9152 (M.D. Fla., 1968). Thereafter, one of the members of the Court of Appeals petitioned for a rehearing en banc, and, on July 29, 1969, the Court, on its own motion, withdrew the opinion. On October 13, 1969, in a 10–3 decision, the Court denied the petition for rehearing. 61 LC ¶ 9342.

[12] On January 29, 1970, Congresswoman Patsy Mink and Mrs. Betty Friedan, author of "The Feminine Mystique," and president of the National Organization for Women (NOW), testified in opposition to the nomination.

accident, and life insurance coverage.[13]

We have stated that, as a general rule, expectant mothers are entitled to a 5–6 month maternity leave of absence with the right of reinstatement to the job vacated, at no loss of seniority or any of the other benefits or privileges of employment.[14]

The EEOC has said that men and women are entitled to equality with regard to optional and compulsory retirement age privileges,[15] and that we would decide questions of differences based on sex in pension benefits on a case-by-case basis.

CLASSIFIED ADVERTISING

The EEOC has long ruled that an advertiser may not indicate a preference or limitation based on sex in the context of classified advertising unless sex is a BFOQ for the job involved. On January 24, 1969, we issued an additional Guideline finding that it is also unlawful for an advertiser to place ads in sex-segregated columns, such as those headed "Help Wanted—Male," and "Help Wanted—Female," unless sex is a BFOQ for the job involved.

Although a lawsuit filed by the American Newspaper Publishers Association—The ANPA—and the Washington, D.C. Evening Star attacking this latter Guideline is currently pending, the appellate court permitted the Guideline to become effective January 1969.[16]

In spite of the Commission's Guideline, most newspapers around the country, including Boston's papers, continue to maintain sex-segregated classified advertising columns. There are a number of reasons for this. The pendency of the ANPA lawsuit has caused some confusion as to the validity of the Commission's Guideline. Furthermore, women initially filed few charges attacking segregated columns, apparently because they were unclear as to who had standing to file such charges.[17]

There are, however, continuing developments in this area. Women in New York City and Pittsburgh filed charges against newspapers in those cities with the city FEP Commissions. As a result, the New York Times and all other major New York City newspapers discontinued the maintenance of sex-segregated columns in December of 1968. The Pittsburgh Commission recently concluded hearings involving the Pittsburgh Press.

Moreover, women are beginning to file charges involving sex-segregated ads with the EEOC. As these charges are decided at the Commission and in the courts, we shall see a crystallization of the law in this area.

STATE PROTECTIVE LEGISLATION

The EEOC issued a number of early Guidelines on the relationship between Title VII and state protective legislation.[18] These state laws prohibit the employment of women in certain occupations, such as mining and bartending; limit their hours of work and the weight they may lift; and require certain benefits for women workers, such as minimum wages, premium pay for overtime, rest periods, and physical facilities.

In August 1969, the EEOC issued its current Guideline on the subject, finding that state laws restricting the employment of women are superseded by Title VII and, accordingly, do not justify the refusal to employ women.[19] Two federal

---

[13] The EEOC's Decisions in the area of sex discrimination and insurance coverage are currently suspended pending a review of the rulings of the EEOC and the Department of Labor under the Equal Pay Act. For a discussion of the problems in this area, see Pressman, *Sex Discrimination and Fringe Benefits under Title VII of the 1964 Civil Rights Act,* CCH Employment Practices Guide, New Developments, ¶ 8004 (Speech of Apr. 16, 1969).

[14] For further discussion of the EEOC's rulings in the area of maternity leave and benefits, see Pressman, *Sex Discrimination and Fringe Benefits under Title VII of the 1964 Civil Rights Act, supra* note 12.

[15] 33 Fed. Reg. 3344 (Feb. 24, 1968), amended in 33 Fed. Reg. 9495 (June 28, 1968). The EEOC's General Counsel issued an interpretation of this ruling that women who had an option to retire within 5, 7, or 10 years after October 1, 1968, under a plan existing on that date which permitted earlier optional retirement by women, might lawfully be permitted to exercise such options. GC Opin. of Sept. 13, 1968, EEOC Press Release 68–60 (Sept. 16, 1968).

[16] *American Newspaper Publishers Assn.* v. *Alexander,* 59 LC ¶ 9203 (C.A., D.C., 1969).

[17] There has been no litigation on this point to date. It would, however, appear that anyone who has *applied* for the job advertised or is interested in *applying* for it, as well as an *incumbent employee* would have standing to attack segregated classified advertising. It may also be found that anyone in the labor force who reads the advertisement has standing.

[18] 29 C.F.R. § 1604.1 (Dec. 2, 1965) ; EEOC policy Statement of Aug. 19, 1966 (unpublished) ; 33 Fed. Reg. 3344 (Feb. 24, 1968), EEOC Press Release 68–14 (Feb. 23, 1968).

[19] 34 Fed. Reg. 13367 (Aug. 19, 1969), EEOC Press Release 69–37.

district courts which had occasion to consider the matter adopted the EEOC's approach.[20]

The EEOC's current Guideline contains no enunciation of the Commission's position with regard to state laws which require benefits for women workers, such as minimum wages and premium overtime pay; the Commission will decide these issues on a case-by-case basis. It would, however, appear that such state laws will likewise not justify a refusal to hire women. They may, however, be harmonized with Title VII where the benefits involved can be extended to men.

Last year, the Attorneys General of South Dakota,[21] Pennsylvania,[22] Oklahoma,[23] and Michigan[24] issued Opinions finding that Title VII and/or their state FEP legislation superseded their state's protective laws.[25]

In December 1969, the EEOC found that Title VII supersedes not only conflicting state legislation, but also prior conflicting federal legislation. In that Decision, the Commission found that Title VII superseded the District of Columbia's maximum hours laws for women.[26] On March 25, 1970, the Corporation Counsel for the District of Columbia issued an Opinion adopting the Commission's view.

In addition to processing charges of discrimination, the EEOC engages in a number of other activities designed to eliminate discrimination, such as conducting hearings, providing grants to state FEP agencies, providing technical assistance to those covered by the Act, research, and analysis of our reporting system. The EEOC financed a report on the rubber industry in Ohio issued in September 1967; and it conducted hearings on the textile industry in North and South Carolina in January 1967, in white-collar employment in New York City in January 1968, and in the aerospace and communications industries in Los Angeles in March 1969. The research study and hearings revealed the substantial under-representation of black women in the rubber industry in Akron, Ohio,[27] and in the Carolina textile establishment studied;[28] and the discriminatory exclusion of women in general from managerial and professional positions in white-collar employment in New York City,[29] and in the aerospace and communications industries in Los Angeles.[30]

Beginning in 1966 for employers, and 1967 for unions and joint labor-management apprenticeship committees, the EEOC has required annual reports on the employment of minority groups and women, their union membership, and their participation in apprenticeship programs. Last year, based on the 1966 reports, we published the first nationwide employment statistics on women.[31] These

---

[20] *Rosenfeld* v. *Southern Pacific Company*, 293 F. Supp. 1219 (C.D. Calif., 1968), appeal pending Nos. 23,983 and 23,984 (C.A. 9); *Richards* v. *Griffith Rubber Mills*, 300 F. Supp. 338 (D.C. Oregon, 1969). But see *Mengelkoch* v. *Industrial Welfare Commission*, 284 F. Supp. 950 (C.D. Calif., 1968), *vac'd and rem'd* 58 LC ¶ 9165 (U.S. S.Ct., 1968), and 284 F. Supp. 956 (C.D. Calif., 1968), *appeal dismissed* 58 LC ¶ 9165 (U.S. S.Ct., 1968), currently pending on appeal in the Ninth Circuit; and *Ward* v. *Luttrell*, 59 LC ¶¶ 9209 and 9210 (E.D. La., 1968) (not appealed). See also state court discussions in *Longacre* v. *State of Wyoming*, 59 LC ¶ 9182 (Wyoming Supreme Court, 1968); *Mating Game, Inc.* v. *The State of California*, Case No. C954160 (Superior Court for Los Angeles County, Jan. 15, 1970), currently pending on appeal to the Court of Appeals for the Second Appellate District; *The Mountain States Telephone and Telegraph Company* v. *Reynolds and The Arizona Civil Rights Commission*, Memorandum Decision of Oct. 22, 1968, in Case No. 196936 (Superior Court of the State of Arizona in and for the county of Maricopa), *aff'g as modified* Opinion of the Arizona Civil Rights Commission in Case No. 17–12E, Dec. 2, 1966, CCH Employment Practices Guide ¶ 20,405.05; and *California* v. *Gardner*, 53 LC ¶ 9015 (L.A. Municipal Court, 1966, *rev'd* in Memorandum Opinion and Judgment (Appellate Dept. of the Superior Court of the State of Calif. for the County of L.A., 1966).
[21] AG Opin., Feb. 27, 1969, CCH Labor Law Reporter, Employment Practices, Transfer Binder. New Developments. Aug., 1968–April 1969, ¶ 8080.
[22] AG Opin., Nov. 14, 1969.
[23] AG Opin. No. 4687, Dec. 30, 1969.
[24] AG Opin. No. 4687, Dec. 30, 1969.
[25] Cf. Opin. of the Attorney General of North Dakota, Apr. 18, 1969, CCH Labor Law Reporter, State Laws, Admin. Rulings, ¶ 49,995.02.
[26] EEOC Decision in Case No. DC 7–6–255 (Dec. 16, 1969), EEOC Press Release 69–69 (Dec. 24, 1969).
[27] Batchelder, A Nearly Free Market for Ohio Rubber Manufacturers But Not for Ohio Negroes (1967); EEOC Press Release No. 67–106 (Nov. 19, 1967); Equal Employment Opportunity Report No. 1, Job Patterns for Minorities and Women in Private Industry, 1966, Part 1, 18–19 (1969).
[28] Employment Patterns in the Textile Industry, North and South Carolina 7; Equal Employment Opportunity Report No. 1, Job Patterns for Minorities and Women in Private Industry, 1966, Part 1, 19–20 (1969).
[29] Help wanted . . . Or Is It? A look at white collar job inequalities for minorities and women (Dec. 1968); Hearings Before the United States Equal Employment Opportunity Commission on Discrimination in White Collar Employment, Hearings held in New York, New York, January 15–18, 1968 (1968).
[30] EEOC Press Release No. 69–9 (Mar. 19, 1969).
[31] Equal Employment Opportunity Report No. 1, Job Patterns for Minorities and Women in Private Industry 1966 (1969).

statistics revealed that while women account for more than 40% of all white collar workers, only 1 out of every 10 management positions, and 1 out of every 7 professional jobs are filled by women.

The statistics revealed by our hearings and our reporting system, as well as similar statistics reported by the Women's Bureau [32] indicate where we are today as regards the status of women in employment. What we have seen in the past 5 years is nothing short of a revolution—a revolution in the legal rights of women to equality on the job, and a revolution in the expectations of women with regard to such equality. There has not yet been a corresponding revolution in the employment status of women—in the jobs they hold and the salaries they earn. Hopefully, with the cooperation of government officials such as those present here today—as well as of representative groups in the private sector—we will be able to convert that legal revolution into a revolution in fact. Thank you.

[News Release, National Organization for Women, June 25, 1970]

N.O.W. President Charges Government Improperly Excludes Equal Opportunity for Women From Federal Compliance Programs; Files Complaint Asking for Labor Secretary To Investigate Federal Contractors Among 1,300 Corporations

National N.O.W. President Aileen Hernandez today scored the Labor Department for weakening sex discrimination guidelines and for accepting corporate Affirmative Action Programs that do not deal with equal opportunity for women.

She called on Secretary of Labor James D. Hodgson to restore the stronger sections originally proposed for the guidelines and to announce and enforce a directive that Order No. 4 shall apply to sex discrimination by all government contractors.

She announced filing of a complaint by N.O.W. with Secretary of Labor Hodgson charging that Federal contractors and subcontractors in a list of more than thirteen hundred major U.S. corporations are not in compliance with the Executive Order (11375) banning discrimination on the basis of sex and demanding that no contracts be awarded to companies filing Affirmative Action Plans that do not provide equal opportunity for women.

She accused the Defense Department, which deals with companies employing half the 14 million workers covered by the Order, of telling companies openly that they do not have to obey the law as far as sex discrimination is concerned—that plans that do not discuss female employment will be accepted.

The complaint filed with the Secretary includes the 100 largest defense contractors (most of which are among the 500 largest U.S. industrial corporations). The complaint asks for compliance reviews of Federal contractors among the 1000 largest industrials, 50 commercial banks, 50 life insurance companies, 50 retail companies, 50 transportation companies, 50 utilities and 47 other companies.

These companies employ over 22,208,241 people. Since the OFCC has authority over companies employing 14,002,075 workers, N.O.W. is confident that this complaint covers virtually all contractors affected by the Executive Order.

At a press conference held today, Mrs. Hernandez stated: "The National Organization for Women is outraged that the U.S. Department of Labor Office of Federal Contract Compliance is accepting Affirmative Action Programs that do not contain equal opportunity for women. The OFCC is not requiring that Federal contractors analyze job categories to determine if underutilization of women exists. Consequently, no goals and timetables are being set to correct deficiencies on the basis of sex.

"N.O.W. believes that it is essential that goals and timetables be required. N.O.W. insists that every covered Federal contractor must set appropriate goals

---

[32] Publications of the Women's Bureau, Department of Labor reveal that many women hold jobs far from commensurate with their abilities and educational achievement. In March, 1968, about one out of six working women who were college graduates were employed in non-professional jobs as clerical, sales, or service workers, or factory operatives. About one-third of the over 29 million women (16 years of age and over) in the labor force in 1968 were employed in clerical jobs, as stenographers, typists, and secretaries.

The median wage or salary income of year-round fulltime workers (14 years and older) in 1967 was:

    men—$7,182
    women—$4,150

In 1967, less than three percent of full-time year-round women workers earned salaries of $10,000 or more; the proportion for men was 23%.

and then direct every effort to increase materially the utilization of women at all levels and in all segments of the work force where they are underrepresented.

"A few contract compliance officers, because of their own concern for equal opportunity for women, have on their own initiative been asking that contractors analyze job categories for underutilization cf women and then set goals and timetables to change these conditions. The majority of contract compliance officers do not even ask for an analysis of the easily identifiable underutilization of women.

"The official policy of the OFCC and the departmental compliance agencies is evident: sex discrimination is de-emphasized in contract compliance. Evidence obtained last week made it obvious that this policy is in fact a stated policy communicated to Federal contractors.

"On June 18, two N.O.W. members attended a workshop conducted by the Defense Department's Office of Contract Compliance for some 200 representatives of major Federal Contractors. The N.O.W. representatives were not invited to the meeting, but learned about it through an employee of one of the participants and believed it would be instructive to hear how Defense Department officials view corporate responsibility and their own responsibility in carrying out the Executive Order.

"The workshop leaders were Seymour Maisel, Chief of the New York Regional Office of Contract Compliance for the Defense Department; Benjamin Collier, his Deputy; and Irving Matlott, Director of Personnel and Industrial Relations for the Bulova Watch Company. It was sponsored by the New York Chamber of Commerce and held in the Chamber's Great Hall at 65 Liberty Street.

"Mr. Maisel told the assembly that the Defense Department has the major compliance office among all government agencies—it has most primary industries under its jurisdiction. He noted tnat written Affirmative Action Programs had been required from government contractors and subcontractors since July 1, 1968.

"Mr. Collier went through each section of Order No. 4, explaining and elaborating on its provisions. He mentioned the word "female" several times in referring to contractors' obligations; most of his discussion and the visual material used in his presentation referred only to racial and ethnic discrimination.

"After the talk, in answer to questions from N.O.W. members, Mr. Maisel stated that: 1. Order No. 4 does not address itself to the "female problem;" 2. The definition of "minority" to include women, as specified in the Federal Register January 17, 1969, has not be "reaffirmed;" minorities are defined as Negro, Oriental, Spanish sur-named and American Indians; 3. Contractors should look at the utilization of women, but they do not have to meet goals for female employment: the obligation to set goals "does not apply" to women; 4. The guidelines do not speak of "Affirmative Action *Programs*" in regard to sex, just as "affirmative action;" and 5. The exclusion of women from Affirmative Action Programs under Order No. 4 would not make a bid "unawardable."

"In effect, minority group women are counted as statistics in setting goal *standards*, but they can be totally excluded from employment, upgrading or training programs without this showing up in compliance reports.

"This outrageous interpretation is a deliberate distortion of the original intent of Executive Order 11375 and of subsequent Labor Department regulations which have made it clear that discrimination against women is to be considered on a par with discrimination against racial and ethnic minorities.

"The government's policy to ignore women in enforcing the Executive Orders against discrimination is evident from the decision made with respect to the McDonnell Douglass Corporation of St. Louis. After holding up some $7.7 billion in contracts from the company, the Defense Department announced that the Pentagon and company officials had reached agreement on goals and quotas for the hiring of Negroes in categories that included professional, supervisory, management and technical positions. The company has 33,000 workers, including 8500 professional and technical and 6390 office and clerical employees. There was no mention of women in the plan.

"Contracts for some 30 other companies are being held up, including a $700 million award for the Newport News Shipbuilding and Dry Dock Company (which has about $7 billion in Defense Department Contracts), and the North American Rockwell Corporation in California must submit a satisfactory plan to obtain the $20 billion contract on which it is bidding. Will these Affirmative Action Programs be accepted without reference to women?

"Instruction to compliance agency staff workers make the Defense Department's position clear. Its Office of Contract Compliance issued an Equal Employment Opportunity Evaluation Report for staff use on April 1, 1970. It instructs staff to provide:

"Information as to the number or percentage of unemployed minorities; the availability in terms of skill levels of minorities and females; the underutilization of minorities and females."

It inquires: "Does the Affirmative Action Plan or did the Contract Relations Officer's review reveal underutilization of minorities and/or females?"

It orders: "Explain whether the Affirmative Action Plan contains acceptable numerical or percentage goals to correct the deficiencies and to increase materially the utilization of minorities and females."

N.O.W. has learned that a revised form, dated May 11, 1970, does not include "female" in any instances.

EEOC ALSO FAILS TO CARRY OUT RESPONSIBILITIES REGARDING WOMEN

Sylvia Roberts, a Baton Rouge attorney and Southern Regional Director of N.O.W., reported at the press conference that lack of concern about women is also apparent in the Equal Employment Opportunity Commission.

She said, "The Report of the President's Task Force on Women's Rights and Responsibilities criticized the Commission for gathering statistics on discrimination that compare the status of minority women to white women and minority men to white men rather than comparing the status of all groups that face discrimination to that of white men.

"The public hearings held June 2 through 4 in Houston (the third set of such hearings in EEOC history) showed little improvement. The announcement for the hearings, issued March 30, made only one reference to women—that "Black females, compared to white females, had the lowest relative occupational standing in 46 urban labor markets studied by the Commission.

"It is an outrage and insult to black women to expect that they should be satisfied with the status of white women in this society. Yet this is the implication of EEOC studies and statements about the status of women workers. Dr. Sally Hacker, President of Houston N.O.W. and a sociologist, re-analyzed all the data in the EEOC staff reports for the hearing to compare the status of white and minority women with white men—the job the EEOC should have done itself."

N.O.W. DEMANDS FEDERAL ACTION

N.O.W. President Aileen Hernandez listed several demands in addition to the demand that Secretary Hodgson announce that Order No. 4 applies to sex discrimination and that no Affirmative Action Programs will be accepted that do not deal with equal opportunity for women. They are that:

1. "The top staffs of compliance agencies and all compliance teams must include women in numbers equal to their representation in the population. The Office of Federal Contract Compliance is opening 11 Agency Technical Compliance Offices around the country. Six of the Directors, Deputy Directors and Community Relations Officers of those offices should be women. The Defense Department's Office of Contract Compliance has only one woman among 110 compliance officers and other departments show similar discrimination. At least half the compliance officers in the country should be women.

"EEOC Commissioner Elizabeth Kuck, the only woman on that body, has been informed that she will not be reappointed by President Nixon. The new appointee must be a woman with substantial experience in the field and with complete dedication to the cause of eradicating discrimination based on sex. The following two appointments to the Commission should also be women of ability and commitment." (Commissioner Kuck was appointed to fill out Mrs. Hernandez's unexpired term.)

"Only 1 of the 13 Regional Area Directors of the EEOC is a woman. Six more women should be appointed to those positions. Half the members of EEOC compliance teams should be women.

2. "The Federal government must give substance to its own Affirmative Action Program—required under Executive Order 11375—by bringing women into top positions in all other government agencies. Although women are 34% of government employees, they are only 5% of employees earning $16,700 and above; 181,-229 individuals are in this category—only 6,556 are women, little more than 1% of all the women in government service. The Federal Women's Programs which are supposed to be set up in all government agencies either do not exist or are not carrying out their mandates. One exception is in the Maritime Agency headed by Helen Bentley.

3. "The Equal Employment Opportunity Commission should hold hearings into sex discrimination in public and private employment in Washington, D.C. In its five years of operation, the EEOC has provided assistance funding to only one local fair employment commission investigating sex discrimination, and that one is more the result of an activist female human rights official than the urgings or interest of the Federal agency. The EEOC should insist that all grants for local investigation and enforcement programs include women and there should be a substantial increase in grants dealing with discrimination where sex alone is a factor."

Mr. Hernandez declared that: "N.O.W. calls upon all members of Congress who are concerned with equal opportunity for women to contact the Secretary of Labor and the President asking for the application of Order No. 4 to women, for the return of the more stringent rules in the original guidelines on sex discrimination and for the other demands we have listed here. We shall not be satisfied until every vestige of sexism in this country is abolished."

Mr. Hernandez's critique of the new guidelines on enforcement of the Executive Order against sex discrimination included the charges that:

"Recruitment at women's schools and colleges and advertising inviting women to apply for jobs are no longer required, just suggested. The reference to creating part-time jobs was totally eliminated.

"The new guidelines do not require that the benefits of protective laws be extended to men. They also create a huge loop-hole by allowing employers to refuse to hire women if they don't have space to build new restrooms—a ludicrous excuse.

"The second defining bona fide occupational qualifications (bfoq) is much weaker than the original, no longer requiring the contractor to prove his justification for refusing to hire women, and the new section on fringe benefits makes it possible to reduce those benefits for women.

"There's no mention of the need to eliminate "ghetto departments" that segregate men and women doing jobs with similar skill requirements into different departments so that women can be paid less, and the ruling says that seniority lines must not be based *solely* on sex, leaving the door open for more "sex plus" decisions.

"One improvement, which wipes out protective legislation as an excuse for denying women jobs, can be attributed to the EEOC ruling that protective laws are invalid when they discriminate against women."

MODEL REMEDIES

[Reprinted from THE AMERICAN SOCIOLOGIST, Vol. 5, No. 1, February, 1970]

3. *Statement and Resolutions of the Women's Caucus:*

For all our commitment to studies of social change the record of the sociological profession has been poor indeed when it comes to predicting and explaining the emergence and the course of major social and political change. We anticipated neither the sharp rise nor the fall of fertility rates in the past 25 years and have only a partial retrospective understanding of why these changes have occurred. We neither predicted nor explained critical turning points in the civil rights or the New Left movements during the past ten years. And unless sociology has a sharp and dramatic awakening rather soon, this predominantly male field will show the same blindness in the late 1960's to the emergence, scale and significance of the women's liberation movement in this country.

Where women are concerned, the majority of men sociologists still engage in the "put down," via ridicule, exclusion masked as sexual flattery, as well as covert denial of the civil rights of women in hiring and promotion. The same white men who experience embarrassment and outrage in old screen stereotypes of the superstitious, foot-shuffling servility of a Stepin Fetchit still accept and act upon a stereotyped set of expectations of male intellectual and social dominance and female intellectual and social dependency that is as outrageous to women as the Negro stereotype is to Blacks. Sociological research and scholarship is rife with a complacent, conventional acceptance of the "what is ought to be" variety, nowhere more apparent than in theory and research on women, marriage and the family. There is a great and pressing need for critical reassessment of many psychological and sociological assumptions in the area of sex role and family structure. To cite but one example: in a world bursting with potential economic and political chaos of population excess, the demographic applied branches of sociology tinker with technological contraceptive gadgetry, despite the fact that research has suggested that the population problem is far more one of how to reduce wanted pregnancies rather than of avoiding unwanted ones. To effect a reduction in wanted pregnancies hinges on the critical issue of what women do with their lives. Any attempts to thwart the aspirations of women for achievement in non-family roles is not only a violation of their basic human rights but a blind encouragement of a bountiful maternity the world no longer needs.

As sociologists we should be capable of distancing ourselves from the dailiness of public and private life, and to work with rather than against any movement dedicated to an expansion of individual opportunity and human rights. It is a failure of the society and of the sociology profession in particular to find as the Women's Caucus survey of graduate departments did this spring, that women were 30 per cent of the doctoral students in graduate school this past year, but only 4 per cent of the full-time full professors in graduate departments; or to find that women were 39 per cent of the research associates in the elite graduate departments but only 5 per cent of the associate and 1 per cent of the full professors in these same top departments. It is outrageous

that a custom persists whereby a woman research associate or lecturer with a Ph.D. and ten years or more of research experience cannot apply for research funds as a sole principal investigator, while a young man with a brand new assistant professorship but no prior responsibility for conducting research can readily do so.

Women are tired of the rationalized litany of their male colleagues—"but women drop out of graduate work to marry and rear a family." In 1969, the question is: what are YOU, the men in graduate sociology departments, doing to retain these highly selected women graduate students? Since these women are carefully selected, else they would not be in your departments, it is more a failure of a department than of the students if they leave without a degree. Do you permit easy transfer of graduate credits to another university? Do you suggest part-time study with stipend support to ease study-home combinations of responsibilities? Has any department studied its Ph.D. drop-outs, much less established policies aimed at reducing this loss of talented young people? Has any sociologist surveyed his own university student, employee and faculty body to gauge the need that might be met by the establishment of university day-care centers for pre-school youngsters?

The Women's Caucus does not seek any new committees. We seek no new symposia. We seek no new conferences on the status of women or the presumed role conflict or identity problems of women. Many of us have attended or contributed to dozens of such ventures already. We have already gathered the empirical facts concerning the distribution of women among students and faculty of graduate sociology departments. What we seek is effective and dramatic action: an unbiased policy in the selection and stipend support of students; a concerted commitment to the hiring and promotion of women sociologists to right the imbalance that is represented by the current situation, in which 67 per cent of the women graduate students in this country do not have a single woman sociology professor of senior rank during the course of their graduate training, and when we participate in an association of sociologists in which NO woman will sit on the 1970 Council, NO woman is included among the associate editors of the *American Sociological Review* or the Advisory Board of the *American Journal of Sociology*, and NO woman sits on the 13-member Committees on Publications and Nominations.

We urge the individual sociologists attending this convention, the departments to which you will shortly return, and the officers, council and committees of this professional association, to consider and to take effective action on the following resolutions from the Women's Caucus:

1. That every sociology department give priority to the hiring and promotion of women faculty on the same salary scale as men until the proportion and rank distribution of women faculty *at least* equals the sex ratio among graduate students, with a long-range goal of increasing the proportion of women among graduate students to 50 per cent. In working toward such a goal, this must supplement rather than detract from depart-

nd promote Black and
dents.

t be given to graduate
oth full- and part-time
l allowances for child
incurred because of

ith others from the
and assisting in the
r pre-school children
at all colleges and

the encouragement
rses on the history
men's movements for
change in all college and university
ogy departments. In departments in which their
male colleagues are sufficiently accessible to personal
education, they should be welcomed as auditors in such
courses.

5. That sex inequality be added as a topic to all courses
and texts which cover social inequality but are now confined to race, religion, and ethnicity.

6. That flexibility guide the appointment of both men
and women to department faculties, facilitating easy
transitions between full- and part-time appointments
to increase the career continuity of women with family
responsibilities or to permit men to play significant roles
in their families and communities. Twenty-six per cent
of the full-time male faculty in graduate departments
today are joint appointments at a senior rank. If a department can thus share a man with another department, it can as readily share a man or a woman faculty
member with a family. It should be noted that an increasing number of young men and women sociologists
wish to contribute significantly to a variety of life areas,
and to avoid a 24-hour-a-day career commitment to
sociology.

7. That women sociologists be added as rapidly as
possible to all committees, advisory or editorial boards
within or related to the American Sociological Association, as the case may be.

8. That sociology endorse the principle of parenthood
leave and family sick leave for all employees, faculty
and students at colleges and universities. Only women

bear children, but men and women rear them. Both sexes
should have the option of taking leave to care for a new
baby, an ill spouse, or a sick child.

9. That sociology consider the findings of their own
research—that school performance predicts school performance but not adult success in work—and examine
the contribution that the present patronage and sponsorship techniques make to these research results. Professors may feel pride in all-round good student perform-
ers and obligation to helpful research assistants, but
this is no necessary harbinger of future success as a
sociologist. We urge the field to dispense with the
patronage system of employment and substitute a strict
adherence to an open employment system based on
performance and creative potential in both scholarship
and teaching. Further, that employers stop violating the
privacy of women and men applicants by inquiries into
actual or potential marital status, fertility plans or political values, and confine interviews to an exchange of
professional qualifications and job characteristics.

10. Lastly, to facilitate communication and assure continuity between annual conventions, we urge the Council,
the Editor, and the Editorial Board of *The American
Sociologist*, to establish a new section in this journal, to
be entitled the "Women's Caucus Newsletter," to
be handled by an editorial representative of the
Women's Caucus.

In the year ahead, the Women's Caucus plans concerted
political action on a departmental and university level
aimed at transforming both the field of sociology and
the status of women within it. But we urge endorsement
from the membership and the Council on either specific
resolutions or the general spirit of these resolutions,
thereby reaffirming sociologists' commitment to social
equality.

It was made clear that the Women's Caucus was seeking
general support and endorsement of the positions taken,
rather than a vote on each separate motion. The general
sense of the statement was approved by both voting and
non-voting members.

Respectfully submitted,
PETER H. ROSSI
Secretary

ACTION RESOLUTIONS PASSED BY MEMBERS OF THE NATIONAL ORGANIZATION FOR
WOMEN AT THE FOURTH ANNUAL CONFERENCE, MARCH 20–22, 1970

HUMAN REPRODUCTION

The basic human right to limit one's own reproduction includes the right to all
forms of birth control (contraception, including sterilization, and abortion),
recognizing the dual responsibility of both sexes. We therefore oppose all legislation and practices that restrict access to any of these means of birth control, and
advocate positive measures requiring:
That all public hospitals offer contraception, sterilization and abortion to anyone requesting these services.
That these services be made accessible to as many people as possible by the
establishment of a network of local public clinics.
That the availability of these services be widely and continuously publicized.
That public funds be allocated for research into new methods of contraception, sterilization and abortion which would increase their safety and availability.
Women should be guaranteed their civil right to an abortion performed by
any qualified person in any suitable setting. We urge the convening of regional
conferences on the repeal of abortion laws.

CHILD CARE

Child care must become a political priority. We therefore propose a coalition
of organizations representing all socio-economic, professional, educational, phil-
anthropic organizations, etc. interested in the establishment of child care facilities
in keeping with the National Organization for Women's goals. The purpose of this
coalition would be to join together to exert pressure on the power structure in
labor, industry, and government to immediately make available facilities, funds,
etc. and to grant tax deductions for quality child care.

In order to make this NOW-sponsored coalition for child care a reality, we call upon the president, chairman of the board, vice presidents of legal, legislation, finance and public relations and the regional directors of the east, south, west and middle west, and chapter and child care committee chairmen to undertake this as an action project of major priority to be organized immediately.

We propose that the fourth annual conference adopt and send the following telegram to Congressman John Brademas (House of Representatives, Washington, D.C.): "The fourth annual conference of the National Organization for Women supports the philosophy behind the Brademas Bill No. HR13520 which addresses itself to child care facilities for children of all economic and social groups. [This was done.]

POLITICS AND LEGISLATION

NOW recognizes the need to act politically to achieve equal rights for women. We are non-partisan: we owe allegiance only to the cause of women's liberation, not to any political party, but we will work through existing political institutions to achieve our aims. We urge women to run for office from any political party and we will work for candidates who support and campaign for our goals.

We support the formation of women's rights caucuses within existing political parties and organizations and the establishment of independent women's political caucuses. These groups would seek out candidates to run for office in support of women's issues and would seek passage of legislation to further the cause of women's rights.

Even when election appears unlikely, NOW members should run for office to educate the public about our concerns. Local chapters should encourage women already active in politics to run on women's issues. Local chapters should set up committees to seek out candidates. Regional conferences should include workshops to train prospective candidates and campaign workers.

NOW urges all political parties to dissolve their women's divisions which have relegated women to servant roles in political life. Women should be included on all levels of party activity on an equal basis with men. In view of the fact that only 2 percent of all elected officials are women, we call on political parties to seek out and run women candidates who represent women's rights and needs.

NOW reaffirms its unalterable opposition to the confirmation of G. Harrold Carswell to the Supreme Court of the United States on the grounds of his sexist action in the Phillips vs. Martin-Marietta case. We understand that the President is committed to a balanced court, and we urge him to appoint a distinguished woman jurist to the present vacancy on the Supreme Court.

We support the New York City demonstration against Rep. Emanuel Cellar in Brooklyn May 9th to protest his opposition to the Equal Rights Amendment.

If possible, the national NOW board meeting should be held in Washington, D.C. May 2–3, immediately before the hearings on the Equal Rights Amendment so that we can call attention to the hearings and urge that national attention be focused on the problems of women.

NOW officers and chapters should seek union support for our legislative goals and work to have unions insure equal rights for women on the job and within labor organizations.

National funds should be earmarked to hire a lobbyist to work on feminist issues in Washington, D.C.

We call a 24-hour general women's strike to commemorate the 50th anniversary of the day women won the right to vote. The strike would focus on the continuing oppression of women and signal the start of a major political effort for the liberation of women.

We advocate that sex discrimination be forbidden in employment, education, housing, public accommodations and government services and that NOW work to add this provision to all local and state laws where it does not appear. NOW should take affirmative action and should insure that enforcement agencies take affirmative action to carry out the law.

We advocate equalizing the legal position of women and men in regard to child care responsibilities, intestate succession and prostitution.

We support United Nations treaties promoting the progress of women, and advocate U.S. government sanctions against any country where women are not enfranchised.

Until our goal of dissolution of women's divisions is reached, we urge the women's divisions of the political parties to run women's candidates for office both within their party and at large.

We urge the Congress of the U.S. to allow Monica Morte and other women to be employed as pages.

EMPLOYMENT

I. Resolve to support and work for legislation to provide equal employment and business opportunities for all women.

We recognize that passage of the equal rights amendment would negate the need for much of this legislation.

Until the amendment is adopted, NOW must work aggressively to achieve the following:

1. The minimum wage act should cover all female employees.

2. All women employees should be covered by Title VII of the Civil Rights Act of 1964.

3. All titles in the Civil Rights Act should contain a provision to eliminate sex discrimination.

4. NOW chapters should institute fair employment practices laws in states where none exist and should work to strengthen those state laws now on the books. Only 22 states have such laws.

5. NOW declares support of the Senate bill S2454 to grant enforcement powers to the Equal Employment Opportunity Commission.

6. NOW endorses Rep. Edith Green's bill HR 15971 and HR 16098 to amend the Federal Fair Labor Standards Act to require equal pay for equal work for female professional, executive or administrative positions.

7. We call upon the government to provide a more practical, realistic and effective way for all federal, state, city and/or public employees to have recourse for filing sex discrimination complaints in employment.

8. We urge repeal of state and local laws which deny women the same freedoms, conditions and privileges as men have for borrowing money, owning real estate and operating businesses.

9. NOW calls for repeal of all restrictive and protective legislation which discriminates against women and requests inclusion of men in all state protective laws.

II. Resolve that NOW provide an affirmative action program to assist women in filing complaints on sex discrimination.

We recognize the need for all chapters to appoint an employment committee chairwoman to spearhead activities.

To assist the programs in each chapter, we offer:

1. New York Chapter employment action plan.

2. A fact sheet on filing a complaint for government and all other female employees and the operation of the EEOC which will be prepared by Eliza Pascal and sent to chapters and submitted to NOW ACTS.

3. We ask that NOW's board of directors appoint an employment coordinator, Aleta Styers, 820 Seward Street, Evanston, Illinois 60202 (Tel: 312–869–4694) who will disseminate information to chapters on the subject; prepare recommendations for actions; compile data on sex discrimination cases filed and won by women. We suggest that pertinent material be printed in NOW ACTS.

III. Resolve that chapters persist in NOW's goal to integrate all newspaper help wanted advertisements.

We recommend continued confrontation with newspaper publishers, picketing, filing complaints with local civil rights commisions. We would like to see a NOW chapter or member prove that a newspaper does exercise judgment in accepting and printing classified advertisements by trying to place a racist and sexist help wanted ad. We ask the board of directors to appoint a coordinator for this project and suggest Joy Sokeitous. Other ideas for chapters to pursue will be coordinated and communicated to NOW chapters by Joy Sokeitous, 1122 Spruce Street, Philadelphia, Pennsylvania 19107.

IV. Resolve to encourage and support women to be economically independent.

We recommend the following chapter actions:

1. Offer career counseling to all women.

2. Encourage and support the formation of businesses for women and women in business.

3. Provide information on securing Small Business Administration loans and obtaining government contracts available to minority businesses.

4. Encourage and suggest procedures for women who wish to pool money to form economic co-ops for businesses, etc.

V. Resolve to make a commitment to help women in poverty.

We recommend that NOW chapters give their support and take action where possible to aid women in poverty. Areas of concern are given below:

1. Whereas we believe in the right of all sisters to employment; and whereas there are not enough jobs to go around; and whereas this situation is expected

to worsen in the 1970's, be it resolved that we support a shortened work week which will open more jobs to women and allow men more time to spend in the home.

2. Be it resolved that we support full employment for our sisters and we believe that when the private economy cannot provide decent jobs, the public economy must.

3. Whereas over 10 percent of women are ill-fed because they are too poor, and whereas this organization is on record as bringing our sisters out of poverty; be it resolved that we look toward the future by supporting in principle a guaranteed income.

WAR

We resolve that NOW shall not take an official position on the Vietnam conflict, feeling that although war is abhorrent, we should not take a position upon this one conflict, since it is not specifically related to Women's Rights.

OVERCOMING SELF-DENIGRATION

We must develop a better means of reaching the many women who are victims of self-hatred. Our anger, so often directed at ourselves, must be focused where it belongs—on the discriminatory laws, policies and attitudes of our society. We can help women to become aware of the need for feminism by approaching the factors that divide and immobilize women:

1. Failure to recognize our sisterhood.

2. Overcoming stereotypes and labels which have socialized us in a male-chauvinist society.

3. Consciousness of the common oppression that affects all women regardless of age, economic status, race or religion.

4. Fear of the feminist movement because of the "sex object" image we have been socialized to believe.

We resolve that:

1. Every chapter and each member of NOW develop skills of communication to large and small groups and on an individual basis. Sensitivity groups could be used to develop support for one another.

2. Training programs be provided to educate women in public speaking, organizing, sensitivity and desexigration techniques.

3. We must trust ourselves and other women approaching new situations. United we stand and progress.

MARRIAGE AND THE FAMILY

We make the following resolutions on marriage and the family.

1. Marriage should be an *equal* partnership with shared economic and household responsibility and shared care of the children.

2. The economic responsibility for the family should be shared proportionately according to income if both partners work outside the home.

3. If only one partner works outside the home, half the income should by law belong to the other partner.

4. All institutions should acknowledge that parenthood is a necessary social service by granting maternal and paternal leaves of absence without prejudice and without loss of job security or seniority.

5. A pamphlet on the legal rights of both partners and divorce and population statistics should be issued with the marriage license.

6. The Social Security law should be altered to provide—

separate social security deductions for employed persons and their dependent spouses in acknowledgement of the fact that the employer is receiving the services of the household spouse as well as the employed person.

full social security payments should continue to children regardless of the re-marriage of their parents.

as long as the present Social Security law is in effect, a dependent spouse should be guaranteed continued coverage regardless of the years of marriage or the financial arrangements of the divorce.

7. Upon dissolution of a marriage, the dependent spouse should be guaranteed health and accident insurance by the government.

8. Government-sponsored child care centers should be available to all in acknowledgement of the responsibility of society toward children.

9. The dependent spouse should be guaranteed government-sponsored retraining for re-entry into the job market.

10. Company pension plans should be expanded to include coverage for the

widow, is she so desires.

11. We encourage insurance companies to issue "end of marriage" insurance. This could be a form of term insurance to be paid to the economically dependent spouse as a form of pension. The sum paid would depend on years of service.

12. The wife should be able to keep her own name or the husband should be able to take his wife's name, and/or there should be the option of both partners choosing a neutral second name to be used also by the children, or the children should use both the wife's and husband's name.

13. A woman's title should be "Ms." without differentiation as to marriage, and a woman should use her given first name.

CONSCIOUSNESS-RAISING IN THE MEDIA

We propose the following actions and reforms:

1. Citizen's suit for equal time for feminist views on TV and radio.

2. FCC complaints against unfair representations about women.

3. NOW Legal Defense and Education Fund; seek grant for commercials for a positive image of women (analogous to anti-cigarette ads).

4. NOW decries sex role stereotypes presented on educational TV and calls for a meeting between producers of Sesame Street and feminist psychologists and writers.

5. Establish a committee for awards to movies, etc. for honest portrayal of women as human beings and for progress toward eliminating male-female stereotypes.

6. Call for more women media executives.

7. Organize and educate women already in media. Work toward getting them into NOW.

8. Call for more women on news and substantive programs on TV networks.

9. At chapter meetings, conduct letter-writing campaigns to companies with particularly obnoxious commercials.

10. Stickers on ads—"this ad is offensive to women."

11. Every member should write letters commending fair coverage of the women's movement (and encourage any effort in that direction).

12. NOW has reached the point where we can complain to newspapers about unfair or dishonest or snickering treatment and the reporter, male or female, who writes such an article should receive no further cooperation. The committee unanimously adopted a motion to urge cooperation with any honest reporter, male or female.

13. Techniques for improving coverage in the media:
    —Picket newsstands urging boycotts of particularly obnoxious newspapers;
    —NOW news conferences should be scheduled at 9 a.m. if possible, and scheduling of other NOW events should take competing news into consideration.

14. Investigate the power of sit-ins to encourage the media to be fairer to women. *Ladies Home Journal* sit-in produced a number of desirable changes.

RELIGION

Since the church bodies have contributed to the development of concepts which encourage discrimination against women and have faithfully reflected these ideas in their own practices, and since the National Council of Churches represents such a large coalition of churches, we urge that the NCC:

1. Challenge and assist church bodies to rethink and restate theological concepts which contribute to a false view of women.

2. Give stronger leadership to efforts to eliminate discrimination against women in society and in the life of the church.

3. Take the lead in uniting women of all denominations and religious groups to work together to support efforts to recognize the right of women to be ordained in religious bodies where that right is still denied.

4. Place the issue of discrimination against women and its relationship to the work of the National Council on the agenda of its general board, its divisions and their departments.

5. Develop personnel policies and practices that will achieve a more adequate representation of women at all levels of the executive staff of the National Council of Churches and of its affiliated churches.

6. Ensure that women are included in significant numbers among the planners, leaders, speakers and participants in all NCC-sponsored conferences.

The national conference of NOW decries the outdated, blatant discrimination displayed by the Roman Catholic Church recently in refusing to accept the credentials of the woman appointed to represent the West German government at the Vatican.

In light of the enslavement of body and mind which the church historically has imposed on women, we demand that the seminaries:

1. Immediately stop and repudiate their propagation of sexist, male supremacist doctrine.

2. Initiate women's studies courses which cut through the traditional male, religious mythology to expose church and other social forces denying women their basic human dignity.

3. Actively recruit, employ and justly promote women theologians and other staff in all departments.

4. Actively recruit, enroll, financially aid and seek equal placement for women theological students.

We demand that the churches desexigrate help-wanted ads in their own publications.

We demand that Title VII of the 1964 Civil Rights Act be amended so that religious groups no longer have legal sanction to discriminate on the basis of sex.

LEGISLATIVE GOALS FOR 1970

The major goal for the national drive is the equal rights amendment. Other goals are:

Equal opportunity in education.

Equal opportunity in employment. NOW advocates action to require all federal contractors and subcontractors to conform to the specific provisions against sex discrimination under Executive Order 11246 as amended by 11375 and administered by the Office of Federal Contract Compliance of the Department of Labor.

Review of Income tax laws, social security laws and retirement plans.

Identifying and reporting on sex discrimination.

Including women in appointive positions in government.

Public accommodations: including sex in Title II.

Goals for state, city level action:

Repeal of abortion laws.

Repeal of states' protective legislation.

Establishment of (or pressuring for action) states' commissions on the status of women.

To promote better legislative activity on the local level, each chapter should make up a local legislative kit which would propose action needed on the local level. For a kit to serve as guidance, see Charlene Suneson of the New York chapter.

STATEMENTS TO THE PRESS

This conference reminds all members who are not completely satisfied with all the results of the democratic processes of this conference that dissent is part of democracy. An equally important part of the democratic process is the willingness and ability to accede to the decision of the majority. We therefore urge that all members who speak publicly on behalf of NOW not make public statements contrary to the decisions of this conference without so specifying.

INTERNATIONAL CONGRESS

We call for a "First International New Feminist Congress" to be held abroad or at home in the summer of 1971.

EDUCATION

Be it resolved that NOW support as priorities in education:

1. The establishment of female studies, which we envision as interdisciplinary courses, both curricular and for credit, and extracurricular, designed to raise consciousness about and expose the biases against and ignorance on women, especially in the fields of history, literature, psychology, sociology, and marriage and family courses.

2. The mobilization of, support for, erasing sex discrimination wherever it exists in education as in admissions, scholarships, fellowships, loans, textbooks, guidance counseling, division of students by sex in home economics, shop, sports and vocational training. We also urge the erasing of sex discrimination in policies on marriage, pregnancy or parenthood as related to students, faculty and staff, stocking of libraries with appropriate books, day care for all students, faculty and staff, in hiring, salaries, tenure and nepotism, in appointments such

as college presidencies, in teacher training curricula, in provision of role models outside the traditional sex role stereotypes, in part-time employment and schooling policies, and in language, which must be restructured to reflect a society where women have status equal to men. We suggest studies of hiring and other forms of discrimination against women faculty on the model of the analysis at Columbia University.

3. The encouragement of any action to require universities and colleges that are federal contractors to end discrimination against women in conformity with the guidelines of the Office of Federal Contract Compliance under Executive Orders 11246 and 11375 or to extend Title VI of the 1964 Civil Rights Act to cover sex discrimination in educational institutions and force compliance with its provisions.

4. The seeking of funding for female studies, scholarships, fellowships, loans and research, from foundations, corporations, alumni and alumnae groups, and such organizations as the BPW, AAUW, and NOW itself, and from bequests and donations from individuals.

PLATFORM ON WOMEN'S RIGHTS, NEW DEMOCRATIC COALITION, NEW YORK STATE, ADOPTED MARCH 10, 1970

1. EQUAL EMPLOYMENT OPPORTUNITY

Women, who are over a third of the State's workforce, have for years been condemned to the lowest paid, least rewarding jobs, and have been denied the opportunity to advance according to their abilities. Men college graduates are welcome in executive training programs; women are asked if they can type.

A 1968 study by the U.S. Equal Employment Opportunity Commission revealed that in 100 major New York corporations, women held only 3.8% of the management posts, and 4.7% of professional jobs. Almost 70% of the City's women workers are in clerical jobs, men got higher pay than women for identical work.

Women in this country no longer work as a diversion, if they ever did. Labor Department studies show that 85% work because they have to, and that the typical worker is 41 and married. Nonetheless, women earn under 60% of what men do. Nationally, women with 4 years of college earn less than half of what men with equivalent training are paid.

Federal, state and city laws outlaw job discrimination against women, but these laws are honored more in the breech than the observance. Even the agencies charged with enforcement have given little emphasis to fighting bias against women.

The New Democratic Coalition calls for a substantial increase in all government efforts to end employment discrimination against women, beginning with hearings by Federal, State and City Human Rights Commissions into the nature and extent of job bias in the major industries. We also call for widespread publicity campaigns to inform women of their rights and to encourage complaints by those who suffer discrimination. Finally, we urge the government to withhold contracts and deposits from firms found guilty of discrimination against women.

Women have always assumed the burdens that go with bearing children in order to carry on our civilization. They are the ones who sacrifice their own dreams and careers to stay home and care for their babies. Even when women find ways to go on with their work, society sets up artificial obstacles and penalties to make their lot more difficult.

Pregnant women can be fired and have no rights to guarantee their rehiring after childbirth. There are no maternity benefits to reflect the contributions of women to the economy and to the companies and institutions for which they work.

We call for laws to make maternity leaves and maternity benefits available to working women. Women should not barred from employment or fired because of pregnancy, and they should be guaranteed the right to return to their jobs after childbirth.

2. ABORTION LAW REPEAL

There are over a million abortions performed in the United States every year. Under 1% of them are legal, 25% of all women in America have had illegal abortions, according to some statistics—one for every four live births. 500 to 1000 women die each year from illegal abortions or suffer brutalizing and degradation at the hands of amateurs and hacks.

The poor suffer most: in New York City, 80% of the women who die are

Black or Puerto Rican. The abortion death rate in the U.S. is 50 to 100 per 100,000, far greater than the 3 per 100,000 in countries where abortion is legal. (The death rate from pregnancy and childbirth is over 29 per 10,000 live births.)

In New York State, abortions may be performed only to save the life of the mother. Proposed reforms would help, at most, 15% of the cases, as 85% of abortions are performed because the woman does not want the child.

The New Democratic Coalition affirms a woman's right to control her own body and to decide whether or not to bear a child. The State Abortion Law denies a woman's right to privacy in her personal and sexual relations, imposes on her the religious beliefs of others, discriminates against the poor, and endangers a woman's right to life. Hospitals which receive government funds or tax benefits should be required to give medically safe abortions to all women who request them. Personnel in schools, hospitals, welfare centers and other government supported institutions should be required to let all women know of the availability of abortion.

The New Democratic Coalition supports the Cook-Leichter Bill.

3. HOUSING AND PUBLIC ACCOMMODATIONS

It is illegal to bar people from housing or public accommodations on the basis of race, creed, color or national origin—but not on the basis of sex. Women suffer serious economic consequences from the policies of landlords and rental agents who have convinced themselves that women are undesirable tenants.

Women also suffer disadvantages in business from the practice of barring women from numerous restaurants, eating clubs, and other places of public accommodation.

The New Democratic Coalition believes that discrimination against women in housing and public accommodations is archaic and unfair, and that it should be illegal.

4. UNIVERSAL CHILD CARE

Almost 40% of the women who work are mothers, and 40% of them have children under 6. Over a quarter of all mothers with children under 6 work. However, nationally, only 2% of the children of working mothers receive group day care. The rest are watched by relatives or look after themselves.

In New York City, over 150,000 children under 5 have working mothers, yet the City's day care centers have space for only 8,000 youngsters from 3 to 5 years old. This crisis situation exists throughout the State, and the few private centers that exist are expensive and inadequate to handle the need.

The government spends billions of dollars in subsidies and experimentation for farmers, in management assistance and technical development for businessmen and industrialists, in research and training grants for academics, and in countless other programs that help certain groups of Americans earn their livings. However, it does not spend a fraction of that sum to give women the most basic assistance they require to earn theirs.

The New Democratic Coalition believes the government should provide child care centers as a matter of right to all children whose mothers need it. These centers should be educational or recreational, or a combination of the two: as the mothers of the children in the community want them to be. We call now for a massive expansion of child care facilities, with priorities for admission given to the children of mothers who are working, looking for work, or enrolled in schools, colleges, or training programs.

It is amazing that working mothers are not allowed to deduct child care expenses, while tax laws recognize the generous deductions claimed for "entertainment" and the ever popular "businessman's lunch". A woman may be unable to work at all without undertaking the expenses of babysitting or nursery school. The New Democratic Coalition believes that this inequity in the law should be remedied on all levels—and applied to widowers and divorced or separated men in similar circumstances.

5. EQUALITY IN EDUCATION

It is illegal for schools and colleges receiving Federal funds to discriminate against students on the basis of race, color, creed or national origin—but nothing stops them from discriminating against women. This practice is particularly onerous in the professions, where women who would be lawyers, doctors, and college professors are faced with long-standing graduate school quotas. However, even secondary schools discriminate: in New York City there are 31 high schools restricted according to sex.

More girls than boys graduate from high school in this country, but more men than women enter college. A quarter of the men aged 20 to 24 are in school, compared to only a tenth of the women. There is also sex discrimination in training programs financed by the government. For example, the State University of New York Urban Center in its Brooklyn Data Processing Program restricts machine operator trainees to men, and keypunch operators to women—again limiting women to the lowest paying jobs.

Millions of dollars of City, State, and Federal money support teachers' salaries, construction, research projects, and operation of schools that deny their opportunities to women, or restrict them to a small quota of the enrollment.

The New Democratic Coalition supports total equality of opportunity in education for women, and favors Federal, State, and City legislation to bar discrimination in education and training programs on the basis of sex, which would make it illegal to grant government funds to schools that discriminate.

The history of women in this country and the rest of the world has been virtually ignored. When women are discussed at all, it is generally because they are famous men's wives. The suffragettes are ridiculed, and the battle to win the vote, which took over seven decades, is passed over with brief comment.

Numerous women who freed themselves from the limiting stereotypes that trapped other women in those times have made great contributions to this country and the development of man. Students barely learn that they existed at all. School guidance teachers continue the stereotypes by shunting girls into secretarial courses; directing them towards the traditional female occupations, and discouraging them from so-called men's jobs. Boys are encouraged to become doctors; girls are told to be nurses.

It is important that girls and boys grow up with the knowledge that sex is no barrier to achievement, and that women have been kept back by discrimination and social convention, not by their lack of ability.

We call for a new emphasis in the schools on the contributions of women in history and culture. We call for new guidance policies that encourage girls to break the barriers that keep them from the more satisfying, better paying jobs and professions. Shop and homemaking classes should be required for all students, and should be integrated.

6. WOMEN'S RIGHTS AMENDMENT

"Equality of rights under the law should not be denied or abridged by the United States or by any State on account of sex." This amendment to the U.S. Constitution has been introduced in the Senate by Eugene McCarthy and John Tower, and in the House by Martha Griffiths (D-Mich.) and Catherine May (R-Wash.). It seeks to overturn laws that restrict the rights of women in business, employment, marriage, divorce, and political activity in virtually every state of the union. (Five states, for example, require court approval before a married woman can go into business on her own. A woman may be refused unemployment insurance if she leaves her job to follow her husband to another city, but she can be divorced for desertion if she fails to go with him.)

The Equal Rights Amendment is a small beginning in the continuing struggle for feminine equality. The New Democratic Coalition endorses it as a necessary protection, and as a statement to Americans that we can no longer afford to limit the opportunities and achievements of more than half of our population.

Legislation has also been proposed to amend the State Charter to prohibit discrimination on the basis of sex. NDC endorses this goal.

7. WOMEN IN PARTY AND GOVERNMENT OFFICE

There are 62 counties in New York State—but only one woman County Chairman (Jean Angel of Tompkins County), and only one woman Acting County Chairman (Catherine Blintz of Oneida County). Traditionally women are made Vice-Chairman—a powerless job given as reward for years of canvassing and envelope stuffing.

Reform Democratic clubs have claimed to be different, with women District Leaders often exerting as much power and influence as men. Yet, with a few exceptions, women are not nominated for public office by local, county, or state Democratic organizations—including those that belong to the NDC.

In the recent New York City elections, there were 85 Democratic candidates for City-wide office, judgeships, City Council, and other posts. Of these only five were women (they all won election).

The position of women in government is nearly as bleak. Only 29 of the 401 top jobs in New York City government are held by women. All of the 12 superagency administrators, and the 17 presidents of boards and commissions are men. All but three of the thirty commissioners are men. Government, which should be setting an example to private industry on equal employment opportunity laws, is itself guilty of denying women the right to hold the jobs they earn by merit of their talents.

The New Democratic Coalition pledges to encourage more women to seek nomination for public and party office, and to press government officials to hire more women in major administrative and policy making capacities.

8. CONTRACEPTION

Last year, there were nearly 2,500 reported pregnancies among New York City high school students; others doubtless went unreported. The Board of Education has a policy of not providing information about contraception to students, and State law forbids prescribing contraceptive devices to anyone under 16. This policy is senseless. It does not prevent young girls from engaging in sexual activity; it only makes it almost inevitable that those who do will become pregnant. Among the general population, many women are unaware of the availability of contraceptive devices; unwanted pregnancies become a special burden for poor women who find themselves trapped even more firmly in the vise of poverty. The New Democratic Coalition urges the repeal of laws that restrict the availability of contraceptives, and calls on the government to make low cost contraceptives available to women who want them. We also call for a public education campaign on contraceptives by the State government which is liberally financed.

9. FINANCIAL DISCRIMINATION

Existing laws and policies regarding taxes, insurance, credit and pension, health, life and other public and private welfare benefits often discriminate on the basis of sex or marital status. Such discrimination should be made illegal.

10. ALIMONY

When equal employment opportunity, child care and programs for preparing women for re-entry into the work force at an equal level with men become realities, the alimony laws should be revised to reflect the changed conditions and needs of women.

11. PROSTITUTION

Prostitution is almost always a result of severe economic and social deprivation. Some 90 percent of the prostitutes in New York are drug addicts. Nevertheless, instead of rehabilitation, the emphasis in the law and the courts has been on punishment. The real victims of prostitution are the women who pass through the revolving doors of the cities' jails.

We call for a revision of the whole approach to the problem of prostitution, starting at once with the end of entrapment by police (who could be better employed fighting crimes that have victims). We call for changes in the laws that punish women but do not punish men. We call for the end of the cynical sacrifice of women by a society which punishes them to assuage its own guilt.

INDEX OF INCLUSIONS

This index lists all the items included in this edition with the exception of the oral testimonies. The parenthetical number refers to the page in the GPO edition; the number following refers to the page in this volume. The titles of statements and prepared testimonies have been simplified.

INDEX OF OMISSIONS

Listed here are items in the original GPO edition that have been omitted from this volume. The parenthetical number refers to the page in the GPO edition. The titles of items have been simplified for easy reference.

INDEX OF PERSONS AND ORGANIZATIONS

This index includes the names of individuals who testified, submitted statements, or wrote articles and the names of organizations they represented. The parenthetical numbers refer to pages in the original GPO edition; numbers without parentheses refer to pages in this volume.

DATE DUE

DATE DUE			
APR 1 8 1988			
NOV 0 1 1989			
DEC 0 8 1989			
DEC 0 7 1990			
MAR 2 8 1991			
OCT 2 3 1992			
DEC 0 9 1994			
GAYLORD			PRINTED IN U.S.A.